Governing the Ungovernable

Institutional Reforms for
Democratic Governance

Governing the Ungovernable

Institutional Reforms for Democratic Governance

ISHRAT HUSAIN

OXFORD

UNIVERSITY PRESS

OXFORD
UNIVERSITY PRESS

Oxford University Press is a department of the University of Oxford.
It furthers the University's objective of excellence in research, scholarship,
and education by publishing worldwide. Oxford is a registered trade mark of
Oxford University Press in the UK and in certain other countries

Published in Pakistan by
Oxford University Press
No.38, Sector 15, Korangi Industrial Area,
PO Box 8214, Karachi-74900, Pakistan

First Edition published in 2018

This edition in Oxford Pakistan Paperbacks 2018

Not for sale in India

ISBN 978-0-19-940897-9

Third Impression 2018

Typeset in Adobe Garamond Pro
Printed on 55gsm Book Paper

Printed by The Times Press Pvt. Ltd., Karachi

Contents

Acknowledgements

This book is a culmination of my residential tenure as Public Policy Fellow with the Asia Program at the Woodrow Wilson Center at Washington DC from June 2016 to March 2017. I wish to thank the President and officers of the Center and particularly Michael Kugelman, the Deputy Director, for providing me this opportunity. The Trustees of the Fellowship Fund for Pakistan and Mr Arif Habib were generous in sponsoring the fellowship. Munawar Noorani and Zaffar Khan deserve my gratitude for proposing and then making this happen. At the Center, I wish to acknowledge Janet Sykes the Librarian who opened up all the resources available at the Library of Congress, Bruce Griffith and Bill Kelly of the IT department, Arlyn Charles, Lindsay Collins, and Krishna Ariel for their support throughout my stay. The participants of the seminar at the Center where I presented the work in progress gave me helpful comments.

Two of my research assistants, Aleena Ali and Hamza Tariq, went beyond their normal duties and responded promptly and diligently to all my requests. Aleena did a superb job in carrying out the literature survey and collating the material in a systematic way. Hamza volunteered to help in preparing the bibliography and verifying the foot notes even after the completion of his assignment. I wish to thank my friend, Steve Radelet, an outstanding scholar in his own right who made the services of one of his graduate students at Georgetown, Rayah Al Farah at my disposal. She worked conscientiously and diligently on the assignment given to her. Two other interns, Divya Sahni and Jamie Liang came to my rescue during the period when I didn't have an RA.

The title of this book was the brainchild of my friend, Shuja Nawaz, who not only had several discussions at different points of time but also provided some unpublished material and offered extensive comments on the Chapter 'The Military'. Lieutenant General Asim Bajwa, Lt Gen. (retd) Khalid Nawaz and their staff, and Major General Chaudhry Sarfarz Ali made material available which added new insights on the defence forces and their businesses. Three persons, among many, need to be mentioned for their contributions. Shahid Yusuf was as usual fierce in his critique of the chapters he reviewed and commented upon. Michael Kugelman not only provided candid feedback himself but also shared the work of the participants of the Conference held in January 2017. Robert Hathaway, a former Director of the Asia Program, took a lot of time out to read the drafts and offered valuable comments.

I am not in a position to acknowledge everyone who participated in the focus groups, filled out the structured questionnaire, and responded to my queries and follow up questions. It was indeed a pleasure that a large number of civil servants—active and retired, corporate CEOs, civil society activists, academics and scholars, and donor representatives shared their views and thoughts candidly and openly. The work produced here would not have been possible without their inputs. Ali Sarfraz and Waqas ul Hasan deserve special mention for getting me the missing data on government employees and following up on the questionnaires. Nasim Beg also pushed some of the C100 members and has helped me throughout the study. Ismail Qureshi deputed one of his staff at the National School of Public Policy to make reports of the training syndicates available to me. Sakib Sherani was kind enough to share his own work in progress on Institutions of Reforms with me. Naseer Rana of the World Bank, with whom I had collaborated earlier, was generous by furnishing very exhaustive notes and substantive comments at the inception stage. To ensure consistency of data, I relied upon the State Bank of Pakistan (SBP), and Farooq Arby and his colleagues were extremely generous in preparing the time series on a large number of variables. I wish to thank them for their outstanding work

My intellectual debt to three of my former bosses who are giants in the profession of economics—Stanley Fischer, Larry Summers and Joe Stiglitz—from whom I learnt a lot, would always overwhelm me but my interest in institutions and economic growth was sparked by Dani Rodrick of Harvard. I have found his work to be both illuminating but also relevant for policy purposes. Thanks, Dani for setting me on this course.

I was very fortunate when one of Pakistan's leading visual artists, Naiza Khan, winner of the 2013 Prince Claus award, volunteered to adorn the title cover of this book with one of her creative designs. Despite her teaching engagements at Cornell she produced several outstanding pieces and it became really difficult to choose one of them. I am greatly indebted to her for this generous offer and for sparing time to produce an excellent piece of work which has enhanced the aesthetic value of this book.

I would like to express my profound thanks to Ameena Saiyid, Nadia Ghani, and Raheela Baqai of the Oxford University Press for their consistent and continuous support, and to my editor, Sunara Nizami, for her hard work and dedication throughout this project.

Finally, I have no words to convey my heartfelt gratitude to my spouse, Shahnaz, and daughters, Farah and Uzma. They have always been fully behind me in whatever I have endeavoured to do, even at the expense of their own inconveniences. Shahnaz not only relocated twice during this period but took care of all the daily chores and allowed me complete space and freedom to concentrate on my work. Farah and Uzma were both interested in my work but equally concerned about the long hours I was putting in and the travels I was undertaking. I felt guilty that this project kept me away from spending more time with my adorable grandchildren. This book would not have seen the light of the day without their love and support.

Preface

Why is Pakistan perceived to be an 'ungovernable' state? A label it never carried in the past? Can anything be done to restore it to the track from which it derailed? These are questions that are often asked by the global community and the public at large in Pakistan. We do not pretend to have either a magic wand to answer these very complicated but relevant questions or a crystal ball to foresee the future. In all humility, what we can do is to figure out why Pakistan was among the top ten performing developing countries ahead of China, India, Vietnam, and many others in economic and social indicators recording an average GDP growth rate of 6 per cent annually for over 40 years until 1990. It was a peaceful country enjoying respect amongst the world community. Tourists and visitors from abroad were able to visit any part of Pakistan freely in what they found to be a safe and secure country of friendly, hospitable, and caring people. Thousands of students from African and Asian countries studied at its universities and professional colleges. What happened then over the following 25 years from 1990–2015? How did Pakistan get left behind both economically and in terms of social development in the region, let alone in comparison to China and Vietnam? The Indian economy was only five times larger than Pakistan's in 1990. According to the latest estimates, it is eight or nine times larger now. Pakistan has, during this period, gained notoriety in the international media as one of the most dangerous countries in the world. Even visitors who need to visit it for business purposes and are assured full security and safety, are reluctant to come. Tourism has virtually vanished. Notwithstanding many excellent institutions of higher learning in Pakistan, there is prevalent a famine of foreign students.

This book is a modest attempt to understand the reasons for this contrast in the performance of Pakistan during two different periods, i.e. 1947–90 and 1990–2015. The choice of the two periods is based on a close scrutiny of the broad economic trends and social patterns. The book strives to analyse the factors that can adequately account for the relatively robust accomplishments in the earlier period and the relative decline and stagnation in the second period. It represents a kind of quasi-natural experiment in exploring the ingredients that contribute to these different results.

The starting point is a survey of academic literature, policy and plan reviews, and popular discourses since 1947 to identify the alternate explanatory hypotheses that have been advanced, and then test them against empirical evidence. This methodology cannot hope to match the rigorous standards set by professional economists as there is no underlying quantitative model underpinning this analysis which is, hence, necessarily ad hoc in nature. The idea was, however, to use a multidisciplinary approach and avoid the limitations of economic modelling, including abstractions from the real world situation; a set of assumptions to keep the model simple and the choices of variables to be included, some of which are not easily amenable to quantification. Using dummy variables was an option that was considered but that could have also led to entanglements with econometric issues of specification, omitted variables, estimation techniques, and the robustness of the results. Data paucity was a further consideration. As this volume is intended for a wider audience than just economists, I decided to follow a more eclectic, qualitative, evidence-based method and capture the richness of the different prisms of political scientists, sociologists, journalists, management and economists, and the like.

This study has benefitted from the insights of influential and thoughtful individuals, focus groups, informal conversations, and consultations with people from a wide range of walks in life. In addition to scholarly research, studies of various government commissions in Pakistan have also been made use of.

There are several features that make this case study distinct from earlier ones. The definition of governance here is not limited to state-centred institutions alone but is multi-dimensional, covering a wide range of them. It is the first of its kind that examines in some depth the complete array of the institutions in a historical context. It blends academic literature with popular opinion on these institutions expressed in the media. Most of the academic literature and popular discourses analyse these institutions in isolation. To overcome this weakness, an attempt has been made to examine the behaviour, norms, and actions of the society, polity, private sector, the military, religious organizations, and external actors that directly or indirectly impinge upon the performance and outcomes generated by these institutions. Emphasis is placed on their interlinkages and interdependencies.

I utilize the broader concept of social, economic, and sustainable development rather than simply economic growth. There are examples where the countries have grown rapidly through indiscriminate utilization of its natural resources, whose benefits accrue to a narrow minority at the top, and which over time become unsustainable. Such countries have witnessed civil wars, social conflicts, a breakdown of law and order, and prolonged periods of economic decline. Pakistan has also been characterized as an economy where the state has been hijacked and markets rigged, with uneven development, pronounced income inequality, and gender and regional disparities. This strategy was pursued by successive governments— whether military or civilian, or a mixture of these—in order to further their own interests and of those belonging to a small elite class. In my definition, development is a more all-encompassing endeavour that results in better education and higher literacy, adequate healthcare, productive jobs and livelihoods, an acceptable level of nutrition and access to clean drinking water, electricity, roads, and infrastructure for ordinary citizens.

Economic growth is critical as it induces investment in human and social development. An educated, healthy, well-nourished, and skilled labour force then enhances productivity and raises output and incomes, resulting in higher economic growth. This virtuous cycle is therefore the key to broad-based development. Over 80 districts of Pakistan rank low on the deprivation index, and the aim of the strategy should be to spread the benefits of development in such a way that these accrue disproportionately to the citizens of these deprived districts.

The growing militancy, and the ascendancy of the jihadist elements and groups can also be explained in terms of the withering away of the state and its institutions. As the people became increasingly disillusioned and disaffected by the state institutions, these non-state actors stepped in to fill the vacuum and operated parallel systems of justice, service delivery, and security. For example, the people in Swat joined or supported the militant group because they were able to provide swift justice against criminals as was earlier the case during the Wali of Swat's rule. Those unwilling to join the jihadists were coerced into doing so as there was no fear of retaliation or punitive action by the dormant and dysfunctional state institutions. The army continues to administer Swat even after eight years of the operation as the civil administration is not yet equipped to assume charge.

This brings us to the instruments, structures, and processes through which the institutions exercise their authority, i.e. civil services, the federal, provincial, and local governments, the police, the prosecutory body, prisons, the parliament, and judiciary. The entire spectrum of institutions is critically evaluated to assess their capabilities and shortcomings but proposals have been developed for reforms of only a few selected institutions concerned with accountability, delivery of services, economic growth, social equity, and security that should have been prioritized. Successful restructuring of these two dozen institutions would have spill-over effects on the other institutions and the islands of good governance would go on expanding over time.

* * *

Going forward, Pakistan's economy has to face a myriad of complex challenges arising from an uncertain global environment, an explosive knowledge economy, disruptive technologies, demographic transition, and climate change. Regionally, the country can take advantage of its strategic location linking South Asia with Central Asia, and Central Asia and China with the Middle East. The China-Pakistan Economic Corridor (CPEC), currently being implemented, can play a crucial role in establishing these linkages.

In the domestic arena, the battle against terrorism and extremism, equipping the youthful population with education and skills for productive employment, bringing about inter-provincial harmony and social cohesion by reducing inequalities and disparities, and managing urbanization need to be aggressively tackled.

***

Is Pakistan preordained to remain 'ungovernable', mired in a state of ceaseless, recurring crises, or can it become 'governable' once more? The long-term agenda for economic revival and social change that could help in transforming Pakistan into a 'governable' state, derived from the analysis and views solicited for this study, is spelt out below, and addresses these global, regional, and domestic challenges. These reforms, if properly implemented over a period of time by successive governments, should enable Pakistan to get back to the trajectory of an average annual growth of six per cent recorded in its first 40 years and achieve the status of an upper middle income country by 2035. However, the successful execution of this agenda will depend upon the willingness of the ruling party and the Opposition to adopt it and assiduously work to maintain political stability, provide a continuity and consistency of policies, and ensure clarity in their sense of direction. The most important factor, as revealed by the findings of this study, is the resuscitation of institutions functioning under the executive, legislative, and judicial branches of governance to enable them to become sufficiently strong to effectively translate these policies, programmes, and projects on the ground. By doing so, it is possible to make up for lost time because effective, responsive, and well-functioning institutions would help to minimize the politics of patronage, unshackle the entrepreneurial energies of the private sector, assure delivery and equitable access to basic services to the citizens, and empower civil society and local governments. It may be recalled that a study by the World Economic Forum had concluded that a slight improvement in governance results in a threefold increase in per capita income in the long run. This is the likely gain which would be accrued by improving the civilian institutions of governance in Pakistan.

The entire ambit of civil-military relations, a highly contentious and emotional issue, ought to undergo a drastic change if the civilian institutions become capable and effective, thus allowing the democratically elected leaders to assert their supremacy over the affairs of the state. The justification for seeking the aid of the army at the drop of a hat and thus opening the doors for their intrusion in the civilian affairs would become redundant (the polls show that they are perceived by the public in Pakistan to be the strongest and most trustworthy institution in the country at present). The armed forces would themselves welcome the opportunity to concentrate on their core functions of ensuring the external security of Pakistan, particularly at a time when it is faced with serious threats from several directions.

Ayub Khan and Zia ul-Haq could not have ruled Pakistan for as long as they did without the active help of competent civil servants and the highly efficient institutions they manned. The military had to withdraw to their barracks soon after the takeover to keep their professionalism intact but also because the command and control system to which they were accustomed was not attuned to civil administration. By the time Pervez Musharraf assumed power, the corrosion had set in. Although his devolution scheme was commendable, the abolition of the offices of the Commissioner, DC, etc. further weakened the institutions of governance. It is no longer possible for an ambitious general to hold the country together with the present cadres of civil servants and the institutional set up in a situation when Pakistan is beset by a magnitude of complex and difficult problems.

These civilian institutions, once strengthened, have to work collaboratively and collectively in a coordinated manner to achieve the goals before them. The federal, provincial, and local governments, the parliament, and the judiciary have to respect the boundaries within which each has to function without encroaching on each other's domains. The current practices, norms, and mind-set that are characterized by confrontation, polarization, fighting for turf, and engaging in 'blame the other' games will need to end. This will indeed be the most challenging undertaking which will either make or break the economic nervous system and the security backbone of the country. The likelihood of this materializing will only be high when the gap between the institutional capability (including the capacity to adapt and change), and the changing development needs and aspirations of the population can be bridged.

It is my contention that the police and law-enforcement agencies, if properly recruited, trained, incentivized, and equipped, along with a responsive judiciary can arrest the inroads of the extremist and jihadist groups and help in implementing in letter and spirit the National Action Plan (NAP) that is intended to eliminate these non-state actors. This, along with the delivery of basic services to the ordinary citizens is the way in which the essential ingredients that had led to the perception of Pakistan as an 'ungovernable' state would slowly and gradually dissipate.

The important question that is often asked in Pakistan is: who will drive this change agenda? The concluding chapter attempts to address this pertinent question at some length. There is almost a consensus in Pakistan that institutional decay, aggravated over the last 25 years, has been responsible for bad governance, and this malaise has to be fixed. Past experience has vividly demonstrated that sweeping reforms across the board that affect the entire system are neither politically feasible nor economically desirable. Therefore, a second best solution has to be tried that limits the disruption and keeps the political noise and resistance to a minimum. The focus of this volume is, therefore, to select a small subset of a core of highly vital institutions for reform and restructuring on a priority basis. The premise of this approach is that if these key institutions can be effectively reformed, it would create a demonstration effect that would help in moving towards the path of overall institutional rejuvenation on a sustained basis. The purpose of this volume is to trigger popular and academic debate and discussion on the proposals developed here and push the envelope further to press forward the actions necessary to arrest and reverse the process of the institutional decay.

1

Introduction

Pakistan was one of the top ten economic performers among the developing countries in the world during the first 40 years of its existence. Beginning with a very weak economic base at the time of Independence in 1947 and a tumultuous period of nation building, marked by continuing political instability in the aftermath of the death of its founder, Mohammed Ali Jinnah, its record of achievement during the first four decades was impressive. It successfully absorbed and rehabilitated eight million refugees, or one fourth of its total population, fought a war with India, a much larger and more powerful neighbour, in 1965, and underwent a painful and traumatic dismemberment of the country in 1971. The emergence of a populist political regime that undertook massive nationalization of private assets in the 1970s, accompanied by an external shock of a major escalation of oil prices, dealt a massive blow to business confidence and led to a complete dislocation of the economy. Close involvement with the US in the Afghan war to oust the Soviet Union in the 1980s and the associated fallout, i.e. the spread of sectarian violence, drugs, and Kalashnikovs, tore asunder the social fabric of the country. Notwithstanding these and many other challenges, both internal and external, Pakistan was able to register an average of 6 per cent annual growth during its first 40 years of existence. Pakistan was ahead of India and Bangladesh in all economic and social indicators.

According to some analysts, Pakistan had reached the threshold of becoming a middle income nation in the late 1980s. According to Burki:[1]

In the late 1980s, Pakistan had begun to exhibit many of the characteristics of a middle income country: it was less dependent on agriculture than most

1

low income countries and had an industrial sector that was comparable in size and diversity to those in many middle income nations; it had a vast reservoir of highly trained labourers; it had a middle class numbering more than 30 million people, and it was as urbanized as the more developed countries of East Asia and the Middle East. In the 1990s, however, the expectation that Pakistan is on the verge of the crossing the threshold to become a middle income country has ceased to exist.

Since 1990, Pakistan has fallen behind its neighbouring countries, and has had a decrease in the potential growth rate from 6.5 to 4.5 per cent[2] with episodes of boom and bust. The booms were short-lived and could not be sustained over extended periods of time. Political instability and frequent changes of government in the 1990s may have created uncertainty for investors, thus slowing down the pace of economic activity. There has, however, been smooth and orderly transition of power from one elected government to the other twice since 2008 but economic and social indicators have not shown much improvement. Growth has been slow, less stable, more volatile, and far less sustained than that of other countries in the region, and also relative to its own performance in the 2000–2007 period. It is only over the past two years that some change for the better is becoming visible but whether it will be stable and sustainable in the years leading up to the general elections is yet to be seen.

Externally, the popular image of Pakistan is that of a fragile or failed state with a large and expanding arsenal of nuclear weapons encircled by Islamic extremists, and a safe haven for nurturing and training terrorists who pose a threat to other countries. There is considerable unease in the international community about the ceaseless rivalry and hostility between nuclear armed India and Pakistan who have thrice fought wars against each other. The eastern part of Pakistan was separated from the western in 1971 as a consequence of a war in which India played a decisive role. Kashmir continues to remain a highly contentious and volatile powder keg. Relations with Afghanistan remain tense, and mutual recriminations and mistrust have vitiated the atmosphere. Although Pakistan is a non-NATO ally of the United States, the general sentiment in both countries about each other is not overly favourable. The US considers Pakistan duplicitous in its dealings with the Afghan Taliban and the Haqqani network, while Pakistan is bitter that notwithstanding it incurring significant losses and sacrificing hundreds of thousands of lives, its role in the war against terror is not fully appreciated.[3] Pakistan is perceived by those beyond its borders as a source of regional instability and as an ungovernable country.

Therefore, the popular hypothesis about Pakistan's economic drift is explained by this increasing influence of religious extremists and terrorists who have threatened law and order and disturbed the peace and security. Economic agents are reluctant to undertake new investments in this environment. This hypothesis may be partially valid but the economic decline had begun in the 1990s, well before Pakistan was embroiled in the war against terror in the post-2001 period. The average growth rate in the 1990s, when the country was relatively peaceful and tranquil, was already down from 6.5 per cent in the 1980s to 4 per cent. Investment ratios, export growth, and social indicators all took a dip in those years. Poverty, which was showing a downward decline until the 1980s, worsened by the end of the 1990s. In contradiction to this trend, the 2002–2008 period, which was a period of acute violence and terror activity in Pakistan—including assassination attempts and terrorist attacks on the sitting president and prime minister—the country recorded a remarkable turnaround. The growth rate touched 6 to 7 per cent on average, the investment/GDP ratio peaked at 23 per cent, and foreign direct investment (FDI) flows exceeded US$5 billion.

The Chief Investment Officer of a Swedish Mutual Fund[4] had this to say:

It was not until the end of 2008 that I first travelled to Pakistan and met with around 30 companies. Some of these companies were family-owned and had been around for 40–50 years. The businesses were growing at an average of ten per cent and the political or security situation was not having much negative impact on their performance.

During the past seven years of tumultuous turmoil resulting from terrorist activities reaching a peak, the corporate sector's earning growth on annual compound average growth rate basis has been around 20 per cent with the return on equity (RoE) in excess of 25 per cent.

The recent experience of the 2013–16 period is illuminating. Macroeconomic stability has been achieved, economic growth rates are moving in an upward direction, and the confidence of domestic and international investors has been restored (Pakistan has been upgraded to the MSCI EM Index from the FM Index and its credit ratings by Moody's and Standard & Poor have also risen), negating the view that Pakistan's security situation and its deep involvement in the war against terrorism is responsible for its poor economic and social performance. Therefore, the security deficit hypothesis does not stand up to serious scrutiny.

It is true that if the huge financial and human costs incurred in combating terrorism, the restrictions on travel to and from Pakistan, and the suspicion with which Pakistanis are regarded were eliminated, the economic upturn would have been even higher in the 2002–16 period.

There is a group of analysts who argue that availability of generous foreign assistance has been the principal determinant of Pakistan's economic success or failure, and that its fortunes vacillate with the ebb and flow of resources from external donors. It has been argued that the three periods of economic spurts in the history of Pakistan, i.e. the 1960s, 1980s, and early 2000s, can be attributed to the heavy infusion of these resources into the country. In the 1960s, Pakistan was a CENTO and SEATO ally and was closely aligned with the US in the Cold War, in the 1980s the country participated actively with the US in ousting the Soviet Union from Afghanistan, and in the early 2000s Pakistan was rewarded for its pivotal role in the war against terror. It is therefore argued that Pakistan was the recipient of large military and economic assistance and that was the major reason for the turnaround in these periods. Notwithstanding this popular perception, the empirical evidence does not prove this assertion.

In the 1950s, Pakistan received huge military, civilian, and food aid, with the PL 480 imports of food from the US keeping hunger at bay. In the 1970s, Pakistan was granted (through debt rescheduling) substantial debt relief; with over two-thirds of the debt payments of US$650 million, due during 1974–7, being written off. Western aid through the World Bank-led consortium amounted to $700 million annually but on top of this, official grants and concessional loans (some of which were subsequently transformed into grants or waived) from oil rich Arab countries and overseas workers remittances financed the huge imbalances in current account.[5]

During 1973–4 to 1977–8, commitments of assistance from Iran and the Arab countries totalled $1.2 billion, largely on concessional terms. Pakistan was therefore comfortably able to meet as high a current account deficit as 10.1 per cent of GDP in 1975, followed by 7.1 and 7 per cent over the next two years. Parvez Hasan has calculated that aid disbursements during the mid-1970s were at a level far above those reached during the 1965–70 period (averaging $600 million annually, which included flows to East Pakistan) after allowing for international inflation.

In the 1990s, the foreign currency deposits of resident and non-resident Pakistanis in Pakistani banks, amounting to $11 billion, were utilized to finance external payments. These deposits, as they had already been consumed, were then frozen in May 1998, causing a huge crisis of liquidity and market confidence. This spilt over into the early 2000s. The IMF, World Bank, and Asian Development Bank (ADB) continued to make loans amounting to several billion dollars between 1988 to 1998, while Japan was the largest bilateral provider of concessional loans and grants until the nuclear test of May 1998.

In the post-2008 period, the Kerry Lugar Bill authorized $7.5 billion US economic and military assistance to Pakistan for a five year period. Multilateral banks and the IMF increased the quantum of their support while Pakistan became the largest recipient of UK aid. In this way, higher volumes of foreign assistance have been received in the post 2008 period but the average growth rate has hovered around 3 to 4 per cent. It can thus be seen that the periods of high growth rates, i.e. the 1960s, 1980s, and early 2000s, did not receive any exceptionally high foreign assistance flows as compared to the periods of the 1950s, 1970s, 1990s, and post-2008 years.

McCartney[6] finds no credible evidence to attribute Pakistan's episodes of growth to foreign aid inflows and circumstances emanating from the global economy. 'Using more rigorous econometrics over a longer period of time, there seems to be little generalised evidence that GDP growth in Pakistan has principally been of the [externally] dependent variety.' McCartney is of the view that acceleration of economic growth occurred when the state successfully created conditions in which high profits were generated for investors and credit was channelled towards them. Therefore, the hypothesis of high foreign assistance resulting in high economic performance is not validated by the facts.

Coterminous with the foreign aid syndrome is the widespread belief that the US and the Western countries in general have supported military dictators at the expense of democratic governments. Their belief is that they are able to manipulate the strongman running the country to follow their agenda and interests, and therefore Pakistan's economy has fared well only under the military regimes with the blessings of the US. The frequent dismissal of elected regimes in the 1990s and the coup to overthrow Z. A. Bhutto in 1977 were all engineered under this compact, and the drop in economic performance was caused by the consequential political instability. While it is true that US national interests did coincide with those of Pakistan during the Cold War, the war against the Soviets in Afghanistan, and that against Al-Qaeda in the 2000s, it must be recalled that the US suspended or curtailed economic and military assistance at crucial times in Pakistan's history when the military dictators were still in power.

US aid was suspended soon after the 1965 war with India, the 1971 separation of East Pakistan, and under the Symington amendment in the early period of Zia ul-Haq's rule. Sanctions were imposed in 1999 when General Pervez Musharraf took over the reins of the government. President Bush's National Security Adviser, Condoleezza Rice has chronicled in her book, *A Memoir of My Extraordinary, and Ordinary Family and Me* (Ember, 2000) the efforts made by the US administration to bring in Mohtarma Benazir Bhutto to take over power from Pervez Musharraf in the post-2007 period. The ambivalent attitude of the US can be gauged from the fact that they have supported dictators in Egypt but have for the past 15 years been engaged in the overthrow of Saddam Hussein, Muammar Gaddafi, and Bashar Al Assad in Syria. The close defence, nuclear, and economic relations between India, the largest democracy in the world, and the US do not lend any credence to this theory either. US national interests in Pakistan have not remained static; US interest has vacillated over time and their support to Pakistan has been opportunistic rather than strategic or deterministic. Whenever these interests converge with those of Pakistan and notwithstanding irritations and quibbles on both sides (1950s—SEATO/CENTO; 1980s—expelling the Soviets from Afghanistan; and the 2001–16 War in Afghanistan), the US has chosen to assist Pakistan irrespective of the nature of the government in power.

We then examine another factor, namely the global economic conditions that may have played a negative role in this outcome. The reality is that the external environment between 1990 and 2008 was an extremely favourable a period in which most emerging and developing countries made great economic strides, as Steve Radelet chronicles in his book *The Great Surge*,[7] while Pakistan fell behind India, Bangladesh, Sri Lanka, Vietnam, and other countries during that period. Since 1995, the real GDP of emerging and developing countries (EDCs) has grown by 4.7 per cent annually on average and per capita incomes have increased by over 70 per cent between 1995 and 2013. On a population weighted basis, excluding China, the increase has been about 90 per cent. Consequently, the relative share of EDCs in the global GDP (measured at purchasing power parity) increased to 57 per cent in 2014. The number of poor living at $1.90 per day has halved from 2 billion in 1990 to 897 million by 2012, bringing down the share of poor people in the total population from 37 to 13 per cent in 2012.

The number of people living at low levels of human development fell from 3 billion in 1990 to slightly over 1 billion in 2014.[8] The share of EDCs in the world exports rose from 24 to 41 per cent during this period and international capital flows jumped from $91 to $1,145 billion. All the social indicators, such as life expectancy, maternal mortality, infant mortality, adult literacy, net enrolment ratios, and average years of schooling have shown significant improvements. We can therefore rule out that the external economic environment was a major factor in explaining Pakistan's poor performance during this 25-year period. Other countries in the neighbourhood who were lagging behind Pakistan have taken advantage of the dynamic global economy to bring improvements in the living standards of the majority of their people.

Some analysts have attributed Pakistan's poor performance to the 'Garrison State' syndrome.[9] As Pakistan has been obsessed with confronting a much larger arch rival India since its formation, it has to allocate a much larger amount of its resources to defence expenditure, and preserve and expand the corporate interests of the military. Hence, the neglect of education, health, and human development in general, and the diversion of resources to meet the demands of defence, nuclear capability, and other security-related expenditure has led to the present economic and social outcomes. The ratio of defence expenditure to GDP has been consistently high in the first 40 years and is now 2.9 per cent of GDP, almost one half of what it was in the 1980s. Most of the nuclear-related expenditure was incurred in the 1970s and 1980s. In FY 2016, the budgetary allocation for education was 2.7 per cent.[10] Combining health and education, the budgetary allocation is 3.7 per cent, higher than that of defence and internal security. In the education and health sectors, it is governance and management issues that are the impediments in the delivery of these services rather than budgetary allocations.

A popular myth that has now become quite entrenched as accepted truth is that of the large corporate interests of the military. It is true that they have foundations and trusts that run enterprises, but the proceeds and profits they earn are utilized for the welfare of army pensioners, particularly the soldiers who retire at an early average age of 45 to 50. The education and healthcare of their families are financed by the income generated by these foundations and trusts. To put this in perspective, the total market cap in November 2016 of all the listed companies owned by the Fauji Foundation, Army Welfare Trust, Shaheen Foundation, and Bahria Foundation represents only 4.5 per cent of the total market cap of the companies listed on the Pakistan Stock Exchange. These are the big players and everyone points fingers towards these companies. All of them pay all their taxes on their income, sales, and imports, and do not enjoy any preferential exemptions or receive any special concessions. The share of other unlisted companies in the total assets of unlisted companies is not known but is likely to be quite insignificant as the universe of privately owned enterprises and businesses is substantial. Therefore, the Garrison State hypothesis too does not meet the test of evidentiary confirmation.

Having ruled out factors such as security and terrorism, inflows of foreign assistance, preference for military rule, external economic environment, and diversion of public expenditure towards defence which may have all played some role but were not the principal determinant of the poor performance, we turn our attention to the institutions of governance. There is by now a great deal of theoretical literature and empirical evidence that points us in this direction.

The principal argument of this study is that the intermediation process through which good economic policies are translated into rise in incomes and equitable distribution of benefits involves the institutions of governance. It is the quality, robustness, and responsiveness of these institutions through which the implementation of social and economic policies takes place. The principal institutions of governance comprise the judiciary, necessary for the protection of property rights, and the enforcement of contracts; the legislature which prescribes laws and the regulatory framework; and the executive which makes policies and supplies public goods and services. If the access to the institutions of governance for common citizens is difficult, time-consuming, and expensive, the benefits from growth get distributed unevenly, for the gainers are only those who enjoy preferential access to these institutions.

The *Human Development in South Asia* reports of 1995 and 2005 lay bare the incidences of unequal access due to poor governance:

South Asia presents a fascinating combination of many contradictions. It has governments that are high on governing and low on serving; it has parliaments that are elected by the poor but aid the rich; and [a] society that asserts the rights of some but perpetuates exclusion for others. Despite a marked improvement in the lives of a few, there are many in South Asia who have been forgotten by formal institutions of governance. These are the poor, the downtrodden, and the most vulnerable of the society, suffering from acute deprivation on account of their income, caste, creed, gender or religion. Their fortunes have not moved with those of the privileged few and this in itself is a deprivation of a depressing nature.

(Human Development South Asia Report, 1999)

Governance constitutes for [ordinary people] a daily struggle for survival and dignity. Ordinary people are too often humiliated at the hands of public institutions. For them, lack of good governance means police brutality, corruption in accessing basic public services, ghost schools, teachers' absenteeism, missing medicines, high cost of and low access to justice, criminalization of politics, and lack of social justice. These are just a few manifestations of the crisis of governance.

(Human Development in South Asia Report, 2005)

It must be conceded that there is no definitive or conclusive definition of governance. I use, for the purpose of this study, the World Bank definition set out in *WDR 2017* (discussed later on in this Chapter). The link between institutions and economic and social development is through investment in physical and human capital. Both the efficiency and the volume of investment could depend upon the quality of institutions. The writ of the state, delivery of services, macroeconomic stability, and equitable distribution of benefits can be effectively achieved only if these institutions are functioning effectively.

Mancur Olson et al. (1998) were among the earlier scholars who demonstrated the link between governance capacity, institutions, and economic growth.[11] Their principal argument was that countries with unstable governance make economic agents act under uncertain conditions, determining weak property rights, and enforcement and protection, and therefore fail in attempting to activate a constant growth process. Property rights protection are an essential ingredient for private sector investment and therefore, overall economic growth. However, in a situation of political, economic, and legal uncertainty, the risk perceptions of investors is heightened. They, therefore, demand higher than normal rates of return and a quicker payoff period before they decide to invest. Their inability to find such investment opportunities results in stagnant or declining investment ratios.

The academic literature on governance and economic growth has empirically examined questions such as: (a) whether there is a positive relationship between good governance and economic growth, (b) whether this relationship is unidirectional or does the relationship run in both directions, i.e. does good governance contribute to economic growth and vice versa, (c) if this relationship holds good, what are the components and aspects of good governance that influence such an outcome, (d) how do countries select among these components because such measures are highly correlated, (e) which public sector reforms will effectively strengthen these measures of good governance, and (f) what are the incentives for the decision-makers to put in place such reforms and zealously implement them.

The available evidence in a number of studies across countries suggests that there is a positive relationship between good governance and economic growth. An IMF empirical study (2003),[12] using geographic variables as instruments, found that governance has a statistically significant impact on GDP per capita across 93 countries, and that governance explains nearly 75 per cent of the cross country variations in income per head. A study by Huther and Shah (2005)[13] found that there is a high correlation between the quality of governance and per capita income. The positive correlation between the 10-year economic growth rate and governance quality supports the argument that it is an important determinant in economic development. As the highest income countries have generally not had the highest growth rates over the past decade, the positive correlation between higher growth and better governance suggests that good governance improves economic performance rather than vice versa. Kaufmann and Kraay (2002)[14] found direct causal effect from better governance to higher per capita income across countries in relation to 175 countries for the period 2000–01. Negative causal effect is also found from poor governance in relation to per capita income, implying that improvements in governance are unlikely to occur merely as a consequence of development. The simple correlation coefficient between per capita income and the quality of governance is significantly positive as the strong positive effects of governance dominate the correlation result. Using the technique of non-sample information (out-of-sample technique) through the Unobserved Component Model, the authors do not find any positive feedback from higher income to better governance outcomes (see Kaufmann and Kraay, 2002).

Barro has reported that better maintenance of the rule of law and political stability affect economic growth (Barro, 1991).[15] Dollar and Kraay found that the rule of law indicator is positively and significantly correlated with the growth in per capita incomes of the poorest quintile. They concluded that greater rule of law may be associated with a greater share of growth accruing to the lowest 20 per cent of the population.[16] Chong and Gradstein[17] discovered that political stability and the rule of law have a negative and significant relation with inequality as measured by the Gini coefficient. Kraay's[18] analysis leads him to conclude that the rule of law and accountability are both positively correlated with growth and distributional changes, while openness to international trade has a positive correlation with growth and poverty, reducing shifts in income. Kimenyi[19] argues that pro poor reforms cannot have the intended impact unless there are significant changes in the institutions of governance.

Cross-country studies by Mauro (1995) and Knack and Keefer (1995) have demonstrated that political instability, corruption, a poor quality of bureaucracy, and absence of the rule of law and the risk of expropriation are strongly correlated with lower investment and growth rates. In response to the critique of these studies by Khan (2002), the relationship between governance and growth for a set—limited only to developing countries— was tested, and it was concluded that governance-caused growth remained statistically significant. The exclusion of East Asian countries from the sample maintained the statistical significance but weakened the results.

Having made some tangible progress in meeting the Millennium Development Goal (MDG) of halving the incidence of poverty between 1990 and 2015, attention is now focused on inequality and the concentration of income. There is a popular feeling that the slowdown in economic growth and rising unemployment, particularly among the youth in advanced countries, can be traced to rising inequality and concentration of income in the hands of a few. This issue no longer remains confined to academic discussion but is now at the forefront of political dialogue and electoral debates in both advanced and developing countries.

The analysis of factors behind the global recession of 2008 and its lingering aftermath received a jolt from the seminal volume by Thomas Piketty.[20] He demonstrated that in contemporary market economies, the rate of return on investment outstrips the overall growth rate, and if that discrepancy persists over time, the wealth held by capitalists increases far more rapidly than other kinds of earnings, eventually outstripping them by a wide margin. Capital wealth is much larger than annual national income; in the case of developed economies it is about five to six times as large. Work by Nobel Prize laureate Joseph Stiglitz, Branko Milanovic, and many other serious economists has brought to the fore the phenomenon of growing inequality, particularly among the developed countries. The evidence to substantiate this viewpoint is overwhelming.

The incomes of the top one per cent of the population in the US, after adjusting for inflation, rose by 275 per cent between 1979–2007, those of the middle class by only 21 per cent, and the poor class a mere 11 per cent.[21] This miniscule group (the top one per cent) earns about a sixth of total income, and the top ten per cent earn as much as half of it. The median household income in the US, adjusted for inflation, fell 6.7 per cent, and was lower in 2009 in comparison to 1997. The top one per cent in the US owns as much wealth as 90 per cent of the population. George Packer notes, 'the more wealth accumulates in a few hands at the top, the more influence and favour the well-connected rich acquire, which makes it easier for them and their political allies to cast off restraint without paying a social price. That, in turn, frees them to amass new money.'

Fifty-eight per cent of economic growth in the US over a 30-year period was captured by this tiny group. The IRS reported in 2007 that the top 0.01 per cent of taxpayers had a combined income of $1 trillion. In Europe, austerity measures in the peripheral countries resulted in cuts in public expenditure, layoffs, retrenchments, a salary freeze, and rising youth unemployment—all adversely affecting those at the bottom of the income distribution scale. The majority of the population is suffering from weak growth, high unemployment, severe austerity, and anxiety about the future in an uncertain, globalized world. At the same time, the chief executives of large firms took home 250 times as much as their average worker as against a differential of 20 to 30 times in the 1970s. The number of millionaires and billionaires is expanding at an unprecedented pace in all parts of the world, even in a country such as India, which has a third of its population living below the poverty line.

The Arab Spring is demonstration of the disenchantment of the educated unemployed with the rapacious lifestyles of the elite, the repression by the él state to maintain the status quo, and the inability of the Arab states to generate productive jobs. The backlash against globalization, trade, immigration, and the flood of refugees entering Europe and the US and the rise of nationalist parties is also a manifestation of the same phenomenon. Whether it is the monarchs, dictators, and elected leaders becoming rich, or highly paid bankers, or big multinationals avoiding payment of their fair share of taxes, the disaffected are using the power of the social networks and the instantaneous communication they offer to coalesce and shake up the entrenched vested interests. The rage and fury of these disenchanted classes is spilling across national boundaries. Contagion is no longer confined to the international financial system but is equally applicable to social movements. There is ample evidence to demonstrate a correlation between elitist capture of economy and politics which is apparent from concentration of income, and the pace of economic development and political stability.

Mancur Olson has argued 'that nations decline because of the lobbying power of distributional coalitions or special interest groups whose growing influence fosters economic inefficiency and inequality'.[22] Jonathan Ostry and Andrew Berg[23] believe that inequality makes an important difference to the level of economic growth, such that more unequal societies have slower and more fragile economic growth. Deep inequality breeds resentment and political instability, and discourages investment. It can lead to political polarization and gridlock as it cleaves the political system between the interests of the rich and the poor. It can make it more difficult for governments to deal with brewing crises and economic imbalances. Growth is faster in more equal societies than in those that are less equal, regardless of whether they have redistributive tax systems. Inequality strongly correlates with a spell of economic expansion and thus less growth over time. For emerging and developing economies, inequality might foster political instability and lead to violence and economic destruction.[24]

Analyses of the factors contributing to this rising income inequality have sparked heated debate among scholars as well as policy-makers and the popular media. Martin Wolf[25] attributes this to globalization, technological changes, and winner takes all markets. Others believe that globalization contributes to inequality by creating a global labour pool that holds down wages while boosting corporate profits. Nigel Lawson is of the view that when businesses are considered too big, too important, or too interconnected, the crucial discipline of the market-place disappears and disaster is almost inevitable. What can possibly be done to cope with this phenomenon of growing inequality and elitist capture? Does this phenomenon arise due to malfunctioning of markets?

New Institutional Economics has advanced economic theories that identify institutional capabilities that states needed to make the markets function efficiently. Douglass North defines institutions 'as humanly devised constraints that structure political, the economic, and social interactions and include the laws, rules, customs, and norms constructed to advance and preserve social order'.[26] In regard to the link of institutions to economic development, his view is: 'How do we account for poverty in the midst of plenty? We must create incentives for people to invest in more efficient technology, increase their skills, and organize efficient markets. Such incentives are embodied in institutions.'[27]

Daron Acemoglu and Robinson in their study, 'Why Nations Fail?',[28] demonstrate that it is institutions that determine the fate of nations. Success comes when political and economic institutions are 'inclusive' and pluralistic, creating incentives for everyone to invest in the future. Nations fail when institutions are 'extractive', protecting the political and economic power of only a small elite that extracts income from everyone else. Institutions that promote good governance and facilitate broad-based and inclusive growth enjoy pride of place in development strategy.

According to Acemoglu and Johnson (2003), good institutions ensure two desirable outcomes: they provide relatively equal access to economic opportunity (a level playing field), and appropriately reward those who provide labour and protect their property rights.

Among the components of good governance, human capital is considered one of the factors that is associated with both economic growth and equity. In a study[29] on human capital and economic growth, the authors, using the data for the 1996–2011 period for 134 countries, found strong evidence in support of the hypothesis that the relationship between human capital and economic growth is much less pronounced in countries with a low quality of governance. Preconditions in the form of good governance are necessary for an educated labour force to contribute to the economic growth of a country. Weak governance, indicated by inadequate law and order, corruption, and maladministration result in inefficient utilization of human resources.

Rashida Haq and Uzma Zia[30] have explored linkages between governance and pro-poor growth in Pakistan for the period 1996 to 2005. The analysis indicates that governance indicators have low scores and rank at the lowest possible percentile in comparison to other countries. They found that the share in income of the bottom 20 per cent has decreased. The results of their study show that there is a strong linkage between governance indicators and pro-poor growth in the country, and econometric analysis showed that there is a strong relationship between good governance and reduction in poverty and income inequality. They concluded that voice and accountability, political stability, regulatory quality, and the rule of law can control corruption and encourage pro-poor policies which ultimately reduce poverty and inequality in the long run.

The model of an elitist economy that was articulated in *Pakistan: The Economy of an Elitist State* published in 1999,[31] sets out the historical context and the drivers of the capture of the state and market-rigging in Pakistan by a small elite—constituting about 1–2 per cent of the population—for self-aggrandizement, neglecting the majority of the population, particularly the poor and the less privileged segments of society. This small minority was thus able to enjoy this accumulation of wealth amidst widespread poverty and squalor. In the absence of a neutral umpire, markets are rigged by the elite for their own advantage, and thus market outcomes and resource allocation are inefficient. The state, which has to ensure equitable distribution of gains of economic growth, is also controlled by the same elite who evade taxes and appropriate the public expenditure for their own benefits. Inequities—interpersonal, regional, gender—become commonplace in such an environment. Over the past decade, there has been a growing concern about the glaring and growing income inequalities and the capture of the economy by small, elite classes elsewhere in the world, both advanced and developing.

Thus, both theoretical and cross country empirical evidence, as well as Pakistan's own experience, lend a great deal of weight to the argument that poor governance manifested by weak institutions, among many other factors, could be the predominant reason for Pakistan's unsatisfactory economic and social performance over the past quarter of a century, in relation to both, its own last four decades and other countries in the region. The evidence for this is the gradual decline in Pakistan's ranking and score on the following indices compiled by international and multilateral bodies, independent think tanks, academics, researchers, NGOS, and others for various years:

World Bank: *World Governance Indicators*
World Economic Forum: *Global Competitiveness Report*
UNDP: *Human Development Index*
Freedom House: *Economic Freedom Index*
Transparency International: *Corruption Perception Index*
International Country Risk Guide
UNESCO: *Education for All Index*
Legatum Prosperity Index

Sakib Sherani (2017)[32] has reviewed the World Governance Indicators for the period 1996–2015. His analysis shows that Pakistan has performed poorly in all six sub-components of governance. The average percentile rank for the 16 years, excluding political stability and absence of violence (extremely low), ranges from 18 to 32. He notes that in four of the six parameters—Government Effectiveness, Control of Corruption, Regulatory Quality, Political Stability and Absence of Violence, the best scores were recorded under President Musharraf (a period during which economic growth was also averaging 6–7 per cent annually). Again, there is some modest improvement in World Governance Indicators, Ease of Doing Business, and Corruption Perception Index for 2015 and 2016, when the economy was beginning to perform well. The same picture emerges by examining other indicators and indices comparing Pakistan with India and Bangladesh. Pakistan has fallen below these countries in the Human Development Index, Corruption Perception Index, and Legatum Prosperity Index, and continues to lag behind India and Bangladesh in Education for All and the Economic Freedom Index. The gap with India has also widened in the Global Competitiveness Index and Global Innovation Index.

The latest nationwide survey,[33] carried out in 2016 by the Pakistan Institute for Legislative Development and Transparency (PILDAT) on Quality of Democracy and Governance in Pakistan, shows that among its institutions, the highest approval rating of 76 per cent was scored by the armed forces and the lowest, at 25 per cent, by the police. Government officers, i.e. civil servants, were second to the bottom with a rating of 29 per cent, and the political parties were third from the bottom with a score of 35 per cent. Following the armed forces, the second top rank was that of the Supreme Court at 62 per cent, and the electronic media at 54 per cent.

A leading thinker, I. A. Rehman, very cogently sums up the state of institutions in Pakistan:

> In a stable democracy, fair elections produce a change only at the top, whilst the rest of the system does not suffer a personnel change. In an unstable state, elections are not fair and the result is a change of personnel along the line—department heads are changed, DPOs are replaced, heads of media organizations are changed, and above all, the *qabza* groups and commission agents that manipulate the sale of land and construction of plazas are replaced. Institutions are handed over to good-for-nothing individuals, merit is derided, and sycophancy rewarded. Can anyone fail to see what

Pakistan has become after six decades of a crusade against its people and their democratic right?

... the disintegration of the basic institutions of the state—the party, the parliament, the judiciary, the executive, and the military—has affected, in varying degrees, all subsidiary institutions such as educational institutions, industry chambers, the trade unions, the media and its commentators who never stop pontificating...[34]

The decay of civilian institutions can also partially explain the nature of civil-military relations in Pakistan and the gradual ascendancy of the military during this period. In the earlier decades of Pakistan's history, its civil services attracted the best talent and enjoyed the highest standards of competence, integrity, and commitment to resolve the problems faced by the citizens. The armed forces, on the other hand, recruited mostly mediocre people at the entry level and their breadth and range were quite limited in their education and exposure. While the civil services abandoned the principle of selection on merit, rigorous training to prepare for the next level, promotion based on performance, regular weeding out of those who did not keep up to the standards, the armed forces adopted and continued to religiously follow these principles. They transformed mediocre individuals into first rate human resource material while the civil services took the crème de la crème and turned the first rate talent either into cynics or self-serving individuals. To illustrate this, one example is quite striking. The IBA, a leading Pakistan business school, was invited by the Pakistan Armed Forces to send their faculty to military bases to provide in-house training. They were also asked to help design their programmes, such as Bachelor of Defence Management, in 1981. This continuing upgradation and rejuvenation of the armed forces was part of the strategy to transform the armed forces into a highly professional, efficient, and effective institution of the state. On the other hand, the sloth, inertia, preservation of the status quo, and alignment with the parochial interests of the ruling parties have made the civil services, and thus the institutions they man, quite unresponsive, inefficient, and ineffective. This is not by any means to suggest that the first period (1947–90) was an idyllic era when everything was hunky-dory, and all institutions functioned efficiently without interference from the politicians or indulgence in corrupt practices. Far from it. Even then there were reports and incidents of political leaders and then some of the military engaging in corruption, nepotism, and favouritism. The allegations of election rigging during General Ayub Khan's presidential election and acquisition of Gandhara Industries by his son, Gohar Ayub reverberated loudly. Zulfikar Ali Bhutto reportedly used the Federal Security Forces (FSF) to settle personal scores against his opponents. Several leading politicians were disqualified under Public Representatives Disqualification Order (PRODA) and Elected Bodies Disqualification Order (EBDO), and the service of thousands of civil servants summarily and arbitrarily terminated by Ayub, General Yahya Khan, and Bhutto on charges of corruption and malfeasance. Petty corruption and extortion by lower government functionaries was rampant during both periods. Patronage, kinship, *biradari,* tribal, and feudal relations pervaded throughout the system. However, on balance, the contribution of the civil servants and the institutions they manned during the first four decades far outweighed the negative damage perpetrated by a minority in their ranks. During informal consultations, focus group participants maintained that out of ten randomly selected higher civil servants in the earlier period, only two or three were found to be corrupt or pliable to extraneous influence. The tables began to turn from 1990 and today, out of a sample of ten such officers, only two or three would be found to be honest, conscientious, and immune to political pressures.

Whenever there is an institutional vacuum, the stronger entity fills in the space. Whether it is fighting the Taliban, clearing Karachi of the criminals and extortionists, evacuating people from the flood-affected or earthquake-struck areas, constructing highways in difficult terrain, or even collecting electricity bills, the army is called upon by the civil administration to take the lead and deliver. The constitutional requirement of holding a census every ten years was not being met because the army *jawans* are not available to assist in this. It is the incapacitation and inability of the civilian institutions of governance that has opened the way for the military to directly or indirectly assert itself and become the dominant player. The institutional imbalance between the military and the civilian structures can, inter alia, be ascribed largely to this growing gap in the capabilities of these two structures. This does not, by any means, absolve some army chiefs and their close confidants, whose personal ambitions to seize power have been a major factor in the disruption of the democratic framework. However, the malaises of corruption, incompetence, mismanagement, personal vendettas, and point-scoring among politicians and their cronies, and the failure to deliver public goods and services to the population at large, provided these generals the opportunity and justification to intervene. Hence, the actions of those who usurped power by removing elected governments and retarded democratic continuity cannot be condoned. This periodic disruption in constitutional rule also contributed to the weakening of political institutions. The institutional imbalance between the military and the civilian structures can, inter alia, be ascribed largely to this phenomenon. The statement by an analyst that 'The Military can be the stabilizer in [a] situation where Pakistan might otherwise falter being a weak state',[35] appears to be largely true.

This study is an attempt to address a difficult question: 'How can this asymmetric and unequal power relationship between the weak civilian institutional set-up and strong institution of the military be reversed for the long-term development of democracy and sustained economic growth and shared prosperity in Pakistan?' The troika of the chief of the army staff, president, and prime minister was perceived to have ruled Pakistan in the 1990s, and in the post-2008 democratic era, it is popularly believed that the army appears to be dictating terms in the areas of defence and nuclear capability, internal security, and foreign policy in relation to India, Afghanistan, and the US. The frequent calls to the military for overt or covert interventions by some politicians and opinion-makers is not in the interest of the long-term political, economic, and social stability of Pakistan. There is a widely accepted belief that if the district administration, law enforcement agencies, and the civilian intelligence agencies were performing their job well, the illegal and unlawful activities of the militant and extremist elements would have been nipped in the bud, and Pakistan would have avoided such a massive dislocation in its economic and social life. Were basic services such as education, healthcare, and justice accessible to common citizens, the drift towards the criminals–extremists nexus would not have taken root in society.

The challenge which is widely recognized by both the political leadership and the bureaucracy is how a vibrant, agile, and effective civilian institution can be rebuilt which is capable of delivering basic goods and services to the people, including access to justice, the provision of security to their life and property, and reigniting the growth impulses that had characterized the first half of Pakistan's existence. As a retired general very succinctly expressed it: 'While the armed forces maintain exceptionally high morale, prolonged involvement is not only putting the army under stress but also keeping it away from its conventional preparedness.'[36]

Any demarcation of boundaries between different periods can be challenged for its arbitrariness. Binary classifications suffer from the inherent problem of everything being painted either black or white. If we adopt a continuum approach, then the shift from grey towards black becomes perceptible sometime in the late 1980s and early 1990s. It must be conceded that the seeds of the institutional weakening were sown much earlier in the 1970s but the past momentum and the intervening period of Zia's rule in the 1980s did create a buffer which unravelled in the 1990s. The dominant tendencies became apparent and the black clouds began appearing during that period. The exception was the brief tenure of Prime Minister Mohammad Khan Junejo which provided an interesting interlude when a feudal politician from Sindh instituted sound government practices but this was not sustained over time. Ironically his successors, who ruled the country between 1988 and 1999, the leaders of two major established political parties, undid all his good work when they assumed power, and the pendulum swung in the opposite direction.

Diagnostic studies, particularly the conference volumes based on the Annual Conferences on Pakistan organized by the Woodrow Wilson Center at Washington,[37] suggest that every single crisis faced by Pakistan—low tax-mobilization, energy shortages, unsatisfactory law and order situation, losses sustained by the public sector enterprises, poor delivery of education and health services, and stagnating trade—can be traced back to this governance deficit and institutional weaknesses. Tax collectors enjoy wide discretionary powers which they utilize to extort money and enrich themselves rather than raise additional revenues for the exchequer. Power and gas companies find a huge gap between the sales revenues they assess, bill, and collect, and the purchases of units which they have to pay. Thefts, leakages, non-recovery, and overbilling have created a huge void between the receivables and payables. Law and order is bound to suffer, and the common citizen bound to feel insecure when police officials are appointed on the recommendations of elected members of the parliament and assemblies or in exchange for bribes rather than on their professional competence. These officials, after appointment in this manner, carry out the bidding of their benefactors rather than arresting, investigating, and prosecuting the criminals. Public sector enterprises are naturally bound to face losses when they become the dumping ground for thousands of surplus, incompetent employees on their payroll at the behest of the ruling party. In competitive markets they lose market share and in public monopolies they fleece their consumers but still incur losses due to inefficiency, waste, and corruption. There is a general consensus in Pakistan endorsed by international organizations that civilian institutions have decayed over time.

The World Bank, in one of its policy notes which forms part of its *Country Economic Memorandum of 2013*, stated: 'In a recent analysis of binding constraints to Pakistan's economy, bad governance and a poor civil service appear to be undermining economic growth. Without improving governance, other efforts in realizing the country's growth potential are destined to be less effective than they would be otherwise.'[38] The same view was echoed in the Framework for Economic Growth, which was adopted by the government of Pakistan during the Zardari period.

The Herald magazine and the Sustainable Development Policy Institute (SDPI) carried out a large-scale survey in 2013, and asked Pakistanis what the most important obstacle to economic progress was. The most frequent answer was 'corruption', followed by 'incompetent leadership', and 'poor governance'. Young entrepreneurs in Pakistan[39] believe that corruption is a major constraint to industrial and economic development.

The National Commission for Government Reforms (NCGR) members drawn from both the private and public sector travelled throughout Pakistan during 2006–08, consulted a range of stakeholders, conducted field studies, made on the spot observations about the delivery of public services, and reviewed research work in compiling their report. The Commission has made exhaustive recommendations regarding the structure, human resource policies, the business process reengineering of the federal, provincial, and local governments, public enterprises and corporations, autonomous bodies, and the like. The recommendations of the Commission have not been accepted or implemented by three successive governments. It would therefore be unrealistic to expect that comprehensive reforms of the civil services and the civilian institutions of governance are feasible. These recommendations have not been implemented even though the top political leadership feels frustrated that the gap between their pronouncements and actual delivery is widening and damaging their credibility. Notwithstanding this recognition, resistance to changing the status quo is strong. Inefficient policies and weak institutions can be easily manipulated by the politically powerful elite.

This study reflects upon the experience of the past five years since the submission of the report, particularly in the light of the Eighteenth Amendment to the Constitution devolving legislative, administrative, and financial powers to the provinces. The recent elections of the local governments provided another opportunity to devolve these powers further to the grassroots level which has been done only in one province, i.e. Khyber Pakhtunkhwa (KP). Other provinces have retrogressed by returning the powers to the provincial governments.

The political economy of reforming policies and restructuring institutions for broad-based growth of the majority of the population is not well understood. 'Lack of political will' has become the catch-all phrase to describe the failure to change, but this is a loose and imprecise term. The question that arises then is: 'How can the incentives of political leaders be aligned to make them compatible with the desired change agenda, and make the "political will" work for a desirable outcome.' The dilemma facing academics and technocratic policy reformers is that inefficient policies and institutions exist and the status quo is defended because it suits the politically influential elite, but the constituency and coalitions for efficient policies and strong institutions do not exist. If the first best solution of comprehensive, across-the-board reforms is not feasible, can a second or third best solution of a selective and incremental approach of taking up a few key institutions of democratic governance be designed, which does not meet the same kind of fierce resistance but has powerful spill-over effects that may over time embrace and occupy a larger space?

In Pakistan, the labelling and characterization of the state as the 'Invisible State', 'Deep State', or 'Garrison State' has become the popular narrative, and all the prevailing ills are attributed to this set of characteristics of the state. A great deal has already been written on the subject by both academic scholars as well as the popular media. This study does however examine the organs of state and at the same time also looks at the society, polity, economy, private sector, religious edifice, and external actors, as they have all played or play a role in the way Pakistan has been governed over time, and economic and social policy choices it has made. It is the interrelation and interaction of all these forces and the state that produces the final outcomes. A preliminary attempt has been made to divide history into several phases and offer subjective judgement about which of these institutions have actually dominated that particular period.

However, I focus on the state-oriented institutions for possible restructuring and reform, and among them a few key institutions that can play a catalytic role in bringing about and restoring the original position of equilibrium from which Pakistan began its journey in the early decades of its existence. This is possible if these key civilian institutions can be put back on the same pathway—merit, integrity, dedicated service, and problem-solving—that historically was their principal asset. Democratic governance can be strengthened only if the supporting institutions regain their lost stature and are able to assert the writ of the state, i.e. government effectiveness, control of corruption, improvement of regulatory oversight, establishment of the rule of law, accountability, and facilitation of the private sector and civil society.

This study also attempts to explore and understand the critical factors which enabled India and Bangladesh, facing an identical external environment with weak institutions, to do so well economically while Pakistan became a laggard and failed to exploit its potential.

India, Bangladesh, and other developing countries have made great strides in growth, poverty reduction, and improved living standards, and moved forward over the past 25 years. Were they able to find safeguards or checks and balances that minimized the adverse political influences on the key institutions of democratic governance? How far did they use private sector and civil society organizations to compensate for the pitfalls of the public sector in the economic revival and delivery of social services to the population? Given the historical, legal, and cultural similarities with Pakistan and the prevalence of widespread corruption in these countries, how were they able to forge ahead? The lessons learnt from these countries' experiences will help Pakistan to sequence and phase the proposed agenda for governance reforms. Identifying the sources of the political compatibility and feasibility of reforms would be a valuable contribution of this study.

The hypothesis underlying this study is that the roots of the decline in the economic growth rate of Pakistan and its diminishing participation in the dynamic global economy can be traced to the gradual decay in its key institutions of governance and their malfunction. This is not to acknowledge many success stories of organizations that have survived over time and succeeded in delivering the desired results. There are already many examples of successful institutions working quite well in the midst of this general atmosphere of institutional decay and their success reflects adherence to the same principles. The performance of the Punjab government in many respects is much superior to that of other provinces and it can be attributed to strong exemplary leadership but its sustainability will only be assured if its institutional infrastructure is also strengthened.

Mahmood Ayub and Turab Hussain, in their study *Candles in Dark*,[40] have documented at least ten such institutions in various sectors run by the government, private foundations, and NGOs, and drawn lessons underpinning their success. In addition, the State Bank of Pakistan, the National Highway and Motor Police, the National Data Registration Authority (NADRA), the Sind Institute of Urology and Transplant (SIUT), Indus Hospital, Aga Khan University and Hospital, Punjab Education

Foundation, Benazir Income Support Program (BISP), HEJ Institute, and the Skills Development Co, are usually considered islands of excellence amidst overall decay. A new form of organizational structure, i.e. companies established by the government of Punjab under the Companies Act, provides an alternate model in the organizational architecture of the government. It is therefore possible that the lessons learnt from these success stories can be applied to other key institutions, and this is critical in achieving the development objectives. The thrust of the argument is, however, that most of key institutions responsible for discharging the functions of security, growth, and equity have fallen behind and are suffering from governance malfunction.

The analytical framework for this study is based on the 2017 *World Development Report* on 'Governance and Law'.[41] The Report uses the term 'governance' as 'the process through which state and non-state actors interact to design and implement policies within a given set of formal and informal rules that shape and are shaped by power'. Power is defined by it 'as the ability of groups and individuals to make others act in their interest and to bring about specific outcomes'. The *WDR* sets out three principles for rethinking governance for development. Rather than investing in designing the right form of policies, the emphasis should be on the functions that institutions must perform. Second, while capacity-building matters, how to use the capacity and where to invest in capacity depends upon the relative bargaining power of actors. Third, in order to achieve the rule of law, countries must first strengthen the different roles of law to enhance contestability, change incentives, and reshape preferences. In practical terms, the framework is translated into a Policy Effectiveness chain that comprises five steps:

1. define the development objective,
2. identify the underlying functional problem (commitment, coordination, cooperation),
3. identify the relevant entry point for reform (incentives, preferences/beliefs, contestability),
4. identify the best mechanism for intervention (menu of policies and laws),

5. identify key stakeholders needed to build a coalition for implementation (elites, citizens, international).

This study will apply, wherever possible, the elements of the policy effectiveness chain to Pakistan and make recommendations that can help in strengthening this chain.

Using the above framework, (1) the development objectives for Pakistan which are broadly shared by a vast majority of people as well as political parties and other stakeholders are Security, Growth, and Equity; (2) for Pakistan, the underlying functional problem is a lack of commitment by successive political and military leaders to replace what suits their parochial interests but not collective public interests in the existing patron-client relationship; (3) the institutions that should carry out these functions will encompass state, society, and markets but this study will limit itself to state-oriented institutions alone; (4) this study proposes a second and third best solution of selective and incremental intervention rather than comprehensive reforms sweeping across the board; (5) the key stakeholders for implementation would be the legislatures, federal, provincial, and local governments, the judiciary, the military, and law enforcement agencies, the private sector and businesses, civil society and citizens' organizations, and international actors

In light of the above, it is important that first the relationship between the state, markets, and society is revisited and the boundaries clearly demarcated. Markets are efficient in producing, exchanging, and trading goods and services and allocating scarce resources but in doing so only those that are already well-endowed are rewarded. If an individual possesses land, capital, natural resources, or skills, the market will do a good job in ensuring a decent return on these assets. If, however, an individual is uneducated, poor, handicapped, or unskilled, the market inflicts pain, for it has little use for such a person. For such segments of the population, the state has to step in by taxing a fraction of the incomes earned by the well-endowed and transfer that to the less well-to-do through public expenditure on education, skill upgradation, healthcare, drinking water, sanitation, and social transfers. Moreover, Dani Rodrik has ably argued that markets are organized around private property and neither property rights nor markets can function on their own. They require other social institutions to support them. Therefore, property rights rely on courts and legal enforcement, and markets depend upon regulations to rein in abuse and fix market failures. State institutions have to therefore set the legal and regulatory framework and the ground rules under which private businesses operate. The regulators have to ensure that competition and not collusion prevails in the marketplace, consumers are protected, and health, safety, and environmental standards are observed, and that a level playing field is ensured for all those participating in the market. The state has to intervene to promote innovation and entrepreneurship by investing in STEM education, vocational and technical training, research and development, technology parks etc. The state is also responsible for maintaining law and order and security, enforcing the rule of law, protecting property rights, and adjudicating and arbitrating in disputes and contracts between the private parties. All these functions are heavily dependent upon the quality of institutions and government effectiveness.

Sensible economic policies do not get translated into action because of the dysfunctionality of the institutions implementing those policies. Society, through the media, NGOs and CSOs, professional bodies, labour unions, citizen groups, human rights and women's rights organizations, and the like, has to play an important role in maintaining vigilance on the state and market institutions, and also participate in the provision of social services such as education and health wherever possible.

Although there are linkages and overlap in the institutions aimed at implementing the three development objectives, a preliminary sketch of the tasks before the predominant institutions to achieve each of these objectives is provided below.

Growth

According to the IMF, Pakistan's potential GDP growth has gradually declined over the years and the output gap has nearly closed.[42] The way forward to improve Pakistan's potential growth is through productivity. In turn, an improvement in productivity requires a business-friendly environment where the government delivers basic services efficiently, promotes the rule of law, reduces corruption, and streamlines business regulation. Pakistan currently ranks 138 out of 189 economies in the World Bank's *Doing Business Report 2016* and 126 out of 140 in the World Economic Forum's *Global Competitiveness Report 2015–16*. Technology Transfer through FDI has been shown to diffuse new technologies and management methods to local firms, raising their competitiveness. Thus, in the ultimate analysis, it is the strength of the institutions centred on markets, the private sector, and businesses that will raise the growth potential of the economy. Creating jobs for 1–1.5 million new entrants to the labour force is a challenge that can be met only through growth rates of around 7–8 per cent annually. Increased female labour force participation would contribute both to growth as well as a reduction in gender disparities.

EQUITY

In a multi-ethnic and multi-linguistic country such as Pakistan, redressal or mitigation of regional and provincial income and social disparities becomes an issue of paramount importance to maintain national and social cohesion.

Punjab, as a province, has progressed ahead of the other three provinces. While there may be some cogent and rational reasons for this outcome, the perception that the majority province is moving ahead at the expense of the smaller ones must be boldly addressed. However, the disparities are not along the provincial boundaries because there are better-off areas and deprived ones within each province. Central and northern Punjab, urban Sindh, Peshawar valley, and parts of Hazara division, Islamabad, and Quetta are relatively better off in terms of their standing as measured by the Deprivation Index and Multipurpose Poverty Index but the situation in southern Punjab, rural Sindh, Malakand and DIK divisions, and the rest of Balochistan is a matter of great concern. Some of the factors responsible for this differentiation are the availability of productive job opportunities and livelihoods, proximity or remoteness from markets, and the supply of basic public services. Access by the poor to basic public services is problematic because of diversion of the scarce resources at the disposal of the institutions supplying these services to the elite. It is here that society-centric institutions have to step in and play the role of watch-dog on the activities of the state and markets, so that no transgressions take place, public services are provided to the poor and marginalized populations, and ensure that citizens' rights are not violated. There have been several instances of non-governmental organizations (NGOs) actively supplementing the state in the provision of public services such as education, healthcare etc. It is also expected that the opening up of the backward districts of Balochistan and KP through the CPEC energy and infrastructure projects will help integrate the people and the markets into the national economy and thus contribute to reducing inequality.

Security

Pakistan's Armed Forces are considered among the best in the developing world, having maintained and imbibed high standards of professionalism. On the other hand, the police, lower judiciary, prosecution departments, and prisons have lost their vigour and effectiveness and enabled serious problems of law and order, and security of person and property. Compliance with the law is, in general, weak and this is exacerbated by discriminatory practices whereby the influential and well-connected escape violation of law, while the poor are harassed and extorted on the basis of unfounded allegations. The judicial process is expensive, cumbersome, and time consuming, and only those who have the financial means can afford to engage with the process. Criminals and offenders get off scot free because of the low conviction rate resulting from weak prosecution. Criminals who are incarcerated and have the resources can enjoy reasonably comfortable lives in the prisons. This entire chain of institutions responsible for the administration of justice needs to be completely overhauled.

Notes and References

1. Burki, S. J., *Pakistan Fifty years of Nationhood*, Westview Press, 1999.

2. IMF, 'Pakistan Selected Issues Paper', *IMF Country Report No.16/2*, 2016.

3. The Haqqani network is part of the Afghan Taliban and the US has accused this terror group of carrying out terrorist activities in Afghanistan against the US and NATO forces; The Pakistan government's participation and facilitation to the US troops has evoked negative and hostile reaction among the extremist groups. All these groups have coalesced to form the Tehreek-i-Taliban Pakistan (TTP) which has publicly declared a war against the state of Pakistan. They have organized suicide bombings in public places, carried out assassination attempts on the president and prime minister, and perpetrated attacks on military installations throughout Pakistan.

4. Martinsson, M., 'Interview of Mattis Martinsson with BR Research', *Business Recorder*, 5 December 2016.

5. Hasan, P., *Pakistan's Economy at the Crossroads* (Karachi: OUP, 1998), 193.

6. McCartney, M., *Pakistan: The Political Economy of Growth, Stagnation and the State, 1951–2009* (New York and London: Routledge, 2011).

7. Radelet, S., *The Great Surge: The Ascent of the the Developing World.* (New York: Simon & Schuster, 2016).

8. UNDP, *Human Development Report 2015* (New York, 2016).

9. Haqqani, H., *Pakistan: Between Mosque and Military* (Washington DC: Carnegie Endowment for International Peace, 2016); Idem, *Magnificent Delusions,* (New York: Preseus Books, Publicaffairs, 2013); Shah, A., *The Army and the Democracy Military Politics in Pakistan,* (Cambridge: Harvard University Press, 2014); Abbas, H., *Pakistan's Drift with Extremism: Allah, the Army and America's War of Terror* (New York and London: Routledge, 2005).

10. Naviwala, N., *Pakistan's Education Crisis: The Real Story* (Washington DC: Woodrow Wilson Center, 2016).

11. Olson, M., 'Big Bills Left on the Sidewalk: Why Some Nations are Rich and Others Poor', in S. Knack (ed.), Democracy, *Governance and Growth* (Anne Arbor: The University of Michigan Press, 1972).

12. Baldacci, E, Kojo, N., Hillman, A., *Growth, Governance, and Fiscal Policy Transmission Channels in Low-Income Countries,* IMF Working Paper WP/03/237, 2003.

13. Huther, J., Shah, 'Ch. 2: A Simple Measure of Good Governance', *Public Services Delivery*, 39.

14. Kaufmann, D., A. Kraay, *Growth without Governance*, World Bank Policy Research Working Paper (World Bank, Washington DC, 2002), 292.

15. Barro, R., 'Economic Growth in a Cross Section of Countries', *Quarterly Journal of Economics* 106, 407–43.

16. Dollar, D., A. Kraay, *Growth is Good for the Poor, Journal of Economic Growth* 7, 2002, 195–225.

17. Chong and Gradstein, *Inequality and Institutions*, Working paper no. 506, Inter-American Development Bank Research Department, 2002.

18. Kraay, *When is Growth Pro Poor?* Working Paper 3225, Cross Country Experience World Bank Policy Research.

19. Kimenyi, M. S., 'Institutions of Governance, Power Diffusion and Pro poor Growth Policies', Paper Presentation. Cape Town, Johannesburg: VII Senior Policy Seminar at Applied Economics Research Centre, 2005.

20. Piketty, T., *Capitalism in the 21st Century* (Cambridge: Harvard University Press, 2015)

21. Packer, G., 'The Broken Contract: Inequality and American Decline', *Foreign Affairs*. Nov–Dec. 2011: 90(6).

22. Olson, M., *The Rise and Decline of Nations: Economic Growth, Stagflation, and Economic Rigidities* (Yale University Press, 1982)

23. Ostry, J. D., A. Berg, *Inequality and Unsustainable Growth: Two sides of the same coin?* (No. 11/08), International Monetary Fund, 2011.

24. Ostry, Berg, H. Tsangarides, *Redistribution, Inequality, and Growth,* IMF Staff Discussion Note, February 2014.

25. Wolf, M., 'Seven Ways to Fix the System's Flaws', *Financial Times*, 23 January 2012.

26. Douglas, N., 'Institutions', *Journal of Economic Perspectives*, 1991, 5(1), 640.

27. North, D., *Institutions, Institutional Change, and Economic Performance* (Cambridge: Cambridge University Press, 1990).

28. Acemoglu, D., Robinson, J., *Why Nations Fail?* (New York: Crown Press, 2012)

29. Muhammad, A., Egbetoken, A., et al., 'Human Capital and Economic Growth', *Pakistan Development Review*, Winter 2015, 529–49.

30. Haq, R., Zia, U., '*PIDE Working paper*', 2009, 52.

31. Husain, I., *Pakistan: The Economy of An Elitist State* (Karachi: OUP, 1999).

32. Sherani, S., *Institutional Reform in Pakistan,* Report submitted to Friedrich Ebert Stiftung (FES), 2017.

33. PILDAT, *Assessment of the Quality of Democracy in Pakistan,* January 2017, Islamabad.

34. Rehman, I. A., 'The Crisis of Institutions in Pakistan', *The News*, 8 February 2009.

35. Personal interview, 23 March 2016 Islamabad.

36. Khattak, M. S., 'The New COAS', *Express Tribune*, 28 November 2016.

37. Diagnostic studies presented at the Annual Conference on Pakistan organized by Woodrow Wilson Center include: R. Hathaway and W. Lee, (eds.), *Islamization and the Pakistani Economy* (Washington DC: Woodrow Wilson Center Asia Program, 2004); R. Hathaway and M. Kugelman, *Education Reform in Pakistan* Washington DC: Woodrow Wilson Center Asia Program, 2005); B. Muchhala, R. Hathaway, and M. Kugelman, (eds.), *Fueling the Future: Meeting Pakistan's Energy Needs in the 21st Century* (Washington DC: Woodrow Wilson Center Asia

Program, 2007); idem, *Running on Empty: Pakistan's Water Crisis* (Washington DC: Woodrow Wilson Center Asia Program, 2009); idem, *Hunger Pains: Pakistan's Food Insecurity* (Washington DC: Woodrow Wilson Center Asia Program, 2010); P. Nayak, and R. Hathaway (eds.), *Aiding Without Abetting: Making U.S. Civilian Assistance to Pakistan Work for Both Sides* (Washington DC: Woodrow Wilson Center Asia Program, 2011); R. Hathaway, and M. Kugelman, (eds.), *Reaping the Dividend: Overcoming Pakistan's Demographic Challenges* (Washington DC: Woodrow Wilson Center Asia Program, 2011; idem, *Pakistan-India Trade: What Needs To Be Done? What Does It Matter?* (Washington DC: Woodrow Wilson Center Asia Program, 2013); idem, *Pakistan's Runaway Urbanization: What Can Be Done?* (Washington DC: Woodrow Wilson Center Asia Program); idem, *Pakistan's Interminable Energy Crisis: Is There Any Way Out?* (Washington DC: Woodrow Wilson Center Asia Program, 2016).

38. Rana, N., Idris, I., Touqeer, I., *Revamping Governance*, Pakistan Policy Note 13, The World Bank Group South Asia Region (Washington DC, 2013).

39. Chamber of Commerce and Industry Islamabad, 2012.

40. Ayub, M., T. Hussain, *Candles in the Dark* (Karachi: OUP, 2015).

41. World Bank, *World Development Report* 2017 (Washington DC, 2017).

42. IMF, 'Improving Pakistan's Competitiveness and Business Climate', Selected Issues Paper, January 2016.

2

Historical Background

Pakistan inherited a well-functioning judiciary, civil service, and military but a relatively weak system of legislative oversight at the time of its Independence. Over time, the domination of the civil service and military in the affairs of the state disrupted the evolution of a democratic political process and further weakened the legislative organ of the state. The judicial arm, with few exceptions, plodded along sanctifying the dominant role of the military and the civil service until the early twenty-first century.

The British had built institutions, both civilian and military, which were both strong and effective but Pakistan entered the path to governance with a serious disadvantage. The financial, organizational, and human resources it inherited at the time of Independence were extremely inadequate in relation to the huge needs of the newly formed state. Ayesha Jalal rightly observes:

> The new state of Pakistan was crippled by its colonial inheritance, a result of its relatively sparse share of colonial administrative resources and structures in comparison with India, where continuity and a ready-made postcolonial state eased the transition to independent statehood.[1]

It was extremely commendable that notwithstanding such a disadvantaged legacy, the civil services inherited from the British era performed extremely well in the early period of Pakistan's history. They were competent, diligent, dedicated, and honest. Millions of refugees from India were settled, new businesses and industries were established as the Hindu owners left the country, basic public services were restored throughout the country, law and order and security of life and property were assured, and institutions of governance and economic development were set up and nurtured.

Muhammad Ali Jinnah, the founder of Pakistan, was quite clear in his mind that the new government in Pakistan would build the foundations of the institutions of governance on the basis of the legacy it had inherited but uproot nepotism and jobbery. Stanley Wolpert[2] quotes his conversation with the governor of Sindh, which shows Jinnah's plans for governance in Pakistan.

Jinnah said at a party given by Sir G. H. Hidayatullah, Governor of Sindh at Karachi Club on 9 August 1947:

> Let us trust each other ... let us judge by results not by theories. With the help of every section, let us work to make the sovereign state of Pakistan really happy, really united, and really powerful ... There is a legacy which has been passed on to us ... the evil of nepotism and jobbery. This evil must be crushed relentlessly. I want to make it quite clear that I shall never tolerate any kind of jobbery, nepotism or any influence directly or indirectly brought to bear on me.

Although he did not survive long after the creation of Pakistan and his close lieutenant, Prime Minister Liaquat Ali Khan, also passed away soon thereafter, Pakistan enjoyed a relatively clean government for a long period of time. Once these two leaders were gone, the Muslim League suffered a series of splits and Waseem[3] believes that 'party careers increasingly depended on bureaucratic patronage rather than organizational promotion'. Frequent changes in political leadership in 1951–58 increasingly placed the onus on the civil servants who had opted for Pakistan, and the new recruits who were groomed and trained by their seniors in the old tradition of commitment, integrity, and goal-orientation. Burki[4] sums up the situation as follows: 'this disintegration of the Muslim League and production of nine highly unstable governments ... admirably suited the Civil Services of Pakistan (CSP). It flourished and thrived in the near political vacuum in which it had been called in to perform'. The politicians were quite content to let the day-to-day administration be handled by it.

The induction of top-ranking civil servants such as Ghulam Mohammad (who subsequently became the governor general), Chaudhry Mohammad Ali (who became prime minister), and Iskander Mirza (who became president) into the higher echelons of government allowed the civil servants unfettered access and support even when the political leaders sought to meddle in their affairs. The secretaries to the government occupying the highest positions in the bureaucracy and their subordinates had the confidence that their decisions would be upheld, and that they would be protected by the higher echelons of power such as the governor general and the prime minister. Khalid Bin Sayeed has characterized this period as one during which politicians were placed under bureaucratic tutelage, and traces this back to Jinnah who 'relied increasingly on the civil service toward the end of his life.[5] The first phase, 1947–58, can be characterized as one of bureaucratic dominance.

The martial law imposed by Ayub Khan in 1958 began with a purge of some senior civil servants and an effective takeover of the administration by military officers. However, Ayub soon realized that he had to rely upon the civil servants to run civil and day-to-day administration. His own colleagues in the military did not have either the training or the experience for the job. After some hesitation in the initial years, his principal advisers were drawn from the ranks of the higher cadres of the Central Superior Services headed by the CSP. The governors of both East and West Pakistan, appointed by Ayub, were from the Police Service of Pakistan (PSP) and the CSP. His finance minister was an officer from the Accounts Service. This military–civil service nexus actually ruled Pakistan for the next seven years, 1962–69. The elections to the national and provincial assemblies were held after the promulgation of a new constitution in 1962, and the cabinets comprising elected representatives were formed. Actual power was exercised by the commissioners, chief secretaries, federal secretaries, and the inspectors general of police. Most of the reforms carried out during this period, which made Pakistan a model developing country in the 1960s, were based on the reports and recommendations[6] of the various national commissions comprising technical experts under the direction of the heads of the ministries and departments. Foreign experts from developed countries were invited to advise and help in creating new institutions.

During the first two decades, the civilian institutions retained their steel frame and were therefore able to play a critical role in meeting multifarious, complex, and difficult challenges faced by the new country. They were instrumental in rehabilitating millions of refugees equalling one fourth of the total population, establishing industries from scratch as few existed in this part of the subcontinent, and reviving agriculture and food production to achieve food security. Successful negotiations with India, and successfully negotiating the Indus Waters Treaty were a key determinant of Pakistan's subsequent achievement of food self-sufficiency. As part of the Treaty, one of the largest construction programmes—the Indus Basin works with large storage dams and link canals, barrages etc.—was carried out by the engineers under the supervision of the Water and Power Development Authority (WAPDA), a strong institution created to harness Pakistan's water and energy resources.

Peace, order, and administration of justice were quite well managed by the law enforcement agencies and the judiciary. The Planning Commission in the 1960s enjoyed stature and autonomy and had the competence to initiate and monitor the implementation of various reforms. Other developing countries followed the example set by India and Pakistan and established their own planning organizations. Malaysia had its Economic Planning Unit (EPU), Indonesia BAPPENAS, Thailand its National Economic and Social Development Board (NESDB), the Philippines a National Economic Development Authority (NEDA), and Korea an Economic Planning Board (EPB) and Korea Development Institute (KDI). Lastly, in China, this task has been performed since 1980 by the National Development Reform Commission (NDRC) aided by a think tank, the China Society of Economic Reforms (CSER).

Several other development-oriented institutions such as, Pakistan Industrial Development Corporation (PIDC) for industrial development; Pakistan International Airlines (PIA), the national carrier; Agriculture Development Corporation (ADC) for agricultural development; Pakistan Industrial Credit and Investment Corporation (PICIC) and Industrial

Development Bank of Pakistan (IDBP) for industrial financing; Agriculture Development Bank of Pakistan (ADBP) for agriculture financing; Karachi Development Authority (KDA), Lahore Development Authority (LDA), and Capital Development Authority (CDA), etc. for urban planning and development; and the provincial planning boards that came into existence during this period, served as models for other developing countries. The civil services' personnel who managed and ran these institutions retained the tradition of an open, competitive, merit-based recruitment; rigorous pre-service training followed by postings in the field for on the job training; mid-career in service training; performance-based promotions and career progression; adequate compensation, perks and a status, and prestige and respect based on personal integrity that was emulated by other professionals. Those selected were not only the best and the brightest but had a deep sense of commitment to public service. They enjoyed security of service guaranteed by the constitution and therefore the exercise of arbitrary and discretionary powers and interference of the ruling parties in their work could be resisted. Young recruits began their careers in the field working at the lowest units of administration but were given assignments that exposed them to a variety of situations. Rotation between field and policy assignments, and working in various provinces, provided them with diverse experience. They, therefore, remained in touch with the real problems faced by the ordinary citizens, and designed and implemented policies to resolve them. This hands-on, diverse problem-solving experience helped them immensely when they rose to higher positions and manned various institutions of governance in the country.

Being assigned heavy and complex responsibilities at a young age, having rotated among different types of challenging jobs, and solving problems relating to millions of people living in their districts, equipped these young men and women with leadership qualities which helped them when they reached top positions in the institutions of governance. If one could construct a composite index of Efficiency, Effective Service, Delivery, and Integrity, the civil services of Pakistan would score quite high in the base year 1960. Goodnow[7] estimated the major accomplishments of the CSP, and found it to have been successful in bringing a degree of order out of chaos and collecting revenues. He, however, pointed out that 'Pakistan's legislature could not control the CSP because the higher services had been given considerable constitutional protection against political influence. To protect competence, responsiveness was sacrificed.'

Authoritarian regimes devoid of legitimate political power are, perforce, impelled to use the instruments of state power to win or maintain coalitions, construct new alliances, or take coercive measures against recalcitrant individuals and groups. The Basic Democracies system, introduced by Ayub Khan to win legitimacy for his continuation in power, was responsible for the loss of popularity and credibility of his regime. The disaffection with the military regime was exploited by Sheikh Mujibur Rehman and his party, the Awami League. Mujib's arrest and trial in the Agartala Conspiracy Case inadvertently facilitated his rise to the height of popularity in East Pakistan. The Six Points agenda of autonomy propounded by him became the manifesto of the Awami League and swept it to a huge majority in the 1970 elections in East Pakistan. The subsequent reluctance shown by President Yahya Khan in transferring power to the elected leader of the majority party, i.e. the Awami League, further reinforced the suspicion and mistrust of the Bengalis against the Pakistan Army and West Pakistan.

The post-25 March 1971 events eventually led to a civil war in which India backed the separatist forces in East Pakistan demanding independence from Pakistan. The civil war ended with the emergence of an independent state of Bangladesh. This rupture between East Pakistan and West Pakistan negated the very concept upon which Pakistan was founded. Although East Pakistan benefited from Ayub's economic reforms and the decade of development, the reality is that his government was perceived to be perpetuating a quasi-colonial military regime in a colony, i.e. East Pakistan, and this proved to be fatal. I. A. Rehman (*Dawn*, 20 July 2009) argues that the central establishment decided on a trade-off between autonomy and development but this manoeuvre failed in East Pakistan and 'it is unlikely to succeed in Baluchistan and the tribal areas'. The lesson is that no federating unit will surrender its right to autonomy in exchange for any development works however huge their economic benefits.

Zulfikar Ali Bhutto, a former foreign minister under Ayub, took advantage of this resentment against the latter's economic policies in West Pakistan and formed his own political party—Pakistan Peoples Party (PPP). He promised to restore the principle of distributive justice and equity to the forefront of Pakistan's development strategy under the slogan of Islamic socialism.[8] Bhutto was a popularly elected, charismatic leader who came to power at the lowest point in the history of the military, and is credited with putting the army generals in their place and abolishing the elite Pakistan civil service but he too missed the opportunity of strengthening the institutional framework of democratic governance. He would have avoided the use of the military in the counterinsurgency operations in Balochistan had he not arbitrarily dismissed the elected government of the National Awami Party (NAP).

To reduce the constant dependence on the military to come to the aid the civil administration, he created a special civilian armed organization called the Federal Security Force (FSF) which ironically led to his own political downfall and later, his sentencing by the Supreme Court. The FSF was purportedly used to settle personal scores and harass Bhutto's political opponents. It was after the FSF opened fire and killed Jamaat-i-Islami (JI) and IJT supporters that nationwide protests began. Curfews had to be imposed in Karachi, Hyderabad, and Lahore and the army had to be called in to restore order. The principal witness against Bhutto in the murder case, on the basis of which he was sentenced to death, was the testimony of his chosen head of the FSF, Masood Mahmood, who had turned approver against his benefactor. It is a shame that his autocratic, highly personalized, and intolerant attitude towards his own partymen and others who dissented or disagreed with him should have been the principal stumbling block to the relative ascendancy of civilian institutions.

Burki[9] has observed:

Over the half century—certainly after the assumption of power in 1971 by Bhutto—Pakistan systematically destroyed the institutions it inherited from the British Raj. India did the opposite; significantly improved upon its institutional inheritance. In the institutional graveyard that Pakistan had become, tombstones carried such names as civil administration and the system of governance; the judicial and legal system; the system for formulating and implementing economic and social strategies; colleges, universities and the system of education.

The trigger point for the gradual decay of the institutions of governance was indeed initiated during Bhutto's populist government. Burki[10] argues that under Ayub, the Planning Commission (PC) had used a variety of devices to direct public and private expenditure but Bhutto found these plans cumbersome, and was not inclined to accept the discipline the PC imposed. Instead, he used prime ministerial directives as the major tool for allocation of development funds. The power of the PM's secretariat increased and the Planning Commission was weakened. Burki[11] terms this as:

> economic decision-making without constraints as the CSP was abolished, the PC was weakened, and the PM Directives became the major tool for development spending. Karachi Steel, Indus Highway, Nuclear Power plant, the Lowari Pass Tunnel, and ZAB Sports and Culture Institute were examples of economic decisions taken for essentially non-economic reasons.

One important consequence of this type of 'decision-making without constraints', according to Burki, was that the sectors that needed development resources and could have helped the country out of a number of its economic difficulties did not receive the attention they deserved.

It would not be unfair to surmise that the process of institutional decay can be traced back to the period in which Bhutto was at the helm of the affairs. His disdain for the civil service's CSP cadre was reflected in the summary dismissal of 1,300 officers soon after he assumed power as Martial Law Administrator. It was for the first time in the history of Pakistan that a civilian leader had taken over the position of Martial Law Administrator. The seeds of recourse to extra-constitutional measures were sown during this period. The dismissal was followed by drastic reforms that led to the abolition of the CSP cadre, introduction of All Pakistan Unified Grades (APUG), removal of the constitutional guarantee of security of employment, etc.

National pay-scales that compressed and pigeonholed all the public servants in Grades 1–22 played havoc with the incentive structure. Lateral induction of persons into higher superior services generated a great deal of frustration and resentment among those who had been recruited through an open, competitive examination and interview system because they felt that their career prospects were being blighted by the lateral entrants selected on the basis of their connections with the political leaders, and that the latter would get preference in promotions. The signalling effect of these reforms upon the young men and women aspiring to make the civil service a career was negative. Until now, there had been a trade-off between job security and lower compensation on the one hand and an accelerated career path on the other. Under the new arrangements there was no job security, no assurance of a defined career path, and also low compensation. The post-1973 period found many young applicants at the CSS examinations giving first preference to customs, income tax, and the police services rather than the previously prestigious cadres of CSP, relabelled the District Management Group (DMG), and the Foreign Service.

Bhutto was quite bitter about the dominance and arrogance of the civil servants during the long period of his ministership under Ayub Khan. He believed that the ill-advised policies that led to the downfall of Ayub Khan were in fact the creation of the top civil servants who occupied the highest positions of government in the 1960s. He believed that these civil servants would be a big hurdle in achieving his grandiose vision of a socialist Pakistan. It was quite ironical that he wanted the executive branch and its institutions to become powerful to execute his agenda but the steps he took eventually weakened their capacity and motivation. His decision to do away with the constitutional guarantee of the security of service in 1973, completely abolish Pakistan's civil service, and entirely reorganize the structure of the civil services which formed the backbone of the administration by bringing in his appointees through lateral entry, proved counterproductive. The industries, banks, insurance companies, and educational institutions he nationalized required professionals to operate and manage them but this was impossible in a setting in which complete subservience to ministers from his political party was the prevailing ethos.

A question that needs to be addressed is why the line for institutional decay is being drawn around 1990, when the actual assault on the civil services, through abolition of the Pakistan Civil Service, the removal of the constitutional guarantee of security of service, allowing induction through lateral entry, and introduction of common training for all those recruited to different cadres through the Central Superior Services examination, was initiated by Z. A. Bhutto in the 1970s. Why did these drastic reforms only have a significant impact on institutional performance in the early 1990s?

As mentioned above, the Bhutto government, having undertaken such a massive agenda of nationalization of industries, banks, insurance, educational institutions, etc. had no option other than to fall back on experienced civil servants to fill in the vacuum created by the withdrawal of the private sector to operate the newly acquired state-owned enterprises (SOEs). The Board of Management, Production Division, and the top management of these SOEs had perforce to be entrusted to the civil servants, and some professionals such as chartered accountants, engineers, etc. were retained or appointed to undertake the task. The past momentum also carried matters forward as Bhutto had very little time to break the back of the civil service because he was distracted by other complex national and international issues. Some of his pragmatic ministers discovered that they couldn't achieve their agenda by antagonizing and cutting civil servants to size because they were necessary for the implementation of the policies, programmes, and projects of the ruling party. The latter also felt that winning the 1977 election required the deputy commissioners to play a cooperative and non-confrontational role as they were key players in conducting the election.

The overthrow of the Bhutto government through a military coup in July 1977, and the assumption of power by a right-wing military leader, General Zia ul-Haq, led only to a halt to the continuation of the socialist policies, not a complete reversal of them. Mahbub ul Haq, who served as planning and then finance minister under Zia, set out the reason for this hiatus:

We have not been able to deregulate the economy as much as I wanted, despite seven years of trying, because the politicians and officials both like the system Bhutto put in place. It suits them both very well, because it gave them lots of lucrative state-appointed jobs in industry and banking to take for themselves or distribute to their relatives and supporters.

Thus the mistrust and suspicion between the private sector and government functionaries remained unabated.

At the political level, Zia ul-Haq first banned political party activity, and wanted to limit participation in government to the local level alone in an effort to win legitimacy through local government institutions. Subsequently, however, he co-opted the Jamaat-i-Islami, a right-wing party, which joined his government. Then Zia revived the Muslim League as a counterforce to the PPP and later formed the federal and provincial governments with its support. This veneer of democracy, however, couldn't mask the centralization of political power in the hands of a single individual.

The question that then arises is why the fallout of these major shocks to the economy—the loss of almost half of the domestic market, transfer of the ownership of industrial units from private entrepreneurs to public servants, and the abolition of Pakistan's civil service and the induction of lateral entrants—caused major dislocations and disruptions during the 1980s.

The incoming military junta had to strike a careful balance between maintaining a professional standing army and shouldering the responsibilities of the civil administration. In the initial period, the martial law administrators and their deputies along with the martial law courts were deeply involved in running the country. The armed forces, keen to preserve their reputation, felt that this close involvement in running the civilian administration was having pernicious effects on them. Rumours and reports were rife about some martial law officers engaging in malpractices and corruption. Notwithstanding the suppression of the press and freedom of expression, questions were raised about the justification for the military intervention if the conduct and behaviour of the present incumbents in office was no different from that of the civilians they had replaced. The armed forces were thus on the brink of losing their justification when

Zia ul-Haq appointed a top civil servant, Ghulam Ishaq Khan, as finance minister with a much larger canvas of responsibilities. He was de facto head of the civil administration and held a strong view that the commanding heights of the economy should remain with the public sector.

The new military ruler needed the civil servants of the old order to help him in running the day-to-day administration and managing the economy, and Ghulam Ishaq Khan provided him that surety. GIK, as he was popularly known, chose some competent and experienced senior civil servants to run the country. Widely respected for his integrity, hard work, and competence, GIK was able to assert himself and thus able to insulate the civil services and the institutions of state from external pressures and influences. It is another matter altogether whether he and his colleagues did anything to dissuade General Zia from the ideological path he had adopted for Pakistan and for which the country is paying a heavy price to this day. GIK also did not reverse Bhutto's policies of nationalization of the backbone of the economy because he shared the latter's distrust of the private sector and therefore managed the economy in an ad hoc, status quo manner without strengthening the institutions of governance.

Zia ul-Haq's own agenda was quite different: the Islamization of Pakistan and active engagement in the Afghan war. According to Haqqani (*Magnificent Delusions*, 244):

> Zia went on to change many aspects of life in Pakistan as part of Islamization of the country. The country's educational system was revamped to ensure that future generations of Pakistanis will be more Islamic and xenophobic than the previous ones. From an early age anti-Semitism as well as fear and hatred of India were instilled in Pakistan's fast-growing populace.

Kamila Hyat describes this period in the following terms:

> Assisted by the Soviet invasion of Afghanistan in 1979, Zia ul-Haq opened up the doors for extremist groups from the Middle East to enter the country, set up seminaries and other centres, and alter forever the face of religion in a country that till then had followed an essentially moderate line of thought.

He also altered laws, introducing into the books and into the constitution his own version of Islam which pushed back the rights of women and minorities.

We still struggle to amend or retract most of these laws. And of course under Zia's watch, arms and drugs poured in from Afghanistan, altering the face of the country forever. A curious attempt was made to push Pakistan across the continent, west into the Middle East, breaking its linkages with the Indian subcontinent and the culture it had inherited from its long association with this region. The crackdown on dance, music and on so much else including forms of art is just one example of this.[12]

Three million refugees from Afghanistan not only created economic dislocation in the Khyber Pakhtunkhwa (KP) and FATA regions but included a large number of trained militants, criminals, and drugs and arms smugglers who posed a challenge to the writ of the state. A culture of violence took root as the arms intended for Mujahideen filtered into Pakistani cities and towns. Drug trafficking had exponentially increased as areas bordering Afghanistan descended into lawlessness. Zia ul-Haq used the state apparatus and select institutions such as the Inter-Services Intelligence (ISI) and Military Intelligence (MI) to perpetuating his regime, and left a legacy that haunts Pakistan almost three decades after his death. He promoted Salafist Islam to keep the country under his control, radicalized the society through madrassas, mosques, and *maulvis*, and used militants to achieve his foreign and domestic policy goals. The popular narrative was changed from an open and modernizing outlook to an obscurantist puritanical world-view that enfeebled the liberal forces in the bureaucracy and society. He showed little or no interest whatsoever in institutional restructuring of the civil order or economic reforms.

The erosion of the quality of recruits into the civil services began occurring gradually since the 1973 reforms but became quite perceptible by the late 1980s and early 1990s. As pointed out earlier, the civil services ceased as hitherto to be the preferred choice for the best and the brightest young men and women in Pakistan after the enactment of the 1973 reforms. There was a time lag in the perception about the desirability of the civil service as a career in the altered reality. The quality of fresh intake in the 1980s and thereafter was nowhere comparable to that of those who had entered the services in the 1950s, 1960s, and 1970s. Both Bhutto and Zia had to assign complex and challenging tasks to the officers of these earlier batches of civil servants who were capable of delivering the desired results. The institutions headed by these individuals continued to perform well.

A renewed ascendancy of the civil service was once again witnessed in the three-year tenure of Prime Minister Mohammad Khan Junejo. Having been a minister in the heydays of the 1960s, he had seen first-hand the value of an efficient and motivated cadre of civil servants. He therefore brought a breath of fresh air in Pakistan's governance structure even though he had his origins in rural Sindh, known for its patronage-based politics. An honest man living a modest and austere personal life, he set an example for others to follow. All key appointments were made on merit, contracts were awarded to the deserving, and postings and transfer of officials were no longer driven by the whims of local politicians. This brief period in the mid-1980s is still remembered as a powerful testimony to the possibility that there is no inherent incompatibility between good governance and democracy. It is ironical that this period of good democratic governance had to end because of the whims of a military dictator who had appointed him to the job. Normally, the popular narrative is that good governance is only possible under strong authoritarian rule and, in Pakistan, that of the military. However, the Junejo–Zia tussle contradicts this narrative. It would be fair to surmise that civilian institutions got some infusion of oxygen during that brief spell of Junejo governance. Some observers speculate that had that period continued and not terminated so abruptly, the quality of institutions would have risen considerably. Junejo was unceremoniously dismissed from office in May 1988 and Zia once again assumed complete control of the government until his tragic death.

The momentum of the 1980s was broken when the two major political parties formed alternating elected governments in the 1988–89 period. There were euphoric scenes in Pakistan when Benazir Bhutto was elected by a popular vote as the first female prime minister. It was believed that the dark days of repression and autocratic rule were over and a young, enlightened, and modern leader with strong grassroots support from the masses would usher in a new era of progress and prosperity. Although she could not completely disassociate herself from the socialist economy agenda of her father or repudiate it publicly, she went along the path set by Zia ul-Haq. She, however, kept struggling to strike an equation with the establishment and her government proved to be so weak and fragile that she did not pay much attention to the economic agenda and the institutions responsible for furthering it. Worse, her government became tainted with scandals of corruption in the award of contracts, sanctioning of loans by the nationalized banks, allocation of land for real estate development, approvals of agreements for independent power plants, and permits for sundry business activities.

In order to fulfil this goal, pliant officers loyal to the government were brought in to occupy top positions as secretaries of the ministries and heads of key institutions, and entrusted with these responsibilities. Appointments, postings, and transfers were, by and large, driven by the considerations of getting 'our' man in place who will do 'our' bidding. These beneficiaries were happy not only to oblige the political leaders but were also able to enrich themselves and their families and friends in the bargain. Objectivity, neutrality, and impartiality, the traditionally acclaimed attributes of the civil services, were completely sacrificed in this Faustian bargain, setting the stage for the decay of the civilian institutions.

The young and inexperienced prime minister was thus unable to face a range of challenges. She was obliged to appease the establishment seeking to dislodge her government, cater to the undesirable wishes of her family and close confidants, and address the grievances of party workers who were not being adequately rewarded for the sacrifices they had made during the Zia's dictatorial regime. She was unable to meet these challenges, and her government was dismissed by the president on grounds of incompetence and corruption. Fresh elections were held and Mian Nawaz Sharif, heading a coalition of rightist parties, became prime minister in November 1990. A petition filed by the former commander in chief of the Pakistan Air Force, Asghar Khan, before the Supreme Court of Pakistan alleged that the Chief of the Army Staff (COAS) and the head of the Inter-Services Intelligence

Agency had forged and supported a coalition of right-wing political parties to defeat the PPP at these elections.

The new prime minister, a businessman himself—generally known as a protégé of General Zia and who had the blessing of the establishment—sparked a new ray of hope that he would be able to put the economy in order. Indeed, he began with a big bang by introducing far-reaching economic reforms with adequate legal cover. The principal thrust of the reforms was to diminish the role of state functionaries in the affairs of the economy, unleash the entrepreneurial energies of the private sector, and allow market forces to operate with minimal government intervention. However, these nascent changes could not be adequately rooted because he got entangled in a tussle with President Ghulam Ishaq Khan. The president accused his government of nepotism, favouritism, and corruption, and dismissed it in 1993, after only two and a half years in office.

The unfortunate tradition of replacing all the previous incumbents of top posts in the executive branch at the federal and provincial governments by loyalists got further entrenched, and the subsequent two terms in which Benazir Bhutto (1993–97) and Nawaz Sharif (1997–99) alternated in power. It is a shame that Nawaz Sharif, during his second term, did not pursue or consolidate the unfinished agenda of economic reforms he had brought about in 1991. This was indeed a great opportunity for his government as he had received an overwhelming mandate from the electorate which could have been profitably utilized to take tough policy decisions and strengthen state institutions. This time, however, he did not pay much attention to the economy because he was distracted by his battles with the superior judiciary, the army chiefs, and nuclear tests in response to India's decision to go ahead with nuclear weapons. As Nawaz Sharif had forced one army chief to resign, his subsequent action to dismiss his successor resulted in a retaliation by the army which toppled him from the office and brought in General Pervez Musharraf as the new chief executive in October 1999.

As both Benazir Bhutto and Nawaz Sharif felt politically insecure and their average tenure of office was around a mere two years, they used the institutions of governance and civil servants to dispense favours and patronage, engaging in a dubious game of co-option or coercion of their opponents and excessive misuse of the discretionary powers of the office. The politicization of the civil services was openly encouraged by them and, for the first time, allegiance to the political party in power was the principal consideration for key appointments, perks, and privileges. Under the British tradition, civil servants did not change their offices when a new government came to power. This tradition was, however, thrown overboard in the 1990s, and the new norm was that with each change of government the elected leaders replaced those appointed by their opponents and brought in a new set of appointees to key positions and heads of institutions loyal to them. The partisan use of state patronage and corruption thus became entrenched during this period, and the incentive structure for career progression was unquestioning acquiescence with the wishes of the ruling dispensation, right or wrong, legal or illegal. The initiative for the formulation of policies, analysis of costs and benefits of policies, and advice to the cabinet, which had always been the prerogative of the bureaucrats, was ungrudgingly ceded to politicians who were not qualified or had the time to examine them critically. Parvez Hasan,[13] summed up this period as follows:

> The political governments were not only weak (the exception being Nawaz Sharif['s] rule during 1997–99) but were dominated by strong vested interests and were not inclined to treat political opposition with much respect. At the same time, there were widespread allegations of corruption, and abuse of power. These factors combined with a lack of financial discipline, ineffective use of public resources, and continued problems in areas such as tax collection led to slowdown in the rate of growth of the economy, a sharp acceleration in inflation in mid 1990s, external payments crises in 1993 and 1996, and an approaching danger of external debt default towards the end of 1990s.

The only exceptions in this long period of eleven years were the two brief interludes of caretaker governments headed by the former senior vice president of the World Bank, Moeen Qureshi, and President Farooq

Leghari. Both of them brought about some improvements in policy and institutions, and tried to reinstate the practice of selection on merit but their tenures were too brief to ensure continuance of these changes in the institutional architecture or practices and processes.

General Musharraf, who came to power in October 1999, selected experts and technocrats as members of his cabinet and they served the country admirably for the first three years. The chief executive paid undivided attention to taxation, tariffs, the financial sector, telecommunications reforms, resumed privatization of loss-making public enterprises, and established an effective National Accountability Bureau (NAB), created a powerful Higher Education Commission (HEC), and also significantly restructured the local government system and the police by revising archaic laws and instituting a new modern system. Had these been fully implemented and survived over time, the institutional architecture would have greatly improved and the process of decay would have at least been halted.

The Musharraf government did the right thing by devolving powers to the local governments, to the elected *nazim*s to whom the provincial governments handed over control of 12 departments in their districts. However, the abolition of the offices of the deputy commissioners and assistant commissioners, and their substitution by the elected *nazim*s in the areas of law and order, land administration, and disaster management was a step too much in advance of its time because the *nazim*s were neither equipped nor trained to shoulder these responsibilities in a non-partisan manner. These functions should have remained in the hands of neutral, impartial, and competent civil servants. Focus group consultations in 2006–8[14] with civil servants of all ranks revealed a deep sense of disenchantment and low morale as a consequence of the decision to abolish the offices of assistant commissioner, deputy commissioner, and the divisional commissioner. Many of them termed the decision as a second blow to the administrative frame, the first being the 1973 reforms under Bhutto.

Ilhan Niaz[15] explains the possible reason for this action: 'the higher bureaucracy led by the CSP/DMG served as the great administrative restraint on military rulers and was able to assert its intellectual and moral superiority over time and time again, often for good sometimes for ill, over their counterparts in the military'. The large-scale induction of retired and serving military officials into civilian institutions by the Musharraf government further demoralized the higher bureaucracy and exacerbated the sense of resentment.

Although there are many detractors and critics of the 2001 devolution, both among analysts and politicians, there is little doubt that the local government system indeed helped in improved provision of basic services at the grassroots level but the premature transfer of powers of administration of justice caused a great deal of disaffection. The Police Order 2001 was also a major step forward but was amended several times at the insistence of Musharraf's political supporters, the provincial chief ministers, that it lost its real transformational power. However, notwithstanding these deficiencies and setbacks, the period 2000–06 is generally viewed as a period of relative good governance in Pakistan. The aggregate governance indicators, according to the World Bank database, peaked during that period and it coincided with the period during which Pakistan recorded high growth rates.

The post-2008 period, which was marked by the return of a democratically elected government, once again witnessed key institutions headed and manned by those who were loyal to the ruling parties. Officials who had fled abroad on self-exile after the dismissal of the second Bhutto government returned and occupied key administrative positions. Personal friendships and loyalty to the leadership were the principal criteria for appointment of heads of institutions. The principle of choosing the right man for the right job was flagrantly violated, leading to an open tussle with the superior judiciary. In that battle, institutions were paralysed, further widening the policy–performance gap. The Supreme Court took suo motu notice of some of these violations and ordered the removal or forced resignation of some of the heads of these institutions. A few others were charged with corruption, malfeasance, and misuse of office. There was, however, no perceptible diminution in rent-seeking activities and patronage by the ruling party in placements and appointments to top positions in public sector organizations. Private investment fell drastically during this period and Pakistan's ranking in the Ease of Doing Business and Transparency indexes slumped.

One of the most encouraging developments that took place during the tenure of the Zardari government was the approval of the Eighteenth Amendment to the Constitution which devolved significant administrative and legislative powers from the federal government to the provinces in many areas relating to the delivery of basic services to citizens: agriculture, education, health, energy etc. This was accompanied by a dramatic shift in the distribution of the divisible tax pool under the 7th National Finance Commission (NFC) award. The share of the provinces jumped from under 40 per cent to almost 60 per cent. Balochistan, the most backward province, was given a higher allocation in the horizontal distribution among the provinces. This highly significant development in the system of constitutional and fiscal federalism could have become a precursor of institutional re-engineering with a clear demarcation of boundaries between the provincial and local governments along with an agreed mechanism for revenue-sharing which would have made a substantial difference and improvement in state–citizen relations. Unfortunately, this opportunity was not only missed but the Local Government Acts of Punjab and Sindh have in fact concentrated more powers at the provincial level. The local governments have become almost impotent in delivering services to citizens as they lack both the authority and the resources for this.

The capacity to formulate policies, implement reforms, and execute projects at the provincial level has not kept pace with the additional responsibilities and functions that have been assigned to them. Education, health, and other social sector budgets of the provincial governments, for example, are not fully utilized, and the funds lapse at the end of the financial year notwithstanding the enormous demand for these resources. This disconnect between the devolved legislative powers and the enlarged resource envelope on one hand, and the limited capacity to implement the programmes is going to worsen unless serious efforts are made to reform the structure, processes, and human resource management policies at the provincial level and further devolve powers and resources to the local governments. The reasons for this lack of capacity and poor governance are several.

The informal, asymmetric power relations within the bureaucracy creates an incentive for poor governance. The accountability of civil servants and public sector employees has been largely limited to the officer class or top and senior managers. In formal terms and in accordance with the distribution of responsibilities within the organization, the onus lies with these officers. In actual practice, however, the informal but effective power rests with the lower echelons of the bureaucracy. The clerks, *patwaris*, SHOs, inspectors, and court readers enjoy enormous discretionary power and engage in institutionalized corruption but remain unscathed from any measures of accountability because they do not have any formal authority and cannot be held responsible in the strict legal sense. All the purges, screenings, and dismissals under the military regimes were targeted at the senior officers as were the NAB inquiries and prosecutions in the recent years. As their superior officers keep rotating while the lower ranking officials remain entrenched almost permanently in their positions, they arouse deep-seated fears among those who file complaints against their high-handed and extortionary practices. In the event of a formal complaint being lodged against these lower functionaries to their superiors, two possible outcomes are likely to ensue. First, if the superiors are in cahoots with the subordinates, the complainant may risk harassment and persecution. In the event that there is an honest officer at the helm, the complainant may incur the wrath of the individual(s) concerned after the transfer of that officer, i.e. a postponed punishment. A resident of the area who depends upon the whims and discretions of the bureaucracy for day to day survival can hardly afford that.

Second, previous army takeovers resulted in the setting up of a parallel hierarchy of military leadership operating under their own laws, leaving civilian institutions dormant and inactive. Serving or retired military officers were brought in to head senior leadership positions in a large number of civilian organizations over a period spanning virtually a decade. This practice denied opportunities to middle-level civil servants to hone their skills, gain the requisite experience, and enhance their performance as they did not see any prospects for career progression for themselves. Their nurturing and grooming was stalled and inertia, indifference, and demotivation took hold, adversely affecting the delivery of public goods and services to citizens. These behavioural lapses contributed to the decay of the institutional capacity of Pakistan, and when democracy returned, the underlying rot began to resurface.

The year 2013 saw the first orderly transition from one elected government to another. Some observers were expecting the poor governance practices of the previous government and the debilitating economic performance of the past five years to end under the new dispensation. After all, it was the impressive track record of the Punjab government under the leadership of Chief Minister Shahbaz Sharif during the 2008–13 period which won the votes for the Pakistan Muslim League-Nawaz (PML-N). There were heightened expectations that the new government would resuscitate the institutions and appoint competent people to head them, restructure the civil services, and usher in transparency but reality fell quite short of those hopes. Loyalty to the person and the party once again figured prominently in the calculus while highly centralized decision-making by an informal coterie of relatives and friends bypassing the cabinet system of collective decision-making became the norm. A transparent, merit based system of screening, interviewing, and selection of the chief executives of 100 institutions by an independent commission comprising people of high integrity and designed in compliance with the orders of the Supreme Court was first side-lined, followed by the disbandment of the commission itself. Civil service and governance reforms were taken up by the government, and the Planning Commission was assigned the task of devising a blueprint and timeline. The actual progress after a lapse of four years has been negligible.

There was another turn in the popular sentiment about the political leadership in Pakistan—especially among the educated youth, the urban middle class, and women—when Imran Khan, a man of integrity who had made his name as a distinguished cricketer and later through his excellent philanthropic work, formed a political party, the Pakistan Tehreek-e-Insaf (PTI). A large number of people who had shied away by exercising their franchise during the general elections decided to come out openly and support him in those held in 2013. His party won a majority in KP and formed the government by defeating the incumbent ANP which had lost its popularity because of poor governance and corruption in the province. Expectations rose that he would focus all his attention in transforming KP into a model of good governance, institutional performance, and delivery of public services to the poor. The voters of KP had rejected the previous ruling party, thus signalling that they were ready for such a transformation. Political resistance to his reform agenda would have been minimal. His government certainly began to bring about some perceptible improvement in police, health, education, and land record management but his distraction because of other issues such as the election irregularities and then escalation of this issue to organizing *dharnas* in Islamabad, caused some disappointment among his newly found well-wishers. They had hoped that he would devote undivided attention in developing a model province, showcasing the essential ingredients of good governance and people's access to public services.

***

Scholars such as Ayesha Jalal, Philip Oldenburg, and Christophe Jaffrelot have undertaken scholarly studies and analysed why both India and Pakistan with a common colonial legacy, and legal and bureaucratic structures, have moved in different directions in relation to democracy. Oldenburg has shed light on the question: what allowed Indian politicians to assert and maintain their dominance over the bureaucratic and military branches of the state, while that has proved to be impossible in Pakistan? The literature is so rich and fascinating that it would be difficult to summarize it here.

Suffice it to say that while Indian politicians right from the outset have been able to effectively assert control over both the bureaucrats and the military, this was not the case in Pakistan. The relative dominance between these two groups has varied in different periods. It is argued by many observers that even in 1988–99, when elections were held and democratically elected leaders were in power, the military was still calling the shots. The same is also true of the post-2008 period when foreign policy, defence policy, and internal security matters fell within the virtually exclusive domain of the military.

Notes and references

1. Jalal, A., *Democracy and Authoritarianism in South Asia* (Lahore: Sang-e-Meel, 1995).

2. Wolpert, S., *Jinnah of Pakistan* (OUP, 2005).

3. Waseem, M., *Politics and the State in Pakistan* (Lahore: Progressive, 1989).

4. Burki, S. J., 'Twenty Years of Civil Service in Pakistan: A Reappraisal', *Asian Survey* (1969), 9 (4).

5. Sayeed, K. B., *Politics in Pakistan: The Nature and Direction of Change* (New York: Praeger, 1980).

6. For a complete listing and summary of the reports and recommendations of the various reform commissions and committees formed since 1947: <ncgr.gov.pk>

7. Goodnow, H. F., *The Civil Service of Pakistan: Bureaucracy in a New Nation* (New Haven: Yale University Press, 1964).

8. Shaikh, F., *Making Sense of Pakistan* (London: Hurst & Co., 2009).

9. Burki, S. J., *Changing Perception, Altered Reality: Emerging Economies in the 1990s* (New York: World Bank Publications, 2000).

10. Burki, S. J., *Pakistan under Bhutto, 1971–1977* (London: Macmillan, 1980).

11. Ibid.

12. Hyat, K., 'All that Glitters', *The News*, 1 December 2016.

13. Hasan, Parvez, *My Life, My Country: Memoirs of a Pakistani Economist* (Ferozsons, 2011).

14. These stakeholder consultations were carried out during the preparation of the Report of the National Commission on Government Reforms (NCGR).

15. Niaz, I., *The Culture of Power and Governance of Pakistan 1947–2008* (OUP, 2010).

3

The Economy

A t the time of Independence, the prospect of the economic survival of Pakistan appeared quite bleak. The following extract from the cover story of *Life* magazine dated 5 January 1948, is reflective of the sentiments on Pakistan's economic future at the time:

When Pakistan suddenly received its freedom last August 15, proud and energetic patriots boasted that they had created a nation with more land than France and more people than Germany. Granting these comparisons, Pakistan still lacks most of the attributes of a modern nation. Today, its capital of Karachi is partly a tent city. And, as the following paragraphs and the picture indicate, it is fighting a close battle with economic bankruptcy.

Labour: Of the approximately 70 million Pakistanis, more than 80% are farmers, very few are wealthy landlords, and the rest are shopkeepers and artisans. Nearly all of Pakistan's financial and professional men were among the approximately four million Hindus who fled to India. From India, Pakistan got about six million impoverished Muslim peasants who, for the most part, left their agricultural implements behind. In return for freedom, Pakistan has huge transient camps full of landless farmers and an almost complete lack of skilled technicians or businessmen.

Industry: As a producing country, Pakistan must quickly industrialize to achieve self-sufficiency or else might establish a cordial interdependence with a processing nation. At present, in all of Pakistan there are only 26,000 workers employed in industry. She has no big iron and steel centers, only 34 railway repair shops, no match factories, no jute mills, no paper mills and only 16 cotton mills against India's 857. Lacking the money or know-how to industrialize, Pakistan obviously requires a commercial rapprochement with Hindu India if her people are to be clothed.

Finances: Pakistan's financial troubles are compounded by her political, trade, and industrial failures. At the time of the division, the Hindu businessmen took all the gold bullion jewels and other liquid assets they could carry with them. With normal trade cut off by rioting and use of railroads for refugees, Pakistan's income probably will not exceed 450 million rupees for the current year against almost certain expenditure of 800 million rupees. Officials talk hopefully of foreign investment or loans but in Pakistan's present conditions, the risks are not very attractive.[1]

PAKISTAN'S GROWTH RECORD

From such a shaky start, Pakistan today is the thirty-fourth largest economy in the world with a per capita income in current US dollars of about $1,500 in comparison to $100 in 1947. Pakistan's overall growth record has been quite impressive: on average, the economy grew at an annual rate of slightly above 5 per cent over the last seven decades. In per-capita terms, the growth rate was 2.5 per cent annually. Per capita incomes in constant terms have multiplied four- to five-fold. Consequently, the incidence of poverty has halved from 40 per cent to less than 20 per cent. The trends in sectoral GDP growth rates indicate that industry, including the manufacturing sector, has been the most dynamic of the economy. In the regional context, Pakistan grew faster than South Asia by an average of two per cent through most of the 1960s and 1970s, and at similar rates during the 1980s. However, since 1990, Pakistan's growth has fallen below the regional average. There are, however, other remarkable achievements that the country can proudly boast about.

A country of 30 million people in 1947 couldn't feed itself and had to import all its food from abroad. In 2016, the farmers of Pakistan were not only able to meet the domestic needs of the country for wheat, rice, sugar, and milk for 190 million people at a much higher per capita consumption level but also export wheat and rice to the rest of the world. Pakistan has emerged as the world's third largest exporter of rice.

Agriculture production rose over five-fold with cotton reaching a peak level of over 14 million bales in comparison to 1 million in 1947. Pakistan has emerged as one of the leading world exporters of textiles.

The manufacturing production index is well over 13,000 with a base of 100 in 1947. Steel, cement, automobiles, sugar, fertilizer, cloth, vegetable ghee, industrial chemicals, refined petroleum, and a variety of other products that did not exist at the time of Independence are now manufactured for the domestic market and, in many cases, for world markets too.

Per capita electricity generation in 2016 was 10,160 kw-h (kilowatt per hour) compared to 100 in 1947.

Pakistan's vast irrigation network of large storage reservoirs and dams, barrages, and link canals constructed during the past seven decades has enabled it to double the area under cultivation to 22 million hectare. Tube-well irrigation provides almost a third of additional water to supplement canal irrigation.

Pakistan's road and highway network spans 260,000 km, over five times the length inherited in 1947. Modern motorways and super highways and four-lane national highways link the entire country along with secondary and tertiary roads.

Natural gas was discovered in Pakistan in the 1950s and supply has been augmented over time. As of now, almost 4 billion cubic feet per day of natural gas is generated and distributed for industrial, commercial, and domestic consumption, and until recently accounted for 40 to 50 per cent of the country's energy needs.

Private consumption standards have kept pace with the rise in income. There were 52 road vehicles for 1,000 persons in 2012 in comparison to only one vehicle for the same number of people in 1947. Phone connections per 1,000 persons have risen to 683 from 0.4 over this period. TV sets, which were non-existent in 1947, cater to 70 out of every 1,000 households.

These achievements in income, consumption, agriculture, and industrial

production are extremely impressive and have lifted millions of people out
of poverty. These, however, pale into insignificance when we consider the
missed opportunities. The largest setback to Pakistan has been the neglect
of human development. Had adult literacy rate been close to 100 per cent
rather than approximately 50 per cent today, it is estimated that the per
capita income would have reached at least $3,000.

There is a virtual consensus among the analysts and economic historians
that Pakistan had three episodes of rapid growth: 1960/61 to 1969/70,
1979/80 to 1988/89, and 2003/04 to 2007/09; and four episodes
of stagnation: 1948/50 to 1958/59, 1970/71 to 1978/79, 1989/90 to
1999/2000, and 2008/09 to 2013/14. McCartney,[2] however, surprisingly
terms the period 1951/52 to 1958/59 as growth years and that of 1970/71
to 1990/92 as a period of stagnation.

The popular notion that the economy prospers under military regimes
and falters during periods of elected civilian leadership is only superficially
valid. Mahbub-ul-Haq, the architect of Human Development Index, who
played an important role in economic policy-making during the Ayub and
Zia governments, in an interview with Anatol Lieven,[3] sums up the reasons
for the faltering economic and social progress during governments headed
by the politicians and the relative success of non-political governments in
accelerating economic growth.

> Growth in Pakistan has never translated into budgetary security because of
> the way our political system works. We could be collecting twice as much in
> revenue—even India collects 50 per cent more than we do—and spending
> the money on infrastructure and education. But agriculture in Pakistan pays
> virtually no tax because the landed gentry controls politics and has therefore
> a grip on every government. Businessmen are given state loans, and then
> allowed to default on them in return for favours to politicians and parties.
> Politicians protect corrupt officials so that they can both share the proceeds
> … As far as development is concerned, our system has the worst features of
> oligarchy and democracy put together. That is why only technocratic, non-
> political governments have ever been able to increase revenues. But they
> cannot stay in power long because they have no political support.

It would be important to briefly recapitulate the economic history of Pakistan which has not been, by any means, smooth or consistent but replete with episodes marked by booms and busts, disappointments and achievements, and crises and resilience. The journey has been bumpy due to domestic policy and institutional failures as well as external and exogenous shocks.

Table 3.1: Growth by Period (Percentage)

FY	Real GDP	Agriculture	Industry	Services
1948–58	3.1	1.6	9.1	3.4
1958–70	5.9	4.4	9.5	6.0
1972–77	4.4	2.4	4.5	6.3
1977–88	6.3	3.8	8.1	7.0
1988–99	4.7	4.3	5.1	4.7
2000–07	5.2	3.4	6.6	5.5
2008–13	3.2	3.3	2.4	3.8
2013–16	4.1	1.9	4.2	4.9

Sources: *Handbook of Statistics*. State Bank of Pakistan; Pakistan Bureau of Statistics; *World Development Indicators*, World Bank; *Haver Analytics*

The 1950s were Pakistan's formative years when the problems arising from the aftermath of Partition and the setting up of a new nation-state preoccupied decision-makers. The disintegration of the subcontinent's economy, and the inheritance of poor human and financial resource endowments proved to be stumbling blocks in laying a solid foundation for the economy during this period. A crisis mode prevailed throughout the decade, exacerbated by political instability. Naturally, overall growth remained subdued as industry took off from a very low base. The principal means to finance investment in the 1950s was via the very high rates of profit earned by the private industry enabled by government trade and exchange-rate policy. The state also made some limited, direct contribution to investment. The principal source of growth over the period was import substitution, and the consequent lower costs and higher productivity in industry.

The major turnaround took place after 1958 under Ayub Khan when Pakistan achieved political stability. Continuity and consistency of policies, combined with incentives to the private sector, a strong Planning Commission setting a clear direction, and the green revolution in agriculture, all made significant contributions. The growth rate hovered around 6 per cent annually, notwithstanding the shock of a war with India in 1965. Industry took the lead but agriculture also saw a revival with high-yielding varieties and increased availability of water for irrigation. The state proved well able to sustain high profit rates in the private sector with reforms to corporate taxation and anti-union policies. The principal sources of growth were domestic demand and a green revolution in agriculture, export growth, and contribution of labour, capital, and overall rise in productivity (TPP).[4]

However, although Ayub's period of governance was a one of high aggregate growth rate, it was also characterized by a substantial increase in income inequalities per se and across regions. The Gini coefficient worsened and the number of people below the poverty line increased. Wage increases did not match productivity gains and the living standards of a large majority of the population remained stagnant or improved only marginally. The index of real wages increased by only two per cent during this ten year period. Investment in the critical social sectors remained very poor and population growth rate remained high, notwithstanding a much-touted family planning campaign. Thus, distributional considerations took backstage to growth performance. The popular perception about concentration of wealth in the hands of 22 families, shared by the chief economist of the government itself, and the wider regional inequalities between East and West Pakistan fuelled resentment among Bengalis who accused Ayub's government of reducing the East to an internal colony.[5]

It can be seen that during the first 20 years following Independence, Pakistan recorded the highest rate of growth in South Asia. According to the World Bank[6] (2002), Pakistan exported more manufactured goods than Indonesia, Malaysia, Philippines, Thailand, and Turkey combined in 1965. Agriculture, which affected the vast majority of the population and was the single largest employer, was also vigorously revived during this period through a combination of public policies, investment, and institutional reforms. The green revolution, brought about by high-yielding varieties of wheat and rice along with large-scale public investment in storage dams and irrigation, made Pakistan self-sufficient in food production and caloric intake. The construction of the Indus Basin Works increased the availability of irrigation water by 40 per cent over the 1960s. Private sector tube-wells augmented surface water by pumping out underground water, lowering the waterlogging and supplementing water supply at critical times in the production cycle. Fertilizer consumption surged by 35 per cent to 40 per cent and the private sector was harnessed to undertake retail distribution of agricultural inputs. The contribution of the total factor productivity (TFP) to the overall growth output increased from 38 per cent in the first five years of the 1960s to 87 per cent in the second half of the decade.

How did Pakistan get derailed from the path it was pursuing? The starting point of this reversal was the paradigm shift in the basic model of development after the break-up of the country. Until the late 1960s, Pakistan relied upon its private sector and achieved very high rates of economic growth. The nationalization of the major manufacturing industries, banking, insurance, education, and the like in 1971 caused a major disruption of the economy and an erosion of private investor confidence that continued for the next 20 years.

Z. A. Bhutto, a highly talented and charismatic leader, rather than consolidating the gains of the 1960s and ameliorating the weaknesses visible in that development model, completely abandoned the model itself and made a complete about-turn. In order to break the stranglehold of the 22 families on the economy, he rushed to take over all the major manufacturing industries, banking, insurance, education, and the like under direct government control, virtually confiscating private property. This experiment with socialism had a negative impact on industrial development, export expansion, and the quality of education, and gave an overarching role to the bureaucracy in economic decision-making. The substitution of a culture of entrepreneurship, risk-taking, and innovation by rent-seeking and patronage suppressed the dynamism of the private sector. The emergence of bureaucrats as business leaders reinforced the new culture. Bureaucratic harassment, problems of law and order, unreliable and expensive power, and inadequate infrastructure also discouraged investment and help explain why the private sector was reluctant to make long-term commitments. The disintegration of the unified economy of East and West Pakistan and the resultant formation of Bangladesh as an independent country also had major economic consequences. The oil price shock of the 1970s, the droughts and floods, and withdrawal of external assistance by the West did not help the situation either.

The growth rate in the 1970s fell to 4.4 per cent per annum from 6.5 per cent in the 1960s. Worst of all, the central plank on which the Bhutto government came to power, that of social justice, proved intractable. Between 1972 and 1980, the Gini Coefficient of overall income increased from 0.291 to 0.355 for farm households and from 0.363 to 0.400 for urban households.[7] Inflation accelerated during this period, averaging about 16 per cent in 1971–77, and thus hurting the poor. Large-scale manufacturing performed very sluggishly, achieving a growth rate of a mere 3 per cent and that too sparked by huge public sector investment. The idea that the government should control the commanding heights of the economy underpinned the industrialization drive. Resources were allocated without proper appraisal at the prime minister's discretion and investment was made in activities that neither stimulated growth nor promoted equity. A newly industrializing economy that was fuelled by private enterprise was placed in an awkward, adversarial position between the government and the private sector. This tense relationship, replete with suspicion of the private sector that lasted for the following two decades, did irreparable damage to Pakistan's economic take-off and pushed it behind its competitors. The lesson learnt from this experience was that good populist politics were eventually detrimental to the economy. The gap between democracy and development widened during this period.

The Zia period (1977–88) was characterized by a surge in economic growth that was back to the over 6 per cent average recorded in the 1960s. It was also a period during which exogenous shocks did not destabilize the economy but in fact proved beneficial. The participation of Pakistan in the campaign to overthrow the Soviet Union from Pakistan brought in a large amount of military and economic assistance from the US. The cost paid by Pakistan for this largesse has been colossal. The seeds of the current Islamic fundamentalism in Pakistan were sown during that period. The spread of the Kalashnikov and drug culture that has nurtured ethnic and sectarian violence throughout the country, the mushrooming of illegal and parallel economic activities such as smuggling of arms and goods, and the promotion of Jihadist parties and elements can all be traced back to the 1980s.

The economic indicators for the period appear on the surface to be quite impressive, with the growth rate up to 6 per cent, inflation down to 7.6 per cent, agriculture growth at around 4 per cent on average annually, and the industrial sector rapidly expanding at a pace of a little over 8 per cent. However, the 1980s also saw an enormous increase in public spending of 9 per cent a year, widening the fiscal deficit which reached 8 per cent of GDP in the second half of 1980s. By 1987–88, defence spending had overtaken development spending and averaged 6.5 per cent of the GDP for the next several years. Development spending was curtailed to 3 per cent of the GDP, resulting in infrastructure bottlenecks and neglect of the social sectors. The large fiscal deficits did not translate immediately into instability or weakened growth rates but the accumulated domestic borrowing to finance these deficits had serious repercussions for public finances in terms of meeting rising debt service obligations and affecting macroeconomic stability. As a consequence, Pakistan had to approach the IMF for assistance in 1988.

Once again the performance of the economy revived under a non-elected military regime and the spurious correlation between military rule and rapid economic growth did gain currency among the intelligentsia wary of the elected political leaders and their conduct, behaviour, and performance.

The opportunity to undo most of the damage wrought by nationalization was missed by the Zia ul-Haq government (1977–78). Rather than taking proactive measures to reverse the state-owned and state-dominated economy, the government maintained the status quo. Although the process of nationalization was abandoned, the orientation towards the public sector did not perceptively diminish. Zia's close aide, General K. M. Arif, the chief of staff,[8] explains the reasoning behind this status quo as follows:

> The [Zia Administration] did not restructure the inherited economic order with a system in which the free market mechanism played a dominant role. The economic policies in the Zia Administration lacked innovative and revolutionary vision and basically moved within safe grooves. Four factors influenced the adoption of the status quo approach in the field of national economy. These were
> - The government's preoccupation with the Bhutto case
> - Pakistan's involvement in the Afghanistan jihad and its fallout effect on her national security
> - The lack of economic expertise of General Zia and his military colleagues
> - And the overly conservative and risk free policies adopted by the Minister of Finance, G. I. Khan, the high priest of economics in the Zia era, whose advice on economic matters had biblical sanctity for General Zia.

While the economic performance was impressive during this period, it was not due to any fundamental policy or institutional reforms. Pakistan benefited from the output that came on-stream from large public sector investments made in the 1970s, the most significant among them being the Tarbela Dam that added considerably to irrigation water availability and hydel power capacity together with the establishment of fertilizer and cement factories.

Nawaz Sharif, after assuming power in 1990, took some very bold steps to liberalize, deregulate, and privatize the economy.[9] His government abolished the much misused import-licensing system, deregulated investment controls, liberalized the foreign exchange regime, and privatized several industrial units and two nationalized commercial banks, marking the beginning of a new economic era. The foresight, courage, and determination showed by him in steering and shepherding these extremely deep-rooted reforms have remained unparalleled. These reforms did not get much traction because his government was dismissed after only two years in office. They were not reversed but were not followed through by the successor government of Benazir Bhutto. In all fairness, Benazir had shied away from her father's economic policies and her own thinking was not very different in terms of liberalizing and deregulating the economy but she got so preoccupied with her political survival that she did not pay much attention to pursuing these reforms. The political credit for the success of these reforms must have gone to her arch rival Nawaz Sharif and so her government did not make much effort to implement them. Benazir did not draw up an alternative economic vision for Pakistan either. Consequently, in the absence of a clear economic direction, private investment and exports stagnated or declined throughout the 1990s. Macroeconomic sustainability remained a serious problem. The financial sector was dominated by inefficient state-owned banks and access to capital was limited. The policy environment in relation to rules, taxes, and import tariffs was unstable and the arbitrary use of statutory regulatory orders (SROs) affected the level playing field which investors required to compete on the basis of business fundamentals rather than their ability to secure special deals.

Economic growth through the 1990s decelerated, showing an average trend of GDP growth of 4.4 per cent per year. Manufacturing—especially large scale industry that constitutes almost 80 per cent of the manufacturing sector output and contributes 11.7 per cent to GDP, and plays a crucial role in the economic growth of a country by helping it absorb most of the urban labour and higher income levels—remained in trouble for quite a long time.

A contrarian view of the benefits of liberalization is expressed by Naved Hamid and Maha Khan, who show that there was some form of 'structural break' around 1990 which adversely affected and slowed down large scale manufacturing (LSM) growth. They argue:[10]

> LSM was clearly the driver of robust GDP growth in the 1960s, 1980s and mid-2000s. In the 30 years prior to 1990, LSM (and GDP) growth averaged over 5 per cent per annum throughout, except for six years in the 1970s. But in the 25 years since 1990, LSM (and GDP) growth has averaged 5 per cent per annum for only nine years, mostly in the 2000s.

The two researchers conclude that the structural break could have occurred because of Pakistan's decision to abandon its proactive industrial policy around 1990 and begin a stop-go process of trade and economic liberalization at the behest of international financial institutions. They, however, insist that:

> trade liberalisation policies do not seem to have had much long-term impact on Pakistan's exports, which, as a percentage of GDP (after reaching a peak in 1992) and world exports (after reaching a peak in 1996), have either declined or stagnated.

They go on to argue that:

> It is possible that, in the last 25 years, Pakistan has managed to get the worst of both worlds. By abandoning its active industrial policy, it lost the benefits of an economic focus on the development of the manufacturing sector, while its lackadaisical attempts at trade liberalization were not enough to start the process of export-oriented manufacturing and economic growth.

Industrial policy, in the sense that the government picks winners and provides them preferential treatment in the form of subsidies below market rate bank credit, and favourable exchange rate has outlived its utility. In a rapidly changing environment of production technologies and consumer tastes, it is no longer possible to lay the future winners in a globalized world. Therefore, the views of Naved and Maha should be taken with a pinch of salt.

Indeed, it was not liberalization but frequent changes in the government throughout the 1990s and the consequent political instability it created that played havoc with the economy. Uncertainty and discontinuity of economic policies, patronage-based economic governance benefiting a small elite to the exclusion of the majority of the population, and exogenous shocks that derailed the economy. The investment ratio plummeted, and persistent fiscal and current account deficits led to an accumulation of large, unsustainable domestic and external debt throughout the decade. The ratio of debt-servicing vis-à-vis foreign exchange earnings reached almost a level of 40 per cent. The freezing of foreign currency accounts of residents and non-residents in the aftermath of the 1998 nuclear tests eroded investor and business confidence in the economy. Sanctions by leading bilateral donors dried up the flows of official aid to Pakistan. International capital was hesitant as the country's risk profile had risen significantly. The level of poverty doubled from 18 to 34 per cent during the decade.

The other contributing factor to Pakistan's lagging performance since the 1990s was the neglect of the social sectors. Pakistan underperformed other countries with similar per capita income in just about all of social indicators: a phenomenon known as the 'social gap'. The discrepancies are especially large for women, i.e. a 'gender gap' reinforced the social gap. These twin gaps stunted the growth rate because no country can hope to make much progress in a globalized world economy without an educated and healthy workforce.

The military government that came to power in October 1999 had set economic recovery as one of its professed objectives. In the face of all manner of sanction, the new government assembled a team of technocrats as part of its cabinet and embarked upon a series of structural reforms during 2000 and 2007. The far-reaching tragedy of 11 September 2001 also changed the geo-strategic importance of Pakistan significantly. The alliance of Pakistan with the US and NATO forces in the war against terrorism not only restored international financial aid but accelerated the volume of the inflows. It was during this period that Pakistan successfully negotiated and implemented a nine months stand-by and three-year Poverty Reduction and Growth Program with the IMF in 2000–4. The Paris Club reprofiled the ODA and non-ODA bilateral debt. The US cancelled $1 billion of Pakistan's debt to it. Investment rose to 24 per cent of the GDP and foreign direct investment (FDI) touched $5 billion in 2007. The exchange rate stability, narrowing the differential between inter-bank and open market rate, helped in channelling workers remittances through banking channels. The foreign exchange reserves of the SBP swelled from under $500 million, equivalent to two weeks' import in 1998, to over $14 billion in 2007—equivalent to five months' import requirements. As a result of economic reforms, the boost in investment, external assistance, and debt relief, the economy bounced back. According to the *SBP Annual Report*,[11] the GDP growth in the 2002–07 period averaged 6.8 per cent annually, surpassing the long-term average.

Devolution to local governments and empowerment of elected officials at the district level improved the delivery of basic public services. Poverty was reduced by 10 percentage points. The unemployment rate fell from 8.4 to 6.5 per cent and about 11.8 million new jobs were created in the FY 1999–2008 period. Gross and net enrolment at primary school level also recorded some improvement, along with child-immunization and reduction in the incidence of diarrhoea and infant mortality.

McCartney[12] analyses the popular argument that Pakistan's support for the US interventions in Afghanistan led to a huge surge in capital inflows and consequently Pakistan's economy prospered. His analysis negates this argument and concludes that:

> the episode of growth between 2002/3 and 2008/9 was better explained by a stronger (military) government able to (briefly) mobilize domestic resources, ensure that they were utilized productively, [and] create institutions that were able (again briefly) to overcome the conflicts associated with economic development. The general statistical evidence fails to relate capital inflows to savings and investment and expenditure and imports, managing domestic and external debt, raising public and private corporate profitability, and boosting public investment.

The reforms and improvement in governance over these seven years were not sustained and some of them were reversed, halted, or modified in the post-2008 period. Constitutional amendments devolving authority from the federal and provincial governments and increased allocation from the divisible taxable pool to the provinces were welcome steps but the local governments were abolished and access to basic services and the quality of governance suffered in consequence. The poor law and order situation and state of internal security resulted in a wait-and-see attitude by prospective investors. Consequently, economic performance during 2008–13 was extremely unsatisfactory, as the following macroeconomic indicators show:

- Average GDP growth under 3 per cent
- Inflation in double digits
- Fiscal deficits at a record high: > 6 per cent of GDP
- Public debt rises to 60 per cent of GDP
- Private consumption 88.3 per cent in FY 11 as against 69 per cent in 2001–08
- Investment declined from 19.8 per cent of GDP to 13.7 per cent

This dismal performance occurred when the US economic assistance disbursements under the Kerry Lugar Bill spiked in 2009–12 to $1 billion annually.

The 2009 IMF programme aimed at macroeconomic stabilization was aborted and later resumed in 2013 and completed in 2016. There was huge expectation that with Nawaz Sharif coming to power, Pakistan would have a pro-business policy approach with less state interventions and intrusions. These expectations have not however been borne out in actual practice. The private sector and businesses apart from traders are not very happy. Cyril Almeida[13] describes this change in the approach of the post-2013 Nawaz Sharif government:

2008 through 2011, Pakistan suffered some of it[s] worst years ever. On top of a declining state were layered economic and security woes that seemed terminal.

Pakistan itself felt like it was unravelling. But the arrival of the PML-N in 2013 did create an expectation that business, the private sector, would get a boost. Maybe a crony capitalism-type of approach, but nevertheless one that looked at the private sector as the engine of growth and where the heroes would be businessmen, big and small. The opposite though seems to have happened. Having established a sort-of macroeconomic stability, the N-League has embarked on a radical economic realignment: championing a state-led capitalism of sorts at the expense of the private sector.

The small businesses and traders, the big industrialists and exporters, farmers and traditional sectors, all seem to have been cast aside as the government itself has lodged itself deeper and deeper into the economy.

Think of every last big economic project inaugurated over the past three and a half years—everywhere and always it is the government that is the star, facilitator or creator.

Economic Reforms

The principal thrust of the reforms undertaken since 1991, albeit hesitantly and falteringly, was to allow greater freedom to the private sector to own, produce, distribute, and trade goods and services while gradually withdrawing the public sector from this ambit. The role of the state in Pakistan was redefined as a facilitator, enabler, protector, and regulator rather than directly managing and presiding over the commanding heights of the economy. Government intervention was justified for the social protection of the poor, provision of public goods, infrastructure, human development, and science and technology. Although the state has not always adhered to the new role assigned to it and has shown dominance in actual practice, there seems an implicit and unwritten political consensus in Pakistan on the boundaries between the public and private sectors. It is another thing that the political party in opposition always makes it difficult for the ruling party to implement these reforms.

Significant efforts were made in unilaterally liberalizing the trade regime. The maximum tariff rate was reduced to 25 per cent with the average tariff rate down to just 9 per cent. The number of duty slabs were reduced to four. Quantitative import restrictions were eliminated apart from those relating to security, health, public morals, and religious and cultural concerns. The statutory orders that exempted certain industries from import duties or provided selective concessions to privileged individual firms were phased out and import duties on 4,000 items were reduced. A number of laws were promulgated to bring the trade regime in conformity with WTO regulations. These include anti-dumping and countervailing measures and protection of intellectual property rights. A stable exchange rate policy helped maintain predictability and the competitiveness of Pakistani exports.

Fiscal policy reforms and consolidation were initiated by raising tax revenues, reducing expenditures, cutting down subsidies of all kinds, and containing the losses of public enterprises. Tax reforms were aimed at widening the tax base, eradicating direct contact between taxpayers and tax collectors, introducing a value-added tax as the major source of revenue, simplifying tax administration, and strengthening the capacity of the Central Board of Revenue. Although these reforms made some progress, other elements such as random audit of selected tax returns, under the universal self-assessment scheme, and automation and reorganization of the tax machinery did not make much headway. The reversal of the tax reforms in 2008, poor enforcement, and compliance have kept the tax to GDP ratio stagnant at around 10 per cent for the past six years or so. There is a huge scope for widening the tax net that has not been vigorously pursued.

As the losses of public enterprises were one of the sources of fiscal problems, every government has actively pursued an aggressive privatization plan. The thrust of this programme was the sale of assets to strategic investors. The sectors where most progress has been made are oil and gas, banking, telecommunications, and energy. Foreign investors were encouraged to participate in the privatization process and a large number of them were successful. The transactions completed in the five-year period up to 2007 yielded $3 billion. Three large nationalized commercial banks were privatized. These banks, after privatization, in contrast to the pre-privatization scenario, are contributing billions to the national exchequer as corporate taxes and dividends as they have all become profitable. Breaking up the monopoly, subsequent privatization of Pakistan Telecommunications Ltd (PTCL) and opening up of the sector to private operators has brought about a revolution in the ICT sector. The speed with which privatization was being pursued has slowed down as the previous PPP government was extremely reluctant to surrender control of the public enterprises which provided them avenues for patronage. The present government has carried out some transactions but the key loss-making enterprises, such as the Pakistan Steel Mills (PSM), Pakistan International Airlines (PIA), etc. have not been touched and the haemorrhage of public finances has not been staunched.

Deregulation of oil and gas, telecommunication, media, and the civil aviation sectors also resulted in significant positive results. Oil and gas exploration activity was stepped up, and constant discovery and production from new gas fields operated by private sector companies added new capacity to meet Pakistan's growing energy needs. Power generation capacity did not, however, keep pace with the rapid demand expansion and reforms in the transmission and distribution of public utility companies did not make much headway. Diversion of natural gas to CNG at subsidized rates and new connections to households on political grounds did create misallocation of scarce natural gas resource, creating a potential gap between supply and demand. The reforms in the energy sector did not make much headway and consequently, Pakistan has been faced with serious energy shortages crippling production and the export sector coupled with the perpetuation of the circular debt problem. The Nawaz Sharif government won the elections on promises of energy reforms but the load-shedding in summer 2017 showed that the desired results have not been achieved.

The telecommunications sector witnessed a boom because private sector companies were allowed licenses to operate cellular phones. The number of mobile phones has reached a figure of over 140 million, or a penetration rate of almost 70 per cent by 2017. The long-distance international and local loop monopoly of the PTCL was broken and new licenses, including those for wireless local loop, were issued. The customers are reaping rich dividends as the prices of phone calls—local, long distance, international— are currently only a fraction of those that previously prevailed. Lower telecommunication costs and increased penetration have had a favourable impact on the productivity of the economy. Internet penetration and broadband wireless connections have been growing rapidly since the 3G and 4G licenses were issued a year ago.

The analysis above indicates that initially, the shift in the economic paradigm under Bhutto initiated the drift but this was subsequently arrested. Economic reforms in many sectors were successfully implemented in bits and pieces. The momentum has however, been lost for a number of reasons, primarily relating to poor economic governance. They range from abrupt changes and reversals, poor enforcement of contracts, unwillingness to take tough but unpopular decisions, to the government's poor implementation capacity, and huge failures of coordination.

WHY GROWTH ACCELERATION

What propels growth acceleration in Pakistan is an extremely contentious question and there is no general consensus. Many believe that it is foreign aid inflows that cause it. A cool and dispassionate analysis shows that there are other factors that can explain the reasons for these episodes of acceleration. Since 1960, Pakistan has experienced three sustained growth accelerations with per capita real growth rates consistently exceeding 2 per cent a year.[14] The first period began in 1961 and lasted 10 years; the second, in 1977, lasted 12 years; and the third between 2002 and 2007. In all three cases, growth resulted from an increase both in capital inputs as well as in productivity.

Importantly, all the growth accelerations were preceded by, or coincided with, a significant increase in the investment ratio. In the early 1960s, the investment ratio rose from just over 12 per cent of the GDP in 1960 to 22.5 per cent in 1964. By 1971, when this ten-year period of strong growth ended, the investment ratio had declined again to about 14 per cent of the GDP. Similarly, the investment ratio rose sharply to 19 per cent of GDP in the 1977–92 period and stayed around this average. The second period ended in 1992 with an investment ratio of 20 per cent. Beginning in 1993, the investment ratio began declining, falling back again to 14 per cent by 1998.

The growth acceleration of 2002–07 was also accompanied by a similar increase in the investment ratio from 15.5 per cent of the GDP in 2001–02 to 23 per cent in 2007–08. Contrary to popular belief that official external aid flows—particularly from the US in the post-11 September 2001 period—were responsible for the economic turnaround of Pakistan, careful empirical analysis indicates that the growth acceleration came largely from an increase in total factor productivity.

Muslehuddin (2007), in his study of the period 1983/4 to 1987/8 and

2002/3 to 2005/6, during which the economy exhibited strong growth, averaging about 7 per cent, finds that the striking similarities between the two growth experiences in these two periods were driven by an improved policy framework and a favourable external environment. However, growth in the latter period differs from that in the 1980s in that growth in the 2000s took place due to better macroeconomic fundamentals, structural reforms, institutions and governance, and private sector dynamism.

Table 3.2: Characteristics of Growth Acceleration

Indicator	1983–84 to 1987–88	2002–03 to 2005–06
Policy consistency	Yes	Yes
Favourable external environment	Yes	Yes
Sound macroeconomic fundamentals	No	Yes
Adequate savings	No	No
Strong human capital base	No	No
High productivity	Yes	No
Structural reforms	No	Yes
Private sector dynamism	No	Somewhat
Strong institutions	No	Somewhat
Good governance	No	Somewhat

Source: M. Din (2007)

Exports of goods and services in the early 2000s rose from $13.6 billion to $21.2 billion—an increase of 55 per cent. Workers' remittances through official channels reached $6.5 billion annually by 2007–08 from less than $1 billion and foreign direct investment inflows rose fivefold during this five-year period. Meanwhile, US assistance as a percentage of Pakistan's total foreign exchange receipts was a paltry 4.5 per cent at its peak and, as a percentage of total budgetary expenditure, never exceeded over 7–8 per cent. These facts do not substantiate the widely-held myth that Pakistan's sustained high growth between 2002 and 2007 was made possible by massive foreign assistance from the US.

Interestingly, the contribution of productivity to growth during this period is similar or even somewhat higher than that in the earlier growth periods. To some extent, this may reflect the growing contribution of the services sector to growth, which usually requires less investment than manufacturing. It may also reflect that following the slump of the late 1990s, there was considerable excess capacity in the economy and therefore less need for new investments to generate growth. The increase in capital utilization translates to higher productivity per unit of capital and is reflected in the higher-than-average contribution of productivity to growth. While the turnaround in the economy post-2000 did put Pakistan on a higher growth path, it is important to understand this phenomenon in relation to earlier episodes of growth acceleration.

A World Bank study on the growth determinants of Pakistan reports that economic growth increases with improvements in education, financial depth, trade openness, and public infrastructure. It decreases when governments impose excessive burdens on the private sector and do not execute policies conducive to macroeconomic stability. An increase in the inflation rate, the volatility of the output gap, real exchange rate overvaluation or the probability of a financial crises all lead to a significant reduction in economic growth.

Growth, Poverty, and Inequality

How has growth affected the incidence of poverty in Pakistan? The earliest published data on poverty incidence available relates to 1963/4; therefore, it is difficult to estimate the proportion of the population that was living below the poverty line at the time of Independence. As the provinces constituting Pakistan were relatively backward in comparison to those inherited by India and there was a large migration of refugees facing dire economic conditions in the early years of its formation, it may be safe to guess-estimate that 50–60 per cent of the population was living below conditions of poverty in 1950.

Although poverty declined from 40 per cent in 1963/64 to 17 per cent in 1987/8, it rose in both the 1960s and 1990s. In the decade of the 2000s there is once again a movement towards reduction in the incidence of poverty. Chart 3.1 shows the declining trend of poverty between 2001 and 2014 as estimated by the Planning Commission The percentage of people living below the poverty line decreased by around 25 points; from a high of 34.6 per cent in 2001–02 to 9.3 per cent in 2013–14. In 2001, some 14 per cent of the population had a real per capita expenditure level of Rs 550 per person. By 2014, this was down to just 2 per cent. When poverty declines, it usually goes hand in hand with other gains in household welfare.

Graph 3.1: Trend in Poverty 2001–14

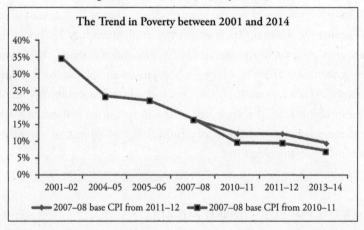

Pakistan saw substantial gains in a number of areas. There was a substantial increase in the ownership of relatively expensive assets like motorcycles and refrigerators among the poorest 20 per cent. Housing quality improved. Homes with some type of latrine (pit or flush connected to a drain) increased considerably, as did school enrolment rates, particularly among girls, during the period of the sharpest poverty decline, from 2001–02 to 2007–08. According to the World Bank,[15] 18 per cent of the poorest households in Pakistan now own motorcycles, in comparison to just 2 per cent 15 years ago; the number of households without any type of toilet has been cut in half—from close to 60 per cent to about 30 per cent among the poorest; and even the least advantaged families in Pakistan have moved towards a more diverse diet, with a greater consumption of dairy products, meat, fruit, and vegetables. This has also brought the rural diet into much closer alignment with that in the urban areas. In fact, rural inequality has actually fallen, while urban inequality has continued to rise. According to Reza Ali,[16] using a broader definition, Pakistan is now almost completely urban or urbanizing.

The most recent survey carried out in 2011/12, based on the basis of caloric requirements indicates that this proportion of the poor has halved to 9 per cent and that the measure of caloric intake to assess poverty is therefore no longer relevant. The cost of basic needs (CBN) poverty line has now officially replaced the old food energy intake (FEI) method. Chart 3.2, derived from the Planning Commission estimates,[17] shows that the direction is the same for both the old and new methods of estimating poverty, i.e. a declining trend. Under the new CBN poverty line, 29.5 per cent of the population in 2013/14 was living below the poverty line in comparison to 9.3 per cent computed by FEI method, i.e. under the old poverty line.

Graph 3.2: Trends in Poverty Incidence (old and new poverty lines)

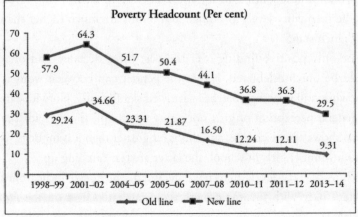

Akbar Zaidi[18] explains the factors underlying the global fall in poverty, which includes Pakistan. These include social and economic interventions in the form of targeted transfers and programmes, the rise in overall incomes, social and physical infrastructure, and development. In Pakistan's case, while a number of factors have played a key role in the fall in poverty, remittances have been singled out as the most significant.

The evidence regarding income distribution is not as clear cut as it is for poverty. The latest *UNDP Human Development Report* shows the value of the Gini coefficient to be 30.7, which is not very different from the past values that have hovered around 29. However, the ratio of incomes earned by the top 20 per cent to the poorest 20 per cent worsened, which shows that income distribution has clearly become less equal over the past three decades. In other words, the rich have become richer, and the gap between them and the rest of the population has increased. The 'middle class' has expanded over the past three decades, the income and asset differences between the richer 40 per cent of the population have grown at a faster pace than those in the lower 60 per cent.

It is not merely income inequality which has worsened, but this has been true also of regional inequalities in Pakistan, notwithstanding measures taken, such as greater provincial autonomy and resources. While the more urbanized Punjab and Khyber Pakhtunkhwa are far more prosperous than rural Sindh, south Punjab, and Balochistan, a surprising finding is that the inequality levels in Punjab and Sindh are much higher than KP and Balochistan.

The only positive finding over the past three decades, and one that should be much celebrated, is that the gender gap between women and men, while still unacceptable, has narrowed significantly. Notwithstanding the general perception of girls not going to school, the data for the last decade shows a huge change, and this is far greater than it is for boys. While boys outnumber girls in school, the latter are fast catching up.

While poverty levels may have declined, the social indicators have not kept pace with income growth. Pakistan ranks 134 on the *Human Development Index* among a group of 177 countries and the value of the index is 0.539, only slightly above the low human development index cut-off point. Almost half the population is illiterate and only one-third of the female population is literate. Over half the population does not have access to decent health facilities. The infant mortality rate of 80 per thousand is still very high. The health status of women and children is particularly low. Female labour force participation rates are the lowest among South Asian countries. The progress has clearly faltered in comparison to countries with similar per capita incomes and growth rates. An above average growth in GDP and per capita incomes was achieved with below average improvement in human development indicators. The picture of the long-term trends of economic growth, poverty, and inequality for Pakistan is very ambiguous, as income inequality has alternately declined and increased during periods of low and high growth. There is, however, a consistent pattern which shows that income inequality does increase when the growth rates are low. Rural–urban income disparities have also risen during the 2000s, a period of high growth. In the early 1990s there was a difference of eight percentage points in the poverty level between urban and rural areas, and this had widened to 13 percentage points by 2004/5. Notwithstanding the remarkable reduction in poverty of almost 10 percentage points in a relatively short period of time, there has been an increase in income inequality as well as urban–rural disparities.

A question that remains unsettled is the relationship between growth and income inequality. While the evidence is overwhelming that rapid growth does alleviate poverty, it is not very clear whether or not inequality is also reduced. There are sceptics who do not subscribe to this point of view. Faisal Bari[19] argues:

A lot of debate, especially from status quo supporters, has been around the fact that it is growth that will eventually address our concerns of inequality and poverty. They argue that if we move to eight per cent to 10 p[er] c[ent] growth per year, poverty will go down. This is the argument that as the size of the pie increases, all will benefit. The other popular analogy is that rising water will raise all boats.

I do not find the argument convincing. Historically, we have seen that while poverty has been going down, even in times of mid-level growth, inequality has been increasing whether growth has been high or low. As we follow the growth agenda, we open up opportunities for all but the ability to benefit from these opportunities is not equally distributed. And there is no reason to think that even over time those who are behind today will catch up. They can fall behind even further.

Education not only helps mitigate income inequality and promote social mobility but is a critical determinant of sustained economic growth and therefore deserves attention. Pakistan suffers from a serious deficiency of human, technical, and managerial manpower. The quality of higher education has deteriorated and graduates produced by our universities do not measure up to acceptable international standards. Those who excel in their fields have been migrating abroad for the past two decades or so. This migration has created a large reservoir of trained and experienced Pakistani expatriates overseas. Some of these expatriate Pakistanis are willing to return to Pakistan and provide the expertise that is wanting. However, those working in institutions where expertise is urgently required (particularly in the public sector) oppose their induction as they feel that this will side-line them. The popular media also unwittingly protects the interests of these less qualified insiders by highlighting differences in the salaries and perks offered to incoming experts without realizing their professional worth. In consequence, these overseas Pakistani experts either refuse to join or leave after a short while. It is paradoxical that a country which is short on highly skilled professionals, cannot attract those who are willing to supply these skills.

PAKISTAN'S RISING MIDDLE CLASS

Pakistan has a youthful population with 60 per cent falling in the age groups below 30. This youth bulge can become a boon for the economy given correct policies and well-organized institutions, particularly those engaged in education and skill formation. If this group can be transformed into a productive workforce for both the country and for labour deficient countries the prospects should be promising. Pakistan's track record of a sharp reduction in poverty in 2001–16 has had the natural effect of a rising middle class. Household income, consumption surveys, and living standards measurement studies indicate a major discrepancy in national income accounts, which may arise due to the large size of the informal economy. Ali Kemal and Ahmed Waqar Qasimi of Pakistan Institute of Development Economics (PIDE),[20] using a combination of PSLM consumption data and mis-invoicing of exports and imports concluded that Pakistan's 'informal economy was 91 per cent of the formal economy in 2007–08'. Afshan Subohi[21] sums up this upsurge of consumption in an article:

> Multiple surveys confirm that consumers' concerns and spending patterns are changing, drifting slowly towards those of their counterparts in developed countries.
>
> More than anything, it is the growing consumer demand that is driving business activity, both local manufacturing and the influx of goods from other countries through formal and informal channels. Most fast-moving consumer goods providers and companies dealing in textiles and garments, mobiles, cars, home appliances, cosmetics, etc. are not only doing well, but expanding. It explains the strong presence of major global players like Lever Brothers, P&G, Toyota, Suzuki, etc. in the local market.
>
> According to a recent Nielsen Consumer Confidence Index, Pakistan scored 104 points against the global average of 98 points, with Africa and the Middle East region trailing at 89 points.
>
> Several consumer behaviour surveys, conducted across the country by different outfits including banks, marketing research firms, and business houses, have reached broadly similar results. More credible ones, with greater circulation, are produced by the State Bank.[22]

Prof. Jawaid Ghani[23] has used the PSLM data and estimated that on the basis of $4–10 per day per person, Pakistan's middle class formed 42 per cent of the total population during 2013–14, rising from 33 per cent in 2001. The data he compiled on the consumer durables owned by the households point it in the same direction. However, the official data on large scale manufacturing does not substantiate this trend. The reason for this disconnect between the LSM data included in the national accounts and the actual consumption and sales data is provided by the State Bank of Pakistan in its annual report of 2014.

> In terms of LSM growth, a number of sectors that are showing strong performance (for example, fast moving consumer goods (FMCG) sector; plastic products; buses and trucks; and even textiles), are either underreported, or not even covered. The omission of such important sectors from official data coverage, probably explains the apparent disconnect between overall economic activity in the country and the hard numbers in LSM.

Homi Kharas,[24] in his study of the global middle class, has estimated that 52 million Pakistanis or 27 per cent of the population in 2015 would meet the global cut-off point of the 'middle class'.

Earlier work done by Durre Nayab of PIDE[25] shows that the size of the middle class in 2007/8, using a weighted composite index, was 61 million or 34.6 per cent of the population. She prefers to use the definition 'Expanded Middle Class' out of the three alternative definitions presented in Table 3.3. If she goes by a stricter definition, the number declines by almost half to 32.5 million or 18.8 per cent of the population. The expanded definition deals with the problem that those in this class are altogether free from the risk of experiencing poverty. The approach of a weighted composite index is attractive in comparison to a single-dimensional income or consumption measure, as it includes several components such as education, housing, lifestyle, and occupation besides income. These sub-indices, comprising the composite index, were then weighted through the principal component analysis (PCA) method and their scores were added up to arrive at the total score for households. The households were then categorized into seven classes based on their total scores on the index. The results of this exercise are set out in the table below.

Table 3.3: Size of the Middle Class in Pakistan Using a Weighted Composite Index

	Proportion of the population (per cent)			Numbers in millions		
	Total	Urban	Rural	Total	Urban	Rural
Strict Middle Class	18.8	32.9	8.6	32.5	22.6	9.8
Expanded Middle Class	34.6	53.7	20.9	61.0	38.5	22.4
Broadest Middle Class	35.0	54.6	21.0	61.6	39.1	22.4

Source: Calculated by Durre Nayab from PSLM, 2007–8

To sum up, the size of the middle class varies a great deal but the three carefully conducted studies indicate that the range would be between 27 to 42 per cent. Durre Nayab's estimate is based on a multidimensional measure, indicative that a figure of about 35 per cent may be the most realistic. Keeping this as the constant, thus assuming that there has been no further expansion in the proportion entering the middle class and applying these to the present population (approximately 200 million), I estimate that the size of the Expanded Middle Class in Pakistan in 2017 would be 69 million. Taking the 'stricter' definition, the numbers would be about 38 million. The estimate of 69 million appears to be more consistent with the rate of increase observed in the demand for cars, apartments, consumer durables, motorcycles, fast-moving consumer goods, area under shopping malls, domestic and international travel, and restaurants and eating places.

International trends in the expansion of the middle class are moving in the same direction as observed in Pakistan and so the country is not experiencing anything that is out of the ordinary. According to Homi Kharas[26] of Brookings, who has been studying the global middle class:

By 1975, 150 years after starting its growth phase, the middle class had reached 1 billion people. By 2006, another 1 billion had joined the middle class, and now less than a decade later, we are at 3 billion. The middle class could surpass 4 billion by 2021, making it a majority of the world's population.

If these global and past historical trends of Pakistan continue to persist into the future, by 2030, according to Kharas's calculations, 65 per cent of the population would consist of the middle class, over twice the size of the 27 per cent in 2015. The following table, based on Kharas's work, provides the future projections of Pakistan's middle class. It assumes that by 2020, the average per capita income in 2011, constant PPP dollars, would be $5,583—an increase of 18 per cent over five years.

A daily income of somewhere around $10 per person, or the equivalent of $10,000 a year for the family of three, can be applied as a rough proxy for middle class status.

A large middle class increases the demand for domestic goods and services, and helps fund consumption-led growth. Middle class parents have the resources to invest in their children's education, building human capital for the country as a whole. They are able to take reasonable business risks, becoming investors as well as consumers and workers. In all these ways, the emergence of a middle class drives economic growth.

Having a large middle class is also critical to fostering good governance. Middle class citizens want the stability and predictability that comes from a political system that promotes fair competition, in which the very rich cannot rely on insider privileges to accumulate unearned wealth. Middle class people are less vulnerable than the poor to pressure to pay into patronage networks and are more likely to support a government that protects private property and encourages private enterprise. When the middle class reaches a certain size, of perhaps 30 per cent of the population, its members can start to identify with one another and use their collective power to demand that the state spend their taxes to finance public services, security, and other critical goods. Finally, members of a prospering middle class are unlikely to be drawn into the kinds of ethnic and religious rivalries that spur political instability.

Table 3.4: Pakistan Headcount and Consumption
(constant 2011 PPP $ billion)

	2015		2020		2030	
	million	$	million	$	million	$
Middle class	52	333	82	536	158	1,146
Total Pakistan	189	683	208	894	245	1,435
Middle class percentage of total	27	49	39	60	65	80
GDP per capita		4,706		5,583		7,623

Source: Homi Kharas, February 2017

It must, however, be recognized as Table 3.4 clearly shows that the middle class in Pakistan is a purely urban phenomenon, and the rapid urbanization and the rising ratio of population living in the cities lends support to this finding. Therefore, only if the migration out of the rural areas continues to exceed the national population growth rate would urbanization take hold. If that happens, the rapid growth of an educated, urban middle class linked with the rest of the world through Internet, social media, and the electronic media would have strong implications for institutional reform and improved governance in Pakistan. Free from the shackles of kinship, *biradari*, feudal landlords, tribal chiefs, and sardars, the urban middle class would demand performance from their elected leaders as they are known to be intolerant of inefficiencies and ineptitude in the delivery of public services. They are the potential drivers of change.

SUMMATION

Pakistan has made much progress in comparison to its inheritance in 1947. It made a very promising beginning and overtook most East Asian countries in growth and exports, and was in performance one of the top ten developing countries in 1950–90. It was way ahead of India and Bangladesh in terms of most of the economic and social indicators. Since then, the economy has seen a downward slope and is lagging behind not only the East Asian countries, which have made great strides, but even in relation to its two neighbours in South Asia. There are many reasons, which we have discussed, which can explain the reasons for this decline but it was the paradigm shift in the economic model adopted in the 1970s, and the politics of patronage, which led to the decay of the institutions of economic governance combined with chronic political instability associated with policy discontinuity and uncertainty that emerge as the most dominant. I tend to agree with Bardhan (1984):[27] 'In the context of economic growth it is rather the capacity of the system to isolate economic management from political processes of distributive demands, rent seeking and patronage, disbursement that makes the crucial difference.'

As the chapter on 'Society' will illustrate, increasing ethno-linguistic fragmentation has dampened the mobility of beneficial factors, retarded economic and social progress, and pushed us in the direction towards which Africa has been set for quite a long time. Easterly and Levine (1997)[28] find an adverse impact of ethno-linguistic fragmentation on income, growth, and economic policies in Sub-Saharan Africa. Easterly (2001c)[29] finds that the effect on growth of ethnic conflict in the original growth regression disappear if institutions are of significantly high quality.

Notwithstanding this setback in terms of growth achievement, there is a surprising outcome, i.e. poverty has been reduced since 2001 and consequently, there has been an expansion in the size of the middle class. Looking to the future, the challenges for the Pakistani economy in the twenty-first century are likely to be more onerous: disruptive technologies, a knowledge economy, a retreat from globalization, and anti-immigration policies in the West. The youth bulge, if properly equipped with the skills required by the knowledge economy and the rising middle class, educated and urbanized, and able to adapt to new realities, can help in accelerating the impulses of broad-based economic growth and social development. The China-Pakistan Economic Corridor (CPEC) provides an alternate course for overcoming energy shortages, developing backward areas, and promoting regional and global integration This agenda needs to be relentlessly and diligently pursued.

ANNEX TABLE I
Sectoral Shares in GDP (fc)

	1950	1969–70	1989–90	2001–02	2007–08	2015–16
Commodity sector	62.8	61.6	51.4	47.9	47.0	40.8
Agriculture	53.2	38.9	25.8	24.1	20.9	20.9
Major crops	27.6	23.4	12.3	8.0	7.1	5.3
Minor crops	6.6	4.2	4.5	3.1	2.4	2.9
Livestock	18.3	10.6	7.7	12.0	10.9	11.8
INDUSTRY	9.6	22.7	25.6	23.7	22.1	21.0
Mining	0.2	0.5	0.5	2.4	2.6	2.9
Manufacturing	7.8	16.0	17.6	15.9	18.9	13.3
LSM	2.2	12.5	12.7	10.4	13.3	10.6
SSM	5.5	3.5	3.3	5.6	4.4	1.7
Construction	1.4	4.2	3.3	2.4	2.7	2.4
Electricity, Gas	0.2	2.0	3.3	3.0	1.7	1.7
SERVICES	37.2	38.4	48.6	52.1	53.0	58.4
Transport and Communication	5.0	6.3	9.5	11.4	10.0	13.4
Trade	11.9	13.8	16.5	17.8	17.1	18.3
Finance	0.4	1.8	2.2	3.5	6.5	3.1
Dwellings	5.1	3.4	5.4	3.2	2.6	6.7
Public Administration and Defence	7.0	6.4	7.1	6.4	6.5	7.4
Other Services	7.7	6.7	7.6	9.8	10.4	9.9

Source for 2015–2016 data: Pakistan Bureau of Statistics at constant basic prices. <http://www.pbs.gov.pk/sites/default/files//tables/Table-7.pdf>

ANNEX TABLE II
KEY ECONOMIC AND SOCIAL INDICATORS 1947–2015

	1947	1970	1990	2001	2015
Population					
In million	33.0	58.1	107.6	142.8	191.7
GDP (current m.p.) Rs. Billion	58.0	62.9	1115.7	4528.0	27493.1
GDP (billion 2010 US$)	3.8	27.5	79.9	119.9	217.7
Income					
Per Capita Income (Constant Rs.) (2005–06=100)	1638.0	24405.0	38295.3	43777.7	59439.8
Per Capita Income (Current US$)	85.0	172.6	371.8	511.8	1429.0
Per Capita Income (Current Rs.)	405.0	821.0	7954.0	29797.0	144945.0
Production Index (2004–06=100)		29.9	62.1	85.7	110.5
Fiber Production Index	100.0	185.0	204.0	254.6	324.3
Water Availability (MAF)	55.0	75.5	117.1	97.0	102.5
Agriculture					
Wheat Production (m. tons)	3.3	7.3	14.4	19.2	25.3
Rice Production (m. tons)	0.7	2.2	3.3	3.9	6.9
Cotton Production (m. bales)	1.1	3.2	8.6	10.6	10.1
Fertilizer per ha. Crop (kg)	0.0	23.0	91.0	134.0	189.0
Manufacturing Production Index (2010=100)	100.0	11.1	36.5	55.8	118.8
Steel Production (000 tons)	0.0	180.0	NA	3453.2	2352.9
Cement Production (000 tons)	292.0	2656.0	7488.0	9672.0	23428.0
Industry					
Chemical Production (000 tons)	0.0	134.1	332.7	446.8	542.5
Sugar Production (000 tons)	10.0	610.0	1857.0	2956.0	4812.0
Veg. Ghee Production (000 tons)	2.0	126.0	683.0	835.0	873.0
Cloth Production (000 Sq. meter)	29581.0	606500.0	294800.0	490200.0	1046500.0
Petroleum Products (000 tons)				8337.0	8300.0
Motor cars production (000)			25.7	39.6	106.1
Motor cycles production(000)			92.8	117.9	1289.5

	1947	1970	1990	2001	2015
Urea Fertilizer (million tons)		206.3	2108.5	4005.1	3806.0
Commercial Energy Production (GW/h)		6380.0	37180.0	68117.0	71712.0
Infrastructure					
Per Capita Electricity production (Gwh)	6.0	109.8	345.5	477.1	374.1
Road Length (km)	22238.0	31673.0	162345.0	249972.0	263942.0
Area under Canal Irrigation(mill. ha)	7.9	9.3	7.7	7.0	6.0
Gas billion cu. Meters	0.0	2.9	443.3	768.1	879.2
Road Vehicles (000 Nos)	1.0	191.9	1989.4	4471.0	13881.1
Consumption					
Phone Connections (000 Nos)	0.4	2.5	922.5	3340.0	5098.0
TV Sets per 1,000 Persons	0.0	92.4	1575.1	3432.0	N.A.
Primary Enrolment Rate (000)	5.0	3910.0	10400.0	14105.0	19935.0
Population per Doctor	23897.0	15256.0	2082.0	1516.0	1073.0
Population per Nurse (population to reg'd nurse)	369318.0	13141.0	6349.3	3567.3	2123.6
Literacy rate, adult female (% of females ages 15 and above)			14.8	29.0	43.0
Literacy rate, adult male (% of males ages 15 and above)			35.3	55.2	69.8
Literacy Rate	11.0	20.0		51.0	60.0
Social indicators					
Infant Mortality Rate	N.A.	141.1	106.1	86.0	65.8
Total Fertility Rate	N.A.	6.6	6.0	4.4	3.6
Population with Access to Safe Water	N.A.	25.0	86.3	88.7	91.4
Mortality rate, under-5 (per 1,000 live births)	N.A.	188.8	138.6	109.8	81.1
Poverty headcount ratio (Population living below $1.90/day)			59.0	28.5	8.3
Share of poorest 20% in income			8.1	9.4	9.6
Life Expectancy		52.9	60.1	63.0	66.2

Notes and References

1. *LIFE Magazine*, 31 January 1948.

2. McCartney, M., *Pakistan, Growth, Dependency, and Crisis* (School of Oriental and African Studies [SOAS], University of London, 2011).

3. Lieven, A., *Pakistan: A Hard Country*, (London: Allen Lane, 2011).

4. Parikh, K. (ed), *Explaining Growth in South Asia: A South Asian Perspective* (New Delhi: OUP, 2006); Kemal, A. R. et al, 'Sources of Growth in Pakistan' *in* K. Parikh (ed); McCartney, M., *Pakistan: The Political Economy of Growth, Stagnation and the State, 1951–2009* (New York and London: Routledge, 2011).

5. Jahan R., *Pakistan: Failure in National Integration* (Columbia University Press, 1972).

6. Poverty Reduction and Economic Management Sector Unit South Asia Region, *Pakistan Development Policy Review A New Dawn?* (World Bank, 2002).

7. Mohammad, F., Badar, Hussain, 'Structure of Rural Income in Pakistan: Some Preliminary Estimates [with Comments]', *Pakistan Development Review,* Autumn/Winter 1985, Vol. 24, No. 3–4.

8. Arif, K. M., *Working with Zia: Pakistan's Power Politics, 1977–1988* (OUP, 1995).

9. For a detailed account of these reforms, see Sartaj Aziz, *Between Dreams and Realities* (OUP, 2009).

10. Hamid, N., M. Khan, 'Pakistan: A Case of Premature De-industrializa

tion?', *Lahore Journal of Economics*, 20 September 2015.

11. State Bank of Pakistan. (Several Years). *Annual Reports,* Government of Pakistan.

12. McCartney, *Pakistan, Growth, Dependency, and Crisis* (School of Oriental and African Studies (SOAS), University of London, 2011).

13. Almeida, C., 'The Revenge of the State', *Dawn,* 17 January 2017.

14. This is the benchmark used by Hausmann et al., 'Growth Acceleration' NBER Working paper 10566 (Cambridge, 2004) for their specification of growth acceleration.

15. World Bank, *Growth: A Shared Responsibility*, Pakistan Development Update, May 2017.

16. Reza Ali, 'Estimating Urbanization', *The Urban Gazette*, Issue December 2013.

17. Communication from Dr Naeemuz Zafar, Member Planning Commission, September 2016.

18. Zaidi, S. A. 'Inequality not Poverty', *Dawn,* 24 January 2017.

19. Bari, F., 'Quest for Solutions', *Dawn,* 26 August 2016.

20. Kamal, A., and A. W. Qasimi, *Precise Estimates of the Informal Economy* (PIDE, 1912).

21. Subohi, A., 'Resilient Despite All Odds', *Dawn,* 31 October 2016.

22. Kamal and Qasimi, op. cit.

23. Ghani, J., *The Emerging Middle Class in Pakistan: How it Consumes, Earns, and Saves,* KSBL Working Paper Series 2014–11.

24. Kharas, H., *The Unprecedented Expansion of the Global Middle Class* (Washington DC: The Brookings Institution, 2010).

25. Nayab D., *Estimating the Middle Class in Pakistan,* PIDE, Working Paper 2011, 77.

26. Kharas, H., *How a Growing Middle Class Could Save the World's Economy* (The Pew Charitable Trusts, 2016).

27. Bardhan, P., *The Political Economy of Development in India* (New Delhi: OUP, 1984).

28. Easterly, W., R. Levine, 'Africa's Growth Tragedy: Policies and Ethnic Divisions', *Quarterly Journal of Economics* Vol 112 Issue 4, November 1997, 1203–50.

29. Easterly, 'Can Civic Institutions Resolve Ethnic Conflict', Economic Development and Cultural Change Vol 49, Issue 4, July 2001, 687–706.

4

The Polity

Empirical evidence about Pakistan's several experiments with strong military-led governments suggests that economic progress, devoid of political legitimacy—however impressive—may prove to be elusive and transient, and leave no lasting footprints. Similarly, those wishing for the installation of a politically neutral, technocratic government of experts underwritten by the army to be installed to bring about the necessary reforms, clean up the political stables, and weed out corruption are also sadly mistaken. Bangladesh attempted this for two years in 2009 but failed to accomplish these goals. In the twenty-first century, with such an active and powerful social media mobilizing public opinion, a free press, a vigilant civil society, and independent judiciary, it is barely conceivable that any non-representative group, however well-meaning and competent, could achieve the intended goals. Political parties would all coalesce and organize their supporters to resist such a government. Rather than the expected economic turnaround, there would be more chaos and disruptions in economic activity. Once such a governmental imposition has also failed, no other option is feasible but the restoration of democracy and a re-run of the general elections. In the interim, the country and its people would have faced needless hardships while gaining nothing in return and the economy would have suffered enormous dislocations and reversals because of the existing political uncertainty.

The economy and economic players require a stable political environment. It is not realized that economic policy decisions are not purely technocratic solutions but affect various segments of the population differentially. There are bound to be winners and losers from these decisions. In a democratic society, there are fora such as the parliament and provincial assemblies, which discuss and debate the implications of particular policies for various sections of the population and areas of the country. Conflicts are resolved through compromise and conciliation. In an authoritarian government a single individual is the final arbiter. His decision may be faulty but there is no recourse available for its reversal. That is why even very sound policies initiated by military governments which had an impact were unable to weather the test of time after their departure. Recent examples of the complete dismantling of the local government system in all the four provinces, the supersession of the Police Order, the reversal of the HR reforms introduced in the Federal Board of Revenue (FBR), the hiatus in the privatization of public enterprises, and the suspension of the order of conversion of B districts which were planned to be covered by the police rather than Levies in Balochistan are illustrative of this. Those who were adversely affected by these policies became quite active and vocal, thereby persuading the newly elected governments that their popularity would rise if these wrongs perpetrated by an authoritarian leader were reversed. Grandstanding by political leaders to paint military dictators in bad light after their exit adds fuel to the fire by accentuating uncertainty about the direction of economic policies.

It can, therefore, be inferred from past experience that without the involvement and participation of the people and their genuine representatives, elegant and technically sound solutions introduced by authoritarian regimes are soon reversed when the form of government changes. Policies—however sound they may appear—are reversed, causing irreparable loss to business confidence. The country pays a heavy price for severe economic disruptions, breakdown of civilian institutions, and a lack of accountability. The other problem with the non-elected governments is that they are not accountable to anyone. When the chief of army staff assumes control of government, all his subordinates fall in line and follow his orders as they are trained and required to do. Dissent, differences of opinion, and/or open disagreements at decision-making forums are rare. The next tier of officers look upon the chief for their promotions, postings, and perks, and it is not in their interest to raise any questions or express scepticism. The data and information the new ruler relies upon for the decisions s/he makes is also based upon inputs from the Intelligence agencies and lower formations of the army. 'Group-think' thus encompasses the entire system and an objective assessment and evaluation of the impact of policies made becomes quite complex.

This widens the gap between the 'perceived reality' as viewed by authoritarian regimes and the 'actual reality' as felt by the population at large. The population, however, feels helpless and hapless because they have no orderly and permissible means of expressing their views or removing the ruler, except through mass protest movements which are themselves inimical to economic order. To the extent that a dictator is benevolent or honest, the damage remains limited. However, if there is a malevolent or corrupt dictator in power, there is no clear exit strategy. However intense the disenchantment or disaffection with his policies may be, there is no legitimate manner in which he can be removed. Gamal Abdel Nasser, Achmad Sukarno, Ibrahim Babangida, and Mobuto Sese Seko were all forced out of office by their own juniors because the latter believed they had overstayed their welcome.

Notwithstanding all its weaknesses and shortcomings, an orderly transition of power at regular intervals through a predictable democratic process is the least damaging means of keeping an economy moving on an even keel. What is the link between political stability and economic growth? Political stability promotes transparency, the rule of law, and predictability of economic policies, thus generating confidence among investors that they can profitably conduct their business in a predictable environment. Efficiency in the allocation of resources and higher capital investment in a stable political environment increases the rate of economic growth. When the political situation becomes volatile and unpredictable, investors adopt a cautious wait-and-watch attitude and are hesitant to invest.

The Indian economy was not faring well during the last few years of Manmohan Singh's tenure although he was an accomplished economist and reformer. The electorate voted him out of power and brought in Narendra Modi, who had built a strong record of performance in Gujarat. The market sentiment took a turn for the better almost immediately after his election and the Indian economy began growing rapidly. The people of

India had evidently exercised their choice wisely at the time of the elections and effected the change. That would not have been possible had India had a dictator who believed in his own indispensability. As a counter-argument to a democratic form of government, many analysts refer to China to substantiate their view regarding the superiority of an authoritarian regime as a catalyst for rapid economic growth. Here, it is conveniently forgotten that the system of governance in China—i.e. the transition from one set of leaders to another—is well known and well understood. The timing of transition is not shrouded in secrecy and although the right of adult franchise does not exist, there is limited franchise exercised by the National People's Congress.

The question that then arises is that if democratically elected governments happen to be the only worthwhile option, how do we break the vicious cycle of political instability, economic stagnation, high unemployment, collapse in demand, low investment, and dissatisfaction with the existing political leadership, and strengthen democratic governance in Pakistan?

In this context it is relevant to trace the evolution of the political parties in Pakistan since Independence, review their present standing and status, identify their weaknesses and shortcomings, and propose reforms that can strengthen the process of democratic governance over time. I begin by critically analysing Pakistan's Muslim League, which was the party that initiated the movement for a separate homeland for Indian Muslims and, under the leadership of Quaid-i-Azam Mohammad Ali Jinnah, successfully accomplished their mission of creating Pakistan.

Anwar Syed, one of the early scholars of politics in Pakistan, does not sketch a very pretty picture of political parties in Pakistan. Although there have been many changes over the past seven decades, the formative nature of the parties does create a path dependency and some of the characteristics have remained unchanged. According to him:

Pakistan's political parties are dominated by a feudalistic ethos that pervades politicians; this ethos results in shifting loyalties, intolerance of rivals, expectation of subservience from lower orders, a propensity for violence, disregard of the law, lack of commitment to public interest and consequent readiness to both corrupt and be corrupted, and subservience to the greater centres of power.[1]

Nothing much has changed since then as is evidenced by the 2016 PILDAT nationwide survey of public opinion, which places Pakistan's political parties second from the bottom, with an approval rating of 35 per cent.[2]

PAKISTAN MUSLIM LEAGUE

The partition of India into two states was spearheaded by the All India Muslim League (AIML) which, on the basis of its overwhelming victory in the 1945/6 elections, became the principal protagonist of a separate Muslim state—Pakistan. AIML was a centrist party and its manifesto promised modern nationalism and 'Modernist Islam'. The Pakistan Muslim League (PML), the successor to AIML came into being in 1947 after the latter succeeded in getting India divided into two countries and creating a new state, Pakistan as homeland for the Muslims of India. The leader of the AIML, M. A. Jinnah, became the governor general of Pakistan, and party affairs were given over to the general secretary, Liaquat Ali Khan, who also assumed the office of the first prime minister of Pakistan. The first convention of the PML was held in February 1948 where a chief organizer was appointed to mould the party and organize the election of its office-bearers. The chief organizer, Ch. Khaliquzzaman, a refugee leader from Uttar Pradesh, was elected the first president of the PML in April 1949. That marked the beginning of the continuing turmoil and frequent divisions of the PML over the following seven decades. Liaquat Ali Khan did not like the separation of the offices of the prime minister and the president of the party, and in this he was supported by the chief ministers of the provinces who also wanted to head the party. This led to an internal struggle within the party and Liaquat Ali Khan succeeded in capturing the office of the president of the PML. The chief ministers became the presidents of the respective provincial branches of the party.

The first fissure appeared in 1949 when a prominent leader of the PML in East Pakistan, Huseyn Shaheed Suhrawardy, decided to quit the party and form a new one, the All Pakistan Awami Muslim League (APAML), which after several mutations became the Awami League. This party formed an alliance with a former PML supporter of East Pakistan, Abul Kasem Fazlul Haq, and their United Front (UF) trounced the PML by capturing 228 of the 238 seats in the first direct elections ever held for the provincial assembly of East Pakistan in 1954 on the basis of adult franchise. This superior performance and the subsequent ascendancy of the Awami League virtually annihilated the PML from the political landscape of East Pakistan. It was the same Awami League that continued to represent the interests of East Pakistan vocally and aggressively under the leadership of Sheikh Mujibur Rahman and won the 1970 general elections with a vast majority. Having been denied the right to form the government as the majority party leader, Mujib and the Awami League led the struggle for the separation of East Pakistan from West Pakistan, which culminated in the break-up of Pakistan in 1971.

In Punjab, Nawab Mamdot, the first chief minister of Punjab, was removed for disobedience of the party and defying the PM's instructions. He resigned from the PML and, along with his supporters, gave birth to the Jinnah Muslim League (JML) in 1949. Suhrawardy and Mamdot merged their two parties to form the Jinnah Awami Muslim League (JAML) but this union did not last long, and in 1953 the word 'Muslim' was removed and the party became Jinnah Awami League (JAL). Mamdot quit the JAL and rejoined the PML. Another splinter group in Punjab led by Mian Iftikharuddin, a provincial minister, transformed itself into a new left-leaning party, the Azad Pakistan Party (APP), in 1949. This party was unable to mobilize much support and eventually merged with the National Awami Party (NAP) in 1957. These party defections, however, did not inflict much damage on the popularity of PML, as in the first direct elections to the Punjab Provincial Assembly held in 1951, the party swept into power, winning 140 of the 191 seats. The Jinnah Awami Muslim League was able to garner only 32 seats and the APP 1 seat.

In Sindh, an attempt to break away from the PML and form a new regional party, the Sindh Muslim League, was made by Ayub Khuhro, the first elected chief minister of Sindh. As a consequence of serious infighting within the Sindh Provincial Muslim League, Khuhro was removed from the post. In protest he formed his own party. In the 1953 elections to the Sindh provincial assembly, the PML was able to capture 76 out of a total of 111 seats, thereby forming the government, while the SML did poorly, winning only 7 seats. The SML folded up in 1954 with its members returning to rejoin the PML. After the four provinces were all unified into one unit, i.e. West Pakistan, General Iskandar Mirza played a vital role in the shaping of the Republican Party when a large number of Muslim Leaguers decided to cross the floor in return for lucrative government positions. The Republican Party remained in power until 1958, when it was dissolved under the martial law regulation banning all political parties. After the promulgation of martial law in 1958 and until the new constitution was framed in 1962, all political activities remained suspended.

When Ayub Khan decided to contest the presidential elections under the new constitution, he needed the support of a political party to back him up and organize the election campaign. He, therefore, convened a meeting of the Muslim Leaguers and the Republican Party and announced the revival of the Pakistan Muslim League. The new party, patronized by Ayub, was called Convention Muslim League as several leaders of the PML—such as Khan Qayyum Khan, former Chief Minister of the North-Western Frontier Province (NWFP), and Mian Mumtaz Daultana, former Chief Minister of Punjab—did not agree with Ayub's proposal and formed their own faction which was called the Council Muslim League. The Council Muslim League supported Mohtarma Fatima Jinnah, the sister of the founder of Pakistan, in her bid to become the president of Pakistan through the indirect elections in which 80,000 Basic Democrats formed the Electoral College. The Convention Muslim League, as expected, threw its full weight behind Ayub Khan.

Z. A. Bhutto, a very close confidant of Ayub at that time, was the general secretary of the party and played a very active role in the election of Ayub Khan. He broke ranks with Ayub after the Tashkent Declaration between India and Pakistan and became one of the fiercest opponents of his mentor. He formed the Pakistan Peoples Party (PPP) in November

1967 on a socialist and leftist electoral platform and swept the country with his emotionally charged speeches and his promise to bring measures for the welfare of common citizens. There was a split in the Council Muslim League when Khan Abdul Qayyum Khan and Mumtaz Daultana developed differences and Qayyum decided to form his own faction, the Qayyum Muslim League. In the 1970 election, the PPP eliminated the Council Muslim League and Qayyum Muslim League both from the national and provincial assemblies, winning a majority of seats from West Pakistan. Against 81 seats won by the PPP in the National Assembly, the Qayyum League and Council Muslim League won only 9 and 7 seats respectively.

As soon as the new constitution was finalized in 1973 and the parliamentary form of government was reinstated in Pakistan, Bhutto became the prime minister. By the time the next general elections were held in 1977, the Muslim League had been completely eliminated from the political scene. It was only during General Zia ul-Haq's time that the Muslim League was once again revived but it soon split into the PML-Junejo, the PML-Functional led by Pir Pagara, and the PML under Nawaz Sharif. Other smaller groups such as PML-Jinnah and PML-Zia surfaced during the period but they did not survive long. The PML-N and the PPP alternated in power in 1988–99 and Pakistan saw eight prime ministers, including four caretaker prime ministers during this period. After the dismissal of the Nawaz Sharif government, when General Pervez Musharraf decided to hold general elections in 2002, the PML-N was further split into two factions: one remaining loyal to the outgoing prime minister, called the PML-N, and the other led by the former interior minister, styled PML-Quaid (PML-Q). The latter remained in power between 2002 and 2007. In the 2008 election, the PML-N formed the government in Punjab but lost to the PPP in the National Assembly elections. The PML-N returned to power once again in the 2013 general elections and formed the government at the federal, Punjab, and Balochistan levels. The PML-Q has been simply decimated and apart from a few districts in Punjab, it no longer exists. Most of the PML-Q leaders and assembly members have crossed over to PML-N. So it is that the circle which began in 1947 with a single unified and strong PML seems to have been completed with PML-N being the only surviving and electorally strong Muslim League in the country with all the other competing factions going into oblivion. Just as in the 1990s, the PPP and PML-N have again alternated in office over the last 8 years. Ideologically, the PML-N has once again become a centrist party, adhering to its original position in 1947. It had remained so until it became an appendage to Zia ul-Haq's government and moved in to support his agenda of Islamization. In recent years, the PML-N appears to be gradually disowning and distancing itself from that ideological disposition and becoming more moderate and broad-minded in its outlook, notwithstanding a number of its leaders still adhering to the old ideology.

The Indian National Congress (INC), the counterpart of the PML which led the Independence movement in India, has remained intact and held uninterrupted power for 30 years until 1977. Thereafter, the INC has remained one of the two major political parties of India and remained in power for 54 out of 70 years, providing political stability and continuity. It recently lost power badly in the 2014 elections, having won the previous two general elections and staying in power for a decade. It seems to be suffering from a crisis of leadership. Had a leader of the stature and calibre of Nehru remained at the helm of Pakistan for several decades during its formative phase, there are good reasons to believe that the political history of Pakistan would have been very different. A commentator[3] summarized the issue as follows:

> The Muslim League (ML) succeeded in creating Pakistan, despite heavy odds, but it could not morph from a nationalist movement to a national party. The main reason for this was the leadership vacuum created by the demise of the Quaid-i-Azam and the assassination of Liaquat Ali Khan within the formative years of our independence.

While India was able to successfully draft a new constitution for itself in 1948, Pakistan was unable to do so. This is why in the nine years following its independence, Pakistan sifted through 7 prime ministers and 8 cabinet changes, which led to the downfall of the PML. While the politicians were busy engaging in a fierce battle for power, the country witnessed the military step in to fill the power vacuum in 1958, 1969, and again in 1977.

Vernon Hewitt[4] describes the period 1988 through 1999 as:

> Eleven years of political instability and constitutional decline, where the Pakistani state was dissected into parallel and disengaged political and legal authorities. The president was pitted against the prime minister, the secular opposed the religious authority, the judiciary acted against the executive, and the executive contrasted the legislature. This paralysed the Pakistani government, and created irreparable instability.

There has been criticism of the PML-N governments in Punjab (holding power since 2008) and at the federal level since 2014 in perpetuating the past practices of patron–client relationships rather than moving away from them. One of Pakistan's top political scientists, Professor Hasan Askari,[5] believes that the PML-N has created a political system of patronage which has subjugated both the bureaucracy and police. Assignments and state resources are distributed to the police and major business companies based on the loyalty to the house of the Sharifs, and no group can afford to alienate them.

> The PML-N has created a patrimonial and patronage-based political order in the Punjab. It has brought the bureaucracy and the police under its firm control. The important bureaucratic and police assignments in the province are assigned purely on loyalty to the House of Sharifs. State resources and patronage are used in a highly partisan manner and no major business group can afford to alienate them.
>
> The PML-N governments at the federal level and in the Punjab have created a class of beneficiaries—government contractors and suppliers, real estate dealers, facilitators for providing services to people, and local influentials—by letting them make money from government tasks and projects or giving them a free hand for making profit in private business or commercial activity or charging money from people for facilitation of their tasks. These 'beneficiaries' have some obligations toward the government,

which include making financial resources available for the activities of the ruling party, building goodwill for the government at the common person level, and securing votes for its candidates.

Thus, the PML could not keep the country on a democratic trajectory during the first decade when it was in power, nor in the decade of 1990s, when it twice got the opportunity. The only redeeming feature was the brief period of Junejo's governance in the mid-1980s when, having been appointed by a military dictator, he challenged the legitimacy of Zia's continuation as president and wanted to know the timetable for his exit. Junejo's merit-based system of governance ushered in a breath of fresh air in the governance structure of Pakistan and it can only be speculated that had he remained in power for a longer period of time, the changes and practices he introduced would have become embedded in the system.

OTHER POLITICAL PARTIES

As the earlier section has shown, the Pakistan Muslim League has passed through several periods of trial and tribulation since 1947. This gave rise to the emergence of other political parties in Pakistan over the last seven decades, some of which have survived while others have vanished. The significant parties can be divided into three categories; (a) national Parties: PML-N, PPP, and PTI; (b) regional parties: ANP, MQM, PKMAP, NP, BNP; and (c) religio-political parties: JI and JUI.

After sweeping the general elections of 1970, the PPP lost its charismatic founder Z. A. Bhutto, popularly known as ZAB, who was hanged in 1979. There was a general expectation that the PPP would usher in a drastic changes in Pakistan's body politic. Mariam Mufti summarizes the rising expectations from the PPP and explains how it has so rapidly let down its supporters. She states that the PPP held widespread national appeal and rose to power in the 1970s by 'adhering to a programmatic representation of voter preferences, manifested in the political slogan of "*roti, kapra,* and *makaan*"'.[6] She however adds that:

It could be argued at that time that the PPP heralded the era of mass-based politics in Pakistan and that the party held widespread national appeal. Yet the party relied more on the charismatic leadership of ZAB to rally support of its constituency and neglected the administration infrastructure and party organization that would help facilitate and deliver the party's mandate. Charismatic leaders tended to consciously disarticulate policy commitments in order to avoid constituency division. Hence the Bhutto regime drifted towards personalism and as the party's organization dwindled, the party turned to more traditional sources of legitimacy from the landholding class.

She then refers to the period during which Bhutto, after assuming power, largely abandoned his left-leaning and progressive-minded colleagues and fell back to wooing the traditional notables: the feudal landlords—Chaudhris—and clan heads—the Khans and tribal chiefs:

> In the 1970s, the PPP retained hold of its constituency not by operation as a programmatic party that engaged in interest articulation and consensus building, but more as a clientalist party that offered direct, selective incentives to those who demonstrated support for the Bhutto family.
>   The PPP relied heavily on charismatic persons of the Bhutto family. The PPP has been unsuccessful in delivering on its agenda, and has not operated in a political vacuum but as part of a party system that has shaped and moulded the way the party has evolved.[7]

The party regained power after the death of Zia ul-Haq in 1988 under the leadership of ZAB's daughter, Benazir Bhutto who was elected prime minister twice, in 1988 and then in 1993. The PPP captured power in 2008 in the aftermath of the assassination of Benazir Bhutto who had returned to Pakistan after a long exile to lead her party to contest the general elections. However, the party was trounced by the PML-N, their traditional rival, in the 2013 general elections. They retained the provincial government of Sindh but were unsuccessful in all the other provinces. The period 2008–13 was marked by allegations of scams and corruption, weak economy, energy shortages, intensified acts of terrorism, and tense relations with the judiciary. President Asif Zardari, however, maintained a spirit of reconciliation and non-confrontation with the opposition parties and successfully steered the smooth democratic transition in 2013.

The Pakistan Tehreek-e-Insaf (PTI) is a newcomer to national politics. Led by the famous cricketer Imran Khan, it was able to attract the educated middle classes who voted in droves for the party in the 2013 elections. The PTI became the second largest party in the National Assembly and formed the provincial government in the KP. They received this support because there was a reignited ray of hope that a new party without the excess baggage of the two major political parties would bring good governance to Pakistan. Since then, the party has lost its lustre and support as evidenced by their losses in the by-elections. The dharnas of 2014, excessive preoccupation with the rigging of elections, too much focus on the Panama Case against Nawaz Sharif and his family, and not playing the role of an effective opposition in parliament are some of the reasons for this disenchantment. The induction of some discredited politicians from other parties, such as the PPP, has also hurt its image as a 'clean' party.

Among the regional parties, the Awami National Party (ANP), an offshoot of the National Awami Party (which was a coalition partner in the NWFP and Balochistan governments after the general elections of 1970), formed the provincial government of Khyber Pakhtunkhwa in 2008. However, it badly lost the 2013 elections because of the allegations of widespread corruption and poor governance. In Sindh, the Muttahida Qaumi Mahaz (MQM) has been in and out of the coalition governments formed both by PPP and PML at various intervals. The party leader, Altaf Hussain, had to take refuge in London after the army action in 1992 against the party for terror, torture, extortion, and intimidation. The party became the target of action by the Rangers in 2014, and has since then split into various factions. The Balochistan National Party (BNP), the Pakhtunkhwa Milli Party (PkMAP), and the National Party (NP) have been the principal regional parties who have been forming coalition governments with the PML, PPP, and JUI. In the 2013 elections, the NP, PkMAP, and PML jointly formed the provincial government. The three leading tribal groups—the Bugtis, Marris, and Mengals—who had been highly influential in the Balochistan politics no longer command much support given divisions among various factions.

The two major religio-political parties, the Jamaat-i-Islami and the Jamiat-e-Ulema Islam, have dominated the political scene from the sidelines but have never been successful at the national level. The best outcome they had was when all six religious political parties joined hands to form the Muttahida Majlis Amal (MMA) in 2002 and won the elections in the NWFP, formed the government there, and entered into a coalition with the PML-Q in Balochistan. The alliance split at the time of the 2008 elections and the two major parties remained on the fringe. JI is currently part of the KP government while JUI has been able to field a few ministers in the federal government. JI has been the most organized and disciplined party which holds intra-party elections regularly and has been free from any taint of corruption.

According to Iftikhar Malik, political parties in Pakistan have been characterized by their 'politics of opportunism',[8] where self-interest has been unified by intermarriage and business ventures. Ideology took a backseat, except in the case of the Jamaat-i-Islami, which is guided by the mission of Islamization of the state. 'Pakistani political parties have been characterized by lack of scruples in the formation of alliances and counter alliances … The self-interests of about fifty dynasties, consolidated by inter-marriage and business ventures, have always dictated a politics of opportunism.' Ideological differences, issue orientation, and a contest of ideas have escaped the parties except in the case of the Jamaat-i-Islami, which espouses a clear mission of Islamization of the state.

One of the disconcerting features of the political evolution in Pakistan has been the gradual disappearance of parties with a nationwide following and presence. The PML and PPP used to be two such parties but in the recent elections, the PML's base was confined largely to Punjab while the PPP had a miserable showing in Punjab but swept the elections in Sindh. The PTI is still in its infancy but has the potential promise of becoming a national party with support across all the four provinces if it plays its cards well and devotes attention to organizing the party apparatus at the grassroots level. The disadvantage of coalition formation is the tendency to make drastic and unpalatable compromises to accommodate the junior partners however unreasonable their demands may be. The survival instinct to remain in power forces them at times to deviate from their own policies and pronouncements. Coalition governments present a slippery slope when it comes to carrying out tough economic reforms.

DYNASTIC POLITICS

A very credible analysis of Pakistan's political parties has been conducted by Ali Cheema, Hassan Javaid, and Farooq Naseer.[9] Their principal argument is that dynastic families enjoy tremendous power in the political system because simply being 'dynastic' substantially increases the prospect of winning an electoral contest. They find that, since 1985, two out of three electoral races in Punjab that have involved a contest between a dynastic candidate and non-dynastic contenders were won by the dynastic contender. These races accounted for approximately 50 per cent of all contests fought from 1985 to 2008 while in another third of the electoral contests, the real competition was between members of dynastic families and there was no effective competition from non-dynastic contenders.

The efforts of the political parties have been directed to winning over the 'electables', which is synonymous with winning over members of these dynastic families. Therefore, parties have, in the past, chosen to forge alliances with dynastic politicians rather than build effective party machinery around a dedicated party cadre. The absence of an effective cadre-based structure significantly increases the likelihood that dynastic politicians will win contests and this expectation perpetuates their power in the system. This vicious cycle feeds both the success of dynasties and the weak organizational structure of political parties.

The authors also argue that the composition of families that constitute the dynastic pool remains stagnant though there was a substantial infusion of new entrants into the dynastic pool after the elections of 1985 and 1988. What is true is that a large share of these individual, non-dynastic entrants into politics throve and formed successful dynastic families in their own right. This suggests that the emergence of a new pool of politicians may not imply a weakening of the dynastic system of politics but rather may only result in the replacement of one set of dynastic families by another.

According to them, there is considerable evidence to suggest that since the elections of 1985, business-owning, trading, and professional elites have been as successful as their land-owning counterparts, if not more, in forming dynastic families, and that the power of capital appears to be as potent as the power of land.

The reason for reliance upon dynastic politics is a pure cost-benefit calculus. Lowering the barriers to entry for non-dynastic political aspirants would also increase the costs of organization for Punjab's political parties, forcing them to invest in building party machines that may or may not be able to deliver votes as effectively as the dynastic candidates. From a longer-term perspective, it must be realized that the investment in building organized, non-dynastic, and non-familial political party structures could deliver much higher electoral returns. What are the sources of change that could potentially lead to a decline in dynastic politics in Punjab and give rise to the need to build organized party machines?

The impetus for this change may come from increased competition in an increasingly urbanizing electorate, the emergence of an educated middle class, and the changing demographic composition of the electorate. The large increase in first-time voters between the ages of 18 and 22—connected to the rest of the world through social media and aware of their own rights and obligations—has the potential to adversely affect dynastic politics in the upcoming and future elections. This is because these voters are weakly integrated into dynastic political networks and may be more open to voting along party rather than factional lines.

Seema Mustafa[10] makes another cogent point against the dynastic politics in India and Pakistan. She believes that 'dynasty brings with it a certain sensibility that does not allow independence of thought and action. It institutionalizes authoritarianism that in turn lives off factionalism'. This appears to be the case even in a democratic country like India, where familial ruling dominates political parties and any deviation can be the basis for disciplinary measures. In Pakistan, people are left to choose between military rule and the stringent control of dynastic parties. Even a democratically elected individual, who is supposed to represent and lead the people, would be held captive by this system. No outside force can guarantee proper governance, as a sound institution was built around the sovereignty of dynasties.

According to I. A. Rehman, who is critical of Ayub Khan's 1962 experiment of a party-less parliament and Zia's monetary rewards to legislators:

The political parties survived Ayub Khan's 1962 experiment of a partyless parliament and executive, and Zia ul-Haq's more resolute effort to finish them off. But the latter did succeed in securing two significant changes in national politics. First, the party nominees in legislatures were elevated (in theory) to the status of its executive. Second, these legislators were given money to ensure their continued electability. This meant that instead of representing the people in legislatures and chambers of power the legislators became the government's agents for keeping the populace quiescent.

The people's exclusion from the management of the state is nearly complete. The rulers have no use for them except for asking them to cast ballots after every few years in elections that are, at best, partly fair.

Having freed themselves from the obligation to consult the party rank and file, and to ascertain the people's aspirations through them, and by relying instead on the legislators, the custodians of power have been moving towards an oligarchy. The matter does not end there.

We are witnessing a strong attempt to stifle the voices of civil society and [the] creation of new legal barriers to the people's right to assent and dissent. After imposing on the people a terrible tool of oppression in the form of the cybercrime act, the authorities have decided to make the right to information law an instrument to deny information.

It is possible that attempts to destroy the people's capacity to build up dynamic and democratic political parties will fail, but the cost of the present drift towards making them empty shells will be too great to be viewed with complacency.[11]

The repeated military interventions brought in the name of disinfecting and cleansing the country had unintended consequences on its body-politic as politicians and political parties continue to look towards the GHQ and the ISI for political engineering to bring them to power through the back door. The dharnas organized by a newcomer to Pakistan's political scene by Imran Khan and his party, the PTI, in 2014, evoked much criticism for their efforts to seek a 'neutral umpire' to raise his finger. I. A. Rehman[12] expresses this succinctly, 'more than anything else what has been exposed is the mainstream political parties' folly of treating each other as worst enemies and thus rendering themselves vulnerable to extra-political intervention that may not be as benign as the Supreme Court's bailout plan on the present occasion. Their inability to learn from history amazes even the most poorly informed villager.'

POLITICAL DYNAMICS FOR REFORMS

The Economist, London[13] has very aptly described the meaning of democracy in the following terms:

> Democracy is far more than just elections. It requires independent courts, non-partisan civil servants, robust institutions, the rule of law and property rights; a free press; constitutional checks and balances, above all a culture of openness and tolerance, especially of minorities. But voters' ability to throw the rascals out at regular intervals is still the indispensable sine qua non.

Evaluated against this definition, Pakistan has passed through the ritual of elections over 36 years out of its 70 years' existence, and the remaining period under the military rule. The other components of democracy could not be nurtured and developed in the prevailing atmosphere of political flux and the only manifestation of democracy in Pakistan was during the eight general elections[14] to the national and provincial assemblies held between 1970 and 2013. Premature dismissal of elected governments under Article 58(2) b of the Constitution in the 1990s before they could complete their full terms was a severe setback to the maturing of democracy. The continuing political instability and uncertainty about the future had serious adverse effects on the structure of political institutions, patterns of leadership, and the dynamics within the political parties, including their support bases. Economic reforms imply important shifts in the balance of political power among contending interests: for example, between the competing export and import sectors and between capital and labour. However, when the political powers themselves are in a constant struggle for survival, they avoid taking unpopular, fundamental decisions that may disturb the existing equilibrium. Similarly, given the sharp squeeze on the government resources, the political leadership has no motivation other than to allocate those resources to maintain and win over popular support for their parties. Market-oriented reforms eliminate the rents collected by the supporters of the ruling parties and thus pose a threat to political stability. Therefore, maintaining the status quo remained the best survival strategy for politicians when in power.

Pakistan's long experience with authoritarian rule promoted a popular and widely held notion that reforms can be effected only under authoritarian or military regimes. This notion too has lost credence. In several countries, military governments undertook economic reforms prior to initiating a transition to democracy. As those reforms yielded tangible benefits, policy gains were not reversed after the transition. The opposite has been the case for Pakistan.

The Ayub and Musharraf governments did undertake some significant economic reforms which, if allowed to continue and are sustained over an extended time period, would have brought about fundamental structural changes. However, in order to gain legitimacy and to ensure their own continuation in office, they had to seek the aid of a group of politicians and select political parties. Ayub formed the Conventional Muslim League and Musharraf forged an alliance between the PML-Q, MMA, and a breakaway faction of the PPP. They, therefore, entered the arena of partisan politics. It was only natural that their opponents, when elected, would reverse these reforms, or make the reforms undertaken by the military rulers appear inconsequential. This experience suggests that economic accomplishments devoid of political legitimacy, however impressive they may be, prove to be short-lived in our cultural context. Without the involvement and participation of the people, elegant and technically sound economic solutions developed by authoritarian regimes have a short shelf life because they are quickly overturned once the form of government changes, causing irreparable loss to the economy.

The inner dynamics of political parties also provides some insights into why economic reforms are not undertaken by democratically elected governments, and if they are, do not survive for long. A personality-cult, an authoritarian style of leadership, centralized decision-making, demand by the leader for absolute loyalty, intolerance of dissent, reliance on a small coterie of sycophants and cronies, and nominees rather than open contests for the party posts beginning from grass-roots have germinated some unhealthy tendencies within political parties. Merit and sycophancy do not go well together because merit by its very definition implies honest assessment and dissent.

Ministers of finance could be natural champions for economic reforms but they fear upsetting their colleagues and leaders and losing their jobs if they vigorously pursue unpopular policies. The constituency for these reforms within the ruling party, therefore, remains weak or non-existent. In absence of a champion, there is barely any room for far-reaching reform.

In the 1990s, the culture of destabilizing elected governments in the midst of their mandated period had taken root as members of the assembly elected on one party ticket were lured away by another party in a quest to capture power at all costs. This culture, therefore, nurtured tendencies for greater rent accumulation by the assembly members who misused the power of their office. This tendency has now been curbed by an amendment in the Political Parties' Act, which stipulates that a member elected on the ticket of a particular party has to resign from his seat in the event of his violating party discipline or is expelled by the party. The pendulum has however swung in the other direction as the scope for dissent, disagreement, and differences of opinion with the party leadership has almost disappeared. The leader has become all powerful given that he awards party nominations, appoints the ministers, and confers other perks and privileges. He is likely to do so only to those whom he considers are loyal to him. This virtually authoritarian power vested in a single individual gives rise to extreme subservience, sycophancy, and a continuing effort to keep the boss happy. The personal shortcomings of their leaders, policy lapses, and poor and ill-informed decisions are neither pointed out nor challenged, negating the very principles of democracy. Elected leaders thus assume the role of authoritarian rulers. Under the veneer of democracy, there is completely personalized and centralized decision-making.

A leading political scientist, Rasul Baksh Rais,[15] believes there is no difference between authoritarian and democratic regimes in Pakistan:

> Pakistan has over the past sixty years been an authoritarian polity under both civilian as well as military regimes. 'Authoritarianism' involves great reverence and obedience to authority and stands opposite to individualism and freedom that come with it. Both the civilian leaders coming from an agrarian and feudal social background and military leaders from the command and control structure of the armed forces have demanded absolute loyalty and compliance with their institutions of origins.

In a democratic dispensation, another check on the arbitrary powers of elected leaders is the exercise of power by the legislature. The opposition parties act as a vigilant watchdog to rectify the errors in judgment and policy made by the ruling party. Notwithstanding their political differences, the opposition should remain wedded to promoting national causes and the well-being of the people at large. A strong and vibrant opposition is certainly necessary in a democratic polity, provided it remains within the ambit of democratic norms and works towards strengthening the system. This is not, however, the case in Pakistan. As Hasan Askari Rizvi points out:

> Most political leaders and groups view democracy more as a weapon against the adversary rather than an operational framework for self-restraint, accommodation and bargain dialogue, and for evolving mutually acceptable solutions. Democracy is a slow consultative process and it is quite messy.[16]

A succinct but apt description of the challenges faced by democratic institutions in Pakistan can be found in the editorial of the leading daily *Dawn*. It avers that 'democracy is only as strong as the people's belief in it',[17] and in Pakistan, the unwillingness to address issues of corruption and the high barriers to entry into politics have tarnished the political system and generated scepticism among too many people. They are managing a system that has a dysfunctional process of accountability, and has already eroded public confidence in it:

> For all the electoral competition and promise of regular elections, the institutions of democracy have not been strengthened in a comparable manner ... Absent is the vital democratic corollary: a belief in and commitment to a system of checks and balances. From dynastic politics to the murky nexus between politics and business, and from dysfunctional systems of accountability to the refusal to embrace regulatory reform, the toll on democratic institutions continues to grow.

Our politicians need to learn from the sound practices and visionary political leadership of other democratic countries on how they have been able to consolidate the gains from democratic order.

INTRA-PARTY DEMOCRACY

Under the law, no political party can be awarded party symbols unless it regularly holds intra-party polls as set out in the party constitution submitted to the Election Commission of Pakistan (ECP) at the time of registration. There is, however, hardly any party, apart from the Jamaat-i-Islami, which has complied with this law. Tasneem Nooran,[18] who was entrusted with the task of holding elections within a leading party, notes that political parties are at the root of a parliamentary democracy, where people who have political ambition can join and attempt to rise through the ranks. While this system has been in place in Pakistan, it is hard to believe that an ordinary citizen who is not a member of the two ruling families can join a political party and rise to the top. Unless democracy is introduced into political parties, family-ruled democracy will continue to proliferate.

Political parties are the basis of parliamentary democracy, which is the format Pakistan politics has been based on under its Constitution. The inspiration comes from the Western models of democracy, especially the Westminster model of UK. Ordinary persons wanting to do public service or having ambitions of political power, join a political party with the hope of rising through the ranks to leadership positions, to get into power in governments.

In Pakistan, while we have been on this format of democracy at least since 1973, the chances of an ordinary member joining a political party and rising to the top are nil. In the 44 years since we set on this course, the system of family hegemony in a political party has become stronger. For the last almost thirty years, two families have been ruling Pakistan, interspersed only by military rulers. Unless meaningful reforms to instil democracy within political parties are introduced, this malaise of family-ruled democracy will not even begin to be addressed.

Aoun Sahi provides additional reasons why there should be a strengthening of democratic process within the political parties. In his words, 'the factor responsible for the failure of democracy in Pakistan is that its most important institutions, the political parties, do not follow the basic democratic process.'[19]

A [d]emocratic political system depends on political parties for the selection of the cadre of people who will run the affairs of the government. But in such a system, parties are also organized democratically. They consist of citizens elected through a tough election process. The office bearers and even the members in different committees and bodies of a party are elected in this manner. This process ensures the upwardly [mobile] organization of parties from the grassroots at the local level which is the most accepted process to form a true democratic institution. In Pakistan, the standard mechanism is to form a party from top downwards, largely by appointing selected individuals to run the affairs of the party at different levels. The power to control the party rests with the leader who is the 'declared' head and selects a group of people who pledge allegiance to him.

Another long-standing commentator and respected analyst of Pakistani politics, I. A. Rehman, has attributed the decline of political parties to lack of intra-party democracy. In a democratic system, the role of political parties is to guarantee a functional legislative and executive system that works in the interest of the public, as well as to provide a system of checks and balances. However, according to Rehman, 'most of Pakistan's political parties look like crowds of the party heads' retainers and errand-boys. They may be ordered to hold *jalsa*s and rallies but there is no record of intra-party discussions on the direction the state should follow and how the genius of the people should be utilized in their own interest.'[20] Rehman emphasizes that what we are witnessing is an attempt by the political parties to assert complete control over party dynamics, and stifle the people's right to construct a truly democratic system. In the end, Pakistani political parties follow the principles of democracy in letter but not spirit.[21]

It is often lamented that ministers do not have the experience of leading and steering their ministries. They either become dependent upon civil servants or they are continually at cross-purposes with them. The problem lies in the kind of people who enter politics. Umair Javed[22] describes the selection process of selecting a candidate for political office in Pakistan.

> In Pakistan ... candidate recruitment takes place outside of any well-defined feeder systems anchored with campuses and community organizations. Here, two major criteria appear to crop up when party leaders pick candidates: first is perceptions about their electability, i.e. a potential candidate's social prominence. The second is their ability to finance their own election campaign, i.e. their financial prominence.

The 'electability' of candidates, which has also engulfed new progressive parties, works in a unique way in the rural areas where kinship and *biradari* are dominant. Sarwar Bari,[23] who has observed the election practises in Pakistan, narrates how this phenomenon actually works:

The family is the primary unit of organization and most *biradari*s have a common ancestry. Hence, elders of *biradari* command much respect. The political elite fully exploit this respect. This is the foundation of parochial politics ... The dependants i.e. employees, peasants, workers or the biradri of early joiners, willingly—or due to pressure—join their master's party. When he switches parties, his dependants follow.

Since party structures and offices do not exist in most districts, a majority of candidates rely on traditional networks for attracting voters. Settlements in the rural areas can be broadly divided into two categories: settled and developed villages and small *jhoks/basti*s or hamlets.

Most of these hamlets consist of residents of the same lineage, while most villages are divided between various factions. Where there are hamlets, the elders reign and in big villages, factional leaders play the same role.

In rural areas, contesting candidates hardly reach out to individual voters. Very often they negotiate with the *biradari* and factional leaders. The outcome of these negotiations is often a mix of personal gain for the local leader and the community's collective interest.

In return, the local leader is supposed to deliver a number of votes to the candidate. If he succeeds, his position is strengthened in the eyes of the candidate. To keep his control over his faction/*biradari*, he tries his utmost to get some benefits for his people.

One of the ways of overcoming this problem is to afford opportunities to hold elections for party offices at the *tehsil* level. The party office-bearers who get elected are then nominated as candidates for the local government elections. After they have gained some experience by discharging responsibilities in administrative and managerial positions in the *tehsil*, municipal, or district governments, and those who have distinguished themselves by proving their competence, should then be given the opportunity to contest the elections to the provincial party and the provincial assembly. The graduation process following this logic would bring to parliament and the federal cabinet only those who have performed well and demonstrated their potential to hold top positions.

This bottom up approach would, over time, produce high quality politicians who are quite capable of running the ministries and departments confidently and competently. This process also encourages young talented individuals without money or family connections or affiliation to *biradari*s, feudal families, or tribal chiefs to aspire to political offices and then make their way up by proving their credentials. This intake of talent of experienced individuals who have proved themselves would improve the quality of political leadership, political institutions, and the delivery of public goods and services. Political parties would also benefit as they would have structures at the grass-root level and voters would be able to link parties with the actual service delivery outcomes. This pressure would force the parties to strengthen the institutions which are responsible for delivering these services. Administrative experience gained by their political operatives would certainly help when they are elevated to become ministers in the provincial or federal cabinets.

One of the other impediments preventing educated and talented individuals from entering politics is the stigma attached to politics as a profession. As Maleeha Lodhi[24] very correctly points out, the media has 'unwittingly promoted public cynicism by caricaturing politics and public life':

> This exposes the media to the risk of being wounded by its own weapon. If all politics is depicted as venal and all political actors as conniving, self-serving and inept, this risks sapping the public's confidence in the political process.
>
> If every problem is depicted as a crisis, each crisis as a drama, a setback as a disaster and a difficulty in policy as an unmitigated failure, the public cynicism that ensues is not just with the political process but directed at the media which is seen as biased and lurching between exaggerating and trivializing issues. This can undercut the media's authority.

SUMMATION

Pakistan's political institutions have not yet achieved the level of maturity that can contribute to the process of improved democratic governance.

The weak foundations of the Pakistan Muslim League, the party which spearheaded the movement for the creation of an independent homeland for the Muslims of India, coupled with the early demise of its charismatic and popular leader M. A. Jinnah a year after the creation of Pakistan, sowed the seeds for inter-party conflict, factionalism, and the rapid succession of formation and dismissal of government. The periodic interruptions of the political process through the imposition of the military rule in 1958, 1977, and 1999 exacerbated the forces of political opportunism and instability. Even during the periods of civilian rule, the army played an active behind-the-scenes role, pulling the strings by favouring certain political parties or politicians. The political parties have done no great service to the evolution of the process by concentrating excessive powers in the hands of the party chiefs, relying on dynastic politics to gain power, and negating the principle of intra-party democracy. Intra-party democracy should be the bedrock of any reform agenda for the strengthening of political institutions. In absence of this, the distinction between a powerful party leader and an authoritarian one becomes indistinguishable.

Electoral reforms that make the ECP an effective and credible institution capable of screening the candidates and disqualifying those who do not meet the eligibility criteria, organize the elections with complete control of the administrative machinery, and set up parameters for campaign-financing reform are some of the steps which need to be acted upon. Money has become a strength for the 'electables', the rich and well to do who have the money to spend to acquire power. In India, the Chief Election Commissioner requires the political parties to file their accounts and returns which are scrutinized by the income tax authorities. Adoption of a similar practice would help in reducing the influence of the money in the elections.

Political stability can be gradually brought about by cleansing the body politic and removing the sword of Damocles hanging over the heads of the political parties. This stability in turn, would have a positive effect on economic performance as policy continuity, predictability, and consistency gain firm ground in place of ad hoc short-term oriented policies.

Notes and References

1. Anwar Syed, *Pakistan: Islam, Politics, and National Solidarity or The Idea of a Pakistani Nationhood* (ABC-CLIO, LLC, 1982).
2. The latest PILDAT nationwide survey of public opinion conducted in 2016 places the political parties second from the bottom with an approval rating of 35 per cent.
3. Khan, R. M., 'Bumpy Road to Stability', *The News*, 10 December 2016.
4. Hewitt, V., *International Politics of South Asia* (Routledge Handbook of South Asian Politics, 2010).
5. Rizvi, H. A., 'The Decisive Confrontation', *Express Tribune* <https://tribune.com.pk/story/1215486/the-decisive-confrontation/>.
6. Mufti, M., *Friday Times,* 1 April 2008.
7. Ibid.
8. Malik, Iftikar, *State and Civil Society in Pakistan: Politics of Authority, Ideology and Ethnicity* (Springer, 1996), 34.
9. Cheema, A. et. al., 'Dynastic Politics in Punjab: Facts, Myths and their Implications', IDEAS Working Paper.
10. Mustafa, S, *Asian Age,* 5 January 2008.
11. Rehman, I. A., 'Decline of Political Parties', *Dawn,* 27 October 2016.
12. Rehman, I. A., *Lessons of the Dharna,* Dawn, 3 November 2016.
13. *Economist,* London, 24 October 2016
14. These general elections were held in 1970, 1977, 1988, 1990, 1993, 1997, 2008, and 2013. The elections held under the auspices of Zia and Musharraf are excluded.
15. Rais, R. B., *Friday Times,* 31 Aug.–6 Sept. 2007.
16. Rizvi, H. A., *Daily Times,* 6 September 2009.
17. Editorial, 'Transition to Democracy', *Dawn,* 23 March 2017 <https://www.dawn.com/news/1322226>
18. I wish to thank Tasneem Noorani, a senior retired federal secretary and a writer for preparing a background note on intra-party democracy.
19. A. Sahi, *The News,* 8 February 2009.
20. I. A. Rehman, 'Decline of Political Parties', *Dawn,* 27 October 2016.
21. Ibid.
22. U. Javed, 'Electoral Patriarchy', *Dawn,* 30 January 2017.
23. S. Bari, 'Elections and Parochialism', *Dawn,* 20 January 2013.
24. M. Lodhi, *The News,* 1 September 2009.

5

The Society

The politics of patronage so widely practised in Pakistan is deeply rooted in Pakistani societal structures. Pakistani society is structured along family, *biradari*, tribe, and ethnicity. The family is male-centred and the patriarchs make all major family decisions although among the urban-educated class, the joint family system is giving way to the nuclear family.

Kinship, i.e. social relations based on blood ties or marriage bonds, is a larger group surrounding a family with which its members are tied with bonds of mutual support, obligations, and common identity. *Biradari*s or clans strike an internal bargain of expectations: support members with your connections and in return they will use their influence on your behalf, particularly in dealing with public officials. At election-time, the candidates in the rural areas approach the clan heads to seek their support in exchange for future favours. A commitment made by the head of the clan is sufficient and avoids the expense and hassle in canvassing and approaching the entire group individually.

This power exchange has become a significant function of kinship. The need for a patron to mediate with the state apparatus has increased in direct relation to the expansion in the role of the Pakistani state and its increasing inefficiency and corruption. However, kinship nepotism is one of the reasons for the erosion of the state's authority and subversion of rules and laws. The culture of patron-client in public affairs is sustained by kinship obligations. Civil society is dualistic in nature and divided along two principal tracks: indigenous (Islamized) and modern.

These prevalent social and cultural norms in Pakistani society also pose a powerful deterrent to reforms, particularly in the area of economic governance, i.e. the bonds of kinship, *biradari,* class, friendship, and familial relations. The operating social behaviour is governed by considerations of '*lihaz, sharam,* and *murawat*' (consideration, respect, and obligingness) ingrained and nurtured right from childhood. Formal organizations are, on the other hand, driven by edicts, evidence, due process, neutrality, and objectivity. This in-built tension between the appropriate social behaviour required of an individual as a member of the society and organizational rules imposed as part of professional responsibilities inhibits the practise of good governance. Nepotism and favouritism are the expected outcomes of demand placed by social and cultural norms, while merit and impartiality are expected to reign supreme under the formal organizational rules of business. Constituency politics and coalitions reinforce the prevalent social norms. It is only with the spread of urbanization, nuclear families, an expanding middle class, professionalism, and weakening of the feudal and tribal hold on the society that the balance will shift in favour of the formal organizational rules. No quick fixes are available as even some highly educated individuals from tribal and feudal families do not deviate significantly from these norms. Therefore, there is a fundamental dilemma: is the impersonal, impartial, non-discriminatory system of governance that is modelled on Western norms compatible with the societal norms that are rooted in reciprocal exchanges of favours and relationships based on kinships and familial affiliations? It is argued that these societal norms are not permanent and dissolve with the passage of time as the forces of urbanization, education, technology, and exposure to the rest of the world take hold.

How has this culture evolved and these norms taken root in our society? At the time of Partition, Pakistan was predominantly a rural agrarian society in which feudal, tribal, and caste relationships were the principal drivers of the society's behaviour and attitude. One of the leading scholars of Pakistani society elaborates this point and adds that the post-Partition period did not bring about any significant change:

Pakistan's social structure has been traditionally stratified in occupational castes, clans, and kinships. In rural areas, this caste/clan hierarchy has coincided with land ownership, affluence, and power. In urban areas, castes/ *biradaris* have overlapped but do not fully correspond to property ownership, income or wealth.

Inherited attributes of caste, tribe or kinship are also woven into economic classes. Class segments also reflect location along the ideological spectrum ranging from traditionalist, Islamist to modern liberal. They range from the global—Westernized muhajirs or Punjabis of middle class standings—on one side of the spectrum to Pashtuns of traditionalist or Islamic bent who are bazaar merchants or transporters.[1]

Like many heterogeneous developing countries, Pakistani society has also many overlapping identities based on ethnicity, language, location, caste, clans, tribes or ideology. Social stratification in the traditional or predominant rural areas is based on tribal affiliation in parts of Balochistan and KP provinces, with clear linguistic divide; on kinship, *biradari,* and caste (*Arain or Jutts*) in Punjab with Potohari, Punjabi, and Saraiki as spoken dialects, and feudal and peasants in Sindh, proud of their native language, along with an affluent middle class in urban areas, mostly Muhajirs or the migrants from India sticking with the language of their ancestors.

In the period following Independence, the sense of newly acquired nationalism did transcend all other affiliations and groupings and kept Pakistan strongly bound together. The absorption of eight million migrants into an economically fragile, moth-eaten country would not have been possible without the devotion and untiring efforts of the local population. The refugees were welcomed with open arms in all the five provinces. The generation that participated in or witnessed the Independence movement, with the passage of time, as events unfolded, gradually became disenchanted.

After the demise of Jinnah, the political leadership in Pakistan fell into the hands of an elite that was more interested in reinforcing characteristics and norms of the society such as feudalism, tribalism, kinships, clans and *biradaris*, castes, and sects for their own narrow, parochial benefit. The political leadership did not act as a countervailing force to diffuse and dilute these retrogressive tendencies by building a more participatory governance structure with institutional checks and balances that would have benefited the majority of the population. The imposition of forced parity of representation between East and West Pakistan in parliament when the east wing had a higher population and the unilateral announcement that Urdu would be the sole national language led to seeds of mistrust being sown in the eastern wing and fanned parochial feelings amongst Bengalis. The merger of the four provinces into a single West Pakistan unit with its headquarters in Lahore against the wishes of the people of three minority provinces generated resentment among them. An unrepresentative military dictatorship, which paved the way for the eventual separation of East Pakistan with India's active assistance, added further fuel to an already smouldering fire.

The younger generation, which reached adolescence in the 1970s and 1980s and had not witnessed the sacrifices and turmoil of 1947, were fed by their political leaders the mantra of injustices being meted out to their linguistic, provincial, and ethnic groups.

The unique composition—where one province has the majority of the population and is also relatively advanced in comparison to the three other provinces—and their nexus with the Muhajirs in the professions and the civil services intensified the tensions and grievances. Christopher Jaffrelot,[2] along with several other authors, attribute many of societal problems afflicting Pakistan to the 'Punjabization of Pakistan'. As Punjabis constituted 80 per cent of the army and held 55 per cent of civil services posts, this stranglehold proved beneficial to their eventual rise to power in the 1950s. They also benefited from the irrigation works, not only in Punjab but by settling in the Barrage areas of Sindh. The other group, the Muhajirs, was over-represented, not in the army but in the bureaucracy as well as in industrial ownership.

After the separation of Bangladesh, Punjab became the most populous province commanding the highest number of seats in the National Assembly. With already entrenched power in the military and bureaucracy, its electoral power consolidated its domineering position vis-à-vis the other three provinces. The situation was further aggravated by the centralized decision-making and concentration of administrative authority in the office of the prime minister.

The dissolution of the single unit and restoration of the provinces in 1970 gave impetus to Sindhi nationalists. The chief minister, Mumtaz Ali Bhutto, although from the PPP, was very keen to establish his credentials with the Sindhis. He introduced a language bill that made Sindhi compulsory in the province's schools. This move was opposed by the Muhajirs and riots erupted in Karachi, Hyderabad, and urban centres, where the Muhajirs were in a majority. Along with the nationalization of industries, banks, insurance, and education, which were the mainstay of the Muhajirs, the language bill brought the disorganized and fragmented Muhajir community on a single platform. They felt an existential threat to the well-being of their community. When Z. A. Bhutto was deposed, and eventually executed, he became a martyr among the Sindhis and a movement was launched against the Zia government in the province.

The Muhajirs were, therefore, wooed by the Zia regime and 'Mohajir Quami Mahaz' (MQM) was formed as a countervailing force against the Sindhi nationalists. The MQM became a powerful voice of the Muhajir community and won a majority of assembly seats in the elections, thereby becoming a political force to reckon with. The PPP and PML could not afford to form provincial governments without their active or tacit support. The urban–rural divide, which propelled the Muhajirs to capture the urban seats while the rural areas remained with the PPP, gave rise to alternating cycles of cooperation and confrontation, and an uneasy coexistence between these two parties. 'Live and let live' policies weakened the Sindhi nationalist parties which never had any success in the general elections. The tension between the two communities lingered on but has to some degree become diffused as Sindhis got educated, entered the civil services and professions, and now occupy key positions in the provincial government thus diluting the earlier dominance of the Muhajirs.

Balochistan, the largest province in area, has its own complex ethnic and tribal/non-tribal, linguistic characteristics. Although the two principal ethnic groups are Baloch/Brahvis, and Pashtuns, there are settlers from

Punjab, Hazaras, and Sindhis living largely in Naseerabad, Jaffarabad, and Jhal Magsi districts. The main tribes in Balochistan were Bugtis, Marris, and Mengals. Baloch tribalism is very different from that of the Pathans: its leadership is hereditary, hierarchal, and even monarchical, whereas the Pathan tradition is meritocratic and in a sense even democratic.

The fourth province bordering Afghanistan used to be called North-Western Frontier province (NWFP) in British days and the name persisted until a few years ago when it was renamed Khyber Pakhtunkhwa (KP). The Federally Administered Tribal Areas (FATA), which separate Afghanistan from Pakistan, were until recently beyond the control of the provincial government. KP consists in the main of Pashto speaking Pathans but there are Hindko speaking people living in the Hazara Division. Khans and tribal chiefs dominate the society in the province. In recent times, the influence of religious parties has gained ground.

Iftikhar Malik[3] believes that Pakistan's dilemma in being unable to establish good governance notwithstanding successive efforts, has largely revolved around a continuing disequilibrium between state and civil society. Although the state has developed since Independence, civil society has not. The moot point is that the development of the state has come at the expense of vital civil institutions including the Constitution, political parties, pluralism, an independent judiciary, a free press, and other think tanks and activist groups outside the public sector. Malik contends that Punjab is the nerve-centre of the Pakistani state and its domination of state institutions has greatly threatened other ethnic groups.

The picture sketched above may have been true a few decades ago but it ignores the profound changes in the texture of the society which once was almost dormant and has become much more vocal and assertive in the recent times. Social change in Pakistan has been driven by a number of exogenous and endogenous factors.

Mass-migration from India, lingering disputes with India, alliances with the US, the Afghan war to expel the Soviets, and the War against Terror in Afghanistan have been the exogenous factors.

Among the endogenous factors, the salient ones are: uneven economic development, a population explosion, mobility, rapid urbanization, and the emergence of the middle class, as well as the spread of communication, particularly through private electronic and social media. These exogenous and endogenous factors have generated a heavy mosaic of benign and pernicious influences on the societal makeup and behaviour.

However, one constant of Pakistan's social change is its commitment to an Islamic identity. Overall, Pakistani society has been visibly Islamized. The Islamic normative order has been forged as a distinct social structure and subculture. Professor M. A. Qadeer[4] explains that Pakistan's society and culture have evolved from a dualistic tripartite structure since Independence. The traditional and modern divide dates back to the colonial period but the third component, institutionalized Islam, has evolved after Independence. These are not three separate belief systems but three parallel ideologies and systems of norms which, although autonomous, are nested together. In one sense, the traditional, modern, and Islamic modes of living are three subcultures, each with distinct values and lifestyles. This division has permeated many social institutions. Education has madrassas, Urdu-medium and English-medium schools. The role of women is delineated along the tradition of women being largely confined to 'char diwarain' (four walls) or the domestic sphere, modern women aspiring to participate in the public sphere, and the more conservative women participating only in segregated activities, covering their heads or clad in the *burqa*.

Most analysts agree that there has been a perceptible change in the orientation of Pakistani society towards Islamization since the 1980s and this trend has become much more perceptible and entrenched since September 2001:

> Islamic observances and pieties have spread to almost all segments of society and [the] Islamic normative order has been forged as a distinct social structure and culture. At the same time the moral fabric of the Pakistani society is fast eroding and Islamic teachings and values of honesty and integrity, tolerance, social justice, observance of peace and order, following rules and ethics, promoting solidarity and brotherhood, [and] taking care of the poor and the disadvantaged are being flouted openly.

However, Prof Qadeer[5] very aptly describes the disconnect between ritualistic behaviour and the substantive teachings of Islam:

While visibly Islam has touched almost all social institutions, it has failed to engender a moral order that would meet contemporary social and economic challenges. The reforms sought are confined to outward behaviour not to truly spiritual or moral change. Consequently, there is now a chasm between how people believe they live and how they actually live or in other, between the imagined and the real.

Babar Sattar,[6] a leading lawyer and thinker, sketches this conflict between the moral values which we ought to observe and our traditional values, and points out its repercussions on the rule of law in Pakistan:

Our culture is defined by a morality wherein loyalty trumps integrity. Simply put, you are expected to lie and disregard principles, if required, to help someone with whom you share bonds of loyalty or love. Such personal morality chokes up our justice system with false testimony, making convictions harder. Two, our collective consciousness is driven by rhetoric, intrigue, emotion, and honour—instead of facts. Often we are more interested in why someone is doing something as opposed to what is being done. This has accelerated our drift to being a fact-free society.

Dr Ali Qasimi[7] explains how, from 1947 till the early-1970s, the state and subsequent governments consciously kept the ulema away from directly influencing government legislation. Qasimi believes that those who ran the state and government at that time were not secular. Rather, their idea of faith and its role in the formation of Pakistani nationalism was different from those held by the ulema and the clerics. Theirs was an extension of the idea of faith and Muslim nationalism developed and evolved by the likes of Sir Syed, Iqbal, and others. These scholars shaped the idea of Islamic modernism in South Asia.

The first departure from the tradition came from a liberal and progressive leader in the late 1970s. Z. A. Bhutto, in his attempt to defuse the political agitation sponsored by the rightist parties and appease them, made some critical announcements, such as declaring the Ahmadis to be a minority and banning the consumption of liquor. The latter decision coming from a person who cherished his drinks every evening was perhaps an act of desperation to remain in power.

That was only the beginning. The biggest shift towards Islamization took place during the 11 years of Zia ul-Haq's rule. General Zia's Islamic laws and policies, particularly the change in the curriculum taught in educational institutions, have brought about a gradual but highly significant departure from the beliefs and practices embedded in the people's world-view. The Hudood Ordinance, a parallel legal code and judicial system—the Shariah, Islamic wealth tax or *zakat,* and levy on farm income or *ushar*—were introduced during that period. Textbooks were revised to indoctrinate children in the Islamists' version of history. Mosque schools and *madrassas* proliferated under state patronage. Public life was transformed, inducing religious observances in everyday life, promoting pieties in verbal/symbolic behaviour layering Islamic laws, and punishments over those of common law institutions.

Mariam Abou Zohaib[8] dwells upon the sectarian consciousness that has developed in Pakistan as a consequence of Zia's Islamization policy. She attributes the state's actions in favouring the Deobandis in bringing theological differences to the fore. At the same time, the Iranian revolution gave a new sense of identity to the Shia community which became more assertive. Saudi Arabia competed with Iran by generously financing mosques, madrassas, and Deobandi preachers in Pakistan. The Shia upsurge in Iran, the Saudi rivalry in Iran, and Zia's pro-Sunni policy stirred up the existing socio-economic tensions.

The mushroom growth of *madrassahs* promoted obscurantism and radical interpretations of Islam in several backward areas of Pakistan and has now become a major challenge to the established education system. Students from poor families are provided with free lodging, boarding, and clothing, easing the financial burden on their parents. Dropouts from Urdu-medium schools with no skills and relevance for the job market also swelled the ranks of *madrassahs* becoming captive audiences for 'charismatic leaders' offering them, through religious violence, 'a means of empowerment' and a 'sacred museum' rolled into one.

Traditional religious parties did not have any systematic control of the sectarian organizations although several *madrassahs*, including the one at Akora Khattak led by Maulana Sami ul Haq of JUI-S, were the training ground for many Afghan and Pakistani Taliban leaders.

In the 1970s, ethnicity had become a substitute identity, but it was branded as treason and violently suppressed. By contrast, it was the state itself that promoted religious identities in the 1980s and in the 1990s struggled to suppress extremist organizations.[9]

The thrust of these changes also continued unabated in the subsequent periods of elected governments. The Pakistan Muslim League, inheritor of the Zia league, was a more conservative party, while the PPP tended to be somewhat more liberal in its outlook.

Musharraf did make an attempt through 'enlightened moderation' to reverse the Zia period trends and make Pakistan a liberal but Islamic society. However, other compulsions, exigencies, and priorities did not allow him to make much of a headway in this endeavour.

Over the past three decades, intolerance and violent reactions to dissent and differences of opinions, particularly relating to issues that have to do with religion, have displaced class, caste, and other divisions and occupied the space of national discourse. Political parties and their leadership, rather than defusing these tensions, have actually proved to be culprits by indulging in these. According to Professor Hasan Askari Rizvi:[10]

Pakistan's politics has become increasingly non-accommodative and conflictual. The competing political interests, especially the PML-N and the PTI, are persistently hostile towards each other in their discourse inside parliament, in public meetings, and TV political talk shows.

These leaders should have worked towards preaching tolerance and accommodation in Pakistani society that has already been suffering from the rise of religious and cultural intolerance over the last three decades. The disposition of the political class is not setting up a precedent to discourage these trends.

As neither the state nor the political parties did much to suppress these tendencies while the uneducated mullahs used their Friday sermons and the *madrassahs* to spread their own distorted version of the religion, some segments of society did get radicalized. The reasons for radicalization have been analysed by a number of observers and scholars. As no single factor can satisfactorily explain this phenomenon, a number of hypotheses have been adduced to throw light on the heterogeneity of the classes involved in terrorist and violent activities. Ziauddin,[11] a respected senior journalist of Pakistan, advances poor governance and alienation of the society from the state as the principal reasons:

> While governance was shrinking in Pakistan, multiple factors had kept spreading radicalization which was occurring on three levels. Firstly, among lower income groups, mainly in poorly governed areas including the tribal areas bordering Afghanistan and nearby districts of Khyber Pakhtunkhwa (KP), as well as parts of southern Punjab and interior Sindh, where poverty, inequality and loose administrative structures spurred radicalization and terrorism. Madrassas and networks of militant and sectarian organizations in these areas acted as catalysts, exploiting these factors to further their extremist agendas, leading to radicalization and sectarian violence.
>
> Secondly, the levels and trends of radicalization were different in middle-income groups. The drivers of radicalisation in urban and semi urban areas, including central and north Punjab, Karachi, and Hyderabad, in Sindh, the settled districts of KP, and Kashmir are mainly political. Thirdly, growing alienation from society is the major driver of radicalisation among upper middle class and the so-called elite in the country.

Prof. M. A. Qadeer adds his voice to those who attribute the growing violence in society to social injustice:

> Our current proneness to violence is the result of accumulated frustrations and sense of injustices arising from widening social disparities, breakdown of the rule of law, and the increasing irrelevance of laws. People see everybody that is powerful get away literally and figuratively with murder.

General Zia's Hudood Law or blasphemy laws—their promised harsh punishments—have reduced the shock value of violence. Who will cringe now at the thought of torturing an accused thief if chopping his hands is the acceptable punishment? Cruelty has been given religious sanction.[12]

He theorizes that three major fissures have appeared in Pakistan's social institutions: (i) development of the material culture and underdevelopment of non-material norms and practices, (ii) disparity between public and private space, and (iii) imbalance between an imagined and lived culture. These divisions within the same structure, on the one hand, and between one institution and another, on the other, have resulted in lopsided modernization and unbalanced development. Modern technology and consumer goods have been readily adopted by all sections of society yet norms of punctuality, work ethic, adhering to rules and laws, and efficiency have not caught on. Expensive and well-manicured homes are surrounded by garbage-strewn streets, vividly contrasting the overdeveloped private space with the backward public space. Social life in Pakistan has thus been simultaneously evolving along two tracks: Islamization of the public sphere and modernization of the private space and economy. These divergent pulls explain the strains in Pakistani society.

There is another viewpoint that discounts the growing influence of Islam in society. According to this view, Pakistani society has gone through a radical transformation during the past 25 years and the state has been unable to adapt itself in to these changes. Akbar Zaidi,[13] the proponent of this view, sums up this transformation as follows: 'Pakistan is a modern, dynamic, capitalist country where a dominant indigenous, badly westernized urban middle class rules. Gone are the days of the feudal and big landlords with their endless hours of leisure.'

The gap between society's aspirations and state capability is therefore becoming a source of dissonance and disillusionment. Social classes excluded from benefits of economic growth are no longer silent spectators to the games being played before their eyes and have become quite assertive. Social and electronic media, which have reached even remote areas of Pakistan, have amplified the sense of deprivation among the majority of the population. The stories of loot and plunder by the ruling classes, highly exaggerated and spiced up, reverberate in the innumerable tea stalls in Pakistani villages. Genuine change will not, however, emanate from the residents of villages, however resentful they may be, but from the articulate, well-informed urban classes.

Prof. Qadeer[14] also believes that 'urbanization emerges as a catalyst for social and economic change and lays the bases for the realignment of social organization and social relations.'

TRUST, SOCIAL CAPITAL, AND CONFIDENCE

Over the past six decades or so, Pakistani society has become more fragmented, highly divisive, excessively polarized, and stubbornly intolerant. Social imbalances, lack of social capital, trust deficit, intolerance, sectarian rivalries, religious division, and ethnicity have together become a major stumbling block to economic revival. In culturally, ethnically, and linguistically homogenous societies, the path to economic advancement is not strewn with these boulders constricting the way forward. In a deeply divided, suspicious, and insecure society, the transaction costs become high and unaffordable. Therefore, the speed of the economic vehicle slows down. The post-2001 developments have exacerbated these cleavages and lent fuel to the fires of violence, extremism, radicalism, and terrorism throughout Pakistan. Accepting the negatives and questioning the positives, and blaming others and not accepting our own responsibility have had dire consequences for economic rejuvenation. Investors listening to this discourse feel disenchanted and uneasy about the feasibility of their investment and shy away from taking the plunge.

Our belief system is premised on the notion that we as a nation cannot do anything good ourselves and all that is good happens through others' goodwill or charity. A cursory glance at our exchanges—social media chat groups and drawing room conversations among the educated—reveals that the preponderant view is that all the scars on our nation have been inflicted by the forces opposed to us. Extremists and radical elements roaming around in our society have been planted, nurtured, and supported by those who wish to destroy us and deprive us of our nuclear capability.

The phobia and excessive preoccupation with the US dominate our national psyche. Governments in Pakistan are widely believed to be formed and removed by the US. Ordinary Pakistanis, although they have exercised their voting rights seven times during the past 23 years, have nothing to do with the changes in government. If Pakistan records a growth rate of 7 per cent or a decline in the level of poverty, these happy outcomes are attributed to a fudging of figures but if the same official data shows an inflation rate of 10–12 per cent, these figures are readily believed and used as a stick to beat the government in power. If the economy turned around in the early 2000s, it was because of the events of 11 September and had nothing to do with the efforts of millions of Pakistani workers, businessmen, and/or farmers who contributed to it.

We have developed a unique tendency to disbelieve and discount any good news about our country or our people and to exaggerate the negatives beyond all proportions. Conspiracy theories have become the staple of the TV talk shows and social media, and it has become difficult to distinguish facts from fiction. 'Fake news' and 'alternative facts' have emerged as a recent phenomenon in the US but they have existed in Pakistan for many decades. According to an observer: 'Conspiracy theory so multi-layered, versions so contradictory, circumstances so murky. Truth has become a casualty replaced by convenience, [and] cynicism. Passionately believed lies that have become so powerful.' Ayesha Jalal[15] believes that 'the vast of majority of Pakistan's literate citizens have opted for the comforts of ignorance, habits of scepticism and most troubling of all, in a contagion of belief in conspiracy theories.'

This lack of self-confidence spurs indifference, inaction, and an unwillingness to resolve our national problems. If we have lost control of the events why should we do anything? What are the repercussions of this lack of self-confidence and widespread prevalence of negativity? According to Samuel Johnson: 'Nothing drains energy more than moaning or having to listen to a moaner. Your consciousness is highly responsive. If you project negativity to those around you, these same negative feelings will reflect back to affect you. You will be derived of vitality. Misery, like happiness, is contagious.'

Prof. Muhammad Abdul Qadeer has very ably described that this mind-set reflects the sense of insecurity and lack of self-confidence. According to him, we blame someone who is thought to be pulling strings or presume that conspiracy is the driving force behind many events. It is not only the default explanation in personal matters but is often immediately presumed to be the cause of adverse national and international events. Lack of acknowledgement of inaction have become the mainstream thinking in Pakistan which is the barrier to objective and inductive thought.

A leading psychologist of Pakistan, Zulfiqar Gilani,[16] explains the phenomenon of blind followership in Pakistan and the urge to have a redeemer to fix societal problems. His analysis of the Pakistani mind-set is summarized in his article:

> In uncertain situations the psychological need to identify with a political leader, or some other figure like a 'Pir', or a person claiming divine entitlement, is greatly increased. As uncertainty has been quite high throughout Pakistan's history, the need for such allegiance in the population is also high. We always seem to be looking for a redeemer, a father-figure in psychological parlance, someone who will solve all our problems or at least promise to do so. The emotional need for such a redeemer gets higher at times when uncertainty is higher, which is also discernible in the current political scenario.

> When the allegiance is based on a primitive emotional need for a father-figure, then it is quite uncritical and blind. The followers idealize their leader and as a corollary demonize the others. Such blind followership has significant costs: there is a destructive suspension of the followers' rational faculties, the common good gets sacrificed for personal gain, rituals of adulation overtake task-related activities and form dominates substance. And our 'good' political leaders seem to recognize this, capitalize on it, and try to ensure that the blind followership continue, and where possible, leaven that with patronage benefits.

Why is trust among people, communities, and regions living in a society or nation important? 'Trust reduces transaction costs, avoids future disputes and litigation, eases settlement of contracts, and acts as a lubricant for facilitating businesses and economic activity.'

Pakistan is among the countries which suffer from a trust deficit or low social capital. The reasons for this phenomenon are historical and structural. As pointed out earlier, the Punjabis and Muhajirs have always been over-represented in the bureaucracy and the army, the two traditional bastions of power in Pakistan, and the demographic balance has heavily tilted towards Punjab in post-1971 Pakistan. With 56 per cent of the population, the national finances were also distributed using population as the only variable for allocation. It was perceived by the smaller provinces that being upper riparian on the Indus river system and holding large underground water resources, the already fertile lands of Punjab receive disproportionate benefits from reservoirs and storage dams. The fierce opposition to Kalabagh Dam, technically and financially a worthwhile investment, by the smaller provinces represents a clear manifestation of this trust deficit.

The over-centralized nature of the federal government (until the Eighteenth Amendment), taking over responsibilities that rightly belong to the provinces, and pre-empting the bulk of the divisible pool of the national finances, further intensified the disharmonious and conflicted character of social order in Pakistan.

The ethnocentrism within the country and ethnic tensions within the provincial boundaries, such as Muhajirs vs Sindhis, Baloch vs Pakhtuns, Saraiki vs Punjabis and Pakhtuns vs Hazarawals, are all derived from the larger struggle for autonomy and fair and just allocation of resources. Sensible solutions equitable for both sides are shelved due to mutual mistrust, suspicion, and a perception of an unjust outcome likely to hurt the community's interests.

According to World Bank research (2005),[17] 'Fairer societies offer their citizens more public goods, more social support and more social capital. Hence they are more capable of sharing the costs and benefits of improving economic policies and in turn facilitating consensus building and decision making.'

What are the causes of this lack of trust and how can this be restored are valid issues for social scientists to systematically analyse. Social capital theory can perhaps shed some light on this subject. The coping mechanisms for this lack of social capital and trust needed to be evolved but these gravitated around narrow parochial interests and self-gratification.

Another social norm impeding economic growth is the poor standard of work ethics that pervades right from the top to the bottom. Promises and commitments made to customers are rarely kept, deliveries are never made on time, cost overruns and overcharging are commonplace, and the quality of goods and services are by and large shoddy. Attendance and timely execution of duties assigned, whether of the labourer, teacher, health worker, or shopkeeper, are the exception rather than rule. The high rejection rates of Pakistani goods by international buyers, along with delayed delivery of orders, have edged Pakistan out of several markets.

Lack of professionalism has also become our hallmark. The same medical doctors in the US, who observe the highest ethical standards and due diligence before diagnosis and prescription, behave in quite the opposite way even in the best private clinics and hospitals in Pakistan. The same is true of lawyers, architects, engineers, pharmacists, and accountants. This malaise has also spilled over to electricians, plumbers, mechanics, sub-engineers, teachers, and also at the level of workers in factories, farms, and the construction industry. Short cuts, cutting corners, misrepresenting facts, adopting a casual attitude, making a fast buck, and becoming rich overnight by hook or by crook have become ingrained in our national psyche. Doctors who can issue false medical certificates, pharmacists who can dispense adulterated drugs, vendors adulterated food, architects and consultants who are satisfied with substandard building materials, and accountants who can help the client to evade taxes, are so popular and widely accepted by the society that people do not realize or care about the material harm being inflicted on the economy.

The attitude and behaviour of private economic agents operating in the markets reinforces the above societal norms and contribute to this destructive culture.

Niaz Murtaza[18] believes that this trust has broken down in the rural areas because of the peculiar structure of society, and advances two reasons for the entrenched traits which perpetuate elite politics and hence misrule:

Firstly, it is deeply fractured, horizontally along ethnic and religious lines and vertically along class and caste lines. This restricts the society-wide flow of the trust and solidarity so critical for just rule. The fractures cause loss of energy, mistrust, and friction across sub-groups. Secondly, we mainly produce low-end goods. In low-end economies, elites require not meritorious but docile, cheap and loyal labour and suppliers to produce low-end goods. The rule of law doesn't suit them. Thus, elites impose the logic of lawlessness and personal loyalty on society. They hog politics too to further their economic interests. Voters too don't look for honest leaders but patrons to take care of them based on social networks. This is the structure of Pakistani society.

However, it must be conceded that the social milieu in urban areas is beginning to function relatively effectively with mutual trust, defined expectations, and common values such as regularity and punctuality.

Why has the past tradition of grievance and defiance survived so long after the end of the colonial rule? The patriarchal British rule (*mai-bap*), where the subject had to supplicate the ruler for redressal of his grievance, has left a strong legacy. It may be recalled that British India comprised several hundred princely states with rajas, maharajas, and nawabs at the helm dispensing favours to their citizens. At the same time, the defiance of authority, particularly in the pre-Independence period, has also left its mark. Gunnar Myrdal, in his exposition of 'the Soft state',[19] has argued that Indians (which includes Pakistanis) had during the freedom struggle got so used to breaking rules and flouting laws that this had become a heroic act of resistance to colonial authority. However, this cultural norm of violation of law and rules has become a debilitating habit. Indians became prey to petty corruption on the slightest pretext. 'Individual's autonomy has been limited not by the state but by kinship ties, caste rules (*biradari*), and religious affiliations. The task of modern citizenship was to convert the partial loyalties of society to a loyalty to the modern, impartial state.'

Another foreign expert on Pakistan, Michael Krepon, comments that 'grievances are deeply rooted in the Pakistani psyche, political culture, and national experience'.[20] Unfortunately, this grievance-oriented political culture focuses on political score settling. It is hard to move forward when so much time is spent on the past. Negative outcomes are widely expected in Pakistan and conspiracy theories exist in abundance, both real and imagined.

The Pakistani societal mind-set has to change from personalizing the impersonal, blaming others, conspiracy theories, double-think, hypocrisy, compartmentalization of beliefs and actions, and the strongman syndrome (the belief that there is a 'fix' for everything: the use of force, right connections, or money), to one which encourages work ethics, doing their jobs professionally, taking initiative and responsibility for their actions, entrepreneurship, and a go-getting culture. Policies, investment, and institutions in themselves aren't sufficient in facing the economic challenges of the twenty-first century as the essential necessity is a change in mind-set, societal values, and norms.

Society's Resilience

Although Pakistani society has faced so many crises and downturns, it has invariably rebounded and demonstrated resilience. How this does happen and how is Pakistani society able to hold together, notwithstanding its ethnic divisions, segmented classes, and fragmented institutions? What are the factors that maintain its social cohesion?

There are many institutional bonds that hold society together. As referred to above, family and kinship as institutions top the list. Those who do better economically have an obligation to share the fruits of their success by helping their relatives and looking after the well-being of kin. This kinship and *biradari* has strong binding qualities of reciprocal relationships of give and take with others and brings segmented sections of the society together.

This is apparent in bilateral dealings and exchanges in which formal contracts and documentation do not figure in business and trade relations.

The *'parchi'* system—an effective method of informal exchange—supervening over legally valid documents.

Material culture has been modernizing rapidly, consumption patterns and mass media have been more open to global influences but business practices, transactional norms, organizational culture, social relations, and the worldview have reinvented traditions and adopted modern forms without incorporating corresponding values and mores.

The evolution of modernizing forces—such as mass-education, urbanization, and the communication revolution—along with some gradual changes in the structure of the economy and its associated fallout are all contributing to this resilience, the most significant being the agrarian economy, which formed the backbone of the economy. Forty-five per cent of the population still depends upon agriculture for their sustenance.

Pakistan inherited a land tenure system where the size of their landholding defined the status and power of landowners. The majority of the rural population, tenants or landless workers, was economically subservient to the landlords. This dependence was skilfully manipulated by the latter to acquire political power. In the absence of any meaningful efforts at land reforms in the 1950s and 1960s, the social and economic inequities remained entrenched.

Subsequently, the laws of inheritance led to the subdivision of landholdings among various heirs and gave rise to the problem of land fragmentation. The introduction of mechanization, tube wells, and tractors led to a greater incidence of owner-operated farms. However, the dependence of landless labour and the peasants—working on these farms, although diluted by the education of their children—on their landlords provided a cohesive bond. In times of need, whether marriage or death, or other occurrences, the landlords do come forward to help their peasants and workers but extract a heavy price for this. The beneficiary not only becomes obligated financially but also politically and would vote at the elections in accordance with the directions of their landlords.

The economic clout of khans, *sardars,* and tribal chiefs have been receding over time due to the speed of education, urbanization, migration to the Middle East, and more democratic forms of relationships amongst the tribes of the KP.

Having outlined the favourable societal resilience of the above relationships, the repercussions for the institutions and the economy of this affiliation and group loyalty are pernicious. Informal networks of connections, nepotism, bribery, and corruption dominate the bulk of the dealings and transactions. People are appointed to government jobs not on merit but to fulfil obligations and promises; contracts are awarded to those who may not deliver but had helped at the time of the elections; and criminals are set free under the pressure from the local MNAs and MPAs.

One of the offshoots of this kinship and familial bonding in Pakistan is the widespread recourse to *benami* (lit. without name) transactions, in which the beneficial owner uses with ease and fearlessness his relatives and extended family members to conceal his own identity. Rampant corruption, tax evasion, drug trafficking, terrorist financing, and other nefarious activities have become possible because of the spread of *benamidar*s. Bank accounts are opened and operated in the names of relatives, earnings are diverted to these accounts, and real estate and assets procured through ill-gotten gains are kept in these people's names so that the actual beneficiary avoids being detected. *Benami* accounts also protect the forfeiture of assets in the event of a criminal case being proved against the actual owner. The recent Panamagate scandal has revealed that a number of Pakistani businesses have transferred funds earned in Pakistan through these means and transferred them to bank accounts abroad. The investment-GDP ratio is low in comparison to other South Asian countries where illicit earnings and rents are reinvested domestically rather than being illegally transferred abroad. Equities markets are manipulated through the use of these *benami* accounts. Nominee directors have also become common-place in the corporate sector which is retarding progress in the consolidation and expansion of companies in the formal sector. Economies of scale and scope do not kick in because the size of the companies is limited and partnerships to set up foreign joint ventures are not consummated because of this fragmentation. Private equity funds keep on looking for investment opportunities in Pakistan but are confronted with this phenomenon of double book keeping and lack of financial disclosure.

It is only recently that the Benazir Income Support programme (BISP), the largest social transfers programme in Pakistan, has been initiated by the government. Under this programme, unconditional cash transfers are made to 4.5 million families living below the poverty line. Whether these transfers will gradually reduce the stranglehold of *biradar*is, clans, landlords, and the tribal chiefs economically and politically is yet to be seen. What is more evident is that the pace of urbanization is weakening these links but creates a new set of problems. In an entirely new environment, with no family or kinship support, economic insecurity hits the poor and lower middle class income groups very hard.

Social Development[21]

A common metric to compare Pakistan's standing in social indicators in relation to its peers is its ranking on the UNDP's Human Development Index (HDI). This index ranks countries on the basis of primary characteristics associated with an adequate living standard. In 2014, Pakistan was ranked 147th out of 188 countries; despite an improvement in its absolute HDI score over this period, Pakistan's relative performance was not at all encouraging.

A number of factors are responsible for this low ranking, and that includes the prolonged war on terror, the policy focus on stabilization necessitated by recurrent balance of payments crises, and, more importantly, inadequate budgetary resources, along with the poor capacity of public institutions to formulate and implement internally consistent policies for social service delivery. Moreover, high population growth, and the social exclusion of a large segment of the female population from education and the labour force also undermined social sector development in Pakistan.

It won't be fair to place the entire blame for low HDI and the Gender Parity Index on the state. Societal barriers play an equally important role in the harnessing of talent of the female population which can reduce gender disparity, increase female labour force participation, and improve the delivery of services. At the tertiary level, females now equal or exceed males in enrolment, graduation, and in achieving distinction. However, their participation rate in the workforce still remains dismally low: about 20–25 per cent, including unpaid workers. It costs the state Rs 5 million to produce a medical doctor and the majority of those admitted to medical colleges are girls because they are able to secure places on merit through open competition. Of the graduating doctors each year, only 20–30 per cent enter the medical profession. Female employment in medicine is resented and therefore discouraged because their economic independence is construed as an act of disobedience towards their husbands and in-laws.

One of the powerful forces for societal transformation is through upward mobility. Umair Javaid[22] believes that going by anecdotal evidence, the time period until the 1980s seemed to be one of greater mobility for the lucky few who lived in Pakistan's cities:

> Public education was of a reasonably good quality, land was cheap, and dignified public- or private-sector employment not impossible to find. It was still possible to chart a way towards middle- or upper middle-class status in the space of one generation.
>
> Since then, all three things have reversed course. Competition for good public-sector universities is astronomical and biased towards big-city students, while high-quality private education is forbiddingly expensive. Speculators and investors rig the land market, while private-sector employment growth is tepid at best. The jobs that are available are often contractual, poorly protected and low-paying. The military and government employment remain the last (unsustainable) bastions of intergenerational mobility, which is exactly why they remain so highly coveted.
>
> In contemporary Pakistan, the father's socio-economic status remains the most crucial determinant of the offspring's economic position. Basically, the initial endowment (or lack thereof) of money, social connections, and cultural outlook weighs heavily on future life chances.

Another reason behind Pakistan's poor economic performance is again linked to poor work ethics. Zeenat Hisham[23] observes that:

> Pakistan has one of the lowest labour productivity rates in the region and suffers from poor work ethics. Anecdotal evidence abounds regarding the violation of ethical values at the workplace by all and sundry, from top to bottom in the organizational hierarchy and in all sectors, be it manufacturing or services, public or private.
>
> Even our parliamentarians and legislators demonstrate poor work ethics. The average attendance rate at the National Assembly hovers around 20 per cent, below the minimum quorum of 25 per cent.

In the manufacturing sector, industrialists recount stories of workers' negative attitudes, inefficiency, irresponsibility, absenteeism, and low productivity. The workers have their own tales to tell of employers' harsh attitude and violation of labour rights. Flagrant disregard for ethical standards (unaccountability, nepotism, corruption, etc.) by all tiers of workers and management in the services and public sector are an open secret. Workers show little respect for the equipment and machinery at the workplace.

The tendency to get away with minimum effort and not abide by the rules is pervasive. The late Dr Akhtar Hameed Khan, renowned development practitioner, described this trait very aptly as *'chori aur kaam chori'*.

CIVIL SOCIETY ORGANIZATIONS

Civil society in Pakistan is dualistic in nature and divided into two main tracks: the indigenous and modern. This taxonomy is, however, changing with the passage of time. A rising middle class has attributes of modernity while retaining elements of indigenous society, i.e. Islamic conservatism. This transition has therefore had an impact on the nature of the civil society organizations (CSOs).

On one hand, there is a rising group of civil society organizations comprising a youthful urban-educated population in step with the rest of the world. On the other hand, at the same time there are many charitable, relief, and welfare organizations affiliated with religious groups which have captured the attention of the poor and marginalized segments of the population. The funding for these religious NGOs is derived both from local traders and businessmen, as well as outsiders. The huge growth in the number of masjids and *madrassahs* throughout Pakistan has been the outcome of aggressive outreach and activities of non-government organizations with religious affiliations.

Naseer Memon, a Sindhi intellectual, traces the origin of the ascendancy of the religious-fundamentalist groups and the spread of their seminaries in Sindh at the expense of the peaceful and harmonious Sufi tradition to their relief activities during the floods of 2010. At a time when the government machinery was unresponsive, these organizations stepped in and filled the vacuum, endearing themselves to the thousands affected by the floods.

At the time of Independence, there were very few non-governmental organizations, the best known being Anjuman-i-Himayat-ul-Islam, which had founded a number of educational institutions for the Muslims. Relief provision in times of natural disasters and other calamities was also organized on an ad hoc basis.

Traditionally, professional bodies such as the bar associations, medical associations, teachers' unions, student unions, labour unions, journalists associations, chambers of commerce and industry, and press clubs were the most organized and active civil society organizations. These were followed by some charitable and philanthropic groups such as the All Pakistan Women Association (APWA), Rotary clubs, Lions clubs, the Red Crescent Society, and others. Later, the Human Rights Commission, Women Action Forum, Aurat Foundation, and many other advocacy groups were set up. International NGOS, such as Oxfam, Action Aid, Save the Children, World Vision, and Amnesty International also established chapters in Pakistan. A new breed of development NGOS, such as national and provincial rural support programmes, the Aga Khan Development Network, Orangi

Pilot Project, and CARE Foundation got involved in social mobilization and community[24] development projects. The Citizens Foundation (TCF), Edhi Foundation, Aman Foundation, and Layton Rahmatulah Blindness Trust (LRBT) have made a significant contribution in the fields of education and health care. The government also helped to set up the Trust for Voluntary Organizations (TVO), Pakistan Poverty Alleviation Fund (PPAF), National Commission for Human Development (NCHD), and Devolution Trust for Community Empowerment (DTCE) with the help of international donors to fund NGOs and enable community development. The number has been constantly growing and the current roster of NGOS and NPOs cover a variety of sectors and activities such as microfinance, rural and urban development, disaster relief, the environment, and the like.

The most impressive manifestation of the spirit of service by civil society was displayed during the earthquake of 2005. Thousands of groups and individuals came from all over Pakistan, bringing in relief goods and volunteering their services. International effort and support too was overwhelming. Collectively, this timely provision of relief, rehabilitation, and reconstruction of the housing infrastructure was a great boon to affected districts in Azad Jammu and Kashmir (AJK) and KP.

The lawyers' movement in 2007–08 against President Musharraf's decision to force Chief Justice Iftikhar Chaudhry to resign from his post is considered a remarkable success of the strength of civil society. However, the subsequent misbehaviour of a group of lawyers threatening and intimidating judges created a great deal of disillusionment amongst the public at large.

Business groups, such as the Federation of Pakistan Chambers of Commerce and Industry (FPCCI),Lahore Chamber of Commerce and Industry (LCCI), Karachi Chamber of Commerce and Industry (KCCI), All Pakistan Textile Manufacturers Association (APTMA), and others are quite active and vocal but they are generally perceived to be lobby groups, promoting their own businesses and protecting their narrow self-interest rather than bodies engaging in non-partisan national economic dialogue and policy development. The Pakistan Business Council (PBC), established a few years ago by the largest business groups in Pakistan, seeks to diverge from the normal business lobbying and present well-researched analysis on critical issues facing the national economy.

I. A. Rehman[25] provides an explanation for the weaknesses of these associations and civil society organizations:

> The climate of suspicion, hate and intolerance (that any witch-hunt generates) suppresses not only dissent but also free thinking. Ordinary people become afraid of associating with fellow beings. Society stops receiving the benefits of productive associations, assemblies and collective endeavours. In a way, the persecution of individuals or groups for their racial identity or political views dehumanizes society to an extent that it consumes itself within a short period.

Concerns have been expressed in the recent years at the government's rigorous scrutiny of NGOs and the strict approval process. This became necessary to screen and purge organizations engaging in terrorist financing. These steps have not been welcomed by the civil society organizations and an analyst described this process in the following terms:

> Space for civil society, civic spaces in general, are under threat both by the state as well as by extremist forces within our society. The intensity of aspersions cast on the agendas pursued by members of civil society has heightened and uses the same surveillance apparatus of the state institutions that is used to check terrorism.
>
> Civil society faces new challenges of registration, particularly since October 2015 when a new NGO policy was announced. The policy gives powers to the interior ministry and intelligence agencies to review NGOs'/ INGOs' registrations on the basis of their work and financing ... Registration has become a horrendously slow process, and deadlines for registration have been extended several times. Overall, civil society organizations have to work in an extremely insecure milieu.[26]

The Media

The role of the media in society has also attracted a great deal of attention since the explosive growth of TV channels in Pakistan initiated in the early 2000s. Ironically, it was a military dictator, generally known for their tendency to suppress the freedom of expression and nurture an intolerance of dissent, who permitted the breakup of the monopoly of state-owned Pakistan TV and allowed private channels to enter the electronic media field. Pervez Musharraf also permitted cross-ownership of the media, resulting in several large and powerful groups to dominate the industry. The proliferation of channels and the rating war for eyeballs had unintended consequences. Rather than performing the role of a watchdog and keeping a vigilant eye on the actions of the government, the owners have aligned themselves with different groups or parties. Many allegations have been circulating about the integrity of well-known TV anchors, some of whom have a large following and viewership and thus influence, directly or indirectly, public opinion. Only those columnists, anchors, and discussants are popular who portray highly negative and pessimistic views and paint doomsday scenarios. Those who present a more balanced and even-handed picture do not find any space or place. This malaise has spread like wildfire and has become an integral part of the national psyche. Students in higher educational institutions trot out the same arguments in their term papers and debates that they have heard on TV and read in the newspapers without verifying their authenticity.

The other problem that has intensified as a consequence of the influence of the media is the highly cynical and negative mind-set of the majority of our population. If anyone says or writes something positive, s/he is taken to task for either having a personal agenda to ingratiate him/herself with the government or already being on their payroll or that of the ISI. The persisting gap between the promise and performance of successive governments seems to have contributed to a lack of credibility and belief. The insecurity of the state generated by the experience of the separation of East Pakistan is another factor which drives our thinking. Pakistan's subservience to the US, Saudi Arabia, the IMF, etc. over time has also given credence to the theory that the policies are being dictated by others and we have no control in shaping the events. A general feeling of helplessness and victimhood has saturated the social discourse in Pakistan.

The print media is no differently perceived. One of the leading editors, Ejaz Haider,[27] has the following views about the op-ed pieces in the newspapers:

Most of those writing in newspapers are hoodwinking readers by presenting feelings, passions and desires as serious analysis. The blame must lie with editors for printing such pieces. The only place for most such pieces is the editor's pike. The dustbin is what I reserve for those pieces that combine some half-baked analysis with what I call roving subjective prose.

A veteran editor, I. A. Rehman points out:[28] 'The media has developed a persecution syndrome that has bred an exaggerated feeling of self-righteousness on the one hand and an aversion to self-criticism on the other.'

Author and journalist Zahid Hussain writes:

The rise of the power of the electronic media works as a double-edged sword. While being the most effective means of disseminating information and for inculcating social and political awareness in all segments of society that are within its phenomenal reach, it is also often used as an instrument for disinformation and falsifying the facts.

Powerful demagogues in control of the mike, and owners of channels only interested in getting high ratings have brought into question the credibility and professionalism of the electronic media. This new and dangerous trend of media vigilantism raises questions about the misuse of freedom of expression endangering the lives and freedom of others. It has become much more imperative now than ever before to enforce a code of ethics to protect the hard-earned freedom of press and democratic rights.[29]

GENDER GAP AND WOMEN'S RIGHTS

Pakistan ranks at the bottom rung among the developing countries in the Global Gender Index. Disparities between males and females are entrenched in the legal, cultural, and social milieu, and it has been an uphill task to overcome the many obstacles that are faced by the women in their day to day lives. Honour killings, acid attacks, and rape are some of the social evils in Pakistan which have attracted worldwide attention as violations of human rights. Notwithstanding these enormous difficulties, it must be admitted that Pakistani women have made a significant progress over the last seven decades but the wide gender gap has yet to be significantly lowered, let alone bridged. Women's participation in the labour force is dismally low: only 22 per cent in contrast to 66 per cent by men and that too largely in the rural areas as unpaid family workers. This low participation in economic activity is attributable to lower educational and literacy rates (only 32 per cent have a higher secondary or higher educational qualification), they shoulder a reproductive burden, care-giving, and household responsibilities, and restrictions on mobility.

There are socially induced discriminatory practices in hiring women and paying compensation for their contribution. Even in cases where both males and females have the same educational qualifications, women are not selected for the job because the employer thinks that they will not stay long and any training imparted to and investment made in them is likely to be counterproductive. They are not offered permanent or regular employment but are hired for contractual positions. Consequently, they do not receive any social security, or medical and old age benefits. The wage gap is also wide and women get paid around 40 per cent less than male employees for the same kind of work. Their career advancement prospects are also poor as they do not form part of the organizational hierarchy and are not trained to shoulder higher responsibilities. Research has also shown that a hostile work environment, harassment at the workplace, social norms discouraging daughters and daughters-in-law from seeking employment, and lack of safe public transport are also important impediments in the way of higher female participation in the labour force.

Recent trends in tertiary education and professional education, such as medicine, are highly encouraging as girls outstrip the boys in enrolment as well as in obtaining top positions in the examinations. Although they acquire the skills and training and are generally believed to be more hard working, the tension in balancing marriage, child rearing, and a career acts as a deterrent. A frustrating practice for policy-makers is that millions are spent on training a medical doctor over a six-year period but a majority of the female doctors tend to withdraw from the profession once they get married. Although it is rewarding for the individual to have succeeded in the marriage market, the loss to the society is huge in terms of financial cost, the foregone opportunities for others who would have stayed on in the profession, and the continuing shortage of qualified female medical practitioners sorely required in conservative communities, and particularly in the rural areas.

The Punjab Commission on Status of Women presents an updated picture of gender disparities in its latest report.[30]

Out of the 146 Punjab MNAs (general seats), only four (2.8 per cent) are occupied by women. In the Punjab Assembly, the 303 MPAs (general seats) include only eight (2.6 per cent) women and only four (14 per cent) are members of the Cabinet of 31.

Female life expectancy has risen to 66.9 years, below the life expectancy for men at 67.7 years while the total fertility rate is still high compared to other neighbouring countries. Women have a lack of access to healthcare facilities.

Female literacy rate has risen to 55 per cent in 2014–15 compared to the male literacy rate of around 70 per cent; the net enrolment rate for girls is 67 per cent (the ratio for boys [is] 73 per cent).

The labour force participation rate for women was a mere 27.8 per cent (for males it was 69.4 per cent); the highest female labour force participation rate—22.8 per cent—is in agriculture (for males [it is] 49.1 per cent); almost 75 per cent of women workers are denied the minimum wage.

Of the 60 Lahore High Court judges, only three (5 per cent) are women; of the 1,703 judges in the district judiciary only 260 (14.5 per cent) are women; there are three female police stations out of a total of 709, [and] there were 7,313 reported cases of violence against women.

SUMMATION

Pakistani societal norms and values of kinship, *biradaris*, and tribal and feudal loyalty have been a source of support in times of adversity, crises, and problems but have had a detrimental effect on the evolution of the formal, structured, state-centric institutions of governance. In the initial post-Independence period, the sense of newly acquired freedom transcended all other feelings of ethnic, linguistic, and/or provincial division but these soon faded because of a series of political developments. Trust and social capital have eroded, religious and sectarian differences have come to the fore, and the strands that constituted the thread of nationalism has begun unravelling.

Social development did not receive much attention and resources and therefore Pakistan lags behind all its neighbouring countries in the human development indicators. Gender disparities and low female labour force participation rates are stifling the realization of Pakistan's full potential.

Civil society organizations have become active and some of them are making useful contributions in education, health, and other fields but new restrictions are being placed in their path which may prove to be a deterrent in the expansion of their activities. The media, freed up and in private hands, can act as a watchdog on the executive and legislature but has developed unhealthy practices of rivalries, sensationalism, negativism, and partisanship.

The institutional landscape cannot be organically nurtured until the disconnect between the prevalent societal values and norms and the ingredients upon which the institutions thrive is bridged.

Notes and References

1. Qadeer, M. A., 'Ruralopolises: The spatial organisation and residential land economy of high-density rural regions in South Asia', *Urban Studies*, (2002), 37(9), 1583–1603.

2. Jaffrelot, C., *Pakistan: Nationalism without a Nation* (Manshar, 2000).

3. Malik, I. H., *State and Civil Society in Pakistan: Politics of Authority, Ideology, and Ethnicity* (Macmillan).

4. Qadeer, *Islam and Social Life* (2006) Accessed at: <http://archives.cerium. ca/IMG/pdf/Qadeer_2006.pdf>

5. Qadeer, quoted in K. Hasan, *The Friday Times.*

6. Sattar, B., 'Rule of Law on Trial' *The News,* 10 June 2017.

7. Qasim, A. I., *Questioning the Authority of the Past* (OUP, 2011).

8. Zahab, M. A., 'The Politicization of the Shia Community in Pakistan in the 1970s and 1980s', in Monsutti A., Naef S., Sabahi F (eds.), *The Other Shiites: From the Mediterranean to Central Asia* (Bern: Peter Lang AG, International Academic Publishers, 2007), 97–114.

9. Mumtaz, S., Ali, I., and Racine, J., *Pakistan: The Contours of State and Society* (Karachi: OUP, 2002).

10. Rizvi, H. A. 'Conflictual Politics', *Express Tribune,* 14 February 2017.

11. Ziauddin, M., 'Good Governance is the Answer', *Express Tribune,* 4 March 2017.

12. Qadeer, 'Brutalization of Society', *The News,* 24 August 2009.

13. Zaidi, A., *Issues in Pakistan's Economy* (OUP, 2015).

14. Qadeer, Paper presented at the Annual Conference of Pakistan Society of Development Economists, Islamabad, 1999.

15. Jalal, A., *Friday Times,* 22 October 2010.

16. Gilani, Z., 'Democratic Political Leaders', *Express Tribune,* 27 May 2017.

17. World Bank, *Economic Growth in 1990s,* (Washington DC: World Bank, 2005).

18. Murtaza, N., 'Grandmother Cause', *Dawn,* 9 May 2017.

19. Myrdal, G., *Asian Drama: An Inquiry into the Poverty of Nations* (Pantheon, 1968).

20. Krepon, M., *The Friday Times,* 30 October 2009.

21. State Bank of Pakistan, *Annual Report 2015–16* (2016).

22. Javaid, U., 'Social Immobility in Pakistan', *Dawn,* 10 October 2016.

23. Hisham, Z., 'Work Ethics', *Dawn,* 5 February 2017.

24. Memon, N., 'How extremism reached Sindh' *The News,* 14 May 2017.

25. Rehman, I. A., 'Shades of McCarthyism', *Dawn,* 24 November 2016.

26. Khan, F. S., 'Shrinking Progress', *Dawn,* 11 October 2016.

27. E. Haider, 'Axing Amb Munir Akram', *Daily Times,* 27 July 2008

28. Rehman, 'Balance of Power', *The News,* 22 March 2009.

29. Hussain, Zahid, 'Media, judge and jury', *Dawn,* 28 January 2017.

30. 'Punjab Commission on Status of Women, Report', *Dawn,* 9 March 2017.

6

Federal and Provincial Governments

Questions such as state vs market, public vs private sector, and neoliberal vs interventionist, usually framed in terms of binary divisions, are not only unhelpful but have created confusion and tension, and have promoted adversarial relationships in Pakistan. These oversimplifications and reductionist labelling have moved the discourse away from the synergetic and symbiotic energies that can be generated by a more collaborative and cooperative approach to steering public policy. In the real world, there are a large number of variants of governance structures and models in which the state, markets, and increasingly civil society play different roles. From the Nordic model to Social Democrat to Anglo Saxon, to the East Asian versions, there is a continuum of functions that are performed by the state, society, and markets in varying degrees. There are broad or narrow grey areas between the extreme white or black that the binary classifications represent and there is no clear demarcation of boundaries fixed for all times to come. Pakistan itself has undertaken several experiments over time. Beginning with a benign state promoting the private sector in the earlier decades, to spearheading the nationalization of private industries, banking, insurance, and educational institutions, there is currently a widely held consensus about the respective roles of the state, the private sector, and NGOs. There is now a broad agreement that a government in a developing country has to:

(1) provide external and internal security for the people
(2) collect taxes
(3) manage the public finances
(4) conduct foreign affairs

(5)   maintain a stable macroeconomic environment including a sound
       and healthy financial system
(6)   make available the basic infrastructural·facilities
(7)   develop an education and training system capable of supplying
       the skilled manpower required by the nation, provide basic health
       facilities, drinking water, and sanitation
(8)   encourage and also undertake research and development and
       promote new technologies, innovation, and entrepreneurship
(9)   ensure an enabling regulatory framework for the private sector and
       community participation in development

The 'Introduction' has already dwelt upon the relative roles of the market,
the state, and society. To recapitulate, markets are efficient in producing,
exchanging, and trading goods and services and allocating scarce resources
but in doing so, only those who are already well-endowed are rewarded.
They do not necessarily benefit the uneducated, poor, handicapped, and
unskilled on whose behalf the state has to step in by taxing a fraction of
the incomes earned by the well-endowed and transferring that to the less
well-to-do through public expenditures on education, skill upgradation,
healthcare, drinking water, sanitation, and social transfers. The state also
has to regulate the markets to ensure that competition and not collusion
prevails in the marketplace, consumers are protected, health, safety, and
environmental standards are observed, and that a level playing field is
ensured for all those participating in the market. Society has to play the
role of maintaining vigilance on the state and market institutions and also,
wherever possible, participate in the provision of social services such as
education and health.

Technological advances have made it possible to reorganize and unbundle
integrated activities into components that can be transformed from public
monopolies to competitive market structures. Telecommunications and
electricity generation and distribution are two such examples which used
to be state-owned monopolies. Now, however, the integrated utility model
has been broken up and there is competition in both these sectors among
privately owned companies benefiting consumers in terms of access,

coverage, and pricing. The long gestation of years to obtain a fixed line phone connection, requiring favours on the part of the provider or paying bribes, has been replaced by access to instantaneous phone connections at a fraction of the prices charged by the state-owned company.

In education and health, there is an obligation by the state to ensure these services are available to citizens as a matter of right. However, the private sector, philanthropic organizations, and NGOs have gotten involved in providing these services in addition to the state. The fee voucher system adopted by the provinces has enabled children from needy families to attend private schools financed by the state.

There has been a continuing process of learning over time regarding the various alternate ways of delivering services which used to be in the exclusive domain of the government/public sector. Today, a variety of mixed models of public–private partnership, public–NGO partnership, private–NGO partnership, and public–private–NGO partnership exist in Pakistan. The existence of these models negates the views of those who believe in the sharp but artificial dichotomous division between the state and the market or the state and society.

Pakistan has been characterized since Independence as a highly centralized unitary state rather than a truly federal form of government. The unification of four provinces—Sindh, Punjab, Balochistan, and the NWFP—within a single unit, West Pakistan, from 1956–70 was a clear manifestation of this trend. The military governments also found it convenient to have a unified system of command and control with which they were familiar and comfortable. The dynastic nature of politics also reinforced the tendency during the tenures of the elected governments as the leader of the party enjoyed and exercised exceptional powers. The 1973 Constitution had two separate lists, i.e. federal, and concurrent, for legislative purposes. The concurrent list, for which the federal government took most of the initiative, remained in force until 2010 and was omitted from the Constitution under the Eighteenth Amendment.

The Constitution directs that the executive powers be exercised by a three-tier system comprising the federal, provincial, and local governments. The federal government is headed by the prime minister and assisted by a cabinet or council of ministers who are given portfolios to run the ministries concerned with specific state functions.

The federal government, after the Eighteenth Amendment, comprises 27 ministries and 35 divisions (excluding the president and prime minister's secretariat), 210 autonomous bodies, and 157 attached departments, corporations, companies, councils, institutes, and subordinate offices. The total number of employees in the federal secretariat, attached departments, and subordinate offices and autonomous corporations in 2014 was 830,459. Table 6.1 below provides a further breakdown of these numbers.

Table 6.1: Federal Government Employees 2014

Secretariat	18,102	Percentage
Grades 1–16	14,866	82.2
Grades 17–22	3,236	17.8
Attached Departments	426,419	
Grades 1–16	407,036	95.6
Grades 17–22	19,382	4.4
Autonomous bodies	385,939	
Grades 1–16	319,029	82.7
Grades 17–22	66,910	17.3
Total no. of federal employees	830,459	
Grades 1–16	740,931	89.3
Grades 17–22	89,528	10.7

Source: Government of Pakistan, Establishment Division, Census of Employees 2014

Among the 444,521 employees serving in the federal secretariat and the attached departments, the cadre of the officer class (BPS 17–22) comprising highly educated and trained professionals accounts for only five per cent of the total workforce while the subordinate or support staff accounts for the majority, i.e. 95 per cent. This skewed distribution of the federal workforce betrays the inadequacy of capable expertise in Pakistan's highest policy-making apparatus. The situation is better in the autonomous bodies where 17 per cent of the staff is from the officer/professional class.

This highly skewed composition of federal employees, which is mirrored in the provincial governments, reveals the relative importance of low grade employees who are neither educated, trained, nor motivated but enjoy vast discretionary powers. The staff work done by them is shoddy, inconsistent, and rarely ever reviewed by their superior officers which is why decision-making is of very poor quality. The increasing tendency to challenge the decisions of the executive in the tribunals/courts, etc. by those aggrieved confirms the general dissatisfaction with government functionaries.

The federal government has taken the right step of transferring education (except higher education and curriculum), health, agriculture, labour, social welfare, population welfare, and local government to the provincial governments. However, the attached departments and autonomous bodies have been retained and there has been no systematic study regarding those that need to be retained at the federal level and those that could usefully be transferred to the provinces. Some of the federal ministries dealing with these subjects have re-emerged in different forms, such as the ministry of higher education and training, ministry of food security and research, and the ministry of national health services regulation and coordination. There is no logic for fully-fledged ministries for these subjects, and the ministry of inter-provincial coordination should have been strengthened with the expertise in these areas to work as the secretariat of the council of common interests.

The national council of ministers, comprising the federal and provincial ministers working under the aegis of the Council of Common Interests (CCI), should formulate the national policies for these transferred subjects. The federal government would retain responsibilities for international relations and inter-provincial coordination in these subjects. In this way, the number of federal ministries can be cut from 27 to 18 and the number of divisions from 35 to 23 through mergers, creation, transfer, and abolition. In view of the new challenges that are facing Pakistan, some new ministries—such as ministries for energy, technology development, regulatory affairs, human resource development, social protection, infrastructure development, and special and underdeveloped areas—should be set up by merging or disbanding some of the existing ministries and replacing others. The autonomous bodies can be regrouped into 177 bodies and the number of executive departments reduced to only 70 under the federal government. All other bodies would be merged, privatized, wound up, liquidated or transferred to the provincial governments.

The performance of the federal and provincial governments in the eyes of citizens is extremely unsatisfactory. PILDAT has conducted a nationwide survey of the quality of governance indicators annually since 2014. These include delivery of services, transparency, law and order, infrastructure, civil services, and others. The PILDAT Survey of Public Opinion for 2016 shows that the respondents rate 10 out of 27 'quality of governance' indicators of the federal government positively in comparison to only 6 indicators in 2015. The overall trend of public approval remains negative.

Governance in Punjab is rated nationwide as the highest across all nationwide respondents with 67 per cent approval ratings. KP, with a positive rating of 38, was the second, while Balochistan and Sindh ratings were 26 and 25 per cent respectively.

The respondents from KP, however, positively rate 18 out of 25 quality of governance indicators, the highest, followed by Punjab (15), and Balochistan and Sindh respondents rated only 12 indicators positively.

Transparency and anti-corruption, merit-based recruitment and promotions, and quality and independence of civil service get consistently low scores, indicating very negative perceptions about these indicators for the federal, Punjab, KP, and Sindh governments. Curiously, transparency and anti-corruption indicators for Balochistan are favourably rated.

According to the Survey, the armed forces remain the most trusted institution in Pakistan with an approval rating of 76 per cent, followed by the Supreme Court/High Court (62 per cent), National Assembly (58 per cent), and electronic media (54 per cent). Police has the lowest public trust with an 18 per cent approval ratings.

The election commission, civil courts, political parties, NAB, and government officers are rated low.

How can these public perceptions be changed? Introducing transparency through simplification of rules and regulations, codification and updating, and wide dissemination through e-governance tools such as a dynamic website, information kiosks, and online access to the government functionaries can help in enforcing internal accountability standards while at the same time making it convenient for citizens to conduct hassle-free transactions. Strong pressure from organized civil society advocacy groups on specific sectors or activities from the media, the political parties, the private sector, and think-tanks can also compel the government departments and ministries to become more accountable in their functioning.

In light of the Eighteenth Amendment to the Constitution and the decline in the share of the federal government from the divisible tax pool, it is important to revisit the size, structure, and scope of the responsibilities of the federal, provincial, and local governments. The overlapping and duplication of functions and responsibilities between different ministries/attached departments/autonomous bodies within the federal government need to be analysed. The relationships between the secretary of a ministry and the heads of the executive departments and autonomous bodies for disposal of business have to be redefined. The hierarchy within the ministry/division has to be trimmed. Fewer hierarchical tiers, delegation of highly centralized decision-making, and introduction of e-governance would save costs and recurrent expenditure. Some organizations, such as the State Bank of Pakistan have made intelligent use of IT tools and improved their efficiency. Measures to computerize records and processes are sorely needed. Besides bringing transparency and efficiency, taking away discretionary powers from lower-level state officers would reduce the incidence of speed-money. The move to transfer the regulatory bodies from the cabinet division to the line ministries is a retrogressive step and must be reversed.

The origin and persistence of the circular debt that surfaces periodically to destabilize the economy is a clear manifestation of the lack of clarity in regard to the location of responsibility in a ministry/agency. There is therefore, for instance, a shifting of blame from the ministry of water and power to that of finance and vice versa, and even within the ministry of water and power, among a myriad of agencies. Accountability for results and performance, or the lack of it, cannot be established when more than 20 different entities are involved.

The role of the planning commission, a body responsible for the long-term direction of the economy, formulation of policies, programmes, and development projects, resolution of inter-ministerial claims in priority-fixing, allocation of resources for these development priorities, and monitoring implementation, has weakened over time. A silo mind-set characterizes the current dispensation and the allocation of resources out of the public sector development programme (PSDP) is simply a reflection of this mind-set. Poor design, cost overruns, and delays in project completion undermine the benefits of development projects. The recent move to transform the commission into a think-tank for policy formulation and monitoring implementation is a salutary step.

IMPROVING INTER-MINISTERIAL COOPERATION

During Ayub Khan's governance, the powers of the federal secretaries were enhanced and decision-making concentrated in their hands. Divisional commissioners in West Pakistan still enjoyed some powers and capable or competent individuals took initiatives and exercised their powers in the best interests of citizens. The administrative reforms of 1973 broke the back of the civil service and the powers enjoyed by the federal secretaries were diluted. The tendencies of over-centralization, personalised decision-making, and listening to the views of a small coterie of loyal officers have become entrenched.

Routine decisions taken by federal secretaries are now made by the prime minister and the chief ministers. Civil servants who have the right connections, the gift of gab, and can impress through power-point presentations, (and) or are obsequious win the day. Deeper analysis and scrutiny of the issues under consideration from different perspectives are shunned.

The secretaries' committee can play an important role in overcoming these flaws. They can provide a common platform for exchanges of views and the presentation of different perspectives, whether legal, administrative, financial, or technical, on the policy issues or individual transactions, as the case may be. This eliminates unnecessary movements of files from one ministry to another and consequent delays in decision-making.

The knowledge of individual secretaries about the subject matter and appreciation of the constraints are much enhanced when they are exposed to different viewpoints, and this will have a positive impact on their decision-making capacity. The cabinet committees and the cabinet will not be overloaded because many decisions would have been taken by the secretaries' committee and their quality of work, the speed of disposal, and focus of attention will be much superior to the current practices. The agenda for the cabinet committees would therefore be limited to unresolved issues alone, i.e. to issues where the differences still persist and a consensus has not been reached by the secretaries. To ensure that these powers are delegated and exercised, a few prior actions need to be taken to smooth the way.

First, the security of tenure for all government officers should be observed in letter and in spirit. If a secretary is appointed for a term of three years he cannot be transferred arbitrarily at the whims and caprices of the competent authority. The reasons for removal should be given in writing and the affected person will have the right to challenge this decision in a court of law. The Supreme Court has already given its verdict on this issue in the Anita Turab case.[1] All that is necessary is to comply with it in the future. This will impose an obligation upon the authority to carefully select a person suitable for the job, to agree on the performance indicators, and to monitor the progress against these. The present practice, where as many as 14 secretaries were appointed and transferred within a period of five years, has led to demotivation, demoralization, political alignments, corrupt practices, and poor outcomes. Lack of continuity of the principal accounting officers and absence of any checks upon their performance[2] are the root cause of poor decision-making, and a sense of inertia and indifference. Delegation of powers would not work in such a working environment.

Second, the rules of business confer enormous discretionary powers upon the prime minister and the chief ministers. In a parliamentary system, the cabinet is responsible for collective decision-making. As practised, the present system has made the ministers ineffective in exercising their powers as all summaries have to be approved by the chief executive. A rebalancing of the powers between the Prime Minister/chief minister, minister, and secretary needs to be immediately evolved to curb this unhealthy tendency of excessive concentration of powers in a single person. All eyes are focused and all approaches made to that single individual negating the accepted principles of collective decision-making and delegation of powers.

Third, a corollary to the excessive concentration of powers in the hands of the PM/chief minister has been the dominance of the principal secretary to the Prime Minister (PSPM)/chief minister as the most powerful individual in the government. These parallel secretariats, in which all the summaries/proposals submitted by the line ministries/departments are again reviewed by junior officials of the PM secretariat, needs to be trimmed down to a few experienced officers/advisers in the PM's office. There is no need to second guess the judgment and wisdom of the secretaries to the government.

Unlike the provinces, the federal government does not have an officer equivalent to the chief secretary who can coordinate among different ministries of the government and also act as the head of the civil service. This role used to be played by the cabinet secretary in the past but has been weakened over time with the gradual empowerment of the private secretary to the Prime Minister. There is a need to appoint the senior-most civil servant as the cabinet secretary, who will play the coordinating role and also attend to the welfare and problems faced by the civil servants. The secretaries committee should also be revived to settle inter-ministerial issues which are now routinely taken by the cabinet and its committees.

The fifth step is to weed out and purge all the existing manuals and rule books of redundant and superseded rules, circulars, directives, and instructions. An exercise was done for Estacode and an updated establishment manual has been prepared. The ministry of finance has also updated all the financial rules. Uploading these manuals and rules on the websites of the respective ministries/departments will go a long way in bringing about transparency and reducing the discretionary powers of the lower functionaries. Some corrupt practices occur because the information about rules and regulations is hoarded by a few individuals who take advantage of this opacity for their self-aggrandizement. An open and transparent system will help minimize such practices.

Sixth, the system of financial advisers (FA) for each ministry in the federal government has proved to be a major stumbling block in orderly decision-making and efficient utilization of budgetary resources. The FA office virtually enjoys veto power in matters of expenditure and although the secretary is accountable for results, s/he cannot do very much as overruling the FA will entail all manner of sanctions. The re-designation of the FA as chief finance and accounts officers is just window dressing. The training, mind-set, and skills of these officers have to be altogether altered. Eligibility criteria and job descriptions should be drawn out for these jobs and suitably qualified persons appointed to these positions with specific terms of reference.

Because of frequent changes in senior policy positions, the ministry tends to lose the institutional memory, continuity, commitment, and thrust of policy. Policies suffer from a lack of complementary changes in rules, structural arrangements of the implementation mechanism, and absent or inadequate budget provisions.

REFORMING PUBLIC ENTERPRISES

According to the Asian Development Bank[3] assessment, there were 191 public enterprises employing about 420,000 workers, which account for 10 per cent of GDP. The total assets of these enterprises in 2014 were Rs 9.4 trillion or $9.4 billion. The outstanding debt and liabilities were Rs 665.9 billion or 2.2 per cent of GDP. Pakistan Railways and the power distribution companies together employed over half the total number of workers in the public enterprise sector. These, along with the Pakistan Steel Mills (PSM) and PIA, are responsible for the losses and the subsidies provided by the exchequer. The magnitude of the subsidies (explicit and implicit), concessions, financing, losses underwritten, bank borrowing guaranteed by the government, foreign loans for all the state-owned enterprises, companies, and entities and corporations owned and managed by the federal and the provincial governments has never been computed but for the federal government alone this would run into almost $6 billion.

Pakistan was among one of the few developing countries in the early 1990s which initiated the process of privatization of state-owned enterprises. Between January 1991 and September 2015, as many as 172 transactions were completed yielding Rs 649 billion (about $6.5 billion).

Successive governments since 1991 have pursued the same policy and the results have been quite impressive in several sectors. Since then, technological advances that made competition possible in industries that were previously considered to be monopolies has negated the concept of retaining vertically integrated monoliths designed to benefit from presumed economies of scale. The shining example is that of telecommunications where a single public sector corporation, PTCL, enjoyed a monopoly of telephony services and the results were disastrous in terms of coverage, service, and pricing. Since the breakup of this monopoly and the entry of the private sector, introduction of mobile technologies, and transparent auction of spectrum, there has been an unparalleled upsurge in the services provided by the sector.

The banking and financial services, and cement and automobile sectors have performed extremely well and attracted substantial investment both from foreign and domestic investors after privatization. For example, HBL and UBL were given a capital injection of Rs 41 billion to compensate for their losses under government ownership. Since 2005, after they were privatized, both banks are paying dividends and corporate tax to the government and the residual value of government shares has risen several-fold.

There was a setback to privatization in 2006 after the Supreme Court nullified the Pakistan Steel Mills transaction. Most estimates prepared by independent analysts have placed the losses incurred by the Steel Mills in the past few years at around Rs 100 billion. The private buyers had planned to expand capacity to 3 million tonnes, which has remained elusive under public ownership.

Had these public enterprises been providing satisfactory services and adequately catering to the needs of the general public, this burden being borne by the taxpayers could have been defended. However, their performance and service standards are so dismal that they have bedevilled the lives of ordinary citizens and proved to be a disruptive element in our economic development.

Notwithstanding the stark evidence of the financial haemorrhaging caused by these corporations, why has the privatization process stalled for the past five years? There are at least three factors that explain this.

First, there are well-meaning Pakistanis who are genuinely apprehensive that these assets will be sold to the cronies of the people in power at throwaway prices at a huge loss to the economy. This is a legitimate concern but can be addressed by conducting the sale transparently, in full public view of the media. Oversight by parliamentary committees and the scrutiny of the judiciary and the media should minimize corruption.

Second, the ministers and the bureaucrats in charge of these corporations enjoy much power, influence, and illegal reward by controlling appointments, transfers, and postings, the award of contracts, and the like. In other words, these enterprises are a source of political patronage and no one would wish to forgo this. This problem too can be resolved by taking these powers away from the ministries and placing all the corporations under an independent holding company responsible to the cabinet division and accountable to the parliamentary committees. Only those that are of a strategic nature should be retained under the direct control of the ministries concerned.

Third, many Pakistanis are opposed to privatization on the ground that the sale of the 'family silver' will result in further concentration of wealth and growing inequities, unemployment, and mean higher prices for consumers. Empirical evidence shows that a strong regulatory agency with competent manpower and enforcement capacity can ensure competition and ensure that consumer interests are protected and the shares divested are distributed to a broad ownership.

There is ample evidence to suggest that under public ownership, there are few incentives for efficiency, returns on investment are low, and in some instances, they contribute to huge fiscal deficits. Overmanning, favouritism, and nepotism in appointments and awards of contracts are a common feature. PIA, Pakistan Steel, and distribution companies (DISCOS) are incurring losses to the exchequer of up to two per cent of the GDP because these organizations have been captured by their workers, managers, and their political and bureaucratic supervisors.

Public sector enterprises and corporations should be revisited and regrouped into those that have to be retained as such for strategic reasons and those that need to be privatized, liquidated, or merged. The decision should be guided by pragmatic considerations rather than for ideological and dogmatic reasons. A hundred of these entities, i.e. public corporations, are running businesses or supplying services. They include some large money-guzzlers such as the Water and Power Development Authority, the Oil and Gas Development Co., Pakistan Electric Power Co., Pakistan Steel, the Trading Corporation of Pakistan, PIA, National Bank, State Life Insurance, etc. Most news stories about the alleged losses incurred by nepotism and favouritism, etc. are not coincidentally focused on this group of corporations.

Some of them are utilities and enjoy monopolies. Notwithstanding the existence of regulatory agencies in Pakistan it would not be advisable to transform public monopolies into private monopolies.

In the event of it being decided to retain the public ownership of a company for strategic reasons, the underlying principle for guiding public-sector corporations should be the separation of policy control and operational and financial control. To illustrate this, let us assume that Pakistan Steel would continue to remain within the public sector. The ministry of industries should then exercise policy control over the company by (a) appointing a board of directors and a chairman of the board, (b) assigning policy objectives or production targets to be achieved during the year, (c) appointing the chief executive of the corporation for a fixed tenure, and (d) holding the board accountable for the results. To exercise the rights of ownership, the government should nominate appropriate persons on the boards and appoint the chief executive but the ministry should not interfere in the company's day-to-day operations. The government can communicate the parameters of policy and performance, as well as hold the company accountable for the results, but it is the board of governors that should monitor and oversee its operations.

If the Boards are saddled with too many bureaucrats representing various ministries, then there won't be much qualitative difference between the direct control of the ministry in-charge of the public enterprise and the board so constituted. Independent non-executive directors who bring expertise and knowledge in the areas of finance, accounting, law, strategy, marketing, and sectoral expertise should be invited to serve on these boards.

The board would be responsible for setting the direction and implementation of government policy, approving strategies, internal policies and procedures, annual business plans and budgets, and monitoring performance. It would enter into a performance contract at the beginning of each financial year with the chief executive. An annual report would be presented on whether the guidelines or targets were achieved and the reasons for the shortfall if they were not. This report would be submitted to the ministry which would study similar reports from the corporations under its control and prepare a comprehensive report for parliament.

Experience of successful public enterprises in Pakistan shows that they were manned by the right people, selected on the basis of merit, and allowed operational autonomy under the supervision of a board of directors and held accountable for the results.

A chief executive should be appointed by the respective Board as laid down in the Companies Act and Code of Corporate Governance. The ministry should specify the qualifications and eligibility criteria for the post of chief executive, invite both nominations and applications to fill in these positions, appoint a search committee of eminent individuals to shortlist and interview candidates, and recommend a panel of three persons to the prime minister for the choice of chief executive.

The selected person would then be asked to appear at an open hearing of the joint National Assembly/senate committee and be approved or rejected by them. Once appointed, the appointee would not be removed from office until the completion of a tenure of five years. Only in cases of proven corruption or malfeasance, mental incapacitation, or consistent shortfalls in meeting performance targets or voluntary resignation could the chief executive be removed.

The chief executive of the corporation would be responsible for recruitment of regular staff; hiring and firing of contract employees; training; promotion; performance evaluation; compensation and benefit packages; and disciplinary actions within the budgetary ceilings and the HR policies approved by the board. This separation of policy and financial/operational control would clarify responsibilities, authority, and accountability and introduce a system of checks and balances.

In the event of requiring budgetary support, the ministry concerned and the ministry of finance should be represented on the board but all operational decisions must be taken by the board itself. The enterprise or the corporation should enjoy the freedom to hire and fire employees, fix the compensation of workers, and conduct day-to-day operations without any interference from the ministry. Their accounts should be audited by the auditor general and examined by the public accounts committee.

Some of the corporations are in such poor shape that it would be difficult to find genuine buyers for them. They must first be restructured without incurring any major financial expenditure. The board of directors and chief executives must be appointed for a fixed tenure and assigned time-bound goals and targets for getting the company ready for sale to either a strategic investor or through the capital markets. They will need to be provided resources and operational autonomy but held accountable for results.

There is a tendency in such cases for the incumbents to prolong their term so that they can continue to enjoy the benefits and power of the office. The tenure should therefore be made coterminous with the completion timeline of restructuring. It should also be ensured that the board and CEOs cannot be transferred or removed arbitrarily and prematurely.

However, for some, such as Pakistan Steel, there is no reason to retain them in the public sector. The construction and the automobile industries would have done much better if we had an efficient steel mill with the capacity to supply the requisite quality products at internationally competitive prices.

If suitably implemented, these reforms would result in an estimated annual budget saving, conservatively estimated, of one per cent of the GDP, thus lowering the fiscal deficit by an equivalent amount. The lower fiscal deficit would in turn have a beneficial impact on government borrowing from the banking system, future debt-servicing obligations, and an easing of inflationary pressures. At the same time, firm political control and oversight would be exercised over their affairs. However, the nature and quality of this control would be transferred from the individual politician to the executive and parliament. Of course, there is no guarantee that the proposed system would not be misused, but at least it would be less amenable to misuse because the individual interests of so many parliamentarians would have given way to collective control.

Fiscal Policy Coordination

The 7th NFC award and the Eighteenth Amendment to the Constitution have brought about a fundamental structural change in Pakistan's fiscal affairs. The federal government is no longer the principal driver of fiscal policy. Power and resources have shifted, and rightly so, to the provinces. The share of the federal government in the net proceeds of the divisible pool has fallen to 42.5 per cent while that of the provinces has risen to 57.5 per cent. Adding direct transfers, grants/subventions, and development loans to the provinces pushes this share up to almost 60 per cent.

Since the award of 7th NFC, there has been a substantial increase in the availability of resources with the provincial governments. In 2008–09, their share in the federal divisible pool was 43.7 per cent and by 2016/17, had risen to 61.8 per cent. Federal transfers have increased fourfold from Rs 565 billion to Rs 2,178 billion. This has enabled the total outlay of the provincial governments to triple from Rs 903 billion to Rs 2,976 billion. On an average, 80 per cent of the current revenue receipts are derived from federal transfers. Punjab and Sindh, the two better off provinces, have increased their own contribution through efficient collection of GST on services which was previously collected on their behalf by the FBR. Only 11 per cent is raised by the provincial governments from their own tax and non-tax revenues. In 2007–08, the provinces' own contribution to the total outlay was 15 per cent.

How has this increase in federal transfers affected the pattern of expenditures? The share of development expenditure in total expenditure has remained almost unchanged.

Table 6.2: Provincial Expenditure on the Social Sectors
Rs billion

	2009/10	2016/17	Percentage increase
Total budgetary expenditure	903	2976	329
Expenditure on social sectors	260	1147	441
Social sectors as a percentage of total expenditure	35.0	38.5	10

Source: Provincial Government Budgets (various years)

It was widely believed that as the provinces spend most of their money on education, health, drinking water, and agriculture irrigation, the ordinary citizen would benefit from this transfer of resources from the federal to the provincial governments. The social sectors are allocated about a third of the development expenditures which are not always fully utilized. Given the dire need to accommodate 22 million out of school children and improve the physical facilities of the existing schools, this amount is insufficient. Of course, the problem in the education sector is poor governance, weak management, lack of accountability, and too much concentration of power at the provincial level. The transition from primary to middle schools is poor and the dropout rates are quite high.

These problems remain unresolved, notwithstanding an upswing in the expenditure (current and development combined) on the social sectors as revealed by the data compiled in Table 6.2. Most of the expenditure, almost 80–85 per cent, is spent on the salaries and allowances paid to teachers of dubious quality and very little is left for curricular activities such as maintaining scientific equipment and laboratories, organizing indoor and outdoor sports, and other extracurricular activities. As the span of control of the supervising authority—the provincial education department—is quite wide, the schools are not properly monitored and inspected. Effective supervision would only be possible if the functions, authority, and resources relating to the primary to high schools, are delegated to the district governments. It is simply not possible for a secretary sitting in the provincial headquarter to supervise the entire network of schools spread throughout 30 or more districts. The same should be the case in relation to primary and secondary healthcare facilities, drinking water supply, sanitation, sewerage, etc.

While the provinces are now quite flush with resources that are derived from the divisible pool, the federal government is in the midst of a difficult fiscal situation. As most of the inflexible expenditures—such as those related to debt-servicing, defence, civil armed forces, and subsidies—fall upon the federal government, it faces financing problems in the face of a declining share in the overall tax pool. The growing fiscal deficit cannot be brought under control because of the asymmetry in the assignment of revenues and location of responsibility for expenditure. The financing of the fiscal deficit by borrowing from the banking system is not sustainable as it crowds out private sector credit and threatens macroeconomic stability, giving rise to investor uncertainty and subdued growth.

We must recognize the new realities of fiscal federalism in Pakistan. Attention and policy objectives have to move from the federal to the provincial governments. The institutional arrangements of the past are no longer adequate to respond to the challenges of the future. New institutional arrangements and policy changes have to be put in place. What are these?

First, the present practice of budget formulation by the federal and provincial governments in isolation must be replaced by an integrated budgetary framework prepared, discussed, and debated at the Council of Common Interests and approved by the National Economic Council. The federal and provincial governments need to formulate their budgets within the parameters approved by the NEC. Sanctions should be put in place for violations, breaches, and deviations. However, the provinces should be allowed to exceed the NEC-approved parameters if they raise additional revenues on their own.

Second, a new fiscal responsibility law should be enacted by each province in which the limits for fiscal deficit/surplus, revenue mobilization, and expenditure on development should be imposed. If the allocation to the provinces from the divisible pool rises or the provinces make an extra tax effort, the incremental resources should be earmarked for development projects or for education and health. The provinces must generate budgetary surpluses in order to offset the federal government deficit.

Third, the provincial governments should not be permitted to borrow from the domestic capital markets or financial institutions. Foreign loans for development projects and foreign grants should be channelled through the federal government and conform to the NEC-approved national plan and annual budget. The advances of the SBP should be strictly used to smooth cash flow problems rather than as additional financing for the budgetary or non-budgetary expenditure.

Fourth, responsibilities for education up to matric level, primary healthcare, rural health centres, *tehsil* and district hospitals, drinking water, sanitation and sewerage, and agriculture and community development should be at the district level and be administered by the elected local governments. The provincial finance commissions should be revived to divide the revenues between the provincial and district governments. Backward districts and rural areas should be given higher weightage in the allocation of resources.

Fifth, education, health, the police, and the judiciary should be taken out of the purview of the national pay-scales as they have created rigidities and distortions, and have reinforced income disparities between the advanced and backward districts. A female science teacher employed at Mithi or Kandhkot should earn a higher salary than the one in Karachi or Hyderabad. Similarly, doctors, nurses, and paramedics serving in remote and inaccessible areas deserve much higher compensation than those living in cities.

Sixth, the tax effort by the provinces has slackened after the 7th NFC Award. Incentives should be built into the 8th NFC award by giving weightage to the tax effort by the provinces. Urban immoveable property tax, agriculture income tax, *abiana* (water charges), and GST on services are some very obvious avenues for additional revenue mobilization by the provinces. Rough estimates show that, if properly designed and implemented, the provinces can raise at least two per cent of the GDP.

International experience has shown that if fiscal federalism is not tackled responsibly, it can create serious economic dislocations and disruptions. Argentina and Brazil suffered from hyperinflation due to the fiscal profligacy of state governments. The institutional and legal arrangements had to be redrawn to overcome this problem and since then, checks and balances put in place have worked well. China had to rework the federation–province tax arrangements, which have now provided adequate fiscal space to the federal government. Spain has been facing the consequences of fiscal excesses of strong regional governments. Domestic and international markets are punishing Spain by either withholding credit or raising the price of credit to levels that may make Spain insolvent. We may be at the beginning of the path towards a similar precipice and ought to take preventive measures at this stage and retreat from the threat it poses.

The federal government is stuck with lumpy, inflexible, and large expenditure obligations such as debt servicing, defence subsidies, and development. At the same time, the revenue base of the federal government is shrinking. In the foreseeable future, it will continue to have deficits of 7 to 8 per cent of the GDP. The provinces together should, on the other hand, be generating budgetary surpluses of 2 to 3 per cent. The overall fiscal deficit should, therefore, remain contained at 5 per cent on average. This arithmetic cannot however be translated into actualization for two reasons. First, there is a structural problem, i.e. no formal arrangement exists to prepare an integrated budgetary framework and to bind the provinces to the parameters agreed upon under that framework. There is no way in which deviant behaviour can be penalized.

The second problem has to do with incentives. The provincial governments are so liquid and cash rich that their own tax efforts have gone into reverse gear. Rather than contributing to equitable burden-sharing of taxes across sectors and income, the provinces have virtually halted any attempt to update the values, and assess and collect revenues from agricultural landowners, irrigation water users, urban immovable property, and services (other than those federally taxed). All these activities are buoyant and the private incomes above the threshold levels are not being brought under the tax net and the recoveries from the existing base are paltry.

FEDERAL–PROVINCIAL COORDINATION

Federal–provincial interactions in formulating national policy matters have no formal anchor after the Eighteenth Amendment. The national council of ministers, comprising the federal and provincial ministers working under the aegis of the Council of Common Interests, should formulate the national policies for the transferred subjects. The federal government would continue to shoulder the responsibilities for international relations and inter-provincial coordination in these subjects. In view of the new challenges that are facing Pakistan, some new ministries are proposed within the revised structure. Ministries for energy, technology development, regulatory affairs, human resource development, social protection, infrastructure development, and special and underdeveloped areas should be set up by merging some of the existing ministries and replacing others. The existing autonomous bodies and attached departments, corporations, companies, councils, institutes, and subordinate offices of the federal government should either be retained, regrouped, merged, privatized, wound up, or liquidated or, where appropriate, transferred to the provinces.

Introducing transparency through simplification of rules and regulations, codification and upgradation, and wide dissemination through e-governance tools—such as a dynamic website, information kiosks, and online access to government functionaries—can help in enforcing internal accountability standards, while at the same time making it convenient for the citizens to carry out trouble-free transactions. Strong pressure from organized civil society advocacy groups on specific sectors or activities from the media, the political parties, private sector, and think-tanks can also compel the government departments and ministries to become more accountable in their functioning.

Proposed Reforms[4]

Structure of Federal, Provincial, and District Governments

a) Devolve powers, responsibilities, and resources for basic public services from the provincial governments to the district governments. A new cadre, a district civil service, should be established on the lines of the provincial and federal civil services.

b) Establish inter-governmental structures with adequate authority and powers to formulate and monitor policy formulation.

c) Separate the policy-making, regulatory, and operational responsibilities of the ministries/provincial departments. Public enterprises retained for strategic purposes should be given operational autonomy with full accountability of their functioning and results.

d) Fully empower each ministry/provincial department and adequately resource it to enable it to take decisions and be accountable for its results.

e) Streamline, rationalize, and transform the attached departments/ autonomous bodies/subordinate offices/field offices into fully functional arms of the ministries, capable of adequately performing operational and executive functions.

f) Reduce the number of layers in the hierarchy of each ministry/ provincial department.

g) The cabinet secretary should be the chief coordinator among the federal secretaries, playing a role akin to that of chief secretary in the provinces.

h) Revive and strengthen the secretaries committee in the federal/ provincial governments as the principal vehicle for inter-ministerial coordination and dispute resolution among various ministries.

i) District level officers, interacting with the general public in day-to-day affairs, should enjoy adequate powers, authority, status, and privileges to be able to resolve the problems and redress the grievances of citizens.

j) Police, revenue, education, water supply, and health are the departments which are highly relevant in the day-to-day lives of ordinary citizens. The internal governance structures of these departments, public grievance redressal systems against these departments, and checks and balances on the discretionary powers of officials need to be introduced.

Business Process Re-engineering

a) All laws, rules, regulations, circulars, and guidelines issued by any government ministry/department/agency should be available in its most updated version to the general public free of cost, in a user-friendly manner, online and in electronic and print forms at public places.

b) Service standards with timelines for each type of service provided at the district, *thana*, and union level should be developed, widely disseminated, and posted at public places in each department.

c) Rules of business at the federal, provincial, and district governments levels should be revised to make them simple and comprehensible, empowering the secretaries/heads of departments/district coordination officers to take decisions without multiple references, clearances, and back and forth movement of files. Post-audit of the decisions taken should be used to ensure accountability rather than prior clearances.

d) Delegation of financial, administrative, procurement, and human resource management powers should be revisited and adequate powers commensurate with the authority should be delegated at each tier of the hierarchy.

e) Estacode, Financial Rules, Accounting and Audit Rules, Fundamental Rules, and all other rules in force should be reviewed systematically and revised to bring them in line with modern management practices.

f) E-governance should be gradually introduced in a phased manner. Technological solutions, and hardware and software applications are an easy part of the process but the most difficult aspect is the training and a change in the culture, attitude, and practices. E-governance should be driven by business needs rather than crafted as an elegant technical solution.

Taxation and Regulation

a) A large number of studies and reports have been prepared, directed towards reforming Pakistan's taxation regime. These include the Taxation Reforms Committee appointed by the present government. There is no need to reinvent the wheel but to implement the salient recommendations of those reports.

b) The regulatory regime has become too intrusive, stifling the initiative and entrepreneurship of the private sector. Effective regulation is a fine balancing act between promoting competition and moderating operating practices to reduce systemic risk.

The agenda outlined above cannot be implemented as a technocratic exercise because it is essentially a political one that takes into account the existing power relationships in which the polity is rooted. Balancing the diverse interests of the various stakeholders involves many politically tough choices which cannot be made by technocrats. The sustainability of reforms requires broad consultation, consensus-building, and communication to articulate the long-term vision. People should see beyond the immediate horizon and take into account likely future changes. Concerns, criticism, and scepticism should be addressed. The scope, phasing, timing, implementation strategies, and mitigation measures for the losers of the reforms should be widely discussed and debated. If things do not proceed the way they were conceptualized, corrective actions should be taken in the light of the feedback received. Citizens' charters, citizens' surveys and report cards, citizens' panels, and focus groups should be used as instruments for receipt of regular feedback about the impact of reforms on society and its different segments.

NOTES AND REFERENCES

1. Rana, A., 'Transferred Woman Officer Pays the Price of Resistance', *Express Tribune,* 22 May 2013.
2. Rana, S., 'Corruption Charges: Presidential Reference against AGP put on Ice', *Express Tribune,* 31 May 2013.
3. Asian Development Bank, *Sector Assessment,* (Manila, June 2016).
4. Reforms based on the report of the National Commission for Government Reforms (NCGR).

7

Local Government

The three major initiatives to devolve powers and resources were taken in the 1960s, 1980s, and 2000s by Ayub Khan, Zia ul-Haq, and Pervez Musharraf—associating the devolution to local governments—with attempts by the military dictators to bypass the established political process and legitimize their non-representative rule by establishing direct links with the officials at the local level elected on a non-party basis. This placed a wedge between the federal and provincial governments, arousing resentment among the provinces. The fact that the three smaller provinces had a very negative experience of the One Unit policy—in which all the four provinces were merged to form a single government of West Pakistan—negatively colours the local government system per se. Most of the analysis of the local government system is, therefore, tarred by this background and precludes a substantive discussion of the positive and negative aspects of devolution.

A scholarly paper on this subject by three highly respected and eminent Pakistani economists,[1] Cheema, Khwaja, and Qadir (CKQ) also conclude that 'our interpretation is that these reforms have been used as a means for a non-representative centre to gain legitimacy by bypassing the political agents at the provincial and national levels'. For the same reason and suspicion, every succeeding democratic government reversed the local government systems of their predecessors, the military dictators, resulting in significant discontinuity and gaps in the delivery of basic public services to citizens. A more dispassionate analysis would reveal that the motivation behind each of the three efforts was not identical and indeed was widely different.

Ayub Khan comes closest to the interpretation offered by CKQ. He did not believe in complete democracy and was a vociferous proponent of 'guided democracy'. He, therefore, legislated the Basic Democracies Ordinance 1959 and the Municipal Administration Ordinance 1960, and introduced a four-tier structure of local government. Only members of the Union Councils, the lowest tier, were elected through adult franchise. The other three tiers comprised people indirectly elected by the union councillors. The controlling authority of the local government system was still the deputy commissioner. The elected representatives at the union council level formed the Electoral College for the presidential election. It is alleged that Ayub used government muscle in the elections he contested to influence and win over these 80,000 councillors.

This was not, however, the motivation that led Zia to introduce the local government system. He wanted to keep the PPP at bay and organized party-less elections for local governments, as well as the national and provincial assemblies. Indeed, the powers entrusted to the local governments under the Local Government Ordinance (LGO) 1979 were extremely limited and so ineffectual that they have been adopted as a blueprint by the elected governments of Punjab, Sindh, and Balochistan in the post-2008 period. Zia's principal levers for exercising political control were the national and provincial assemblies where he had succeeded in forming an alliance with Pakistan Muslim League. He appointed a prime minister from among his allies but this experiment proved very costly for him; subsequently, he contrived to remove his own chosen appointee from office.

The most radical shock to the existing system was effected under the Musharraf government. He was politically under no obligation to opt for a local government system to acquire legitimacy because the Supreme Court had categorically given him a three-year period to hold general elections for the national and provincial assemblies. He was, therefore, under no compulsion, as in Ayub's case, to substitute the authority of these assemblies with the local government (LG) system. Musharraf not only made the drastic decision to abolish the century-old traditional offices of the commissioner, deputy commissioner, and assistant commissioners and replace them with a much weaker district coordination officer (DCO) who reported to the elected District Nazim (this arrangement was engineered on the analogy of the chief secretary reporting to the chief minister at the provincial government level); the police were also placed under the Nazim. The DCO, unlike the DC, did not exercise any control over the police.

The Local Government Ordinance 2001 was thus a significant departure from the existing provincial–local government relations system which transferred twelve provincial departments such as education, health, water supply, roads, agriculture, and the like, to the district governments. This transfer of functions and administrative authority was accompanied by huge re-allocation of financial resources and fiscal decentralization. The office of the district nazim became so powerful that some MNAs and MPAs resigned to contest the elections for the post. On the lines of the National Finance Commission, provincial finance commissions were formed to divide the revenues between the provincial and the district governments.

Thus, unlike Ayub and Zia, who neither empowered local governments nor provided constitutional protection, Musharraf went ahead and accomplished both these goals. The transfer of functions, authority, and resources were of substantial nature and the Seventeenth Amendment to the Constitution explicitly recognized the local government as the third tier of government. The Local Government Ordinance was given protection for a limited period of time under the constitution as no changes could be made by the provinces without the prior approval of the president. The substitution of a non-elected provincial bureaucrat by an elected politician in the reporting and accountability had unintended consequences for the morale and attractiveness of the civil services. The LG reforms, together with the police reforms, could have been a game-changer in governance had they been allowed to be implemented in letter and spirit and not subsequently been distorted through the ill-will of the provincial governments. That would have been a major step forward in bringing the government closer to the people. Accessibility and accountability would have improved over time had the system not been prematurely dismantled.

To meet his political requirements, Musharraf was able to win over breakaway factions of the Pakistan Muslim League and the PPP, and formed an alliance with a group of religious religious parties, the Muttahida Majlis-e-Amal (MMA), and the Sindh urban-based ethnic party, the MQM, and succeeded in forming the government at the federal and provincial levels. He appointed and removed prime ministers and chief ministers at will and therefore had no political compulsion to utilize the local governments for that purpose. He had such smooth sailing until March 2007 that he brought in an unelected technocrat as the prime minister, ignoring a number of aspirants who had the right political credentials and background and were equally qualified for the job.

I, therefore, differ with the CKQ assertion that:

Musharraf's local government reforms represent a continuity of the central historical tendency or that the local governments have not been given complete autonomy by design so [that] the non-representative centre could retain political control over local governments or [that] local governments were never financially empowered which weakened their ability to meet even their own restricted expenditure mandates.

The evidence set out above does not seem to corroborate these findings in relation to the 2001 reforms. However, the central historical tendency remains quite valid for the Ayub regime and, to a limited degree, for the Zia regime.

There were many flaws in the 2001 system, including the fact that the functions of law and order, revenue records, and land administration and disaster management should have remained with neutral civil servants and not been transferred to the nazims. In that event, the offices of the deputy/assistant commissioner should not have been abolished, thereby diluting the writ of the state. Two innovative features of the 2001 system are worth mentioning. The reservation of one-third seats for women and others for peasants, workers, and minorities—the marginalized classes of our society—was an extremely commendable step. Similarly, the integration of the rural and urban administrative units at the *tehsil* level would have allowed the rural areas to benefit equally from the larger envelope of pooled resources available to the Tehsil Council.

CKQ correctly cautioned in their paper that the conflict between the provincial representatives and local governments did not bode well for the future of the decentralization programme. They were proved right when Musharraf lost out and elected governments assumed power in 2008.

WHY DEVOLUTION IS NECESSARY

The World Bank in its report[2] asserts that governments are more effective when they listen to businesses and citizens, and work in partnership with them in deciding and implementing policy. Where governments lack mechanisms to listen, they are not responsive to people's interests. The devolution of authority to local tiers of government and decentralization can bring in representation of local business and citizens' interests. The visibility of the results achieved by the resources deployed in a specific geographic area maintains pressure on government functionaries. Public–private partnerships, including NGO–public partnerships have proved effective tools in fostering good governance.

Increased Accountability

Empirical literature shows a strong, unconditional, and positive relationship between decentralization and accountability. Bardhan and Mukherjee[3] have advocated that electoral decentralization and devolution of the public service provision are complementary to pro-poor governance reforms in developing countries. The *World Development Report*[4] (*WDR*, 2004) has argued that the accountability of governments to local communities and marginalized social groups will increase by assigning service delivery functions to politicians who are closer to the people and make them electorally accountable. At a micro level, Cheema and Mohmand[5] analysed a dataset of 364 households in the rural *tehsil* of Jaranwala in Faisalabad District to gain some insights regarding the types of households which gain and lose through electoral decentralization and whether the change in the post-reform provision between different household types is equitable. The empirical results of their study showed that increased access to development funds and heightened mandates for union nazims have resulted in a significant increase in union level provisions within a short span of time. However, the villages to which nazims belong have had a substantial increase in comparison to non-nazim villages. They further found that the increase in the post-reform provision in nazim villages is less elite-based as it encompasses small peasants, minority peasant *biradaris*, and non-agricultural castes.

Devolution of service delivery functions, delegation of financial powers, decentralization of authority to take decisions, and de-concentration of executive powers together will lead to better accountability of results. The prospects for delivery of public services to the poor and the marginalized groups under such a system would certainly improve. Even if the underlying patron–client relationship persists, the scope for inclusion of clients traditionally denied access under a MNA-/MPA-centred system will be much wider under a decentralized and devolved system. The representation of the marginalized groups—such as women, peasants, and labourers—in electoral politics enhances the prospects of these groups to improved access to public services.

The allegations of corruption of the local governments, advanced as a justification for their removal, could have been investigated and those found guilty should have been punished. An audit, monitoring, and evaluation system could have been effective in addressing this problem.

Enhanced Delivery of Public Goods

The Deprivation Index[6] shows that at least 80 districts suffer from low access to basic services. The population of Pakistan has risen from 30 million in 1947 to 180 million today. There is no way that such a large population can be served from Islamabad or the four provincial capitals. The unique circumstances and needs of each district require an understanding of its unique problems and the design of interventions that can address these. The criteria of backwardness and poverty should be given due weight in the distribution of resources out of the provincial divisible pool. The better-off and well-endowed districts do not deserve the same quantum of public resources proportionate to their population as their private incomes are reasonably high. Local level public expenditure should be utilized to promote equity and welfare.

It has been observed that access to basic services in Pakistan can be obtained either through payment or by approaching the elected representatives. Members of the National Assembly or provincial assembly are largely absent from their constituencies and are not always easily accessible. The local government nazims and councillors, on the other hand, spend most of their time within the areas from which they have been elected and an ordinary citizen can easily access them. Hasnain[7] reports on the basis of a survey carried out in 2005 that over 60 per cent of the households stated that they would approach a union councillor or nazim to resolve their problems, in comparison to only 10 per cent who said they would approach members of the provincial or National Assembly. This reflects the increase in accessibility of policy-makers after devolution. A system in which the bureaucrats control the development departments provides neither access nor accountability. Having a system of elected nazims and councillors who remain responsive to the needs of their citizens is better because these officials are liable to lose their offices if they do not fulfil their responsibilities and duties. The best one can do with a recalcitrant bureaucrat is to transfer him out of a particular district but that does not resolve the inherent problem of access to the poor.

Governments have found a variety of methods of delivering essential public services. The *World Development Report 2004* catalogues successful examples, ranging from direct provision by the government, contracting out to the private sector and NGOs, decentralization of local governments, community participation, and direct transfers to households. Both the successes and failures of these experiments provide some useful lessons. First, accountability needs to be strengthened between the poor and the service providers, between the poor and government institutions, and between government institutions and the service providers. Second, the poor people's choices and participation in service delivery will have to be expanded. It is not necessary that the children of poor families remain stuck with the substandard instruction provided at government-run schools. These children can be provided financial means by the government to pursue their studies at non-governmental schools of their choice. The same applies to health clinics and hospitals. Mexico and Brazil have lifted millions out of poverty by making cash transfers to the poor families, conditional upon participation in education, immunization, vaccination, and the like. In Pakistan too, the Benazir Income Support Programme has begun a programme (Waseela-e-Taleem, or resource for education) of conditional cash transfers to children attending school. Third, it is not the availability of financial resources that alone makes the differences in the outcomes. Out of the central government's budget allocations for running a school, studies have shown that the actual amount reaching the school after passing through the various government channels is only one-tenth of the original allocation. The exclusive preoccupation with expenditure on education and health, while ignoring the myriad problems of governance of these sectors at all levels, is palpably wrong. Reforms in the governance structure of the public sector and regulation of the non-governmental sector will have a much stronger impact on the access and quality of these services by the poor.

In cases where the government takes upon itself to deliver these services through direct provisions, studies have shown that seeking improvements in the efficiency of that spending is the key to substantial benefits accruing. On average, the relationship between public spending on health and education and the outcomes is weak or inconsistent. Most of the public spending on health and education goes to the non-poor. School buildings are constructed by government departments at an exorbitant cost, and teachers are hired but nepotism, corruption, leakages, weak supervision, and lack of accountability do not allow effective delivery of education to the intended beneficiaries. Anecdotal evidence and surveys of primary healthcare and educational facilities have consistently shown high absentee rates among doctors and teachers. In contrast to this, examples can be found where teachers and health workers in non-governmental schools and clinics deliver timely, efficient, and courteous services often in difficult circumstances while drawing much lower monetary and fringe benefits in comparison to their counterparts in the government-run institutions.

It has also been found that for direct delivery by the government, the transfer of responsibility for these services to lower tiers of governance improves access by the poor. Local government management of schools and hospitals involving communities and demand-side subsidies to the poor, monitored and under the oversight of the government, results in a favourable outcome in education and health.

Improved Policy Design

Local governments form an integral part of the democratic governance framework and allow greater participation by the citizens in the management and control of their day-to-day affairs. The trade-offs and assignment of priorities among various development projects are managed more realistically and pragmatically under local governments. Their intimate knowledge of local problems and solutions to resolve these lead to better outcomes and more efficient utilization of resources in comparison to a more centralized system of resource allocation. Decentralized decision-making has proved to be the cornerstone of democratic governance. The cost–benefit analysis, and, therefore allocative efficiency, are superior under a decentralized system.

Generation of Revenue

Empirical evidence shows that raising taxes or charging user fees for services at the local level is relatively easier. The taxpayers can see the visible benefits of such payments. They are reluctant to make contributions to a remote, central pot whose purpose is not known. Pakistan, with its low tax–GDP ratio, can mobilize additional resources by gearing up provincial and local taxes through the urban immovable property tax, capital gains tax, agricultural tax, and user fees and charges.

Fuelling Greater Political Participation

The increased representation of a neglected segment of the society—the female population—in the local government system has made participation more broad-based. Political empowerment of women is the first step towards the path of generating greater economic opportunities and contribution to economic progress. Given the interest of female representatives in the social sectors, education, health, water, and sanitation received greater attention and resources under the vigilant watch of women councillors. Pakistan has a very low female labour force participation rate; therefore, the political empowerment of women is a precursor to raising this.

ASSESSMENT OF REFORMS

CKQ, in their study,[8] found three types of changes brought about by the 2001 Devolution: (a) changes in the decision-making level of the service, i.e. from provincial bureaucrats to the district level bureaucracy; (b) changes in the decision-maker's accountability, i.e. from bureaucrats to the elected representatives at the district level; and (c) changes in the fiscal resources available to the service. The education department, primary healthcare, and the management of district and *tehsil* hospitals experienced a change of type (a), where the decisions previously made by the provincial secretariat and the provincial cabinet were transferred to the district nazim and executive district officers. The municipal services provided by the local government, the rural development department, and the public health engineering departments of the provincial government became the sole functional responsibility of the *tehsil* municipal administration. This was a fundamental change because the power to allocate resources, prioritize projects, and deliver results moved away from 48 provincial departments to 6,000 units of local government, whereas prior to devolution, the deconcentrated provincial bureaucracy at the district level was accountable to their non-elected provincial secretariat. The 2001 devolution made them accountable to the elected heads of districts and *tehsil* governments. Under the previous system, the de facto head of the district administration was the district commissioner who would report to the non-elected commissioner while after devolution, he reported to the elected district nazim.

Their study also found that a 'rule based' fiscal transfer system between the provinces and the local governments was established under the 2001 Devolution Plan. Approximately 40 per cent of the provincial consolidated fund was distributed among local governments with due weightage given to backwardness in order to ensure some form of equity across districts in the allocation of development funds. The other innovation was that these budgetary transfers did not lapse at the end of the year but continued to be retained by the relevant local governments, providing for flexibility and presumably some improvement in the efficiency of resource allocation.

Fiscal Transfers

The degree of fiscal decentralization remained limited because the districts continued to depend upon the province for resources, didn't have the powers to collect new taxes, and didn't have the capacity to levy service or user charges. On the expenditure side, the fixed and growing expense of salaries, wages, and allowances paid to the staff devolved to the district governments (although they continue to be provincial servants) did not leave much surplus for either maintenance, operational, or development expenditure.

Over 90 per cent of the expenditure of local governments was financed by transfers from the provincial governments. Lack of enhancement in local fiscal powers was a major weakness in the process of fiscal decentralization. The share of local governments in the provincial allocable pool was about 40 per cent but their share in total public expenditure was only 13 per cent.

The largest share in the current expenditure of local governments was on primary and secondary education, in excess of 60 per cent. On the development side, a significant part was allocated for construction of roads. Health was the most neglected sector, receiving, in most cases, under 10 per cent of the development allocation.

While current transfers did not lead to significant fiscal equalization, development transfers were the prime instruments for removing inter-district differentials in access to services over time. However, their role was limited by the relatively modest scale.

Resource mobilization at provincial and local levels remained substantially under-exploited. Land revenue accounted for less than 1 per cent of the agricultural income while the effective rate of property taxation of rental incomes was about 5 per cent as opposed to the statutory rate of 20 per cent or more.

Service Delivery

The functioning of the district governments during the first two years was quite promising. However, the conflict between provincial elected representatives and local elected representatives that surfaced after the 2002 provincial and national elections created an adversarial rather than cooperative environment. Until then, the nazims, under the supervision of the army monitoring teams, were carrying out some useful activities for the welfare of their constituents. However, as soon as the provincial ministers assumed office, they realized that there was a substantial shift in the power of patronage from them to the district nazims. This led to a number of amendments, particularly in the police ordinance, which diluted the powers of the police command and once more made the police force subservient to the chief minister and the home department. The police rules were never allowed to be finalized, the district services were never established, and the powers of recruitment, transfers, and postings of the staff working at the district level remained centralized at the provincial level. The balance of power, authority, and resources between the provincial and the local governments was, in practice, gradually moving away from what had been envisaged in the devolution plan. The perpetual state of flux, the unease in political relations, the lack of clarity for the civil servants working in the districts, and the incomplete transition all adversely affected service delivery.

Policy Formulation

The internal dynamics arising from the flawed design of the local government system also took a toll. The integration of rural and urban areas within a common framework led to lopsided decision-making. District headquarters, for example, which were predominantly urban centres, were neglected because a majority of the members of the district council decided that the allocations for development projects should go to the rural areas. The integration had exactly the opposite effect: the fragmentation of development projects into small schemes catered to the narrow interests of the local communities without any sense of priority, linkages, or widespread coverage. Ideally, the transfer of resources from the urban to rural areas should be a welcome move but such a transfer—in the absence of a district-wide plan, without specifying the goals to be achieved, and assessing the cost-benefits of the approved schemes—can be counter-productive. Urban–rural integration did not recognize or cater to the needs of growing urbanization. Residents of urban areas and cities within the districts resented what they described as the tyranny of the rural majority that deprived them of the services and infrastructure they deserved.

The indirect election of the district nazim through the union council and *tehsil* council reinforced the tendency of fragmentation of the development schemes. According to Hasnain,[9] there were 17,000 development schemes in the development portfolio of the districts in Punjab. These were typically neighbourhood-specific schemes: the construction or rehabilitation of a small road or drains. The average size of a typical scheme varied between Rs 0.3 million for water and sanitation to Rs 1.5 million for a road. This was not the entire picture as it did not include the block allocation to the union councils and the Citizens Community Boards' (CCB) schemes. In order to keep his voters happy, the district nazim would have very little choice but to acquiesce to the pressures exerted by the union and *tehsil* Nazims to allocate resources equally. The difference between 'equal' and 'equitable' distribution of resources should be understood as it is at the crux of the problem. Under an 'equal' distribution scheme, there is no clear relationship between the needs of the community and the intended interventions. Rich and poor communities will receive the same amount, irrespective of the intensity of their need. 'Equitable' distribution takes into account the differences in the initial endowments and conditions of the intended beneficiaries. Those who are poor, marginalized, and living in remote or geographically disadvantaged areas and cannot earn decent incomes on their own should receive higher allocations than those who are better off. Public resources thus supplement the private incomes of the poor to help them out of poverty.

It is interesting that while the provincial governments did take 'backwardness' into account in the allocation of development funds across districts and, therefore, the allocation was to a degree equitable, the district governments were unable to do the same within the district given the inherent flaw in the design of the system pointed out earlier. The district nazim became hostage to being blackmailed by the members of district councils who would either withhold approval of the budget or threaten to move a vote of no confidence. Under these circumstances, the nazims were unable to do justice to their fiduciary responsibilities.

An analysis of the district development priorities in Punjab by Hasnain (2008) revealed four distinct realities. First, the physical infrastructure, in particular roads, was by far the highest priority of the district governments. Second, these infrastructural schemes were small and largely neighbourhood-specific. Third, district policy-makers appeared to attach a lower priority in operation and maintenance than their provincial counterparts. Finally, provincial interventions in education and health appear to have provided additional incentives for districts to prioritize the physical infrastructure sectors.

Transfer of Administrative Authority

The alienation of the powerful district management group (DMG) and the provincial civil services (PCS) cadres—which resulted from the abolition of the posts of commissioner, deputy commissioner, and assistant commissioner—was also a stumbling block in the smooth functioning of the new local government system. On the one hand, the police force was perceived to have become much stronger after having been taken out of the supervisory ambit of the district coordination officer and made directly accountable to district nazim. On the other hand, the executive authority of the DCO was diluted as magisterial powers were taken away from him or her although s/he was expected to perform duties relating to maintenance of law and order, removal of encroachments, price controls, and the like. The provincial secretaries from the DMG and PCS retained considerable administrative authority over the district bureaucrats and used these powers to undercut the efficacy of the elective nazims. A tripartite confrontational mode, in which the provincial ministers and secretaries aligned themselves against the district Nazims, was responsible for most of the practical difficulties faced by the citizens in access to services.

The accountability of the local governments assigned to the local government commissions proved to be perfunctory and almost non-existent. The provincial governments used backhanded tactics to assume effective control of the departments devolved to the districts. As the powers of recruitment, transfers, postings, and disciplinary actions continued to remain vested in the provincial departments, the diarchy proved to be fatal for the effective functioning of the devolved departments. The gap between the law and actual practices remained wide to the detriment of the public at large. Corruption at the district government level could not be contained given the inadequate supervisory arrangements evolved by the provincial governments.

Political Participation

Gurcharan Das[10] believes that 'participation at the local level is a school of democracy in which people learn civic habits, duties, and attitudes. These civic virtues help build the self-restraint that eventually strengthens the rule of law.'

The union councils and district councils could have acted as nurseries for hands-on training for higher positions in the provincial and federal governments. One common complaint is the inexperience and incompetence of the elected ministers and legislators. The lower tier leadership positions could have provided such an experience and some of them would certainly have excelled. Those performing well could then have been selected for the ministerial positions.

The significant increase in reservations of seats for peasants and women was a salutary move under the 2001 devolution plan. The higher representation, particularly of women (one-third of the total seats were reserved for them), could have changed, and did, the quality and the composition of expenditure. This would have resulted in increased allocations for education, drinking water, health, and sanitation in comparison to the male preference for infrastructure projects. The empirical evidence on this correlation is, however, difficult to obtain and therefore this assertion remains purely conjectural based on my visits to the districts.

Impact of Devolution on Service Delivery

The latest *Social Audit Survey 2009–10*—of 12,000 households drawn from 21 districts in all four provinces—found that 56 per cent favoured the continuation of the local government system, with high proportions in Punjab and Sindh. The level of satisfaction with the union councils was 33.8 per cent but the situation regarding support and social acceptability of women's participation seemed to have improved. 60 per cent of female union councillors were of the view that people in their constituencies were happy with them.

The satisfaction levels of households with various public services varied but by 2009–10, satisfaction with roads, sewerage and sanitation, garbage disposal, water supply, health, and education had improved. Although, in percentage terms, only less than half of the households expressed satisfaction with the services. Public education, at 58 per cent, showed the highest level of satisfaction.

The Social Policy Development Centre (SPDC)[11] carried out a survey of 12 districts in the four provinces and found that the rate of enhancement in literacy of the population and access to water supply and sanitation had perceptibly increased during the post-devolution period. However, there were no indications of any impact of devolution on health indicators.

The process of devolution was beginning to contribute to a quicker improvement in enrolment at the primary level and literacy in Pakistan. The SPDC report observed:

> if this effort at enhancing human capabilities is sustained, then it augurs well for achieving more reduction in the incidence of poverty during the coming years. However, the lack of significant change to date in the trend of health indicators, gender equality, and regional disparities limits the potential impact of local governments on poverty in the post-devolution scenario.

According to this report, while most of the functions of a local nature had been devolved to the local governments, a number of issues had to be resolved in the design and speed of implementation of the devolution plan: the need for the intermediate tier, the Tehsil Municipal Administration, was questioned; a wide range of services were transferred in one go to local governments which stretched the governments' capacity to the limits—a more gradualist strategy could have minimized such challenges; the provincial governments, even after six years, were not fully prepared to devolve power to local governments; institutional structures to improve accountability and people's participation in the system were either not operational or not performing according to the mandate given by the LGO; and 'state capture' by local elites was an important and persistent challenge— the overwhelming influence of family, *biradari*, tribal ties, and political manoeuvring of union councillors in return for lucrative benefits was quite evident.

Education

The district governments were made responsible under the 2001 devolution plan for all primary, secondary, and higher secondary education. They could recruit teachers up to basic pay scale BPS-16. The authority for staffing (hiring, firing, and transfers) for BPS-17 and above remained with the provincial governments. The ban on wholesale recruitment of teachers by the provincial governments and the authority to relax the ban in individual cases rested with the chief minister. This backdoor tactic made the district governments wholly dependent upon the whims and caprices of the chief minister. In the event of the latter being from the same political party or being a close political ally of the district nazim, relaxations were granted. In other cases, the authority was exercised to penalize the nazim so the posts remained unfilled for quite a long time. As many teachers owed their appointments to the members of the provincial or National Assembly, they did not adhere to the discipline of the Education District Officer (EDO), and teacher-absenteeism was rampant in such cases.

The funding for education came principally from the provincial allocations but was mostly spent on salaries and allowances, leaving very little for other expenses. A USAID team found that in Sialkot district, as much as 95 per cent of the budget funds were allocated for salaries and only 5 per cent for non-salary expenses. The physical condition of the schools were poor, with no electricity or water available. Teacher-training had become a popular hobby horse for donors, to the extent that the teachers in Thatta were reported to be spending as many as 17 days on different training courses organized by various donors. Notwithstanding such a heavy investment in teacher-training, the outcomes were not very encouraging.

The devolution of primary and secondary education and healthcare to the districts remained on paper and was patchy and incomplete. Through a variety of measures, including control on finances, the actual delivery of these services remained sub-optimal, given the tension between the provincial and the district governments. A more supportive rather than an intrusive role by the provincial governments, together with effective monitoring and accountability, would have made a great and salutary difference. The data shows that 21 per cent of the funds for Punjab's annual development programme for education and health remained with the respective provincial departments. Provincial recurrent expenditures in education and health also grew annually by 48 per cent and 16 per cent respectively during the post-devolution period (2001–07).

The Punjab government launched a high-profile Punjab Education Sector Reform Programme with a number of interventions for primary and middle schools. The funding for the provision of facilities that were lacking was transferred to local governments as tied grants. The centralized decision-making in the hands of the provincial education department and the local MPA reduced both the availability of funds as well as prioritization by the district governments. Implementation of the projects under this programme was entrusted to the National Logistics Corporation in 2006. The districts therefore served principally as a conduit for funds with no role in the identification, planning, and execution of these schemes. The same situation prevailed in the Health Sector Reform Programme and the CMAPSD (Chief Minister Accelerated Programme for Social Development).

HEALTH

The LGO 2001 devolved health services (basic and rural health, child and maternal health, population welfare, and district and *tehsil* hospitals) to the district governments with the exception of the large teaching hospitals and medical and dental colleges, which remained under the direct control of the provincial government. The fundamental structural discrepancy in the system was that the control over the health manpower was exercised both by the provincial health department and the elected district nazim. The EDO Health at the district level was answerable for service delivery to the elected district nazim and for his career progression to the province. All medical staff reported to the EDO Health but their postings and transfers were controlled by the provincial health department. The procurement of medicines was also within the purview of the provincial government, which resulted in delays, mismatches in demand and requirements, and non-availability of medicines when required by patients. The nominal fees collected by each health facility, although not sufficient to cover even

a fraction of total costs, were not allowed to be retained by the district
government and had to be deposited in the provincial government account.
This dual control also led to lax supervision and weak accountability,
with posts lying vacant and a high rate of absenteeism amongst health
staff. These factors limited the impact of devolution on the delivery of
health services. Sania Nishtar,[12] a leading international health sector expert,
explains the reason for this limited impact:

> The success of a fiscal policy implemented through a budget instrument
> is deeply dependent on the quality of governance and institutional ability
> to effectively and transparently implement policies in their stated spirit.
> This is where the biggest gap lies in Pakistan. Exceptions notwithstanding,
> issues of capacity and performance are widely recognized in Pakistan's public
> management process; years of under-funding of state institutions and the
> culture of patronage and collusion have eroded the technical capacity of our
> ministries. Limited accountability, poor governance, and mismanagement
> have led to the institutionalization of a number of behaviours detrimental
> to equitable deployment of resources. As a result, evidence-guided choices
> are bypassed, motivations other than welfare of the people dominate
> decisions, and considerations other than equity and social justice become
> the cornerstones of institutional performance.

The picture sketched above indicates that there was a wide disparity between
the intention, promise, and content of the laws and the actual functioning
of the local governments. As stated, the dynamics of political struggle did
not allow dilution of the powers of the provincial secretaries, ministers,
and legislators—the traditional holders—at the expense of the newcomers,
the nazims. The former ensured that through their complete control over
finances and legislative instruments, the nazims were weakened.

LOCAL GOVERNMENTS AFTER 2008

The local government system introduced by President Musharraf's government in 2001 was short-lived and was abolished in 2008 as soon as the new government came into power. The principal motivation for the rejection of the system was the usual objection that it had been designed by a dictator to legitimize his own rule and to build a constituency to garner support for himself. This is for the fourth time that the local government system had been discarded in Pakistan. It takes several decades for any new system to take root and mature, and it is most unfortunate that we take so much time in setting up a new system and then, without testing it over a reasonable period, we ditch it, leaving a vacuum. Then we begin the entire exercise ab initio and devise a new system, only to see it consigned to dust after a few years.

A comparative analysis of the new local government acts of the four provinces, conducted by the SPDC,[13] reveals that the system in Khyber Pakhtunkhwa is inspired by the LGO 2001, whereas the structure of local government legislation promulgated in the other provinces closely resembles that of the LGO 1979:

> In general, the current process of local government reform initiated by the provinces can be termed as 'devolution without delegation', with the exception of Khyber Pakhtunkhwa where offices of several social and economic service departments, including education, health, social welfare, water supply and sanitation, have been devolved to local governments. In the other provinces, only basic municipal functions are delegated to local governments such as water supply and sanitation, solid waste collection, roads and streets, streets lighting, parks and playgrounds. As far as the potential implications of devolution for social service delivery are concerned, keeping in view the trend during the Devolution Plan 2001, it can be expected that the new local governments will be able to play a significant role in improving the deteriorating condition of social services if they are provided with sufficient authority and resources. Progress in social indicators may nevertheless vary according to the degree of decentralization in each province. In this respect, prospects of improvement in delivery of social services appear to be higher in Khyber Pakhtunkhwa as compared with other provinces.

It was expected that after the Eighteenth Amendment giving enhanced powers to the provinces, and 7th National Finance Commission award, under which the provinces receive 60 per cent of the revenues, the process of devolution to the districts would have deepened and accelerated. The reality is however that the contrary is happening. There is a reversion towards greater centralization and concentration of powers in the provinces. The Punjab government has retaken control of 11 of the 13 departments devolved to the district level under the LGO 2001. Education and health will be run indirectly through its proxies in the district authorities. In major cities, the province has also taken control of a number of local functions through the creation of SPVs such as the Lahore Solid Waste Management Co. Babar Sattar,[14] a leading lawyer, makes the following comments on the Punjab system:

> Article 140-a of the constitution after the 18th Amendment, mandates the provinces to establish local governments and 'devolve political, administrative and financial responsibility and authority to the elected representatives'. It was the relentless prodding by the Supreme Court that caused the reluctant promulgation of local government laws across provinces, including Punjab. And just when local governments were finally coming to life, the PML-N has revived the retrograde commissionerate system through the Punjab Civil Administration Ordinance, 2016.
>
> None of the local government laws devolve political, administrative, and financial authority to elected local governments. The rules framed under these laws have been used by the provincial governments to claw back power instead of delegating it to the third-tier of government. But with the Punjab Civil Administration Ordinance, the PML-N isn't even being coy any more. It has vested administrative and financial authority in the DC and commissioners who will lord over districts and divisions, while elected local governments will remain useless debating clubs.
>
> In 2013, the PML-N was voted into power in the centre, Punjab, and Balochistan and had a real opportunity to build local governments in at least two provinces as an effective third-tier of government most relevant to ordinary people. Instead, it used all the power and the devices at its behest to

sabotage the idea of the local government. The Punjab Civil Administration Ordinance will ensure that leading up to the 2018 elections, districts are under the control of DCs, who themselves have no security of tenure and are kept on a tight leash by the CM's office.

In Sindh, the Karachi Building Control Authority, Karachi Water and Sewerage Board, Karachi/Lyari/Malir development authorities, and other urban development authorities and water and sewerage agencies have been taken over by the provincial government. What is the government doing with the infusion of large funds? An answer is sketched out by Afshan Subohi, business editor at *Dawn*, from an interview with members of the provincial hierarchy:

> Sindh has plenty of funds since money transfers improved after the 7th NFC award. Do you ever wonder about ghost employees or schools or basic health units, etc? Every year projects appear on paper, funds are released but monies are deposited in personal accounts and shared in the ring of the corrupt officers and politicians. … Believe it or not there are multiple projects where less than 5pc of the allocated amount was spent and the remaining 95pc was pocketed by politicians and their cronies. In Punjab, according to anecdotal estimates, corruption cost is 45pc of the total project cost.[15]

Karachi witnessed a significant turnaround in construction and remodelling of roads, underpasses, flyovers, improved traffic and transport management, availability of water, sanitation, and solid waste disposal in 2002–08. What has happened since then is described by an observer, after visiting Karachi in recent years:

> Among the first impressions that non-residents of Karachi get of the city when they arrive here is that Pakistan's largest metropolis is one large garbage dump. For the residents of Karachi, it is more than a garbage dump—it is a forever looming health hazard.
> Why the city's roads and drainage are in perpetual need of repairs and why the quality of construction [is] always so poor are questions that are

never really answered. As things stand, Karachi fails on all measures of providing a decent living standard to its residents. It produces around 20,000 tonnes of solid waste, with at least 18,000 tonnes of it burnt in drains and open spaces. Hardly 2,000 tonnes of garbage makes it out of the city while the remaining keeps piling up on the streets, roads and other open spaces.

It is difficult to disagree with one of the leading architects and serious scholars of Karachi, Arif Hasan,[16] who thinks that in the absence of new and effective institutions of governance at the local level, there is very little hope of delivering the services demanded by the citizens:

> For the poor, and now also for the lower middle class, needs related to transport, water, land, and housing are catered to by an exploitative, unreliable informal sector, while land use is controlled by a powerful developers' lobby through bribes and coercion, devastating the city.
>
> In 1998, 30 per cent of Karachi's primary school students studied at government schools. This dropped to 6pc in 2015. Most of these schools, including the 600-plus KMC ones, are on the verge of collapse. Many of them have more teachers than students. For curative health, the vast majority of Karachiites rely on quacks as there is no comprehensive preventive health plan in place.
>
> One-time events and short term funded projects are important but they alone cannot overcome the problems of the city which needs new and effective institutions of governance.

Management, recording, zoning, land titles, and computerization of urban land is an area which requires major reforms and decentralization to local levels as urban land has become a major source of windfall capital gains. First, the conversion of agriculture and urban use adds value and increases land prices. Second, changes in the zoning laws—in which urban areas are divided into residential, commercial, and industrial zones—are another source of capital gains. Finally, the difference between the allotment price, which is actually subsidized, and the market price reflects a scarcity premium and has made fortunes for the allottees.

The conditions in the rural areas have become even worse. Just 23 per cent of schools in rural Sindh have electricity, water, toilets, and boundary walls, according to Alif Ailan. Teachers are found absent from the schools, rural health clinics do not have an adequate supply of essential medicines and are usually manned by unqualified compounders, and children are surrounded by filth and dirt, as Naween Mangi,[17] who runs a successful NGO in rural Sukkur, describes. 'Most kids spend their days playing barefoot on trash heaps without any form of constructive engagement.'

A comparison of key social indicators or the periods before the 2001 LGO reforms and after their replacement by the post-2008 local government system is very revealing. All the four key indicators showed impressive growth during the period 2002–08 in comparison to the earlier or later periods when they were either stagnating or declining.

Table 7.1: Selected indicators of social development in Pakistan

	1996	2002	2008	2014	Annual growth rates		
					1996–2002	2002–2008	2008–2014
Literacy Rate	39	45	56	58	2.4	3.7	0.7
Net primary enrolment rate	44	42	55	57	-0.8	4.6	0.7
Child immunization		53	73	76	-	5.5	0.8
Access to tap water	25	25	36	26	0	6.3	-6.3

Sources: Pakistan Integrated Household Survey 1995–96; Pakistan Living Standards Measurement Survey (2004–05, 2007–08 and 2013–14); Pakistan Economic Survey (2014–15) culled from SPDC, Annual Report 2016

PROPOSED REFORMS

As most of the interaction between an ordinary citizen and a government functionary takes place at the district level—and the present level of the latter are ill-trained, poorly paid, unhelpful, and discourteous individuals enjoying arbitrary powers—a new set up is required at the district level. A district service should be constituted comprising all employees serving in Grades 1–16. These employees will serve in the districts of their choice throughout their career. Direct recruitment to Grades 11 and above will be made on merit through the Provincial Public Service Commission. The district service will consist of two cadres: generalist and technical. This will minimize the political pressures for transfers and postings as two-thirds out of 2 million employees working in the provinces will remain in their respective district governments. Training in technical and soft skills will be made mandatory for all members. The district government needs to be strengthened by establishing administrative linkages between the union councils, town committees/*tehsil* councils, and district governments. The post of executive magistrates will need to be revived. If the system of district nazims is revived, which it ought to be, law and order, disaster management, and land record management should be taken out of his purview and transferred to the deputy commissioner. This office should be transformed into that of a district chief operating officer with an enlarged scope of responsibilities. The devolution of developmental projects, programmes, and departments was working satisfactorily until 2007 and should remain with the district governments.

SUMMATION

The system of local government has not taken firm root even after 70 years. The ignominious association of the LG revival and strengthening with military dictators has created a popular narrative that has undermined the potential usefulness of devolution and decentralization. The Basic Democracies System under Ayub got a bad name because it was used as an electoral college for his election. Zia ul-Haq did not confer any significant powers on the LGs apart from the routine municipal functions. The most radical change was brought about under Musharraf in 2001 which transferred 12 provincial departments to the district governments, abolished the post of deputy commissioner, and made an elected nazim head of the district administration. Forty per cent of the provincial budgetary resources were placed at the disposal of the districts. As the local nazims became powerful this caused a stir amongst provincial ministers and legislators who, with their control of financial resources and legislative authority, did all they could to weaken the district governments. This tussle was still in play and the system had not reached a point of equilibrium, when the new governments after 2008, instead of amending the 2001 Ordinance, took the drastic step of abandoning the system altogether and once more began the process from scratch. Apart from KP, which continued to retain some of the features of the 2001 system, the other three provinces opted for the much weaker 1979 Ordinance which is a negation of devolution. Thus the provincial governments, having become relatively sound financially after the 7th NFC and themselves assuming all the powers, have caused a severe setback to the process of bringing the government to the doorsteps of citizens. The future of the LGs does not look at all promising.

NOTES AND REFERENCES

1. Cheema, Khwaja, Khan, 'Decentralization in Pakistan: Context, Content and Causes', in P. Bardhan, D. Mookherjee (eds.), *Decentralization in Developing Countries: A Comparative Perspective*, (MIT Press, 2006).

2. World Bank, *World Development Report 1997: The State in a Changing World* (1997).

3. Bardhan, Mukherjee, *Decentralization and Local Governance in Developing Countries: A Comparative Perspective* (Delhi: OUP, 2007).

4. World Bank, *World Development Report* (2007).

5. Cheema, A., Mohmand, S., *Account-ability Failures and the Decentralisation of Service Delivery in Pakistan* (2006).

6. Jamal, H., *Districts' Indices of Multiple Deprivations for Pakistan, 2011*, (SPDC).

7. Zahid, H., *Devolution, Accountability, and Service Delivery: Some Insights from Pakistan*, Policy Research Working Paper No. 4610 (World Bank, Washington DC, 2008).

8. Ibid.

9. Ibid.

10. Das, G., *India Grows at Night* (Penguin, 2012).

11. SPDC, *Annual Review of Social Development* (Karachi, 2007).

12. Nishtar, S., 'Equity, Social Justice and the Social Sector', *The News,* 22 June 2009.

13. SPDC, *Devolution and Social Development: Annual Review 2011–12* (2012).

14. Sattar, B., 'Race to the Bottom', *The News,* 7 January 2017.

15. Subohi, A., Sindh's 'Second Chance', *Dawn,* 29 August 2016.

16. Hasan, A., 'Ugly Karachi', *Dawn,* 6 November 2016.

17. Mangi, N., 'Rural Sindh Agenda', *Dawn,* 20 September 2016.

8

The Civil Services

The channel through which governance affects development is its civil servants, their quality, incentives afforded to them, and their accountability in terms of results. The key to quality and high performance lies in attracting, retaining, and motivating civil servants of a high professional calibre, and their integrity. It is therefore instructive to trace the evolution of the civil services in Pakistan, assess their current performance, and propose reforms that can help revive the services to become effective, efficient, and responsive.

Pakistan inherited the British civil services as its administrative apparatus at the time of the partition of India. The hallmark of those civil servants was constitutional protection, political neutrality, permanency, anonymity, and merit-based recruitment. This permanent civil service provided the indispensable element of continuity and a source of expertise to the administration. Jinnah wanted to retain these positive features of the British period and wanted an 'apolitical, neutral, and independent' civil service structure for Pakistan. The founder believed that politicians and bureaucrats would need to work together and respect each other's lawful autonomy and role in the state. In an address to ministers and the bureaucrats in Peshawar, he made it clear that the bureaucracy constituted the backbone of the state. Ilhan Niaz aptly comments, 'the weight borne by this backbone and the speed with which it managed to restore order, taxation, and communications and even began working on [a] long term development plan was stunning'. According to Ilhan,[1] there is little evidence that indicates Jinnah 'aimed at reforming the bureaucratic order inherited from the British Raj'.[2]

At the time of Independence, there were only 101 Muslim officers in the entire cadre of 1,167 in the Indian Civil Service.[3] Of these Muslim officers,

210

95 opted for Pakistan. In all, there were only 300 Class I civil servants at the time of Independence. This small group formed the core of the new state's administration and was called upon to meet the challenges of the formative phase of the newly carved-out country with very little financial resources, no industry, and primitive agriculture as the dominant sector of the economy.

Braibanti[4] pays tributes to this small group of dedicated officers as follows:

> Pakistan had to create de novo a state from two culturally disparate, physically separate, strife torn areas. The odds against success were enormous. To have constructed a nation for several years with 50 experienced government officials of reasonable maturity in policy-making positions is a singular tribute to the British administrative heritage and Muslim perseverance.

Dennis Kux[5] too has high praise for them: 'American diplomats in Karachi admired the small band of overworked, highly motivated and idealist civil servants who struggled to establish their new country.'

The new government of Pakistan, therefore, decided to continue the system inherited from the British and in the same vein, set up the Central Public Service Commission and entrusted it with the task of recruiting young officers to fill in the cadres of the Civil Service of Pakistan (CSP), the Foreign Service, Police Service, Audit and Accounting Service, Income Tax Service, Customs Service, Railway and Military Accounts Service, Railway Service, and Postal Service. These officers—grouped under the Central Superior Services (CSS)—were selected through a competitive examination, an interview, and a battery of psychological tests conducted to assess their competence, potential, and aptitude. The standards were so high that only the best and brightest 100 young men and women (the average age at the time of entry was 24 years) from several thousand applicants were able to make it to the final selection.

The Superior Civil Services became the profession of choice for Pakistan's talented youth as selection to any one of these services conferred prestige, status, security, career progression, and job satisfaction. Remuneration was not particularly attractive in comparison to the very few private multinationals but alternative employment opportunities were almost non-existent. Besides, the lifelong job security and a sense of idealism to serve the country in key positions in different public organizations and institutions compensated for that shortcoming and acted as a powerful magnet. The larger role assumed by the state in the post-Independence period and the challenges of laying the foundations of a new developing country provided both the opportunities as well as motivation to this high calibre group. Most of the new entrants had at least a Master's degree and had secured the highest division from one of the leading universities in Pakistan, and several of them had graduated from Oxford, Cambridge, the London School of Economics, and the like. A study of the civil servants, published in 1964, revealed that out of the sample of 31 CSP officers, as many as 14 had obtained foreign qualifications.[6] Until the late 1950s, CSP probationers were sent to Oxford or Cambridge for a year after completing their training at the Civil Service Academy. This crème-de-la-crème formed the backbone of the higher civil service of Pakistan. Their continuing development as future leaders was carefully planned through on the job training, rotation of jobs, delegation of authority, mid-career training at the National Institutes of Public Administration, and advanced management training at the Administrative Staff College.

By the mid-1960s, Class I officers expanded to 3,000, with 500 belonging to the top CSP cadre. These officers filled in the positions of deputy commissioners and commissioners in the field, heads of the departments in the provinces, and secretaries in the central government ministries. The heads of the newly established organizations, such as Pakistan Industrial Development Corporation (PIDC), Water and Power Development Authority (WAPDA), Agriculture Development Corporation (ADC+, Planning Commission, Development Authorities—such as KDA for Karachi, CDA for the Capital, and the Pakistan Industrial and Investment Corporation (PICIC), which played an instrumental role in turning the economy around, were drawn from this cadre of officers.

Although the selection process was based on merit, an innovative approach was introduced in the form of affirmative action for the candidates appearing from Pakistan's less advanced provinces. As they could not secure the top positions purely through merit, a quota system was introduced, ensuring that the top candidates from their respective provinces were represented in the final selection. In recent years, 10 per cent of the seats have been reserved for women and 5 per cent for the minorities. This merit-cum-quota based system has survived all attempts at reform to this day. It has been relatively successful as there are officers from Balochistan and rural Sindh, and women occupying top positions in the civil service. Given the wide regional and gender disparities, this innovation has, with few exceptions, not compromised the quality of the overall intake as it has incentivized young, bright, and talented students from the backward areas of Pakistan to prepare themselves to compete in the examination. In absence of this reservation system, it is doubtful whether this incentive would have actually worked.

The practice—where most of the positions of secretaries, heads of department, autonomous bodies, public corporations, and other state-centred institutions were reserved for members of the CSP—continued uninterrupted until the reforms of 1973.

The CSS officers, along with a large number of specialists in the fields of agriculture, engineering, medicine, education, health, animal husbandry, and forestry who were recruited for the attached departments were from Class I services. While the ministries of the central government and the secretariat departments in the provinces were responsible for policy formulation, the attached departments implemented and oversaw the policies and projects. Other administrative and technical persons, who provided support to Class I officers, were placed in Class II and the crossover from Class II to Class I could occur either by appearing at a direct recruitment examination or to a limited degree through promotion on merit cum seniority. Their remuneration was much lower and the opportunities for career progression were much more limited and slower on the time scale. Class I and II officers were called Gazetted officers—their appointments were notified in the official Gazette of the Government of Pakistan—and were therefore assured some sense of stability, security, and entitlement.

Class III officials in the main clerical staff engaged in the bulk of routine, repetitive tasks, maintained the records, initiated the movement of files, and dealt with the public at large. The lowest cadre was Class IV which comprised peons, messengers, tea boys, cleaners, attendants, labourers, and the like. Class III and IV employees were non-gazetted and not recruited by the Public Service Commission. The provincial governments were allowed to recruit their own provincial cadres along the same lines except that they could not recruit officers of the All Pakistan Services, i.e. the Civil Service of Pakistan (CSP) and the Police Service of Pakistan (PSP), and the Federal cadres. CSP and PSP officers could be posted at the Centre as well as in any one of the provincial governments. The rotation among different provinces was aimed at developing a national, cohesive, and informed outlook on policy matters as they acquired hands-on experience, working in diverse geographical areas with different ethnic and diverse populations at many levels of responsibility, i.e. both in the field and the secretariat. This concept was a departure from the British legacy which has been retained by the Indian government. The IAS and IPS officers are assigned to a particular state cadre and they serve throughout their career in that state or on deputation at the Centre. They have no exposure to, or experience of, any other state.

This strict stratification inherited from the British remained in place until the early 1970s when it was replaced by a Unified Pay and Grade Structure, moving from the lowest Grade 1 to the highest Grade 22. In reality, the new structure did still correspond to the old stratification. For example, Class I officers were now directly recruited at Grade 17 and gradually rose to the highest positions in Grade 22. Class II officials were placed in Grade 13 to 16, Class III in Grades 6 to 12, and Class IV in Grades 1 to 5. Their pay-scales, methods of recruitment, and career advancement opportunities strictly mapped those of the four classes from which the 22 grade structure was derived. Changes in nomenclature and designations were also periodically introduced and the upgradation of posts from one grade to another have become a constant feature, continuing to date but the spirit behind the original rigid class structure has remained intact.

The 1964 study[7] revealed that the elite nature of the superior services cadre was not due to the socio-economic background of those selected but due to their intellect and educational excellence. In fact, both the civil services and the armed forces proved to be the major vehicles for social mobility of individuals from families in the lower and middle income strata of society. The study shows that only 13 per cent of the members of the highest ranking CSP cadre were from landed families while 64 per cent were from families with long histories of government service.[8]

A popular criticism of the CSP cadre has been the enormous powers they enjoyed in Pakistan's early period. An observer has opined that 'internally, incompetent politicians and their factionalism generated conflict and instability, while the civil servants and later the military, came to represent stability.'

One of the earliest reforms of any significance was undertaken in the 1960s by Ayub Khan on the recommendations of the Administrative Reorganization Committee.[9] The section officers' scheme was introduced in the central ministries and the provincial secretariat departments. The hierarchical tiers were reduced from seven to four through which the files moved and decisions were made. The role of assistants and clerks in noting and initiating a file was curtailed and assigned to the section officer. The logic underlying this reform was that a better qualified and trained officer would contribute towards the improvement in the quality of input that goes into policy-making, reduce the time-span in the disposal of official business, and accelerate the decision-making process. Financial control, budgeting, and accounting was overhauled by building in financial advisers within each ministry. An economic pool, based on selection from various cadres and non-cadre officers, was created to fill senior positions in economic ministries. A noteworthy move by the Ayub government was to establish an Administrative Staff College to train senior civil servants and the National Institutes of Public Administration at Karachi, Lahore, and Dhaka to train mid-career civil servants. Foreign training of civil servants at leading universities in the US and UK was also made part of career development. Training was linked to promotion by taking into account the evaluation reports of the training institutions at the time of promotion.[10]

The Planning Commission was strengthened and converted into a fully-fledged division directly under the president. This elevation in status, as well as the selection of highly qualified professionals, institutionalized the planning and policy process. The Commission played a key role in the impressive economic turnaround of Pakistan in the 1960s.

It was not until 1972 that a popularly elected government decided to break up the frame of the civil services and make them more pliable and flexible. The constitutional protection ensuring the civil servants' independence and neutrality was revoked. The service cadres were replaced by occupational groups and a unified grading structure was introduced, ranging from Grades 1 to 22. All Class I positions relating to cadre, non-cadre, or ex cadre were lumped under Grades 17 to 22. A former Establishment secretary found, after this structure had been in place for some time, that 'the new system introduced rigidity, distortion, and grade consciousness'.[11] The unified pay-scales embedded in this structure were tilted in favour of lower grade employees. The difference in salary between an officer in Grade 22, which used to be 285 times that of the Grade 1 at the time of Independence, shrank 10 times after the 1972–73 reforms. One of the reasons for the higher civil services becoming unattractive for young talented individuals and for the increasing tendency to engage in corrupt practices can be largely ascribed to this reduced financial remuneration.

The elite cadre of the CSP was split into the Secretariat Group, District Management Group, and Tribal Areas Group. The Secretariat Group was opened up for lateral and horizontal movement of officers from other cadres or groups. Thus, the quasi-monopoly of the Civil Service of Pakistan in senior appointments and exclusive reservation of top management positions came to an end. The CSP Academy, which previously used to exclusively train pre-service probationers of the CSP cadre, was abolished and in its place a Common Training Programme for all occupational groups was set up. The entire bureaucratic machinery was amalgamated into a hierarchical framework of 22 pay-scales.[12] All the different superior service cadres (now termed occupational groups) were brought at par and unified with a uniform pay-scale, recruitment, and training.

The federal and provincial secretaries and additional secretaries could be retired from the service without assigning any reason. Summary procedure was introduced as part of the Efficiency and Discipline Rules. Omar Noman[13] argues that 'the new procedures of dismissal accentuated the insecurity of bureaucrats and further undermined their authority.'

The reforms curtailed the autonomy and supremacy of the Civil Service of Pakistan. Policies were now being outlined by elected representatives, a significant demotion for civil service. The genesis of the reforms can be traced back to the following statement made by Mr Bhutto: 'No institution in the country has so lowered the quality of our national life as what is called *naukarshahi* (rule of civil servants). It has created a class of brahmins or mandarins unrivalled in its snobbery and arrogance, insulated from the life of the people and incapable of identifying itself with them.'

The numbers of those actually inducted through lateral entry vary greatly. Some authors say that 5,476 persons were appointed to Grade 16 and above positions in the federal (2,800) and provincial governments (2,676). 'Lateral entry of 1,374 officers at the higher echelons—three times greater than were required to fill in the vacancies—and their selection on the basis of the recommendations of party stalwarts shook confidence in the public institutions under the new government.' Ilhan Niaz[14] believes that 'Bhutto wanted to create a body of officials personally loyal to him and abjectly dependent on his favour for their elevation. Through them, the career bureaucrats could be controlled and marginalized.' The out of turn promotion policy introduced as a result of these reforms prompted ambitious civil servants to align themselves closely with the politicians in the ruling party. The line between the party and the state was further blurred in 1977 when members of the civil services actively participated in the rigging of the parliamentary elections.[15]

A strong, popular, and highly intelligent leader with an abundance of charisma, who could have laid the foundations for the establishment of civilian democratic institutions on sound foundations, missed that great opportunity. His autocratic style and the personality cult he built around himself overwhelmed his instincts for an enduring long-term solution which could have provided an institutional base for democratic sustenance in Pakistan. It is ironical that his failure to strengthen the institutions of democratic governance and neutral civil and police services for short term political ends led to his deposition from office by the armed forces.

Zia continued with the same structures and did not undo the administrative reforms of the Bhutto period. A Civil Service Commission was formed by Zia ul-Haq in 1978 but it chose to leave the 1973 reforms intact. 'Unlike Yahya or Musharraf, [Zia] quickly grasped that the higher bureaucracy represented the most competent element in Pakistani society and should be relied upon to carry out the civil administration.'

The 1988–89 period was a turning point in the history of the civil services and the process of institutional decay. The reforms of the 1970s began permeating as incompetence, politicization, and corruption began surfacing like a hydra's head. The following 25 years witnessed a significant decline in the quality of new recruits to the civil services as the implicit trade-off between job security and low compensation ceased to operate and the expanding private sector, including multinational corporations, offered more attractive career opportunities. Job insecurity, combined with an erosion of real wages in the public sector, also led to low morale, demotivation, inefficiency, and resorting to corrupt practices among the civil servants at all levels. The abuse of discretionary powers, bureaucratic obstructionism, and the delaying tactics adopted by government functionaries became part of the manoeuvring to extract rents to supplement their salaries. In real terms, the compensation paid to higher civil servants was only half the 1994 package.

The low wages meant that the civil service no longer attracted the most talented young men and women. Some of the incumbents of the civil services, in their instinct for self-preservation, fell prey to the machinations of the governments in power and many of them got identified with one political party or another. They willingly participated in and benefited from the culture of patronage practised by the politicians. During the 1990s, the replacement of one political party by another in the corridors of power was followed by changes in the higher bureaucracy. This growing tendency of informal political affiliation to hold on to key positions was also responsible for the end of an impartial, neutral, and competent civil service responsive to the needs of the common man. Loyalty to ministers, the chief minister, and prime minister took ascendancy over accountability to the general public. The frequent takeovers by military regimes and the consequential screening of hundreds of civil servants led to subservience of the civil service to the military rulers, erosion of the authority of the traditional institutions of governance, and loss of initiative by the higher bureaucracy.

A former senior civil servant[16] describes this period in the following terms:

> the marginal recovery in terms of neutrality, independence, and nonpartisanship of public services made under Zia collapsed in the face of the unrestrained political patronage. The persistent interference from the elected representatives in the transfers and promotions of officials high and low allowed 'unscrupulous and dishonest bureaucrats' to rise and reinforced a pervasive 'culture of corruption. Such arbitrary acts eroded to a very considerable extent the 'autonomy of all departments' and adversely impacted the district administration.

It has become a new norm that civil servants who were perceived as being loyal to one particular political regime when it was in power came to grief when the opposition party assumed office. The number of officers on special duty (OSDs), which was the summary punishment for these individuals, swelled at the time of regime change. Rewards in the form of promotions, prize jobs, plots of land, and other perks including highly subsidized housing in government estates were bestowed exclusively upon those who were pliable and towed the line of the political party in power. Frequent transfers at the instance of the minister in charge of the portfolio have become a highly abused tool to harass, victimize, intimidate or win over recalcitrant civil servants. Lack of continuity in the top job adversely affects the performance of the department, erodes accountability for results, and results in failure of delivery of services to the public at large. At the policymaking level, job insecurity forced the civil servants to go along with the whims and caprices of their political masters rather than render independent advice. Successive governments brought in their favourite civil servants to occupy key positions. Loyalty rather than competence became the acid test for survival. The winners in this game included political leaders and acquiescent civil servants while the losers were ordinary citizens who ceased to have access to the government and had no way of having their grievances redressed and honest officers who did not want to play this game.

Another far-reaching change took place under the Devolution Plan of 2000 prepared by the National Reconstruction Bureau under the chairmanship of Lieutenant General Tanvir Naqvi. The 2001 Local Government Ordinance and the Police Ordinance 2002 abolished the post of deputy commissioner who formed the single-point anchor for both citizens and government leaders. These powers were transferred to the elected nazims. Hitherto, whether it was law and order, security and safety, land records, revenue collection, or development work, the DC who was considered a neutral, impartial, and fair officer had been assigned responsibility and held accountable for the results. The DC–SP duo played a crucial role in enforcing the state's writ in the district. The executive magistracy system was also replaced by judicial magistrates and the police administration was brought under the control of Public Safety Commissions with the elected nazim reporting on the performance of the district superintendent of police. The level of demotivation and disillusionment among the younger civil servants touched its peak because they did not see any future for themselves. Many of them opted for postings outside the government, thereby further depleting the pool of honest and competent officers.

The repercussion of these changes in the civil service structure and incentives over time has been seen in the deterioration in the quality of new entrants. The following table shows that the competition has slackened as talented and bright students no longer opt for the Central Services examinations which once used to be considered a dream job for bright young men and women.

Table 8.1: Recruitment through Central Superior Services Examination

Year of the examination	Number of Candidates Appeared	Number of candidates passed the examination	Number of jobs open	Number of candidates for each job
1990	10,000	1,000	126	7.9
2006	4,125	273	180	1.5
2016	9,643	202	199	1.0

Source: *Federal Public Service Commission Annual Reports* (various years)

An examination of the data shows that the number of candidates appearing at the CSS examinations has fallen drastically in comparison to 1990 at a time when the number of graduates coming out of the universities has multiplied manifold. The other point that emerges is that the pass percentage has fallen so low that anyone who passes is assured a job as the number of vacancies are almost equal to the number who pass the examination. In the 1960s and early 1970s the competition was fierce and as many as eight to ten candidates qualified for each job opening but only those who made it on the merit-cum-quota criteria were selected.

Another contentious issue that has remained unresolved, notwithstanding many deliberations, relates to the role of specialists—engineers, doctors, lawyers, accountants, agricultural experts, economists, scientists, and others—who feel like second class citizens in the government hierarchy. The specialists think that a generalist should not be appointed as head of a technical department because they are neither interested in nor understand and have the skills and knowledge to adequately manage projects on hand and have to be educated on the job. As soon as they have mastered these, they are transferred to another department and everything has to start from scratch once more. The opportunities for career advancement for technical specialists is therefore always limited and they feel demoralized and demotivated, and lose interest in their work. In the long run they also lose their technical skills and expertise because they hardly get to utilize their skills or get opportunities to refresh their knowledge. Professor Paul Beckett noted, after visiting Pakistan, that the technical judgement of mature and well-qualified technical personnel was generally subjected to modification by junior secretariat officers of very limited maturity and experience. He observed that he could think of few more effective ways in which to dampen the enthusiasm and to stifle the initiative of the specialists or to impede economic development programmes which must depend heavily on technical skills and judgement. According to him, experience and maturity should be the decisive factor and not the cadre to which they belong.

The generalists argue that the administrative head should be a person who is impartial and unbiased; specialists drawn from the department who have spent their career there develop favourable or unfavourable attitudes towards their peers and subordinates. The postings, promotions, and perks are then assigned by them on the basis of merit, impartiality, and objectivity. They further argue that decision-making does not involve technical knowledge alone but is broad-based, taking into account also economic, social, and financial considerations. The specialist head of a department lacks the knowledge of these dimensions and therefore the outcome may be too narrowly focused on technical considerations alone resulting in unintended but adverse consequences. The departmental head has to coordinate with other departments and agencies of the government and the generalist can perform this function better because of his wide network of contacts serving in other departments. The downside is that, apart from a couple of thousand officers recruited through the Central Superior Services, the majority of civil servants remain confined to ex-cadre or non-cadre jobs with limited opportunities for career progression. In the twenty-first century domain, expertise has become important and needs to be harnessed to enhance productivity, foster innovation, and assimilate and diffuse technology for the general welfare of the population. The public sector will not be able to attract and retain this expertise unless the present adversarial system is so altered as to bring about synergies between generalists and specialists for the common good.

The resultant demotivation, demoralization, and despondency among a majority of civil servants is reflected in the poor service delivery, indifference, inaction, and apathy towards clients, and a mind-set resistant to change becoming ingrained in their psyche. A survey of the civil servants carried out by PIDE in 2007[17] confirms this observation. 93 per cent of respondents, i.e. all civil servants, agreed that civil service performance had deteriorated over the years They acknowledged that the service is corrupt and their public approval rating is low. They were demoralized and did not have faith in their human resource management as connections played a major part in the selection for foreign training and their independence was curbed by repeated political interference. In contrast, a survey carried out in 1961 of the various categories of civil servants in Pakistan by Muneer Ahmad found that the most attractive profession for young men and women in Pakistan was government service. The reasons for this choice were:(a) prestige of the office and rapid career progression; (b) security of tenure guaranteed in government service; and (c) and post-retirement benefits.

At an informal poll conducted at the IBA, Karachi, the students were asked, after a presentation made by a member of the Federal Public Service Commission in 2010, why they did not opt for the civil services. They advanced the following reasons: (a) poor salary and remuneration; (b) poor perception of the civil servants amongst the public; (c) insecurity; and (d) lack of opportunity for professional achievement.

The question as to whether the best and the brightest talent should be attracted to the civil services or the public sector in general has been debated at official, private, and public fora. There is a great deal of variance in the views of the civil servants themselves. A serving young officer is of the view that:

> Since its inception as the Imperial Civil Service in the nineteenth century, the civil service (via bureaucrats) has acted as a linchpin in administering the everyday affairs of the government and ensuring continuity of service delivery irrespective of political upheavals. As such, it is imperative that the civil service consist of the best, brightest, and most competitive individuals who possess a passion for public duty. As part of the recruitment process, competitive exams then form the backbone of civil service given that the quality of Pakistan's future governance hinges upon it.

Over the years, however, the decline in the quality of new recruits has resulted in poorer governance. Politicizing the service further weakened the institution, and bureaucracy was blamed for its perceived facilitation of malpractice by being hand-in-glove with corrupt politicians. This has tarnished the image of the once prestigious CSS to the point that the general public has become increasingly discontented with its performance.[18]

A contrarian view has been expressed by another civil servant who became so disenchanted that he decided to resign from the service. He feels:

The question is: do we really need extraordinary individuals in the civil service? Exercise helps make muscles stronger and more powerful; inactivity renders them limp and powerless. The same can be said of intellect. Even if able-minded, dynamic individuals join the civil service, the system is designed to blunt their cutting edge. The current system places a lot of focus on the politician (the temporary executive) and very little on the civil servant (the permanent executive). There is no need to have brilliant minds when all you are going to do with them is throw their potential away or leave them to rust indefinitely.

For example, civil servants in this country are hardly ever involved in policymaking. When it comes to town planning or development projects, it is generally the wishes of politicians that prevail. Prudent civil servants can continue to amass their offices with plans but, at the end of the day, the plan most likely to see the light of day will be the one that gets the nod from politicians. Political mileage is key.

Then comes foreign policy; the government also sometimes appears to be at sea on this front despite the fact that the prime minister himself holds the portfolio of foreign minister and also has the counsel of a couple of very senior advisers. Civil servants hardly have an input in foreign policy, they are mere paper pushers.

Pakistan Railways claims to have turned things around for good. Even if we are to believe their claim, does this so-called turnaround have anything to do with the intake of civil servants? The answer is a simple 'no'—the only thing that changed in the department from the previous government was the minister.[19]

One of the reasons for the waste and non-utilization of talent is the neglect of in-service training for the upgradation of the skills of the civil servants and preparing them for the next level of responsibilities. There is an elaborate system of training institutions and no promotions are possible from Grade 18 upwards unless the officers have attended the relevant courses. This has unfortunately become a formalistic ritual rather than a substantive undertaking. Afshan Subohi, a senior official who has been associated with training institutions, believes:

> there appears little motivation to undergo training for skill development, and professional growth … Attracting and retaining the best faculty positions remains the greatest challenge for public sector training institutions. Unlike the Armed Forces where being selected for an instructional assignment is a matter of prestige, a civil servant opting for the training institute is generally looked upon as having failed in the mainstream.[20]

In the 2007 perception survey, 80 per cent of the respondents cited foreign training as being superior to the domestic variety, identifying the quality of faculty and better training content and methodology as the principal reasons. The irony is that while the training evaluation reports are rarely used for matching the skills and competencies acquired by the trained officers with their postings and assignments (the government having spent millions of dollars on their training), there is a hue and cry over severe capacity constraints in public sector institutions. There is a huge disconnect between investment in and proper utilization of human resources in the public sector. Specialized training institutions are doing very little to enhance the technical skills of the officers. The present network of training institutions cater to the cadre officers only while the vast majority of the professional and technical experts working in the government outside the cadre services have no opportunity to learn new techniques and upgrade their domain knowledge at all during their careers in government service.

One of the major reasons for the poor image of the government amongst a majority of citizens is the antiquated system of primary interaction between the state and citizen. This interaction occurs through low-paid, ill-equipped, poorly educated, and rude functionaries such as the *patwari, thanedar,* and sub-divisional officer enjoying enormous discretionary powers and engaging in rampant corruption, inefficiency, and poor governance.

The officials at the local level do not enjoy the authority and powers to act expeditiously but keep on referring the matters to their superiors and the citizens are forced to move back and forth among different offices. The clerks and assistants in the offices of their superiors are neither courteous nor responsive.

Donor agencies have also been engaged in reviews of the civil services and the organizational structure of the government. The World Bank in its report, *A Framework for the Civil Service Reform in Pakistan,*[21] identified three major shortcomings:

An over-centralized organizational structure, as well as rigid, often irrelevant, and unevenly enforced rules and management that are inappropriate for most public sector activities, result in delays in responding to clients and distract senior officers from strategy formulation, policy making and results-oriented management

Seriously eroded internal accountability and lack of accountability to the public. As a result of its colonial heritage and long years of military dictatorship, the civil service accountability to the public has always been very limited

and

Politicization of civil service decision making. Political interference has reduced the effectiveness and professionalism of the civil service, while at the same time politicians have failed to exercise their oversight role in the wider public interest.

The constant refrain of politicization of the civil services and a growing culture of loyalty and patronage is also confirmed by academic research.

In a case study of Pakistan published in a refereed journal, Ayesha Hanif, Nasira Jabeen, and Zafar Jadoon[22] came to the following conclusion:

> According to the interviewees, political meddling and interference was highlighted as the most important factor affecting not only performance but also the entire functioning and working of civil service. One senior bureaucrat viewed that merit starts deteriorating when no matter how sluggish or dim witted the officer is, he/she gets good scoring on Performance Evaluation Report (PER) and also better transfer and places of posting on the basis of political connections. Lack of merit based transfers and postings make officials unconditionally loyal to their political masters and this fear factor heavily influences performance of the civil servants.
>
> In essence, the servants of the state, reduced to the condition of personal servants of the politically powerful, have become miniature reflections of their masters. It means that all too often, the officers with integrity do not get sufficient opportunity to gain experience in important positions while those subservient to the rulers are placed in key positions where they can effectively promote the personal interests of their masters. Thus, on one hand Pakistan has many honest but inexperienced bureaucrats while on the other it has a greater number of dishonest ones who invest their time not in performing their statutory functions but in pleasing the boss.

The views expressed above concur closely with the findings of the previous Commission/Committee reports,[23] which have carried out in-depth studies in the field and through interviews and presentations made by a variety of stakeholder. Their major findings are:

(1) Absence of a long-term human resource development and management policy, which has resulted in a neglect in harnessing the potential of civil servants and providing a transparent, predictable, [and] level playing field for all civil servants.

(2) Civil servants have by and large become risk averse individuals, who avoid taking timely decisions, as the need for catering to the personal whims

of the ruling classes takes precedence over observing and implementing the rule of law.

(3) Pressures and compulsions from the political leadership in power push ambitious civil servants into taking partisan positions, favouring the ruling party rather than adopting a neutral position.

(4) A small group of cadre civil servants has been given preference in terms of training, development, promotion, and status, to the exclusion of a large majority of others, particularly professionals and technical experts.

(5) Decision-making has become highly centralized and fear of delegating powers to the lower tiers is very pervasive.

(6) Rapid turnover and transfers of key civil servants, particularly in the police and district administration at the behest of the politicians in power has adversely affected implementation capacity and equality of access.

(7) Less than adequate compensation packages have encouraged widespread rent-seeking activities by the civil servants, particularly at the lower levels, where most of the interactions take place between citizens and government functionaries.

(8) Creation of isolated, parallel, project units and organizations in order to meet donors' conditionalities, has fragmented and weakened the existing capacity of the civil service.

(9) Reliance on antiquated and outdated rules, procedures, and regulations has led to failure in adapting to the changed circumstances and promoting a problem-solving approach.

(10) The fight for turf and self-preservation, perpetually adversarial relationships, and a silo mentality amongst the ministries, between the federal and provincial governments, and between the provincial and district governments delay grievance redressal and confuse the citizens.

(11) Redressal of grievance- and complaint-resolution mechanisms for the citizens against civil servants remain unsatisfactory and time-consuming, notwithstanding the existence of the Federal and Provincial Ombudsmen's offices.

(12) An absence of internal accountability for results/outcomes, convoluted and formalistic accountability before the public have shorn the incentives for improving performance and behaviour.

While the evidence about these weaknesses and deficiencies in the human resource management and development of the civil servants is so overwhelming, no action has been taken to rectify the malaise. Sakib Sherani, a former economic adviser to the government, believes that:

> The most anti-reform constituency in Pakistan, contrary to popular perception, is not the politicians but the bureaucracy. Barring occasional individual reform champions, the bulk of Pakistan's Civil service has become an entrenched vested interest that is protecting unimaginably huge rents and for whom serious and meaningful reform that will alter the status quo for the better is anathema. While the FBR bureaucracy is the most obvious example, it is not an outlier: the entire civil service has over the years appeared to align itself to protecting the 'empire of rents'. This empire straddles everything from public procurement to land allotment to tax exempt or concessionary plots, perks and privileges, to re-employment on contract.
>
> With the politicians becoming wiser since 2008, these rents are being shared but the pie appears to have grown to accommodate new demands.
>
> Hence, any reform effort that attempts to ignore the 'elephant in the room' institutional reform will have little chance of succeeding. And if institutional reform is the elephant in the room, the 700 pound gorilla setting in the corner is the civil service reform. Without slaying these dragons, Pakistan's quest for a modern, vibrant, globally connected, and inclusive economy will remain a pipe dream, CPEC notwithstanding.[24]

This line of thinking is shared by Zafar Jadoon[25] who writes:

> The bureaucracy, specifically the top layer of central superior services is well entrenched and considered as a major force resisting any structural reform which may involve lowering its status and prestige. Any reform initiative which comes as a shock therapy that is not owned by the bureaucracy is either bound to fail or get modified and diffused.

Proposed Reforms

The reforms that have so far been effected have not addressed the larger question of the delivery of public services to the population at large. Pakistan was unable to meet most of the Millennium Development Goals and is now committed to Sustainable Development Goals (SDGs). Writing about these goals, Ignacis Artaza of the UN[26] expressed this forcefully:

> This need for efficient service delivery is greater for developing countries that face issues of poverty, inequality, hunger, limited access to quality education and health services, lack of clean drinking water and sanitation facilities, and other issues that the SDGs aim to address. The state cannot resolve these development challenges without an effective civil service, which, in turn, cannot perform its functions in a manner that helps meet the SDGs, without continuous reform. The increasing demand for service delivery (and accountability) calls for realigning public administration with the broader goals of development. Effective civil service is characterized by good governance which means sound policymaking, efficient service delivery, and accountability and responsibility in public resource utilisation. Given the fact that government provides public goods to which market mechanisms often do not apply, an efficient public administration remains the only option for addressing citizens' needs. Efficient and capable public service is therefore crucial for both economic and social development. Certainly, an efficient and transparent civil service is far more likely to be able to address the 2030 Sustainable Development Agenda.

The focus of the reforms and reorganization should be aimed at this goal. There are several ways through which this can be achieved.

One of the lingering legacies of the past which has contributed to sub-optimal utilization of civil servants and demoralization of the majority among them has to do with the existence of superior and non-superior services. The concept of the superior services should be replaced by an equality of all services at federal and provincial levels. The terms and conditions of all the services in matters of recruitment, promotion, career progression, and compensation, would be similar. The specialists and professionals working in ex-cadre positions should be brought at par with the cadre services in terms of promotion and career advancement. To provide equality of opportunity to all deserving civil servants, the National Executive Service (NES) and Provincial Executive Services (PES) ought to be constituted to man all the federal and provincial secretarial positions. Any officer serving the government at the federal or provincial level or autonomous body in Grade 19 or equivalent—and other professionals meeting the eligibility criteria—should be able to appear at a competitive examination held by the Federal or Provincial Public Service Commission. Those qualifying at this examination will be selected to the NES. To redress the grievances of the smaller provinces for lack of representation at the higher decision-making level, provincial and regional quotas should be introduced for entry into NES. The NES should have two streams, General and Economic, thus promoting some limited specialization among our civil servants.

As most of the interaction between an ordinary citizen and the government takes place at the district level, and the present level of functionaries comprises ill-trained, poorly paid, unhelpful, and discourteous individuals enjoying arbitrary powers, a new set up is required at the district level. A district service should be constituted for each district government. All employees serving in Grades 1–16 will become part of the district service and serve in the districts of their choice throughout their career. Direct recruitment to Grades 11 and above should be made on merit through the Provincial Public Service Commission. The district service should comprise two cadres, generalist and technical. This will minimize the political pressures for transfers and postings as 1.2 million out of 1.8 million employees working in the provinces will remain in their respective district governments. Training in technical and soft skills should be mandatory for all members of the district services. The district government should be strengthened by establishing administrative linkages between the union councils, town committees/*tehsil* councils, and district governments. The post of executive magistrates should be revived.

All Pakistan Services will consist of the National Executive Service, the Pakistan Administrative Service (the present District Management Group), and the Police Service of Pakistan. The federal services will comprise the Pakistan Foreign Service, Pakistan Audit and Accounts Service, and Pakistan Taxation Service. Direct recruitment to the other existing services through the Central Superior Services examination should be discontinued in a phased manner. The provincial services should include the Provincial Executive Service, Provincial Management Service, Provincial Technical Services, and Provincial Judicial Service. All direct recruitment to positions in Grade 17 and above should be merit-based, with due representation to the regional and women quotas. Recruitment in all cases should only be made by the Federal and Provincial Public Service commissions through an open, transparent, and competitive examination and interview process.

One of the principal weaknesses of the present system is that once you have entered the civil service at a young age, there is no compulsion to upgrade your skills or knowledge. Career advancement is divorced from skill and knowledge acquisition and application. Promotion and placement policy should be aimed at rewarding those who perform well and demonstrate potential for shouldering higher responsibilities. Promotion policy should lay down the criteria, including the weightage given to PER, training and skills acquisition, rotation of assignments, diversity of experience, complexity of jobs, and the like, for each level. Training of all civil servants at all levels, cadre or ex-cadre, should be mandatory and explicitly linked to promotion to the next grade. For this purpose, the existing training institutes should be autonomous and provided with the requisite human and professional training for engineers, scientists, accountants, health experts, educators, economists, and the like, and new institutes established to fill the gaps.

Corruption amongst the majority of civil servants cannot be curbed by moral persuasion but by providing them with an adequate compensation package. The present compensation structure, under which officers are grossly underpaid in relation to their compatriots in the private sector and do not earn a decent living wage, has given rise to poor morale, a sense of indifference to work, and a sense of apathy. None of the reforms proposed in the Report can succeed unless the compensation package offered to the officer cadre is substantially upgraded. To keep the wage bill of the government within the limits of fiscal prudence, it is proposed that a freeze should be imposed on fresh recruitment to lower grades apart from teachers, health workers, and police personnel. Although this is a politically difficult decision, it should also be borne in mind that high fiscal deficits result in high rates of inflation which undermine popular support for the political party in power. After all, government employment accounts for under six per cent of total employment in Pakistan and makeshift employment in the public sector cannot satisfy voters.

A fair and equitable compensation system cannot work well unless it is accompanied by an objective performance appraisal system. The current system of the annual confidential report (ACR) has outlived its utility and should be replaced with an open performance evaluation report (PER) system, in which the goals and targets are agreed to at the beginning of the year, key performance indicators to measure the achievements are established, and a frank discussion is held between the appraisee and the supervisor on the identification of development needs to be addressed. A mid-year review should be held to assess progress and provide feedback and the annual evaluation held jointly through a discussion between the appraisee and the supervisor. The appraisee can then sign the report or appeal to the supervisor next in line against the findings of his immediate supervisor. In this way, the PER will be used largely as a tool for the development of the individual to meet the needs of the organization. Poor or under-performers should be particularly focused upon to enable them to achieve higher levels of performance outcomes.

In order to improve the interaction between the citizen and government functionaries at the grass-roots level, the present oppressive and highly arbitrary system has to be drastically reorganized. The officials selected to man the revenue, municipal, police, and other service departments should be well educated, trained, courteous, and responsive and be held accountable for nepotism, favouritism, and corruption. This can be accomplished by introducing the same principles that are applied to the higher bureaucracy, i.e. minimum acceptable qualification for selection, a merit-based recruitment system, continuing training and skill upgradation, equality of opportunity in career progression, continuing training in soft and domain skills, adequate compensation, proper performance evaluation, financial accountability, and citizen feedback mechanisms. There is at present no system of post-induction, on-the-job, or soft skills training available for these officials.

Notes and References

1. Niaz, I., *The Culture of Power and Governance of Pakistan 1947–2008* (OUP, 2010).
2. Shafqat, S., (1994): 'Pakistani Bureaucracy: Crisis of Governance and Prospects of Reform', *Pakistan Development Review* 38: 4 part II (Winter 1999), 995–1017.
3. Maddison, A., *Class Structure and Economic Growth* (Allen & Unwin, 1971).
4. Braibanti, R., *Research on the Bureaucracy of Pakistan* (Duke University, 1996).
5. Kux, D., *The United States and Pakistan, 1947–2000: Disenchanted Allies* (John Hopkins University Press, 2001).
6. Ahmed, M., *The Civil Servant in Pakistan* (OUP, 1964).
7. Ibid.
8. Ibid.
9. *Administrative Reorganization Committee Report.* Government of Pakistan.
10. Khan, M. J. R. (ed.), *Government and Administration in Pakistan* (Pakistan Public Administration Research Centre).
11. Ijlal Haider Zaidi cited in Ilhan Niaz, *The Culture of Power and Governance of Pakistan* (Karachi: OUP, 2010)
12. Noman, O., *A Political and Economic History of Pakistan* (OUP, 1998).
13. Ibid.
14. Niaz, 'Corruption and the Bureaucratic Elite in Pakistan: The 1960s and 1970s Revisited', *Journal of the Royal Asiatic Society,* October 2013.
15. Ibid.
16. Siddiqui, T. A., *Towards Good Governance* (OUP, 2001).
17. Haque, N. U., Khawaja, I., *Public Service through the Eyes of Civil Servants* (PIDE Series on Governance and Institutions, 2007).
18. Ghumman, A., 'Revitalising CSS Performance', *Dawn,* 31 October 2016.
19. Sadat, S., 'The Bitter Truth', *Dawn,* 27 October 2016.
20. Subohi, A., 'Public Sector Training', *Development Advocate,* vol 3, issue 3.
21. World Bank, *Pakistan: A Framework for Civil Service Reform in Pakistan,* Report no. 18386-PAK, 15 December 1998.

22. Hanif, et al. 'Performance Management in Public sector: A Case Study
of Civil Service in Pakistan', *South
Asia Studies* 31 (1).

23. Government of Pakistan, *Report of the
National Commission for Government
Reforms,* vol I.

24. Sherani, S. 'Poverty of our Reform
Ambition', *Dawn*, 5 August 2016.

25. Jadoon, Z., *'Administrative Reforms
in Pakistan'*, in M. Sabharwal, and E.
Berman (eds), *Public Administration
in South Asia* (CRC Press, 2013).

26. Artaza, I. 'Civil Service Reform',
Dawn, 15 November 2016.

9

The Judiciary

mong all the three organs of the state set out in the constitution,
a well-functioning judiciary is crucial to democracy, governance,
security, economic growth, and equity. No other institution has
such a pervasive influence on so many aspects of the daily life of a citizen
and also on that of the government. The executive has perforce no choice
but to comply with the directives of the courts, however unpalatable they
may be. The legislature can take a cue from the courts' decisions and
bring about changes in the laws or amend the constitution but the process
required for this is cumbersome. The judiciary, particularly the Supreme
Court of Pakistan, enjoys unfettered powers under the constitution.
Hasan Askari Rizvi describes the relationship between democracy and the
justice system:

> Democracy is based on liberal constitutionalism. It needs a well-established
> constitutional and legal system that recognizes civil and political rights,
> equality of all citizens irrespective of religion, caste, ethnicity, or language
> and region. An independent judiciary ensures that the Rule of Law is
> available to all citizens. The civil and political rights have to [be] protected
> not only from the excesses of state institutions and functionaries but also
> secured against powerful interest groups that resort to violence or a threat
> thereof against any particular community or region.[1]

One of the principal components of governance is the rule of law, which
carries significant weight in the overall structure. It also shapes societal
behaviour and conduct. Another component, i.e. accountability, is also
underlain as an independent judiciary would not tolerate any conflict

of official and private interests on the part of those in power, be they politicians or bureaucrats. Accountability courts form an integral part of the value chain with the appellate authority vested in the higher courts.

Security of person and property, and the excesses and arbitrary actions of those in power, are safeguarded by a vigilant judiciary. The Supreme Court has taken suo motu notice of many incidents in which the fundamental rights of individuals have been violated.

The most direct link between an effective judiciary and economic growth is the protection and enforcement of contracts. A market-based economy is driven by various kinds of contracts reached between private parties. If these contracts are reneged upon or openly violated, the exchange of goods and services would come to a grinding halt. It is the courts who are the custodians of these contractual obligations.

Finally, the poor do not have the resources to pay for prolonged litigation and are therefore vulnerable to exploitation and suppression by the financially well-endowed members of society. Inexpensive, affordable, and expeditious justice and simplified alternate dispute resolution mechanisms can come to the rescue of the poor.

CONSTITUTIONAL ROLE

Under the Constitution, Pakistan's judicial system comprises three tiers. At the apex level is the Supreme Court of Pakistan followed by a High Court in each province and in Islamabad. The lowest tier comprises the courts at the district level. These courts also follow a hierarchical order. The civil judge or the magistrate's court is where most original petitions are filed or criminal cases are presented. Additional district and sessions judge is the second rung, and the district and sessions judge sits at the top of the ladder of the lower judiciary.

The Supreme Court's record over the decades has been, at best, mixed. In the earliest period of the 1950s the court, headed by Justice Munir, endorsed the action of the governor general in dissolving the elected assembly and declaring a state of emergency. By invoking the doctrines of necessity and revolutionary legality, the Supreme Court subsequently upheld the dismissal of the elected governments through extra-constitutional means—martial law, or supersession or suspension of the Constitution—and endorsed the amendments to the constitution introduced by the military rulers. The court ruled against the doctrine of revolutionary legality in 1972 when it declared General Yahya Khan (to whom Ayub Khan transferred power in 1969) as a usurper and held all his actions illegal. Yahya Khan was no longer in power at that time.

Martial law was suspended and arrangements for drafting a new constitution for Pakistan were initiated. This judgment did not, however, create an irreversible precedent as the same court upheld the imposition of martial law by General Zia ul-Haq in the Nusrat Bhutto case in 1977. In the Zafar Ali Shah case in 2000, the same court endorsed the intervention of the armed forces through extra-constitutional measures on 12 October 1999. The doctrine of necessity was invoked once again to justify the takeover by the military. In 1990, the court also upheld the dissolution of the National Assembly and the elected government of Benazir Bhutto by the president.

It was only in 2007, after General Musharraf declared an emergency in November, that the Supreme Court, headed by Justice Iftikhar Chaudhry, swung into action and declared the Provisional Constitutional Order (PCO) illegal. The judges who passed this judgement were removed from office and fresh oaths under the PCO were administered to the judges who chose to serve under the new dispensation. The newly constituted court reversed the earlier decision. Soon after that, lawyers launched a movement protesting against the removal of Chief Justice Iftikhar Chaudhry. This movement eventually forced Musharraf to step down as army chief. The lawyers' movement helped the Supreme and high courts to assert greater independence.

The conviction of Z. A. Bhutto by the Lahore High Court in 1979, and the decision by the Supreme Court, proved to be a highly controversial and contentious issue in the judicial history of Pakistan. A number of jurists questioned the validity of the court decisions and openly blamed some of the judges for bias against the former prime minister.

Another avenue that exposed the superior judiciary to criticism was the judicial activism aggressively exercised by the Iftikhar Chaudhry court after his reinstatement in office. To many observers in Pakistan, the court appears to have gone overboard, stifling the working of the executive organ of government. Suo motu cases initiated by the Supreme Court were justified in many instances but excessive display of judicial activism did adversely affect the political and economic conditions in Pakistan, causing disruption and uncertainty in the orderly conduct of the business of the state. A continuing battle with the executive arm of the government in matters of appointments, promotions, award of contracts, etc., and the eventual removal of an elected prime minister at the orders of the Supreme Court in 2012 engendered a new type of jurisdictional ambiguity and policy unpredictability. The most worrying development was the unintended consequences of judicial activism on the economy.

JUDICIAL ACTIVISM AND THE ECONOMY

How did judicial activism and suo motu actions impact the economy?

There is a strong relationship between the rule of law and investment and business development. In absence of a conducive legal environment, the uncertainties created by other factors such as political instability, security, law and order, energy, and the like, worsen the situation. However, a well-functioning judicial system can reassure the investor and act as a countervailing force to the other negative attributes. An investor will part with his financial savings and share his expertise and experience only when he is assured that a firm is profitable. For profitability, arbitrary and discretionary actions on the part of state actors need to be kept at bay. To achieve this, non-discriminatory and impartial application of law, enforcement of contracts, protection of property rights, and speedy disposal of legal cases are necessary and need to be seen to be happening.

Judicial activism and suo motu actions taken by the Supreme Court and high courts, particularly between 2009 and 2013, could have been profitably utilized to address some of the structural issues plaguing the judiciary and attention could have been focused on reforms that could, (1) do away with the procedural and process difficulties in ensuring broad-based access to justice; (2) revise outdated and redundant laws and processes; (3) maximize the employment of modern technology to improve case management; (4) encourage the establishment of Alternative Dispute Resolution (ADR) mechanisms; (5) track and enforce the National Judicial Policy 2009; and (6) direct and ensure that the special courts and tribunals adhered to the deadlines for disposal of cases. These measures would have had a more enduring and fundamental impact on the economic governance of the country and would have helped remove some of the obstacles in the way of investment and equitable economic growth.

The reverse was the case and the economy had to bear certain costs because of the proactive decisions of the Supreme Court in matters of economic policy during that period. At least four examples can highlight this problem.

Pakistan's already high risk profile was further elevated with the addition of the litigation risk. Even if investors and businesses are able to surmount all the different hurdles imposed by the federal, provincial, and local governments, they are then faced with an additional constraint that adds to uncertainty and unpredictability of investing and doing business in Pakistan. After all the approvals have been obtained there is the fear that the Supreme Court or high courts might take suo motu notice of the transaction, issue a stay order, and decree long-drawn, time-consuming proceedings to decide the case. Alternatively, some other party aggrieved with the outcome of an executive decision may file a petition that is readily admitted by the courts. A large number of frivolous petitions are filed every year that have dire economic consequences. The penalty for filing these is insignificant but their cost to the economy is enormous.

A decision passed in January 2013, declaring void the Chagai Hills Exploration Joint Venture Agreement (CHEJVA)—signed between the Balochistan government and Australian mining company BHP in 1993—has led to the suspension of mining operations by Tethyan Copper Company, a joint venture of Barrick Gold of Canada and Antofagasta Minerals of Chile. This decision has scared away a potential $3 billion investment by the world's two leading gold and copper mining companies for exploring and developing the mining resources in a part of Pakistan difficult to access. In addition, it has given Pakistan a bad name amongst the international investor community and millions of dollars had to be spent at international tribunals to defend these actions. In the meanwhile, the mining operations have been at a standstill for over six years and whatever little foreign exchange Pakistan was earning through exports is no longer accruing at a time when it is so sorely required. Pakistan does not have the technical knowhow, financial resources, and organizational ability in the public sector to run such a sophisticated operation but foreign investment and knowhow are in this way thrust aside.

The second blatant example is that of the LNG project. Any country facing an acute shortage of energy, and particularly natural gas, would take exceptional measures to exploit alternative sources. Four years were wasted in a repeated issue of tenders, biddings, and awards but the project came to a halt due to the intervention of the courts. It is quite legitimate for the courts to ascertain that the process is transparent and no favours were done in the award of contracts. What is needed, however, is expeditious disposal of these suo motu cases or petitions filed so that the projects are implemented and the economic costs—in terms of foregone production, missed export orders, and laying off of employees—is avoided.

The third example is that of the privatization of the Pakistan Steel Mills which was cancelled by the Supreme Court. Since that historic decision, there was a complete hiatus in the process of privatization and according to PRIME, a think tank:

> The Privatization Commission—largely mandated to save public exchequer money from wasteful spending on inefficient and loss-making state-owned entities (SOEs)—has not privatized any such entity in the last three and a half years, though the priority list has 31 companies. The commission has not plugged even a single rupee loss that has been burdening public finance.[2]

The debt and liabilities of the state-owned corporations to the banking sector have reached a figure of over $8 billion or almost 3 per cent of the

GDP. Losses of over $1 billion or more have been incurred in keeping the Steel Mill alive but its production is barely a small fraction of its installed capacity. The products which the mill uses to fabricate have to be imported to meet the domestic demand and valuable foreign exchange expended for this purpose. There are no sales or revenues being generated but the salaries and wages of the employees who are currently providing no productive services have to be paid each month in addition to other fixed costs. The more pernicious fallout of this decision has been the sense of fear it has generated among the civil servants and political leaders, who are reluctant to put any other public assets for sale or transfer to the private sector to avoid the wrath of the judiciary.

The fourth example of judicial activism that is hurting the smooth operations of the civil services is its interference in the appointments, promotions, and terminations of the executive. The Anita Turab case judgement—in which the security of the tenure of civil servants has been made a justiciable right—is commendable. However, invoking the fundamental rights ambit to review the validity of individual decisions and staying the decisions taken has weakened the powers of the executive and resulted in unnecessary and inordinate delays in the process of filling in these key positions. There was, therefore, a state of paralysis in these bodies. Many of the petitions filed by those who are superseded are frivolous but they linger on for a long time in the courts. The judiciary should certainly ensure that the rules, procedures, and processes are in place and have been observed but the application of these rules and processes should be left to the executive.

Economic decision-making is highly complex and its repercussions are interlinked both in time and space. For example, prices are determined by interactions among hundreds of thousands of economic agents and no administrator, planner, economist, or judge can ever improve or better the market mechanism. Only in cases of market failure, monopoly, or external factors should the regulator intervene. Tampering with this natural way of determining prices seriously distorts the allocation of resources. It is simply not feasible for any individual or group to acquire and command the enormous information that is necessary to decide on what the price levels should be. Administered prices or prices fixed by any means other than those determined by the market result in winners and losers and have distributional consequences.

Private sector and profit-making are not dirty words. They form the backbone of market-based economy, growth, and poverty alleviation. Where undesirable practices are detected, the judiciary has every right to intervene. For example, it should curb rent-seeking through collusion between private players, where favours are being bestowed by the executive on their cronies, or the pre-determined rules and processes for tenders and contracts are being violated and awards not being transparently made. In other words, if there is any attempt made to dilute or weaken the forces of competition, the judiciary has every right to intervene. However, simply opposing privatization on sentimental, ideological, or subjective grounds that the family silver, i.e. public assets, are being sold to private profit-makers without taking into account the larger economic impact does more harm than good to an economy.

The situation is not dissimilar in neighbouring India which has a similar legacy. Pratap Mehta (2005)[3] terms the Indian judiciary as a deeply paradoxical institution. The courts have accumulated great power, even managing to limit parliament's right to amend the constitution. They have, however, also become an institution of governance, in effect enacting laws which are in the sphere of parliament, pronouncing on public policy, and have even directly taken over the supervision of executive agencies.

Going beyond the economy, Benazir Jatoi[4] discusses the impact of judicial activism and suo motu powers of the Supreme Court in another important area, i.e. of parliamentary sovereignty:

The constitutional suo motu, otherwise known as 'on its own motion', powers of the Supreme Court have been increasingly utilised in Pakistan. This was particularly so under the ex-chief justice of the Supreme Court, Chaudhry Iftikhar. His Court was action filled with pending important concerns, certainly of public interest and importance. But the questions that arise are whether this power should be used more sparingly? Is this judicial activism impinging on the administrative duties of the executive?

Is this imbalance because Parliament and its committees are defunct? And importantly, does an overactive judiciary blur and diminish the important impartial constitutional role to be played by it? The suo motu powers of the Supreme Court are often driven by a media frenzy resulting in popular activism and public support. However, an under-monitored media often acts irresponsibly and sensationally and should not drive the highest court in the land. Popular in their actions, yet the possibility of partiality should not be the legacy of the judiciary. The Supreme Court must use its power so sparingly that it creates the merited impact.

Pakistan's Supreme Court must be recognized as a central institution in our democracy. It should not be personality-based, or seek to grab the headlines otherwise it will eventually lose its essential characteristic, impartiality, prudence, and discretion. The essence of justice requires the judiciary to remain relevant and powerful, beyond and above party politics. It also requires the judiciary to understand and respect parliament and its supremacy as being above all branches of the administration.

We are poised at a juncture in history, and 2018 is likely to see the second democratic transition from one elected government to another. As a young democracy, the only judicious way forward is for all its institutions and state apparatus, elected, appointed, and those in uniform, to recognise and adhere to the first basic and most imperative principle in a democracy: a recognition of parliamentary supremacy.

Paula Newberg admirably sums up the balance between prudence and impunity that the judiciary in Pakistan should strike:

Pakistan's judicial history reflects a calculus of conflict and convenience that highlights the incomplete resolution of the country's fundamental political disputes and deep structural tensions between the judiciary and the Executive. The regular imposition of military or emergency rule has consistently skewered constitutions for short term political gain, systematically undercutting citizens' rights. As parliamentary leaders have sparred with presidents and military leaders in their continual effort to re-equilibrate executive-legislative relations, the courts have been left to dangle between them, sometimes as victims of intra-governmental strife, occasionally as arbiters in the case of constitutionality. When they have failed, the courts have contributed to an evolving culture of executive impunity in which anti-constitutional behaviour regularly overrides promises of future good governance. This poisonous combination has repeatedly diminished the rule of law, limited access to justice and deeply injured democratic development.[5]

She has gone on to note that under military rule, the courts have acquiesced to executive actions that might otherwise be deemed unconstitutional. According to her, 'Pakistan's jurisprudence remains inconsistent and idiosyncratic—long on prudence, occasionally short on justice, often compromised, and always intensely, if retrospectively, political'.

JUDICIAL GOVERNANCE

A debate in Pakistan concerns the procedures of appointment, grant of remuneration, and accountability of judges. Although the parliamentary committee is involved, its role is restricted by the judicial committee which virtually takes all decisions concerning the appointments of judges to the high courts and their elevation to the Supreme Court. The remuneration of judges of the superior courts also fall outside the purview of the National Pay Scales which are applicable to all public servants. Similarly, the jurisdiction of the NAB does not extend to judges.

Salahuddin Ahmed has made the following comments on the procedures of appointments, remuneration, and oversight:

> The SC has brooked no interference from any quarter in any matter relating to performance. Long ago, it wrested away—from the government—all powers to appoint judges. When parliament asserted its right to scrutinize judicial appointments, the SC forced Parliament to amend the Constitution rendering the parliamentary committee toothless. The apex court refused to allow its accounts to be audited by the public accounts committee and

refused to allow its registrar to appear before the committee. When it felt that judges and their staff were underpaid, it issued a judicial policy, which gave them a threefold enhancement and directly or indirectly compelled various federal and provincial governments to approve such enhancements. It is neither a coincidence nor an inflation-related phenomenon that the monthly remuneration of superior court judges has, in the past 20 years, crept up from around Rs 35,000 to more than Rs 1,000,000.[6]

Under Article 29 of the Constitution, the judges of the higher judiciary can only be removed by the Supreme Judicial Council (SJC), presided over by the Chief Justice of the Supreme Court. The Council is composed of judges of the Supreme Court and the chief justices of the high courts. A system of internal accountability is good in theory to protect the independence of the judiciary and the SJC can recommend the removal of a judge or dismiss the complaint. The national accountability law excludes the military and the judiciary from the purview of the National Accountability Bureau on the plea that both these institutions have their own internal accountability mechanisms and therefore there is no need for an additional layer to be superimposed.

However, Faisal Siddiqi,[7] a leading lawyer, has written that this internal accountability system of a superior judiciary has barely worked because not even a single judge of the Supreme or High Court has been removed by the SJC since the enactment of the Constitution in 1973. The transparency of procedure and process, which is routinely examined in relation to the executive branch, is not so in the case of the judiciary. It is not within public knowledge, for example, how many complaints have been filed against judges and what has been the end result of these. Siddiqi is of the view that 'sadly, the potential threat to judicial independence, has become an excuse to keep back transparency in judicial accountability'.

Babar Sattar articulates his views on why the role of the judiciary in Pakistan has become controversial:

What rule of law is meant to do is inject certainty into affairs of the state and society by defining the rules of the game and meticulously following them without exception. We are not a rule of law society because no one around here can be certain what the rules are and that they won't be changed midstream to accommodate the interests of one power elite or another.

In a polity where rules aren't entrenched, the law isn't certain, and cynics see judicial outcomes flowing backward from consequences desirable for the winning power elite, any court verdict—whether motivated by law or morality—will attract controversy.[8]

LEGAL PROFESSION

The legal profession is regulated by the Pakistan Bar Council (PBC) established under an act of parliament in 1973. The Attorney General is its ex-officio chairman and 22 members are elected by the members of the provincial bar councils. The PBC is responsible for the entry of lawyers into the legal profession, and to adjudicate in cases of professional and other misconduct by lawyers. The fact that the Council members are to be elected by the votes of the lawyers themselves imposes some constraints in its ability to take penal action in relation to the conduct and behaviour of lawyers. On both counts, the performance leaves much to be desired. The standards, methods of assessment, and quality of legal education are so lax that they produce every year a surfeit of lawyers. By and large, the profession comprises responsible individuals but the unrestricted entry has brought a bad name for the irresponsible behaviour of a few. Some of the brief-less lawyers, in order to attract attention, resort to means that are not altogether professional. The politicization of the PBC has not allowed it to assert itself in taking disciplinary action against those lawyers violating the code of ethics. The behaviour of some lawyers after the 2007 movement— engaging in hooliganism, beating up their opponents, and insulting and harassing judges—has also been a subject of concern but no action was taken by the PBC. The new chief justice of Lahore High Court, Justice Mansoor Ali Shah, seeks to introduce some reforms of the system for the convenience of the litigants but these proposals have met stiff resistance from a group of lawyers. Tufail Malik,[9] himself a lawyer, elaborates these issues in a newspaper article:

> The recent episode of a courtroom soap opera (where a lawyer disrespected an additional sessions judge), highlighted the challenges faced by the judiciary on a regular basis. This strain between the bar and bench, if left unchecked, is bound to prophesy bad tidings for the independence of one of the most important pillars of the state.
>
> There are stories of some lawyers adopting threatening attitudes towards judges up and down the country. Why do some lawyers stoop to such an approach? It appears that such tactics ensure that the requested relief is granted to a client of a relatively powerful lawyer from a relatively weaker judge. On the other hand, sheer reliance on one's intellectual abilities or case preparation may not have the desired outcomes.
>
> As far as the working of an effective justice system is concerned, the bar and bench must ensure that there is no compromise on the independence of the bench. The first principle of the United Nations' Basic Principles on the Independence of the Judiciary clearly states that 'the independence of the judiciary shall be guaranteed by the state and enshrined in the constitution or the law of the country. It is the duty of all governmental and other institutions to respect and observe the independence of the judiciary.
>
> The bar, in its role as the standard-bearer for the independence of the judiciary must ensure that 'any source' does not involve lawyers and that any such involvement should be met with the strictest disciplinary measures.
>
> In Pakistan, we are mired in a situation where there are literally no effective policies adopted by governments to ensure the vibrancy and strength of state institutions. The stability of institutions must come from the institutions themselves, including the judiciary, and must be supported by the bar.
>
> At the same time, to avoid criticism, the judiciary needs to ensure that there is a little room for complaints against the appointments and competence of judges. The judiciary's conduct must be exemplary at all levels. This must be evident in the approach of judges hearing the cases

who must be fully prepared to deal with any situation with dignity, professionalism, and composure.

At the end of the day, the public needs an effective 'justice system' and not just 'a system' which seems to have been in place for the past seven decades.

Sameer Khosa[10] is also critical of the indiscipline publicly demonstrated by the lawyers following the 2007 lawyers' movement in favour of the restoration of CJ Iftikhar Chaudhry. He says:

> It should be unacceptable for bar institutions to turn a blind eye to incidents of mob behaviour and hooliganism by lawyers, simply to preserve their electoral alliances. It is even worse that they have now gone one step further to actively protect such behaviour. Ironically, this protect-at-all-costs mentality hurts the legal fraternity at large. By protecting mob behaviour and hooliganism, the bar councils destroy their own credibility and that of the legal fraternity. Therefore, in 'protecting' the few, they harm the many.
>
> Yet it is essential that such disciplinary authority be effectively exercised. Bar associations and bar councils are important to the administration of justice.
>
> The world over, they work as bodies that further professional development, and ensure that the highest standards are maintained. By doing so, they maintain the trust of the public in the administration of justice. Therefore, they perform not just a service to lawyers, but to the public at large. Their disciplinary authority over lawyers is given to them to protect the public—which has the most important stake in the administration of justice—against lawyers.

While the issues of internal governance, accountability of judges, and the behaviour of legal profession are quite significant, the most important issue from a citizen's perspective is how easy, inexpensive, and expeditious it is to seek relief from the courts in disputes, i.e. access to justice. This is the linchpin of any judicial system.

ACCESS TO JUSTICE

Access to justice continues to remain a worsening problem for the poor. S. R. Khan,[11] in a benchmark study on law and order and the dispensation of justice, shows enormously and unnecessarily drawn-out proceedings: cases pursued to establish prestige, with many in the end being abandoned or in an in or out of court settlement after years of court appearances. Influential people use the courts to settle scores and the police and the courts oblige and appear to collude with them in harassing the poor. Over half the respondents said that it was difficult to register a case with the police and most indicated that this was the case because the police were seeking a bribe.

A graphic description is provided by the convention organized in India on 'The Judiciary and the Poor' by the Campaign for Judicial Accountability and Reform. It is very applicable to Pakistan. The convention noted:

> The judiciary of the country is not functioning as an instrument to provide justice to the vast majority of the people in the country. On the other hand, most of the judiciary appears to be working in the interests of wealthy corporate interests, which are today controlling the entire ruling establishment of the country. Thus, more often than not, its orders today have the effect of depriving the poor of their rights, than restoring their rights, which are being rampantly violated by the powerful and the State. [The judicial system] cannot be accessed without lawyers ... And the poor cannot afford lawyers. In fact, a poor person accused of an offence has no hope of defending himself in the present judicial system and is condemned to its mercy.

Even if we set aside the great injustice meted out to litigants through these delays, the impact is greatly detrimental to the law-abiding fabric of society in general. Individuals in civilized societies are able to peacefully coexist through mutual observance of agreed upon rules.

They are motivated to observe and internalize those rules when punishment for transgression are swift and certain. When this assurance is lost, when punishment is uncertain and long-delayed, or when the innocent are punished as frequently as the guilty, the entire fabric underpinning civilization and the rule of law unravels. The failure to provide such assurance explains the unrest and anarchy prevailing in every segment of society. It is a useful exercise to gather together the views of both, insiders—lawyers and the judges—and outsiders—civil society and human rights' activists—to make an objective assessment of the citizens' access to justice. Some of the practitioners have indeed already diagnosed and prescribed the remedies for this malaise.

We begin with a research report that was prepared for the German Cooperation Agency in 2015. The report finds that:

98.2 per cent of respondents in a survey opined that the poor and lower classes do not have access to justice in the formal justice system. In the same survey, 42.8 pc felt that women and 25.2 pc that landless peasants and agricultural labourers similarly lack access. One of the reasons for limited access to the formal justice system, as perceived by half the respondents, is the high legal fees charged by lawyers.

The World Justice Project Report, 2016, on the Rule of Law Index, ranked Pakistan's criminal justice system as being at 81 out of 113 countries, above Bangladesh (97) but below India (71), and clearly very low down among the 113 countries surveyed. In the civil justice system, the same report ranked Pakistan even lower (106/113), below Bangladesh (103), Sri Lanka (96), and India (93). On 'accessibility and affordability', Pakistan scores slightly higher than India, but lagging behind Sri Lanka and Bangladesh. A comparative analysis of the legal aid systems of Bangladesh, India, and Sri Lanka shows that these countries, although struggling like Pakistan in many ways in developing effective legal aid systems, have at least established organized aid structures.

In Bangladesh, the Supreme Court Legal Aid Office was established in 2015 to provide legal aid in both civil and criminal cases. The structure of legal aid in Bangladesh is organized under the watch of the Supreme Court at four levels: (a) Supreme Court legal aid, (b) district legal aid committees,

(c) *upa-zila* (sub-division) legal aid committees, and (d) union council legal aid committees.

India's National Legal Aid Services Authorities Act, 1987 provides for an organized structure of legal aid and services. The chief justice of the Supreme Court of India is the patron-in-chief of NALSA and a retired judge of the Supreme Court works as its executive director. Similarly, there are state, district, and sub-divisional legal aid service authorities organized on a similar pattern.

In Sri Lanka, the Legal Aid Act, 1978, set up the Legal Aid Commission comprising nine members, three nominated by the justice ministry and six by the bar council of Sri Lanka. The LAC provides legal aid services through regional, district committees and clinics, and also works to promote legal awareness, training, and reforms.

The existing legal aid structures in Pakistan lack ownership at the relevant levels and performance management mechanisms. For example, district legal empowerment committees (DLECs) constituted by the Law and Justice Commission of Pakistan (LJCP) in 2011, in a well-meaning attempt to provide legal aid to deserving litigants at the district level, lack (a) ownership at the most relevant level: the high courts and the district judiciary, (b) effective oversight, and (c) performance management mechanisms.

An efficient legal aid system can significantly help to improve access of vulnerable sections of society to justice and reduce legal exclusion. It is crucial to build the trust of millions of poor people with the justice sector and importantly, with the political system of the country.[12]

We now turn to a leading human rights activist, I. A. Rehman, and put across his view point:

> The law has ceased to be a deterrent to crime. The state's effort to meet this situation by making penalties for offences harsher misses the point that the majesty of the law rests not so much on punishments as it does on the public belief that nobody can escape paying for his misdeeds. In today's Pakistan, most wrongdoers believe they can get away with anything.[13]

Tufail Malik, an insider, i.e. a leading lawyer and writer, points to the outdated procedures as one of the principal culprits for the delays in court proceedings:

> One of the main reasons for the delays in the disposal of cases is the archaic court procedures that have remained intact for over a century.
>
> The criminal procedure code is 118 years old while the civil procedure code is 108-years old. While our court/case management rules vary from province to province, they are generally about 70 to 80 years old.
>
> A product of the British Raj, the nature of criminal and criminal disputes was altogether different and the resources and technologies available to courts, lawyers, and the litigant public were incomparable.
>
> They are overly technical, allow for endless rounds of appeals, reviews and revisions, and generally tilt towards sacrificing efficiency at the altar of thoroughness.
>
> It makes sense to introduce greater efficiency and update these rules in keeping with current realities and new developments in global practices.[14]

Another scholar, Umar Gilani, reports the findings of a pilot study and sketches the current situation quite aptly:

> A pilot study conducted with the Supreme Court concluded that the average high-stakes civil case which ends up in the apex court takes over two decades to conclude. Justice Khosa's posthumous acquittal cases suggest the situation is similar for the criminal system. This can be compared with, for instance, the UK where the average criminal trial for a serious offence takes no more than one year. The same situation applies with the average civil trial involving more than £10,000. Less serious criminal and civil proceedings take, on the average, under seven months.
>
> The illusion must never be entertained that the systemic reform of Pakistan's judiciary is simply a technical problem—a neat and clean job. Were it a technical problem, the ADB-funded $350 million Access to Justice Project and various subsequent donor-funded multi-million dollar projects would have resolved it. Any form of judicial reform is a political struggle, an

ugly job which is bound to create winner and losers, just like former chief
justice Iftikhar Chaudhry's movement did.

While Article 37(d) of the constitution ensures 'inexpensive and
expeditious justice' to all the people of Pakistan, no chief justice in our
history has ever delivered upon this promise. If the incoming chief justice
wants to do something different, he or she should be willing [to] take on
everybody who is responsible for the delays. These include senior judges and
lawyers, powerful bar association leaders and, perhaps, the legal fraternity
as a whole. The only durable friends an honest chief justice can afford to
have are the people of Pakistan—the obstinate, resilient millions who have
never seen a glimpse of 'inexpensive and expeditious justice' and yet, to their
credit, have never stopped dreaming about it.[15]

Justice Saqib Nisar, the new chief justice of Pakistan, said in one of his
judgments in 2015: 'a judiciary which … is tardy … and has no urge …
and ability to decide the cases/disputes before it expeditiously … is a danger
to the state and the society'.

In *MFMY* v *Federation*, Justice Nisar also went on to prescribe the
remedy for addressing delays which many countries in the world have
adopted: proactive case management by judges. He said, 'the courts must,
thus, exercise all the authority conferred upon them to prevent any delays
which are being caused at any level by any person whosoever'.

Another leading lawyer, Salahuddin Ahmed depicts the reality vividly:

It takes between 20 to 30 years to eventually resolve any moderately complex
civil suit through the litigation system after exhausting numerous rounds
of appeals, revisions, and remands. Criminal cases may take marginally less
time to finally resolve. These are not headline-worthy aberrations, this is the
norm. If one even puts aside the injustice on litigants wreaked through these
delays, the impact is greatly detrimental to the law-abiding fabric of society.
Individuals are able to peacefully co-exist in civilized societies through the
mutual observance of certain agreed upon rules. They are motivated to
observe and internalize those rules when punishment for transgressions
are swift and certain. When this assurance is lost, when punishments are

uncertain and long-delayed, or when the innocent are punished as frequently as the guilty, the entire fabric underpinning civilization and the rule of law unravels. The failure to provide such assurance explains the unrest and anarchy prevailing in very segment of society.

Delays in the judicial system are not due to any 'external factors' but are endemic; pointing fingers at 'external factors' is nothing more than blame-shifting. The most glaring causes include outmoded court procedures and inefficient case management techniques. It was reported in a newspaper article that at [the] end of June 2010 the Sindh High Court had 13712 civil cases, 7180 civil appeals, 6606 constitutional petitions, and 4,266 criminal matters in all 31, 764 cases before 18 judges. 1133 fresh cases were instituted that month. A judge is assigned 60 to 70 cases daily but he will not be able to hear more than 10% of these cases, the remaining being adjourned. Then, with a culture—among judges, lawyers, prosecutors, and the police—that is lackadaisical about procedural rules and timelines, further delays become inevitable. To add, inadequate physical and human infrastructure is unable to keep up with the growing population and litigation demands. These causes can be addressed by a resolute judiciary, but that does not factor in the obdurate refusal of the legal community to recognize systemic flaws in the system.[16]

Anatol Lieven, a scholar on Pakistan, makes another relevant point about the disconnect between the laws and the ordinary citizens:

The state's law is felt by many advisory people not just to be rigged in favor of the rich, and hopelessly slow, corrupt, and inefficient, but also to be alien—alien to local tradition, alien to Islam; the creation of alien Christian rulers, and conducted by the elites for their own benefit.[17]

Mansoor Hasan Khan,[18] another senior Pakistani lawyer, draws our attention to the problem which has to do with the outdated laws governing our judicial system and emphasizes the need to review them:

Legislations in Pakistan which purportedly recognize and enforce these sacred concepts (property rights and the sanctity of contracts) are once again totally outdated. These include the Transfer of Property Act 1882; the Stamp Code 1899; the Registration Act 1908; the Contract Act 1872; the Evidence Act 1872 (Qanun-i-Shahadat Order 1984). It is simply not possible to establish a modern society where trade and commerce may flourish upon the ruins of the outdated laws mentioned. TPA does not apply to rural areas. Registration and [the] Stamp Act do not compulsorily apply to any side of purchase or sale of lands in rural areas. Land Revenue Act has been held to be of no legal consequence. Small wonder then that these matters hardly get resolved inside the Courts and virtually no investment is made in our agriculture sector.

Both India and Pakistan continue to groan under outdated laws such as the Code of Civil Procedure 1878, considering it the gospel truth while ignoring the fact that the formalistic English model on which it was based was discarded even in English a long time ago. The English model which is followed in the CPC 1908 preferred form over substance. On account of this fundamental flaw, litigations continue in Pakistan for decades while lawyers squabble over issues of virtually no consequence. In each litigation there is a lawyer seeking justice for his client and an opposing lawyer who will successfully prolong and delay the litigation while liberally drawing upon various dilatory provisions of CPC. Knockouts on the basis of hyper-technicalities and the causing of abnormal delays are in fact appreciated and considered assets and qualities of astute lawyers.[19]

REFORMING JUDICIAL FUNCTIONS

Why is it necessary to reform the judiciary? Justice Douglas[20] made a very apt remark which is very relevant to the role of the judiciary: 'Law has reached its finest moments when it has freed men from the unlimited discretion of some ruler, some civil or military official, some bureaucrat. When discretion is absolute, man has always suffered.' The judiciary acts as a check on the exercise of unlimited discretionary powers of the executive in the conduct of the affairs of the state.

The objective of the reforms is not with abstract concepts such as judicial independence, judicial activism, and judicial acquiescence but with the access, affordability and speedy disposal of cases, protection of property rights and freedoms, and the fundamental rights enshrined in the Constitution for the common citizens of Pakistan. There is a widespread belief that the law has ceased to be a deterrent to deviant behaviour and most wrongdoers can get off scot free. The inordinate delay in judicial proceedings has emasculated the state by indefinitely protecting tax evaders, loan defaulters, illegal occupants of public land, and other delinquents frozen by stay orders issued by the courts. Access to justice has been denied to the poor and marginalized segments of the population as it has become expensive, cumbersome, and prolonged. Private sector contracts are held up because of the excessive time taken in the execution of court decrees. The World Bank Enterprise Survey found that 38 per cent of Pakistani firms find the court system a major constraint to an average of 14 per cent in South Asia. An investment climate assessment reported that a third of Pakistani firms view the low quality of courts as an obstacle in comparison to only one-fifth in Bangladesh.

It is argued in some quarters that there is no point in reforming or disciplining courts unless other actors in the judicial system—lawyers, state counsels, prosecutors, and police investigations—are simultaneously reformed. Given that none have shown any great inclination towards self-discipline, it is pointless trying to effect judicial reform in isolation.

Judges drive and control the judicial process while other actors follow their lead, sometimes reluctantly and grudgingly; in the case of the bar, they may even show their pique through strikes. In the final analysis, if these participants really want to achieve their desired objectives they must inevitably follow the judicial lead.

Rather than waiting for other reforms to occur, the Supreme Court is well placed to take a lead in this area. The power, prestige, and resources it has under its command are unparalleled. When it initiates suo motu inquiries and passes directives regarding provincial policing systems, land revenue record-keeping, appointments, and promotions and transfers in the civil service generally it would appear more credible if it reformed the judicial system itself. The National Judicial Policy Committee, which comprises the chief justices of all the high courts presided over by the chief justice of the Supreme Court, is an ideal platform for the formulation, design, and implementation of these reforms.

First, access to judiciary is limited to only those who can afford good lawyers and pay their enormous fees and expenses. An ordinary litigant, however genuine his or her claim may be, therefore bows before the influential or resorts to non-conventional methods of dispute resolution. Unequal access to justice is one of the principal factors perpetuating the patronage capacity of politicians and, in turn, leads to poor economic governance. The feudalistic ethos that pervades our governance structure cannot be altered until all citizens are treated equally by law. Today, it is only the rich who can manipulate the system to their advantage.

Second, the laws governing economic transactions such as the Contract Act, the Evidence Act, the Registration Act, the Transfer of Property Act, and the Stamp Code, were devised in the nineteenth and twentieth centuries. They are not only deficient, defective, and outdated but in some instances their applicability is limited. The most important law that needs updating is the Land Revenue Act to make it more germane to the modern demands of agriculture, agro-business, industry, commerce, infrastructure, and the like. Land use for industrial, commercial, and agricultural purposes is critical to the production of goods and provision of services. Land disputes on the title and possession of land both in the urban and rural areas form the bulk of civil litigation at the local level with appeals escalating all the way to the Supreme Court. The process of adjudication is not only tedious, cumbersome, and expensive but also time consuming. Transparency of land sales through clear land titles and market-based transactions would reduce the volume of litigation and promote efficient use of land, both urban and rural.

Third, the capacity of judges to deal with the substance and content of economic-related processes and that of lawyers engaged in this line of specialization should be continually upgraded. A large number of defective decisions are delivered because of the inability of judges and lawyers to grasp the intricacies of the principles underpinning a transaction. The entry into and standards of legal education, in general, have to be raised to the same level as other professions such as medicine, engineering, and accountancy. Expert witnesses or amicus curiae should be invited more frequently to intervene to help the court in complex and technical matters.

Fourth, case-load management in our courts, particularly at the lower level, is ridden with discretion, corruption, delays, and inefficiencies. For the last decade attempts are being made to manage the load through a transparent computerized system but the results have been sporadic. Unless the top judicial leadership fixes strict deadlines there is little prospect of anything concrete being achieved. Rigorous supervision of the lower courts and penal actions against non-performers and rewarding those who are quick and fair in disposal of cases should be institutionalized.

Fifth, while we all rightly criticize the informal *jirgas*, *sardari* practices, and *qazi* courts, the fact remains that we have been unable to extract the essential ingredients of these informal systems to enrich the formal legal systems. The uprising in Malakand division was inspired by the mullahs who contrasted the speedy and expeditious justice of the Shariah courts in the days of the Wali of Swat with the established judicial system applied in the area since the merger of Malakand in the NWFP. The FBR had implemented an ADR mechanism until 2008. As soon as the new government assumed power it abolished the mechanism rather than plugging its defects and weaknesses and making it more effective. Small Causes courts and properly functioning village level Masalahit Committees and other aspects of ADR can take a lot of the load off the present congestion in our courts and also provide access to justice at very little cost.

The ADR Bill 2016, a welcome move, needs to be implemented in letter and spirit. Pervez Rahim[21] describes the features of the ADR Bill, and holds that:

> it will facilitate dispute settlement without resorting to formal litigation for adjudication by the courts. This includes arbitration, mediation, conciliation, neutral evaluation, and dispute resolution through panchayat.

A panel of 'neutrals' will be notified by the government, which includes a conciliator, evaluator and mediator or any other impartial person. A panchayat will be a conciliatory body constituted by any law for the time being in force. The court may refer a matter pending before it to ADR with the consent of the parties. If the parties agree before initiating formal proceedings, they may make an application to the court or an ADR centre (notified by the federal government), or a panchayat for resolution of their dispute.

A 'neutral' will have to dispose of the matter within a maximum of 45 days. If the matter is referred to an arbitrator, the process must be completed within a maximum of 90 days.

If a settlement is reached, it will have to be submitted by the 'neutral' or arbitrator to the court, which will announce a verdict and pass decree in terms of the settlement. A list of 23 types of matters and (civil and commercial) disputes that can be referred for ADR are mentioned in the schedule to the bill. The objectives behind the formation of an ADR system are to settle disputes effectively, overcome delays, provide inexpensive justice, and reduce the burden on courts. As litigation is a lengthy and expensive process, there is a worldwide trend to adopt ADR.

Sixth, there was a ray of hope in 2009 when the National Judicial Policy was announced. The policy made some very radical pronouncements such as the rule that cases relating to banking and different taxes and duties such as income tax, property tax, etc., should be decided within six months. All stay of judgements should be decided within 15 days of the grant of an interim injunction. Cases relating to rent should be decided within four months in the trial courts and appeals within two months. Cases relating to suits on bills of exchange, *hundis*, and promissory notes should be decided through summary procedure within 90 days. However, the progress in achieving these stated goals after a lapse of eight years has, regrettably, been disappointing.

Seventh, the banking system can simply not work if wilful defaulters can obtain stay orders from the courts and hundreds of billions of rupees of bank loans remains stuck. Even where the courts have decided cases in favour of the lenders the execution of the decree takes a long time. Unscrupulous borrowers are happy that they can use the borrowed money for decades or years without servicing the loans. The same is true of income tax, sales tax, and customs pendency. Special courts are either without judges or some of the judges do not have the competence to deal with specialized laws and regulations. The cases are adjourned and remain undecided for decades. The NJP should involve a more proactive monitoring mechanism. According to the *Annual Report of 2012*, the disposal by the banking courts was 23,694 out of 68,973 outstanding cases, i.e. 34 per cent disposal which is lower than the 42 per cent disposal by all special courts and administrative tribunals. Conviction rates for insider trading, tax evasion, loan default, and other economic crimes are quite low. The deterrent effect of the laws on the books is then virtually absent and the behavioural change towards better observance and compliance is almost non-existent.

As a leading Pakistani lawyer has so aptly commented, the British model on which the Code of Civil Procedures (CPC) 1908 was based was discarded even in the UK a long time ago. The British model preferred form over substance; on account of this fundamental flaw, litigations continue in Pakistan for decades while lawyers squabble over issues of virtually no consequence. In each piece of litigation there is a lawyer seeking justice for his client and an opposing lawyer who will very successfully prolong and delay the litigation while liberally drawing upon various dilatory provisions of CPC. Knock outs on the basis of hyper-technicalities and the causing of abnormal delays are in fact appreciated and considered 'assets' and 'qualities' of astute lawyers.

To conclude, the National Judicial Policy has very relevant and valuable elements which if implemented can make the judiciary a major contributor towards good governance. The problem as usual in Pakistan is the lack of implementation. The honourable members of the committee overseeing the policy will be performing a great service to the nation if they regularly monitor and ensure that it is being implemented both in letter and spirit. This single outcome will be a hundred times more valuable than hundreds of disparate cases of judicial activism.

SUMMATION

The system of checks and balances enshrined in our Constitution assigns a critical role to the judiciary for upholding the rule of law. The latter also plays an equally important part in promoting economic and social development. The IMF, in the *World Economic Outlook 2017*, has confirmed that higher quality of legal systems and strong protection of property rights are associated with better medium-term growth outcomes in emerging and developing countries (EMDCs).[22] However, in reality, like other institutions, preservation of the interests of the elites has not escaped the judicial history of Pakistan. Babar Sattar[23] has rightly concluded that:

> the history of rule of law in Pakistan is a discreditable one of using the law and its processes to strike deals between competing power elites, as opposed to defining the boundaries of right and wrong and holding the guilty to account. In the past when courts waded into the political thicket and produced partisan consequences, they did so at the expense of public faith in the neutrality and integrity of rule. That is why many see the law as a tool for the powerful to settle scores, and not as an instrument of justice ... Our system of checks and balances is neither potent nor functional. Our power elites don't like public officials exhibiting autonomy and independence.

In matters relating to economy and finance, much damage was done in the post-2007 period of judicial activism and there is still no respite. A World Bank 'Enterprise Survey' reported that 38 per cent of Pakistani firms find the court system a major constraint in doing business in comparison to 14 per cent in South Asia as a whole. Under 'Investment Climate Assessment' a third of Pakistani firms perceive the low quality of courts as an obstacle in comparison to a fifth in Bangladesh.

Policy-makers, leaders of the legal profession, the National Judicial Policy Committee, and others involved in the chain providing justice and the rule of law in the country should realize how much good they can bring about in the lives of ordinary citizens and facilitate the spread of shared economic prosperity among them by introducing and implementing the necessary judicial reforms.

NOTES AND REFERENCES

1. Rizvi, 'In Search of Genuine Democracy', *Express Tribune*, 18 September 2016.

2. Salman, A., 'Privatisation Commission failing to plug losses', *Express Tribune*, 20 February 2017.

3. Mehta, P, 'India's Judiciary: The Promise of Uncertainty' *in* D. Kapur, and P. B. Mehta, (eds.), *Public Institutions in India: Performance and Design* (OUP, 2007).

4. Jatoi, B., 'Parliament or Judiciary: Who is the Grand Inquisitor?', *Express Tribune*, 29 December 2016.

5. Newberg, P., 'Balancing Act: Prudence, Impunity and Pakistan's Jurisprudence' *in* P. R. Brass (ed.) Routledge *Handbook of South Asian Politics* (Routledge, 2010).

6. Ahmed, S., 'Justice delayed is justice denied', *Dawn*, 19 December 2016.

7. Siddiqi, F., 'Judicial Independence', *Dawn*, 1 August 2016.

8. Sattar, B., 'Not Guilty vs Not Proven', *News*, 21 January 2017.

9. Malik T., 'Judicial Freedom', *Dawn*, 1 November 2016.

10. Khosa, S., 'Indiscipline Ignored', *The News*, 16 October 2016.

11. Khan, S. R., et al *Initiating Devolution*

for Service Delivery in Pakistan, (OUP, 2007).

12. Shinwari, N. A., *Understanding the Informal Justice System: Opportunities and Possibilities for Legal Pluralism in Pakistan*, cited in M. A. Nekokara, 'Access to Justice and Legal Aid', *Dawn*, 12 December 2016.

13. Shinwari, *Understanding the Informal Justice System* (2015) <Camp.org.pk>

14. Ibid.

15. Gilani, U., 'The Pace of Justice', *The News*, 31 December 2016.

16. Ahmed, S., 'Justice Delayed is Justice Denied', *Dawn*, 20 December 2016.

17. Lieven, A., 'Pakistan: A Hard Country' *Public Affairs April 2011*

18. Khan, M. H., 'Judicial Reforms', *Dawn*, 1 April 2011.

19. Ahmed, S., 'Justice Delayed is Justice Denied', *Dawn*, 20 December 2016.

20. Douglas, W. O., *United States Supreme Court* (1951). quoted in A. G. Noorani, 'Civil Society', *Dawn*, 20 August 2016.

21. Rahim, P., 'Justice for Labour', *Dawn*, 24 January 2017.

22. IMF, *World Economic Outlook, 2017*.

23. Sattar, B., 'Rule of Law on Trial', *The News*, 10 June 2017.

10

The Legislature

Pakistan has experimented with both the presidential and parliamentary forms of government under different constitutional arrangements. Thus the position of the legislature has also ebbed and flowed during these different periods. The Constitution of 1956 envisaged a parliamentary form of government with a single house, i.e. the National Assembly elected directly on the basis of adult franchise but the Constitution was soon thereafter cast aside by the military coup of October 1958. The 1962 Constitution under Ayub Khan switched to a presidential form of the government with the National Assembly at the centre and two provincial assemblies, one for east and the other for west Pakistan.

The election of the president, on the one hand, and the national and provincial assemblies, on the other, were held indirectly by an electoral college of 80,000 Basic Democrats. The 1973 Constitution has remained in force except that it has been suspended twice, in 1977 and 1999, when General Zia ul-Haq and General Pervez Musharraf dismissed the elected governments and assumed power. In both these periods, amendments were made that shifted executive power from the office of the prime minister to the president. Although parliamentary democracy was restored, first in 1988 and then in 2008, the powers to dismiss the elected prime minister and the National Assembly continued to remain vested in the president under Article 58(2) (b). These powers were exercised by Ghulam Ishaq Khan in 1990 and 1993, and by Farooq Leghari in 1996.

The Nawaz Sharif government successfully abolished this power under the Thirteenth Amendment to the Constitution in 1997. However, it was once again revived in 2002 under the Legal Framework Order (LFO). The authority of parliament was further diluted under the two military regimes making the executive relatively more powerful, with legislative initiatives resting with the executive. It was not until April 2010 that the Eighteenth Amendment to the Constitution, approved unanimously by parliament, withdrew the powers of dismissal of the national and provincial assemblies and dismissal of the prime minister from the president and the primacy of the elected leader of the house was restored. However, the same amendment also gave exceptional powers to the leaders of the political parties who could ask any individual legislator to resign from their seat if they violated party discipline. This is a significant departure from the days of the 1990s when crossing the floor at will posed a threat to political stability. Under the present law, the casualty has been dissent and difference of opinion engendering a culture that induces sycophancy, loyalty to the leader, and yes-manship. The expansion of the electronic media has also diverted the interest of individual members from the affairs of the parliament.

Tasneem Sultana[1] provides an interesting perspective on the behaviour of individual legislators:

> The growth of a strong party system (in particular two party system) has undermined the independence of individual assembly members. It has nearly guaranteed that the party with a majority in the assembly will succeed in passing any legislation that it initiates. Another factor which has affected the role of the assembly is the increasing importance of the electronic media. The commentator and the anchors have now become influential analysts and the populace looks to the media for their contact with politicians. Furthermore, politicians are also preferring to address the nation or make policy statements in front of TV cameras rather than in parliament.

Under the 1973 Constitution that remains in place notwithstanding many mutations, the Pakistani legislative system comprises the president as the ceremonial head of the state, the National Assembly, and the Senate at the federal level and four provincial assemblies in each of the provinces. All the assemblies are elected directly through adult franchise while the Senate is elected indirectly by the national and provincial assembly members, and the president elected by the joint meeting of the National Assembly and the Senate.

Parliament is the supreme legislative body which enacts all the laws on the subjects listed in the fourth schedule of the Constitution as federal legislative subjects. The second important function that parliament performs is to function as watchdog on the actions of the executive, maintaining checks and balances on the government, and restraining it from exercising excessive discretionary powers that result in abuse or misuse of office. The third function of parliament is financial accountability, beginning with approval of the budget, scrutiny of public expenditure, and consideration of the audit reports prepared by the Auditor General of Pakistan. Parliament can take action on these reports where necessary, including recovery of dues. In this context it forms part of the larger accountability mechanism.

The principal instruments utilized by the legislature to discharge its constitutional obligations and keep check on the government are Standing Committees, debates, adjournment motions, and the question hour.

As pointed out earlier, the most significant among them is the standing committee system in which the committees have the powers to examine the expenditure, administration, delegated legislation, public petitions, and the policies of the ministry concerned and its associated bodies.

Dr Fazal Kamal[2] has conducted a comparative study of the functioning of the parliamentary committees of Pakistan, India, and Bangladesh. The committees comprise all shades of the political spectrum represented in the parliament which helps to develop a consensus of opinion amongst diverse political parties. In Pakistan, the current parliament has established 34 standing committees. Their findings and recommendations do not become decisions until approved by the larger body (i.e., the assembly). In addition to standing committees, non-departmental standing committees can also be constituted by the house. These include: the Public Accounts Committee and the committee on government assurances.

There are several other committees such as the Committee on Rules of Procedure and Privileges, House and Library Committee, Business Advisory Committee, and Special Committee on Kashmir.

Dr Kamal conducted an analysis of the 13th National Assembly to assess the working of the committees. Out of 49 standing committees, 17 have been devolved to the provinces and the remaining 32 held a total of 429 meetings over three years, a dismal performance. The most active were the standing committees on health, finance, planning, revenue and development, and food and agriculture.

Beside these parliamentary standing committees, there are senate committees, established under different Acts and with different mandates. The senate has 37 committees relating to various departments and ministries. These committees have suo motu powers to examine expenditure, subordinate legislation, and administrative matters of the respective ministries. A committee normally has 12–14 elected members of the senate. No member can be a member of more than 3 standing committees.

Dr Kamal made the following recommendations to make the standing committees more effective:

(a) The ruling party or the opposition should use legislative deliberations or conduct enquiries into the matters of public importance through the respective parliamentary committees.

(b) Capacity-building measures should be undertaken, for instance, through the creation of a dedicated pool of researchers and expert staff within the committee secretariat.

Ahmed Bilal Soofi[3] provides an updated picture as of 2016:

At present, the Senate has almost 49 committees, the National Assembly 47; the number of committees in the four provincial assemblies range from 18 in Balochistan to 51 in Punjab. The activism of a committee usually depends on the committee chair but committee members can exercise a great deal of influence too, including the power to requisition a committee meeting by 25pc members of a committee .... The committee system in our legislatures is an elaborate arrangement and the state spends a considerable sum to support them. One may argue that a greater degree of research and administrative support needs to be provided to the committees to do a better job, but the scarcity of this is more a matter of lack of demand by the honourable parliamentarians than constraints of state funding.

I. A. Rehman[4] offers some suggestions on how the standing committees can be made to function more effectively:

Now that this system has been in practice for many years it may be time for parliament to review its working and find ways of increasing its part in deepening democracy.

The first issue is the manner of selecting members, especially presidents of standing committees. If members are selected on the basis of their understanding of, or at least interest in, the thematic charge of a committee as well as some training in lawmaking they will make a greater contribution to an efficient performance than otherwise. Particularly necessary is to avoid using leadership of standing committees as prizes or rewards to junior partners in coalition governments because these offices do carry, besides prestige, attractive perks.

It should not be difficult to imagine the consequences of having as chairman of a standing committee on finance a person who has no idea of public finance or who is too rigidly committed to a particular economic theory to permit free debate. Or the consequences of allocating the chairmanship of a committee on human rights to a person who has no understanding of the rights of women, children, religious minorities, or who does not have a clean record as a law-abiding citizen.

Secondly, there should be some method of ensuring that a standing committee gets sufficient time to discuss a legislative proposal or the performance of a ministry/department. In Pakistan, we have seen laws made without screening by standing committees, and also the phenomenon of bills pending with standing committees for inordinately long periods. Both instances call for corrective action.

Pakistan's standing committees have won considerable credit by seeking public/civil society views on matters before them. This is of course as it should be provided that the government, which has a tendency to claim a monopoly on wisdom and integrity both, is open to conversion and change of conviction.

One particular aspect of parliament's function i.e. the executive's accountability to the assembly was scrutinized by PILDAT in 2011 using a number of indicators. The highlights of the results of this study are:

a. The weakest aspect was the ineffectiveness of the National Assembly's involvement in foreign policy which was given a score of 41 per cent.

b. The highest percentage of 74 per cent was given on the freedom of journalists in reporting on the National Assembly's activities.

c. The ineffectiveness of the National Assembly's oversight over the executive was given a score of 47 per cent.

d. The National Assembly's control over the budget, agenda, and timetable, etc. was scored at 58 per cent.

e. The effectiveness of specialist committees in conducting their oversight functions showed a negative score of -11.32 per cent.

f. The effectiveness of the committees' procedures for scrutinizing and amending legislation also showed a negative score of -12.28 per cent.

The broader performance of the national and provincial assemblies is also now regularly monitored by independent non-governmental organizations. The head of one such organization, Ahmed Bilal Mahboob,[5] published their findings recently which provide a succinct appraisal:

During the 135 days in which the Assembly is deemed to have met (it actually met for just 99), the lack of quorum was pointed out 26 times. The quorum is merely 25pc which means that only 86 members have to be present out of a total of 342 to maintain it. But most of the time when the quorum was found lacking, the proceedings had to be suspended. Many a time, assembly proceedings were allowed to continue because of the understanding reached between the treasury and opposition benches, even though there was no quorum. In the parliamentary year that ended in June 2016, the average duration of one Assembly sitting came to a little less than two and a half hours. For roughly the same period, the Indian Lok Sabha met for an average six hours per day ...

The Punjab Assembly frequently faces lack of quorum. During the third parliamentary year, lack of quorum was pointed out about 30 times for 75 sittings and most of the time the proceedings had to be suspended.

The instances of gross indiscipline like the recent brawl, lack of substantive business in the house and committees, members' dwindling attendance and interest in parliamentary proceedings, and an embarrassing token attendance for the sake of daily allowance are all symptoms of a major problem. The crux of the matter is that the quality of parliamentary democracy has hit a plateau or may even be deteriorating.

The core issue is that one individual or at best a few individuals at the top have come to control all the levers of decision-making rendering the collective fora of consultation and decision-making such as the legislatures, cabinets, party councils, and executive committees almost redundant. Unless the voters stop pledging allegiance to individuals instead of institutions and unless the top leaders find a way to correct the situation, taxpayers may start questioning the need and desirability of paying for such misbehaving entities.

At the next tier, the provincial assemblies elected directly by adult franchise have begun enjoying considerable autonomy since the enactment of the Eighteenth Amendment. The abolition of the concurrent list, which had 47 subjects, was a source of tension between those who aspired to greater provincial autonomy and the centrists who wanted strong control by the federal government. Under the concurrent list, both the federal and provincial legislatures are entitled to frame laws. The federal government, with greater resources and relative strength, used this provision largely to its advantage, weakening the jurisdiction of the provinces and diluting their legislative capacity. As the federal government enjoyed the powers of dismissing the chief minister and the provincial assembly, its strength and influence created a sense of de facto subordination and aroused a deep feeling of resentment. The surrender of this power has fortified the autonomy of the provinces. Functions previously performed by 17 federal ministries were also devolved to the provinces.

However, in comparison to the National Assembly and senate, the performance of the provincial assemblies requires very substantial improvement. The committee system has not been effectively utilized either in the process of legislation or for oversight of the executive. An accountability mechanism does exist in form of the public accounts committees but they lack knowledge and incisiveness. The audit reports presented are not for the most recent years and relate to the period for which it is difficult to take action because the officials who had committed the irregularities have either retired or are dead by the time the reports are tabled before the committees. Specialist assistance is also not available to the members of the provincial assemblies.

ROLE IN ECONOMIC GOVERNANCE[6]

The parliament has so far remained lax in many of its functions, particularly in terms of developing an economic vision, long-term planning, oversight of policy-making, and in monitoring the implementation of projects and the accountability of the executive. Had parliament been more active, it is possible that the judiciary would not have taken suo motu cognizance of many cases linked to economic governance. It is a pity that although the major political parties do not differ much on the content of the policies and programmes, those that would have proved beneficial to the economy at large have not been allowed to complete their natural life-cycle. This track record of discontinuity, patchwork, postponement or cancellation of key projects, sudden reversals of otherwise sensible initiatives, and weak implementation has inflicted serious loss to the economy. One way of avoiding our past mistakes is to strengthen the role of parliament and its committees. After all, the National Assembly's public accounts committee has proved to be quite effective. How can this be achieved?

First is the question-answer session. These sessions should have filled in the gap in the knowledge of the citizens with regard to essential facts about government performance but, in actual practice, they have proved to be no more than perfunctory and ritualistic. Alertness and thoroughness in providing answers have been substituted by evasiveness. Revelation of facts on the floor of the house is one way of removing the mistrust between the government and the public at large.

Second, there is the appointment process of the chief executives of constitutional, quasi-judicial, and key public sector corporations. The nominations by the executive to the key positions of auditor general, governor of the State Bank of Pakistan, the chairman of the Federal Public Service Commission, etc., should be reviewed by parliamentary committees. The latter should hold public hearings where testimonies by experts can be heard to testify to the suitability of the candidates for these positions. Once confirmed, it should not be possible for the executive to arbitrarily remove these functionaries till they complete their tenure. This transparent mode of selection and guaranteed tenure of office will ensure that many of problems that the public sector enterprises and regulatory bodies face today in their management and financial affairs are not repeated.

Third, the annual budgetary process is more an exercise in going through the motions rather than a serious examination of the options and alternatives available. The annual budget should be anchored in the Medium Term Budgetary Framework (MTBF) and the executive has to justify the deviations, variances, and slippages between the goals committed in the MTBF and the actual outcomes in the budgets each year. The parliamentary committees should consider the draft budget proposals before they are finalized, only excluding specific revenue and tax measures, or any other information that is market-sensitive.

Fourth, the economic vision, long-term perspective plan, strategy, and medium-term plan and policy documents should be discussed by the parliamentary committees and then presented before the senate or the National Assembly for approval. The bipartisan support given to the final plan or policy would ensure to a considerable degree that a successor government would not reverse or abandon it. This assurance of continuity would, to a considerable extent, clear much of the uncertainty and unpredictability from the minds of investors, whether domestic or foreign.

Fifth, all major international agreements, such as with the IMF, with long-term implications for the economy, should be presented before a parliamentary committee for an in-depth review and scrutiny. Independent experts should be invited to provide their assessments. The committees should then prepare and present the recommendations to parliament.

Sixth, there are important pieces of legislation that have repercussions for the economy, for example, the Fiscal Responsibility and Debt Limitation Act which places limits on the maximum extent of public debt. In the event of these limits being exceeded, parliament should question the executive. Once the bill amending the SBP Act and placing an explicit ceiling on budgetary borrowing by the government from SBP is approved, parliament should take the government to task for any violation.

These steps should substantially strengthen the hands of the standing committees and the parliament in fill in the gap that exists today, i.e. the lack of a long-term economic vision and a strategic plan to achieve it.

Some criticisms can be raised about the approach proposed above. For example, by involving the parliamentary committees in the government's decision-making mechanism may slow it down or paralyse it. This risk can be minimized if the procedures and rules for it are so crafted that the power to delay or veto decisions by parliament is circumscribed. Voting will not be across party lines on these issues, either at the committee level or at the full parliament level. Joint sittings and sessions should be encouraged to debate policies and plans. This process will take more time but as most snags will have been sorted out beforehand, their implementation could proceed fairly smoothly.

The criticism that the parliamentary committees may not have the necessary expertise on the matters at hand can be overcome by the committees employing full-time professional staff to assist them. The committees can always summon experts to advise them. This combination of in-house staff, outside experts, and some parliamentarians already having the necessary experience and competence should overcome this problem. Another risk is that the committees may split across party lines and engage in point-scoring rather than coming to an amicable resolution of the problems. The limited experience with the existing committees does not lend credence to this view. Convergence and compromises have been reached in many instances by people from different political parties as is evidenced by the passage of the Eighteenth Amendment. Intense vigilance by media and civil society and the public nature of the discourse should also act as a deterrent to this tendency.

Initially there may be some discord but with the passage of time, the process, practice, and public exposure is likely to strike an equilibrium; and a healthy balance between execution, responsibilities, and oversight will be reached.

It should be reiterated that the popular disaffection with the state of governance can be countered only if there are institutional checks and balances, as Charles Kupchan[7] very cogently sets out in an essay:

> Growing demand for good governance and its shrinking supply; the inability of the democratic governments to address the needs of their broader publics has only increased popular disaffection, further undermining the legitimacy and efficacy of representative institutions.
>
> Democracies can be nimble and responsive when their electorates are content and enjoy a consensus born of rising expectations, but they are clumsy and sluggish when their citizens are downcast and divided.
>
> Popular participation, institutional checks and balances, competition amongst interest groups appear to be better at distributing benefits.

PARLIAMENTARY SUPREMACY

The question of the supremacy of parliament has gained increasing attention over the past 50 years. Parliament's right and ability to make a law on any subject, so long as it is within constitutional bounds, are well established. Therefore, the doctrine of separation of powers between the legislature and the judiciary is in theory quite clear: parliament legislates while the judiciary interprets the laws passed by parliament rather than challenging them, provided of course that such laws do not infringe any constitutional provisions.

Benazir Jatoi[8] sheds further light on the interdependence of the parliament and the judiciary. She argues that a sovereign and truly democratic parliament should result in a more focused judiciary, i.e. when the parliamentary machinery is truly democratic, representative of society (including minorities and all genders), and functions well, it should lead to a more subservient judiciary that does not challenge the legislature's intentions but interprets the law within the context of the constitution. There seems to be much merit in her view that if the parliamentary committees, which comprise all party and independent candidates, function across party lines, they could be an effective check on the executive branch of government by scrutinizing its acts and proposed legislation and their execution. They can, therefore, enhance good governance, or, differently expressed, if properly formed and functioning, parliamentary committees can help eliminate bad governance.

She then attempts to address the question of whether the supremacy of parliament and the powers granted to the Supreme Court under the Constitution are contradictory:

> I do not believe that any such contradiction exists. In fact, they are complimentary. But the essential rule to understand is that a democratic Parliament should always be supreme. This does not take away from the grandness of the judiciary, nor does it diminish its key constitutional role. Supremacy of Parliament in fact enhances the role of the judiciary by allowing it to carry out its primary responsibility—to adjudicate, interpret the law, and ensure justice, as the final court of appeal.

However, some reservations have been expressed about the capacity of Pakistan's parliament to perform its assigned role. Saeed Shafqat[9] thinks of the National Assembly as 'being more a rubber stamp than a genuine forum, and the rule being hostility and confrontation between leading parties rather than bargain and compromise, extra parliamentary tactics have dominated Pakistani politics'. Pierre LaFrance[10] comments that: 'An average Parliamentarian is a man of property so aloof from the populace and from the middle classes that the Pakistan Parliament has sometimes been defined as a House of Lords and a Senate with no House of Commons'.

One of the strong pillars of a parliamentary democracy is the opposition parties which keep a check on the ruling party so that they adhere to the mandate given to them and do not engage in excesses and practices favouring themselves and their party supporters to the exclusion of others. Regrettably, the bickering, sparring, and bitterness between the contesting parties spills over to parliament even after the elections. The recent events, in which the PTI organized *dharnas* and street protests outside parliament demanding the resignation of the sitting prime minister and filed cases in the courts against him, do not help in building healthy traditions of parliamentary supremacy. The blame for such behaviour does not accrue to the opposition alone but, as Anwar Syed tells us, the ruling party is equally responsible:

> Illiberal politics; the commitment of Benazir, Nawaz and ZAB to liberty and equality before the law was tentative and conditional for they treated the opposition arbitrarily and lawlessly. Each initiated bogus criminal cases against the other, and each was accused of electoral malpractice in the form of elections in which they participated.[11]

Another area that would enhance parliament's supremacy in the context of its constitutional obligations has to do with a credible accountability mechanism which is currently wanting. There is both too much and too little accountability of those involved in public affairs in Pakistan. On one hand, the plethora of laws and institutions such as the anti-corruption bureaus, NAB, Auditor General's reports, Public Accounts Committees, parliamentary committees, judicial activism, and the Ombudsman system have created an atmosphere of fear, inertia, and a state of paralysis in decision-making among civil servants.

On the other hand, instances of rampant corruption, malpractices, nepotism and favouritism, and waste and inefficiency have become part of common folklore in Pakistan's administrative culture. There is an excessive emphasis on ritualistic compliance with procedures; rules and form have tended to substitute substantive concerns with results and outcomes for welfare and justice. The NAB should be made a truly independent body reporting directly to the prime minister and its chairman should be jointly selected by the prime minister and the leader of the opposition on the basis of competence, integrity, and independence. The responsibilities for investigating and prosecuting white collar economic crimes and corruption should be entrusted to the NAB. However, the oversight of the NAB by the Public Accounts Committee should be institutionalized. Accountability courts should be manned by honest judges who are free from influences and pressure. The provincial anti-corruption establishments should also be reorganized on the lines of the NAB.

The Supreme Audit Institution of Pakistan (SAIP), which should replace the Office of the Auditor General of Pakistan (OAGP), should be the apex body for the financial accountability mechanism and an integral part of the institutions of accountability in Pakistan to promote accountability and good governance. The SAIP must be concerned not only with the proper and effective use of public funds but also in overseeing a sound public financial management system, comprising budgeting and revenue collection, accounting, internal controls, audit, and legislative oversight. As part of the overall framework of institutions of accountability, the SAIP should assist the NAB, FIA, and the anti-corruption agencies in the detection and investigation of misuse and leakage of public funds. The SAIP should submit objective reports to the Public Accounts Committee to support parliamentary oversight of the management and use of public resources.

Many countries have established independent budget offices as part of the parliamentary oversight process. The members receive advice from the experts working in these offices on the budget proposals submitted by the executive. The current budgetary review and approval process in Pakistan is shoddy and superficial and goes through the motions without any substantive inputs from parliament. A Parliamentary Budget Office should be established to assist the members and also provide an objective appraisal of the budget to the public at large

The powers of the president in Pakistan have also swung from one extreme to another. From an all-powerful arbiter of the fate of the elected assemblies which he could dismiss under his constitutional powers to a ceremonial figurehead, as in the 1970s and the present; we have to strike a balance. A better configuration could be a leaf from the 1956 Constitution. Article 42 of the 1956 Constitution enjoined the PM to explicitly communicate to the president all decisions taken by the cabinet relating to the affairs of the nation and proposals for legislation; to furnish to the president such information relating to those matters as the president might call for; and if the president so required to submit to the cabinet any matter on which a decision has been taken by a minister alone.[12] There is a general perception, whether true or unfounded, that the principal organs of the state—the executive, judiciary, legislature, and the military—spend much of their time in creating formidable hurdles for one another rather than facilitating and complementing each other. Can the president play any useful role in resolving these conflicts amicably and facilitate a harmonious relationships among the three branches of state and the military to the nation's benefit?

ELECTORAL REFORMS

The current process of holding general elections suffers from several weaknesses and has led to serious dislocations in the smooth functioning of the government as manifested by the *dharna* of 2014. The list of weaknesses is long but stems from the powers, authority, resources, and capacity of the Election Commission of Pakistan (ECP). Unlike India, where the EC is a highly respected constitutional authority and is headed by an administrator, the ECP comprises five retired judges lacking in administrative experience. Organizing elections primarily requires managerial abilities rather than those of a judicial nature. This has repercussions throughout the process. Questions are raised about the registration, preparation, scrutiny, and verification of electoral rolls.

If the lists of voters are incomplete or compromised or tampered with, then there is a possibility of some genuine voters not being able to exercise their franchise. Lack of confidence in the functioning of the returning officers, presiding officers, etc. and their ability to manage logistics for simultaneous polling on the same day throughout Pakistan are also matters of concern. For example, schoolteachers are appointed as polling officers but it is alleged that they owe their appointments as teachers to the local politician and therefore, are likely to oblige their benefactors on the day of polling to discharge their debt. The powers of the ECP to screen and disqualify candidates who do not meet the eligibility criteria, the reform of campaign finances, and the slow and protracted process of grievance redressal and dispute resolution have also been matters of concern.

Tasneem Noorani,[13] a retired senior civil servant makes the following assessment of the current process and proposes some measures to reform the ECP:

ECP seems convinced that its only task is to physically conduct the elections. The implementation of rules pertaining to holding free and fair party elections within the political parties is taken so perfunctorily, that a report of having held elections from political parties has never been known to be scrutinized critically. No one has even been show caused, what to talk about punishment for conducting fixed party elections. This indolence of ECP can only be explained by a very low level expectation threshold of the ECP.

ECP has styled itself as a judicial forum by ordaining that Members will only be from the judiciary and each member including the Chairman will have one vote in joint decision making. Recently amendments were introduced when all four provincial members' tenure was coming to a close. The requirement of being from the judiciary was dropped.

But no reforms to convert the ECP from a judicial forum to an executive forum was taken. Presently the Chairman of the Commission, who is selected through an extensive search process requiring the consent of both the government and the opposition, has only one vote amongst the five members. He is only a Chief in name, as any three members from the provinces can disagree and get their way.

So the reforms that need to be taken to improve the political party system in my view are:

1. Change the law and the rules to place the CEC as an executive head with the powers of CEO, with the Commission acting as the BOG.

2. ECP has to take intra party elections seriously and ensure that they are held as per democratic principles, to enable an ordinary citizen to rise through the ranks of the party and in the process challenge the increasing hegemony of an individual/family owning a political party.

3. The time taken to settle an election petition laid down by law, needs to be implemented, to make the process of accountability meaningful.

4. Rather than having interim governments conduct elections, the ECP should be empowered with powers to stop the government from taking any non-essential and controversial decisions after the process of elections is announced. Also, they [should] be given powers to make the bureaucracy look towards them rather than the government.

The above set of electoral reforms should be able to remedy some of the weaknesses of the present arrangements and transform the ECP into a respected, non-partisan, professional organization capable of delivering credible election results. A parliamentary committee on electoral reforms was constituted in July 2014. While its full report is awaited, some proposals made in redefining the qualifications of the Chief Election Commissioner (CEC) and the members of the ECP were included in the Twenty-second Amendment, which was passed by the National Assembly in May 2016. To what extent this amendment has made a difference forms the centrepiece of an article by Zarrar Khuhro:[14]

Steps have been taken to strengthen the ECP, and the government will no longer be able to transfer or suspend election officials, a power that rests solely with the ECP. However, the ECP has no say in preventing the transfers of other government officials, such as local police officials or district commissioners during the poll process, which is alarming given the role such officials have historically played in influencing elections on the local level.

Ironically, while the ECP can suspend such government officials it deems to be violating election laws, there is no prescribed penalty for such officials, meaning that they can ride out their suspension in bliss and then get reinstated as a 'reward' for services rendered.

Another step in the wrong direction is that the ECP can no longer disqualify elected members found to have submitted false statements of election expenses or false wealth statements. Instead, such matters are now to be referred to the session court, and experience tells us that—given lengthy court procedures and appeals—the offending member can retain his seat for months if not years while the gears of the legal machinery grind on.

Anyone who recalls the general frustration with the pace of election tribunals in the recent past can easily imagine the consequences of turning the process over to the already burdened 'mainstream' judicial system.

But perhaps the biggest problem with this bill is that it limits freedom of information and access in significant ways. Take the process of scrutiny; in a break from the past, this process can now no longer be observed by the media (media personnel are not included in the list of persons authorized to be present during the process) and thus, by extension, the public.

Further, it is not clear whether media will have access to polling stations, be able to observe vote counting or access the returning officer's office during consolidation of votes—all of which are points in the electoral process where the possibility of rigging is high. Given that the right to this access has not been clearly defined, it is now the discretion of the ECP as to which parts of the process media will have access to.

The issue of excessive expenditures incurred by the candidates, and lately by their parties on electronic media ads during the election campaign, has drawn a lot of flak. It is postulated that the present system is intended only for the rich and well-to-do to contest elections. Other talented persons belonging to the middle class do not stand a chance. An article in the leading daily of Pakistan, *Dawn*,[15] makes the following comments:

According to the law in vogue, political parties and elected representatives have to file returns of their income, expenditure, and assets, but there is no mechanism to check the veracity of those statements. A proper mechanism to punish those filing bogus returns is also absent.

... According to the judgement, the ECP is empowered to check not just illegal actions relating to the election (including violations of limits set for campaign finances) or corrupt practices (such as bribery), but is also empowered to review all election activities, including corner and public meetings as well as the use of loudspeakers.

Moreover, the official said, a careful reading of Article 218(3) of the Constitution shows that the clause gives wide-ranging powers to the ECP to check all sorts of corrupt practices and it was for the commission to decide on how to proceed.

The article in question reads: 'It shall be the duty of the Election Commission to organize and conduct the election and to make such arrangements as are necessary to ensure that the election is conducted honestly, justly, fairly and in accordance with law, and the corrupt practices are guarded against.'

Talking about the scrutiny of parties' statements of accounts, he said the ECP had already ruled that it had the jurisdiction to do so in PTI's foreign funding case, as the power is clearly defined in the Political Parties Order of 2002.

There are other areas of reform that would go into the heart of the existing system but require some reflection. These have to do with the present first-past-the-post election by constituency and the appointment of the cabinet members. In Egypt, for example, the 2011 elections—the first democratic elections held after 1952—were conducted under a parallel voting system. Two-thirds of seats were elected on the basis of a party list proportional representation. The remaining one-third were directly elected through the constituencies. The party list comprised the youth, women, minorities, labourers, farmers, and professionals. The law stipulated that half the representation in the new parliament must consist of 'labourers' or 'farmers', while 'professionals' should constitute at most half of the parliament. This arrangement made it possible for a large number of candidates holding doctoral degrees in their respective fields to get elected.

The Egyptian model may be able to address the concerns of Fahd Hussain[16] who expresses two different kinds of reservations on the present mode of elections:

> This constituency-based electoral system adopted from the British model is, within the Pakistani context, essentially exclusionary in nature. It will only throw up winners who can manage constituencies based on either *biradris*, tribes and/or a long history of local patronage/kinship. It automatically excludes a vast majority of Pakistanis who do not fall in this category, and who do not have the wealth to neutralize the deep roots in the constituency
>
> Yes there are other models of electoral democracy—various forms of proportional representation among them—that can offset the negative effects of the present one and that can at least attempt to break the vicious electoral stranglehold of families over this system. It is indeed kosher to be a democrat and criticize this parliamentary system of exclusionary democracy.

His second, but related point, is about the exclusivity of the cabinet members drawn only from among the elected members of the assemblies. He poses this:

> What is also deeply flawed in this system is the requirement to choose the Cabinets from the elected people. Is it not a farce for example to have as the minister of Science and Technology a politician who cannot even in his wildest imagination claim to have any background or expertise on the subject? He then becomes dependent on the Secretary who himself is there for a stint till he gets posted to yet another completely different ministry dealing with something totally different. It is a system running on empty because it is fuelled by the awesome mediocrity of the civil servant combusted with the magnificent incompetence of your average constituency politician.[17]

However that may be, the seats in parliament and the provincial assemblies are allocated on a dual basis of both proportional representation and direct constituency-wide elections and the reservations expressed above can be tackled. Those who are suitably qualified but cannot afford to contest constituency seats can be included in the party list for proportional representation, as is currently the case for women and minorities. As the party list would include experts and professionals drawn from various fields they should be able to discharge their ministerial functions ably and competently.

SUMMATION

The taking off point of the discussion of the legislature is the premise very ably enunciated by Nobel Prize winner Amartya Sen: 'While democracy is not yet universally practiced nor uniformly accepted, in the general climate of world opinion, democratic governance has now achieved the status of being taken to be generally right.'[18] The legislature forms an integral part of democratic governance and needs to be fortified to fulfil its specified role.

For this to occur, we need reforms of the electoral process, delimiting constituencies afresh on the basis of the new population census. Fresh electoral rolls must be prepared from the new data on households generated through this census. The Election Commission and Chief Election Commissioner must be given unfettered powers to organize the elections by directly taking over the administrative apparatus of the provincial and the district governments. This will obviate the need to induct caretaker governments which have only shown themselves to be disruptive of the smooth process of conducting elections. Electronic machines should be used for voting. Candidates for the national and provincial assemblies should be carefully screened and those who do not meet the eligibility criteria should be disqualified from contesting elections by the Election Commission. The sources of campaign finances should be transparently disclosed by each party and the elections held in a fair and free atmosphere. Once the right candidates are elected the quality of parliamentary conduct should improve.

The parliament would then be able to exert better checks on the excesses of the executive and also enact legislation to preserve the rule of law, and protect the fundamental rights of citizens. This is, however, currently hardly the case in Pakistan. There is little legislative accountability to citizens, weak market oversight, and indifference in responsiveness to the citizen demands. The parliamentary committees such as the Public Accounts Committee, through public hearings, can exert a sobering pre-emptive influence on government departments, ministries, and agencies. They could ensure that public expenditure is underpinned by value for money and waste, inefficiencies, and irregularities are minimized. However, the partisanship demonstrated in the committees' deliberations and the lack of technical expertise amongst the staff assigned to these committees has weakened their watchdog and oversight functions. Strengthening of these committees would help to exert effective control over the misuse of power and resources by the executive.

The functioning and the capacity of the committees at the provincial assembly level would require greater effort to bring them at least at par with those at the National Assembly and the senate.

Notes and References

1. Sultana, T., 'Montesquieu's Doctrine of Separation of Powers: A Case Study of Pakistan', *Journal of European Studies*, 5 May 2014. Accessed at: <pgil.pk/wp-content.uploads/2014/05/5>.

2. Kamal, Dr F., *Comparative Functions of Parliamentary Committee System in Pakistan, India and Bangladesh.*

3. Soofi, A. B., 'Parliament's Inertia', *Dawn,* 30 August 2016.

4. Rehman, I. A., 'Standing Committees', *Dawn,* 10 November 2016.

5. Mahboob, A. B., 'Who Pays for the Brawl?', *Dawn,* 7 February 2017.

6. This section draws heavily on the following article: Husain, I., 'Parliament's Role in Economic Governance', *The Express Tribune,* 1 December 2011.

7. Kupchan, C., 'The Democratic Malaise', *Foreign Affairs,* Jan–Feb. 2012.

8. Jatoi, B., 'Parliament or Judiciary', *Express Tribune,* 29 December 2016.

9. Shafqat, S., 'Democracy and Political Transformation in Pakistan' *in* Sofia Mumtaz, et al., *Pakistan: The Contours of Society and State* (OUP, 2002).

10. Pierre Lafrance, UNESCO Special Envoy, France's Special Representative for Afghanistan and Pakistan.

11. Syed, A., 'Liberal Tradition in Pakistan', *Dawn,* 8 July 2007.

12. Article: 46 Duties of Prime Minister in relation to President. Accessed at: <https://pakistanconstitutionlaw.com/article-46-duties-of-prime-minister-in-relation-to-president/>

13. Noorani, T., Background Paper, December 2016.

14. Khuhro, Z., 'Reformation', *Dawn*, 23 January 2017.

15. 'ECP Reactivates Political Finance Wing', *Dawn*, 3 October 2016.

16. Husain, F., 'Wisdom Without Expiry Date', *Express Tribune*, 5 February 2017.

17. Ibid.

18. Sen, A., 'Democracy as a Universal Value'. *Journal of Democracy*, 1999, 10.3, 10.

11

The Military

The overwhelming influence of the military in directly or indirectly steering the governance of Pakistan should be viewed in a historical context. Pakistan was a major source of recruitment for the British Army. The Potohar region of Punjab and some districts of the former NWFP were the principal recruiting grounds for soldiers and officers. At the time of Independence, the armed forces of Pakistan comprised 120,000 men. By the mid-1960s, the number had risen to 300,000, and today its strength is around 520,000. If we add the reserves and the civilian members of the armed forces, the total number would be around 1 million.

The armed forces of course comprise three branches: the army, navy, and air force; the army being by far the largest among them. Unlike some other countries where these soldiers are conscripted, Pakistan's forces comprise volunteers selected through an open, highly competitive process. The other two wings, the navy and the air force, are much smaller and lacked, at the time of Independence, the necessary equipment such as ships and planes.

The Pakistan Army, as the largest service, has occupied a special place in the defence services. It is headed by Chief of Army Staff with its headquarters at Rawalpindi and is divided into two broad functional categories: the fighting force (infantry, armoured units, artillery, aviation, engineers, and signals) and the services (medical, ordinance, EME, administrative support, education, military, police, and veterinary units). Currently the army has 46 major military training establishments. At the time of Independence only the Staff College, Quetta, and five schools of lesser significance were situated in the areas which fell under Pakistan. It had to, therefore, begin establishing a number of training institutes from scratch, and has developed a highly impressive array of these at various levels and different functional capabilities.

The Pakistan Military Academy was established in 1948 to train officer cadets. The army command consistently emphasized high quality training for officers and personnel at all levels. Exercises were held regularly to assess the standards of training and effectiveness.

The Army Planning Board was established and reconstituted in 1955 directly under the commander-in-chief (C-in-C) to analyse and make recommendations on how an efficient, mobile army could be established within the limited resources available.

In February 1954, the army received a big boost when the US decided to provide military assistance to Pakistan to strengthen its defence capabilities. Pakistan's membership of CENTO and SEATO also proved beneficial in professionally strengthening and modernizing the army.

The assumption of power by the C-in-C of the army, General Ayub Khan, in October 1958 was a turning point in Pakistan's history. Not only did it set a precedent of the army ousting civilian governments but led to an enhancement in the capability of the armed forces through increased budgetary allocations for defence expenditures. In 1960, defence accounted for 30 per cent of the total budgetary expenditure. This was further supplemented by the infusion of defence assistance from the US in the form of equipment and training of officers by the US.

A central organization known as Inter-Services Intelligence (ISI) Directorate exists in addition to the intelligence agencies of each service to develop and implement strategies to counter internal as well as external threats. The ISI gained eminence after its active participation in the Afghan war under the Zia regime, and for its involvement in political activities in the 1990s and later under the Musharraf government. In relation to Afghanistan and India in particular, the ISI is perceived to play an exceptionally crucial role, sometimes even overruling the established chain of command. The DG ISI is appointed by the prime minister, generally on the advice of the army chief, and is invariably a senior serving general. The ISI however operates under the army C-in-C although as a joint services body it ought to come under the command of the chairman of the Joint Chiefs of Staff.

The period 1958–71 was marked by the control of the military as the heads of the state in that period were both army chiefs. The 1962 Constitution, which was enacted by Ayub Khan himself, had devolved the powers of acting president to the speaker of the National Assembly but this provision was flagrantly violated in March 1969 when power was handed over by Ayub Khan to General Yahya Khan, the army chief.

The loss of East Pakistan in 1971 and the detention of 92,000 prisoners of war (largely from the army) by India was the first blow to the prestige of the army. Within the army, the younger officers did not want Yahya Khan to continue in power and forced him to hand over the presidency and the office of Chief Martial Law Administrator to the democratically elected leader from West Pakistan, Zulfikar Ali Bhutto, leader of the PPP. The Simla agreement with India, which facilitated the release of these prisoners, added to the stature of the civilian prime minister and it was for the first time that the army was de facto brought under civilian control. Bhutto felt so confident of his position that he sacked the army and air force chiefs who had played a crucial role in bringing him to power.

This was the background against which the 1973 Constitution was enacted. Under the constitution, the principle of civilian control of the armed forces was fully established. The constitution gave control and command of the armed forces to the federal government. The prime minister is responsible for the allocation of the necessary resources to the defence ministry, to establish, expand, and/or re-organize institutions to ensure the coordinated application of such resources, ensuring the raising and development of armed forces commensurate with requirements, determining the resource requirements and priorities, and coordinating defence with domestic and external policies. The PM is assisted by the minister of state and minister of defence. A cabinet committee, the Defence Committee of the cabinet (DCC) headed by the prime minister, comprises the defence, finance, and interior ministers, the three service chiefs, and the chairman of the Joint Chiefs of Staff Committee (JCSC) is the most important body that makes assessments and plans for the fulfilment of defence policy which are reviewed by the DCC. As there is no secretariat for the DCC, in actual practice, the ministry of defence carries out this function. Joint operations planning, joint logistic planning, and joint training planning are carried out and reviewed by the Directorate General Joint Staff. The Strategic Plans Division (SPD) and the National Defence University function directly under the supervision of JCSC. The army chief plays a key role in the appointment of the president of the NDU as well as the head of the SPD.

The Constitution also provides parliamentary standing committees on defence affairs comprising members drawn from different political parties. The committees are entrusted with monitoring defence development and reviewing budget inputs. As discussed in Chapter 10, the performance of these committees leaves much to be desired.

It is another matter that the constitution was violated by Zulfikar Bhutto's own hand-picked army chief who he thought was so loyal and subservient that he would carry out his orders. This rude shock was an awakening to the civilian leadership that the army always acts as an institution and that personal affiliations did not matter much.

The 1979–88 period was once again a time of military rule. In the early stages, army officers were placed in key positions such as those of martial law administrators at the provincial level with the entire hierarchy stretching down to the district level. Although the offices of the commissioner and deputy commissioners continued to exist, they took orders from their counterparts in the parallel martial law administration. Martial law courts were established for speedy disposal of cases for violation of martial law. Public flogging was resorted to in certain cases which aroused resentment against military rule. This arrangement was reorganized when politicians were inducted into the government.

In October 1999, the army once again assumed power by deposing the elected Prime Minister Nawaz Sharif and installing the army chief, General Pervez Musharraf in power. The difference this time was that the president of the republic was allowed to remain as a figurehead, and the army chief became the chief executive, exercising the powers of prime minister as set out in the constitution. This time, there was no formal promulgation of martial law and the civilian institutions remained intact, fulfilling their normal responsibilities. It was only after a few years that General Musharraf assumed the office of the president and a strong presidential form of government was established. The constitutional issue that ended up in an open confrontation between the executive and the judiciary was whether the army chief in uniform could contest the general elections. The court was opposed to the idea, which prompted the president to declare a state of emergency. After the general elections of 2008, he had to resign from the office of president under threat of impeachment by the Pakistan Peoples Party and the Pakistan Muslim League-Nawaz, the two leading political parties.

PROFESSIONAL GROWTH OF THE MILITARY

The Pakistan Military Academy (PMA), the Command and Staff College, and the various other training establishments were given high priority and allocated resources to develop professionalism, leadership qualities, and skills. After serving for a few years and acquiring the rank of major, selected officers are sent to the Staff College at Quetta which provides an almost year-long course in tactics, administration, staff duties, and command functions. At least one joint exercise is conducted with officers of the air force and navy, along with several field exercises and a study tour abroad. At the apex of the training process is the National Defence University (NDU) which runs two courses. The first is a national defence course in which most participants are of brigadier or equivalent rank from other services and joint secretaries in the case of civilian administrators. The second is the war course in which most participants are of colonel or equivalent rank. Selection for either of these courses reflects positive attainments in the career of an officer. The NDU courses prepare officers for planning at the higher levels of national strategy, including national, economic, and political systems and related issues that widen the worldview of military officers.

The entire training system comprises specialty arms schools/colleges, special warfare/skills courses, and advanced learning institutions. The aim of the Junior Leaders Academy is to train non-commissioned officers to become an integral link between officers and troops. The guiding philosophy of training is to achieve excellence in combat, which is translated into a system of continuing, pre-planned, skill-enhancing, targeted training courses through the life cycle of an officer and the lower ranks.

Apart from the PMA and a wide variety of specialist training schools, a university—the National University of Science and Technology (NUST) in Islamabad with several affiliated colleges—has been established which caters primarily for the needs of the defence services in the fields of engineering, science, and technology.

In the case of the navy, all officer cadets spend a year and a half at the Pakistan Naval Academy, and on passing out they are appointed midshipmen which entails a further six months of training at sea. After qualifying at their final fleet examinations, they are commissioned as acting sub-lieutenants and sent to various branches of the navy. After allocation to the various branches, they continue their training at the Naval Engineering College or at the Supply and Secretariat Schools. Once this phase is completed, they undergo sea training for a year. Having completed this phase, each officer is entrusted with independent responsibilities. The training period for the various branches varies from four years for operations to four and a half years for the technical branches. After serving for a few years, the officers are sent to staff courses at the Pakistan Navy College, Lahore, or the Staff College, Quetta, or the Air War College, Karachi, or the Joint Staff College, Rawalpindi. A few mid-career officers are sent to the Quaid-i-Azam University (QAU) for defence study courses. Selected senior officers regularly undergo the war course at the NDU in Islamabad. Most senior captains and commodores attend the coveted defence studies course. Some of them are sent to various suitable training institutions.

Very high standards of training have acquired a very important place on the priority list of the Pakistan Air Force (PAF) with emphasis on technical advances. The initial selection of candidates is extremely strict. Of about 1500 applicants for various branches, only 300 or so are selected.

The PAF picks candidates at an early age. After having passed their intermediate examinations, candidates undergo a selection process which is conducted by the Inter Services Selection Board.

The selected candidates then undergo five and a half years of rigorous professional training at the PAF College, Risalpur. For pilot cadets, the attrition rate is set very high. Up to 65 per cent fail to meet the rigid requirements for flying, but they can then choose other branches of the air force. After completing their training at PAF College, the successful candidates are posted to Mianwali for advanced tactical training to become fighter pilots. Of 100 candidates only 15–20 survive the rigours of this training. After qualifying, most of them are posted to various squadrons. After having served for a few years, some are selected for training at the Combat Command School at Sargodha, where, for five months, they learn the finer techniques of air combat. Those who excel are often retained for two years as instructors.

The College of Aeronautical Engineering, established in 1965, provides training in avionics, engineering, aerospace engineering, industrial engineering, and humanities and social sciences. A Transport Conversion Squadron trains pilots, navigators, flight engineers, loadmasters, and scanners to work with a range of aircraft.

In 1993–94, a basic staff school was set up in Peshawar to hold three-month courses for flying officers and flight lieutenants. In addition, a College of Staff Studies, established in the early 1970s, offers courses to flight lieutenants and squadron leaders. Senior officers are selected to attend a war course at the PAF Air War College to prepare them for the assumption of key command and staff appointments. Many higher rank officers are sent to the National Defence University for a year's comprehensive training. In the PAF, emphasis is placed on training through operational exercises. These help senior officers to evaluate the operational readiness of the service and also to evolve new concepts. Training in the PAF is not only accorded a very high priority but is a continuing process for both officers and airmen, regardless of the role they play.

There has been international recognition of the capabilities and effectiveness of Pakistan's armed forces. They have been invited to participate in UN peacekeeping operations where they have made significant contribution. Saudi Arabia, Jordan, the UAE, and other countries have on many occasions called upon them to assist in combat and noncombat training and organizational development of their own forces. The Pakistan training establishment receives military officers from over 50 countries around the world each year.

The high degree of professionalism and investment in human resources by the armed forces has been widely acknowledged by civilian leaders, scholars, analysts, and outside observers. Even the most vocal detractors of the military agree with this assessment.

On human resource development in the military, the former Prime Minister, Shaukat Aziz,[1] recorded his impressions in a book in the following words:

The Military has a professional meritocratic system for hiring and promoting officers. I witnessed this first hand when President Musharraf invited me, as Prime Minister, to attend the Army's Promotion Board. Even coming from the corporate world and seeing internal human resource processes in many leading private companies, I was impressed. The Army's system of promotion is professional, transparent, and merit driven. Every proposed case was discussed in various independent committees and there was a frank debate about each candidate. The Military also has a rigorous system of managed attrition, operating on a strict pyramid structure, where at each level, people are let go instead of automatically progressing. Reviewing the HR and personnel processes in civilian institutions would be useful and relevant aspects of the Military's process could be adapted.

He goes on to add: 'the Military became distinguished by its discipline, efficiency, and structure and perceived as a respectable career path which treats its soldiers well post-retirement.' According to him, the military—collectively comprising the army, air force, the navy, the intelligence agencies—has since developed into one of the strongest and most effective institutions. Similar sentiments are expressed by other scholars who have studied the Pakistan military. Shuja Nawaz[2] has commented: '[the] Pakistan Army also kept itself adapting and preparing for the new challenges. After the Tehrik Taliban Pakistan (TTP) became a strong force in the FATA, the Army made changes in equipping its combat and supporting arms. With the capability to force the counter insurgency (COIN).'

According to Nawaz, the army made a rapid shift after the Swat operation by introducing COIN training at the Pakistan Military Academy, the School of Infantry and Tactics, and made it a part of the syllabus at the Command and Staff College and National Defence University.[3] While the army still retains its conventional force structure and approach vis-à-vis India, its arch rival and neighbour, it appears to have used the insurgency to rotate its forces in and out of FATA and Swat in such a way as to expose most of its regular troops to irregular warfare. The Frontier Corps (FC) is being trained by US trainers at Warsak in KP, and this is being supplemented with overseas courses for officers.

Mahmud Ali Durrani, a former diplomat and a retired general, describes the institution in the following terms:

The army is not the monolith it is normally perceived to be. No, the army is a collection of people who come from all kinds of backgrounds. This collection may have someone like me who studied at an English medium school run by Christian missionaries and it may have someone from Toba Tek Singh who studied at a government school. The army does put you in a straitjacket; it gives you discipline and provides you with a perspective on geopolitics but the individual thoughts developed at school and home stay with you. It is because of the discipline that people in the army do not voice their personal feelings and follow the given line or narrative. The military is not as hard-line today as it was in 1948 or 1965. Subtle changes have come about; if all the other institutions fail then the army goes in to control the situation. It is going in on the invitation of the federal government or the provincial governments in aid of civilian powers.[4]

Anatol Lieven[5] dwells upon the reason for the relative strength of the army as an institution:

> In fact, one reason why the army is by far the strongest institution in Pakistan is that it is the only one in which its real internal content, behaviour, rules, and culture match more or less its official, outward form. Or to put it any other way, it is the only Pakistani institution which actually works as it is officially meant to—which means that it repeatedly tries something that it is not meant to, which seized power from its weaker and more confused sister institutions.

One of the topics in Pakistan that is widely discussed is the personality of the chief of army staff. In recent years, the exit of General Raheel Sharif has attracted much comment. A group of commentators was critical of his exposure to the media and the wide publicity given to him and his activities by the ISPR. It is in this context that Imtiaz Gul[6] provides a useful insight about the relative importance of individuals and institutions in the army:

> General Sharif's exit may ease off pressures that had hamstrung the government, yet it resonates an unambiguous message to the political leadership: individuals don't matter for institutions. It is their collective wisdom, professionalism, and commitment that keeps the institutions evolving. The system keeps throwing up leadership through the consultative process that is known as the Corps/Formation commanders' conference. General Sharif's conduct offers some soul-searching for the civilian leadership; rather than scheming and intriguing, let us focus on the job that the voters and the institutions place on you.

MILITARY INTERVENTIONS AND TAKEOVERS

This very high degree of professionalism and efficiency is also believed to be the principal factor behind the ouster of weak civilian governments by the army chiefs at various points of time. The armed forces have seized governance in Pakistan and directly ruled it four times since Independence. Ayub Khan (1958–69) assumed power after seven civilian governments were unable to maintain a coalition between 1951 and 1958. Yahya Khan (1969–71) was chosen to the government by Ayub Khan. Zia ul-Haq (1977–88) dismissed the elected government of Z. A. Bhutto in the wake of charges of rigging the elections that were levelled by the opposition. Pervez Musharraf (1999–2007) refers to his takeover as 'being thrust into power'[7] because Prime Minister Nawaz Sharif dismissed him from the office of army chief while he was abroad and did not allow his plane to land in Pakistan. Earlier, a previous chief had been forced to resign and, therefore, on this occasion the top army command considered this act as an affront to the dignity and morale of the armed forces in the face of which the generals moved in to oust the Sharif government and install Musharraf as Chief Executive.

Lieutenant General Mahmud Ahmed, in an interview with Shuja Nawaz, has stated that had General Musharraf not been prematurely replaced on 12 October 1999, 'then 12th October would have been another day like 11th October before, like 10th October was, like 9th October was'. Musharraf characterized his generals' actions as a counter-coup against Sharif's coup against him. The fact however remains that whatever the motivations there have been for these coups, the military has led Pakistan for a total of 32 of the 70 years of its existence, casting a heavy shadow over its history as a nation. A large number of books, treatises, and articles have analysed the reasons for this direct and indirect political intervention by the Pakistan Armed Forces. These can be summed up as follows:

1. The armed forces emerged as a superior, disciplined, and highly professional organization and continued to hone their efficiency and skills.
2. The political institutions remained entangled in continuing wrangling and became weak over time and some of them enlisted the support of the military to dislodge their adversaries.
3. The civilian institutions were mired in corruption, nepotism, and favouritism, resulting in wide disaffection and dissatisfaction among the public at large with the state of governance.

4. In the absence of an organized and informed civil society, there was very little public outrage.

5. The relatively improved economic performance during the three military regimes, of Ayub, Zia, and Musharraf, compared favourably with the dismal performance of the civilian leaders.

6. The periods preceding the army takeovers were characterized by political instability of the civilian governments in power.

7. The US and Western nations found it convenient to deal with a strongman rather than a group of bickering politicians who could not deliver on their commitments.

A more sceptical view about the military takeovers is expressed by several scholars. In the opinion of Monshipour and Samuel:

> For the most part, military rulers have been the final arbiters of Pakistan's destiny. Dominated by Punjabis and representing the landed and industrial interests, the military regards its dominance of Pakistan politics not only as a right but as a duty based on the need to safeguard the territorial integrity of the country in the face of lingering ethnic, linguistic, and religious fissures.[8]

Aqil Shah[9] thinks that Bhutto, by 'letting the institution of military off the hook at a time when there was direct public support for holding the generals accountable, reinforced officers' presumption of impunity'.

The central argument is that the military's tutelary beliefs and norms, a legacy of its formative experience under conditions of geopolitical insecurity and nation building problems, have profoundly shaped its political interventions and influence by justifying the authoritarian expansion of its role in state and society. Security threats and crises can subdue civilians and pass all powers to the generals.

In another piece he refers, like many other critics of the Pakistan Army, to its corporate interests:

> The military's corporate identity and interests are linked to projecting itself as Pakistan's only saviour against the evil designs of India. The military high

command's apparent patronage of LeT, JM etc. certainly signal its resolve to keeping the pot boiling in Kashmir in the future hope that the international community will take the bait.[10]

A more benign view on this subject is expressed by Talbott and Cohen in their books. Ian Talbott[11] attributes the military's taste for power in the following way: 'The civilian dependence on the military to provide internal security had already enabled the men in uniform to renew their taste for power and drew them back into politics.'

Stephen Cohen also articulates similar views:[12]

The very fact of calling in the military implies civilian incompetence or a failure to apply corrective measures before things get out of hand. Is the military obligated continually to rescue civilian politicians and administration for their own mistakes[?] Does the military dare to pick and choose the times when it will provide support, and if it does, will it make the government dependent on them[?]

The government's reliance on the army, either to perform tasks within the civil sphere or bailing out the civilian leadership from transient governmental crises emboldened them.

The question that then arises is: When military dictators are welcomed so warmly upon assumption of power, why do they all meet the same fate?

Mancur Olson[13] ascribes the downfall of the military dictators in Pakistan to the following factors:

a) In order to gain legitimacy they adopted the tactics of coercing or co-opting some of the same political leaders whom they had discredited in the first instance, thus losing the raison d'etre for their intervention.

b) There was a gap between the heightened expectations of the people and the state's capacity to deliver as the same elite class now extended to include high-ranking military officials benefiting from economic growth.

c) There were increased external pressures to reinstate democracy in Pakistan as violations of human rights and suppression of civil liberties became commonplace under these regimes.

d) The military used these periods to strengthen and consolidate their grip on power by inducting serving and retired officers in civilian institutions giving rise to resentment by those directly affected.

e) Accountability was promised by every single rule but became a selective tool for rewarding those who crossed over to support the regime and penalize those who remained opposed to it.

In recalling the history of Pakistan's military's rise and fall on four different occasions, their unpopularity and people's discontentment can be traced to a variety of exogenous and endogenous factors. The popular myth that it is manipulation by the US, which is largely responsible for both their coming to and exiting power, is simply a myth. There is hardly any evidence to corroborate this 'conspiracy theory' explanation. It is, however true that the Bush administration, with Condoleezza Rice in the lead, made efforts to bring about a compromise that would let Benazir Bhutto return to Pakistan to contest elections with Musharraf remaining in office as president.

Ayub's political fortunes took a nosedive because of the 1965 war with India and the perceived rise of income inequality between East and West Pakistan. Yahya Khan was forced to relinquish power because of the loss of East Pakistan in 1971. Zia ul-Haq died accidentally but his zealous pursuit of the Islamization of Pakistan and severe restrictions on established political parties had led to popular movements against him. Pervez Musharraf lost power due to his confrontation with the judiciary which precipitated into a nationwide movement led by lawyers against his continued rule.

Anwar Syed advances the following reasoning for the downfall of the military dictators:

A military coup d'etat is inherently illegitimate. The law regards it as treason. A coup maker may have done his deed in a spirit of righteousness. His action may initially be met with general approval. But as time goes and it transpires that he is unable to deliver the good things he had promised he falls in public esteem and encounters a general disapproval of his right to govern. As this process of public disenchantment with him goes on, he is shaken and he becomes ambivalent and indecisive. His will to act forcefully to counter adversity may be breaking.[14]

What of future takeovers? Since 2008, there have been constant murmurings as well as a yearning from certain quarters and certain sections of the media about the army removing the corrupt and incompetent politicians who have made such a mess of Pakistan. However, Shuja Nawaz[15] is correct in asserting that:

...extenuating circumstances today have made it difficult for direct army take over. The composition of the army today better represents the society in which it operates than the army at independence. It has also [become] more professional and better trained than ever before. It now represents a broader range of the country's rapidly urbanizing population. The emergence of a new and vibrant mass media and public discourse has also challenged the military's ability to rule the country with an iron hand. Control, when applied, can only work temporarily. Today's emerging technologies have introduced ways of bypassing authoritarianism.[16]

However, a contrarian viewpoint is espoused by Ayesha Siddiqa,[17] who believes that the military has developed a vested interest which would discourage the armed forces from allowing democratic institutions to function, 'and since its economic enterprise has been constructed on the basis of its economic power, further encouragement for the military to enhance its economic power would lead to increasing its entrenchment in politics'.

The assertion above needs to be dissected. First, empirical evidence shows that the claim of the military's large economic enterprise is highly exaggerated, as shown later in this chapter. It pales into insignificance in comparison with the conglomerates owned by other leading Pakistani private sector tycoons. Second, every government, elected or authoritarian, has been equally well-disposed towards the foundations and trusts which own these enterprises because their proceeds are utilized for the welfare of the soldiers and their families. This burden-sharing by the foundations relieves the government of its obligation to provide these services to this segment of retirees from its own budgetary resources. Third, the cost of disrupting the orderly process of democratic governance for the sake of an illusory and unfounded fear of curtailment of its economic power far exceeds the profits to be made by the military or officers belonging to this cadre. The allotment of urban and agricultural land and other perks enjoyed by these officers would continue unabated irrespective of the nature of the government in power.

EVOLUTION OF PAKISTAN'S DEFENCE POLICY

In a country where there is barely a national consensus on any major issue, there has been one policy on which all political leaders of different persuasions have agreed, i.e. to ward off the threat that India presents and strengthening the defence services with the requisite resources for this. Similarly, the nuclear programme has received continuing and overwhelming support from successive governments in Pakistan without any questions being asked. Under the most adverse circumstances and severe resource constraints, the armed forces have received consistent financial support. They have not only steadily grown but kept pace with modern developments, including the development of domestic capability in nuclear, missile, weapon, and aircraft technology.

Pakistan's foreign policy has also been intertwined with its defence policy. The decision in the early 1950s to align with the US during the Cold War, followed by the close cooperation with the CIA in ousting of the Soviets from Afghanistan in the 1980s, and the 'war against terror' following 9/11 in the post-2001 period, were guided by Pakistan's desire to keep its defence forces strong and equipped with modern arms. That motivation arose from the threat perception of a much larger but unfriendly neighbour, i.e. India.

Pervaiz Iqbal Cheema explains this evolution in terms of the inherited asymmetry in compatibility between a much larger arch-rival India and a greater sense of insecurity on the part of the latter that led to the alliance with the US:

Pakistan inherited much of British India's external defence problems but with drastically lower defence capabilities. A combination of this and other factors were to make the strategic environment extremely depressing. First, for the British Indian government the main defence problem had concerned control and defence of NWFP. Second, Pakistan inherited extremely insecure borders. Pakistan emerged as an independent entity comprising two wings separated by large tracts of Indian Territory. The then East Pakistan was and is surrounded by India on all sides except for a small strip that borders Myanmar. Pakistan's inherited borders were not only very long but not properly demarcated. Third, the birth of two extremely hostile rather than friendly neighbours as a result of partition. Pakistan decided to align itself with the West to cope with Indian threats. India forged a close relationship with the Soviet Union. The subsequent arms race and the three wars the two countries fought, along with countless border clashes resulted from these alliances. A fourth factor was the behaviour and policies of Afghanistan towards Pakistan. On recognition of Durand Line as the official boundary between the two countries has been a source of major contention.[18]

The loss of East Pakistan in 1971 as a consequence of Indian intervention convinced the Pakistani leadership that the military's conventional strength was far less than a necessary counter (600,000 armed forces personnel vs. 1.2 million in India; 1.1 million active paramilitary personnel in India vs. 300,000 in Pakistan) and this pattern was likely remain so, merely because of the difference in the size of the two economies. India's domestic defence industries are able to produce rockets, mortars, anti-tank guns, anti-aircraft guns, long range and short range missiles, ships, and aircraft. This imbalance, coupled with the lead taken by India in 1974 through a nuclear test in Rajasthan, triggered an examination of various options by

Pakistan's defence establishment and political leadership. Their efforts to secure a protective nuclear umbrella from one of the existing major nuclear powers and for the promotion of the concept of a nuclear-free zone under the auspices of the UN failed. It was argued and agreed among the decision-makers that the only feasible way to keep an equilibrium between the two countries was to develop a nuclear capacity. They, therefore, embarked on a very difficult and time-consuming path of developing their own nuclear capability which culminated in a test on 28 May 1998 in response to the Indian testing of 11 and 13 May. Tensions with India had eased in the 1970s and 1980s following the Shimla Pact signed by Z. A. Bhutto and Indira Gandhi in 1974, but these could not be sustained. The high volatility of Indo-Pak relations provided ample justification for the pursuit of this objective. The revival of a populist movement in Kashmir against India in 1989 once again witnessed an upsurge in the tensions in the 1990s as India blamed Pakistani non-state actors as being responsible for inciting violence in Kashmir.

Some critics of the Pakistan Army consider this response to be arising either from a sense of embattlement or paranoia: 'The sense of strategic disadvantage and embattlement has been with the Pakistani military from the start. Relative size and geography have contributed greatly to the sense of danger, often spilling over into paranoia, which characterizes the Pakistani security establishment.'

Ahmed Rashid adds weight to this line of thinking:

The narratives that have seeped into the national psyche decree the army must maintain a permanent state of enmity with India; controlling influence in Afghanistan and the deployment of Islamic extremists or non-state actors as a tool of foreign policy in the region; and it commands a lion's share of the national budget alongside its control of Pakistan's nuclear weapons. U.S. attempts to change this course with either carrots or sticks are rebuffed while the civilian government cowers in the background.[19]

A similar view is espoused by Hussain Haqqani in his book: 'The focus on building an ideological state has caused Pakistan to lag behind in almost all areas that define a functional modern state ... The military has sought the US support by making itself useful for the concerns of the moment while continuing to strengthen the Mullah-Military alliance.'[20]

The current situation—in which the Pakistan Armed Forces are overstretched in defending the borders with India and Afghanistan while at the same time also conducting counter-terrorism operations within the country—would dictate that its defence policy will continue to remain intertwined with its foreign policy. Much to the dismay of those who feel that the latter should be the exclusive domain of the foreign office, the political realities in the current circumstances do not permit this. After all, the Pentagon and CIA have equal weight in the foreign policy-making process in the US as the State Department and the Treasury have.

CIVIL–MILITARY RELATIONS

There is no other topic that is debated as hotly and fiercely in Pakistan than that of civil-military relations, particularly when state power resides with elected democratic governments. The 1990s were characterized as the rule of the Troika: the president, prime minister, and the army chief. The post-2008 period is termed, among many other labels, with that of co-governance. The proponent of this term, Talat Husain,[21] believes that Pakistan is even at present not fully under civilian control, and has a semi-civilian rule. He postulates that:

> From carrying out national census to securing cricket stadiums, from holding national elections to convincing foreign governments that good things are happening in Pakistan—so much is left to the army that it practically co-governs this country besides running its defence and foreign policy.

He goes on to explain his thesis in terms of the:

> unwillingness of civilian governments to carry out painful but much needed institutional reforms to strengthen the civilian supremacy. The public

argument that all governments have to do this because the army is too powerful is primarily a ruse to hide incompetence and sheer laziness in carrying the institutional reform needed to reduce dependence on the army. As a result, the ... government is as dependent on General Bajwa as it was on General Raheel and General Kayani. Similarly, the PPP leadership is as keen to please the army leadership in good humor as the PTI leaders are in playing the khaki gallery. Other parties have similar scores on this board.

The popular narrative is that it is the military which has stifled the growth of democratic institutions in Pakistan. Aqil Shah,[22] for instance, believes that the:

> expansive professional development of the military [has] inculcated a belief that they should take over the governance of the country if needed. The military's corporate identity and interests are linked to projecting itself as Pakistan's only saviour against the evil designs of India. The military high command's apparent patronage of LeT, JM etc certainly signal its resolve to keeping the pot boiling in Kashmir in the future hope that the international community will take the bait.

These variable explanations of the domination of the military in Pakistan are unsatisfactory. While ambitions of individual generals in assuming power cannot be discounted, the counter-view is that the fractious politics of Pakistan, unprincipled political competition, lack of intra-party democracy, advancement of personal and parochial interests of the leaders, partisan use of state patronage, and the dynastic nature of political leadership have also played an equally important part. In between 1951 and 1958, Pakistan witnessed six different prime ministers and cabinets. General elections were held only in East Pakistan in 1954. The frequent changes in party loyalties led to political instability and the framing of Constitution of the new country was delayed for almost nine years. Ayub Khan in his book justifies the military coup of October 1958 in the following terms: 'The Army could not remain unaffected by the conditions around it. Nor was it conceivable that officers and men would not react to all the political chicanery, intrigue, corruption, and inefficiency manifest in every sphere of life.'[23]

Moeed Yusuf has a more balanced view to offer. He believes the civilian-political enclave continues to side-track the issue by suggesting that the military has never accorded them the space to act independently. This may be true in the domain of security and foreign policy but to argue that the military forced the civilian governments to produce poor economic and social outcomes, which encouraged corruption under civilian rule and pressured the politicians to maintain a non-transparent developmental model is absurd.[24]

In a similar vein, Babar Sattar compares the civilian and military institutions and gives his reasons for the army's influence in the country's affairs:

> The reason an army chief wields the power and influence that he wields is that he sits atop a well-oiled, resourceful, and functional institution which focuses on merit, training, and human resource development, wherein self-correction and new ideas come along with succession planning and regular change of guard. The perennial problem of Pakistan has been its failure to develop functional and accountable institutions of governance and service delivery in the civilian side.[25]

In another article, Babar Sattar[26] poses a very basic question: whether the Pakistan Army enjoys a supra-constitutional role to keep the civilian institutions under control. He goes on to clarify that the army is not a countervailing institution but is a subset of the executive branch of the state:

> The idea of civilian control of the military is anathema to many who imagine the army as a supra-constitutional body meant to keep constitutional institutions in check. Notwithstanding that the constitution is the source of all authority and the only authority a state institution can claim to wield is that vested in it by law, some still view the army's ability (and willingness) to use brute force within the country as a self-legitimizing

reality ... The executive, judiciary, and the legislature are the three pillars of state. The military is a subset of the executive. But the distance in our constitutional journey that remains to be covered can be gauged from the fact that we view the civilian government as the executive and the army as an independent countervailing institution. To bridge the gap and antagonism between the civilian and military arms of the government, we must address the process of identity formation in which the civilian is stigmatized as the 'other'.

The Pakistan military's development, discipline, and functionality surpass that of civilian institutions. The military can be the stabilizer in situations where Pakistan might otherwise falter being a weak state.[27]

Mazhar Aziz,[28] in the vein of Siddiqa Agha, Aqil Shah, and others, asserts that the military coups in Pakistan were aimed at protecting and extending the institutional interests of the military and were not a response to political mismanagement or corruption. He believes that the military has come to identify itself with the state rather than see itself as just one of the key components of a constitutional state. A powerful military has penetrated and exercised control over political developments and arrogated to itself the task of nation-building.

A former president of the National Defence University presents the perspective from the military's viewpoint:

The military and civilian leadership should share similar perspectives on fundamental matters of national interests, threat perception, and response parameters. If this is not the case, affability between the two institutions can vanish instantly. In Pakistan, the concerns of the military are generally the same as those of any informed and patriotic citizen. It is also difficult to discern if the military entered the political arena by intent or by default. Forgoing [sic] in view, the judiciary had to legitimize the non-democratic forces to avoid chaos in the country. The international climate at the time and continuous division among the politicians allowed the military to remain in power longer than needed. This proved to be damaging to the growth of genuine democracy and its long-term dividends in the country.[29]

He then goes on make a list of suggestions of things which would cement the relations between the two institutions, including greater use of the cabinet committee on national security to reduce dissonance over internal and foreign policies. He also pleads that 'those who lead the country cannot be unscrupulous, corrupt, or power-hungry. The articulation of national interests should be worked out by the parliament which also ensures civilian control of military authorities.'

The above viewpoint needs to be further parsed. 'National interest' can be articulated by the elected political rulers as they have been entrusted with this power by the people of Pakistan. However, it should be debated in the legislatures, discussed by civil society, and arbitrated in case of conflict by the judiciary. The practical difficulty with such an idealistic approach is that the term itself does not remain static and changes with the passage of time. Repeating such a laborious exercise at different intervals of time defies both logic and reason.

As the views on this subject are extremely varied and polarized, it would be fair to conclude that Hasan Askari's characterization is a more apt description of the current state of civil–military relations in Pakistan:

Pakistan represents a civil–military hybrid where an elected civilian government rules but it cannot command the political system to the exclusion of the top military brass, which exercises clout over policymaking from the side-lines.

Governance involves balancing the imperatives of participatory democracy and good governance with the pressures of national security. External security pressures and internal political and social incoherencies, rampant extremism and an incessant use of violence by competing politico-religious interests. Periodic civilian demands on the military to undertake tasks outside of its professional domain to aid civilians leads to a leadership crisis resulting in incoherence and inaction and personal preferences of the rulers.[30]

DEFENCE EXPENDITURE

One of the popular explanatory hypotheses about Pakistan's lagging economic and social performance is the garrison state or security state syndrome. As a smaller country in relation to its perpetual arch-rival India, with which it has fought four wars since 1947, it has had to spend an exceptionally high percentage of its budgetary resources on building up its defence capability. Military alliance with the US since the 1950s was also motivated by the consideration that the superpower would provide modern equipment and weapons to its ally. Acquisition of nuclear capability was also part of this strategy. As a consequence, resources that ought to have been spent on human development—education, health, and other social sectors—have been diverted to fund defence spending. There was a trade-off between development spending and defence (the typical guns vs butter problem discussed in economics textbooks) in the face of scarce resources which was resolved in favour of defence. This is an unproductive form of expenditure which does not contribute to economic growth and social development. That is a primary reason why Pakistan has fared poorly. Defence spending was quite high during the period 1950–90 and touched 7.3 per cent of the GDP in 1988.

The annual growth rates of defence expenditure for the two periods, 1950–90 and 1990–2015 are, however, quite divergent. The fastest GDP growth in Pakistan was during the 1950–90 period, when defence expenditure was growing at the very rapid pace of 9 per cent annually, while the period that recorded a slowdown in defence spending, 3 per cent annually, was the same when the GDP growth rate fell much below its long term trajectory. The 4.3 per cent GDP growth rate for 1990–2015 masks the contribution of the impressive 6.6 per cent annual growth rate registered between 2003 and 2007. Excluding those four years, the average falls below 4 per cent. Ironically, it was the military government under President Musharraf that brought down defence spending from 3.3 per cent of GDP in FY 2002 to 2.7 per cent in FY 2008 and increased development spending from 2.1 per cent to 5 per cent during that period.

Table 11.1: Growth rates of Defence Spending and GDP

	Annual growth rate of Defence expenditure (percentage)	Annual growth rate of GDP
1950–1990	9.0	5.9
1990–2015	3.0	4.3
1950–2015	5.4	4.8

Source: Economic Survey of Pakistan (various years)

During Zia ul-Haq's rule, there was a huge increase in defence spending—9 per cent of the GDP a year—with development spending at a meagre 3 per cent. By 1987, 8 per cent of the GDP spent on defence had overtaken development spending. Following the Soviet withdrawal from Afghanistan, defence spending dropped by 26.8 per cent of public expenditure in the 1980s to an average of 19.3 per cent for the years 2008–2015 according to World Development Indicators.

There are a number of conflicting numbers floating around with regard to defence spending. Depending upon the predilection of the author and the point he wishes to prove, several variants are presented with adjustments and assumptions creating confusion in the mind of the lay reader or viewer. The exclusion of military pensions from military expenditure is advanced as an example to conceal and understate the true expenditure. When it is pointed out that this is to conform to public accounting standards, fingers are raised on the actual motives behind it. Some observers have also alleged that some components of defence are also hidden under different heads to escape public attention. Very few know that defence expenditure is audited by officers of the Military Accounts Service, who are selected through the Central Superior Services examinations like all other civil servants, and form an independent cadre under the control of the Auditor General of Pakistan; a constitutional position. The expenditure series presented in Table 11.2 is based on the audited accounts and are reported in the annual budget documents and annually reproduced in the *Economic Survey of Pakistan*. Any attempt to tamper with this series is likely to introduce an element of subjective bias and should therefore be avoided.

Table 11.2: Defence Expenditure, Social Spending, and Development

End June	Defence		Health and Education		Development Spending	
	% of GDP	% of Total expend-iture	% of GDP	% of Total expend-iture	% of GDP	% of Total expend-iture
1960	5.8	28.3	1.3	6.2	10.3	49.8
1970	5.8	22.6	1.6	6.3	14.8	58.1
1980	5.4	23.1	2.1	8.9	9.3	39.9
1990	6.9	26.5	3.3	12.7	6.5	25.3
2000	4.0	21.5	2.0	10.7	2.5	13.5
2010	2.5	12.5	2.3	11.3	4.1	20.4
2015	2.5	13.0	2.9	14.8	4.0	20.7

Source: Economic Survey of Pakistan (various years)

Comparing the defence spending with that of education and health, the picture is almost identical. The ratio of defence expenditure to GDP has been consistently high during the first 40 years and that of education and health was much below that of defence. The defence–GDP ratio has now fallen to 2.5 per cent of the GDP, almost a third of what it was in the 1990s. Most of the nuclear-related expenditure was incurred in the 1970s and 1980s. In FY 2016, the budgetary allocation for health and education was 2.9 per cent[31] and the budgetary allocation for 2016–17 is 3.7 per cent, which is higher than that of defence and internal security. In the education and health sectors, the impediments to delivery of these services are issues concerning governance and management rather than budgetary allocations. It is true that development expenditure has declined from the 1970s, when the public sector commanded the heights of the economy but there are cogent reasons for this decline. As the private sector has entered the telecommunications sector (the monopoly of PTCL was broken), the energy sector (IPPs were allowed to set up generation plants), and highways and motorways (through public-private partnership), their investment previously listed under a public sector development programme now forms part of private investment. Organizations such as Water and Power Development Authority (WAPDA), National Highway Authority (NHA), Frontier Works Organization (FWO), and National Logistic Cell (NLC) provide partial financing from their own resources for development spending. This structural change is naturally reflected in a lower ratio of development expenditure/GDP compared to the past trends. However, it is heartening that after the 7th NFC, which enhanced the share of the provinces in the divisible tax pool, a gradual rise is observable in the health and education allocation and the development budget in general.

MILITARY BUSINESSES

A popular myth that has now become quite entrenched and accepted as the truth concerns the large corporate interests of the military. It is factually accurate that the military has foundations and trusts that run enterprises, but the proceeds and profits they earn are utilized for the welfare of the army pensioners, the families of soldiers who retire at an early average age of 45 to 50, and those who have lost their lives in combat, the *shaheed*. The education and healthcare of their families are financed by the income generated by these foundations and trusts.

Fauji Foundation was set up in 1967 to provide welfare services to retired soldiers and their families. The justification for setting it up was that about three-fourths of Pakistan Army officers and soldiers retire young, after 23 years of service, at an average age of 45. By setting up businesses, their training and experience is utilized by the foundations and trusts. However, professionals in their respective areas of business are also employed by the foundation as these companies have to compete with others in the same sector. The net profits from the enterprises are utilized for the welfare of the soldiers and their families. The military businesses play a central role in boosting the morale and fighting spirit of the soldiers who are assured that they and their immediate families will receive excellent services even after they retire from service or are killed in action. The effect has been to make the military—a voluntary service—very attractive indeed for many ordinary Pakistanis and to ensure a high quality of recruitment.

By early 2010, over 2,000 Pakistani soldiers and para-military personnel had been killed. Also, the families of the men in active service are helped by the Welfare Trusts with assistance in the form of health care, recreational facilities, and the like.

The Fauji Foundation had earned dividends (their share of the appropriated profits) of about Rs 13.5 billion in 2016 from its enterprises out of which it spent Rs 11 billion for the welfare budget, Rs 1 billion on administrative expenses, and Rs 1 billion saved for future/new investments. Rs 0.5 billion were spent to fund corporate social responsibility activities such as public health and educational institutions outside the Forces. The welfare budget provides healthcare, education, and vocational training for the children and dependants of ex-servicemen and for parents, widows, and families of soldiers killed or disabled in action. It is estimated that the welfare services provided by the military foundations and trusts can potentially benefit 9.6 million people, or 7 per cent of Pakistan's total population.

In 2015, the Foundation ran 11 hospitals, 103 medical centres, dispensaries and mobile dispensaries, 104 schools, 2 colleges, and 77 technical and vocational training centres. It also provided Rs 3.5 million stipends to the children of soldiers. It also runs a private university, with a proportion of funded places for the children of ex-servicemen.

The Army Welfare Trust (AWT) has total assets of Rs 50 billion ($590 million) and owns, among other things, 16,000 acres of farmland, rice and sugar mills, cement plants, and an insurance company. There have been, in the past, both poor investment choices by the AWT and also operational lapses. This however, happens in all enterprises engaged in business. Some of the losses of AWT enterprises were squared off by disposing of plots of land owned by it. The management of some of the AWT enterprises has not been at par with that of the Fauji Foundation which is more professionally run. It would be advisable for the GHQ to review the performance of the AWT in relation to operational autonomy, composition of the boards, competencies of the staff, and the market niche in which these enterprises are operating. It would be quite acceptable if the cement sector was faring poorly and the AWT cement plant was making losses but if the banking sector is faring well but the AWT equivalent company is losing money, then hard questions should be asked about the latter's performance. The AWT was quite right in divesting many of its holdings and, more recently, offloading Askari Commercial Bank which has been bought over by the Foundation.

The AWT is much smaller in size and scope of business activities in comparison to the Foundation. It owns 18 enterprises but only one is a public listed company, i.e. Askari General Insurance. Two are unlisted public companies (MAL Pakistan and Askari Securities Ltd), four are private limited companies (Askari Aviation, Askari Guards, Askari Enterprises, and Fauji Security Services). The remaining seven are business units and, apart from the sugar mill, would fall in the medium enterprise category. Similarly, the air force has set up Shaheen Foundation and the navy the Bahria Foundation on the same lines. Shaheen Foundation has 11 enterprises, mostly in services sector such as airport services, education, medical, commercial and residential real estate, etc. Bahria Foundation, a charitable trust, owns 15 businesses, principally real estate development and construction, maritime services, boat-building, specialized paints, and security services. Neither of them belong in the same league in terms of assets as the AWT.

Defence housing authorities have also sprung up in all the major cities of Pakistan with large tracts of urban land allotted to them by the provincial boards of revenue or the Military Lands and Cantonment Directorate. Officers of the defence forces are allotted plots at lower than market prices which they sell at a premium. Similar housing schemes have also been set up by the navy and the air force.

Fauji Foundation's assets have grown from Rs 52 million ($11 million) in 1970, to Rs 342 billion ($3.28 billion) in 2015. The foundation operates 18 enterprises, four of them fully owned (Fauji Cereals, Foundation Gas, Overseas Employment Services, and FF Seed Multiplication Farm). 14 are associated companies, of which six are public listed companies (Fauji Fertilizer, Fauji bin Qasim, Fauji Cement, Mari Petroleum, Askari Bank, Fauji Foods) and another 9 are public unlisted companies (two wind energy projects, three power generation plants, two marine terminals, one cement factory, and one joint venture in Morocco). The total investment in these nine projects amount to slightly above $1 billion.

The total market capitalization in November 2016 of all the listed companies owned by Fauji Foundation, Army Welfare Trust, Shaheen Foundation, and Bahria Foundation was Rs 395.6 billion, i.e. 4.5 per cent of the total market capitalization of the companies listed on the Pakistan Stock Exchange (PSE). The largest company is Fauji Fertilizers (Rs 135 billion) followed by Mari Petroleum (115 billion), Fauji Cement (54 billion), Fauji bin Qasim (50 billion), Askari Bank (30 billion), Fauji Foods (10 billion), Askari General Insurance (1.5 billion), and Shaheen Insurance (400 million). It may be pointed out that there are many other shareholders in these public listed companies and the shares held by the Fauji Group itself would be approximately 60 to 70 per cent of this reported total.

These companies are the big players and everyone points fingers at them. Their major assets are in the fertilizer sector which is a highly competitive business both domestically and in terms of imports. All of them pay full taxes on their income, sales, and imports, and do not enjoy any exemptions or concessions of a preferential nature. The Fauji Group's net worth in 2015 was Rs 104 billion ($1 million), and it earned net profits amounting to Rs 27 billion ($265 million) or 6.7 per cent of profits after tax of all non-financial listed companies.[32] The Group paid Rs 178 billion ($1.7 million) in duties, taxes, and levies. Only the welfare activities are tax exempt, as is the case with all other charities in Pakistan. The Group employed 4,551 ex-servicemen and 7,972 civilians.[33]

Table 11.3: Growth in Assets of Fauji Foundation 1970–2015

1970	2005	2009	2015
Rs. 52 million	Rs 10 billion	Rs 125 billion	Rs. 342 billion

Source: Fauji Foundation Annual Reports 2005–2015

Ayesha Siddiqa has estimated that the military's private wealth could be as high as $20 billon: 10 billion in land and 10 billion in private military assets. This figure could not be verified despite efforts to gather information from various sources and cross-check them. Housing in the Defence societies is owned preponderantly by civilians with only a sprinkle of the original allottees from the armed forces. There must have been capital gains earned by the original allottees when they sold their plots and homes at market price. It is not possible to quantify these gains. There are varying estimations of the probable capital gains earned by the original allottees from the armed forces but the dynamics of the real estate market, non-availability of accurate data, and the timing of entry and exit make it difficult to even hazard any informed guesses. Those of us who have bought land or property in the Defence housing societies have equally benefited from this appreciation in the value. Whether the proportion of the civilians in capturing these gains is higher than that of the original military officers is again anyone's wild guess. Suffice it to say that the elites of Pakistan, which include both civilians and military personnel, have been the major beneficiaries of this windfall gain while the poor have been the losers from this flawed public policy.

Another argument advanced against the military businesses is that they are crowding out the private sector. First, as indicated earlier, their relative market share is too insignificant to displace the ten privately owned conglomerates which have a net worth higher or comparable to that of all the combined holdings of the military. However, in comparison to PIA—which is crowding out private airlines—or Pakistan Steel—which stunted the expansion of private steel mills—the effect of the military enterprises pales into insignificance. Fertilizer, cement, banking, oil and gas, energy, and cereals are all competitive sectors and to the extent that these enterprises are not given any special preferences or concessions relative to others, they may be contributing to capital formation in Pakistan in the form of their retained earnings and their creditworthiness in the debt market.

However, the role of two military organizations which have been actively engaged in the construction and transportation sector, i.e. the Frontier Works Organization (FWO) and the National Logistics Cell (NLC), needs

GOVERNING THE UNGOVERNABLE

to be reviewed. A level playing field should be provided to private sector contractors in accessing finance, providing bid and performance bonds, tax rates, regulatory oversight, and the like. No special concessions or privileges must be granted to the FWO and NLC.

FWO has successfully completed roads and highways in treacherous terrains such as the Karakoram Highway (KKH) and dangerous areas such as FATA, and they should continue to perform these functions. However, their prices should be driven by market conditions and determined by an independent board. For other civilian contracts, they should compete along with others and sole source awards to them should be avoided or made transparent for the underlying reasons. NLC was established in 1978 in response to a congestion problem at the Karachi Port. It then became a big player in the trucking industry and captured a significant market share.

Today, the NLC—a Rs 5 billion average annual revenue-earning enterprise—undertakes tasks ranging from the construction of mega-structures, to providing pragmatic logistics solutions, management of a chain of well-equipped dry ports and border terminals, and collection of toll revenue on national and provincial highways. Although it works under the Planning Commission, most of its personnel is drawn from the armed forces. It has responded very well in times of crises, such as earthquakes, floods, droughts, and other natural and manmade calamities. That being said, its core corporate activities and its other duties in times of emergency have to be separated. There should be no difference between the NLC vis-à-vis other private sector firms in terms of preferences or concessions. At least this perception should be addressed by making its corporate activities transparent in all its aspects. Competition would bring about lower cost to the end users, and promote the formation of private sector corporate entities, mergers and acquisitions to achieve scale, thus benefiting the economy. The NLC filled an important gap in the logistics value chain when it was needed but it is time to examine the rationale for its continuance in its present form as it might be hurting the growth of the railways and organized private trucking industry.

SUMMATION

The nature of civil–military relations is perhaps the most debated and controversial issue in Pakistan and abroad. The military has directly ruled for 32 years out of the 70 years of Pakistan's existence, under four different army chiefs and indirectly through the troika that included the army chief in the 1990s. The post-2008 period of restoration of democracy and the succession of two elected governments has not eased this uneasy relationship, creating uncertainty for investors and denting business confidence. I have to agree with what Shuja Nawaz had to say in his book *Crossed Swords* back in 2008 which remains true to this day:

> For the most part, military rulers have been the final arbiters of Pakistan's destiny. Dominated by Punjabis and representing the landed and industrial interests, the military regards its dominance of Pakistani politics not only as a right but as a duty based on the need to safeguard the territorial integrity of the country in the face of lingering ethnic, linguistic, and religious fissures. As past experience shows, when politicians run to the army chief for help, it upsets the balance of civilian system of government and eventually brings the army into power. Even Ayub Khan, the army man, learnt this lesson to his discomfiture. As did Z. A. Bhutto and Nawaz Sharif. If this cycle of a civilian interregnum followed by a period of military rule is to come to an end in Pakistan, the civilian politicians have to play their part faithfully and in national interest. If they do, then the army may play its part too and Pakistan may break out of this vicious cycle that has kept it from developing into a true democracy and a truly progressive nation.[34]

The other myth exploded in this chapter is that defence expenditures have crowded out social sector spending in particular and development expenditure in general. It is true that up to 1990 defence expenditure was inflicting a heavy cost on development expenditure and social spending but it has now fallen to under 3 per cent of GDP and constitutes less than 15 per cent of public expenditure but the growth performance in this period of declining defence spending has been dismal.

Another popular argument advanced is that the continuing military intervention is in order to defend, preserve, and expand their corporate business interests. Empirical evidence shows that they are competing in the sectors where there are several other conglomerates operating, their market capitalization is insignificant, and they are paying full taxes and duties just like other companies. In addition, they are supplementing government efforts by providing education and health facilities to millions of soldiers and their families.

NOTES AND REFERENCES

1. Aziz, S., *From Banking to the Thorny World of Politics* (Quartet, 2016).

2. Nawaz, S., *Crossed Swords* (OUP, 2008).

3. Idem, *Learning by Doing: The Pakistan Army's Experience with Counterinsurgency* (Atlantic Council, 2011).

4. Humayun, F., 'Interview of Mahmud Ali Durrani', *Dawn*, 28 July 2016.

5. Lieven, 'Pakistan: A Hard Country', *Public Affairs*, 2012.

6. Gul, I., 'The Sharif Exit', *Express Tribune*, 23 November 2016.

7. Musharraf, P., *In the Line of Fire* (Free Press, 2006).

8. Monashipour, M., Samuel, A., 'Development and Democracy in Pakistan', *Asian Survey*, xxxv, no. 11, November 1995.

9. Shah, A., *The Army and Democracy: Military Politics in Pakistan* (Harvard University Press, 2014).

10. Shah, A., 'Why do coups happen in Pakistan', *The Diplomat*, 31 August 2016.

11. Talbott, I., *Pakistan: A New History* (OUP, 2015).

12. Cohen, S., *The Pakistan Army* (OUP, 1998).

13. Olson, M., 'Dictatorship, Democracy and Development', *American Political Science Review* (3), September 1993.

14. Syed, A., 'Extremism on the Loose', *Dawn*, 8 April 2007. Accessed at: <https://www.dawn.com/news/1069994/dawn-opinion-april-08-2007>

15. Ibid.

16. Ibid.

17. Cheema, P. I., *The Armed Forces of Pakistan* (New York University Press, 2003).

18. Ibid.

19. Rashid, A., 'Ten Years of Rising Resentment', *International Herald Tribune*, 10–11 September 2011.

20. Haqqani, H., *Pakistan: Between Mosque and Military*, (Carnegie Endowment for International Peace, 2005).

21. Husain, T., 'Semi-civilian Rule', *The News*, 6 March 2017.

22. Shah, A., 'Why do coups happen in Pakistan', *The Diplomat*, 31 August 2016.

23. Khan, A., *Friends not Masters* (OUP, Karachi, 1967).

24. Moeed Yusuf.

25. Sattar, B., 'Is the Silly Season here?', *The News*, 14 May 2016. Accessed at: <http://tn.thenews.com.pk/print/119826-Is-the-silly-season-here>

26. Sattar, B., 'The Anti Climax', *The News*, 14 May 2017.

27. Ibid.

28. Aziz, M., *Military Control in Pakistan* (Routledge, 2008).

29. Khan, R. M., 'Bumpy Road to Stability', *The News*, 10 December 2016.

30. Rizvi, H. A., 'Civil Military Relations', *Express Tribune*, 17 October 2016.

31. Naviwala, N., *Pakistan's Education Crisis: The Real Story* (Woodrow Wilson Center, 2016).

32. All the data presented here is drawn from the annual reports of the Fauji Foundation, Army Welfare Trust, Shaheen Foundation, and Bahria Foundation.

33. The profits of Fauji Foundation of Rs 27 billion include those of the non-listed companies owned by the Foundation. Thus the actual profits of listed non-financial companies would be lower than Rs 27 billion. The data of profits for all non-financial listed companies is drawn from the State Bank of Pakistan's balance sheet analysis of non-financial companies 2011–2015.

34. Nawaz, S., *Crossed Swords* (Karachi: OUP, 2008).

12

The Religious Edifice

The critical role played by religion in Pakistani society raises a fundamental question of whether religion will facilitate Pakistan's onward journey towards economic and social development or retard it. Islam as a religion teaches us to lead a pious personal life, work hard, care for and reach out to the poor, and share a part of our wealth and income with the poor. As such, it can play a positive role. However, if religion is interpreted in a narrow, ritualistic sense that promotes isolation and withdrawal from the rest of the world, an inward-looking and insular mind-set, intolerance of others' points of view, and dogmatic beliefs, then the chances are that the country will lag behind the rest of the world and not benefit from the buoyant world economy.

Misbah Islam alludes to this tendency for the decline of Muslim states and societies:

> We believed in the notions of Kismet, predestination and ritual prayers so much, that it has affected all incentive and endeavours to improve. We have involved ourselves in intercessory conflicts and schisms that have sapped our energies, rendering us vulnerable against the relentless onslaught of enemies striking at the very heart of Muslim states. Our elite and professionals have not all been totally incompetent or ubiquitous. It is all the fault of the Mullah, and nobody else, and the one-liners never end.[1]

He defines civilization as an all-encompassing term that characterizes the cumulative intellectual, cultural, and social achievements evolved over a considerable span of time.

Some scholars outside Pakistan assume that the ascendancy of religion over the past three decades is an obstructive force in the way of Pakistan's efforts to modernize and its natural corollary is the decay in its institutions which are modelled in the Western tradition and shaped by the colonial heritage. This disconnect between the way of life, according to Islamic edicts propagated by the religious clerics that the majority of the population wishes to pursue, and the small minority prescribing retention and rejuvenation of Western-rooted institutions of the state, is pulling Pakistan in two opposing directions. Aasim Sajjad Akhtar postulates that:

> The religious establishment is probably the single biggest force sustaining the status quo in as much as it actively prevents debate on major social ills by issuing what are effectively unchallengeable religious edicts. The clerics enjoy a monopoly in interpretation of religion and anyone who ventures from what is considered proper religious conduct is subject to sanction of the religious establishment. Yet the religious right is part of a bigger problem.[2]

However, as the Chapter on 'The Polity' shows, the religious political parties have never won over 11 per cent of the popular vote in any general election in Pakistan. There is undoubtedly growing religiosity and Pakistani society is becoming increasingly conservative but it is not obvious that the religious establishment has all that much influence on the majority of the population. To the extent that the existing institutions in Pakistan are able to deliver basic public services efficiently and effectively, ensure fair play, ensure the rule of law, equity, and speedy and inexpensive justice and welfare to the less-privileged segments of the society, there would hardly be any deviation from the Islamic precepts, and indeed a congruence would be found between the two. Religion therefore, is not an obstructive force but indeed reinforces the goals of the institutional reforms being proposed. There are others who attribute religion to be the very basis on which Pakistan was created. Farzana Sheikh[3] is one of such scholar who has postulated: 'It is the country's problematic making sense of Pakistan and contested leadership with Islam that has most decisively frustrated its quest for coherent national identity and for stability as a national state capable of absorbing the challenges of its rich and diverse society.'

Babar Ayaz[4] also believes that Pakistan was born with a genetic defect and the numerous problems faced by Pakistan today have arisen because the country's foundation was based on religion. He thinks Islamization of Pakistan's laws is in conflict with the twenty-first century value systems.

A great deal of literature has also emerged that seeks to link the religion of Islam with militancy, terrorism, and obscurantism. The recent ban by the Trump Administration in the US on the admission of Muslims from seven states in the Middle East and the restriction on Syrian refugees there and the strong anti-refugee sentiment in Europe are the public policy and social manifestations of this widely shared sentiment.

In this connection, Pakistan, being formally called an Islamic Republic, with terrorists present in its areas bordering Afghanistan, and several terrorist attacks in the UK and US launched by persons of Pakistani origin, has attracted a great deal of attention. This narrative has to be placed in the historical context. Although called an Islamic Republic, the contest between two ideas—democratic norms versus puritanical Islam—remains an unsettled issue in Pakistan even after 70 years of its existence. The proponents of each contesting idea draw upon their own interpretation of Pakistan pronounced by the founder, M. A. Jinnah, in support of their viewpoint. Those who advocate Islam as the 'ideology of Pakistan' refer to the slogan of *'Pakistan ka matlab kia: La Illaha Il Lilha'* (Pakistan means affirmation of one God). They argue that Pakistan was intended to be a theocratic state enforcing Shariah laws but are unable to clearly define which particular model would be applicable, given several interpretations of the Islamic order. The sharp divisions between Shias and Sunnis, and within Sunnis, Deobandis, Barelvis and Ahl-e-Hadees, and more recently the rising influence of extremist groups such as Al-Qaeda, Taliban, and ISIS who want to establish Islamic states practising their own beliefs, have in practice further complicated the application of the model of a cohesive Islamic ideological state. This lack of unanimity existed even prior to the partition of India and, as Ayesha Jalal puts it:

Muslims shared a common religious identity but were hardly united in their politics, which were more defined by class, regional, and ideological affiliation. An absence of unanimity in Muslim politics, not the commonalities of religion, allowed the Indian National Congress to cut the All India Muslim League down to size.[5]

She therefore deduces[6] that in absence of this lack of consensus over Pakistan's ideological and territorial contours, the ambiguity in the dedicated struggle for Pakistan was vital to its establishment. This ambiguity paid off when the Muslim League swept the 1945–46 general elections, demonstrating that it was the sole representative of the Muslims of India and Jinnah their sole spokesman.

The contrary view to the Islamic ideological state proposition is that Pakistan was not an Islamic movement but a movement by the Muslims of India to seek greater social and economic opportunity for themselves. Jinnah was a protagonist of a national democratic order of liberal and modern tenets and Muslim identity. According to the proponents of this view, Pakistan was achieved to protect and safeguard the economic and political interests of the Muslim minority population from the vast Hindu majority, which necessitated a separate homeland for that purpose. This idea of Pakistan as a 'political unit where Muslims govern themselves and thrive as a cultural and economic community' was articulated in the Two Nation Theory. They are willing to buy in the Islamic ideology concept so long as it helps to promote efficiency, fairness, and justice in society. There is no doubt in anyone's mind that Islam could be a source of ethical and spiritual guidance for the achievement of the goal. The grievance of this group is that those espousing the cause of puritanical Islam have been focusing too much on the ritualistic and formalistic aspects rather than the substantive and ethical aspects of this great religion.

Ziad Haider[7] dwells on the schism between the Aligarh tradition, which selectively balanced Western notions of modernity and learning with a retention of an Islamic identity, and the Deoband tradition, which reflected Western mores as a deviation from religious orthodoxy 'as the main reason for the contested ideas underpinning Pakistan's birth'.

Akbar Zaidi is of the view that:

> Culturally and socially Pakistan is a Muslim state. It is not an Islamic state
> ... While Islam is probably the most significant marker in the lives of almost
> all Pakistanis, their politics and social relations are not strictly determined
> by this marker, although perhaps cultural practices are ... Islamic beliefs do
> also very comfortably sit with modern, even western beliefs and practices.
> They are accommodated without much tension and contradiction.[8]

For the past three decades, the role of religion in state governance has assumed an important but highly divisive role in popular discourse as well as in public policy.

The campaign for the Shariah is not so much about the content of the law as about popular access to the law, the speedy execution of the law, and who gets to enforce it. Different Islamic groups cannot agree on which form of the Shariah is in fact valid. There are a multi-faceted collection of different forms of Sunni Islam and there is no monolithic version of it. Those who believe in the ideology of Pakistan, that there was no separation of state and religion in Islam, were fortified by the chain of constitutional developments that began soon after the founder's death.

The Objectives Resolution that was adopted in March 1949 by the Constituent Assembly proved to be an important milestone in the subsequent discourse on the nature of the Pakistani state. The Resolution was criticized at that time by representatives of the minorities who, along with a few others, voted against its adoption. The Resolution was made a part of the Constitution by Zia ul-Haq through a presidential order. The Supreme Court has now recognized it as a part of the basic structure of the constitution and Islam is 'one of its salient or defining features on the basis of Article 2A that cannot be repealed, abrogated, or substantially altered'.[9]

Those who believe that this Resolution has created more problems show that the state has 'since employed ideological puritanism triggered by the Resolution to curtail space for dissent'. Although the Objectives Resolution states that equality, tolerance, and social justice—as enunciated by Islam—

would be its cornerstone, in practice this has not happened, and particularly so since the 1980s.

The adoption of the Objectives Resolution, according to those who opposed it, went against Jinnah's pronouncements in his first address that Pakistan was a modern Muslim-majority state but 'where the state would remain religiously neutral and where citizens would transcend their personal faiths to become Pakistanis'.

Scathing criticism of this ceaseless debate over the national identity and ideology of Pakistan comes from a former US Ambassador to Pakistan, William Milam, who says:

> Nations have usually been able to establish a coherent national identity or ideology, which is the foundation for an organic national narrative.
>
> Pakistan is a weak state with an invented nationalist ideology that is still up for grabs. Its national narrative has been to a large extent hijacked, first by the military which constructed a self-serving defensive national narrative and later by fundamentalists who have morphed into a defensive and exclusionist one. Pakistan as a country has not yet and may never come to terms with modernity, a country whose elite has no interest in education for the under classes, a country whose contorted, out of date national identity and distorted national narrative are both cause and effect of its weakness as a state and sow the seeds for possible failure.[10]

With the state's backing that began in the Zia period, the Islamic discourse in Pakistan has privileged the Sunni-Deobandi-Wahabi sect. Other sects and minorities have been marginalized, thereby sharpening denominational differences and fostering sectarian strife. Zia ul-Haq allowed the *maulvis* a space totally incommensurate with its political support base. The state changed laws, tampered with textbooks, and utilized the media to this end. The jihad moved Pakistan away from a diffused religious identity to a well-defined and concrete manifestation of self-destiny. The state's enterprise of Islamizing Pakistan sought to change the very nature and identity of an average Pakistani.

Those who were opposed to Zia's policies felt that 'a premium was placed on displays of piety without stemming the growing rot in social morality'. Zaigham Khan believes that:

Zia ul-Haq opened the floodgates to Middle Eastern ideological and political influence in Pakistan. Zia's regime adopted a laissez faire attitude towards the Arab and Iranian sectarian public diplomacy in Pakistan and allowed both sides to cultivate influence among political parties and sectarian groups. It did not take long for the laboratory of Islam to turn into an assembly line of Frankenstein's monsters.[11]

Zahid Hussain adds:

The enforcement of so called Islamic laws reinforced obscurantism in society, discouraging any enlightened discourse. The Afghan resistance war against Soviet Occupation gave rise to a new 'jihadi' culture that threatened to tear apart the nation's social fabric. Escalation in sectarian and religion based violence made it much more difficult for the left to mobilize mass support. Universities and other educational institutions were purged of progressive elements. Student and labour unions were clamped down upon and freedom of expression was curtailed in the name of the so called national interest.[12]

There is a school of thought which believes that broader development and social interventions such as equality of opportunity, equal access to basic public services, and expeditious, inexpensive, and fair justice can provide a sustainable basis for the eradication of the root causes that give rise to frustrations, and repulsions leading finally to acts of violence, militancy, extremism, and terrorism. Military force alone in absence of such interventions would prove short-lived.

Abid Burki and his colleagues emphasize that:

Social marginalization and subservience, as well as violence and vulnerability, then, have to be looked at through the prism of the interlocking inequalities of market opportunities ... This point is underlined if it is considered that, according to the 1998 census, non-Muslims are half as likely to be able to read as Muslims and that in Punjab the non-agricultural classes are often the poorest and most exploited. In addition, as already noted, gender inequalities remain very significant.[13]

Abdul Basit attributes the emergence of educated urban jihadists to their identity crisis and alienation from the state, and expands on this thesis:

The path to violent extremism for these jihadists has been triggered by an identity crisis, the quest for a sense of belonging, a struggle for recognition and resentment towards their respective states due to unemployment, corruption, and bad governance. They suffer from double alienation from unresponsive states which have failed them as citizens and societies where a lack of consensus on what constitutes a 'good Muslim' pushes them towards extremist discourses to seek answers. This set of grievances fall within the broader parameter of contemporary political Islam and the Salafist narrative.[14]

Traditionally, the jihadist and sectarian organizations in South Asia have been grass-roots movements linked to *madrassahs* and mosque networks whose target audience remained the poor and lower-income segments of society. Meanwhile, the educated middle and upper-middle class sections in the urban areas have been targeted by evangelical and missionary organizations whose teachings and lectures revolve around contemporary discourses on political Islam. Prior to their engagement with violent extremism, these educated militants from the urban areas had some exposure to the so-called non-violent extremist narratives.

There are three reasons which account for the emergence of educated and urban militants in South Asia. First, deeper Internet penetration and the spread of social media have decreased the distance between local and global developments, accelerated the flow of communication, democratized violence, and eroded a state's monopoly on information. The unregulated cyberspace in South Asia, with 480 million users, is the second largest in the world. The Islamic State (IS) has exploited it to further its ideological narrative. This has had a huge impact on the patterns of violent extremism and terrorism.

The IS's ability to universalize local grievances in its meta-narrative of global jihad and offer a putative solution in the revival of the so-called caliphate has resonated with the educated audience of urban areas. Other than addressing individual grievances, such rhetoric also provided them with a stronger sense of belonging and empowerment.

Second, the low threshold of radicalization and violence because of the IS's violent and well-publicized tactics has also played a critical role in mobilizing South Asia's educated and urban youth. They may have harboured radical thoughts but did not find Al-Qaeda and its associates' jihadist platforms attractive. The IS's radical message provided them with an alternative jihadist platform, coupled with the excitement of creating a global 'Sunni Caliphate' and the spiritual experience of fighting for the glory of Islam as its hero-warriors and saviours.

Third, with the changing times and circumstances, social, political, and religious movements undergo a generational shift, creating a rift between the old and the new generations. This rift can result in dissension, leading to the creation of splinter factions of young and rebellious members. The younger generation views the older generation as status quo-oriented, rigid, and resistant to change. Meanwhile, the younger generation tends to be impatient, hungry for quick fixes, and driven by grander ambitions.

Characteristically, this generation of South Asian urban militants is technology and media savvy, overambitious, and, in comparison to the traditional South Asian jihadists, better aware of the political and religious history from which it cherry-picks. Generally, this generation has Salafi-Takfiri leanings.

Most of the militants of this generation are between 18 and 30 years old and have undergone a relatively shorter period of radicalization. While the motivational factors may vary from individual to individual and area to area, they all seem to be obsessed with ideas of the so-called caliphate, *hijrah*, and the end-of-time narratives. It is extreme in its methods, unapologetically brutal, and morally consequentialist. For them, the ends justify the means.

In the rapidly changing global and regional environment—especially the reshaping of the Sunni–Shia conflict in the Middle East due to civil wars in Yemen, Iraq, and Syria—the disaffected and disenfranchised Muslim youth in South Asia are facing an ideological dilemma. This unique challenge, in addition to operational and traditional law-enforcement responses, requires counter-narrative and counter-ideological responses.

A senior Pakistani journalist very cogently argues that the weakening of local government at the grass-root level and, therefore, lack of access to basic services by ordinary citizens has contributed to the spread of terrorism in Pakistan. He believes that:

> Good governance immediately following one single focused all-encompassing military mission, can do the job. But that is what we have been lacking—good governance. And that is the reason why even after so many military campaigns we are still living under constant threat of terrorism.
>
> The basic physical ingredient of good governance is the irreducible minimum governing unit at the grassroots known as local government. Powers devolved from the federal government through the 18th Amendment, even after the passage of over half a decade since have either been denied by the bureaucratic red tape or whatever little that has been devolved has been monopolized by provincial governments.
>
> The lack of a local governance system for decades has given rise to exploitative forces that have virtually taken over power at the grass-roots. Weak governance and its effects on the quality of services to the people have been denting public trust in the ability of the state and its institutions to deliver, and this in turn has been conceding moral space to those that use religion to package their militant views.
>
> If the people of a state are living a good life with all the fundamental rights and the basic necessitates secured, they would themselves ensure that their lives are not disrupted by violent ideologies. A state when healthy at the grassroots would also be vigorous in its defence of the basis of its politico-economic establishment.
>
> Terrorism has however been on the boil in Pakistan for the past 36 years because the country has for years been suffering from an acute crisis

of governance. People at large have for decades been denied affordable education, health cover, transport, and housing. This has led to citizens losing faith in the state and losing too any sense of belonging to the country. Such people readily embrace ideologies that promise a better life, no matter how militant these appear to be.

The governance crisis has resulted in declining public health, illiteracy, and conditions conducive to poverty, providing fertile ground for militants to sow their disruptive seeds of terror. Another important way [of] judging the crisis of governance in Pakistan is the weak state institutions and mismanaged state-controlled enterprises. The law-enforcement agencies, administrative institutions, and judiciary all have been politicized and serve the executive branch like servile minions. Also, there has always been a rift at some level between the civil and military leadership in Pakistan. This accounts for a major factor behind the crisis of good governance in Pakistan which comes in shape of clash between the state institutions thus adversely affecting their performance.[15]

Religious parties have taken advantage of this neglect and indifference of the state institutions and moved in to occupy the vacuum. They are always found to be highly proactive in all natural disasters and emergencies, providing much-needed relief to the people. Amir Rana narrates how this has helped them to win the sympathy of the public:

> Religious politics survives on continuous social activism, which keeps workers of religious political parties active and their support bases intact. Issues linked to religion or regional and international politics appear worthwhile to religious political parties ... The religious forces can only create limited turmoil, mainly because of internal compulsions and differences ... Barelvis do not have organized structures and networks. The *pirs* and influential scholars constitute local power centres and seek strength from the followers of their respective shrines.[16]

Tom Friedman is of the view that Saudi Arabia helped 'transform the face of Sunni Islam from an open and modernizing faith to a puritanical, anti-women, anti-shiite, anti-pluralistic one'.[17] This puritanical Salafist transformation of Islam mutated into the ideology that inspired the 9/11 hijackers, 15 of 19 of whom were Saudis.

M. Amir Rana, a security expert, is of the opinion that:

Some militant groups reoriented existing nationalism and further narrowed it to religio-nationalism and generated hyper religio-nationalism. This happened so slowly that the risks were not assessed until the damage was done. Religious nationalism is similar to 'purification'—it moves towards religious extremes to attain enriching 'self-righteousness'.

It is an exclusionary process that does not shape or follow the course of traditional nationalism. Instead, as it becomes more exclusionary, elements of religious sectarianism and socio-political hate narratives become part of its defining characteristics. Many religious nationalists become more faith-centric and 'nationalism' becomes meaningless for them. Al Qaeda and the militant Islamic State group would be examples of such extreme entities.

As far as the probability of mainstreaming or re-integrating non-state actors is concerned, the characteristics of non-state actors in Pakistan first need to be identified. There are five types of militant groups existing in the country: foreign, tribal, sectarian, new urban militants, and conventional militant groups. All these have many commonalities, but it is the conventional militant groups that are considered the proxies once used in Afghanistan and India-held Kashmir.[18]

Malik M. Ashraf echoes the oft-heard views in Pakistan that external actors are involved in creating these problems. He believes that:

The external aspect pertains to support by the Afghan agencies and government to the TTP operatives based on Afghan soil for carrying out terrorist acts within Pakistan in connivance with RAW. Some countries are also reportedly promoting sectarian violence in the country. The involvement of Afghanistan, India, and other countries in acts of terrorism and sectarian violence is the trickiest aspect of the problem. It is also felt that the presence of 3.2 million Afghan refugees in Pakistan over the last thirty plus years is the real cause of Afghanistan related terrorism in Pakistan.[19]

After his interview with Rashid Ghazi of Lal Masjid, Anatol Lieven sums up his impressions as follows:

> They [Islamic Militants] may be able to exploit US and Indian actions to mobilize much larger numbers of Pakistani behind their Islamic and Pakistani nationalist agendas, which have some degree of sympathy from the great majority of their fellow countrymen.
>
> Ghazi's views illustrate the very great differences between different strands of Islamism in Pakistan, except on their mutual hostility to the US, India, and Israel.[20]

ISLAM AND THE ECONOMY

Unfortunately, most of the assumptions and premises on which the hypotheses about the Islamic economic system have been constructed are seriously flawed. Pakistan is and will remain a responsible member of the international community and is committed to utilizing the vast opportunities provided by globalization and financial integration of world markets for the benefit of its population. There is no suggestion whatsoever by any significant group of people or political parties in favour of isolation or withdrawal from the international economic system. Secondly, the preconditions for a robust and well-functioning Islamic economic system are missing in Pakistan. Islamic moral values which emphasize integrity, honesty, truthfulness, full disclosure, and transparency are not yet widely practised by Pakistani businesses. Once these preconditions are established, the adoption of a real Islamic economic system will lead to a superior welfare outcome for a majority of the Pakistani population.

How can the Islamization of the economy affect this future direction of Pakistan's economy and improve the welfare of its people vis-à-vis the present system? The extensions that the true practice and application of an

Islamic economic model can bring about will, in fact, help in overcoming the weaknesses inherent in the capitalist model of economy. Before coming to that, let us recapitulate the basic principles upon which the Islamic economic system is built.

Unlike positive economics, the entire edifice of Islamic economics is built upon a set of objectives or *maqasid*. In other words, Islamic economics is normative in nature, with the objective of the Shariah being to promote the wellbeing of all, concerns safeguarding their faith, their human self, their intellect, posterity, and wealth.

At the micro level, the precepts of profit maximization and utility maximization are retained intact but are supplemented by a set of interlinked objective functions. An Islamic system attempts to promote a balance between market, family, society, and the state. It does so by promoting both the material and the spiritual urges of the human self in order to foster peace of mind and enhance family and social solidarity. Some Western thinkers and anti-globalization activists decry the Western economic model as being suppressive of collective human rights and community and social well-being, disruptive of family values, and too focused on selfish individual interests. Behavioural economists have also begun challenging the assumption of rationality in the choices and preferences an individual makes in day-to-day life. Thus, the merit of the Islamic economic model lies in its extension of the Western model in some fundamental and beneficial ways. It introduces into the objective function an additional argument which keeps self-interest within the bounds of social interest by limiting individual preferences to conform with social priorities, and eliminating or minimizing the use of resources for purposes that frustrate the realization of a social vision. This may help promote harmony between self-interest and social interest.

This approach complements the market mechanism by subjecting the allocation and distribution of resources to a double layer of filters. It attacks the problem by first changing the behaviour and preference scale in keeping with the demands of the normative goals. Claims on resources are then exposed to the second filter of market prices. In this process, the influence that initial resource endowments are able to exercise in the allocation and distribution of resources may be substantially reduced. Faith seeks to accomplish this by giving self-interest a longer-term perspective, i.e. stretching it beyond the span of the world to the Hereafter. This interest in the Hereafter can only be served when an individual serves his/her social obligations. This may induce individuals to voluntarily restrict their claims on resources within the limits of the general well-being of society and thus create harmony between self-interest and social interest even when the two are in conflict.

The promotion of simple living and the reduction of wasteful and conspicuous consumption may help reduce excessive claims on resources and thereby release a greater volume of these for the need-fulfilment of others who are not so well off. It may also help promote higher savings and investment and thereby raise employment and growth.

At the macro level, the Islamic economic model in its ideal form tends to combine the positive aspects of the capitalist economy and the socialist economy while minimizing their negative consequences. A capitalist economy based on private property and market mechanisms allocates resources efficiently but as it takes the initial resource endowment as given, equity considerations do not figure in this system. The socialist system is acutely concerned with equity and the welfare of its population and ensures benefits to its citizens from the cradle to the grave. It however relies on state ownership and bureaucracy, it is wanting in allocating resources, thus creating inefficiency, waste, and value subtraction. The Islamic system overcomes the deficiencies of both the systems because it is firmly based on private property and the market mechanism but also has explicitly built in equity and distribution through the compulsory deduction of *zakat*, i.e., transfer payments from the asset holders to the deprived segments of the population. The Western economic model is criticized today as being unable to address the issues of unemployment, poverty, and income inequalities in developing countries. The Islamic economic model explicitly addresses the distribution issues after the market has allocated the gains. It does so through a compulsory deduction of 2.5 per cent of tangible wealth and net asset holdings from the income generated by market mechanisms for transfer among the vulnerable, sick, handicapped, and indigent segments of society.

Although the deduction is compulsory, the transfers are made voluntarily by the well-to-do to their poor relatives, neighbours, and others whom they know have legitimate needs. Thus the leakages, waste, and corruption that are inherent in a state-administered system of welfare payments are conspicuous by their absence under such a system. Only really deserving persons and families or *mustahaqeen* receive these payments. In Pakistan, it is estimated that private transfers made voluntarily to the poor account for two per cent of GDP annually. These welfare payments are a potent force in reducing poverty, helping the vulnerable to earn their own livelihoods, and lowering income disparities.

At the sectoral level, the introduction of Islamic banking should result in a deepening of the financial sector and promotion of financial inclusion, so acutely needed in a world where inequalities are creating a serious polarization between the top one per cent of the population and the rest. There are believers in the Islamic faith who do not use the conventional banking system because of their strongly held views against *riba* (usury). They will willingly deposit their savings in Islamic banks and borrow from these banks for expansion of their businesses or new investment. Thus a significant segment of the population that is currently outside the organized financial sector will be brought into its fold.

The primary principle of Islamic banking is the prohibition of *riba*, which is believed to be a means of exploiting the common man. Trade is the preferred mode of business in Islam. The goal of banking is the general economic improvement of the public at large rather than that of a few groups.

Below are some of the distinguishing features of Islamic banking:

• As part of a faith-based system, it is obligatory on Islamic banks not to pursue activities that are detrimental to the society and its moral values. Thus Islamic banks are not permitted to invest in casinos, nightclubs, breweries, and the like. It is relevant to note that casinos are among the prime vehicles for money-laundering, and dealing with them could expose the conventional banks to such risk. Islamic banks have to deploy their deposits for financing small and medium enterprises, small farmers, and low-cost housing, all areas that have been traditionally neglected by conventional banks.

• The second distinguishing feature of Islamic banking is that, in addition to the rules and regulations applicable to the conventional banks, Islamic banks have to go through another test, i.e. fulfil exhaustive requirements to be Shariah-compliant. This requires that the clients of Islamic banks must have businesses that are socially beneficial, creating real wealth, and adding value to the economy rather than making paper transactions. Therefore, a stringent 'Know Your Customer' (KYC) policy is inherently an inbuilt requirement for an Islamic bank, as it has to know the customer and his/her business before engaging in a socially-responsible, Shariah-compliant transaction. KYC is the first line of defence against money-laundering in any banking system.

• Third, by their very nature, Islamic modes of financing and deposit-taking discourage questionable/undisclosed means of wealth that form the basis of money-laundering operations. The disclosure standards are stringent because Islamic banks require their customers to divulge the origins of their funds in order to ensure that they are not derived from un-Islamic means, e.g. drug trading, gambling, extortion, subversive activities, or other criminal activities. On the financing side, Islamic banks must ensure that funds are directed towards identifiable and acceptable productive activities. Most Islamic financing modes are asset-backed, i.e. are used to finance specific physical assets such as machinery, inventory, and equipment.

• Fourth, the role of the bank is not limited to being a passive financier concerned only with timely interest payments and loan recovery. The bank is a partner in trade and has to concern itself with the nature of the business and its clients' profitability. In the event of a loss in business, the Islamic financier has to share that loss. To avoid such loss and reputational risk, Islamic banks have to be extra-vigilant about their clientele.

To sum up, it can be said that banks that judiciously follow Islamic banking principles are less likely to engage in illegal activities such as money-laundering and financing terrorism than conventional banks. However, the existence of rogue elements cannot be ruled out in any form of organization. It is the responsibility of the state and regulators to ensure that notwithstanding these built-in safeguards, there is adequate legislation, sufficient regulations, and enforcement mechanisms in place to take action against potential offenders.

Pakistan has taken a policy decision that it will allow both the conventional and Islamic banking systems to operate in parallel. The choice will be left to consumers to decide whether they wish to migrate from the conventional banking system to Islamic banking or not. The State Bank of Pakistan has a transparent system of licensing, regulating, and supervising Islamic banks in Pakistan. There are three ways in which this type of banking can be set up: (a) a stand-alone exclusive Islamic bank; (b) existing conventional banks establishing a subsidiary; or (c) earmarking some of their branches for Islamic banking. A Shariah board comprising scholars, economists, accountants, and bankers will determine whether or not the products and services offered by these institutions are compliant with Shariah.

To sum up, Islamization, if adopted and practiced in its true form at any time in the future, will strengthen the economy, particularly income distribution and poverty alleviation, which have proved elusive under the present economic model. This will, indeed, have a dampening effect on the sources of instability, violence, and propensity towards terrorism arising from a sense of deprivation.

MADRASSAHS

One of the popular perceptions outside Pakistan that has attracted much attention is that the Islamic seminaries, i.e. the *madrassahs*, have spread like wildfire and have become recruiting centres for the extremist elements and groups. Studies conducted by independent scholars show that the total enrolment in these *madrassahs* under the most optimistic scenario does not exceed five per cent of all school enrolment. These are largely concentrated in KP and Balochistan in areas bordering Afghanistan and cater to the needs of poor families who cannot afford to send their children to regular schools. *Madrassahs* provide free lodging, boarding, and clothing and thus take a substantial burden off the shoulders of these families. Although several of them have trained Taliban and members of other extremist groups, this sweeping generalization does not apply across the board. It is true that these seminaries have imparted an obscurantist understanding of Islam with no marketable skills or modern knowledge but taking action against them is quite difficult. Irfan Husain underlines this:

> To be fair, taking on the religious right is not easy in a country that has seen a post-Zia generation grow up in an environment of increasing intolerance and religiosity. Many have been radicalized. Upwards of 25,000 *madrassas* churn out graduates who are unequipped to get jobs in today's complex world. And a poorly informed and hysterical electronic media, in a hunt for audience share and advertising, constantly misguides millions.

That is why several attempts at reform of *madrassahs*, initiated by President Musharraf and subsequent governments, have got little traction. Amir Rana is of the view that three challenges face the government in relation to *madrassahs*. The first is the registration process and identifying those seminarians which pose security threat. The second is one of regulating the educational standards of the *madrassahs*. The third is curriculum reform for providing students with the necessary skills to find gainful employment. Vigilance must be exercised to ensure that the *madrassahs* aren't offering any out-of-syllabus courses that preach against a particular religion, sect, or community. Some of the religious schools are merging religious and modern formal education.[21] If the government can reform the madrassas along these lines, it could minimize the risk of these institutions being misused by sectarian or extremist groups.

There are other critics who believe that action is required because there is a relationship between madrassas and the spread of fundamentalism and militancy in Pakistan. Among them is Zahid Hussain who has written:

> The education imparted by traditional madrassas often spawned factional, religious, and cultural conflict. It carried barriers to modern knowledge, stifled creativity, and bred bigotry thus laying the foundation on which fundamentalism—militant or otherwise—was based. Divided by sectarian identities, these institutions were, by their very nature, driven by their zeal to outnumber and dominate rival sects. Promoting a particular sect inevitably implied the rejection of other sects, sowing the seeds of extremism in the minds of the students. The literature produced by their parent religious organizations promoted sectarian hatred and was aimed at probing the rival sects as infidels and apostates. The efforts by the successive governments to modernize the *madrassa* curricula and introduce secular subjects failed because of stiff resistance from the religious organs that control the religious schools.[22]

Hasan Askari Rizvi is of the view that it is not only *madrassahs* but also the regular education system that is responsible for the change in mind-set that has taken place over the past 25 years:

> The skewed mental and emotional disposition has been created not only by madrassa education but also by the regular education system starting in the mid-1980s under the Zia regime. [The] Zia ul-Haq government also used state patronage to promote Islamist groups and militancy; the media was also used to propagate Islamic orthodoxy and militancy. The socialization of young people along these lines continued even after the death of Zia ul-Haq.
>
> Thus, a generation and a half has been socialized into religious orthodoxy and militancy, and has internalized hard-line Islamist discourse on national and international affairs to the exclusion of other perspectives. This socialization downplays the notion of Pakistan as a territorial nation-state, Pakistani citizenship, and Pakistan as a political community. Their main reference points are transnational Muslim identity; western injustices against Muslims, non-resolution of the Palestine and Kashmir issue, the west as an

adversary of Muslims, and the role of the Islamic movement rather than Muslim states as the liberators of Muslims from Western domination.[23]

William Darlymple, in his study of *madrassahs*, published in 2005, found:

Across Pakistan, the tenor of religious belief has been correspondingly radicalized: the tolerant Sufi-minded Barelvi form of Islam is now deeply out of fashion in Pakistan, overtaken by the sudden rise of the more hard-line and politicized reformist Deobandi, Wahhabi, and Salafi strains of the faith.

The sharp acceleration in the number of these *madrassahs* first began under General Zia ul-Haq at the time of the Afghan jihad in the 1980s, and was financed mainly by the Saudis. Although some of the madrasas so founded were little more than single rooms attached to village mosques, others are now very substantial institutions: the Dar ul-Uloom in Baluchistan, for example, is now annually enrolling some 1,500 boarders and a further 1,000 day-boys. Altogether there are possibly as many as 800,000 students in Pakistan's *madrassahs*: an entire free Islamic education system running parallel to the moribund state sector.

There is now almost a consensus that the indoctrination of the younger generation began in the 1980s when the textbooks taught at and curriculum adopted by the government schools were revised. The history books described Pakistan's formation as 'an inexorable culmination of the arrival of Islam on the sub-continent', skipped the British colonial period and the shared Hindu-Muslim heritage, and contained material fanning hostility against Hindus and India. The authors of the textbooks on Islamic studies and Pakistan studies made compulsory for all schools and colleges were directed 'to demonstrate that the basis of Pakistan is not to be founded in racial, linguistic or geographical factors, but rather in the shared experience of a [full out] common religion and to guide students towards the ultimate goal of Pakistan—the creation of a completely Islamicized state.' The ideas propounded in these textbooks subsequently moulded the world-view of the younger generation subjected to such schooling.[24]

The jihadi culture that engulfed Pakistan was the product of this indoctrination of the younger generation, the use of proxy-Islamic groups in the fight against the Soviets in Afghanistan in collaboration with the US, and the growing influence of the Sunni Wahhabism promoted by the Saudi Arabia that nurtured sectarianism. The influx of over three million Afghan refugees into Pakistan brought in not only some of the militant elements but also arms and ammunitions and drugs.

SECTARIANISM

Sectarianism grew in parallel with the Islamization process and became a source of endemic violence, largely through acts of terrorism the practice of violence, and violation of women's and minority rights in the name of religion over the past decade or so has alienated the rest of the world and placed Pakistan in a highly negative light internationally and at grave risk.

The roots of the growing sectarian divide can be traced to the Iranian revolution led by Ayatollah Khomeini in 1979. In its aftermath, Saudi Arabia took upon itself the responsibility for limiting the influence of Shias in the region and Pakistan became a battleground in the transplanted war between Saudi Arabia and Iran. The Tehrik-i-Nifaz-fiqh Jafria, a Shia religious group, and the Sunni extremist group, Sipah-e Sahabah (SSP), got embroiled in a violent struggle which has continued fiercely since then. Subsequent governments have failed to come to grips with this problem, although these sectarian organizations have been banned but periodically re-emerge under different names and banners. The jihadi culture reinforced sectarianism and the conservative PML-N formed electoral alliances in the 1990s with the Islamic parties which were soft on the jihadis and sectarian groups After the withdrawal of the Soviets from Afghanistan, some of the jihadi groups diverted their energies, resources, and trained manpower towards Kashmir. New configurations such as Lashkar-e-Tayyiba (LeT) under the leadership of Hafiz Saeed and Jaish-e-Mohammad (JeM) led by Maulana Masood Azhar emerged as splinter groups from the original sectarian organizations and became quite active. India has placed the responsibility for the Mumbai carnage of 2008 on Hafiz Saeed and his new group Jamaat-ud-Dawa (JuD). The other anti-Shia organization which has played havoc in Pakistan is Lashkar-e-Jhangvi (LeJ), formed as an offshoot of Sipah-e-Sahabah, after the death of Maulana Haq Nawaz. The top leaders of this group have been eliminated in several encounters but they periodically regroup under new leadership.

The Muttahida Majlis-i-Amal (MMA), a joint alliance of the six mainstream political parties, came to power in the NWFP and formed a coalition government in Balochistan after the 2002 elections. The two principal components of the MMA, Jamiat Ulema-e-Islam (JUI) and Jamaat-i-Islami (JI), both followers of the Deobandi school, had a soft corner for the jihadi, sectarian elements because there existed an overlapping membership and common training at the *madrassahs*. The MMA used their electoral success to introduce rigid Islamic rule in the Frontier province, creating an enabling environment for the extremist elements to flourish as the state institutions were either indifferent to or supportive of their activities. These groups were able to publicly raise funds, openly recruit volunteers, and arm their cadres and paramilitary wings without any hindrance from the authorities. These extremist groups became so strong that they became a nuisance to public order even in Islamabad. Red Mosque (Lal Masjid) and its associated *madrassahs* formed vigilante groups to enforce codes of Islamic morality. When the army stormed the mosque and arrested Maulana Aziz there was a hue and cry by the media. Malala Yousafzai[25] describes the Lal Masjid incident in her book:

In 2007, Lal Masjid students began terrorizing the streets of Islamabad. They raided houses they claimed were being used as massage centres, kidnapped women they said were prostitutes and closed down DVD shops, making bonfires of CDs and DVDs. The mosque also set up its own courts to dispense Islamic justice. Their militants kidnapped policemen and ransacked government buildings. The situation was so bad that people began to worry [that] the militants could take over the capital.

On July 3, 2007 commandos with tanks and APCs surrounded the mosque, cut off electricity, blasted holes in the walls, and fired mortars at the compound. There was exchange of fire between the militants and troops outside. The siege went on until late on July 9 when the Commander of the Special Forces outside was killed by a sniper in one of the minarets. The military finally stormed the compound. By nightfall July 10 the siege was finally over, around 100 people had been killed including soldiers, [and] children.

Some observers speculate that the coalescing of all the jihadist elements and 40 militant leaders—commanding some 40,000 fighters in the form of the TTP—in December 2007 took place as a reaction to this attack on Lal Masjid. The sectarian organizations and jihadi groups in Pakistan formed a nexus with the TTP and supported each other. Lashkar-e-Jhangvi continued to commit abhorrent acts of cold-blooded murders of the Hazara tribe in Quetta and the killing of Shia doctors and professionals in Karachi led to the out-migration from Pakistan of many Shia families.

The former interior minister, Chaudhry Nisar Ali, sparked a serious controversy when he tried to draw a distinction between terrorists and sectarian groups in Pakistan. Amir Rana responded to him by terming this a dangerous approach. Rana believes that this flawed threat perception by state functionaries was our real enemy and expounds this point by arguing:

The militant landscape in Pakistan is very much sectarian in nature; sectarian tendencies flow like blood through the veins of religiously inspired extremism and militancy.

All local and foreign terrorist organizations such as the Taliban, Al Qaeda, and the militant Islamic State (IS) group follow sectarian agendas at varying levels.

The Afghan Taliban recognize sectarian differences and support sectarian outfits both in Afghanistan and Pakistan but avoid using the concept as a political tool because it could hurt their movement in Afghanistan.

While Al Qaeda has used sectarian groups as strategic allies in the region, IS has an even more aggressive sectarian agenda.

The Tehreek-e-Taliban Pakistan (TTP) remained close to the Punjabi Taliban, Jundullah, and Lashkar-i-Jhangvi; all these groups take pride in their sectarian credentials.

The TTP's splinter Jamaatul Ahrar also has strong sectarian credentials.

Overall, under the influence of Al Qaeda and IS, sectarian and jihadist groups underwent a radical transformation into global jihadist entities.

From where such groups draw their human resource is no secret. Given this background, flawed threat perceptions on the part of the state are likely to adversely affect its approach to countering extremism and terrorism.

A flawed threat perception is our real enemy and it is based on certain stereotypes that many state functionaries also appear to believe. These notions do not distinguish between a religious scholar and a sectarian leader. This weak threat perception has failed to grasp the political dynamics of sectarian violence in Pakistan.

Many of the banned sectarian organizations wear political hats and have been participating in electoral politics, whether under different names, through independent candidates, or through alliances with mainstream political parties. Through such tactics, these groups have acquired political legitimacy. Both the TJP and SSP, now known as the Ahle Sunnat Wal Jamaat, have promoted sectarian hatred and intolerance.[26]

TALIBAN

One of the major unsettled issues that touches on the fringes of religious extremism has been Pakistan's involvement in Afghanistan since late 1970s to date. The Taliban movement filled a vacuum left in the governance of Afghanistan soon after the US withdrew from there after the Soviet ouster and the Mujahideen leaders engaged in an internecine struggle for power. It was an indigenous movement aimed at providing expeditious and fair justice to the people at a time when the existing institutions had all crumbled. The Taliban themselves did not realize that their movement would spread like wildfire. As a small group of their followers moved from one district to another, people joined them of their own volition without any coercion or bloodshed. They faced no resistance except in the north where Shah Ahmed Masud, supported by the Tajiks and Abdul Rashid Dostum, supported by the Uzbeks, formed the Northern Alliance and refused to accept the hegemony of the Taliban. There was an ethnic colour to this conflict as the Taliban were largely Pashtuns. Adversarial lines were drawn between the two groups with the Taliban controlling a very large area and population and the Northern Alliance confined to the Panjshir Valley. Pakistan came into the picture much later. The 'War against Terror' launched after 9/11, which Pakistan joined on the side of the US and NATO, pushed the Taliban out of power but created severe existential problems for Pakistan which have lingered on for the last 15 years:

> For militants, the Western presence in Afghanistan and Pakistan was a threat to Islam. This view became the ultimate rationale for jihadist militancy in Pakistan. Anybody allied with the enemy or those who seemed to be complicit in the war on the side of Western forces such as soldiers charged with safe passage for NATO convoys, civilians, moderate clerics, and more recently the government officials, were regarded as safe game.[27]

As far as the battle to oust the Soviets from Afghanistan was concerned, there wasn't any ambivalence in the minds of ordinary Pakistanis as a 'jihad' had been launched to expel external occupiers from a neighbouring, brotherly Muslim country. Confusion, however, arose when Pakistani soldiers were asked to take arms against their Muslim kith and kin across the border after 9 September 2001 in support of foreign US and NATO troops who had acted exactly as the Soviets had done in the 1980s. This apparent contradiction and sense of injustice at the atrocities committed through drone killings of innocent women and children led to the formation of the TTP under a single umbrella. They used religion as the unifying banner to coalesce disparate factions fighting independently. A large number of people from the rest of Pakistan who felt aggrieved by the US actions joined the ranks of the TTP and strengthened the organization.

Saleem Safi[28] sketches a picture of what Pakistan had to undergo as a consequence of its participation in the Afghan War in support of the US and NATO:

More than 50 thousand people, including security personnel, have lost their lives. And Pakistan has also sustained a monetary loss of about $107 billion.

… Soon after the overthrow of the Taliban regime, Islamabad extended unconditional support to the Karzai government and worked zealously for its stability and strength. For the first time in our history, we even moved the army into the tribal belt and tried to eliminate the Taliban.

However, Pakistan now feels betrayed and thinks that the US and Afghan governments have, in return, started sheltering Baloch insurgents, renewed the Pashtunistan and Durand Line issues, and given a free hand to RAW to use Afghan soil to destabilise Pakistan.

… Similarly, Pakistan is sheltering million of Afghan refugees with proper documentation.

… But in Afghanistan, portraying Pakistan as the enemy state has become a litmus test of patriotism. Anti-Pakistan propaganda is in full swing and hatred against Pakistan can be seen on the floor of parliament as well as on media.

… In contrast, in Pakistan while there may be some anti-Kabul voices, those voices also criticise other countries with whom Pakistan has close ties—like the US and countries of the Arab world.

… When a minister from Balochistan used derogatory words regarding Afghan refugees, he was immediately countered by politicians and the media and forced to take back his words.

… In addition, Pakistani intelligence also claims that TTP head Mullah Fazlullah frequently visits Kabul and Hakeemullah Mehsud would use Kabul hospitals for treatment.

A case study of a self-proclaimed 'second line of defence of every Muslim state', Harkatul Jihad-i-Islami (HJI), may provide some insight. Once the largest Pakistani jihadist groups active in Afghanistan and India-held Kashmir, it became a parasite of Al-Qaeda and the Afghan Taliban pre-9/11 owing to internal rifts. Its founder, Qari Saifullah Akhtar, was killed while fighting against the Afghan security forces. It is significant that the once mythical jihadist leader's death did not receive much coverage in mainstream or the militants' media. The first Pakistani group to launch attacks on its own soil was HJI. Before the Lal Masjid siege in 2007, HJI and Lashkar-i-Jhangvi factions were behind most of the terrorist attacks carried out in Pakistan, largely between 2002 and 2006. The Pakistani state had decided to dismantle HJI in 2003, although it took nine years to defang the small group. During that time, HJI not only caused enormous damage to Pakistan through terrorist attacks but also provided trained militants to other terrorist groups. It contributed towards the formation of the Punjabi Taliban groups, which comprised HJI's splinter terrorist cells besides others. Militants from HJI also joined the ranks of Al-Qaeda and the TTP.

Afghanistan was ruled by the Taliban between 1996 and 2001 when the US troops uprooted their government and helped in the formation of a new one with Hamid Karzai as president. Although many jihadist and sectarian organizations from Pakistan were linked with the Afghan Taliban and provided them with recruits and material support, they operated, by and large, independently. It was only in December 2007, after the formation of the TTP, that they all began working together under a commonly accepted leader and on a single platform, heavily influenced by the Al-Qaeda and Salafi ideology espoused by them. According to Zahid Hussain: 'What brought them together was the military assault ordered by Musharraf on Islamabad's Red Mosque in July 2007.' They, therefore, declared a jihad against the Pakistan military. They also declared their allegiance to Mullah Omar, the leader of the Afghan Taliban commanded by Osama bin Laden. The eight point charter of the TTP demanded enforcement of Shariah law, thus drawing together the disparate jihadi elements from Pakistan which had thus far—by and large—been functioning independent of one another. This force multiplier and the paradigm shift in their thinking about the military and extending their war to Pakistan turned the TTP into an extremely ferocious and brutal grouping.

Militant activity in Pakistan accelerated after the formation of the TTP, beginning with the assassination of Benazir Bhutto after her return from exile. Suicide bombings targeted at both the military and civilians became commonplace, occurring virtually every five or six days, killing around 90 people a month. The attack on Marriott Hotel in Islamabad, the capital, in September 2007 scared off foreigners who stopped coming to Pakistan after that incident which resulted in the death of 60 people. Over 3,000 people, including senior army and intelligence officials, lost their lives or were seriously wounded between 2007 and 2009. Through fear and intimidation, the Pakistani Taliban were able to neutralize the local population—who were forced to help them in their militant activities—and were virtually able to take control of and rule in all the seven agencies of the FATA. South and North Waziristan, in particular, became safe havens for the terrorists from other parts of the world: Uzbeks, Tajiks, Chechens, Arabs, and others. They set up IED (improvised explosive device) assembling facilities, dug tunnels, set up training camps, and the like. They also took control of Swat, a settled district of KP province, in 2009. This set off alarm bells throughout Pakistan because they were less than 100 miles away from the capital, Islamabad. Malala Yousafzai, the Nobel Prize winner, recounts this episode in her book:[29]

> In Swat, Mullah Fazlullah started his campaign through radio broadcasts in which he openly preached revolt against the State. Soon his followers attacked the Police and took over many villages. The militants would enter villages with mega phones and the police would flee. In a short time they had taken over fifty-nine villages and set up their own parallel administration. Policemen were so scared of being killed that they took out ads in the newspapers to announce that they had left the force. All this happened and nobody did a thing.
>
> In January 2007, an ANP leader was kidnapped by eight masked men and his body was found dumped in his family's graveyard. It was [the] first targeted killing in Swat. The authorities turned a blind eye.
>
> The Taliban switched off the cable channels so that people didn't watch TV, [and] shops selling music, CDS and DVDs were attacked. By the end of 2008, around 400 schools had been destroyed by the Taliban. They announced that all girls' schools would close and from January 15 girls must not go to schools.

The Army conducted a major operation involving 30,000 troops and evicted the TTP from Swat, and assumed control of the territory. The militants, however, retaliated by stepping up their activities in other parts of Pakistan. They made a daring attack on the general headquarters of the army in Rawalpindi and held 39 officers hostage for almost 24 hours. This attack prompted the army to deploy a massive force of 45,000 soldiers, backed by the air force, to drive the Taliban out of their stronghold, South Waziristan—a mission which they successfully accomplished by December 2009. Subsequent army operations in Bajaur, Mohmand, Khyber, and Kurram were successful in recapturing these agencies from the TTP and the army has held on to them since then. The most difficult and challenging task was to penetrate and reclaim North Waziristan. This was due to a variety of reasons: its difficult terrain, widespread presence of militants and terrorists from all over the world throughout the area, and a lack of political will. A group of politicians was urging the government to enter into a dialogue with the TTP.

Political consensus on such an operation could be reached only after the tragic 16 December 2014 attack on the Army Public School, Peshawar, in which 140 young children lost their lives. Soon after, it was decided to launch a full-scale attack on the militants hiding in North Waziristan. Operation Zarb-e-Azb was launched by the army in conjunction with the Pakistan Air Force. Over a million residents had to be displaced from their homes to keep them out of harm's way during the operation. After two years of serious conflict, the 4,000 km area of North Waziristan was freed from the terrorists and militants who were either killed in the encounters, arrested, or slipped away across the Afghan border.

Following the operation in North Waziristan, the Rangers carried out another against the Taliban and their allies in Karachi where they had congregated after being evicted from South and North Waziristan. Action was taken simultaneously against a leading political party, the MQM, which was also alleged to be involved in acts of violence in Karachi and was able to shut down the city at will. The *Global Terrorism Index* (GTI) 2015 report has testified to the success of the Zarb-e-Azb operations. Subsequently, suicide attacks in Pakistan fell significantly, Civilian fatalities, dropped 40 per cent in 2014, 65 per cent in 2015, and 74 per cent in 2016. A prominent critic of the present government, Ayaz Amir, wrote in one of his newspaper columns:

Terrorism has not been eliminated but its roots have been shaken. Terrorist incidents can still occur in Karachi but terrorism and violence are not what they were before. Extortion in the MQM's heyday had become one of Karachi's leading enterprises. It may not have ended completely but Karachi's atmosphere, compared to two years ago, has vastly improved, its citizens breathing easier. And they, and the nation at large, are finally rid of that burden of having to listen perforce to the leader's menacing speeches ... this after a court order stopped TV channels from airing them.[30]

Counter-Terrorism Strategy

According to open-source databases, a variety of perpetrators—including the TTP, other Al-Qaeda-inspired groups, sectarian militants, and nationalist insurgents in Balochistan—have succeeded in carrying out 7,311 terrorist attacks in Pakistan from January 2011 to mid-August 2016. These attacks claimed 9,689 lives and left 18,812 others injured. Fatalities among security force personnel, including paramilitary forces and the police, were 2,672. The percentage of collateral damage was quite high.[31]

Amir Rana[32] classifies the militants in Pakistan into four broad categories: Kashmir-focused groups operating under the cover of charities; tribal militants (TTP, Lashkar-i-Islam, etc.); sectarian groups; and breakaway factions of the classical militant groups and reactionary groups of urban youth, which emerged after 9/11 in reaction to the US invasion of Afghanistan and Pakistan's alliance with the international counterterrorism coalition.

Well-structured groups based in urban areas behave differently from those in the tribal areas. Some of these groups had established connections with smugglers, criminal gangs, and mafias, and developed a symbiotic relationship with them. The criminals provided money in exchange for protection and safe havens furnished by the militant groups. In Karachi, the situation was further complicated as some of the political parties engaging in extortion from businesses or kidnapping for ransom had to enter into loose and informal understandings with the Taliban living in 'no-go' areas, i.e. beyond the reach of the law-enforcement agencies. In Balochistan, the nationalist militant groups added to this equation and the mafias involved in drugs and arms. Smuggling of oil, vehicles, and goods from across the border had the backing and support of unscrupulous politicians, Frontier Corps (FC) staff, and bureaucrats. The entire picture of the militants–criminals– politicians nexus remains fuzzy and highly speculative. No concrete evidence exists on the basis of which any meaningful analysis can be undertaken.

The federal and provincial governments and the law enforcement agencies did not develop a coherent and coordinated strategy to respond to the threats from each of the above groups. The reactive and undifferentiated response did not help. The Pakistan government did form a national counterterrorism agency during the Zardari period but the delays in decisions on manning, resourcing, and reporting relationship, and the coordination of Intelligence through the newly formed Directorate of Intelligence Services took a toll on the government's ability to effectively tackle terrorism threats and deal with the fallout from the military operations.

Soon after the military launched the Zarb-e-Azb operation in North Waziristan to flush out the militants and demolish their infrastructure and control and command structure, a 20-point National Action Plan (NAP) was announced. There has been a great deal of criticism by several analysts and commentators against the slow, lacklustre, and indifferent implementation of the NAP. Imtiaz Alam is of the view that:

> the performance of civilian authorities remained dismal, having been unable to ban active banned outfits, eliminate religious extremism and sectarianism, curb hate material, and stop funding and communication networks (appeals for and collection of funds are again on the rise). Recruitments for jihad are yet again picking momentum for Kashmir, with eye-catching Wani posters on the streets to attract youth to jihad. Reforms in the criminal justice system and civilian armed forces, the police in particular, are yet to be launched.[33]

In the areas that have been cleared of militants, such as Swat, and North and South Waziristan, the civil administration has not yet been put in place and the army is still holding the fort. Roads and highways are also being constructed by the Frontier Works Organization, an army organization, and schools and hospitals are being established by the army. This situation is not tenable and the population and their representatives along with the civilian administration must assume this responsibility.

Irfan Husain[34] compares Pakistan with Turkey:

> While in Turkey, the military's natural partners have been the secular elites, in Pakistan the defence establishment tends to reach out to the religious parties. The latter have no chance of winning power through elections, and thus seek to gain influence by riding on the army's coat-tails.
>
> In Turkey, the laws are enforced far more zealously. And while it has suffered a spate of terrorist attacks in the last few months, clerics are not free to preach whatever they please in mosques. The Friday sermon is faxed to every mosque from Ankara, and prayer leaders are employees of the state. In Pakistan, we have been unable to even regulate the curricula taught in the thousands of madrassas that have mushroomed over the last four decades or so.

Ayaz Amir[35] offers a radically different view about the spread of terrorism in Pakistan and ascribes the responsibility for it to Pakistani elite. He says in support of his contention:

> The *maulvi*, the cleric, the doctor of the faith did not create the mess Pakistan is in. The *maulvi* was never in command of politics and power. He was always, and still is, a figure on the sidelines ... a nuisance at best, the creator of too much noise, the specialist with the loudspeaker, but he never was the driving force behind national policies.
>
> That was the prerogative, the monopoly, not of the *maulvi*, not of the Tableeghi Jamaat, but of the English-speaking classes, the real rulers of Pakistan. Who runs Pakistan even today? The army, the civil service, the political class, the enterprising *seth*, [and] the sharp-eyed real-estate tycoon. Where is the Islamic warrior in this distinguished coalition?
>
> Pakistan needs a transformation of state and society. How long can it live with plundering robber barons who have democracy on their lips and

exploitation in their hearts? This transformation can only come from a strong and radically-inclined leadership, with the strength and outlook to clean the national stables, knock heads together, lessen some of the hypocrisy which is the republic's leading currency, and change the Pakistani landscape for the better.

The extremism of the Taliban is primitive extremism, the product of narrow minds. Pakistan needs the extremism of the pathfinder, the pioneer, the searcher of the depths, the climber of the highest mountains. Of quaking moderation, belting out empty slogans and mouthing empty promises, it has had enough. Seventy years is a long enough time to test any experiment. It is time to give that a decent burial.

SUMMATION

Pakistan continues to struggle with the rationale for its formation: whether it was conceived as a state where Muslims could lead peaceful independent lives in a sovereign nation or as an ideological state where Islam would be the guiding principle. The debate has continued fiercely and although the religious parties have not won a majority of the votes at any general election during the last seventy years, they have succeeded in changing the narrative in their favour. Religious groups received a big boost during the Zia ul-Haq period with a man at the helm who openly used Islam as a tool for personal rule and to gain legitimacy for his non-representative governance. The fundamental changes he brought about in the Constitution, laws, and educational curricula have fundamentally altered the essential form of Pakistan from a moderate, modern state to a religiously conservative one. The Afghan wars of the 1980s and post-2001 have also made a huge contribution to the formation of terrorist groups such as the Tehreek-e-Taliban Pakistan, who have let loose a reign of violence throughout the country. Saleem Safi[36] presents a cogent picture of the problem:

> The use of religion for politics and strategic goals has been one of the prime causes of extremism. Since the inception of the country, religion—a message

of peace—has been exploited and used for politics and other vested interests. In the 1980s, thanks to cold-war politics, it began to be used for strategic goals as well. That proved to be a risky gamble since the country failed to extract anything positive from it. What is even more unfortunate is the fact that we have failed to learn from our past strategic blunders. The misuse of religion for political ends—not only by the traditional religious forces but also by newer forces—is still a common practice.

There is also a lack of unity and trust among state institutions. The military has reservations against politicians while the government and other institutions question the role of the judiciary. In return, the judiciary is angry at and even sceptical of the government machinery. The executive, judiciary, and legislature also have reservations against the media. Instead of jointly fighting against terrorism, every state institution seems busy in a struggle for self-survival.

NOTES AND REFERENCES

1. Islam, M., *Decline of Muslim States and Societies* (Xlibris Corporation, 2008).

2. Akhtar, A. S., 'Structural Violence', *Dawn*, 29 May 2014.

3. Sheikh, F., 'Making Sense of Pakistan', *The Independent*, 20 July 2009.

4. Ayaz, B., *What's Wrong with Pakistan?* (Hay House, 2013).

5. Jalal, A., The past as present *in* M. Lodhi (ed.) *Pakistan: Beyond the Crisis State* (Columbia University Press, 2011).

6. Jalal, A., *The State of Martial Rule* (Cambridge University Press, 1990).

7. Haider, Z., 'Ideologically Adrift', *in* M. Lodhi, (ed.) *Pakistan: Beyond the Crisis State* (Karachi: OUP, 2011).

8. Zaidi, A., *Issues in Pakistan's Economy* (OUP, 2015).

9. Ziauddin, U., 'The road not taken', *Express Tribune* 26 January 2017.

10. Milam, W., 'Abstraction to reality', Dhaka Tribune 30 October 2014.

11. Khan, Z., 'The New Raheel Sharif', *The News*, 16 January 2016.

12. Hussain, Z., 'A Quintessential Rebel', *Dawn*, 3 August 2016.

13. Burki, Abid A., Rashid Memon, Khalid Mir (2015), *Multiple Inequalities and Policies to Mitigate Inequality Traps in Pakistan*, Oxfam Research Report, Lahore University of Management Sciences and Oxfam Pakistan, Lahore and Islamabad.

14. Basit, A., 'Urban Jihadists', *The News*, 7 January 2017.

15. Ziauddin, M., 'Good governance is the answer', *Express Tribune*, 3 March 2017.

16. Rana, M. A., 'In search of relevance', *Dawn*, 13 March 2016.
17. Friedman, T., 'Backing Up Our Wager With Iran', *The New York Times*, 22 July 2015.
18. Idem, 'Between the intervals', *Dawn*, 9 October 2016.
19. Ashraf, M. M., 'Taking the Fight to Terror', *The News*, 7 January 2017.
20. Lieven, 'Pakistan: A Hard Country', *Public Affairs*, 2012.
21. Rana, A.,'Unfolding Madrassah Challenge', *Dawn*, 1 January 2017.
22. Hussain, Z., *Pakistan* (Vanguard, 2007).
23. Rizvi, H. A., 'Can Pakistan cope with terrorism?', *Daily Times*, 12 April 2009.
24. Darlymple, W., 'Inside the Madrasa', *New York Review of Books,* November 2005.
25. Yousafzai, M., Lamb, C., *I Am Malala* (Orion, 3013).
26. Rana, M. A., 'A Dangerous Approach', *Dawn*, 15 January 2017.
27. Hussain, Z., *Battling Militancy in Pakistan: Beyond Crisis* (Columbia University Press, 2010).
28. Safi, S., 'Afghanistan: Our Case', *The News,* 2 August 2016.
29. Yousafzai and Lamb, *I Am Malala* (Orion, 2013).
30. Amir, A., 'The Altaf Cure', *The News* 26 August 2016.
31. Rana, A., 'The Myth of Soft Targets', *Dawn*, 28 August 2016
32. Rana, A., *Layers of Complexity, Dawn,* 23 September 2013.
33. Alam, A., 'Taking Stock in Increasingly Dangerous Times', *The News*, 18 August 2016.
34. Husain, I., 'The Turkish Model', *Dawn*, 15 October 2016.
35. Amir, A., 'Pakistan's Problem is Moderation not Extremism', *The News*, 27 December 2017.
36. Safi, S., 'How to Strike the Root of Terror', *The News,* 21 February 2017.

13

The Private Sector

As has already been pointed out in Chapter 2 on the economy, Pakistan had no industry worth the name at the time of Independence and, therefore, no organized private sector as we know it today, barring the agriculture sector which was dominated by big landlords and *jagirdar*s. A majority of the population subsisted on small landholdings as tenants, or small shopkeepers. The government, therefore, had to play a catalytic role in nurturing the development of the private sector by pursuing liberal and imaginative economic policies in the 1950s, and more systematically in the 1960s. This had the effect of the emergence of a dynamic and vibrant private sector which became the engine of growth. Naturally, in the initial stages of capital formation, there was bound to have been some concentration of incomes and wealth. But this proposition, without firm empirical basis, was so blatantly exploited for political opposition to the Ayub regime that it had the effect of stunting overall development and fortifying the widely held perceptions among the East Pakistanis to a sense of deprivation.

Although still in its infancy, private sector development suffered a great setback when large industries, along with banks and insurance companies, were nationalized in the 1970s. The recovery since that big shock has been quite patchy and the tradition ingrained at that time of intrusive government interventions in the form of taxation, regulation, inspection, permits, licences, clearances, etc. have persisted in one form or way or another with varying degrees of intensity. A breakdown of the different sectors of the economy shows that public sector ownership is confined to only 10 per cent of the GDP and government investment and consumption together constitute around 16–17 per cent of the GDP. The public sector, including the federal and provincial governments, corporations, and the defence forces, employ under 10 per cent of the labour force. Thus, the bulk of the incomes, ownership, and employment are in the hands of the private sector. Within this sector, small and medium enterprises contribute almost 70 per cent to the national income and account for the bulk of formal and informal employment.

The imperatives of globalization in the twenty-first century have highlighted the importance of the growth of the private sector in powering the economy facilitated by enlightened economic reforms which enable the widest participation of Pakistani businesses in the larger world economy, thereby spurring development. The pathway for countries to successfully compete with in the international economy is by now well understood. In this the state has to play an equally important but different role by nurturing and creating markets that foster competition and provide information about opportunities to all participants. It has also to act against collusion and monopolistic practices, generate among its people the skills to engage in productive activities, transparently determining the rules and adjudicating and resolving disputes fairly and equitably. To adequately perform these functions the capacity, competence, and responsiveness of the institutions of market governance have to be upgraded along with the rules, enforcement mechanisms, organizational structures, and incentives.

According to Acemoglu and Johnson,[1] good institutions ensure two desirable outcomes: that there is relatively equal access to economic opportunity (a level playing field) and that those who provide labour or capital are appropriately rewarded and their property rights protected.

Even after 70 years, collaborative and cooperative relations between the government and the private sector have not taken root. There is a huge trust deficit between the two which, in turn, is hurting the economy and is constraining Pakistan from achieving its potential. The government blames the myopic mind-set of many risk-averse businessmen who fail to think ahead, do not capitalize on Pakistan's comparative advantage, nor innovate or invest in improving the quality of their merchandise. There is a tendency on their part, i.e. private businesses, to opt for easy and instant solutions and become rich overnight by whatever the means.

Manufacturing industries entail a great deal of hard work, supervision, management of resources, and relatively low margins in competitive sectors. New investment is not taking place in the manufacturing and export industries, and major business houses have branched off into trading, retailing, shopping malls, and the services sectors where less effort is involved, the risk is lower, the hassles are fewer, and profits are high. More recently, they have entered the power sector where the returns are guaranteed, whether or not there is full capacity utilization.

This indictment is made not only by government officials but is echoed by the popular media. Afshan Subohi, the business editor of *Dawn*, makes the following observation in her weekly column:

> In Pakistan, the business class did not go through the grind. They leaned too much on the government that accommodated them to a level where, instead of focusing on market demands, they relied more on their links to high placed officials to succeed in business. The outcome is for everyone to see.
>
> 'The manufacturers in Pakistan produce sub-standard merchandise at a high cost and then blame everyone but themselves for not faring well in domestic and global markets. Look at cars. Do you think the quality justifies the price?' said an official who headed the commerce ministry at one point and championed free competition through liberalization to force locals towards improving their production and management practices.[2]

Governments are accused of indulging in crony capitalism through concessions, exemptions, and bank loans that are subsequently written off, preferential allocation of land at subsidized rates, import licences on a priority basis, etc. to their political supporters, friends, family members, or in blatant exchange for favours. Rent-seeking rather than normal returns on capital and effort then becomes the norm. The attitude and behaviour of private economic agents operating in such a distorted environment are likely to be affected. Competitive forces are repressed under a plethora of public policies, taxation measures, regulatory prescriptions, and other such unwarranted interventions.

Competitive markets are characterized by economic outcomes that benefit consumers, producers, and others in the economic chain. However, when the processes are not determined by forces of supply and demand but are distorted by administered prices, manipulations, collusion, speculation, and excessive rent-seeking, the markets fail to perform their function, i.e. efficient allocation of resources. A wedge is created between 'observed prices' and their fundamental determinants. Investors shy away from sectors and activities that the economy really needs for growth and sustenance and shift to those unproductive ones where quick, short-term gains can be achieved in an environment of market distortions and imperfections. Private profits keep accumulating at the cost of benefits to society. Overall low economic growth coexists with excessive returns pre-empted by selected market players.

An effective taxation system should be able to capture some of these returns to finance public goods and services. However, here again the connivance of tax officials who receive a small share for their 'services' by these 'potential' taxpayers negates even that. Over-invoicing, under-invoicing, misclassification, understatement of valuation, misrepresentation and concealment of data, contrived shortages in inventories to suppress actual production, inflated purchases to exaggerate expenses and show losses, unrealistic tender bids to win contracts and then claim large cost overruns, supplying low quality goods below the original specifications, theft during transport of goods, particularly petroleum products, misuse of price-equalization surcharges, and claim for bogus refunds and rebates are some of the common tactics deployed by these market fraudsters.

Michael Walton,[3] in his examination of the origins and sources of wealth of 46 billionaires in India, found that 20 of them had drawn their primary source of wealth from sectors that can be classified as 'rent thick' (real estate, construction, infrastructure or ports, media, cement, and mining). The situation in Pakistan is no different in this respect. The sectors in which the government and not the market enjoys disproportionate powers in determining the financial health of a company through administered pricing, award of contracts, tariff determination, grant of licences or permits, and allotment of land have been the principal source of wealth creation. In addition, if the government is the single buyer of goods and services, as in case of power or the principal guarantor of raw material or input supplies, such as in the fertilizer industry, rent thickness becomes even more pronounced. That is why there is a strong case for multiple buyers and multiple sellers competing in the power market and determination of tariffs through an open, transparent, auction bidding system rather than the present upfront tariff determination by National Electric Power Regulatory Authority (NEPRA). After all, the successful open spectrum auction for telecommunications, which has fetched a billion plus dollars to the exchequer and intensified competition, is something worthy of emulation.

Economies are in the long run transformed by weeding out inefficient firms and outdated products, embarking upon innovation, risk-taking, and entrepreneurship, and abandoning old ways of producing goods and services. In Pakistan, competitive markets have not emerged because powerful interests, through their connections, influence, and money power have found lobbying and rent-seeking to be more profitable than taking risks and setting up new ventures. Pakistan's export structure has remained largely unchanged from 1990 and its market share in world trade has declined significantly. Both India and Bangladesh have kept up with the rising demand in the international market and doubled and tripled their market share. Even in textiles, Pakistan is still stuck with low value goods and does not for instance produce the man-made cotton fibre mix that is demanded by the market. Research and development grants and technology upgradation funds have been used as a financial subsidy for the existing products rather than changing the product mix.

The state is unable to perform its functions partly because of its own inefficiencies and the parochial interests of the elite classes but also because for private economic agents non-payment of taxes has become a widespread ingrained habit. Government enterprises have been captured by their workers, managers, and political and bureaucratic supervisors. Trade unions and bureaucrats in public sector enterprises have made privatization difficult to achieve. Whenever any government wishes to take some tough measures, they are immediately confronted by strikes, shut-downs, and suspensions of transport, causing immense hardships for indigent workers and ordinary citizens. The government in question backs down and the status quo ante is restored.

LAND AND LABOUR MARKETS

Markets for land and labour are both highly inefficient and inequitable. It is not realized that land can be used to create wealth for the benefit of society and contribute to an eradication of poverty. During British rule, in each district revenue officials would update the status of current land utilization and land records. Land revenue collection was thus easy as the payable liabilities were clearly defined and documented through systematic cadastral survey delineating land boundaries and recording the current tenure holders. All mutations and changes that took place in the intervening period were incorporated to present an updated picture at the end of the settlement period. No such settlement has taken place in Pakistan for over half a century and the land records are murky, land ownership is unclear, and therefore a competitive land market is virtually non-existent.

Inefficient landholders are under-utilizing this scarce asset while those who can use land more productively cannot get access due to non-competitive prices. Excessive rent-seeking does not allow reallocation of resources, a prerequisite for economic transformation. The same is true for water rights. Irrigation flows in a water-stressed country ought to reflect its scarcity premium. Water charges recovered today in the form of *abiana* cannot cover even a small fraction of the operational and maintenance expenditure. Land-acquisition laws are outdated and confer a great deal of discretionary and arbitrary power to petty officials of the revenue department in determining compensation for land acquired by the government. State lands and forests are under the occupation of influential and politically connected *zamindars* who do not pay market-determined lease money or taxes to the state. Litigation in land disputes accounts for 80 per cent of the cases in our courts.

As mentioned earlier, urban land allotment at prices lower than market prices and liberal conversion of residential to commercial land use have been a consistent source of enrichment of the elite class in Pakistan: civil and military officials, politicians and legislators, influential businessmen and landlords, religious and tribal leaders, media anchors and owners, real estate developers, and the like. Low property taxes assessed on extremely understated (one-tenth of the prevailing market price) valuation and almost negligible capital gains tax have further incentivized the mad race to acquire urban land from the state. The news reports about the head of Sindh Building Control Authority becoming a billionaire and living abroad comfortably testify to the enormous discretionary powers enjoyed by those entrusted with the utilization of land. Stark inequality in incomes and wealth reflect this unjust allocation of scarce state resources thus generating huge resentment.

In urban areas, state land is also continually encroached upon by land mafias patronized by the political parties. Prices of land have, therefore, shot up because of the scarcity created by these land-grabbers and are beyond the reach of the middle and lower income classes who earn an honest living. Property titles, outside the defence housing authorities, are not clearly established or documented. Insecure titles prevent people from taking full advantage of the productive use of the land. Zoning regulations are commonly violated in collusion with municipal officials. The most blatant example is that of the residential areas in Islamabad which have a large number of offices, commercial enterprises, schools, health clinics, and laboratories in clear violation of the zoning laws.

Mortgage loan markets cannot function in an environment where titles are not secure and properly documented, values of collaterals offered differ significantly from the registered deeds, encumbrances on the property are suppressed or misrepresented, and evidence of payments made and received in exchange of property are missing. In comparison to other developing countries, the share of mortgage lending in Pakistan is miniscule, accentuating the problem of the huge backlog of housing units available. Punjab and Sindh have recently completed the computerization of land records. This Land Record Management system, regularly updated through cadastral surveys of urban immovable property, can capture, store, and retrieve data on land rights and ownership, and can also be used to issue land titles. Geographic Information systems (GIS) and Google maps can be useful tools in this process. Land transactions can thus be facilitated and uncertainty removed, making the land market more efficient.

Digital records are less amenable to fraud and manipulation and provide easy access to key information. The accuracy of information can also help in avoidance of potential disputes and reduce the congestion in our courts, improving the functioning of our legal system. Alternative dispute resolution mechanisms can then be used to settle the disputes. Similar arrangements should be made by regularizing *katchi abadi*s and transferring land titles to long-term occupants thus adding a huge amount of 'hidden capital' to the stock.

Turning to the market for labour. Employment in the informal sector is expanding over time for a variety of reasons, including the formal labour market rigidities, insider-outsider conflict of interest, and wages below efficiency level. Some of the rigidities arise due to public policies and cost-enhancing regulations such as social security charges, workers' participation fund, employees' old age benefits contribution, and the like, the multiplicity of inspections by different agencies and the arbitrary powers enjoyed by petty officials. Informality is generally associated with lower productivity which can be increased if these distortions are eradicated. Economic transformation takes place when more productive jobs are created and less productive jobs disappear through constant reallocation of resources, including labour.

Changes in labour earnings are the largest contributor to poverty reduction. Increasing earnings from work has made the greatest difference in poverty reduction. In Pakistan, however, the movement is pacing in the opposite direction and the share of the informal economy is on the rise.

Private employers, by utilizing contractual labour and daily wage-earners, have no incentive to invest in training their workers. Besides, they are exposed to poor work environments and deprived of adequate health and social protection benefits. These practices have indeed reinforced the trend towards low productivity informal employment. Laying off their workers during economic downturns and downsizing the labour force are counterproductive measures. The additional costs of locating and training new workers on the job far exceed the savings made through severance and downsizing.

The economy of scale is not realized because many small and medium enterprises prefer to operate at the current scale and do not want to expand because of labour market regulations. Static and myopic views of owners of enterprises, who believe that the premium paid for entering the formal sector and expansion is high, leads to a low level equilibrium in which the large informal and limited formal sectors coexist. It is not realized that rural youth, after completing even a high school education, do not wish to return to farming. Similarly, the children of urban slum-dwellers who receive some education are most reluctant to join the informal trading, vending, or servicing jobs that their parents engaged in. The changing labour supply conditions dictate a more flexible and less rigid labour market.

While core labour standards such as avoidance of child labour, forced labour, and discrimination, and freedom of association and collective bargaining should be implemented, the harassment and extortionary practices associated with their compliance should be avoided. Unions should not be permitted to benefit insiders at the expense of new entrants. Job security for insiders discourages job flows for youthful workers.

The skills gap between the requirements of the economy and the output produced by our educational institutions is also retarding productivity. While mobile phones, Internet broadband, and fibre optics have made impressive inroads, they have not yet been utilized for training and skill upgradation. Chambers of commerce and trade associations, in conjunction with technical and vocational training institutes, should have organized job training courses, certification, and diploma courses in the trades for which there is perceptible demand both locally and regionally. It is not feasible for any individual firm to incur the costs of training when the benefits cannot be utilized by the company itself. Government-run institutions have proved a failure and therefore an innovative model of partnership should be experimented with in which design, delivery, curriculum, and testing are undertaken by the private operators while infrastructure, certification, and accreditation are the responsibility of the government.

Another major cause for low productivity is that academia and research institutions have not been able to make any contribution in the diffusion and upgradation of technology throughout the economy. Notwithstanding a rapid rise in the number of PhDs in science and engineering at our universities and research institutions, the link with industry remains very weak. Business schools too have not done much to improve organizational efficiency and the strategic directions taken by our large and small enterprises. In our public sector universities, professional colleges, and institutions of higher learning, teachers are engaged in politics for acquisition of strategic administrative positions rather than being absorbed in teaching and research. Tuition centres and individual coaching preoccupy the teacher at all levels while those who cannot afford to pay these exorbitant charges remain disadvantaged. Groupings, rivalries, and agitations characterize the culture in these institutions. The younger faculty members, who return with advanced degrees and enthused with the goal of achieving something satisfying, are either blocked entry, ostracized, or co-opted. In this way, any hope for the regeneration and rejuvenation of our academia through the infusion of new blood is dashed.

The productivity of labour, capital, land, and organization in Pakistan are the lowest among the developing countries and are on a constant downward spiral. The cumulative cost of sub-standard goods, supply chain inefficiency, poor work ethics, low skill sets, lack of professionalism, fake receipts and certificates, under-invoicing and smuggling, evasion of taxes, and the like, arising from the prevalent societal norms and culture and private economic agents' behaviour and practices are estimated to reduce productivity to an extent amounting to a loss of 2–3 per cent of GDP annually. Notwithstanding all the imperfections and weaknesses of government policies and governance, it is possible to reach a 6 to 7 per cent growth rate by altering the behaviour, attitudes, and practices in our society and private economic agents. Is this possible? Because it will transfer the responsibility to our shoulders rather than blaming the government of the day, this appears to be a herculean task. We must not, however, forget that responsible citizenship is a prerequisite for a buoyant economy.

FINANCIAL MARKETS

Financial markets in Pakistan have been liberalized and have become competitive and relatively efficient but continue to remain shallow. The array of financial instruments available for various types of transactions in the market has widened. The banking sector, of which 80 per cent was earlier in the public sector, is now dominated by private banks and has become financially sound, profitable, service-oriented, and efficient, with high capital adequacy and liquidity ratios. The financial infrastructure has been strengthened but the legal system remains too time-consuming and expensive for ordinary market participants. The regulatory environment has improved and the capacity of regulators to oversee and monitor is much better today than in the past but enforcement and prompt corrective action capabilities need to be further enhanced. The financial soundness indicators of the system show an upward trend in almost all dimensions but there are weaknesses and vulnerabilities that need remedial action. Corporate governance rules have been clarified and conform to the best international practices but their consistent application and voluntary adoption by the industry remain uneven.

Much, however, remains to be done:

1. Broadening Access to Middle and Lower Income Groups

Agriculture and SME lending have not kept pace with the public sector corporate and personal lending, as both are risky. The banks have to reach out to at least three million households in the agricultural sector and two million small, medium, and micro enterprises over the next five years if it is to achieve the goals of financial inclusion.

2. New Liability Products

The industry has so far paid adequate attention to developing new products on the asset side but neglected the savers and depositors. It is myopic for us to have such a one-sided approach as it is savers and depositors who provide the wherewithal for the industry to perform its basic function of intermediation. The banks and non-bank institutions need to devise innovative solutions tailored to the needs of Pakistan's 28 million depositors and savers. Development of new liability products should be on the top of the agenda for the next five years. This is a serious weakness that we cannot afford to live with any longer.

3. Corporate Restructuring

Financial sector reforms, in absence of corporate sector restructuring, i.e. pruning costs, reducing debt, and increasing efficiency, will have only short-term beneficial effects. The ratio of total corporate debt to GDP should be lowered, capacity expanded, and labour productivity raised. Firms have to be healthier and invest in productive activities while new firms should enter the credit markets.

The bankruptcy law must provide a mechanism for an orderly settlement of obligations. Bankruptcy separates bad managers from potentially valuable assets, lifts debts from shoulders that cannot support them, and preserves value that alternatives such as liquidation might destroy.

4. Infrastructure Financing

The traditional method of financing infrastructure projects only through the Public Sector Development Programme has resulted in congestions, shortages, and bottlenecks. There are institutions such as insurance, provident and pension funds that are seeking long-term instruments. Infrastructure financing can match the assets and liabilities through infrastructure financing in the public–private partnership mode.

5. E-Banking/Digital Financial Services (DFS)

With the deregulation of the telecommunication sector in Pakistan, and introduction of 3G/4G technologies, smartphones, and broadband Internet, the opportunities for further value-added services to underpin banking transactions have multiplied manifold. Bank-less branching has made quite a promising beginning but an e-payment gateway needs to be established to meet the growing demand for e-commerce. There is a much greater scope for Fintech and DFS to bring the banking excluded population within the ambit of financial services.

6. Private Equity, Pension, and Provident Funds

There remains a mismatch between the growing appetite for institutional and contractual saving institutions for long-term investment vehicles and the demand for long gestation mortgage, infrastructure, real estate, and project financing. Private equity and venture capital funds, private pension and provident funds, and insurance companies are stripped of profitable investment opportunities to meet their obligations while the rate of capital formation in Pakistan lags behind that of its neighbours. Debt capital markets can also flourish if the demand for issuers are matched by the needs of these investors whose pool of savings is expanding.

7. Investment Banking

The role of investment banking in Pakistan has so far remained quite murky. The spread of a universal banking model has led to a certain degree of ambiguity in terms of the market niche in which investment banks can operate. Corporate institutions will always require investment banks to provide services such as investment advice, corporate restructuring, distressed assets acquisition and disposal, mergers and acquisitions, and equity and debt financing. These services can best be provided by specialized financial institutions.

8. Risk Management

The advent of the Basel III regime imposes a sense of urgency on both the regulators as well as the financial industry to put their act together so far as risk management is concerned. The large banks have to attract human resources of the right kind, set up internal rating systems, and the supporting technology to continually monitor their portfolios and conduct stress testing.

9. Promotion of Islamic Banking

Islamic Banking has been making significant progress but is still functioning in the shadows of conventional banking. Islamic banks have to come up with different products, services, and target groups to come into their own and make a difference.

AGRICULTURE[4]

No other sector in Pakistan falls so completely in the private sector as agriculture but it is unfortunate that the conventional analysis of the private sector usually lacks any substantive discussion of it. Almost half of Pakistan's employed labour force derives its livelihood and sustenance directly or indirectly from agriculture. It also plays a pivotal role in poverty-alleviation and reduction in urban–rural income disparities, provides nutrition and food security, and contributes to export expansion and therefore to Pakistan's overall economic prosperity and social uplift.

Like all other countries undergoing transformation, in Pakistan, agriculture contribution to the GDP has declined to 20 per cent from more than 50 per cent but it takes care of the food and fibre needs of Pakistan's 200 million people. Its direct contribution in employment and downstream activities—processing, transportation, and the supply chain—remains quite significant. Pakistan's agriculture-based exports, direct and indirect, using agricultural raw materials, still account for over half the total earnings. As per capita incomes have risen and the middle class has expanded, there has been a gradual shift towards high value products such as dairy, meat, eggs, fruits, vegetables, and fisheries. The four major crops—wheat, cotton, rice, and sugarcane—which used to form the bulk of agricultural produce, now account for a little more than a third of the produce of the agricultural sector. Notwithstanding the overwhelming importance of agriculture in Pakistan's economy, the recent stagnation in agriculture growth rates and farmers' yields, the declining availability of water, and high rate of malnourishment have become sources of major concern.

Table 13.1 shows agriculture sector growth rates in Pakistan over the past five decades.

Table 13.1: Agriculture Sector Growth Rates 1960–2010

Deacade	Growth Rate (%)
1960s	5.1
1970s	2.4
1980s	5.4
1990s	4.4
2000s	3.2

Source: Pakistan Economic Survey 2009–10

From an average growth rate of 5.1 per cent a year, among the highest in developing countries, it has slowed down to 3.2 per cent, or a little over the population growth rate. The principal reason for this decline and stagnation lies in the gradual erosion of productivity gains. Two-thirds of the growth in the 1980s was contributed by increases in productivity. By the 1990s, the rise in productivity accounted for a third and in 2000s it fell to only one-fifth of the average growth. The gap between the national average yields and those of the progressive farmers has been widening over the past two decades. In the case of rice and wheat, the gap is about 45 per cent of progressive farmer yields while in sugarcane it is about 73 per cent.

Among the many factors responsible for losses in agricultural productivity and the widening gap between the national average yields and those of the progressive farmers, the one that stands out at the top of the list is the inefficiency of Pakistan's national agricultural research system. After the great impact of the Green revolution technology of fertilizers and seeds tapered off in the 1980s, there has hardly been any major breakthrough in agricultural technology. The agenda for research is quite vast and includes development of high yielding heat and cold tolerant, drought resistant, and short duration varieties of field crops, water and soil conservation technologies, moisture management, green manuring, precision levelling, tunnel farming, bio-fertilizers, reclamation of saline and waterlogged soils, zero tillage, intercropping, and ridge sowing. Some of the progressive farmers who are using some of these technologies together with drip and sprinkler irrigation have obtained higher returns on their investment. The agricultural credit system and crop insurance targeted at small and medium farmers could induce them to adopt these techniques on their farms. The national agricultural research system has suffered not only because of the budgetary allocations being curtailed but also because of the lack of human resource capability, organizational inertia, bureaucratic procedures and processes, and lack of clarity in the roles of national and provincial agriculture research institutions.

Another critical constraint is the poor utilization of the vast irrigation system. Per capita availability of water has decreased to 1066 cubic metres, placing Pakistan in the category of high water-stressed countries. Any other country, with about 95 per cent of arable land cultivated under irrigation, would have been a major player in the global food and commercial crops market by utilizing this scarce resource more efficiently. This potential has not, however, been realized as the total water productivity in Pakistan in 2011 remains only half that of India. Pakistan produces only 0.13 kg per cubic metre of water. This shows the enormous scope that exists of a much higher GDP and agricultural production if this gap in water productivity is narrowed and irrigated crop intensity enhanced.

Although the rate of irrigation has been expanding by 1.4 per cent a year, the cropland has been shrinking at an average 0.4 per cent a year. Mismanagement, mis-governance, and poor maintenance of the irrigation system have limited farmers' access to water, particularly those at the tail-end of the water courses. Influential and politically well-connected farmers receive excessive supplies and waste water by over-irrigating their land, while the poor farmers are starved of water. Studies have shown that 60 per cent of the water delivered at the head does not reach the farms due to transmission losses in the distributaries, canals, watercourses, and fields. There is also the issue of timing between the supply and demand for water. Supply peaks during the summer; demand is spread throughout the year. Storage capacity that would be able to collect excess water in the peak season and release it according to the demand is inadequate and no large dam has been constructed since Tarbela in the 1970s. Political controversy has vitiated the overall atmosphere for the construction of storage dams in Pakistan.

The financial sustainability of the irrigation system is another major area of concern. Water user charges, collected from the farmers, amount to a paltry 0.5 per cent of crop revenue and do not cover even 25 per cent of the operational and maintenance expenses of the irrigation canals, channels, and watercourses, accentuating the vulnerabilities and risks to the integrity of the system. The collection rate of these charges is also low, at about 60 per cent of the receivables, obliging the government to subsidize irrigation water users. Moreover, the large farmers are also, for all practical purposes, exempt from paying agriculture income tax. Therefore, the irrigation system suffers from serious underinvestment in terms of modernization, expansion, storage, lining of canals, drainage etc. The present flat rate of irrigation charges is both inefficient and inequitable. Consumption by volumes should be the basis for assessment of charges. This would lead to both water conservation and fairness in burden-sharing.

The impending risks associated with climate change have not yet caught the attention of the policy-makers. Climate change is in all likelihood going to melt glaciers, affecting downstream water availability, adversely impact the annual rainfall pattern, and raise the sea level. Pakistan's irrigation system draws its sustenance for fresh water from the glacial melt of the Himalayas as 70 per cent of the flow of the Indus River is contributed by this glacial melt. Global warming will accelerate the melting of the glaciers, increasing the risk of floods in the short run due to greater runoff into the rivers. In the long run, there are likely to be shortages of water as the run-offs decline. A study has shown that by 2050 almost 35 per cent of the glaciers will disappear and river runoffs will increase. Following that, the resultant glacial recession will result in a decrease in river flows by 30 to 40 per cent over the next 50 years. Simulation studies depicting various scenarios of climate change, indicate that Pakistan's agricultural GDP could decline by 5 per cent from its base value. However, if an additional 12 MAF of canal water out of the existing 106 MAF could be saved and utilized for irrigating cropland, agricultural GDP could be boosted by 4.2 per cent.

Monsoon rains are a vital resource for agriculture production supplementing canal and groundwater use. Warmer temperature caused by decreasing rainfall and increasing variability in the magnitude and timing of rainfall can result in greater water stress. Rain-fed agriculture is the principal source of livelihood for the poor population of the arid and semi-arid zones of Pakistan. The negative impact of this changing weather pattern would have disastrous consequences for their existence. It is projected that in Pakistan, there is likely to be a decrease in monsoon precipitation of about 20 per cent.

The other risk from climate change is the probability of increased incidence and frequency of extreme weather events such as floods, droughts, cyclones, and the like. Floods in Pakistan in 2010 affected over 20 million people and were followed by the floods in the Sindh province in 2012.

In an environment of system-wide water stress, declining per capita water availability for agriculture and food production, the growing need for hydropower development, the likelihood of trans-boundary disputes and conflicts between the upper riparian and lower riparian, are also likely to develop with greater intensity. The retention of water upstream in India for energy generation has already given rise to serious apprehensions in Pakistan that this will restrict water flows for the downstream Pakistani farmers. The Indus Water Basin Treaty provides the framework for the resolution of these disputes but in the coming years the overall shortages of supplies resulting from glacial melting and precipitation losses will give rise to greater tension between the two countries. A new mechanism will have to be evolved and agreed upon to resolve future disputes.

Climate change will thus impact the agricultural sector by negatively affecting crop yields with serious consequences for food security. Rice and wheat yields would be reduced and the overall decline would be between 2 to 4 per cent by 2020. There may be a shift in the sowing season due to heat stress while increased humidity will heighten the threat of pest attack. Physiological stress may reduce the reproduction of animals affecting livestock production in Pakistan. A study conducted by the IUCN suggests that livestock production could decline by 20–30 per cent due to the rising temperature resulting in a crises in milk, meat, and poultry production and pushing prices beyond reach of the average Pakistani. On average, rough estimates indicate that Pakistan's agricultural sector could lose $2–16 billion per annum due to change in climate by the end of the twenty-first century.

The other burning issue that requires attention is that of food security. Public policy has so far focused exclusively on increasing the aggregate food production and self-sufficiency in wheat, the staple food of most Pakistanis. Food security has never been an explicit objective of policy-makers. The average per capita daily consumption which was 2,375 Kcal in 1990s has fallen to 2,250 Kcal by 2007, compared to an average of 2,630 Kcal in developing countries. Lack of access rather than lack of food supply is the principal factor underlying food insecurity because the per capita food production index increased from 99 in 1991 to 106 in 2008 but has since then stagnated. It is estimated that about 15 per cent of the wheat crop is lost annually due to wastage, inefficient handling of procurement, distribution, transportation, and inadequate and poor storage facilities.

The other factor is income inequality as almost half the population spends less on food than is necessary for a healthy and active life. The situation is worse for those in the lowest income quintiles. The average monthly household consumption in the lowest quintile in urban areas is only a third of that of the highest quintile and less than half of the average. This disparity in the consumption pattern is an outcome of several factors: open and disguised unemployment and underemployment, high inflation, lagging real wage rates, absence of social safety nets, poor access to healthcare, and unhygienic practices relating to nutrition and child and maternal care. In the last six years, food inflation in urban areas has outpaced growth in income. In the rural areas, 60 per cent of the rural population buys food from markets. Inflationary pressures therefore hit them equally hard. Although the government pays substantial amounts towards wheat subsidy in the name of poor urban consumers, the beneficiaries are the flour-mill owners. Similarly, the subsidies on fertilizer are also captured by producers and large farmers rather than those for whom the subsidy is intended, i.e. small and marginal farmers.

In the case of the sugar industry, political patronage rather than consumer welfare has been the major determinant of public policy. When there is surplus production, the government takes upon itself the responsibility to purchase the surplus sugar from the mill-owners and sell it at a loss in international markets. When there are shortages, domestic imports are delayed until the sugar mills have realized windfall gains by selling at higher market prices.

The Millennium Development Goal (MDG) to reduce the number of undernourished population by half by 2015 was not achieved. The latest numbers indicate that one in every four of the population is still malnourished and child nutrition has not shown much improvement either. Pakistan has the highest rate of stunting among the children in South Asia, at around 44 per cent. This is a highly disturbing trend for the future mental and physical well-being of its youth.

To sum up, there is a need to rethink our agricultural sector strategies away from the past emphasis on production and supplies alone and to address the new challenges that we are likely to face in the next three to four decades. Climate change, water productivity, and food insecurity are the emerging issues that need the focus and attention of public policy-makers.

TAXATION[5]

One of the worrying trends that has become highly inimical to private business development and investment in Pakistan is the rising burden of taxation on those who are already in the tax net. Corporate organizations are paying as much as 40–50 per cent of their profits in the form of various taxes, super taxes, cesses, fees, Employees Old-age Benefit Institution (EOBI), social security, workers' welfare fund, dividends, and the like. While they are expected to invest, the tax regime requires them to distribute at least 40 per cent of their profits in the form of dividends. Pakistan is stuck with a low investment–GDP ratio of 15–16 per cent while in India it exceeds 30 per cent and in Bangladesh stands around 30 per cent. Capital formation will not occur if the level of tax penalizes effort and entrepreneurship and acts as a disincentive to future expansion. The government is also in a bind as tax–GDP ratio, hovering around 10–12 per cent, is inadequate to meet the demands of development, debt–servicing, and defence.

Provinces now receive almost 60 per cent of the divisible tax pool and are quite content with that, mobilizing only 1 per cent of the GDP in the form of provincial revenues. The World Bank[6] has estimated that the potential of own taxes in Punjab alone is at least four times the present level of tax collection.

As tax revenues are inadequate, the government is obliged to borrow internally from the banking system and externally from international financial institutions to fill the gap between its revenue and expenditure. High indebtedness leads to a rising cost of debt-servicing which currently consumes 40 per cent of tax revenues. Another 25 per cent goes towards defence expenditure, and another 20 per cent towards subsidies, leaving very little for development expenditure. Thus mobilizing tax revenues is the top priority for the country's economic managers.

The important question that needs to be addressed is: Why is Pakistan's tax–GDP ratio so low? To analyse the reasons for this intractable nature of the tax regime, we have to adopt a systemic approach by dividing the economy along several parameters such as rural and urban; formal, informal, and illicit; agriculture, industry, and services; salaried and unsalaried; and corporates vs non-corporates.

Of Pakistan's potential labour force of 75 million, 18 million are not participating, 5 million are unemployed, and 52 million are employed. The rural labour force accounts for approximately 70 per cent of the total. 10 per cent families hold over 12.5 acres of irrigated and 25 acres of non-irrigated land, of which only a third hold over 50 acres of land and fall within the tax net. 90 per cent of families are subsistence farmers, landless peasants, unpaid family helps, casual workers, and small vendors, exempt from direct taxes. The yields in tax revenue from the agricultural sector are unlikely to exceed 2 or 3 per cent of the total. The principal burden therefore falls on urban incomes earned by 30 per cent of the labour force or non-agricultural incomes in the rural areas.

Studies on sectoral incidence show that industry bears over two-thirds of the tax realized, the services sector around 21 per cent, and agriculture 3 per cent. In the services sector, transportation and trade together account for one-third of the GDP. Apart from a few companies, the transport sub-sector is dominated by small- and medium-size operators. Only air and shipping yield some revenues. Similarly, out of 1.5 million wholesale and retail trade units (employing a population of 9 million), 85 per cent are small family-run stores. The entire direct and sales tax collection from the trade sub-sector constitutes 0.5 per cent of federal taxes. The scope from the services sector also remains limited.

As two-thirds of the tax collected is in the form of indirect taxes and one-fourth of the entire amount comes from petroleum and petroleum products at various stages (which is passed on to consumers), the overall incidence is regressive. Even in the case of direct taxes, two-thirds are evaded as they pay only withholding taxes (WHT) for sectors covered by the WHT regime but do not discharge their full and final tax liability on all sources of incomes Therefore, in terms of the impact of taxes on different income groups, the burden falls disproportionately on the poor and middle-income groups.

To top this up, policy-makers, in their attempt to achieve revenue targets, impose additional levies on the existing taxpayers. This disincentive leads to the quest for various loopholes in the complex tax code, beset as it is with enormous discretionary regulations, to understate incomes, claim exemptions, and avoid paying full taxes.

Direct evidence and hard facts regarding the informal and illicit economy are difficult to gather. Casual observations point to a gradual expansion in the informal sector's share through workers' remittances, understated property income, a proliferation of unregistered enterprises such as boutiques, tuition centres, schools, clinics, beauty salons, restaurants, etc. In the rural areas, the informal sector includes *arthis*, or intermediaries in *mandi* towns and agriculture produce markets, and other input and services providers. Their common feature is that they are all outside the tax net.

Over the past five to six years, illicit incomes earned through corruption and bribery by public office holders, extortion, robberies, ransom, extortion by land, water, and other mafias, prostitution, gambling dens, and other illegal and criminal activities have multiplied manifold. Therefore, the taxable base, even in urban areas, is shrinking because of the transfer of income from the formal to the informal/illicit economy.

As a consequence of the enlarged scope of the informal and illicit economy, under 1.1 per cent of the GDP is collected as actual direct income tax. The top 20 per cent of the population or 6 million households receive 50 per cent of the national income. The potential taxpayer base for individual income tax is 3.5 million. Some 118,000 firms are registered in the sales tax system but only 15,000 actually pay any tax. In FY 2013, only 21 per cent of registered companies paid any income tax while 80 per cent of the total amount was collected from multinationals and a few large Pakistani companies. As much as 82 per cent of the total sales tax and federal excise duty is collected from only 100 companies. In the formal sector, documented companies coexist with undocumented ones. As the former evade payment of sale tax either by remaining below the threshold level or misrepresenting their true turnover they are able to sell at lower prices than the documented firms, the aggregate sales of the latter decline and consequently tax collection is lowered.

The analysis here shows that the present taxation regime that is highly skewed towards the urban, industry, and formal sectors is narrow, inequitable, regressive, and distortive. Unless there is a structural transformation of the economy—one that expands the formal sector, makes the rural sector and agriculture more efficient, raises middle-class numbers, and makes taxes more progressive and less patronage-ridden—attempts to reform the tax regime will continue to be unproductive.

Tax reforms that should be continued and undertaken are:

1. Withdrawal of Statutory Regulatory Orders (SROs) which provide concessions, waivers, and rebates to specific firms or sub-sectors. Some progress was made under the 2014 IMF programme but these are now gaining currency, particularly under the China-Pakistan Economic Corridor (CPEC).

2. Out of 3.2 million potential taxpayers, only 1.1 million are actually filing tax returns. New taxpayers should be brought into the net through enforcement and audit.

3. A risk-based audit system should identify those found understating or concealing their incomes. They should be heavily penalized as a deterrent to others.

4. Provincial tax collection remains abysmally low at 1 per cent of GDP. Urban property tax and agricultural income tax have a high potential that is not being tapped.

5. Presumptive and withholding taxes, which are then taken as full and final settlement of tax liability, should be replaced by mandatory filing of tax returns along with payments.

6. The system of tax refunds has to be replaced by a single stage non-refundable tax at a reasonable rate.

7. The tax code, which has become overly complex and convoluted, giving rise to the exercise of discretionary powers by tax collectors and leaving many loopholes exploited by tax practitioners, needs to be revised and simplified.

8. The powers of the Federal Tax Ombudsman (FTO) have to be expanded to detect, investigate, and take action against those found engaging in malpractices, misuse of office for personal gain, and causing revenue leakages.

9. The number of taxes and levies collected by the federal, provincial, and district governments should be reduced and consolidated.

Currently, labour levies such as EOBI and Social Security are being collected by different agencies. From the taxpayer's point of view it is the combined burden of all taxes, fees, levies, and contributions which is relevant. If this burden is excessive, then there will be a natural temptation for them to evade taxes and then there will be collusion between them and the tax collectors to minimize this burden. In that event the state exchequer is the ultimate loser. Thus the reduction in number of taxes and an appraisal of the total tax burden on individual firms and businesses are essential to generate realistic revenue stream.

10. The dispute resolution and adjudication process for taxes is too lengthy, cumbersome, and time consuming. There are multiple tiers through which the taxpayer can entangle the department in litigation and postpone the payments due. In this way the deterrence effect of non-compliance is nullified. There is a need to streamline this process and only one appeal should be allowed to either parties after the original jurisdiction has exercised its mind.

11. The recruitment, training, remuneration, progression, and incentive structure of the tax administration should be completely revamped with a view to transforming the FBR into a highly professional and performance-based organization. Currently there are too many unqualified and redundant staff occupying non-technical positions. They pre-empt a large proportion of the salaries and wages with the result that high level professionals cannot be recruited, retained, and paid the remuneration that they merit.

REGULATION

Besides taxation, another function that is performed by the state is to regulate the private sector, particularly in areas where there are natural monopolies, market failures or imperfections, missing markets, or a pronounced tendency for collusion. Regulatory structures should be evaluated in the context of the market structure prevalent in the industry.

In this context, the most critical regulator is always in the financial sector. The State Bank of Pakistan has to ensure that the interests of the depositors who provide the bulk of the bank financing are protected and safeguarded against the egregious behaviour of the owners of the banks. As the shareholders provide only a small fraction of the total capital of a bank they have an incentive to take excessive risk in deploying the capital as the upside gains are appropriated by them while the losses are disproportionately borne by the depositors with no say in the matter. Effective regulation of financial markets is a balancing act between competition and moderating operating practices to reduce systemic risk. Both the speed and complexity of transactions have pushed the risks of market failure progressively higher.

Other regulatory agencies are the SECP, Competition Commission of Pakistan, and the Federal Board of Revenue (which is both a tax collection agency and a regulatory body). According to IOSCO, the core objectives of securities market regulation are:

1. Investor protection from misleading, manipulative, or fraudulent practices including insider trading, front running, misuse of client assets, and trading ahead of customers. Full disclosure of information, accounting standards are key.
2. Fair, efficient, and transparent markets to ensure that investors are given fair access to market facilities and market and/or price information.
3. Reduction of systemic risk.

Outside the financial sector, we have the National Electric Power Regulatory Authority (NEPRA), Oil and Gas Regulatory Authority (OGRA), Pakistan Electronic Media Regulatory Authority (PEMRA), Drug Regulatory Authority of Pakistan (DRAP), Civil Aviation Authority (CAA), etc. In each of these cases, the motives are different, ranging from protecting consumer interests to safety, health, and environmental protection.

A question that is often asked is: Why is regulation needed in the first place when the declared government policy is deregulation?

The most common argument for regulation is to correct market failures and inefficiencies and ensure a level playing field. Market failures can arise due to economies of scale, technological or network characteristics, and a monopoly structure giving rise to abuse of power.

Another underlying reason behind independent regulatory agencies is the desire to distance the political executive from the inevitable and unpopular hikes in tariffs as one of the means of increasing revenue generation. The idea of keeping the regulatory agency under the direct administrative control of the concerned ministries is therefore a negation of this motive. Agencies such as DRAP and PEMRA should either be placed under the cabinet division or under a separate ministry of regulatory affairs.

There is no inherent inconsistency between deregulation and regulation. The choice depends entirely on the market structure of the industry. If the markets are competitive and functioning efficiently as they ought to, then there is no reason for intensive regulation. As much should be left to market forces as possible and the task of the regulator is simply that of watchdog to ensure that there are no market distortions or collusive practices. In other sectors, as pointed out earlier, such as the financial sector, effective regulation is absolutely critical because of the asymmetries in the behaviour of the owners and the depositors in tolerating risks and in order to avoid systemic collapse.

SUMMATION

To achieve sustained economic growth, a competitive private sector must be nurtured and relied upon. Therefore, a major area of reforms in Pakistan is to create space for the growth of new entrants in the private sector by eradicating the constraints created by the state to their entry and smooth operations. Notwithstanding the pursuit of policies of liberalization, deregulation, de-licensing, and disinvestment over the past twenty years, the overbearing burden of government interventions in business life-cycle looms large. Rent-seeking in those sectors where government is heavily involved either as a single buyer or guarantor of supplies, granter of permits and concessions, or the award of contracts, has become an obstacle to new entrants. The difficulties faced by new businesses in acquiring, getting a title to, pricing, transferring, and possessing land, in obtaining no-objection certificates from various agencies, in obtaining water and gas connections, sewerage facilities, a reliable electricity supply, access roads, in securing finances for greenfield projects, or new enterprises utilizing emerging technologies are still overwhelming and nerve-wrecking.

The powers wielded by petty inspectors from various departments/ agencies are so vast that they can make or break a business. The growing trend towards 'informalization' of the economy, particularly by small and medium enterprises, is a testimony to the still dominant nature of the government. Over 96 per cent of the establishments reported in the economic census 2005 fall in this category. The attitude of middle and lower functionaries of the government in the provinces and districts towards private business remains ambivalent. Either the functionaries harass the business to extract pecuniary and non-pecuniary benefits for themselves or they are simply distrustful of or hostile to private entrepreneurs. The multiplicity of agencies involved and clearances required and avoidable delays at every level raise the transaction costs for new entrants. Unless the ease of entry and exit is facilitated, competitive forces will not emerge and the collusive and monopolistic practices of large businesses will continue to hurt consumers.

The bulk of popular discussion on the economy remains obsessively focused on the government, its policies and institutions. While it is true that these policies and institutions play a critical role, we tend to forget that productivity gains which form the cornerstone of economic growth and better living standards are achieved under a given factor endowment through interactions between public policies and institutions, private sector response and behaviour, social norms and culture, and the external environment. The private sector contributes 90 per cent to the national income and leads the way in capital formation, employment, and growth. An enabling environment that eases the path to business is therefore the sine qua non for unleashing entrepreneurial energies and productivity of private businesses. Taxation and regulatory regimes should therefore be supportive of rather than a constraint on private sector activity. Agriculture is still critical to the economy for its impact on food security, nutrition, employment, poverty, and regional disparities. The gap between progressive farmers and national averages can be bridged through better allocation and utilization of resources. Small and medium enterprises that account for 70 per cent of the economy have not performed up to their potential and public policies should be geared to assuage their problems.

Notes and References

1. Acemoglu, D., Johnson, S., *Unbundling Institutions* (Massachusetts Institute of Technology, 2003).

2. Subohi, A., 'Productivity', *Dawn*, 23 January 2017.

3. Walton, M., 'Where do India's billionaires get their wealth?', *Economic and Political Weekly*, vol 97(40), 6 October 2012.

4. This section has benefited from the various chapters compiled in the IFPRI publication: Spielman, et al. *Agriculture and the Rural Economy in Pakistan* (University of Pennsylvania Press, 2016).

5. A large number of studies have been carried out on the Pakistan taxation system and its reform. This section draws upon the findings of those studies to underpin the analysis and recommendations provided here.

6. World Bank, *Punjab Development Update*, 2017.

14

Administration of Justice

Pakistan's system of administration of justice comprising the police, prosecution, prisons, and the courts is the principal vehicle for ensuring the rule of law, dispensation of justice, and enforcement of contracts. These institutions have assumed even greater importance in the post-2001 period because of the fight against terrorism and extremism that have engulfed Pakistan and severely damaged the economy. As the role of the courts has already been discussed in Chapter 9, the discussion here will focus on the police, prosecution, and prisons. A large number of scholarly studies on this subject have been produced over time both in Pakistan and abroad.[1] It would serve little purpose here in repeating their findings and therefore I will address the contemporary issues facing the criminal justice system in Pakistan and what can be done to improve it.

The most troublesome part of the system is the shifting of responsibility from one component to the other with the result that the conviction rate is only 5–10 per cent. Even in terrorism cases, tried under the Anti-Terrorism Act by special courts, 282 out of 447 high profile terrorists were acquitted in Punjab in 2011. The courts find the investigation to be shoddy, crime scene management to be sub-par, scientific collection methods missing, and the prosecution to be flawed. They therefore have no other alternative than to discharge the case on the basis of benefit of doubt. The police and the prosecutors believe that the court procedures are lengthy and cumbersome, and adjournments are granted too frequently on flimsy grounds and are tilted in favour of the criminals defended by highly paid and well-connected lawyers. Witnesses are intimidated or their evidence tampered with. As the probability of the accused being set free is high, the witnesses and their families are scared of retaliation. The witnesses either do not come forward to testify, or if they do, their evidence is too weak and insufficient to establish guilt.

A blatant example was that of Malik Ishaq, the head of Lashkar-e-Jhangvi, a sectarian group that was professedly involved in the killings of Shias in Pakistan. He had 70 murder cases against him but was not convicted for any one of them. Those who had given evidence against him lived in fear of retaliation as there is no credible witness protection programme.

POLICE

The Pakistan police force was formed in 1947 with a mere 12 Muslim Indian police officers and 14 British officers who opted to stay. The police force, which in each province is controlled by the respective provincial governments, has grown to a strength of 400,000 comprising constables, junior and non-commissioned officers, and senior gazetted officers. There are now around 1,500 police stations spread throughout Pakistan, headed by a station house officer (SHO) who is the principal contact point between the citizens and the police. In addition, there are over 26 law enforcement agencies under the direct control of the federal government, with a total strength of over 250,000. The important federal agencies are the Rangers, Frontier Constabulary, Frontier Corps, Federal Investigation Agency (FIA), Intelligence Bureau, and the National Highway and Motorway Police, among others.

Notwithstanding the huge expansion in the numbers of the police force, it still remains undermanned, is poorly trained, possesses inadequate equipment, and functions under antiquated laws, rules, procedures, and practices. Other extraneous duties, such as the protocol duties and the security of a large number of VIPs, further reduces the strength of the effective force and dilutes the quality of service. Politically motivated recruitment, postings, and transfers have taken the sting out of their professionalism.

For the ordinary citizen, it is the police force which represents the face of the state; and it is an ugly face. The word 'police' in Pakistan is synonymous with oppression, extortion, and high-handedness. The force is plagued by stories of false cases being filed, patronage of criminal activities, and contrived encounters where the accused are tortured and killed. The prosecution capacity of the state is weak, often venal and shoddy. Witnesses can often go missing or be gunned down. Prisons have no set of rules. Those who can afford to keep the warden happy receive preferential treatment. It is also not rare to hear of convicts escaping from prison. In short, the state of our police service, prisons, investigation and prosecution capacities, and administration of justice is scandalous. Pakistan is stuck with antiquated Raj-era laws. The parallel situation in India is not very different. Gurcharan Das[2] describes the Indian police and lower judicial system, which does not sound very different from its counterpart in Pakistan: 'The Police are a tool in the hands of the political leadership and often used to settle scores against rivals. The lower judiciary is mostly corrupt and judicial delay is the commonest form of injustice.'

Prof D. H. Bayley,[3] the author of a definitive work on the subject, observed that 'a dual system of criminal justice' emerged. 'The one of law, the other of politics ... the rule of law in modern India, the frame upon which justice hangs, has been undermined by the rule of politics. Supervision in the name of democracy has eroded the foundations upon which impartiality depends in a criminal justice system.'

Initiatives have been taken by various commissions and committees for the reform of the police. Most of the reports have made very practical recommendations, which can quite easily be put into effect, on the legal framework under which the police function, the replacement of outdated procedures and manuals, strengthening the numbers, the recruitment process, training, equipment, mobility, communication, and welfare of the personnel. Very little was done to implement those recommendations until 15 years ago. A ray of hope was seen when Police Order 2002 replaced the Police Act 1858 and came into force on 14 August 2002. Originally, the spirit behind the reforms initiative was to transform the police from a 'force' into a 'public service'. As implied in the documents, the vision underlying the Police Order 2002 was to develop a police system that was professionally competent, operationally neutral (not politically motivated), service-oriented, and accountable to the people.

Amir Husain[4] describes the salient features of the Police Order 2002:

Some of the key features of the Police Order 2002 were, one, financial, administrative and operational independence with an enhanced role of the Inspector General (IG) of police in the provincial governance structure. This entails that an incumbent IG had to act as secretary to the provincial government rather than being subservient to the provincial home department. Two, tenure protection of police personnel for three years (every officer to be posted at his/her service area for at least three years to reduce politically induced transfers).

Three, in case an officer was to be removed before the expiry of his/ her tenure it was to be through a transparent process where each party had to explain their position in writing to the higher authority. This aimed to insulate the police from political pressures.

Four, establishment of the National Public Safety Commission. With twelve members, six of whom were to be selected under the supervision of the chief justice of Pakistan as the head of the selection committee. The other six were to be elected members (three from the treasury benches and three from the opposition). The committee was to be responsible for decisions regarding the structure, recruitments, and operational remit of the police.

Five, establishment of an accessible Police Complaints Authority at all levels, for the citizens to report their grievances to the authority and hence make the police accountable to the public for their conduct and service.

Six, establishment of a Federal Agencies' Coordination Committee at the district and range level including sessions judges, public prosecutors, and public representatives. The committee, thus constituted, had the autonomy to discuss the localized challenges to law and order, crime, and other public safety issues and to recommend a devolved mechanism for the enforcement of actions.

And finally, functional specialization of the police service by inducting experts for watch and ward (operations), security and investigation rather than relying on the discretionary powers of an SHO.

Unfortunately, these reforms, including the application of the Police Order 2002, were suspended and put on hold by all the four provinces once the new governments came to power in 2008. New versions have been tried or ad hoc measures have been put in place but KP is the only province which has decided to retain the 2002 Police order in letter and spirit while Punjab is still bringing its new law into shape. Hassan Khawar[5] makes the following assessment of the KP situation:

The K-P Police Ordinance 2016 has definitely minimized the discretion of political masters by giving tenure security to the Provincial Police Officer and fully empowering him to transfer and post officers of his choice. By abandoning the powers previously enjoyed by the chief minister, the K-P government has set a commendable precedent towards ensuring autonomy of police and prevention of political interference. Furthermore, through various commissions and bodies, the law has attempted to create a system of police accountability to the public. The public safety commissions will review performance of the police and will approve policing plans, whereas regional complaint authorities will enquire into citizen's complaints. The district assemblies will be able to recommend the premature transfer of district police officers on grounds of unsatisfactory performance, but only after passing a resolution with two-thirds majority and only once during their tenures.

What lies at the heart of policing systems in developed countries is robust performance management based on quality inspections and measurement of crime incidence, conviction rates, etc. In the absence of such information, the chief minister, IG, or even the safety commissions are expected to manage the problems in a knee-jerk manner, relying either on unauthentic newspaper reports or delayed bureaucratic inquiries. The solution, therefore, lies not in shifting control from one person to another but rather in reducing discretion and making decision-making objective.

A very insightful example of the reversal of some sensible reforms undertaken by the government in Balochistan in the early 2000s is provided by the former IG Police, Balochistan, Tariq Khosa:[6]

It is unfortunate that a sound legislative framework established by Police Order, 2002—along with extending the writ of the state in the entire province by replacing ineffective levies with a well-trained, fully equipped police force, established in all 30 districts on Aug 14, 2007—was frittered away at the altar of expediency by tribal political chiefs and a scheming, power-hungry bureaucracy. The resultant void in the absence of a well-oiled law-enforcement machinery has seen sectarian and militant outfits proliferate in lawless regions of the vast province. Civil armed forces and military cannot be a substitute for a long-term and enduring law-enforcement framework.

Pakistan has the dubious distinction of being one of the 10 most lawless countries according to the World Justice Project's 2016 Rule of Law Index. Our companions are Venezuela, Cambodia, Afghanistan, Egypt, Cameroon, Zimbabwe, Ethiopia, Uganda, and Bolivia.

Such a situation is all the more puzzling in the context that Balochistan has been facing grave security and law and order problems, to put it mildly, for quite a long time. The police, which is in charge of internal security, is missing from areas outside Quetta and it is the Frontier Constabulary, a border security force, which has been heavily involved in combating nationalists, extremists, and sectarian elements. A lack of political consensus on converting levies' (an irregular force under the control of tribal chiefs) districts to police districts has perforce obliged the FC to assume these duties. This is, however, by no means a sustainable or desirable situation.

The police force is, in general, held in very poor esteem but there is one specialized police cadre that commands high respect for its efficiency, integrity, and courteous service with courtesy to the public: the National Highway and Motorway Police (NHMP). It is, therefore, instructive to learn lessons from this highly successful example of reforms which have remained in place even after two decades under different political dispensation. A founding IG of the Highway Police, Iftikhar Rashid,[7] explains the reasons for its success and why this example has not been emulated in the police forces in the provinces:

In 1997 the Government tasked me to raise a[n] efficient and honest force for the newly constructed Motorway from Lahore to Islamabad. Due to time constraint, fresh recruitment was not possible therefore all provinces and other territories were asked to provide serving traffic policemen on deputation. It was no surprise that semi-literate, routinely trained and unwanted policemen were provided for the proposed model force. To the bewilderment of everyone it was this lot of rejects which pioneered a unique policing culture on the motorway which has weathered the vicissitudes and turmoil of the last two decades. This practical demonstration of metamorphosis shatters to pieces all theories of reforming police through better pay, good recruitment, adequate resources, and training ... The theory of good recruitment is not applicable as a reason for the acknowledged good performance of the Motorway Police, based on public service.

A pivotal factor in the performance and conduct of Motorway Police was unity of command. There was no magistrate and police officers were empowered. In my judgment the main reason for police high-handedness, corruption and failure is dual control. It is essential that authority and responsibility must be inculcated in each individual, to ensure good results. Formal training was dispensed and the subject taught to the trainees was Public Service. Practical training was given in first aid, minor repair of vehicles, rescue procedures, and handling all conceivable situations where a commuter in distress needed help.

It is perceived that in our part of the world it is neither possible to establish Rule of Law nor have a police force free of nepotism, corruption, and apathy. Probably for the first time in the history of Pakistan these accepted norms were torpedoed on the Motorway and law was applied to all motorists. When the public saw generals, judges, inspectors, and ministers being prosecuted they were pleased and started abiding [by] the law. A crucial factor for the success of Motorway Police was complete delegation, blind trust, and full independence of action. Within a few months the force started performing and responding to the beck and call of their officers. Alongside delegation and trust, speedy and stringent accountability was ensured for any misdemeanour established. This was possible because every officer knew his subordinates intimately and there was tremendous peer pressure for efficient work. Over and above all this was the fact that in all matters IG Motorway was the final authority.

One of the key ingredients identified in the success of the National Highway and Motorway Police was its emphasis on training. Unlike the military, where only outstanding officers with high potential are selected for instructional assignments, the faculty at the police training centres and the academy were for the most part the problem: children or rejects from the main cadre. Instead of looking forward to the opportunity of positively influencing entire generations of future police officers, the faculty regarded their postings as a cruel and unusual punishment. This had a perceptible impact on the morale and motivation of young officers who began their careers by learning to become cynics. Rather than demonstrating energy and commitment to serve the public, they followed the wrong path set by their seniors.

Police officers were engaged in illegal acquisition of property, making deals with local businesses, manipulating cases, and living beyond their means. The senior officers were protecting and facilitating corrupt and servile subordinates, acquiring property, and accepting hospitality from local notables in exchange for favours. This in turn meant that the restraining influence of a clean officers' corps upon the intermediate and lower ranks of the police significantly diminished.[8]

As long ago as 1986, a survey of 21,000 respondents found that the police was considered the most corrupt institution in Pakistan, with only 43 per cent of 21,000 respondents willing to turn to the police for help in the event of encountering a personal problem.[9]

The internal structure and processes have much to do with this outcome. Unlike the commander of any armed force, the inspector general of police being the commander of the force couldn't do much even when aware of malpractices among his subordinate officers. He had no legal authority and no powers to discipline them as it was either the Establishment Division in the federal government or the home department in case of the provincial officers who enjoyed these powers. The home secretary could also overrule his decisions in regard to postings and transfers, one of the tools frequently employed by politicians to get officers of their choice posted to their districts. It was reported by a former IG Police: 'A senior police officer in Punjab told me that around half of the 648 station house officers (chiefs of local police stations) in the province are chosen by local politicians through influence on the Punjab Government, to serve their local interests.'

As recently as 2016, inquiries were held against senior police officers of Sindh into the recruitment and promotion, transfers and postings, procurement, purchase of uniforms, CCTV cameras, arms and ammunition, and investigation and security. These inquiries revealed massive corruption in the police department.

The situation sketched above was not limited to Sindh alone but was equally applicable to Balochistan. Chief Justice Anwar Zaheer Jamali[10] remarked—during the hearing of a corruption case against Balochistan's former food minister—that 'they were living in a country where police stations were auctioned and the officials appointed there were earning huge amounts of money'.

The root cause of this dismal performance of the police can be traced back to the weakening of the institutional architecture, starting with recruitment to the central superior services and ending in the increasing politicization of the police. A retired civil servant, Saeed Khalid,[11] sums this up to a nicety:

> Today's administrative service is a mere shadow of the powerful structure inherited in 1947. Bit by bit, its power was diluted to the benefit of the rulers. They like nothing better than a weakened permanent bureaucracy to serve at the master's whims.
>
> Those at the helm never seem to realize that weakening of the administration—district management or the police service—also means weakening of the state writ and inevitable deterioration of law and order, accompanied by a phenomenal rise of mafia rule. If weakening of civil structures means rule of assorted gangs then the cost of pushing the bureaucracy against the wall is not really worth it. How can anyone run police, education, health or other government departments when elected representatives exert their energies on getting teachers and officials transferred or try to block those very transfers?
>
> Our worthy ministers, MNAs, and MPAs are least concerned about rule of law in their constituencies as long as their own interests are safeguarded. If

the police exercise their duties, political heavy-weights are ready to sponsor raids to free the offenders from police custody.

Another issue that needs careful attention is review of the mandates, legal powers, and capacity of the existing law enforcement agencies. Given the constraints of human, financial, and organizational resources it is better to have fewer but capable and effective institutions by eliminating, merging, and/or expanding the mandates. There appears to be overlapping, duplication of efforts, parallel intrusion resulting in turf-battles and rivalries, frittering away of scarce resources, and inadequate manpower which all benefit the criminals and mafias at the expense of security and order. We should be mindful of the experience of the 1970s when Z. A. Bhutto, disgusted with the performance of the existing law enforcement agencies, created the Federal Security Force (FSF). In the words of General K. M. Arif:[12]

> Bhutto created parallel institutions that can do his personal bidding. One such institution was the Federal Security Force (FSF) which became a 'dreaded and detested' organization. It had earned notoriety for clandestinely committing acts of violence and terror. The government then attributed those misdeeds to the opposition. It is inimical that Mr Bhutto's handpicked Director General of FSF, Mr Masood Mahmood, turned approver in the murder case against Mr Bhutto. He confessed that he was mentally scared of the vindictive nature of Mr Bhutto. The Prime Minister made life hell for those who did not fall in line with his desire.
>
> General Zia might not have had political ambitions in September 1977. He decidedly developed them soon thereafter.

Counter-terrorism

Pakistan has suffered over 30,000 casualties of civilians and law enforcement and security agency personnel, and has lost over $123 billion in fighting insurgency in the FATA and other parts of Pakistan.

Notwithstanding the huge proliferation of law enforcement agencies in Pakistan, none of them is mandated or equipped to tackle the growing menace of terrorism and violence unleashed by the extremist elements. The police force was not trained for counter-terrorism.

The National Action Plan, which was devised in the aftermath of the Army Public School, Peshawar mayhem, was the first concerted effort to launch a multi-pronged attack to counter the influence of terrorist groups, their sources of financing, and their links. One of the requirements was the formation of a strong National Counter-Terrorism Authority (NACTA) which would coordinate the intelligence from all the various agencies and act as the nodal point for action including the surveillance of the banned groups. There is very little evidence to show that the activities of the banned groups and other jihadist and sectarian organizations have been curbed to any substantial degree, or that the distribution, dissemination, and propagation of hate material and speeches have been curtailed, and funding and communication networks (appeals for and collection of funds) are again on the rise. Reforms in the criminal justice system and civilian armed forces, the police in particular, are yet to be undertaken.

Imtiaz Alam,[13] a senior journalist, gives his assessment:

We are yet to see the establishment of a rapidly deployable counterterrorism force, except the army, doing the job all over. Banned outfits continue to dominate the streets of Pakistan since they somehow are still not considered 'bad Taliban', and the Afghan Taliban are yet to be pressurized enough to either opt for a ceasefire and negotiate or leave, despite the COAS' strict prohibitive directions which he unequivocally issued in July.

Without a peaceful neighbourhood and cooperative neighbours we cannot even defeat our own terrorists who are freely available in the free terrorist markets to be hired to commit crimes against the humanity. Therefore, even if you fully implement NAP, without peace with neighbours, terrorism cannot be defeated without joint efforts by Pakistan, Afghanistan, Iran, India, Central Asia, China, Russia, and Nato. The continuity of the democratic dispensation and war-tested commander is essential—but with a changed security paradigm for a peaceful neighbourhood.

Similar views were echoed by a former DG FIA and IG Police, Tariq Khosa:[14]

> Counterterrorism and countering violent extremism are essentially law-enforcement domains in which the police should play the lead role, with civil armed forces, intelligence agencies, and military playing a support role. It is teamwork that wins wars. Turf battles and information silos do not strengthen the state and democratic institutions. In fact, since 2015, a federal civilian intelligence agency has been instrumental in giving great support to the provincial CTDs in identifying, locating and arresting terrorists. No one can perform a better job than the police at the grassroots in the state's fight against militancy. The essential point of NAP regarding reforming the criminal justice system has been sadly ignored by the federal and provincial governments.

Imtiaz Gul[15] seriously questions whether, under these circumstances, citizens can ever count on the hope of restoration of the rule of law and justice for all:

> Events of the last few months only inject a sense of despondency and helplessness, prompting even people like us to wonder whether issues such as moral integrity, transparency, and the rule of law should at all be discussed in this country, where the mighty ones get away with broad-day murders while the weaker ones are made to pay even for small deviations from law, a country where tax frauds worth billions by the elites go unpunished and are vehemently defended by cronies, while the honest and powerless ones are made to run from pillar to post to extricate themselves from the clutches of the corrupt bureaucracy.
>
> A country for the rich and influential politicos, journos, generals and their legal associates indeed.

The same refrain is repeatedly and periodically echoed. If the newly formed agency for counter-terrorism is to be drawn from the existing police force and shaped and structured along the same lines, there is not very much that can be expected from it. After all, the civilian police have lost their capacity to deal with law enforcement and maintenance of order, and that will continue unless measures are taken to completely end political interference in administrative matters of appointment, training, promotion, and posting. If this malaise is not remedied the government will have to continue to rely upon the civilian armed forces—the Rangers and the Frontier Constabulary—in order to bring an end to the activities of the terrorist-criminal nexus. Their record speaks for itself.

In Karachi, for example, the law and order situation got out of control in 2013, the deadliest year on record, with 2,700 casualties, mostly targeted killings and a large number of businesses moving out of the city to the north to avoid unbearable extortion rackets. The Anti-Terrorism Act was amended to give special policing powers to the Rangers to detain suspected high-profile criminals and terrorists for a period of 90 days. Raids were organized by the Rangers without taking the police in confidence. The latter precautionary step was taken because certain police officers and ranks were suspected of having affiliations or sympathies with one political party or the other which, in turn, had close links with the criminal gangs, land and water mafias, terrorists, and extremist groups. The extortion and ransom for kidnappings, the media alleged, was divided as the criminals received protection from both the terrorist groups and the political parties. The Sindh government was always found to be reluctant whenever the question arose of extending the services of the Rangers for another quarter. *Newsline*,[16] the magazine, reported:

> a confidential report presented to the Army Chief last year revealed that there was a nexus of politicians, government officials, and the police with terror networks like Al-Qaeda, the TTP, and Lyari gangs. It was alleged that terrorists were working with officials in the Sindh Building Control Authority (SBCA) to collect extortion money.
>
> It was this briefing which led to the decision that the war against militancy in Karachi and elsewhere could not be won without breaking this nexus and eradicating corruption.

The Rangers were entrusted the task of cleaning up Karachi and getting rid of the criminals and different factions of the TTP who provided protection to them in exchange for a share of the loot, extortion, and ransom money collected. Since the last three years, Karachi is once again calm and peaceful and life is back to normal. A conscientious IG Police wanted to establish the writ of the Police in the province so that the Rangers could go back to their duties but he has been stymied by his political bosses.

It was also reported that the Punjab Government was also reluctant to confer the policing powers to the Rangers and insisted upon joint teams drawn from the Elite Police of Punjab and the Rangers. It was only when the army announced the Operation Zarb-al-Fasad that the Government yielded to this demand of the Rangers.

PROSECUTION

The Prosecution Service became independent in the early 2000s as a follow up to the police reforms in which the functions of watch and ward, investigation, and prosecution were unbundled. The provinces passed Criminal Prosecution Service acts to establish 'an independent, effective and efficient service for prosecution of the criminal cases'. A prosecutor general, appointed by the chief minister, heads the service. He is assisted by a hierarchy comprising additional, deputy, assistant prosecutors general, and district prosecutors with their own battery of prosecutors. A prosecutor has to formally approve a case for it to go forward to trial. This requires him to scrutinize case files so that legal lacunae, if any, are addressed before they come to court.

Depending upon the level of the working relationship between a prosecutor and investigator, if the preparatory work is done collaboratively, it results in eventual success at the trial. In most cases, adversarial relations, the 'pass the buck', 'blame the other' syndrome prevails with very negative results. Prosecutors blame the investigators for poorly recording, storing, falsifying, and losing critical pieces of evidence that can help in establishing that the offence was committed. Crime scenes, even in important cases such as the assassination of Benazir Bhutto, are washed away or contaminated. Investigators think that the prosecutors do not make sufficient effort or take adequate interest in familiarizing themselves with the nitty-gritty of the case enabling them to satisfy the questions raised by the opposing lawyers or the judge. They sometimes do not raise the appropriate arguments that would have strengthened the case.

A well-respected police officer, M. A. Nekokara, had the following comments to offer on the nature of the relations between the prosecution and the police:

> Training of investigators, a functional and professional relationship between police and prosecutors, and a leading role for the judiciary would significantly help reduce the use of illegitimate and violent tactics by police to control crime[17]
>
> An equally troubling aspect is the disconnect between its various actors including the police, judiciary, lawyers, prosecution, and prison personnel.
>
> This disconnect is very evident in incidents such as lawyers assaulting police investigators and judges of the lower courts. This creates pressure for other important actors of the system. The courts blame the police for defective investigation and lawyers for seeking endless adjournments. The lawyers complain of poor training, low rewards, and insufficient facilities in the courts. Police officers grumble about the difficult standards set for evidence collection; non-availability of witnesses; the dearth of witness protection programmes; and ridiculing and humiliating behaviour in court. Prosecutors bemoan their status as 'poor relatives' of the CJS. This generates a narrative which has a paralysing effect on the wheels of justice.
>
> Importantly, it pushes people towards desperation instead of giving them hope.[18]

This dysfunctional relationship has serious social and legal costs: the acquittal of terrorists, conviction of the innocent, and fast-tracked justice for the powerful and inordinate delays for those with no connections.

It was heartening to see that a code of conduct for prosecutors has been prescribed.[19] Some of the guidelines, reproduced below, make a lot of sense:

(a) Prosecutors must cooperate and coordinate with police to ensure fair and just prosecutions. This would entail guidance to police regarding possible lines of enquiry, evidential requirements, and pre-charge procedures.

(b) To assist police and other investigators to complete the investigation within a reasonable period of time and to build the most effective prosecution case.

(c) The decision to prosecute is a serious step that affects suspects, victims, witnesses, and the public at large, and must be taken with the utmost care and caution after a review of the police case once it has been finalized.

(d) Acquaint themselves with the facts and circumstances of the case and work to ensure that the right person is prosecuted for the right offence and no one else.

(e) Ensure that the law is properly applied, that relevant evidence is placed before the court and that obligations of disclosure are met. Prosecutors must also consider whether trial is the best solution.

(f) Lawfully direct a police officer to rectify evidential weaknesses at any stage of the investigation; ensure forensic analysis of items collected, additional evidence collected, follow a line of enquiry, provide additional information about the collection of evidence and additional information about the circumstances of a witness, and explain why a key witness was not examined.

> The prosecution should have a significant impact in terms of deterrence of crime and/or boosting the community's confidence in the rule of law.

If this code of conduct is faithfully adhered to, most of the problems identified above are likely to disappear and the criminal justice system will be rejuvenated. However, like other laws, rules, and codes on the books, the disconnect between what is prescribed and what is practised remains wide.

One of the lingering problems, notwithstanding the creation of this independent service, is that the incentive structure for the induction of talented young lawyers into the service remains unattractive. Criminals have sufficient financial muscle to hire eminent lawyers to defend them. In addition, they have contacts, professional standing, influence, and outreach to quash the efforts of young, low-paid government lawyers' attempts to aggressively build up a case. Even those who do not engage in any malpractices are poorly trained and inexperienced, and not fully on the top of investigation methods and material. The situation is further aggravated by some members of the lower judiciary who are alleged to enjoy a bad reputation for accepting bribes or favours and entertain *sifarish* from influential individuals.

PRISONS

Prisons are overcrowded, with under-trial prisoners accounting for over 80 per cent of the prison population. According to the statistics compiled by the ICG[20] in 2010, only 27,000 of roughly 81,000 prisoners have been convicted. The capacity of the major prisons in Lahore was 1,050 but it held 4,651 prisoners. In Sindh, prisons held 18,234 prisoners, twice their capacity of 9,541, among them only 2,641 convicts. Only 155 prison vans were available to ferry 13,000 prisoners to court. Prisoners are seldom transported to the courts on the date of their hearing.

The conditions in the prisons are abysmal, and prisoners' rights regularly violated. Those without any means remain in jail for several years and the trials keep dragging on. 'The generally barbaric and brutal behaviour of the jail staff produced hardened criminals instead of repentant sinners.'[21]

On the other hand, those with financial resources or political connections lead a comfortable life and are frequently transferred to the private wards of hospitals on the basis of fake medical certificates furnished by the jail staff. There are allegations that these rich prisoners have an unrestricted flow of visitors and other luxuries such as food from home, air-conditioning, TVs, and other amenities provided to them in jail.

Prisons have become a hotbed of criminal activities from where operations are planned and managed, facilitated by mobile phones and a generally permissive environment. They have also become major recruitment grounds for jihadi organizations.

A raid on the Karachi Central Jail by officials of the Rangers and the Frontier Constabulary uncovered a large number of banned items. According to newspaper reports,[22] they confiscated millions in cash, hundreds of TV sets, 100 mobile phones, 400 cigarette packs, 45 daggers and knives, speakers, remote controls, memory cards, LCD screens, scissors, and five packets of heroin. The raid took place after two hardened terrorists belonging to the banned Lashkar-e-Jhangvi escaped from the judicial complex within the jail. It was reported that security is so lax that the prisoners are able to communicate using their mobile phones with the aid of anti-jammer devices and the jail staff. Some of the terrorist attacks are believed to have been planned from within the jail.

The ICG, in its report,[23] has sketched the following picture of the prison system in Pakistan:

A corrupt and dysfunctional prison system has contributed to—and is a manifestation of—the breakdown of the rule of law in Pakistan. Heavily overpopulated, understaffed, and poorly managed, the prisons have become a fertile breeding ground for criminality and militancy, with prisoners more likely to return to crime than to abandon it. The system must be examined in the context of a deteriorating criminal justice sector that fails to prevent or prosecute crime, and protects the powerful while victimizing the underprivileged. Yet, while domestic and international actors alike are devoting more resources to improve policing and prosecution, prisons continue to be largely neglected.

Pakistan lacks a systematic program for the capacity building of prison staff, while existing regulations on postings, transfers, and promotions are frequently breached because of nepotism and political interference. Given weak accountability mechanisms for warders and prison superintendents, torture and other brutal treatment are rampant and rarely checked. Moreover, with outdated laws and procedures, bad practices and poor oversight, the criminal justice system is characterized by long detentions without trial. As a result, prisons remain massively overcrowded, with nearly 33,000 more prisoners than the authorized capacity. The large majority of the total prison population—around 50,000 out of 78,000—are remand prisoners awaiting or on trial. With more than two dozen capital offences, including many discriminatory provisions that carry a mandatory death penalty, the death-row population is the largest in the world, though the current government has placed an informal moratorium on executions.

Circumventing the justice system, the military has detained thousands of people, ostensibly suspected of terrorism but including thousands of political dissidents and others opposed to the military's policies, especially in Balochistan, Khyber Pakhtunkhwa (KP), and the Federally Administered Tribal Areas (FATA). Its methods include torture, collective justice, and extrajudicial killings. By swelling public resentment, such practices are more likely to create terrorists than counter them. Instead of establishing parallel, unaccountable and illegal structures, countering militancy requires the reform of a dysfunctional criminal justice system. The separation of low-level offenders and suspects, particularly impressionable youth, from the criminal hardcore is particularly urgent.

Like the police and courts, the prison system is a major contact point between citizen and state, reflecting the public's access to justice. Major reforms are necessary to restore public confidence in the government's ability to enforce the rule of law while protecting the rights of all citizens. The government should allocate the necessary human and financial resources and meet its obligations under these international treaties, so as to ensure that torture and other ill-treatment of detainees are stopped and that officials and institutions responsible for such practises are held accountable. If Pakistan's prison system remains brutal, opaque and unaccountable, it will continue to aggravate rather than help resolve the country's major internal security challenges.

SUMMATION

J. M. Buchanan[24] has surmised that the rule of law is not a public good but social capital. A public good can be provided by the government whenever it wants to do so. Social capital will have to be built over time, and that involves numerous actors in the society, starting from the police and judges, to lawyers, the governments, civil society, and the people at large.

As I showed in the chapter 'The Society', it would take some time to build social capital in Pakistan. In the meantime, efforts should be focused on improving the public good aspects of the administration of justice. The key components of this chain—the police, prosecution, and prisons—are malfunctioning in themselves but the relationship between the police and the magistracy has degenerated into collision as well. The end result of this ceaseless tussle between the police, prosecutors, and the courts is the low conviction rate. A low conviction rate, in turn, has very little deterrent effect on the criminals or likely offenders, giving them the impression that they can get away scot-free. M. A. Babakhel[25] elaborates this point in relation to terrorism:

> The low conviction rate in terror cases has eroded the confidence of the community in the criminal justice system. However, an increase in the conviction rate is not possible without the cooperation of witnesses. In a society where witnesses feel insecure, how can judges be expected to convict terrorists? The ultimate beneficiaries here are extremists.

Another major problem is the generally abysmal quality of the members of the legal fraternity. Standards are lax, exams often a formality, and it was observed by many interviewees that a large number of lawyers are almost as dishonest as the criminals and policemen with whom they interact. The results are an expanding circle of alienation of the credibility of the national justice system.

The principal reason for the decay of these institutions is that they have fallen prey to the machinations and manipulations of politicians and well-to-do sections of society. There are two standards: one for the rich, privileged, and well-to do; the other, for ordinary citizens. Law and order and security cannot be entrusted on a permanent basis to the civilian armed forces as it is not their duty. Continuing deployment of the military will not only thin out its resources but will also unnecessarily embroil it in the needless political controversies.

The government, in its larger interest, and politicians to rehabilitate their credibility, have to assume full responsibility and desist from political interference in policing. The solution lies in ensuring that the rule of law prevails in the operation of a fully accountable and neutral police force which is insulated from all extraneous interference.

As an immediate measure, the police chiefs should have legally ensured tenures with total operational autonomy, including powers to post, transfer, and take disciplinary action against those engaging in malpractices and malfeasance or neglecting their duties. Financial resources should be made available so that each *thana* has its own budget and does not have to rely on the complainants or others to enable them to make their visits and conduct interrogation. Forensic and modern investigation tools should be adopted as early as possible because cases which do come to court often fall at the evidence stage because the process of evidence gathering and case building is weak. Criminals then are acquitted, which in turn scares off potential witnesses from testifying. Crime scene management techniques, including forensics, have to be gradually brought in to match global standards. The process of collecting DNA and other evidence, and the analytical and investigation process need to be bolstered.

The prosecution service in Pakistan needs improvement, as well as analytical and technical support. Like all government employers, those in the prosecution and investigation service are not paid sufficiently, making it difficult to attract the necessary talent. More training, modern technology, and technical assistance are needed. There is need for an institutional arrangement at the provincial and district levels to watch and evaluate the performance of the entire chain of judicial administration. Punjab and Sindh need to reinvigorate and amend Police Order 2002 along the lines of the KP Police Order 2016.

The system of administration of justice has to be strengthened throughout its entire value chain. Simply tinkering with one component without fixing the others would hardly produce any tangible results. The need for greater coordination among various agencies is not so strongly compelling as is in the case in the police, prosecution, prisons, and lower judiciary. District level committees, headed by the Deputy Commissioner/District Magistrate, should be empowered to monitor and take remedial measures. Citizens' easy and inexpensive access to basic justice and rule of law is one of the most powerful tools for restoring trust between the state and the ordinary citizen. This growing trust and satisfaction will act as one of the glues that bind the forces of good democratic governance together.

Notes and References

1. Khan, J. R., *Government and Administration in Pakistan* (Pakistan Public Administration Research Centre, O&M Division, Cabinet Secretariat, Government of Pakistan, 1987); N. H. Shah, *Judicial Administration*; Yasin, and Banuri, *Dispensation of Justice in Pakistan* (OUP, 2004); LaPalombara, *Bureaucracy and Political Development.* (Princeton University Press, 1967); Shafqat, S., *Civil-Military Relations in Pakistan* (Westview, 1997); Kennedy, C., *Bureaucracy in Pakistan* (OUP, 1987).

2. Das, G., *India Unbound: The Social and Economic Revolution* (Penguin Books, 2000).

3. Bayley, D. H., *The Police and Political Development in India* (Princeton University Press, 2015).

4. Hussain, A., 'Public Safety and the Police', *The News,* 30 August 2016.

5. Khawar, H., 'KP Police Law: Reform or Rhetoric', *Express Tribune,* 30 August 2016.

6. Khosa, T., 'Between the Devil and Deep State', *Dawn,* 1 November 2016.

7. Rashid, I., 'Fundamental Reform Required in Our Police Force', *Express Tribune,* 22 November 2016.

8. Government of Pakistan, *Report of the Pakistan Police Commission 1969–70.*

9. Government of Pakistan, *Report of the Committee for the (Stopping) of Corruption.*

10. 'Police stations are auctioned here: CJ' *The News,* 21 July 2016.

11. Khalid, S., 'Mature CSS', *The News,* 28 August 2016.

12. Arif, K. M., *Working with Zia* (OUP, 1995).

13. Alam, I., 'Stocktaking in Increasingly Dangerous Times', *The News,* 18 August 2016.

14. Khosa, T., '*Sleeping on the Job*', *Dawn,* 22 August 2016.

15. Gul, I., 'Integrity and Character', *Express Tribune,* 26 January 2017.

16. Abbas, M., 'Corrupt to the core', *Newsline Magazine,* 2016.

17. Nekokara, M. A., 'Crime of extra judicial killing', *Dawn,* 25 January 2017.

18. Idem, 'Rickety Justice System', *Dawn,* 27 August 2017.

19. 'Public Prosecutors Code of Conduct', *Dawn*, 3 October 2016.

20. International Crisis Group, *Reforming the Criminal Justice System in Pakistan* (December 2010).

21. Committee for the Study of Corruption, 1986.

22. *The News*, 20 June 2017.

23. International Crisis Group, *Reforming Pakistan's Prison System* (ICG, Islamabad/Brussels, October 2011).

24. Buchanan, J. M., *The Limits of Liberty*, (Chicago University Press, 1975).

25. Babakhel, M. A., 'Building Community Resilience', *Express Tribune*, 26 August 2016.

15

The Role of External Actors

Many Pakistanis and a large number of foreign observers are strongly convinced that from its birth Pakistan has been propped up through external assistance. In the formative stages, the Pakistani leadership made a deliberate choice to ally with the US. Liaquat Ali Khan, the first prime minister of Pakistan, was invited by the Soviet Union but decided instead to visit the US. During the Cold War, the US was seeking allies in Asia and the Middle East and found a mutually convenient arrangement in forging an alliance with a newly established country that was seeking sustenance and struggling for survival. As was pointed out in Chapter 3, there was a widespread belief that the partition of India was a hasty and unfortunate decision by the British. The massive displacement and migration—involving 10–12 million people from one country to the other—combined with widespread violence, killings, and atrocities against Muslims in India, and the Sikhs and Hindus in Pakistan was a tragedy greater than the world war. The numbers of lives lost vary between several hundred thousand and two million.

Pakistan, the newly established country—divided in two wings and physically separated by a thousand miles of Indian territory—with its poor resource base and backward population was not considered economically viable. The popular narrative was that sooner rather than later it would have to reunite with its much larger neighbour, India. In the meantime, a heavy cost would have to be paid for this unnatural experiment in political engineering, resulting in untold human misery. The proposal of the last viceroy of British India, Lord Louis Mountbatten, to have a single governor general for the two countries during the transition was not acceptable to M. A. Jinnah. Under this proposal, the British Army would remain united for some period of time. Jinnah was quite clear in his mind that he and his party wanted to completely sever Pakistan's umbilical cord from the British Raj, particularly as the Muslim League did not trust Mountbatten. It is highly speculative whether the bloodshed in the aftermath of Partition could have been avoided if there had been a unified military command and control structure in place.

Soon after Partition, the question of the accession of the state of Jammu and Kashmir became a serious bone of contention between the two countries. A majority Muslim state ruled by a Hindu *maharajah* should have become a part of Pakistan on the principle followed for the partition of British India. The *maharajah* however decided to accede to India, causing uproar in and a strong retaliatory action by Pakistan. The first war between India and Pakistan in 1948 resulted in a division of the state of Jammu and Kashmir, with Gilgit-Baltistan and several districts adjoining Pakistan captured by Pakistani troops while a larger territory remained under Indian occupation. The seeds of hatred between the two countries sown by Partition were further nurtured by this dispute which has continued to sour relations between the two countries even after the lapse of seventy years. The asymmetric economic and military power calculus forced Pakistan to align itself with the US with the twin objectives of strengthening its economy and modernizing its military. Pakistan became a willing and active member of SEATO in 1954, along with Thailand, the Philippines, the US, the UK, France, Australia, and New Zealand. The purpose of the organization was to prevent communism from gaining ground in the region. In 1955, Pakistan joined the Central Treaty Organization (CENTO) or the Baghdad Pact, whose other members were Iran, Iraq, Turkey, and the UK. One of the aims of CENTO, formed at the behest of the UK and US, was to counter the threat of Soviet expansion into the vital Middle East oil-producing region.

Pervaiz Iqbal Cheema points out the differences in the expectations of the US and Pakistan in becoming members of these alliances:

> The implications and consequences of the choices Pakistan made in entering
> into alliances with the US and getting entangled in the Cold War were not

fully understood. Pakistanis thought that they were entering into alliances with the US in the belief that when their security was threatened the US would come for their help. There was huge disappointment when the Americans imposed an arms embargo in its war of 1965 and did not do anything to stop India from taking over East Pakistan in 1971. Under the alliances between the two countries the Americans had not committed or contemplated the deployment of the US troops or authorized the use of American supplied equipment for this purpose. Although Pakistan withdrew from the formal membership of the CENTO and SEATO in the 1970s, it came to play once again a very decisive role as a front line state in the US attempts to oust the Soviets from Afghanistan in the 1980s and later in the War against Terror after 9/11. Pakistan got a rude shock once again when the US, after the withdrawal of the Soviets from Afghanistan, invoked the Pressler Amendment to suspend aid to Pakistan on the plea it had refused to abandon its quest for nuclear capability.[1]

Pakistan's arch rival, India, under the leadership of Jawaharlal Nehru, chose to join Nasser of Egypt, Tito of Yugoslavia, Soekarno of Indonesia, and Kwame Nkrumah of Ghana in forming the Non-Aligned Movement (NAM). These leaders advocated a middle course between the Western and Eastern blocs during the Cold War, but were wedded to the principles of anti-colonialism, anti-imperialism, and the like, and declared themselves to be non-aligned to either bloc.

India's growing overtures towards the Soviet Union were in fact a reaction to the US–Pakistan alliance and provided the Soviets an opportunity to gain influence in India. The Soviets also expected that India's status as a leader in the non-aligned movement (NAM) would allow the USSR to bolster Soviet policy in the Third World. Following the 1962 Sino-Indian war, the Soviets began providing massive military aid to India, which culminated in a formal treaty of friendship and cooperation signed in August 1971.

This division into two opposing camps, India in the Soviet camp and Pakistan in the Western, and the continued rivalry between India and Pakistan, has and continues to inform Pakistan's external relations.

A corollary of this political alliance with the West was the warm relationship between the Bretton Woods institutions and Pakistan, particularly with the IMF. A significant number of Pakistanis believe that the two most powerful external actors guiding the country's economic and foreign policy are the IMF and the US. How far the proposition that nothing of substance happens in Pakistan without the acquiescence of these two players holds true needs to be examined. We begin with the foreign assistance flows.

Foreign Assistance Flows

Many analysts and scholars argue that the availability of generous foreign assistance has been the principal determinant of Pakistan's economic success or failure and the country's fortunes vacillate with the ebb and rise of the flows from external donors. T. V. Paul, for example, is of the opinion that:

> [The] geostrategic curse is at the root of Pakistan's unique inability to progress. Since its founding in 1947, Pakistan has been at the centre of major geopolitical struggles: the US–Soviet rivalry, the conflict with India, and most recently the post 9/11 wars. No matter how ineffective the regime is, massive foreign aid keeps pouring in from major powers and their allies with a stake in the region. The reliability of such aid defuses any pressure on political elites to launch the far-reaching domestic reforms necessary to promote sustained growth, higher standards of living, and more stable democratic institutions.[2]

It has been vehemently asserted by several Pakistani and non-Pakistani scholars that the economic spurts witnessed in the history of Pakistan, i.e. in the 1960s, the 1980s, and early 2000s, can all be attributed to the heavy infusion of this money into Pakistan. In the 1960s, Pakistan was a CENTO and SEATO ally and was closely aligned with the US in the Cold War. In the 1980s it actively participated with the US in driving out the Soviet

Union from Afghanistan, and in the early 2000s Pakistan was rewarded for its front-line role in the war against terror. It was the recipient of large military and economic assistance and that was the primary reason for the economic turnaround during these periods. Notwithstanding this popular perception, the empirical evidence does not prove this assertion. The slow growth periods of the 1950s, 1970s, 1990s, and the 2008–2013 period were also marked by similar volumes of foreign aid flows. This point needs to be emphasized and reiterated.

In the 1950s, Pakistan received huge military, civilian, and food aid. It was the PL 480 imports of food from the US that kept hunger in Pakistan at bay. In the 1970s, Pakistan was granted (through debt rescheduling) substantial debt relief; over two-thirds of the debt payments of US$650 million, due during 1974–77, were waived. Western aid through a consortium amounted to $700 million annually but in addition, official grants and concessional loans (some of which were subsequently transformed into grants or waived) from oil-rich Arab countries and the workers' remittances did not pose major problems and financed the huge current account imbalances.[3] Between 1973–74 and 1977–78, commitments of assistance from Iran and Arab countries totalled $1.2 billion, mostly on concessional terms. Pakistan was therefore comfortably able to meet as high a current account deficit as 10.1 per cent of GDP in 1975, followed by 7.1 and 7 per cent during the next two years.

Parvez Hasan has calculated that aid disbursements during the mid-1970s were at a level far above that reached during the 1965–70 period (average $600 million annually, which included flows to East Pakistan) after allowing for international inflation. In the 1990s, foreign currency deposits of resident and non-resident Pakistanis in Pakistani banks, amounting to $11 billion, were utilized to finance external payments. These deposits, as they had already been consumed, were then frozen in May 1998, causing a huge liquidity and confidence crisis. This crisis spilled over into the early 2000s.

The IMF, World Bank, and the Asian Development Bank continued to disburse loans amounting to several billion dollars between 1988 and

1998, while Japan was the largest bilateral provider of concessional loans and grants until the nuclear test of May 1998. In the post-2008 period, the Kerry Lugar Bill authorized $7.5 billion of economic and military assistance from the US to Pakistan for a five-year period (the actual disbursement figure were approximately $4.6 billion). Multilateral banks and the IMF increased the quantum of their support while Pakistan became the largest recipient of UK aid. Thus, higher volumes of foreign assistance have been received in the post-2008 period but the average growth rate has hovered at around 3 to 4 per cent. It can thus be seen that the periods of high growth rates, i.e. 1960s, 1980s, and the early 2000s, did not receive any exceptionally high foreign assistance flows in comparison to the 1950s, 1970s, 1990s, and the post 2008 years.[4]

Box 15.1 presents the binary comparisons of the annual average flows by the periods, regime type, and growth outcomes. The 1960s vs 1970s, the 1980s vs 1990s, and 2002–08 vs 2009–14 comparisons show the opposite results.

Mcartney[5] finds no credible evidence for attributing Pakistan's episodes of growth to foreign aid inflows and circumstances emanating from the global economy. In the early 2000s, 'using more rigorous econometrics over a longer period of time, there seems to be little generalized evidence that GDP growth in Pakistan has principally been of the [externally] dependent variety'.

McCartney is of the view that acceleration of economic growth occurred when the state successfully created conditions in which high profits were generated for investors and credit was channelled toward them. Thus, the hypothesis of high foreign assistance resulting in high economic performance is not validated by the facts.

The data presented in Table 15.1 indicates that foreign aid flows to Pakistan have gradually declined from 7.4 per cent of gross national income (GNI) in the 1960s to 1.3 per cent by 2014. Other aid dependence indicators, such as aid as a percentage of total investment, aid as a percentage of total import, aid as percentage of budgetary expenditure, and aid as a percentage of development expenditure also show a similar tapering off. Net official development assistance includes all loans and grants from multilateral agencies, bilateral government aid, and other donors of all types. Therefore, the aid dependence hypothesis is not borne out by actual facts. The other corollary is that Pakistan has received relatively more aid during periods of the military rule which led to high growth rates. This correlation is also proved wrong if we compare the total annual average flows computed in Box 15.1. The popular myth that Pakistan would cease to survive economically in absence of these flows is contradicted by hard evidence. The differential outcomes resulting in economic spurts and slippages faced by Pakistan during its 70-year history have to be explained by variables other than foreign assistance flows.

Box 15.1			
Period	Government type	Growth outcome	Annual average flows (million)
1960s vs.	Military	High growth	$ 385
1970s	Democratic	Low growth	$ 588
1980s vs.	Military	High growth	$ 870
1990s	Democratic	Low growth	$ 1,110
2000–2008 vs.	Military	High growth	$ 1,653
2009–2014	Democratic	Low growth	$ 2,851

Table 15.1: Net official development assistance to Pakistan

Years	Percentage of Gross National Income
1960–68	7.4
1969–71	3.9
1972–77	5.1
1978–88	2.9
1989–99	2.2
2000–07	1.7
2008–14	1.3

Source: World Bank Indicators

Table 15.1a: Net Official Development Assistance to Pakistan
(in US million dollars)
Net ODA Flows and Transfers

	1970	1980	1990	1999	2001	2002	2003
Net flows	433	1,021	1,228	1,071	1,622	1,066	1,247
Net transfers	369	819	778	263	525	511	596
Net flows/ National income	4.3	4.0	2.9	1.5	1.7	1.5	1.5
Net transfers/ National income	3.6	3.2	1.9	0.4	0.8	0.7	0.7

Table 15.2: Net Official Development Assistance
(from all sources; includes loans and grants)
(in US billion dollars)

Period	Total flows	Annual average
1952–58	0.320	0.102
1959–68	3.845	0.385
1969–71	1.175	0.395
1972–77	3.525	0.588
1978–88	9.574	0.870
1989–99	12.206	1.110
2000–2008	14.877	1.653
2009–2014	17.106	2.851

Source: World Bank Indicators

PAKISTAN AND THE INTERNATIONAL MONETARY FUND

One of the most misunderstood and controversial subjects in Pakistan's popular discourse relating to the economy is its relationship with the IMF. It is considered a sin to approach the IMF for assistance as this is perceived to be an infringement of its sovereignty and dictation by an external agency which takes its orders from the US and the Western powers. It is believed that if these powers, who hold a majority of the shares and thus influence decision-making, are happy with Pakistan then the IMF is soft in its conditions and increases the amount of assistance. In the event of its being in their bad books, it becomes difficult to access those resources or alternatively, the conditions are so unfavourable that it cannot meet them and the agreement falls through. Khurram Husain, in his article on Pakistan and the IMF, cogently sums up these perceptions:

> Every time I tell someone that I am working on the history of Pakistan's relationship with the IMF, there is one question that always comes up: ... 'They say once a country borrows from them,' said one particularly keen questioner, 'that country can never repay the debt and remains in their clutches forever; is it true?' ... The better off try and connect it with some imperialist ambitions: it is a tool of US foreign policy, used to reward those who serve the imperial masters and punish those who disagree. It engineers the overthrow of governments and works in cahoots with the CIA.[6]

Opposition parties consider any approach for assistance from the IMF as a failure of the government of the day although they themselves do exactly the same when they are in power.

As there are many misperceptions and misgivings about the IMF, it might be useful at the outset to recapitulate its essential purpose and practices. The IMF is a cooperative institution, with a membership of developing and developed countries, established at Bretton Woods in 1945 to provide stability to the international financial system. Today, with 189 member countries, it has almost become a universal institution. It was established to provide member countries short term balance of payments support when they experienced temporary liquidity shortfalls in meeting their payments obligations. The right to access the Fund's resources was governed by the individual countries' quota in the Fund. Upper tranche releases were contingent upon a set of actions that would restore the equilibrium between inflows and outflows. Unlike its twin, the World Bank, which is a long term development partner of developing countries, the IMF comes into the picture only when a country faces dire short-term financial difficulties. The Fund's mandate has, however, evolved with the passage of time in response to changing economic conditions, and now no longer limits itself to short-term financing alone.

Pakistan has borrowed from the IMF 16 times since December 1958, seven times during 1958–88 (three times during Bhutto's stewardship notwithstanding his allergy towards the West and the US), and five times since December 1988, i.e. five times during the Sharif–Benazir period, twice by the Musharraf government, once by Zardari, and the most recently by the PML-N government. Against this record, India has borrowed only once in 1991 and never again, Bangladesh thrice, and Sri Lanka twice since 1990.

The principal motivation behind Pakistan's decision to approach the IMF has been quick infusion of funds required to sustain and support its balance of payments when it was almost on the brink of default of external payments. Other multilateral banks piggy-backed on the IMF programme and provided quick disbursal loans. The IMF loan also implied a seal of approval for seeking commercial and export credit facilities. The IMF thus provides an anchor support and hence its relative importance or notoriety.

However, Pakistan's track record in implementation has been patchy. Sometimes reformist economic managers used the IMF programmes to restrain and block the pursuit of populist policies by political leaders. The IMF was also used as a scapegoat by politicians to shift the blame for some of the politically unpopular decisions to the pressures exerted by external donors. The most common reason for the failure of the recommended policy was the ascendancy of vested interests of those who were slated to lose from the reforms and conditionalities of the IMF programme. They were so powerful that they ensured that these difficult decisions were reversed, modified, or diluted to such a degree that their purpose was nullified.

Adjustment was adopted as a short-term palliative measure rather than introduced as a particularly desirable policy and direction of institutional changes. Some cosmetic changes were made to meet the minimum requirements and money drawn in the first or second lower tranches from the Fund along with disbursements from other external donors contingent upon the Fund programme. The Fund was then taken to task for its rigid 'one shoe fits all' approach, oblivious of the peculiar conditions prevailing in Pakistan and its dogmatic adherence to the neoliberal 'Washington Consensus' prescriptions which did not fit in with the ills faced by the Pakistani economy. When the time came to implement tough structural reforms that threatened to upset the apple-cart, the programme was abandoned citing the above grounds.

Out of the ten programmes since 1988, only three were successfully completed, i.e. the 2000–01 standby agreement, the 2001–04 Poverty Reduction and Growth Facility (PRGF), and the 2013–16 Extended Fund Facility (EFF). All the other programmes were terminated prematurely and therefore, Pakistan has earned the reputation of a 'one tranche' country. It signs an agreement, agrees to the conditionalities, draws down the automatic release of the first tranche, and then abandons the programme either because the immediate crisis has receded or the policy actions required were politically difficult to implement. Ehtesham Ahmad and Aziz Ali Mohammed,[7] both ex-IMF staffers, in their analysis have come up with a very novel and interesting idea. On the analogy of oil revenues giving birth to a Dutch disease for the producer countries, they think that the Fund's role appears to have produced an effect similar to Dutch disease in Pakistan. According to them, the Fund resources have provided a continuing inflow of easy money that prevented a broadening of the revenue base as well as hindered the accumulation of reserves through a broadening of the export base. In this way, the status quo is maintained and the impetus for structural reforms is negated.

There is an element of truth in the above line of thinking but it may also be relevant to point out that apart from the three programmes cited, full disbursements of the committed amounts were not made by the IMF, as found by the IEO[8] in its report on prolonged users. During the 1988–99 period, a large portion of the committed financing was not disbursed in Pakistan because of policy slippages. The cumulative amount drawn by Pakistan between 1958 and 2000 has been Special Drawing Right (SDR) 2 billion out of the total committed amount of SDR 4.1 billion. This amount formed a small fraction of Pakistan's total revenues. Surely, such a small amount cannot be compared to a country characterized by the Dutch disease such as Nigeria, where oil revenues account for 90 per cent of the total revenues.

The IEO report also acknowledges that there is difficulty in reconciling the Fund's role as a provider of temporary balance of payments support with the long term requirements necessary to undertake complex institutional reforms necessary to achieve sustainability. Even the three-year facilities are not congruent with the time span necessary for such reforms. Besides, all the loans had to be paid back with interest after a certain interval of time.

Why has the IMF assumed such importance? Credit rating agencies, fund managers, foreign investors all look at the state of IMF relations with a country to assess its economic viability and make financing decisions on that basis. In the absence of a satisfactory seal of approval, they tend to be reluctant to provide financing. There is a domino effect of suspension or incomplete review by the IMF. Other multilateral and bilateral donors, who agree to take part in the financing package under the umbrella of the Fund programme, also draw back. The country in question is thus caught in a dire situation with a balance of payments crisis at hand with no relief in sight. This particular aspect of the IMF's dominance in international financial relations has been widely criticized by developing countries. The recent rupture between the EU and the IMF on assistance to Greece shows that the problem is no longer confined to the developing countries but also afflicts developed ones.

On the other hand, prolonged association with the IMF shows that an economy is suffering from chronic ailment and has not been able to heal. This carries a stigma in the international financial markets, which become reluctant to provide financing to such IMF-dependent economies. The sooner a country is able to sever its financial programmes from the IMF, the better off it is in signalling that the economy has become normalized and is healthy.

It is wrong to place all the blame on the IMF and plead helplessness. Skilful and adroit management of relations with the organization by the policy-makers can indeed bring enormous benefits to Pakistan. For example, the September 2000 agreement was carefully designed to bring about enduring change in Pakistan's debt profile. It was determined, after careful analysis, that rather than approaching the IMF every three years or so for a rescheduling of money flows, stock re-profiling should be sought that would align debt payment capacity with the new profile of payments.

It was quite clear from the outset that the implementation of the Fund conditionalities, a prerequisite for debt re-profiling, would not be easy and the people of Pakistan would have to endure pain in the short term. The idea was that after undergoing this period of tribulations and averting the payment crisis, Pakistan would emerge on a stronger economic footing and regain flexibility in economic decision-making. The authorities would no longer have to run to the IMF or the US government with a begging bowl every now and again to bail them out of one crisis after another. This was the objective with which the standby agreement of 2000 and the Poverty Reduction and Growth Facility (PRGF) agreement of 2001 were negotiated with the IMF.

As the agreements with the IMF remained on track and the performance was impressive, the Paris Club—a group of officials of bilateral creditors— agreed to re-profile the entire stock of external bilateral debt of $12 billion on a long-term basis. The grace period for the re-profiled debt was fixed at 15 years and the repayment period was extended to 38 years. Thus, in terms of net present value, the stock of the debt was reduced by a third. This treatment was exceptional and only four other countries had received such a generous package. Pakistan was no longer obligated to negotiate further debt-rescheduling agreements with the IMF. At a go, it was able to find a permanent and durable resolution of the bilateral external debt problem by cutting back on bilateral debt. Those who argue that debt re-profiling simply postpones the D-day are seriously mistaken. The payments due after the next 15 years will be miniscule in relation to Pakistan's expanded earning capacity.

This was one of the first of this kind of debt stock restructuring undertaken by Pakistan in place of the traditional rescheduling of flows normally carried out under IMF programmes without altering the basic structure. Therefore, the sense of despair and helplessness, and alluding to the asymmetric power relationship between a strong lender and a weak borrower can be negated by examples of this kind.

The other objective of the 2000 and 2001 programmes, besides debt reduction, was building up foreign exchange reserves. These reserves, which were $1.5 billion in January 2000, jumped almost threefold to $3.5 billion by December 2001, stemming from a speculative attack on the rupee. The programmes had the effect of stabilizing the currency and calming the foreign exchange markets.

At the end of September 2004, the termination date of the PRFG with the IMF, the reserves had climbed to a comfortable level of the equivalent to six months' merchandize imports. SBP reserve accumulation continued even after the expiry of the IMF agreement and reached $14.6 billion in October 2007, when the caretaker government refused to take remedial measures in response to price increases in international oil, food, and commodity prices. Reserve depletion set in rapidly in 2008, reaching a low of $4 billion by October. The new government had to approach the IMF for assistance once again in December 2008.

World Bank

In the public mind, the World Bank and the IMF are identical, or painted with the same brush. There is, however, a fundamental difference between the two institutions. A country approaches the IMF when its economy is reaching a crisis situation while it has a long term engagement with the World Bank for development, growth, and poverty alleviation. By all counts, the World Bank has played an important and essential role in Pakistan's development process right from the 1960s. Throughout this six decade partnership, the Bank has contributed to alleviating poverty, mitigating the social effects of economic adjustment programmes, and provided the poor with greater access to healthcare, education and physical infrastructure, environmentally sustainable development, and improving the condition of women in Pakistan. The largest social safety net programme of unconditional cash transfer, i.e. the Benazir Income

Support Programme, which benefits over 5 million poor households, has also been partly financed by the Bank. It was also the principal financier of Pakistan's Poverty Alleviation Fund (PPAF), which provides assistance to poor communities throughout the country. The PPAF has been working with nearly 40 local organizations and has extended micro-credit loans to over 275 thousand borrowers, among whom 45 per cent are women. During the last three years, the annual commitments to Pakistan by the World Bank Group have averaged $2 billion.

In 1960, the World Bank organized the first Aid-to-Pakistan Consortium to facilitate coordination among the major providers of international assistance. The meetings of the Consortium were held every year and pledges were made by the donors regarding the quantum of assistance they would provide to Pakistan. This consortium was Pakistan's principal financial nerve line for several decades, and held 92 per cent of Pakistan's outstanding disbursed debt at the end of June 1991. The consortium's members included the US, Canada, Japan, the UK, Germany, France, and international organizations such as the World Bank and the Asian Development Bank (ADB). The World Bank accounted for 26 per cent of the outstanding debt, and the ADB, which was the largest lender in the early 1990s, accounted for 15 per cent. A news story, published in *Dawn* in 1964, reported that Pakistan had sought $500 million in aid and the consortium granted $450 million. That was the extent of the influence of the Bank in the early days as all the other donors relied upon the analysis and advice of the Bank staff. The Bank has contributed in building infrastructure such as airports, ports, highways, gas pipelines, power-generating plants, transmission lines, and the like. Project lending constituted the bulk of lending assistance for the first few decades.

The Bank was also instrumental in brokering the Indus Waters Treaty, dividing the five western rivers between Pakistan and India, and then led the investment for replacement works in the form of link canals, barrages, and reservoirs in Pakistan. This treaty, despite three wars and many points of no return between the two countries, has withstood the test of time. Water from the Indus Basin works helped in the dispersal of high-yielding varieties of wheat and rice making Pakistan self-sufficient in food production.

The strategic approach shifted away from infrastructure lending during the McNamara years towards poverty reduction, and in the 1980s a new lending instrument, termed a structural adjustment programme, was initiated to promote growth by addressing structural rigidities and market distortions. This was a move for budgetary and balance of payments support in exchange for reforms. In the 1990s, the Bank realized that the social sectors were being neglected and designed a Social Action Programme (SAP) to increase enrolment in schools but the SAP did not meet expectations and was considered a failure. The Bank's assistance strategy keeps changing in response to Pakistan's requirements. In the early 2000s, the focus was on supporting the government's development strategy organized around three mutually reinforcing pillars which were: 1. Strengthening macroeconomic stability and government effectiveness, 2. strengthening and enabling the investment climate, and 3. supporting pro-poor and pro-gender equity policies. The current Country Partnership Strategy (CPS) for 2014–19 has four strategic pillars: 1. Transforming the energy sector, 2. supporting private sector development, 3. reaching out to the under-served, neglected, and poor, and 4. accelerating improvement in services. The CPS envisages an indicative financing envelope of about $11 billion, including $3–3.5 billion from the International Finance Corporation (IFC) for investment in private businesses.

The World Bank has lent Pakistan $31.4 billion and provided grants of $9.3 billion since its inception. Of the total loans contracted, $21.5 billion were soft credits under IDA, repayable without interest and an average grace period of 10 years, with repayment spread over 30 years. Pakistan has so far repaid $9.3 billion to the World Bank and has an outstanding debt of $14.6 billion; of this amount $13.4 are IDA soft credits at highly concessional terms.

Asian Development Bank

While the World Bank is a global development bank, established soon after the Second World War, the ADB is a regional development bank with a mandate to economically assist its member developing countries of Asia. Operational since December 1966, the Bank's principal functions are: 1. to disburse loans and equity investments for the economic and social advancement of member developing countries, 2. provide technical assistance for the preparation and execution of development projects and advisory services, 3. promote investment of public and private capital for development purposes, and 4. respond to requests for assistance in coordinating development policies and plans of member countries. The Bank's operations cover the entire spectrum of economic development, with particular emphasis on agriculture, energy, capital market development, transport and communications, and social infrastructure.

The ADB in Pakistan is currently undertaking various initiatives to promote social protection and social safety mechanisms, capital market reforms, reforms at the provincial level, support for devolution, and the like. The CPS 2015–19 for Pakistan is designed to support the government in improving connectivity, productivity, and access to markets and public services. It has a provisional assistance package of at least $1.2 billion a year on average, which will focus on infrastructure upgrades and institutional reforms. Assistance will target six sectors: energy, transport, and agriculture; natural resources and rural development; water and other urban infrastructure and services; public sector management; and the financial sector. The bulk of the assistance is earmarked for infrastructure developments in the power, transport, agriculture, and urban services sectors.

How Critical is US Assistance for Pakistan?

Economic and military assistance to Pakistan has been pouring in since 1951. It comprised military, economic, and humanitarian assistance. According to the data compiled by the Center for Global Development, Washington, the US has provided nearly $67 billion (in constant 2011 dollars) to Pakistan between 1951 and 2011. The appropriations for economy-related assistance for four years, between FY 2011 and 2014, are $4 billion.[9]

There has been an acceleration in US assistance to Pakistan since September 2001 but it is estimated that only 30 per cent of the funds were appropriated for economic purposes and 70 per cent for security-related assistance. Under the Kerry–Lugar–Berman authorization of $7.5 billion over five years for FY 2010 through 2014, the allocation for economic-related activities was still 41 per cent of the total. It is relevant to point out that all disaster assistance, including that provided by international agencies, is included in this economic assistance fund. There was a large diversion from other programs to provide emergency funding for relief to flood victims in 2010.

In order to examine the importance of these flows to Pakistan's economy and evaluate the dependence of our economy on the US, four key indicators are selected: 1. US assistance as a percentage of Pakistan's total budgetary expenditure, 2. US assistance as a percentage of Pakistan's total foreign exchange receipts, 3. US assistance as a percentage of Pakistan's total current account receipts, and 4. US assistance as a percentage of the total value of imports by Pakistan. These indicators have been carefully chosen to see as to how much damage will accrue to our balance of payments and fiscal accounts if the US, for one reason or another, abruptly decides to completely withdraw all types of assistance.

The results of this analysis for one specific year, 2006–7, shown in Table 15.2, indicate that even under the worst case scenario of zero aid flows and no reimbursements for logistics services provided to US troops, the diminution in foreign exchange receipts or budgetary resources would be insignificant, varying between 4.5 per cent of total foreign exchange receipts to 7.2 per cent of total budgetary expenditure. The other two indicators, i.e. the proportions of total value of imports and current account receipts financed by US assistance, account for 6.4 per cent and 5.8 per cent respectively; not altogether worrying amounts.

Table 15.3: Key Indicators of US Assistance (US$ million)

Indicator	2006–07 (percentage)
1. Annual US assistance (of all forms) as a percentage of total budgetary expenditure ($25 billion)	7.2
2. Annual US assistance (of all forms) as a percentage of total foreign exchange receipts ($40 billion)	4.5
3. Annual US assistance (of all forms) as percentage of total imports ($28 billion)	6.4
4. Annual US assistance as a percentage of current account receipts ($31 billion)	5.8

Source: I. Husain, 'How Critical is US Assistance to Pakistan', Dawn, 17 April 2007

Some observers would argue that the World Bank and ADB assistance to Pakistan would also be reduced if the US takes action to suspend its financial aid. Although this assumption is open to question and debate, even if it is accepted at face value, the total gross flows of foreign aid from all official bilateral and multilateral sources (excluding reimbursement for services) amount to 8.5 per cent of Pakistan's foreign exchange receipts in 2006-07 and 10.8 per cent if the reimbursement for services is included. As a proportion of the GDP, these gross flows from all sources work out to only 3 per cent. Using a more appropriate indicator, i.e. net transfers on account of all foreign assistance, the impact is even more negligible: only 1.1 per cent of the GDP.

In light of the persistent and continuing threats by several US Congressmen and the think-tank pundits of cutting off all US aid to Pakistan under the KLB bill, an exercise was undertaken to assess its impact on the Pakistani economy. The results of this showed that there was no cause for any alarm or panic in the event of US aid flows drying up. In the post-KLB period, the volume of US assistance has significantly tapered off and apart from a few areas such as education, it is channelled primarily through non-governmental organizations or US-based contractors and consultancy firms. The actual financial flows accruing to Pakistan's public finances are marginal. The consistent threat by the US Congress to withhold even the Coalition Support Fund, which is actually reimbursement of Pakistan's expenses incurred in providing logistics support to the US troops in Afghanistan and the incremental expenditure incurred by the Pakistan Armed Forces in the war against terror, creates in Pakistani minds a negative perception of the US.

It is also less well known that the UK government provides a much larger volume of economic assistance to Pakistan than does the US. The Department for International Development (DFID) of the UK has raised its annual grant aid to Pakistan from £240 million ($480 million) to £480 million ($960 million). Most of this aid is targeted at education, health, and social development, i.e. largely on the development of the people of Pakistan. Notwithstanding these huge amounts involved, exceeding the entirety of US economic and military assistance, there are very little noises from the British parliament or think-tanks, or even the influential media, that Pakistan should be penalized 'as it is not doing enough to help meet the British objectives in Afghanistan'. There is a sense of maturity in the UK that recognizes that such tactics have, in the end, the effect of alienating and antagonizing public opinion in the recipient countries rather than altering their behaviour. Ill-will rather than goodwill is generated against the donors if they continue to threaten with the stick. A better way is to engage in dialogue, listen to and understand the perspectives and limitations of the recipient countries on the reasons for the divergence of views of the two sides and what can be done to remedy matters.

Overall, the actual experience of US bilateral assistance has not been very positive, either in improving the economy or in creating better understanding between the two countries. Pakistan's fiscal troubles have persisted because very little has entered the exchequer from this source. Pakistan's energy and infrastructure weaknesses have become more acute as the investment needs of the sector remain unattended. US assistance has proved to be more effective and responsive to natural disasters such as earthquake and floods and has won kudos from the people affected. Other than that, US economic aid has become a highly contentious issue due to the widely differing perceptions held in the two countries.

The above analysis debunks the popularly held myth that Pakistan is so dependent on foreign assistance for its economic survival that pulling the plug would force it to yield under pressure. These sages and their followers in Pakistan are well advised to seriously reconsider their basic premise. Successive governments in Pakistan since 1974—whether military, democratically elected, or transitory—have successfully resisted all kinds of pressure exerted on them to discontinue the nuclear programme under worse economic conditions than are currently prevalent.

However, there is no doubt that the government and people of Pakistan greatly appreciate the financial and moral support provided by the US government at this critical moment of Pakistan's economy, such as the US bilateral debt cancellation, the US EXIM Bank and OPIC's very positive initiatives towards Pakistan, and the withdrawal of all the various forms of economic sanctions earlier imposed. The US administration has played a helpful role in ensuring a larger volume of concessional assistance to Pakistan through the IMF, World Bank, and Asian Development Bank. The prompt and generous response to the earthquake of October 2005 by the US government, the private sector and non-governmental organizations in the US left a very favourable impressions in the minds of Pakistanis.

DOMESTIC PERCEPTIONS OF PAKISTAN–US RELATIONS

The bumpy ride of Pakistan–US relations over an extended period of time has been characterized as a marriage of convenience in which the two parties do not wish to file for divorce. This rocky marriage, though, has been affected by the Pakistanis' and the Americans' differing perceptions about each other. This public opinion is an important ingredient in the policy formation.

The popular narrative in the US—as articulated by the media, a few think-tanks, and congressmen—rests on the premise that Pakistan is not an ally but an enemy. The penalty for deviant behaviour on Pakistan's part should be severe and aid should be suspended, curtailed, or withdrawn as it is only through such punitive measures that Pakistan can be compelled to mend its ways. This view, prevalent amongst segments of American political, diplomatic, and civil society, is premised on the notion that Pakistan is unreliable and is playing a double game in the war against terror. This view holds that while Pakistan receives huge financial resources from the US, it still provides a safe haven to the militants, who carry out attacks against the US and NATO troops and the Afghan government across the border and then return to their sanctuaries in the tribal areas of Pakistan.

Many other Americans believe that helping Pakistan is simply not worth the time or money, and that by doing so, their hard-earned tax money is being wasted. Given the high domestic unemployment rate and growing fiscal deficit in the US, it is considered better to stop giving aid to Pakistan. A more benign variant prevalent among some US politicians and scholars is that Pakistan has been let down too many times by the US in the past and the best way to demonstrate the US long-term strategic commitment to Pakistan is to help it in its pursuit of economic development.

Jeffrey Goldberg and Marc Ambinder[10] succinctly summed up US perceptions in 2011 when the relations took a nosedive:

1. Kayani, the chief of army staff, is the most powerful person; there is semblance of civilian government with only limited powers.
2. The Pakistani nuclear arsenal is growing; exports to rogue states. Terrorist theft of a nuclear weapon a distinct possibility. Instability or splintering of the state create a risk of weapons takeover and thus keeping the weapons out of the hands of jihadists is crucial.
3. The Pakistani military and security services are infiltrated by an unknown number of jihadist sympathizers
4. Pakistani statements contain large doses of deceit.

Ahmed Rashid[11] addresses the US policy towards Pakistan in terms of the popular perception of the Pakistan Army:

The narratives that have seeped into the national psyche decree that the army must maintain a permanent state of enmity with India; controlling influence in Afghanistan and the deployment of Islamic extremists or non-state actors as a tool of foreign policy in the region; and it commands a lion's share of the national budget alongside its control of Pakistan's nuclear weapons. US attempts to change this course with either carrots or sticks are rebuffed while the civilian government cowers in the background.

Both these approaches, whether stick or carrot, are based on the tacit assumption that the quantum of US assistance is so significant that it would have the capacity to alter Pakistan's behaviour. The reality is that US aid does not help the government's precarious fiscal situation in any meaningful way as only 12–15 per cent of the total amount goes into budgetary support.

DOMESTIC PERCEPTIONS IN PAKISTAN

In Pakistan there are several viewpoints about the efficacy and impact of US aid. A large number of Pakistanis are deeply resentful that the US has been able to obtain a disproportionate leverage on Pakistan's policy space given the paltry sums they provide. The sovereign autonomy and dignity of the country has been sacrificed and it has been relegated to the status of a client state or 'rent-a-state'. The long-term stability of Pakistan is at risk because of this painfully obsequiousness alliance.

Another group believes that by entangling itself in the war on terror, Pakistan has suffered enormous losses financially, economically, socially, and psychologically, and that the compensation being paid by the US for this colossal damage amounts to virtually nothing. It is estimated that since 2001, the US spent $2,000 billion in Afghanistan, Iraq, and on beefing up domestic security. Pakistan's share of this amount was 20 billion or 0.1 per cent, while the country has lost 35,000 civilians and soldiers, in addition to suffering disruption and dislocation of its economy, a displacement of population, a several fold increase in expenditure on military operations and internal security, a virtual boycott of Pakistan by external visitors and a state of perpetual fear, etc. Of the amount received, $8 billion under the Coalition Support Fund was simply reimbursement of the expenditures incurred on logistical support and supplies to NATO and US troops.

A third group believes that despite the late Richard Holbrooke and Secretary of State Hillary Clinton's best efforts, the divergence between the development priorities of the government of Pakistan and US aid remains wide. This is borne out by the report of the Centre for Global Development, a leading US think-tank on development issues (I must in all fairness disclose that I was a member of the Study Group that produced this Report). In assessing US assistance to Pakistan, the report notes that:

> the integration of development, diplomacy, and defence has muddled the development mission and left the programme without a clear, focused mandate. The Kerry–Lugar legislation lists no fewer than 11 different objectives of US policy. As a result, the aid decisions are too often politicized and subject to short-term pressures. Overall, the programme ends up trying to do too much, too quickly. Goldberg and Ambinder are of the view that 'Pakistanis believe the US has designs on the Pakistani nuclear program, and have the technical means to stage simultaneous raids on Pakistan's nuclear sites'.[12]

Strengthening Pak–US Ties

Notwithstanding the prevalence of contentious domestic perceptions regarding US–Pakistan relations, the US remains for Pakistan an important trading and investment partner and we should continue to remain friends with this superpower. We should expand our relations with the US in the areas of higher education, transfer of science and technology, trade, investment, and labour flows. We should also seek duty-free market access for products exported from the tribal areas as part of our joint strategy to provide economic benefits to the 3 million population living on the porous border with Afghanistan.

The best way forward to strengthen US–Pakistan economic relations is through the following measures.

First, the US should finance only such infrastructure, education, and health projects that are included in the government's development programme and that too by co-financing these projects with the World Bank and Asian Development Bank, which possess the required expertise and experience. This would be the most effective use of the US taxpayers' money.

Second, the US Chamber of Commerce has rightly called for an easing of access to American markets of Pakistani textiles. American tariffs on Pakistan's leading exports average approximately 10 per cent, about four times the average US tariffs on imports from other countries. A reduction in the level of tariffs would not confer any favour on Pakistani exporters but provide them with a level playing field. For a country that so strongly believes in marketplace competition, this is a correction not a concession.

Third, Pakistan needs foreign direct investment in power-generation, transmission and distribution, gas pipelines, oil and LNG terminals, refining capacity, and petrochemical complexes, among others. US investors should be encouraged, through export–import bank loans and Overseas Private Investment Corporation guarantees to participate in Pakistan's energy development plans.

Fourth, the US leads the world in higher education and scientific and technological research. They should resume their assistance in training our teachers and scientists in leading US institutions, forging links between Pakistani and American universities, and strengthening the capacity of our research organizations in agriculture, water resources, renewable energy, and low-cost building materials.

Fifth, Pakistan should charge transit fees on fuel and other supplies for NATO troops travelling to Afghanistan from Karachi port. These will not form part of US aid but a commercial charge for the use of our infrastructure. Much misunderstanding on both sides will be dissipated if these fees replace the Coalition Support Fund.

CHINA

China is the one country which has been a steady and trustworthy friend of Pakistan over the past six decades. Although Pakistan was an openly declared ally of the US during the Cold War against communism and China was a leading communist power, there was hardly any occasion where there was even an iota of friction between the two countries. Right from the time of Mao Zedong and Zhou En-lai—the architects of Sino-Pakistan friendship—every Chinese leader from Deng Xiaoping to Xi Jinping has contributed to strengthening bilateral relations. When Pakistan was in a difficult position, facing US sanctions and those of the Western powers, China came to its rescue in providing military assistance and helping it to acquire nuclear and missile capability. The current state of preparedness of the Pakistan military owes a great deal to Chinese support.

There has been a gradual intensification of cooperation in almost all areas: economy, trade, academia, science and technology, and the like. The most dramatic move in taking China–Pakistan relations to a virtually stratospheric level was the offer by President Xi in 2015 to invest over $50 billion in energy, infrastructure, the Gwadar Port, and industrial zones along the China–Pakistan Economic Corridor (CPEC). This constellation of diverse projects, to be completed over a 15-year period, should be a game-changer for Pakistan's economy. By adding 10,000 MW of power generation, Chinese investors will immensely help Pakistan to overcome its energy shortages which have been crippling the economy for almost a decade. The road and highway network between Gwadar and Kashgar will help Xinjiang province to cost-effectively and speedily export and import goods to and from Pakistan. It will integrate the backward districts of Balochistan and KP, situated on this corridor, with the national market, thus providing livelihoods to the citizens of these districts and enhancing the earning potential of their citizens.

Rehabilitation and upgradation of the main railway line between Karachi and Peshawar will eradicate the logistical bottleneck in transporting goods from the sea ports to the rest of Pakistan, reduce the turnaround time, and lower the costs of distribution. Demand for construction materials and skilled and unskilled labour for these projects would have a strong multiplier effect on the rest of the economy. However, these beneficial outcomes can only be realized if the policy and institutional reforms are put in place to implement these projects on time and without cost overruns.

The construction of the CPEC has caused quite a stir in neighbouring countries, particularly in India. The latter has publicly expressed their opposition to the project and did not participate in the summit on the One Belt and One Road (OBOR) initiative held in Beijing in May 2017. A number of sceptics and naysayers within Pakistan are also providing a lot of ammunition to the detractors of the CPEC by spreading misinformation and falsehoods. This is reason for even greater efforts on part of the federal and provincial governments to make detailed information available in the public domain.

INDIA

The relations between India and Pakistan have been quite tense and sometimes hostile over the past 70 years, with some bright moments of light and reconciliation. The Bhutto–Indira Gandhi, Benazir Bhutto–Rahul Gandhi, Nawaz Sharif–Vajpayee, and Musharraf–Manmohan Singh periods did open up avenues for dialogue for a peaceful resolution of the issues dividing the two countries. As the political relations have not shown any improvement given some intractable problems, it is advocated by certain analysts that an attempt should be made to improve economic relations first and then move on to the more difficult political ones. Trade offers a powerful vehicle through which business interests can create a constituency for peace and friendly relations between the two countries. The normalization of trade relations also offers excellent opportunities for regional connectivity, as is happening in the case of China and Pakistan.

Overview of India–Pakistan Trade

India–Pakistan trade has recorded a virtually tenfold increase between 2001 and 2011, reaching a level of $2 billion. Unofficial trade, including that through third countries, is also estimated at almost an equal amount.

India's exports to Pakistan multiplied almost three times in 2004–05 to 2008–09, from $835 million to $2,234 million, while during the same period, Pakistan's exports remained virtually stagnant, with a very modest gain of only 11 per cent. The volumes actually fell in 2011–12, but even at its peak, Indian exports to Pakistan represented only 1 per cent of its total exports and is much lower now. Similarly, imports from Pakistan accounted for only 0.12 per cent of its total imports. Our projections show that even if Pakistan is able to triple its exports to India, it will remain an insignificant player with no threat of any consequence to the vast and expanding Indian market. It is unlikely that in the near future, the share of Pakistan in India's total trade will exceed 1 per cent.

The Pakistani mirror image shows that India accounts for 1.7 per cent of the Pakistani export market. Indian imports, however, have a 6 per cent share in Pakistan's total imports and in all probability, this share is expected to rise, given the phasing out of the negative list, the MFN status granted by India, and the preferential duty structure under the South Asian Free Trade Agreement (SAFTA). To the extent that the imbalance in bilateral trade is gradual and not abrupt and disruptive, and has had a visibly positive impact on the Pakistani economy—consumers, producers, and government—there will not be much resistance.

Most studies calculate that because of low transport costs, dismantling of tariff and non-tariff barriers, grant of MFN status to India by Pakistan, and improvement of logistics arrangements, the total volume of bilateral trade should be able to rise to approximately $8–10 billion annually.

Pakistan and India together ship over $300 billion worth of goods throughout the world. This increased volume of trade between them would still account for about 3 per cent of the two countries' trade volume. Therefore, the expectations, at least in the short run, should be tempered with a sense of realism on both sides. Large scale realization of the potential of trade will take some time, but like a newly planted sapling, it will require careful nurturing and protection from the buffeting winds of politics.

Pakistan realizes that liberalization of bilateral trade between Pakistan and India would not only lend beneficial impetus to both economies but also dissipate the barriers to regional integration within South Asia. The potential advantages to Pakistan from broader regional economic integration appear to be large. Going well beyond the immediate creation of trade flows, capital investment, and joint economic ventures, cooperation in the fields of IT, science and technology, and research and development would, in all likelihood, boost the productivity of domestic industries and stimulate economic growth.

AFGHANISTAN

Pakistan has been heavily involved in two wars in Afghanistan, against the Soviet Union in the 1980s and as an ally of the US in the War against Terror since September 2011. The damage and the losses Pakistan has suffered financially, economically, socially, psychologically, and internationally in the aftermath of these wars are well known and documented. The entire texture of Pakistani society has changed, with intolerance, violence, extremism, and criminal activities tearing apart its entire social fabric. It is highly debatable whether Pakistan should have played such an active role in these two cataclysms. Whether or not Pakistan would have been better off by remaining neutral is difficult to establish. The migration of three million refugees as a spill-over from the first war and the threat of the US to raze Pakistan to ground if it did not cooperate make it even more difficult to weigh the pros and cons of alternative strategies. A sobering assessment is provided by Adnan Adil:

> When big powers like the Soviet Union and the US with their full military might failed to pull Afghan society out of tribal culture, how can Pakistan do the job? Islamabad has no option but to side with the overwhelming majority in its neighbouring country.
>
> For 15 years, Taliban groups have survived the military operations of international troops led by the US forces. Following the withdrawal of the troops of the US-led coalition in 2014, the Taliban have expanded their writ. Out of 408 districts, the writ of the government-allied tribal lords is 258 while the Taliban control 33, most of which are in the south. The remaining 116 districts are contested zones where government forces are on the retreat.

The US still maintains nearly 9,800 troops in Afghanistan as part of the international troop presence. In 2014, the main responsibility for fighting the Taliban was transferred to the Afghan forces, including the military and the police but the US forces provide critical domain awareness, intelligence, surveillance support, and air power. Further, the US and Nato provide around $5 billion per annum to sustain the Afghan forces.

The Afghan army has been constantly crippled by incompetence and nearly 90 per cent illiteracy. It has a desertion rate of 25 per cent. If not supported by the US troops, this army is incapable of preventing the Taliban from regaining Kabul. The question that now arises is: when the US could not rout Taliban groups with nearly 100,000 troops, how can it defeat them with merely one-tenth of that force? How long can Washington and its allies dole out billions of dollars year after year to the Kabul administration to keep it in power? There is no way out of this situation—except a power-sharing arrangement between Taliban and non-Taliban forces.[13]

Relations between Pakistan and Afghanistan have not been amicable in recent years. Cross-border infiltration, repatriation of Afghan refugees, control of the borders to stop militant groups crossing it, disputes over counterterrorism policy, and the harbouring of each other's terrorist networks in their respective countries have contributed to an entrenched trust deficit and have eroded relations. These issues have impacts beyond the security sector, complicating efforts to build stronger trade and economic ties. Notwithstanding these tensions, Pakistan today is Afghanistan's largest trading partner, and Afghanistan is Pakistan's second-largest trading partner.

Trade between Pakistan and Afghanistan has increased substantially, from $0.83 billion in FY 2006 to $2.1 billion in FY 2013. Pakistan supplies the largest share of Afghan imports, at 24.3 per cent as of FY 2013, but this share has declined since 2011 due to a combination of factors, including political instability, customs delays, suspension of NATO supply shipments, and other issues. While Pakistan's share in transit trade has declined, Iran's share has steadily increased. India, Iran, and Afghanistan recently drafted a new transit trade agreement envisaging a trade route between Iran's

Chabahar Port in the Gulf of Oman—connecting Afghanistan to the Persian Gulf—and allowing the movement of goods from South Asia into Afghanistan and Central Asia.

Afghanistan's total reported exports are currently equivalent to only 5 per cent of total imports, with exports amounting to $363.70 million in FY 2013. Pakistan is the largest export destination, accounting for 32.2 per cent of all Afghan exports. Even without direct transit access, India constitutes the second-largest destination for Afghan exports, at 27 per cent of the total.

Afghanistan's landlocked status means it relies on neighbours to facilitate the transit of its trade with the broader global economy. The two countries initially signed the Afghanistan–Pakistan Transit Trade Agreement (APTTA) in 1965. The APTTA was redesigned in 2010 to allow the transit of Afghan exports through Pakistan to the Wagah Border with India, and to the seaport cities of Karachi and Gwadar. Pakistani trucks are, in turn, permitted to move products to all regions of Afghanistan. The agreement also led to the formation of a joint chamber of commerce. In July 2012, Afghanistan and Pakistan agreed to extend the APTTA to Tajikistan, a final step in the establishment of a north-south trade corridor. The proposed agreement would allow Tajikistan to use Pakistan's Gwadar and Karachi ports for its imports and exports, while Pakistan would enjoy trade with Tajikistan under terms similar to the transit arrangement with Afghanistan.

During his visit to Pakistan in November 2014, Afghan president Ashraf Ghani had highlighted Afghanistan's potential to function as a land bridge between Pakistan and Central Asia, and sought the same facility from Pakistan for trade with India. Ghani set a goal of increasing Afghanistan–Pakistan bilateral trade to $5 billion by 2017. Pakistan, in turn, agreed to take measures to clear 95 per cent of Afghan goods imported under the transit trade agreement within 24 hours, and to lower tariffs and charges for port and storage facilities. However, subsequent political tensions have caused a severe setback to bilateral trade between the two countries and it appears that the trade volumes would, in actuality, move on a downward path.

SUMMATION

The US and multilateral institutions, such as the World Bank, have always been considered to be major external actors influencing Pakistan. This chapter has demonstrated that the claim that foreign economic assistance, and particularly that from the US, has represented the life-blood of Pakistan's sustenance is highly exaggerated. Bilateral relations with the US have improved when there is convergence of their national interests. When their paths diverge, difficulties and alienation result.

With regard to India, Pakistan's perpetual arch-rival since its very inception, there have been very few and far between breakthroughs. Much of the time, there has been hostility and adversity between the two countries, missing the great opportunities of trade, economic cooperation, and people-to-people contacts to foster mutual goodwill.

Afghanistan–Pakistan relations have also taken a dip in recent years even though Pakistan has sacrificed a great deal by being host to over three million Afghan refugees displaced by the war, losing over 50,000 soldiers and civilians in terrorist attacks, and suffering financial and economic losses exceeding over $100 billion.

China has emerged as Pakistan's sole steadfast, reliable, all-weather friend over a prolonged period of several decades. The recent move under the China–Pakistan Economic Corridor project to invest over $50 billion has further strengthened the ties between the two countries.

NOTES AND REFERENCES

1. Cheema, P. I., 'Pakistani Perspectives on International Security', in Donald H. McMillen (ed)., *Asian Perspectives on International Security* (MacMillan, 1984).

2. Paul, T. V., *The Warrior State: Pakistan in the Contemporary World* (OUP, 2013).

3. Hasan, P., *Pakistan's Economy at the Crossroads* (OUP, 1998), 193.

4. Ibid.

5. McCartney, M., *Pakistan: The Political Economy of Growth, Stagnation and the State, 1951–2009* (Routledge, 2011).

6. Husain, K., 'Pakistan and the IMF: The Ties that Bind Pakistan', *Dawn*, 11 January 2015.

7. Ahmad, E., A. A. Mohammed, *Pakistan, the United States and the IMF*, LSE Working paper, 2012, 57.

8. IMF and IEO, *Evaluation of the Prolonged Users of the IMF*, September 2002.

9. Center for Global Development, *Aid to Pakistan by the Numbers* (Pakistan: US Development Strategy).

10. Goldberg, J., M. Ambinder, 'Pakistan: The Ally from Hell', *Atlantic*, December 2011.

11. Rashid, A., 'Ten Years of Rising Resentment', *International Herald Tribune*, 10 September 2011.

12. Goldberg, Ambinder, Pakistan: The Ally from Hell, *Atlantic*.

13. Adil, 'A Balancing Act in Afghanistan', *The News*, 21 January 2017.

16

Restructuring Key Institutions

Acemoglu and Robinson[1] provide a useful analytical framework of the pitfalls that lie in the path of institutional reforms. These relate to the fact that patterns of relative economic performance are very persistent. That is not to say that change does not occur: it does, and some countries accomplish it successfully. It is difficult to change institutions and there are powerful forces at work maintaining the status quo.

Their principal argument is that direct institutional reform in itself is unlikely to be effective and that instead it might be more beneficial to focus on understanding and reforming the forces that keep bad institutions in place. It is, therefore, important to focus on political institutions and the distribution of political power as well as the nature of economic institutions when thinking about potential institutional reform or institution building.

Acemoglu and Robinson believe that making or imposing specific institutional reforms may have little impact on the general structure of economic institutions or performance if they leave untouched the underlying political equilibrium. Political power will, of course, to a degree reflect economic institutions so it is possible that a change in economic institutions may induce a change in de facto power and eventually in the broader political equilibrium.

Just as reforming economic institutions without changing the political equilibrium may not improve the institutional equilibrium, and therefore changing *de jure* power while leaving the sources of de facto power intact, may have little impact on economic performance.

It is because even if *de jure* and de facto power change, those who acquire the power in the new political equilibrium may themselves not have the correct incentives. More importantly, their incentives to use their power, and the institutions they find it convenient to create, may be fundamentally shaped by the status quo they replace—they may be path-dependent. If an elite with power is initially structuring economic institutions to extract rents from society, then the very fact that it is doing this may induce a new elite to do the same. The replacement of one elite with another may therefore do little to improve economic performance.

Applying this framework, it is possible to focus on reforming some key institutions that may alter the current de facto and *de jure* political power equilibrium over time. This attempt to restructure such key institutions ought to fit into a clearly defined agenda of structural political and economic reforms over a long-term horizon aimed at achieving the desired development objectives. I agree with Acemoglu and Robinson that although we recognize the importance of political institutions, we are still at the outset of understanding the complex relationship between political institutions and political equilibrium. Sometimes changing political institutions may be insufficient, or even counterproductive, in achieving better economic outcomes.

The authors use the example of China to substantiate their view of the importance of institutional and policy reforms. According to them:

It can hardly be denied, for example, that the rapid take-off of growth in China after 1978 was a result of policy and institutional reforms. These were a direct result of the defeat of the 'Gang of Four' and a dramatic shift in those who controlled the Communist Party. Growth did not occur because the culture of the Chinese changed, or because some geographical constraint was lifted. Growth also did not occur because previously the Chinese were mistaken about the correct form of policy. They did not suddenly discover what to do. Rather, growth occurred because the political equilibrium changed in a way that gave more power to those who wanted to push through reforms. Said in this way, our analysis is an optimistic one. The institutional approach opens the promise that if we can understand the determinants of political equilibria then we can really design interventions that make poor societies prosperous.

Having analysed the various obstacles and constraints to reforms in the previous chapters and conscious of the above caveats, an attempt is made here to prioritize and spell out the essential ingredients of the necessary reform agenda.

The pace, sequencing, and implementation of reform would depend upon the consensus among the major political parties as the time horizon would cover several electoral cycles. No government in power can afford to take upon itself the sole responsibility to carry this forward, well aware as it is that there will be resistance by their opponents or the process would be disrupted after a change of government. Partial, incomplete, and half-hearted actions would not alter the course set out.

The Long-term Structural Reform Agenda

The long-term agenda is derived from the analysis presented in the previous chapters of this volume and highlights the salient reforms in various areas that can begin to make a difference in Pakistan's economic landscape. This list is by no means exhaustive and there are many other areas that can be included. These have been purposely omitted because of the capacity constraints of the organs of state. Non-state-centric institutions are also not discussed here although these should be able to have some positive impact.

Below are some of the key issues and necessary steps required:

1. There is a need for reforms of the electoral process. Constituencies should be delimited afresh on the basis of the new population census and electoral rolls should be prepared from fresh data generated through this census. The election commission and chief election commissioner should be given unfettered powers to organize the elections by directly taking control of the administrative apparatus of the provincial and the district governments. This will obviate the need to induct caretaker governments which have only proved to be disruptive of the process of conducting elections smoothly. Electronic machines should be used for voting. Candidates for the national and provincial assemblies should be carefully screened and those who do not meet the eligibility criteria should

be disqualified from contesting elections by the election commission. The recent Supreme Court judgment on 'Panama Gate' has provided an opening for the determination of the eligibility of the candidates under Articles 62 and 63 of the Constitution. The unsettled question is about the scope of the jurisdiction of the Supreme Court and the correct process in reaching a conclusion on the disqualification of candidates under these articles.

2. The political parties themselves must institute democratic contests within their organizations. In the 1950s, for instance, the elections for party office-bearers were held at the grass-root level. Those who were elected by the members through popular and transparent voting were in a position to stand up to their leaders. Since the 1970s, this process has been substituted by the discretionary choice made by a powerful party leader at all levels, nominating the central working committee members, allocating party tickets for the national and provincial assemblies, and the senate. He also selects the ministers for the federal and provincial governments if his party achieves power. Such a high concentration of power in the hands of a single individual is inimical to the essence of democratic governance which is based on debate, consultation, and consensus.

Constitutional amendments have stripped an individual member of the assembly from voting according to his conscience. Thus dissent and differences of opinions within a party have given way to sycophancy and pleasing the boss at all costs. The pendulum has swung from horse-trading and changing party affiliations to obeying the dictates of a single individual. The combination of the offices of the party chief and the chief executive being vested in a single individual has withered away whatever little accountability could be expected.

3. The Eighteenth Amendment and 7th NFC have very rightly devolved administrative, legal, and financial powers and authority from the federal to the provincial governments. However, this devolution remains incomplete as the provinces have not transferred the powers and resources further down to the local governments where most of the interaction between an ordinary citizen and the government takes place. Whether it is law and order and security, schooling for the children, immunization and healthcare, supply of drinking water, and sanitation, it is the local government that delivers

these essential services. Since 2008 the powers of the local governments have been reassumed by the provincial governments. The proposed laws setting up the local governments are a big step backward from the Local Government Ordinance 2001.

With the exception of KP, the provincial governments enjoy enormous powers under the proposed laws to keep the elected local governments subservient to them. Under such a set-up, the elected representatives at the local level will remain impotent. The disconnect between the wishes of the provincial governments, along with the members of the provincial assemblies, to centralize all powers in their hands and the aspirations of the people to access basic public services at their doorsteps must be resolved. Attempts to strengthen democratic governance are bound to fail in the absence of decentralization of decision-making, delegation of powers, devolution of authority, and de-concentration of resources.

4. The administrative machinery of the government, i.e. the civil services as a whole, has broken down. As pointed out earlier, every crisis that Pakistan has faced for the last many years, i.e. the security of person and property and poor law and order, energy shortages, delays in the administration of justice, ghost schools and absentee teachers, missing drugs and malfunctioning health facilities, and piles of garbage in the urban areas, can all be traced to institutional decay and governance deficit. Reforms in police, of the civil service, revenue administration, land management, judiciary, and delivery of social services must be undertaken to set the country in the right direction. A road map has already been prepared and the Report of the National Commission for Government Reforms (NCGR) sets out detailed recommendations. The civil services of the early days used to attract the best and brightest talent until the late 1970s. Their security of tenure guaranteed by the constitution was withdrawn and since then politicization of the bureaucracy has seriously impaired its capacity to remain neutral and objective which is the hallmark of an efficient civil service. The challenge is to revitalize them to enable them to regain their earlier lustre.

5. The dispensation of justice in Pakistan has become time-consuming, expensive, convoluted, and unnecessarily layered. Criminal and Civil

Procedure Codes and the Evidence Act have been modified in the UK itself, where they had their origin, but have remained unchanged in Pakistan. The backlog of millions of cases pending in the lower courts has nullified the deterrent effect of punishment on criminals, defaulters, and other violators of the law. State revenues, amounting to hundreds of billions of rupees are stuck up due to litigation by tax violators and the grant of indefinite stay orders. Bank loan defaulters enjoy a free ride because of the unending stay orders and appeals and lack of progress in execution of decrees granted by the courts themselves. Property titles and exchanges of deeds have lost their sanctity because of the prolonged disputes and complex processes prescribed by the courts. Detection, investigation, and prosecution of cases are so sloppy that the conviction rate is miserably low. Criminals get off scot-free and continue to engage in their nefarious activities without any sense of fear.

6. The Freedom of Information Act promulgated by the federal government is overly diluted and defanged. It indeed does nothing to facilitate the flow of information into public hands. The Right to Information Act in India has played a major role in keeping public servants and political leaders on their toes because of the fear that their actions and misdeeds could become public knowledge and embarrass them. Civil society organizations and the media have played a crucial role in accessing information and data under the Act. A similar, effective, piece of legislation in Pakistan and curtailment of the Official Secrets Act can be an effective tool in ensuring transparency in governance. Provincial legislation, particularly those in KP and Punjab, are an improvement but the requisite institutional arrangements have not yet been made. Governments that do not have much to fear and believe in transparency will benefit.

7. Parliament is expected to ensure that checks and balances are in place to curb the excesses of the executive. But this, however, is hardly the case in Pakistan. There is little legislative accountability to citizens, weak market oversight, and indifference in responses to citizen demands. The parliamentary committees, such as the public accounts committee, through public hearings can exert a sobering pre-emptive influence on the government departments, ministries, and agencies. They could ensure

that public expenditure is underpinned by value for money and that waste, inefficiencies, and irregularities are minimized. However, the partisanship shown in the committees' deliberations and the lack of technical expertise among the staff assigned to these committees have weakened their watchdog and oversight functions. Strengthening these committees would help in exerting effective control over the misuse of power and resources by the executive.

8. Finally, the management practices in the government need to be modernized and overhauled. Over-centralization, concentration of power in the hands of the prime minister and the provincial chief has resulted in diffused responsibility, absence of clear accountability inertia, and lack of commitment. Elongated hierarchical chains, consultation for the sake of form and procedures rather than substance, turf-building and turf-protection, and a tendency to pass the buck has created a big wedge between promise and performance. The rules of business have to be rewritten to assign clear responsibilities to the ministries and providing them with the requisite authority and resources to fulfil their obligations and hold them accountable for results. There should be inter-ministerial coordination and conflict resolution at the level of the cabinet secretary, secretaries' committees, cabinet sub-committees, and the cabinet.

The catalogue of comprehensive reforms set out above is easy to visualize but extremely complex and difficult to implement. The challenge of reforming these institutions is formidable because the vested interests desirous of perpetuating the status quo are politically powerful and the relations between them and the political leadership and beneficiaries of the existing system are so strong that they cannot be easily wished away. Elected governments with an eye on short-term electoral cycles are not inclined to incur the pains that such reforms are likely to inflict when it is quite likely that the long-term gains are likely to accrue to a different political party. Authoritarian governments are not effective because they do not enjoy legitimacy and therefore cannot sustain reforms. Changing the form in which institutions function is a slow and difficult process requiring, in addition to significant political will, fundamental measures to reduce the opportunity and incentives for particular groups to capture economic rents.

It will not be possible to execute these reforms unless all the major political parties agree to them and reach a consensus so that partisanship and point-scoring do not come in the way of their implementation. Civil servants who have retreated into passivity can be reactivated, motivated, and mobilized if they are certain that the risks of retribution and penalties entailed in implementing these reforms are likely to be minimal. Politicians of all persuasions must realize that the growing disaffection against political parties and leaders in Pakistan, the rapid spread of violence and intolerance, the rising popularity of and respect for the armed forces, and the widening gap between the expectations of the general public and delivery by the government demand a drastic change in their past conduct, practices, and behaviour. The ultimate beneficiaries of such altered behaviour would not only be the citizens of Pakistan but also the political parties themselves. The cynicism and wide distrust of politicians in society at large could be replaced by improved access and delivery of essential basic services, thus bolstering people's confidence in their politicians.

Assuming that this long-term agenda receives broad-based acceptance by the political parties and their willingness to implement it is demonstrated, the next question is: how to execute such an agenda? This would require strong institutional support across all different sectors. Institutional strengthening, therefore, becomes the *sine qua non* for building the capacity to implement the reform agenda in an intelligently phased sequence of actions.

Institutional Strengthening in Support of the Reform Agenda

A vibrant democracy, with adequate checks and balances, needs to reshape and revamp its institutions of governance to implement the long-term reform agenda of achieving development outcomes of security, growth, and equity. The prerequisites for this are: a functioning bureaucracy, strong and effective institutions at the federal and provincial levels, and local governments working under the watchdog of elected legislatures at the federal and provincial levels. An accessible, inexpensive, and speedy judicial and dispute-resolution system, particularly at the grass-root level along with a decentralized and devolved system for the delivery of basic services such as education, healthcare, potable water, sanitation, and transport, would motivate ordinary citizens to participate in the affairs of the state. A dynamic and efficient private sector that operates in a competitive market environment and maintains high standards of corporate governance and social responsibility would propel the engines of the economy.

These read like utopian goals, and indeed they are, but it may be useful to define the ultimate destination to chart the desired path forward. Pakistan would certainly be a far better place if such an institutional landscape could be created but the ground realities—the legacy of a past with deeply rooted and entrenched interests; the power dynamics; and human, organizational, and financial resource constraints—militate against it.

Key Institutions Requiring Restructuring and Strengthening

Following the analytical framework of the *WDR 2017*, this study focuses on the drivers that can change the political equilibrium in a way that gives power to those who seek to push through the reforms. The design of institutional reforms proposed here is based on an understanding of past pitfalls. Selective interventions in certain key institutions that would not totally unsettle the existing political dynamics but gradually allow for a change in the status quo, are addressed. The blowback and resistance are likely to be much more subdued than would be a sweeping, across-the-board approach. The report of the National Commission for Government Reforms, which recommended comprehensive administrative reforms of the civil services and the structure, and the processes and policies associated with it, found no traction during the past seven years under three different governments. An attempt has to be made to lower the sights and aim for a second best or third best solution entailing an incremental approach, involving the careful selection of few key institutions with large spill-over effects. Reforms of these institutions should create a ripple effect and may, over time, produce a cumulative impact, making a substantial difference. At the very least it may arrest the process of decay that is spreading rapidly in the absence of any corrective measures.

Institutions of Accountability, Transparency, and Oversight

- Parliamentary committees
- Auditor General of Pakistan (AGP), and the Public Accounts Committees (PACs)
- National Accountability Bureau (NAB)
- Election Commission of Pakistan (ECP)
- Higher Education Commission (HEC)
- Public Service Commissions (FPSC/PPSCs)
- National Science and Technology Commission (NSTC)
- Information Commissioners
- E-Government Directorate General

Security

- Lower Judiciary
- Police
- Federal Investigation Agency (FIA)
- National Counter-Terrorism Agency (NACTA)
- Prosecution Departments

Growth

- State Bank of Pakistan (SBP)
- Securities and Exchange Commission of Pakistan (SECP)

- Federal Board of Revenue (FBR)
- Trade Development Authority of Pakistan (TDAP)
- Board of Investment (BoI)

Equity

- Pakistan Agriculture Research Council (PARC)
- SBP
- HEC
- Benazir Income Support Programme (BISP)
- Irrigation authorities
- Urban development authorities
- National Vocational and Technical Education Authority (NAVTEC)

How would changes in these institutions translate into actual economic benefits for Pakistan? Economists believe that incentives play a large part in altering human behaviour. It is important first to describe the current incentive structure in Pakistan faced by firms, farms, households, and individuals, and then to suggest how these incentives can be modified by appropriate institutional interventions that are likely to have positive effects on growth, equity, and security, the three development outcomes set out in the Policy Effectiveness Chain. The selective approach suggested here should contribute towards an easing of the binding constraints facing the economy. I would like to map these interventions to each of the development outcomes. The first, a favourable and benign environment for doing business, would affect growth; the second, boosting agricultural productivity and rural income distribution, would have a salutary effect on equity; and the third, improving the administration of justice and protection of property rights on security and with secondary links to growth and equity.

(a) Growth Outcome: A Favourable and Benign Environment for Doing Business

Market forces, by and large, determine the allocation of scarce capital, labour, formal credit, skills, and technical knowhow among various competing demands and players. So long as this occurs through competition without any other consideration, the economy will remain efficient and contribute to rapid growth. However, if different kinds of artificial barriers are erected and access to these resources are subject to bureaucratic discretion rather than on the basis of a level playing field for all market players, the economy will end up in a sub-optimal equilibrium. Pakistan ranks 147 on the World Bank Ease of Doing Business Index. It takes, on average, three years and lot of upfront costs for an investor to obtain 30 clearances from the various federal, provincial, and local governments but some privileged individuals are able to use their connections and influence to get these much sooner than others, thus tilting the field and creating distortions. Similarly, the burden of high regulatory costs, unsecured land titles, inadequate and expensive infrastructure services, particularly energy, and a slow and cumbersome contract enforcement system are the major constraints for both new and established businesses and are not shared uniformly.

The general attitude of a lack of responsiveness and coordination between different agencies of the government can also be quickly turned on its head if the intended beneficiary has an influential background. Lower functionaries in the labour, health, environment, food, social security, and taxation departments usually harass and extort rents from the small and medium enterprises, further adding to their cost of business. Small and medium enterprises cannot afford these rents, and are defeated by these protracted processes. It is thus in their best interest to remain confined to the informal sector and the same scale of operations and forgo any ambitions for expansion.

A World Bank study shows that the entry and exit of firms in Pakistan's export sector is extremely limited. Institutions such as the SBP, SECP, BoI, TDAP, and FBR, if revamped, can make a substantial difference in removing these hurdles, enforcing a level playing field, and thus easing the cost of doing business for a majority of small- and medium-sized firms and entrepreneurs. Dynamic websites and applications which allow downloading, uploading, and approval of the various forms can cut down both the costs and the lead time significantly. Inspections by different agencies should be pre-announced, at specified intervals of time, based on risk ratings and conducted in presence of neutral observers.

(b) Equity Outcome: Boosting Productivity and Income Distribution

Upward social mobility in Pakistan has not made much headway because of the poor indicators such as literacy, access to health care, maternal and child health, drinking water, and sanitation. Steve Radelet[2] shows that advances in education and knowledge improve health, better health helps improve learning ability, and both together contribute to economic growth. This form of growth would help to reduce inequities because increases in income lead to better education and health, and with these a positive self-reinforcing cycle sets in. Delivery of these basic public services to the poor segments of the population, remote and backward districts, and the disadvantaged should be given the highest priority with both growth and equity objectives in view.

In the agricultural sector, the average productivity of land is 50–60 per cent lower than that of progressive farmers. This cannot be currently raised because irrigation water is diverted from the water-course heads to over-irrigate the land of large and influential landlords, in collusion with irrigation department officials, depriving the poor tail-enders of the quota to which they are entitled. Large subsidized tube-wells are a source of groundwater for the same class. Public procurement of food-grains at higher than market prices is also made from the ranks of the same group of influential and well connected individuals. Electricity and other inputs in times of scarcity are allocated to individuals on the basis of their connections or in exchange for favours to officials. The Gini coefficients in the rural economy are naturally much higher because of this preferential access to scarce public resources and untargeted subsidies. There is hardly any motivation for non-elite farmers to raise their productivity in highly tilted circumstances. Theoretical calculations show that Pakistan can earn $300 billion through proper allocation and utilization of irrigation water and groundwater on the basis of a combination of, one, cultivating higher value crops and two, realizing the average productivity level which is only one-sixth of the potential value.

The scarcity premium of the key public resource—water—is pre-empted by a few thousand private individuals and families. Water use charges do not cover even one-tenth of the operational and maintenance costs, and the subsidy is borne by the general taxpayers. Realistic pricing of water usage and targeted subsidies for those below a landholding threshold would do much to change the perverse incentives which reward waste and inefficiency and forgo potential productivity gains. Rural infrastructure, such as storage godowns, farm-to-market roads, and institutions such as empowered and devolved district governments, along with the SBP for credit availability to small farmers and micro-enterprises, provincial irrigation departments, and national agricultural research institutes can play a major role in bringing prosperity to the rural countryside.

Pratap Mehta,[3] an Indian scholar, has commented that 'the discretionary power the state has with respect to land is the single biggest source of corruption in India.' This statement applies equally to Pakistan where the military, civil services, politicians, and other real estate developers have used land acquisition, land allocation, and contrived changes in the land use regulations to enrich themselves. The land market is over-regulated and the discretionary powers enjoyed by the urban development authorities—such as Capital Development Authority (CDA), Lahore Development Authority (LDA), Karachi Development Authority (KDA), etc., and the defence housing authorities—are used to acquire land.

These bodies allocate land acquired from their original owners at a fraction of the market price to individuals or developers at highly subsidized price while collecting rents for themselves and their political bosses. These new owners then dispose of the same plots of land in the market at five to ten times their allotted price or build and sell residential and commercial property at highly inflated prices. The change in classification of land, i.e. from residential to commercial, is another point at which rents are extracted and shared. These developers who have benefited from the discretionary favours then pay back at election time by contributing to the campaign financing of their patrons. The vicious cycle continues after the patrons get elected and occupy public offices. As a consequence of this unholy nexus, the housing societies and schemes catering to the needs of the well-to-do segment of the population have sprung up in all the major urban areas but the poor continue to live in *katchi abadi*s without basic amenities and services because land prices are beyond their reach. Therefore, reform of the urban development authorities is essential to minimize this huge source of corruption and inequity.

(c) Security Outcome: Improving the Administration of Justice, Rule of Law, and Property Rights

Incentives for a better security outcome are also vitiated by the anachronistic laws, rules, practices, and institutional malfeasance. Victims of crimes do not report them to police stations because they do not believe that their complaints will be redressed. Should they do so, they have to go through an endless routine of harassment and extortion at the hands of the policemen. The criminals get off scot-free and are emboldened to continue with their antisocial activities as the prospect of their getting apprehended is low and, in many instances, they are in cahoots with the police officials who act as their protectors in return for a share of the loot. A percentage of these illegal earnings is then passed on to the higher echelons of bureaucrats and politicians who had posted them to these stations in the first place. The principle of reciprocity is also observed at the time of elections when these police officials reciprocate by helping their benefactors. Land mafias, water mafias, drug peddlers, arms merchants, and prostitution and gambling dens, all, consequently, thrive under the eyes of the custodians of law.

In a few cases, where reports are registered and cognizance is taken of the crime committed and the accused are apprehended, the investigation methods are antiquated, high handed, and sloppy. The staff is not properly trained, forensic techniques are not properly utilized, and the linkages are not established. Witnesses are either tutored or coerced, and confessional statements do not stand the scrutiny of the court. The prosecution is conducted by lawyers who are low paid, ill-educated, and otherwise unable to get any other decent jobs in the profession and have been appointed on the basis of the recommendation of people in the higher echelons. Court procedures relating to evidence date back to the 1850s and have not been revised since; the time and costs of these antiquated procedures are beyond the means of ordinary litigants. Sons and relatives of the elite classes who commit heinous crimes such as murder get away by engaging high-paid lawyers, winning over or intimidating the witnesses, and bribing the investigators, prosecutors, and judges from the lower judiciary. Those few cases where conviction does take place, and the accused are sent to jail, the conditions in prison are pathetic for ordinary individuals but with every comfort provided to the well-to-do. The entire chain of institutions involved in the administration of justice breeds more crime. Criminals and violators of the law get away with minimum or no punishment while the common citizens pray to Allah that they will not have to face the police, prosecutors, or judges.

It is not just the criminal justice system that is loaded in favour of the elite classes; the property rights and contracts regime meets the same fate. The rich feudal lords and large real estate owners dispossess the poor from their lands and homes because they can obtain stay orders for indefinite periods and their lawyers can file adjournment motions or raise frivolous procedural or technical reasons in court. Well aware that their opponents do not have the means to resist, they resort to dilatory tactics which favour them. Banks have decrees granted by the courts for recovering outstanding loans but the execution rate is so low that those who have misappropriated the loans have nothing to worry about. Several hundred billion rupees of these loans remain stuck. Tax dodgers, evaders, and concealers of income resort to a ceaseless process of appeals before various tiers, tribunals, appellate courts, and high courts. The disposal rate is so slow that the delinquents can roll over the money, which actually belongs to the tax authorities or the banks, for their businesses or for highly conspicuous consumption.

The key institutions that can make a significant difference in this space are the police, Federal Investigation Agency, National Counterterrorism Authority (NACTA), lower judiciary, prosecution departments, and intelligence agencies. The frequent recourse to calling the civilian armed forces for law enforcement and counterterrorism would be minimized by raising the standards of recruitment, training, postings, performance management, promotion, and career progression, and bringing disciplinary rules of the police, FIA, and NACTA at par with those of the CAF.

Institutions of Restraint/Accountability, Transparency, and Oversight

One of the major areas of reform has to do with the absence of accountability for performance. There is both too much and too little accountability of those involved in public affairs in Pakistan. On one hand, the plethora of laws and institutions such as anti-corruption bureaus, national accountability bureau, auditor general's reports, public accounts committees of the legislature, parliamentary oversight, judicial activism, and the ombudsman system have created an atmosphere of fear, inertia, and lack of decision-making amongst civil servants. On the other hand, instances of rampant corruption, malpractices, nepotism, and favouritism, and waste and inefficiency are common folklore in the administrative culture of Pakistan. Excessive preoccupation with ritualistic compliance with procedures, rules, and form has replaced substantive concerns with the results and outcomes for welfare and justice. Therefore, restructuring the National Accountability Bureau and the provincial anti-corruption bureaus is important.

Critical to the overall policies of human resource management are the federal and provincial public service commissions; for financial integrity the Auditor General of Pakistan, for ensuring fair and impartial elections the Election Commission of Pakistan, which should screen and disqualify undesirable candidates; to develop the skills and technology of the future, the Higher Education Commission and a proposed National Science Commission need to be reorganized, strengthened, and provided with operational autonomy and resources. All these institutions should be manned by competent and impartial individuals of integrity with security of tenure but held accountable for the results. The UNDP has developed a Better Governance Index (BGI) to measure institutional performance.[4] A variant of the Index adapted to each type of institution can be used to gauge whether these revamped institutions are meeting the goals assigned to them. E-governance tools should be embedded in the institutional architecture to improve transparency, curb discretionary practices, monitor progress, and obtain feedback.

Together, these 25 state-centric institutions, if allowed to work independently without any undue political interference in their functioning, can become the precursors of a strong democratic governance structure and processes. In addition to these institutions, civil society organizations including NGOs engaged in the delivery of basic social services, particularly in the backward districts and communities, rural and remote areas, should be facilitated, encouraged, and incentivized, as in Bangladesh, to step up their outreach activities and coverage.

Why have these particular institutions been chosen out of a myriad of so many for reform and restructuring?

a) **Institutions of Market Governance:** Whether they will be able to enable private businesses to operate without hassle or high costs of transactions and facilitate governance.

b) **Institutions for Delivery of Services:** Whether they will be able to improve the delivery of basic services such as education, health, drinking water, sanitation, and the like, to ordinary citizens effectively and at affordable cost.

c) **Institutions of Administration of Justice:** Whether they will be able to provide security of life and property of the citizens and access to expeditions and inexpensive justice.

d) **Institutions of Accountability:** Whether they will be able to take action against malfeasance, corruption, and misuse of public office for personal gain.

e) **Institutions for Equality and Human Opportunity:** Whether they will be able to strengthen the capacity of those who do not have assets or skills to fully participate in market-based economic activities.

Another aspect that figures prominently is the relative strength of cross-over linkages and spill-overs. For example, the reform of the Public Services Commissions will be able to attract, select, and retain young men and women based on an open, merit-based competitive system of entry into the civil services. The higher quality of these civil servants will help to raise the level of performance of the institutions that deal with service delivery, market governance, and administration of justice.

Drivers of Change

As the previous chapters have shown, societal, political, and economic interests and priorities have so far stoutly resisted any scheme of bureaucratic and administrative reform. Imperceptible changes driven by a growing middle class, urbanization, a youthful population connected to the rest of the world, technological advances, an assertive civil society, and the influence of social and electronic media are already beginning to gradually manifest themselves. Professor Iftikhar Malik[5] alluded to this phenomenon as long ago as 1997 and his prognosis is beginning to be proven right:

People have overwhelmingly supported the moderate forces in consecutive elections, and rapid urbanization and consumerism, mingled with more mobility and unlimited access to print and visual media, have already unleashed new processes of communication. A comparatively youthful society, most of whose members have been brought up as Pakistanis, are not only raising [their] voices against a monopoly of feudal interests over politics. They are not comfortable with the existing oligarchic tri-polar relationship between the bureaucracy, the military, and politicians which smacks of age-old dynastic elitism and so the demands for accountability are becoming louder.

More recently, a seminal work by Ali Cheema, Farooq Naseer, and Hassan Javid,[6] on the dynastic politics of Punjab, seems to have endorsed Professor Malik's proposition. Their study finds:

> The urban areas of Punjab have begun to witness a weakening of dynastic politics. In comparison with their rural counterparts, urban dynastic politicians are 40 percentage points less likely to win in the constituencies where they stand for election. Furthermore, the number of races without any dynastic contender is almost 10 percentage points higher in urban areas than in rural areas.
>
> The ties of kinship and economic dependence that often characterize rural social relations are weaker in cities, thus decreasing some of the electoral advantage that underpins the electability of rural dynastic candidates. The physical space of cities, consisting of high population density levels, as well as the presence of a relatively mobile and fluid population of inhabitants, is less conducive to the mobilization of vote blocs similar to those that characterize local-level village politics. Cities are also more plural spaces than villages, with a diverse range of organizations and interest groups facilitating a freer exchange of information and ideas that can make it harder for dynastic politicians to rely upon their traditional sources of power when campaigning for votes. Given the changing demographics of Punjab, with the province becoming increasingly urban, we may see a decline in dynasticism over time and the emergence of political party machines.

Thus the driver of change for this restructuring to be sustainable and endurable has to be endogenously induced rather than externally driven. The virtuous cycle envisaged would be propelled along the following path.

The emergence of a vocal, assertive, educated middle-class, based in urban areas free from links of kinship, caste, tribal affiliations, and feudal subservience, has a high probability of triggering this driver. *WDR 2017* has shown that when the middle class grew in Latin America, people began demanding better quality services and demonstrating for better governance. Urbanization improves the overall productivity and growth rates of the economy through reallocation of labour from low productive sectors such as agriculture to high productive manufacturing and formal services sectors. High density of populations reduces the cost of provision of infrastructure and services. Agglomeration economies allow for a scaling up of production, spill-over of skills and transfer of knowhow, availability of intermediate inputs, and reduction in the length of the supply chain.

Pakistan has had no census since 1998[7] (the results of the census conducted in 2017 are still provisional) but, taking the last census as the base and extrapolating inter-censal growth rates derived from surveys, it was estimated that Pakistan's urban population in 2015 would be 72.5 million or a 38.6 per cent increase. Casual empiricism and serious studies have challenged the definition of 'urban' areas used in the 1998 census as it covers only those living in the municipalities and cantonments. Raza Ali,[8] using a more broad-based definition of urban and urbanizing areas, has shown in his studies that the attributes of administrative areas do not adequately reflect the process of urbanization and agglomeration. Using density, urban core, and distance to city, his re-estimation of the 1998 census shows that the urban population is likely to increase by at least 20 per cent to 48 million, i.e. 36 per cent of the total population. Assuming 4 per cent to be the average growth rate between 1998 and 2015, the current urban population would be 87 million or 46 per cent of the total population today.

This mixture of an urban population comprising a growing middle-class, demographics favouring a younger, better-educated, more self-confident population, a vibrant social media, and an active, vocal civil society can have a serious transformational impact on Pakistan's politics, governance, and delivery of basic services. The latest census should therefore result in a fresh delimitation of constituencies for the national and provincial assemblies, shifting the balance of power from the dominance of rural electorate (70 per cent) to an even-handed division of the population (55:45). The rural constituencies are, by and large, driven by the politics of *biradri*, kinship, familial ties, tribal affinity, and obligations to the feudal lords, and are characterized largely by the traditional patron–client relationship.

On the other hand, the expectations of the urban electorate are related to delivery of tangible results and promised parameters of performance. Those who are unable to meet these expectations are usually shown the door as the threshold of the urban population's tolerance for incompetent, self-serving, and corrupt individuals is relatively low. A comparison between the candidates contesting the elections over five decades shows a persistence of a dynastic element and family orientation as significant determinants in the rural constituencies with low turnover. In the urban constituencies, the fatality rate is relatively high and new faces are more common. Changes in party affiliations are relatively more common in the rural constituencies because the parties chase 'electables' and bring them into their fold. The same long dominant families in rural Pakistan are found to be more prone to changing party loyalties than their urban counterparts. However, this tendency has been curbed since the constitutional amendment that forces a person to resign from his seat if he crosses the floor.

The complexion of parliament and the provincial assemblies and the electoral outcomes in 2018 is, therefore, likely to be quite different from that in 2013 if the elections are held in freshly delimited constituencies. The induction of a large number of urban elected representatives is also likely to help to alter the governance structure. Accountability, transparency, right to information, financial disclosure, and audit are likely to be demanded by the urban electorate. They are more likely to be interested in getting access to public services such as education, health, water supply, sanitation, transport, land for housing, and security. These services are delivered largely by the local governments.

The MNAs and MPAs will therefore, perforce, have to work with the municipal corporations, municipal committees, town committees, and cantonments to satisfy their voters. The impetus for reforms of institutions delivering these services will therefore be shared by all three tiers of the government. The present tension and in-built conflict that is the main hurdle in adopting reforms would thus be eased and give way to a harmonious and synergistic relationship that would affect the quality of governance. An important side effect will be that the state would be able to assert its legitimacy through a demonstrated record of effectiveness in delivering basic public services to the population. This would allow it to collect taxes from individuals who question the government's moral authority to tax the people when they are unable to deliver essential services.

The sequence of events that can minimize the current mess associated with urbanization and unshackle its hidden potential is clear. The constituencies should be delimited on the basis of the 2017 census results, and administrative powers and resources should be devolved to the local governments. Once the new elected representatives come to office, their survival instinct would force them to reform the institutions that deliver basic public services for fear of being thrown out of office by an informed and demanding electorate. These changes will not occur during one five-year period but at least a beginning ought to be made now by holding the census and delimiting the constituencies. This appears to be the best possible prospect for driving institutional reforms in Pakistan.

BOX 16.1

Essential ingredients for restructuring and strengthening the proposed institutions

- Select and appoint on basis of open competition and merit a widely respected, strong, and competent individual of known integrity and demonstrated leadership qualities to head the institution for a fixed tenure. Removal from the office can take place only under pre-specified conditions.
- Agree on the mandate, terms of reference, responsibilities, functions, powers, objectives, framework agreement, and key performance indicators (KPIs).
- Appoint an independent Board of Governors wherever necessary, consisting of eminent persons for oversight, supervision, strategic planning, and budgetary allocations, holding the management accountable for results.
- Grant one line budgetary allocation to resource the organization and allow financial autonomy subject to internal controls and external audit.
- Delegate the powers to the head of the organization to appoint the professional staff and human resources of calibre through an open, transparent process.
- Submit an annual performance report to the Parliament and appear before the relevant Parliamentary committee to answer questions.
- Government can provide policy direction but not interfere in day-to-day operations.

Notes and References

1. Acemoglu, Robinson, *The Role of Institutions in Growth and Development*, Working paper 10, Growth Commission (2008).

2. Radelet, S., *The Great Surge: The Ascent of the Developing World* (Simon & Schuster, 2016).

3. Mehta, P. B., 'It's Land, Stupid', *Indian Express*, 19 August 2010.

4. UNDP, *Development Advocate Pakistan: Civil Service Reforms in Pakistan*, vol. 3, issue 3, 2016.

5. Malik, I. H., *State and Civil Society in Pakistan* (Macmillan, 1997).

6. Cheema, Javid, Naseer, *Dynastic Politics in Punjab: Facts, Myths and their Implications*, IDEAS Working Paper 1/13, 2013.

7. The latest census was held recently in 2017.

8. Ali, R., *The Urban Edge*. SPDC, 2015; Acemoglu and Robinson, *The Role of Institutions in Growth and Development*; Radelet, *The Great Surge: The Ascent of the Developing World*; Bokhari, F., 'Poor Food Insecurity', *Dawn*, 20 November 2016; Mehta, P. B., 'It's Land, Stupid', *Indian Express*, 19 August 2010; UNDP, *Development Advocate Pakistan: Civil Service Reforms in Pakistan*. vol. 3, issue 3, 2016; Malik, I. H., *State and Civil Society in Pakistan* (Macmillan, 1997); Cheema, et al., *Dynastic Politics in Punjab: Facts, Myths and their Implications*, IDEAS Working Paper 1/13 2013; Ali, *The Urban Edge* (SPDC, 2015).

17

Lessons from the Experience of Other Countries

A question that may be raised in the context of the theme explored in this volume is whether Pakistan is unique in the impact of its governance infirmities. Aren't there other countries with weak or frail institutions and poor governance that have performed quite well? Table 17.1 presents a comparative picture of Pakistan, Bangladesh, and India in relation to various governance rankings compiled by different organizations. Yes, it is true that Pakistan has slipped steeply since 1990 but the rankings for the other two countries are not very encouraging either. Bangladesh was rated by Transparency International for five consecutive years in the early 2000s as the globally most corrupt country. It was only in 2006 that it moved from the last position to the third last amongst 163 countries. The two *begums* have been constantly engaged in unseemly political battles for over two decades. Matters came to such a pass that the military had to intervene in 2007 and set up a caretaker government for two years to cleanse the political system but without much success.

The result after the two year hiatus was the same: The Awami League (AL) and the Bangladesh National Awami Party (BNP) continued to remain the two dominant parties, with AL winning the elections. Since then, the ruling party has crushed the opposition party with a heavy hand and gradually tamed all institutions of the state, including the judiciary, and is on the path toward a one-party government. Nonetheless, Bangladesh has done remarkably well over the past 25 years, growing economically at a respectable rate and showing improvement on social indicators. India, for its part, has not fared well on some of these indicators.

A study of India's public institutions reached the following conclusion: Many of India's institutions—bureaucracy, political parties, universities, investigative agencies, public enterprises—have markedly deteriorated and institutional decay, and its causes and consequences for governance, has been an important subject and enquiry for concern.'[1] A recent study has focused on the nexus between crime and politics in India.[2] M. P. Singh in his study[3] concludes that 'India's record of administrative reforms is shown to be glacial and unimpressive. This is attributable to the vested interest of the political and bureaucratic classes, the weakness of the class of bourgeois, fragmented electoral mandates, and divided governments.' Several ministers of the union government and chief ministers along with senior bureaucrats were accused, indicted, or convicted of corruption and other malpractices in recent years. Notwithstanding this frailty of institutions and weak governance, India remains one of the top performers among the emerging economies. Devesh Kapur[4] explores what he calls this paradox posed by the Indian experience: more rapid and less volatile growth despite greater governmental instability.

Indonesia under Suharto was cited as a striking example of crony capitalism. The family was involved in most of the large projects and business transactions along with their business partners and no major deal could be consummated without the blessing of the Family. This notwithstanding, Suharto's record in turning around Indonesia's economy and lifting almost 100,000,000 people out of poverty by 1998 was quite impressive.

A careful comparative analysis of binary pairs of Pakistan vs these other three countries is beyond the scope of this chapter but some tentative and preliminary explanatory hypotheses can be offered. All three countries—India, Indonesia, and Bangladesh—enjoyed macroeconomic and political stability over a prolonged period of time with a continuity of economic policies. Successive governments did not deviate from the basic policy anchor, i.e. promotion and support of the private sector, signalling to investors that changes of government would have no shock or unanticipated effect on economic policies. This imbued a sense of confidence and predictability which permitted an uninterrupted and orderly journey in a predictable direction. Rent-sharing among private businesses, government officials, and politicians was commonplace and got entrenched as a standard norm of doing business. There were no surprises or abrupt disruptions when governments changed hands and therefore the rent-seeking was growth-enhancing,[5] in the sense that the owners used the surplus to invest and expand their domain while the government facilitated and paved the way by removing the bottlenecks and hurdles, thereby enabling the businesses to become internationally competitive. This relationship unshackled the entrepreneurial energies of the private sector in contributing to higher national growth. Investment rates remained high.

Civil society organizations (CSOs) in Pakistan remained dormant and inactive until the 2007 lawyers' movement which eventually led to the resignation of President Pervez Musharraf in August 2008. Larry Diamond[6] points out that in democracies, growing accountability is coming from a combination of older civil society organizations—student associations, trade unions, and religious bodies—alongside newer groups working for good governance and democracy such as think-tanks, bar associations, human rights groups, women's groups, and the like. These newer groups have played a prominent role in Bangladesh and India, and much less so in Pakistan.

In India, the reforms of 1991 almost completely unshackled the private sector and allowed it to compete in the domestic and international markets for goods and services. Although there is a great deal of ambivalence[7] towards private businesses in India, a legacy of the Mahalanobian thought, Indian entrepreneurs must be given credit for taking advantage of liberalization and deregulation. Once it was clear that these reforms were irreversible, they invested in expansion and the development of new productive capacity. Their learning by doing under the constraints of the protected import-substitution regime helped them to achieve efficiency. India has a large domestic market and as disposable incomes rose and poverty declined, manufacturing firms were able to reduce their unit cost of production through economies of scale. Some other sectors were able to prosper on their own because of the state's benign neglect, a well-known example of this being the IT sector and its dynamic growth. The post-1991 period also witnessed the return of Indian nationals who had received an academic education at the best educational institutions overseas and had worked in the most advanced companies around the world. A number of Indians who had prospered economically in the Silicon Valley set up venture capital funds and angel investor funds to support the start-ups. They were followed by international venture capital, angel investors, and private equity and hedge fund managers who made beeline to India.

Foreign direct investment shot up and investment–GDP ratios exceeded 30 per cent, demonstrating a renewed confidence in future economic prospects. Multinational companies were attracted to India's low cost talent, vast market, and the newly liberalized business environment. They decided to set up joint ventures with well-known Indian companies bringing in technology, marketing know-how, and their global networks. The diffusion of technology and knowledge then permeated Indian-owned companies too when managers and technicians of the multinationals were lured by the former, thus raising the general productivity levels. India was thus not only able to cater to the large and burgeoning middle-class domestically at competitive prices even after imports became freely available but also doubled its share in the global export market. Indian business houses acquired assets abroad and invested in foreign markets and thereby diversified their portfolios. IT exports rose dramatically, making India the largest outsourcing services centre in the world.

The other unanticipated but favourable side effect of the 1991 reforms was the changed nature of the relationship between the union government and the states, as Raja Chelliah[8] aptly puts it, 'The relative spheres of the two levels of the government have been thrown into flux. The scope for real decentralization of economic power has been greatly increased and new vistas have opened for creative and innovative activities by the subnational level of government.' A new 'federal market economy' emerged, the distinguishing characteristic of which was competitive federalism. The state chief ministers vied with one another to attract investment, holding conferences, road shows, receiving delegations, and persuading investors to locate their industries or business projects in their states, with the lures of incentives, tax breaks, land at subsidized rates, public utility connections, and the like. The more enterprising states, such as Tamil Nadu, Gujarat, Maharashtra, and Andhra Pradesh under Chandrababu Naidu, became role models for rapid economic growth which would then be emulated by the laggards.

The 11th Finance Commission's supplementary report also strengthened the fiscal powers of these progressive states by altering the priorities for allocation from need and social justice to effective utilization of resources and economic growth. Rudolph and Rudolph[9] go to the extent of attributing India's high growth rate in large measure to state-level initiatives and entrepreneurship.

In addition to the private sector dynamism and competitive federalism, there were some public institutions too that contributed to India's economic resurgence and resilience. Kapur[10] is of the view that India's polymorphic institutions provide a kind of institutional safety net that has limited the downside and given it a systemic resilience. There is large variance and some public institutions have played a critical and vital role amidst 'a thick institutional web'. The diversity of this institutional portfolio may reduce both risk (systemic stability) and return (rates of economic growth). He believes that this diversity reduces covariance risk across institutions which minimizes systemic risk, and that these features of the institutional landscape have given India a systemic resilience. According to him, 'this resilience weakens the downside risks of political instability— political volatility neither results in economic volatility nor amplifies into systemic collapse'.

M. B. Alam[11] is of the view that e-governance in India has made a significant contribution in monitoring and implementing various government schemes and projects and this has resulted in bringing accountability and transparency in governance and improved the quality of life of citizens both in the rural and urban areas.

Several former senior Indian policy-makers interviewed for this study identified some of such institutions. They were of the view that the independence given to accountability institutions such as the Chief Election Commissioner, Central Vigilance Commission, Union Public Service Commission, Comptroller and Auditor General of India, Central Bureau of Investigation, Reserve Bank of India, Securities, and the Exchange Board of India has gradually improved their performance and made them relatively effective. They also added that the Right to Information Act, the Information Commission, and Citizens' Charter are positive developments which have strengthened the hands of the civil society organizations (CSOs) in ensuring transparency in the public sector.

The most effective gatekeeper of Indian democracy which has emerged in the last 25 years is the Chief Election Commissioner who enjoys virtually unfettered powers to disqualify candidates and parties from contesting elections. The post gained a lot of attention and public confidence since the appointment of the no-nonsense T. N. Seshan in 1990. The traditions set by him were forcefully emulated by his successors. The elections in this extremely socially heterogeneous and ethnically and linguistically divided country have been free, and fair, and the results are rarely challenged.

India's competitive federalism was also greatly assisted by the politically far-sighted decision to reorganize the administrative structure on the basis of ethnicity and language, in this way demonstrating flexibility in accommodating the demands of the various segments of the population in carving out new states. This helped in lowering the temperature, diffusing grievances, and forging trust in the central government. All the noise and protest died down and the creation of the Telangana state, carved out of Andhra Pradesh, was the last of such demands to be met.

Pakistan, on the other hand, has followed a highly centralized approach, first unifying all the four provinces into one unit, i.e. the province of West Pakistan, causing a great deal of heartburn and dissatisfaction in the smaller provinces. The alienation of East Pakistan was triggered by the decision to declare Urdu to be the sole national language while the majority in East Pakistan spoke Bengali. Imposing parity in political representation on a province which had a majority of the population was also perceived to be a blatant violation of democratic principles and a betrayal by a minority of the West Pakistani elite seeking to retain control. In a country divided physically by a distance of 1,000 miles of territory of a not over-friendly neighbour, logic demanded that greater autonomy should have been given to the provinces. Rather, the opposite was the case, with greater centralization and all important decisions being taken in Islamabad. The six-point agenda of Sheikh Mujibur Rahman, which galvanized the Bengali population and then led to the emergence of Bangladesh, was a reaction to this system of over-centralized governance that neglected the genuine interests of East Pakistan. After 1971, a confidence-building measure to forge trust and allay the fears of the three smaller provinces would have been to divide the largest province of Punjab into three provinces. Punjab currently dominates the Pakistani landscape politically and being relatively more advanced, this gives rise to unnecessary rivalries and unproductive tensions. A further reorganization of the existing four provinces could be a more sensible and durable solution by accommodating the distinct ethnic and linguistic identities of the people living in these areas.

A scholar of South Asia has correctly observed:

> Far from opening the doors to fragmentation and weakness, the redrawing of state boundaries on linguistic basis has on balance probably strengthened India's unity and thus the platform for its democracy. Creating and maintaining some fundamental institutions of democracy proved to be more difficult in Pakistan than in India. The rule of law, on balance, is significantly sturdier in India than it is in Pakistan at the highest levels of the system, but equally filled with holes at the lower levels.[12]

THE INDIAN REFORM EXPERIENCE[13]

The credit for this must be go to P. V. Narasimha Rao who, as a prime minister heading a minority government after the tragic assassination of Rajiv Gandhi in May 1991, was able to establish the necessary political coalitions in support of the reforms. Rao was successful in conveying to his political opponents and to the people at large that India would be faced not only with an unprecedented economic crisis but also a potentially great political one if the population failed to unite in support of the reforms. His principal secretary, A. N. Verma, marshalled a highly sceptical bureaucracy in support of the effort. This unity of purpose amongst the political class and senior bureaucracy provided the necessary conditions for the Rao government to successfully reverse the three decades of steadily rising state intervention in all aspects of economic activity which expanded the scope of state capitalism, central planning, and bureaucratic overregulation.

In sum, the best testimony to the success of the 1991 reforms is reflected by the rate of growth of per capita incomes in the 25 years preceding the reforms and those succeeding it. Between 1965 and 1990, India's average annual GDP growth was a mere 4.1 per cent, which translated to a per capita income growth of 1.9 per cent per annum. In the subsequent period (1990 to 2015), this increased to 6.3 per cent and 4.6 per cent respectively. The reforms allowed India to completely jettison the so-called Hindu rate of growth. It would not be misplaced to say that without these reforms, India could have faced acute social and political unrest that would have arisen due to the economy's inability to generate sufficient wealth and employment had economic growth remained at pre-1991 levels.

A related achievement of the reforms, characterized by making the Indian economy more open to foreign financial flows and markets, was to integrate the Indian economy more deeply with the global economy. During the 25 years prior to the reforms, the share of the trade (export and imports of goods and services) in the total GDP was a low 11.5 per cent on average. This increased fourfold to reach 48.7 per cent in 2015.[14] This was a direct outcome of policy reform measures being focused largely on the 'tradable sectors' of the economy. The average import tariffs have been brought down from about 82 per cent in 1990 to under 10 per cent in 2014, giving Indian consumers and producers the benefit of the lower prices prevalent in global markets. Exports of goods and services (taken together) have increased from a mere $2.0 billion in 1965 and $22.6 billion in 1990 to $522 billion in 2014.

The higher level of integration has allowed India to benefit not only from easier access to foreign markets and relatively cheaper intermediate inputs but also from higher inflows of foreign direct investment (FDI), portfolio investments, and technology. This has enhanced the investment capacity and raised productivity levels in the economy. In sum, the 1991 reforms put India on a higher trajectory of economic growth by removing some of the dysfunctional controls and regulations, facilitating the import of intermediate inputs, technology, and financial inflows, thereby moving the economy towards greater integration with the world economy and de-reserving some key sectors from exclusive public sector ownership. During the 25 years after the reforms, India has been successful in reducing the percentage of its population living in abject poverty. 56 per cent of the total population lived below the poverty line in 1973 and 46 per cent in 1993 but by 2011 it was down to 22 per cent. This means that over 150 million people were brought out of rank poverty as compared to an increase in the number of poor from around 326 million to 416 million, between 1973 and 1993, in the period prior to the 1991 reforms.

However, reforming governance is a necessary condition for improvement in the delivery of public services and thereby making it more inclusive. Better (accountable, consistent, and transparent) governance is also at the heart of improving the conditions for doing business and making India a more investor-friendly environment.

More accountable governance also reduces the distance between the governors and the governed, thereby deepening democracy and liberating it from the feudal overtones that currently characterize it.[15] Prime Minister Modi and the BJP government are deeply concerned with probity in public affairs and their record in office for the past three years has been a great improvement over the previous government which was stigmatized by one big scam after another. Casual empiricism suggests that corruption at the higher levels at the Centre has indeed taken a nosedive since 2014. Both politicians and senior bureaucrats are afraid of serious consequences if they are found indulging in malfeasance. However, that does not by any means indicate that corruption has disappeared from the citizen's day-to-day dealings with the lower level government functionaries.

The Indian experience demonstrates that tough economic reforms become politically feasible in times of crisis. The role of leadership in seizing that particular opportunity and biting the bullet is critical. Another factor for success is that the credibility of reforms is established only when the party in opposition to the one that introduced the reforms also fully endorses them and carries them forward when in power. This perception of irreversibility acts as a strong signal to domestic and international economic actors that a paradigm shift has taken place and changes in the political dispensation would have very little effect on the broader economic policies.

Bangladesh

Since 1990, Bangladesh's economic growth has averaged 4 per cent per annum. Its national income doubled in real terms within two decades between 1990 and 2010. The share of extreme poverty fell to 40 per cent by 2011 from 59 per cent in 1990. Life expectancy rose from 55 to 69 years. The percentage of children dying before their fifth birthday dropped from 14 to under 5; over 90 per cent girls are enrolled in primary school.

By contrast, the period 1970–90 was characterized by a zero growth rate per capita. An average citizen had the same income in 1990 as in 1970. Extreme poverty had risen from 46 per cent in 1970 to 59 per cent in 1990. Disease was widespread. Bangladesh, which did not grow a single bale of cotton, has become one of the world's largest exporters of readymade garments (RMG) in less than two decades. The development of the RMG sector in Bangladesh is a fascinating story that needs to be explored and understood.

The multi fibre agreement (MFA) quota system provided entrepreneurs with promising opportunities to start a high profit business. The problem of foreign market entry was solved when Bangladeshi entrepreneurs negotiated business alliances with large foreign garment producers and buyers. The class to which the RMG industrialists belonged[16] enabled them to have great influence on policy matters and that, in turn, led to the formulation of policies and incentives that were RMG-sector friendly; the problems associated with stifling government control and regulations were thereby sidestepped by the industry. Moreover, the operation of the government's incentive scheme, along with quota rents, created large profit opportunities for the RMG industrialists, and this was further enlarged by the government deliberately overlooking some illegitimate activities engaged in by the RMG exporters, such as selling fabric imported on a duty free basis into bonded warehouses in the domestic tariff area and violations of labour laws.

The higher than normal profits they earned not only made it possible for the RMG producers to absorb the higher cost of doing business attributable to poor governance, but also allowed them to spend heavily on 'speed money' and also to reinvest and expand production facilities. It is often observed by critics of the garment industry that bribery in Bangladesh, prevalent in a relatively mild form before the establishment of the cotton garment industry, increased manifold and became firmly embedded in the country's administration's psyche with the birth and growth of the industry.

Faisal Ahmed, et al.[17] explain that the successive military governments between 1976 and 1991 introduced economic reforms which created favourable external conditions for the RMG's take-off. Since 1990, political competition has operated in a moderately stable but vulnerable equilibrium of democratic institutional rules with competitive clientele-ism. The fiery political differences between the Bangladesh National Party (BNP) and the Awami League (AL) have had no tangible implications for economic policy. Both parties maintain sufficiently large coalitions of support to remain in power via the redistribution of informal and formal rents. For both parties, these coalitions increasingly comprise legislators with financial stakes in the garment industry (10 per cent of the country's legislators directly own garment factories or have financial interests in the garment industry).

The government policy has been to facilitate the sector's growth through non-interference and a decentralized industrial policy. The state decentralized and delegated responsibilities to private organizations such as the various garment associations (for example, BGMEA, BKMEA, and others). This consensus on liberal economic policies has occurred in the face of a politico-economic environment that rewards political rent-seeking and fosters a regulatory state. Notwithstanding a rotation of governments every five years, economic policy has remained consistent because both parties favour privatization, liberalization, and export-led growth. In contrast to other developing countries, the approach of each party's industrial policies has been relatively hands-off. The government decided to delegate authority to issue import customs certificates to the BGMEA which streamlines the procedures for manufacturers to acquire imported raw material and technology. An abiding feature of Bangladesh politics is patronage-based corruption. However, as an astute observer pithily commented: 'In the event stationary bandits dominate the raving bandits, the harmful effects on economic growth in Bangladesh would be limited.'

M. Ali Rashid[18] examines how, in the face of such inadequate infrastructural facilities such as power and transport, bureaucratic delays and inefficiency, political instability marked by frequent strikes and interruption of services, all contributing to very high cost of business in Bangladesh, the readymade garment industry has grown so rapidly and succeeded in generating three quarters of Bangladesh's aggregate exports.

The answer is threefold. First, the industry earned extraordinarily high profits originating from the MFA quota system, collaborative arrangements with foreign importers and their representatives in Bangladesh for assistance and guidance in meeting the specifications, standards, and quality required for overseas markets, and foreign investment in export-processing zones.

Second, the entrepreneurs were drawn principally from the elite or ruling class, that is, retired civil or military officials and politicians, all with sufficient connections with and influence over government policy decisions favourable to the industry. Export subsidies, tax rebate on imported components, bonded warehouse, and a back-to-back licensing system greatly economized on working capital requirements; the poor working conditions due to inadequate or non-enforcement of labour and safety, standards which added to the abnormal profits, persisted partly because the entrepreneurs had sufficient influence over the regulatory authorities who ignored violations and partly because high profits enabled them to buy off the enforcement agencies.

Third, the high cost of business, stemming from poor or lax customs, a sea, and airport administration often ridden with corruption, were overcome through the necessary illicit payments, the former, in turn, encouraging corruption. Some observers believe that the most successful institutionalized system of corruption in Bangladesh was established by the garment industry.

M. A. Taslim[19] points out that certain economic policies adopted by the governments in Bangladesh, especially those concerning private sector-led growth, were instrumental in accelerating growth notwithstanding poor and deteriorating governance in certain areas. Bangladesh's experience shows that wholesale improvement is not essential for high growth. There, professionals, particularly lawyers, formed the most important group in the first parliament. However, by the eighth parliament, 51 per cent of the elected members were businessmen. Taslim argues that even if many of these members engaged in corruption, much of this money would find its way directly into legitimate business. This would ensure that government policies were in the personal and collective interests of influential business groups. Protection of legitimate business enterprises and their incomes now became a priority for the ruling elite. For example, opposition leaders owning banks keep their banks open during *hartals* when they forcibly shut down virtually everything else. There has not been much determined resistance to financial sector reforms in the recent past because poor governance could jeopardize the health of the entire sector. Policies and practices intended for private sector were introduced in consultation with them.

Mushtaq Khan[20] argues that what is critical for economic growth is a high level of growth-enhancing governance, the most important elements of which are: (a) management of weak property rights, (b) provision of incentives for technological progress or 'catching up', (c) management of political stabilization in an environment of personalized power relationship and patron–client politics, (d) performance-linked state assistance measures to domestic enterprise, and (e) records of property ownership titles, registration, public disclosure, and display, and allocation of state land to the landless. Only when growth occurs are adequate fiscal resources available for transfer through transparent, accountable, and participatory processes to balance a multiplicity of competing interest groups in order to achieve political and social stability that is conducive to capital accumulation.

In Bangladesh, there was growth-enhancing governance as the efficiency of investment and returns were high because the transaction costs of exporting were lowered by an investment-friendly environment. Starting and engaging in business was relatively easy and higher returns and lower transaction costs promoted a greater volume of investment. What were those policies that led to a lowering of the transaction costs?

Banking Reforms allowed the private sector to expand and take over the share of the Nationalized Commercial Banks (NCBs). The share of the NCBs in total deposits fell to 40 per cent by 2005 while that of private banks exceeded 50 per cent. The same was the case for advances, with the NCBs share declining to 35 per cent and the private banks capturing 55 per cent. Consequently, private sector credit to the GDP ratio rose to 44 per cent, a much higher percentage than in Pakistan, thus meeting both the working capital and fixed investment needs. Bangladesh's currency has been stable and has not depreciated, thus avoiding inflation of the imported inputs which represents 40 per cent of the export output.

An overall improvement in the banking sector, along with an unfettered access to associations, trade bodies, and chambers of commerce and industry of the private sector, allowed prompt redressal of their grievances and bottlenecks.

The tax rate in Bangladesh is low in relation to other countries. Industries competing with imports enjoy a very high level of protection. There is trade protection for RMG in developed countries in the form of quotas, duty free access, import bars, high import taxes in the domestic markets, and generous cash incentive schemes.

A large pool of unemployed or under-employed workers and a largely ineffective trade union movement maintained an effective lid on demands for higher wages and allowed employers to reduce labour protection standards with impunity. Minimum wages were not revised for long periods; real wages nearly halved. The hourly labour cost is thus amongst the lowest in the world. Domestic and industrial credit have grown robustly.

Gherzi,[21] in their report to the ministry of commerce, summarize these developments:

> In the 25 years, the private sector's contribution to GDP has grown to more than 7 times that of the public sector. Rate of decline of the public sector was 18% in the 1990s.

- RMG succeeded in creating a cocoon around itself for protection against existing governances-related problems. The industry attracted a fairly large number of well-educated people including former bureaucrats and military officers who had the skill, contact, and influence to bend the government machinery and regulations to this advantage. A series of innovations such as back-to-back L/C, duty drawback, and the bonded warehouse system created a virtual economic enclave that mimicked a free trade environment. It helped to eliminate the anti-export bias of the extant trade policy. A weakening of left politics and trade unionism afforded the manufacturing a highly flexible labour market with very low wages and lax labour standards. There were virtually no industry-wide movements until very recently.

Low wages because of an excess supply of labour and poor labour standards and high product prices owing to quotas and duty free access ensured large profits for the industry.

The other dimension of rural poverty alleviation was the spread of micro-credit principally to women. This has revolutionized the rural landscape. 16.1 million beneficiaries of micro-credit programmes are being served by 721 NGOs disbursing TK 339 billion annually.

An additional factor that was missing in Pakistan but played a pivotal role in Bangladesh was the subservience of the judiciary to the executive. Ali Riaz[22] points out this particular feature of the Bangladesh governance framework:

The 4th Amendment served the very root of the independence of the judiciary and made it subservient to the executive branch. Under the new constitution, the President could remove a judge including the CJ simply by an order of the grounds of misbehaviour or incapacity. The President also assumed the authority to appoint additional judges to the Supreme Court (SC) without any consultation with the Chief Justice.

The power and authority of the SC was severely curtailed. The authority of the SC in matters of appointments to, and control and discipline of, subordinate courts was withdrawn and vested in the president. The power of the High Court Division in respect of the enforcement of fundamental rights and to issue certain orders and directions was circumscribed.

The Fourth amendment established the supremacy of the executive over the legislative and judicial organs of the state.

Survi[23] includes the anti-corruption institution to this process of the executive capture:

In Bangladesh, not only does the political class oppose but actively frustrates any efforts to build institutions that will be the source of horizontal accountability. In 2013, the outgoing chief of the anti-corruption commission described the commission as a 'toothless tiger'. These institutions are considered by the political class, irrespective of their party affiliations, as unnecessary, burdensome, and detrimental to the political mission.

What are the lessons that can be learnt from the Bangladesh case? It may be safe to assume that in Bangladesh, the leadership was convinced that maximizing the long-term growth of the economy provided greater political dividends to the larger business community rather than confining patronage to a narrow group. A symbiotic relationship brought about a stable equilibrium between businesses, politicians, and bureaucrats. Politicians receive money from large businesses for their election campaigns, bureaucrats supplement their incomes with gifts and payoffs, while the businessmen enrich themselves and expand their businesses by investing their inordinate profits made through the largesse they receive from and the friendly environment provided by the government. Everyone is well off, including the public at large, which benefits from high investment rate and economic growth. Increased participation of women in the organized labour force has had a favourable impact on health, education, family planning, and nutritional intake.

Liberal out-migration policies help to resolve the unemployment problem and add to foreign exchange earnings and better living standards for the families of the poor. An alternative to the present policies looks is not obvious. Members of the general public would lose trust in politicians in absence of employment, migration, and growth, and political discontent, and violent uprising would be the eventual outcome. The social and electronic media have made free, unvarnished, and also sensational flow of information possible which helps in arousing unrest and discontent. The objective of the ruling parties to maximize the probability of their continuing in office does seem precarious if the latter were to occur. The very people who are the perpetrators of poor governance also have the ultimate power to salvage the situation.

The principal lesson to be drawn from the Bangladesh example is that the opening up of the economy to greater private sector participation, trade liberalization, bank credit growth, lax labour standards, and facilitation rather than obstruction by government functionaries were critical success factors in the achievement of a high growth rate. The second prong in the strategy was to allow NGOs to fully participate in social development and the provision of micro-credit to address rural poverty.

SUMMATION

Acceleration in economic growth does not require wholesale improvement in governance, as the experience of Bangladesh, India, and other countries suggests. Hausman[24] is of the view that some institutions are more helpful to economic growth than others because they remove binding constraints, e.g. sensible economic policies are put in place, and the private sector is unfettered.

Notwithstanding poor governance, in India and Bangladesh they were able to perform better than Pakistan since the 1990s for a variety of reasons, i.e. political stability, macroeconomic stability, continuity, and predictability of economic policies despite changes in political avatars, promotion and encouragement of the private sector, and private investment. The investment rates in both these countries were twice as high as that in Pakistan.

In India, competitive federalism and administrative reorganization of states lowered political tensions and mistrust, infusing a sense of unity and common purpose which proved beneficial to the economy. Bangladesh also allowed non-governmental organizations to play an active role in the provision of basic social services such as education, health, and micro-credit, thus improving the social indicators. Female literacy and female participation rates were higher in Bangladesh in comparison to India and Pakistan which also contributed to lowering the incidence of poverty. Pakistan had a relatively dormant and inactive NGO sector but there have been some positive developments in the recent years in the education and health sectors.

Political uncertainty in Pakistan lowered the time horizon of the private economic actors who used their returns for investment in real estate and the stock market, or capital flight. Investment in productive activities slackened in consequence but also due to the extremely intrusive character of the lower bureaucracy which increased the transaction costs of doing business. Insecurity of life and property because of the terrorism during the post-2001 period also played havoc with the economy.

The comparative governance indicators for the three countries discussed in this chapter are not particularly impressive but those of Pakistan have deteriorated relatively more rapidly over the past two decades.

APPENDIX

Table 17.1: Comparative Indicators of Governance

Report	Pakistan	India	Bangladesh
Global competitiveness Report			
Earliest year (2004)	91	55	100
Latest year (2015)	122	39	106
Human development indicators			
Earliest year (1990)	120	123	136
Latest year (2015)	147	130	142
Ease of doing business			
Earliest year (2006)	60	116	65
Latest year (2016)	138	130	174

Report	Pakistan	India	Bangladesh
World governance indicators			
Earliest year (2005)		"	"
Voice and accountability	17	60	29
Political stability and its Absence	5	18	4
Government effectiveness	40	55	21
Regulatory quality	26	47	17
Rule of law	22	58	18
Control of corruption	14	43	5
Latest year (2005)		"	"
Voice and accountability	27	61	31
Political Stability & Absence of Terr.	1	17	11
Government effectiveness	27	56	24
Regulatory quality	29	40	**17**
Rule of law	24	56	27
Control of corruption	24	44	18
Perception of corruption index			
Earliest year (1998) - Score Format	2.25	N/A	2.78
Latest year (2015) (out of 168)	117	76	139
Global innovation index			
Earliest year (2007)	73	23	98
Latest year (2016)	47	31	112
Education for all index			
Earliest year (1980)	0.161	0.24	0.202
Latest year (2013)	0.372	0.473	0.447
Legatum Prosperity Index: Governance			
Earliest year (2007)	46	47	48
Latest year (2016)	100	47	109
Bertelsmann Stiftung: transformation index			
Earliest year (2006)	84	24	54
Latest year (2016)	100	23	73
Freedom House: Economic Freedom Index			
Earliest year (1998) Freedom Rating 1–7	N/A	2.5	3

Report	Pakistan	India	Bangladesh
Latest year (2016)	41	77	49
Polity IV: Intl. Country Risk Guide			
Earliest year (2009)	–	–	–
Latest year (2010)	5	9	5
Global Food Security Index			
Earliest year	–	–	–
Latest year (2016) on 113	78	75	95

NOTES AND REFERENCES

1. Kapur and Mehta, *Public Institutions in India* (OUP, 2005).
2. Vaishnav, M., *When Crime Pays: Money and Muscle in Indian Politics*. (Yale University Press, 2017).
3. Singh, M. P., 'Administrative Reforms in India', *in* Meghan Sabharwal and Evan Berman (eds), *Public Administration in South Asia* (CRC Press, 2013).
4. Kapur, D., 'Explaining Democratic Durability and Economic Performance: The Role of Indian Institutions', *in* D. Kapur and P. B. Mehta, *Public Institutions in India* (OUP, 2007).
5. Khan, M., Jomo, K. S., eds. *Rents, Rent-Seeking and Economic Development: Theory and Evidence in Asia* (Cambridge: Cambridge University Press, 2000).
6. Diamond, L., *Democratic Governance and the Performance of Democracy*, CDDRL Working Paper no. 117, November 2009.
7. *World Values Survey 2010–2012* depicts a less favourable picture of the private sector in India vis-à-vis that of Pakistan.
8. Chelliah, R., *Towards Sustainable Growth: Essay in Public Finance and Financial Reforms in India*, (New Delhi: OUP, 1999).
9. Rudolph, L., Rudolph, S. H., 'The Old and the New Federalism in Independent India', *in* Brass, P., (ed) *Routledge Handbook of South Asian Politics* (Routledge, 2010).
10. Kapur, D., Nangia, P., 'A Targeted Approach: India's Expanding Social Safety Net', *World Politics Review*, 24 September 2013.
11. Alam, M. B. 'E-government in India', *in* Meghan Sabharwal and Evan Berman (eds.), *Public Administration in South Asia* (CRC Press, 2016).
12. Khan, S. R., et al., *Initiating Devolution of Service Delivery*, (OUP, 2007).
13. This section is drawn from Rajiv Kumar, 'Making Reforms Work for the People', *Economic and Political Weekly*, 2016. Accessed at: <http://www.epw.in/journal/2016/29/makingreformsworkcommonpeople.html0#>

14. Kumar, R., 'Making Reforms Work for the Common People', *Economic and Political Weekly*, 2016. Accessed at: <http://www.epw.in/journal/2016/29/makingreforms-workcommonpeople.html0#>

15. Ibid.

16. The above paragraph is the gist of the various chapters in the volume authored by Nurul Islam and M. Asaduzzaman, *A Ship Adrift* (Dhaka: Bangladesh Institute of Development Studies, 2008).

17. Ahmed, F., Greenleaf, A., and Sacko, A., 'The Paradox of Export Growth in Areas of Weak Governance: The Case of the Ready-Made Garment Sector in Bangladesh', *World Development*, 2013, vol. 56, 258–71. Accessed at: <dx.doi.org/10.1016/j.worlddev.2013>

18. Rashid, M. A., *Governance Policies and Development in Bangladesh* (Dhaka: Bangladesh Institute of Development Studies, 2009)

19. Taslim, M. A., 'Governance, Policies and Economic Growth in Bangladesh', *in* N. Islam and M. Asaduzzaman (eds.), A *Ship Adrift: Governance and Development in Bangladesh* (Dhaka: Bangladesh Institute of Development Studies, 2008).

20. Khan, M. H., *The Political Settlement and its Evolutions in Bangladesh*, SOAS Working Paper. Accessed at: <http://eprints.soas.ac.uk/12845/1/The_Political_Settlement_and_its_Evolution_in_Bangladesh.pdf>

21. Gherzi Textile Organization, *Executive Summary of the Initial Report on Post-MFA Development Strategy and Technical Assistance for the RMG Sector*, Report submitted to the Ministry of Commerce, Govt. of Bangladesh, 2002.

22. Riaz, A., *Bangladesh: A Political History Since Independence* (New York & London: I. A. Taurus, 2016).

23. Survi, K. C. et al. 'Support for Democracy in S. Asia', Global Barometer Surveys Conference, Taipei, 15–16 October 2010.

24. Hausman, *Economic Growth: Shared Beliefs, Shared Disappointments?* (CID, Harvard, 2006).

18

Conclusions

Pakistan's economic rise in the course of the first 40 years of its history and subsequent decline in the last 25 has puzzled a number of analysts, observers, and policy-makers. This study was an attempt to shed some light on this conundrum. The principal conclusions from the chapters in this volume can be summarized as follows:

Single factor explanations are simplistic and misleading, although each of them is a contributory factor. This study demonstrates that it is the interplay of many internal and external factors that has led to the present predicament. At least seven internal and six external factors cumulatively are responsible for the present situation. This list is by no means exhaustive and additions and deletions are possible.

INTERNAL FACTORS

In Pakistan, the relationship between state and market has been turned upside down. The market efficiently allocates resources while the state equitably distributes the gains from economic growth. In Pakistan, the market has been rigged by a small elite which has also captured the state. This lethal concentration of political and economic power in the same hands—although the composition of these hands has changed at different times—has given rise to both an inefficient economy and inequitable income distribution.

An interrupted, discontinuous political order which prevented the nascent democratic form of government from nurturance and growth into a healthy tree: When Pakistan returns to democratic governance, what that amounts to is procedural democracy rather than substantive democracy. Political representation is dominated by the *biradari* and kinship ties prevalent in the rural areas. Politicians win over the heads of *biradaris* at election time and they ensure that their followers vote en bloc at the behest of their heads, thereby disenfranchising individual members. An absence of institutional checks and balances, personalized, centralized, and authoritative decision-making, with a concentration of powers in the hands of the party head—along with weak political parties where dissent is not tolerated—have enfeebled the polity. Then there is the structural factor, with one large, well-developed province with a population exceeding that of the three other provinces of the federation, is seen to completely dominate the latter. There is acute mistrust and hostility between the largest province and the other three which is not conducive to stable and harmonious relations. 54 per cent of the seats out of a total of 342 seats in the National Assembly are reserved for Punjab. The province has done well in improving its economy and reducing poverty while other provinces have not been able to catch up.

The dominant role of the military in assuming power four times and the unsettled contours of civil–military relations during the period of democratically elected governments has given rise to an asymmetrical power structure. This finding will be elaborated later in this chapter in greater detail.

The growing demand for good governance and its shrinking supply: The principal reason is the deterioration in the quality of the civil services and their politicization, thus profoundly impairing the capacity of state institutions to maintain law and order, collect taxes, deliver basic services, and thus exercise the writ of the state. The Chinese government is built around a long tradition of meritocratic recruitment, civil service exams, a high emphasis on education, deference to technocratic authority, and a highly qualified bureaucratic government. Its leaders have managed a hugely complex transition from a centralized, Soviet-style planned economy to a dynamic open one and have done so with remarkable competence and have the capacity to take far-reaching, complex decisions quickly. The inability of democratic governments to address the needs of the broader public has increased popular disaffection, further undermining the legitimacy and efficacy of representative institutions. The withering away of state–society relations and people's disillusionment with the state and its institutions provide space to non-state actors to operate parallel systems of justice, service, delivery, and security. The radicals among them exploit the people's unfulfilled desires to their advantage, receive public support, and are able to and recruit people to their ranks.

Economic management: Pakistan has lacked continuity, predictability, and consistency of policies. Investors are not certain about the long-term position of the government. In consequence, investment rates are low and growth extremely low. Much of the time, finance ministers, after allowing inappropriate policies to continue and the economy to reach virtually the brink of crisis, then appeal to external donors to bail out the country.

The Zia government sought to develop Pakistan into a centre for global Islamic resurgence and to promote Islamist groups and militancy. The media at the time was utilized to propagate orthodox Islam and militancy. Oppression, lack of justice, and politico–economic inequalities also contributed to extremism and militancy in Pakistan. A sense of humiliation, political grievances, and a breakdown of the existing culture or political structure exacerbated this tendency. The educated middle-class did not prove a sufficiently strong countervailing force to match this extremism. To quote Ayesha Jalal:

> The vast majority of Pakistan's literate citizens have opted for the comforts of ignorance, habits of scepticism and cynicism, and most troubling of all, in the contagion of belief in conspiracy theories. The modern education system inherited from the British was altered during this period and never reversed subsequently to suit this goal. Thus, a generation and a half has internalized hard-line Islamic discourse to the exclusion of other perspectives. This socialization has its reference points—transnational Muslim identity, Western injustices against Muslims, non-resolution of Palestine and Kashmir, the West as an adversary of Muslims, and the role of the Islamic movement rather than the Muslim status as the liberators of Muslims for Western domination.[1]

EXTERNAL FACTORS

Pakistan's long-standing alignment with the US during the Cold War, the Afghan war against the Soviet Union, and the recent war against terror in Afghanistan has severely limited the scope for independent decision-making. The factors Pakistan has had to contend with could be itemized as:

- A perpetual fear of India as a hostile neighbour and the Kashmir dispute have led to a state of national insecurity with disproportionate space occupied by the military. We have felt compelled to defend our nation and constantly define and redefine our identity vis-à-vis Hindu India.

- The regional proxy war between Saudi Arabia and Iran, and Pakistan's overt alignment with one or the other of these contesting parties in the 1980s, has led to an intensification of sectarian and extremism within the country.

- The remnants of the Afghan war against the Soviets in the form of Kalashnikovs and other armaments, drugs, criminals, and religious fundamentalism have fragmented the society into many factions.

- The consistent bailing out of Pakistan by external donors at a time when it was on the brink of an economic crisis has vitiated any effort and weakened the political will to bring about fundamental structural reforms in the economy and governance.

- Pakistan's domestic constraints and capacity have not allowed it to benefit from the international wave of globalization. India, Bangladesh, Sri Lanka, and Nepal have all overtaken Pakistan which in the 1960s was a model developing country.

Several alternate hypotheses have been advanced which were all tested in this study but the dominant explanation that stands out has to do with the relative performance of the institutions of governance. A survey of these institutions—and the foundations upon which they derive their sustenance: the state, society, polity, economy, and the like—conducted by this study maps a zigzag course, alternating between military and civilian governments in Pakistan's 70-year history.

The four transitions from elected to military governments and vice-versa have created political instability and uncertainty but the lessons have not been learnt. Governance under a democratic dispensation has been under attack in Pakistan for a long time. The yearning for a messiah or strong authoritarian leader who can fix the 'mess' created by democratically elected leaders still remains quite strong. Political uncertainty leads to a wait-and-see attitude on the part of investors. Lack of investment—both domestic and foreign—retards the pace of economic growth. Low growth rates result in high levels of unemployment and rise in poverty. The consequential collapse in demand discourages investment in capacity-utilization or new assets, perpetuating the uncertainty and thus retarding the pace of economic development. Besides, if the gains of even this modest growth are concentrated in the hands of a narrow privileged elite or in one or two regions rather than widely shared, the forces promoting social and national cohesion are at risk.

Detractors of democratic governance point to the 1960s, 1980s, and early to mid-2000s as periods which were characterized by rapid growth, reduction in the incidence of poverty, and lower levels of unemployment. The temptation therefore, at a superficial level, would be to attribute these successful economic outcomes to military leaders such as Ayub Khan, Zia ul-Haq, and Pervez Musharraf who were then at the helm. It is not, however, realized that the transfer of power from military to civilian governments in 1971, 1988, and 2008 were marked with macroeconomic instability, a slowdown in economic activity, rising unemployment and poverty, and high inflation. The 1970s, 1990s, and 2008–13 have witnessed crises in balance of payments, a depletion in foreign exchange reserves, a depreciating exchange rate, flight of capital, below average growth rates, and serious economic difficulties, forcing Pakistan to seek IMF assistance.

This problem arises because of the ephemeral nature of economic policies under these governments which remained preoccupied in establishing their legitimacy by demonstrating that they could achieve rapid economic growth. According to one analyst:

Zia's economic policies represented a rather sharp contrast between reasonably satisfactory short-term economic management and an almost total neglect of long term policy issues. The long period of political stability and sustained growth under Zia ul-Haq offered major opportunities for dealing with the underlying structural issues but these were never exploited.[2]

Once well-intentioned and honest military leaders in Pakistan decide to co-opt political leaders in order to gain popular support and legitimacy for their continuing rule, they have to abandon their principled stand and reluctantly make compromises and concessions to which they themselves may be opposed. The first three years of Musharraf's rule in Pakistan represented one of the best periods in the history of Pakistan's governance. However, the following five years under a quasi-political government, when he had to enter into a coalition with a group of politicians, were quite different.

Empirical evidence suggests that economic accomplishments devoid of political legitimacy, however impressive, may prove to be elusive and transient, and do not leave any lasting footprint. Similarly, those wishing that a politically neutral, technocratic government of experts underwritten by the army should be installed to bring about the necessary reforms, clean up the political stables, and weed out corrupt elements are also sadly mistaken. In the twenty-first century, with the social media so active and powerful in mobilizing public opinion, a free press, a vigilant civil society, and an independent judiciary, it is hardly conceivable that any non-representative group, however well-meaning and competent, can succeed. Political parties would all coalesce and organize their supporters to resist such a government. Rather than the expected economic turnaround, there would be greater chaos and disruptions in economic activity. Once the imposition of such a government also fails, there would be no alternative other than to restore democracy and once more hold general elections. In the meanwhile, the country and its people might have to face hardships for nothing and the economy would have suffered enormous dislocations and reversals purposelessly as a consequence of the political uncertainty so created.

The economy and economic players require a stable political

environment. It is not realized that economic policy decisions are not purely technocratic solutions but affect various segments of the population in different ways and to different degrees. There are bound to be winners and losers from these decisions. In a democratic society, there are forums such as parliament and provincial assemblies which discuss and debate the implications of various policies. Conflicts among winners and losers are resolved through compromise, conciliation, and give-and-take. In an authoritarian regime, one person is the final arbiter. S/he may have taken a faulty decision but there is no recourse available for its reversal. That is why even very sound policies initiated by military governments which had made an impact could not withstand the test of time after their departure.

The examples of the post-Musharraf period of a complete dismantling of the local government system in all the four provinces, the supersession of the Police Order, the reversal of the HR reforms introduced in the Federal Board of Revenue (FBR), the hiatus in the privatization of public enterprises, the weakening of the higher education commission, and the suspension of the order of conversion of B districts that were planned to be covered by the police rather than levies in Balochistan are illustrative of this tendency. Those who were adversely affected by these policies became quite active and persuaded the newly elected governments that their popularity would rise if these wrongs perpetrated by an authoritarian leader were reversed.

It can therefore be inferred from these examples that without the involvement and participation of the people and their genuine representatives, elegant and technically sound solutions introduced by authoritarian regimes or competent technocrats are quickly thrown overboard once the government changes. Policies, however, sound as they may appear, are reversed, causing irreparable loss to business confidence. The country pays a heavy price for the severe economic disruptions, complete breakdown of civilian institutions, and lack of accountability that ensues.

The problem with non-elected governments is that they are not accountable to anyone. As a new chief of army staff takes over, all his subordinates fall in line and follow his orders as they are trained to do throughout their careers and this is the requirement of the job. Dissent, open differences of opinion at decision-making forums are rare. The next tier of officers look up to the chief for their promotions, postings, and perks, and it is not in their interest to raise any questions or express scepticism. When the same army chief takes over the civilian government, he finds himself at a loss because the control and command structure to which he is accustomed does not exist. He finds that even the data and information which he needs for decision-making is not in a form that is of any value to him. There are no clear black and white choices and plenty of grey areas. The ambiguities that have to be resolved require familiarity and hands-on experience in the civil administration. He, therefore, perforce, relies upon the intelligence agencies and lower formations of the army.

'Groupthink' thus permeates the system and an objective assessment and evaluation of the impact of policies becomes quite challenging. This widens the gap between the 'reality', as perceived by authoritarian regimes and the 'actual reality' confronting the population at large. In such a situation, the population feels helpless because they do not have any means at their disposal to express their views or remove the ruler. To the extent that a dictator is benevolent or honest, the damage remains limited. However, in the event of a malevolent or corrupt dictator seizing power or a benevolent one changing his stripes over time, there is no clear exit strategy. However intense the disenchantment or disaffection may be, there is hardly any prescribed way of removing such leaders. Nasser, Sukarno, Babangida, and Mobutu were all forced out of office by their own juniors as the latter believed their leaders had overstayed their welcome.

There is another danger which has to do with the sustained efficiency, integrity, discipline, and order which are the hallmarks of the military. Past episodes of martial law in Pakistan remind us that the military officers had to be withdrawn from civil administration and court duties because there were allegations of corruption, favouritism, and nepotism against them. As one senior ISI officer narrated to Anatol Lieven, the reasons were quite persuasive. According to him:

Under the British, the military was kept ... very separate from society.

That was a good model, because in Pakistan there is a permanent threat of politicization and corruption of the military. We fear this very deeply and try to keep ourselves separate. Within purely military institutions, things are honest and closely controlled. This is a matter of honour for officers and people keep tabs on each other. Corruption comes whenever there is interaction with civilian bodies.

We have a great fear of the politicians interfering in military promotions and appointments. This could split the army and if you split the army you destroy the country.[3]

Lieven also believes that the Pakistan military's discipline, efficiency, and solidarity have repeatedly enabled the Pakistani military to take over the state, or to dominate it from behind the scenes. Their ideology was, first and foremost, Pakistani nationalism.

However, the political parties on their part have to prove that they are capable of exercising responsible and responsive control over the armed force. Stephen Cohen[4] is of the view that the mere repetition of the slogan 'civilian control' is not sufficient to guarantee its existence: that a civilian leadership's demonstration of its capacity to rule is no less important than the maintenance of the tradition of the military's apolitical professionalism. Just as important as an obedient military is to the maintenance of liberal–democratic relations, is the existence of a competent, respected, and democratically committed political elite. Najam Sethi (2008)[5] is of the view that 'the civilians must establish their credentials for responsible democracy and functional governance before they can safely and effectively tame the military.'

One of the critical factors contributing to the weakness of the political parties in excelling in governance has to do with the inherent nature of society–state relations. Pakistan, as a predominantly rural economy, inherited the complex web of patron–client relations. Under this system, villages, families, groups, and individuals 'secure protection, security and the necessities of existence based on reciprocal exchange of mutual dependency and obligations. Those with higher ranks, wealth, and status command the services and support of those of lower rank and the lower ranks receive the support and protection from their patrons in return.'[6]

This system of client-ship or reciprocal exchange plays a critical role in governance outcomes. Clients fulfil their obligations by voting for those who have benefited them while the patrons, once elected with the support of their clients, use the resources of the state to continue conferring privileges and favours upon the latter. This is one of the major societal factors that has proved to be an obstacle in harnessing political will to bring about the desired changes in the governance structure and processes in Pakistan. Therefore, to expect that such an entrenched web of relationships will be easy to untangle in the short term, is very unrealistic. Biting and nibbling at the edges may be a more feasible option.

The contrast between the countries of the Middle East undergoing serious turmoil and destruction, and Pakistan facing severe terrorism over the past 15 years, is that the armies in those countries have split due to sectarian or other divisive factors while the Pakistan Army has remained a highly cohesive, unifying, and nationalist institution maintaining a high degree of professionalism. One of the principal reasons for such fierce condemnation and violent reaction against the military among Pakistan's detractors is this particular attribute. It would, therefore, be against the larger national interest of Pakistan's security for the scope of the military being extended to tasks which are expected to be performed by civilian institutions, diverting them from undertaking their core responsibilities. The first prime minister of Pakistan, Liaquat Ali Khan, had aptly said: 'the defence of the state is our foremost consideration. It dominates all other considerations.' Those well-meaning Pakistanis who express a desire that the military should eliminate the corruption and incompetence of civilian institutions are unwittingly inflicting severe damage to this concept.

Notwithstanding all its weaknesses and shortcomings, an orderly transition of power at regular intervals through a predictable democratic process is the least damaging means of keeping the economy moving at an even keel. What is the link between political stability and economic growth? Political stability promotes transparency, the rule of law, predictability, and continuity of economic policies, thus generating confidence among investors so that they can conduct business in the normal course and earn a decent return. Efficiency in the allocation of resources and higher capital investment under a stable political environment increases the rate of economic growth. When the political situation becomes unstable, investors adopt a wait-and-watch approach.

The Indian economy was not faring well during the last few years of Manmohan Singh's tenure although he was an accomplished economist and reformer. The electorate voted him out of power and brought in Narendra Modi who had a strong economic track record in Gujarat. Market sentiment in India took a turn for the better immediately after his election and the Indian economy has begun growing rapidly once again. The people of India exercised their choice wisely at the time of the elections and effected the change. This would not have been possible if India had been ruled by a dictator who believed in his own indispensability.

As a counter-argument to a democratic form of government, many analysts refer to China to substantiate their belief in the superiority of an authoritarian regime as a catalyst for rapid economic growth. It is, however, conveniently forgotten that the rules of the game, i.e. the transition from one set of leaders to another in China, are quite well known and the process well understood. The timing of transition is not shrouded in secrecy and although the right of adult franchise does not exist, there is limited franchise exercised by the National People's Congress. The question then arises that if governments happen to be the only viable form of governance, how can the vicious cycle of political instability, economic stagnation, high unemployment, collapse in demand, low investment, and further dissatisfaction with the existing political leadership be broken and democratic governance strengthened in Pakistan.

The proposals set out in the chapter entitled 'Restructuring Key Institutions' are intended to draw the attention of political parties and their leadership in Pakistan to discuss and debate the future course of action necessary to strengthen democratic governance in Pakistan and arrive at a consensus on the desirable road ahead.

DRIVERS OF CHANGE

The moot question is who is going to take the lead in taking action on these recommendations? Why have the previous attempts for reform not been successful? Here, the role of leadership is quite critical. Pakistanis, in general, have been disappointed that after the death of the founder of Pakistan, the Quaid-i-Azam, and the first prime minister, Liaquat Ali Khan, Pakistanis have not been able to find a national chief executive, either elected or from the military, with the courage, foresight, and integrity to provide transformative leadership. Ayub Khan's period of leadership is generally considered a golden period in Pakistan's history and he did indeed do a great deal for Pakistan's economic development but he lacked the legitimacy and broad political support necessary to continue with his mission. The failure to bring East Pakistanis along was his great drawback. He also did not fulfil the obligation under the Constitution of 1962 which he himself devised, to hand over the power to the elected speaker of the National Assembly. Instead, he called upon the chief of army staff, General Yahya Khan, to assume power.

This was a major setback to an orderly transition of power envisaged in the constitution. His successor deserves credit for holding fair and transparent elections but his inability or unwillingness to appoint the elected leader of the majority party and opt for the minority party leader because he was from West Pakistan led to the formation of Bangladesh. Z. A. Bhutto was a very capable and charismatic leader who could indeed have helped to transform the country but he moved it in the wrong direction by nationalizing private industries, banks, insurance, and educational institutions. By doing so, he failed to realize his goal of equity and stifled the growth impulses of an otherwise dynamic and vibrant economy and undermined high quality manpower and skill development. His personal ego and intolerance came in the way and the new Pakistan missed an excellent opportunity at a critical juncture in its history.

General Zia ul-Haq was an individual with a single-point agenda of Islamizing Pakistan and was not interested in either economic or social development programmes which would improve the lives of the common people. There was great fervour and high expectation when the young, highly educated, and articulate Mohtarma Benazir Bhutto assumed office as the first elected woman prime minister. She enjoyed popular support and also had the competence to bring about the desirable changes in Pakistan's economic landscape. Her governance was, however, short-lived because her party deviated from its professed path and failed to deliver on popular expectations notwithstanding the two opportunities it had in the 1990s. The other key leader in the 1990s was Nawaz Sharif, the former prime minister.

The future looked promising when he decided in the 1991 to carry out a major programme of liberalization, deregulation, and privatization which was so essential. India followed a similar set of reforms after PM Nawaz Sharif had made this announcement. His first term in office was full of promise but it soon came to a sudden and premature end when he became embroiled in a power tussle with the president of Pakistan. In his second term however—second term when his party was elected with a large mandate—he could have done a great deal to implement his unfinished reform agenda and put Pakistan on a sound economic footing. His attention was, however, diverted to other issues such as relations with the judiciary, the army, and the like and he failed to pay much attention to his economic agenda.

General Musharraf, who came to power in October 1999, pursued a vigorous agenda of reforms during the first three years which made a significant difference. After the elections, during which he had to seek the support of political parties to establish the legitimacy of his government, the reform process slowed down and some of the politically unpopular decisions were either delayed, postponed, or shelved, and some of the desirable provisions of the Local Government Act and Police Order were reversed. His attention was later diverted to other issues such as the judiciary, imposition of the emergency in 2007, the National Reconciliation Ordinance, etc., and the most important task of restructuring the civil services and the federal and provincial governments was set aside.

The subsequent PPP government, which was elected by a popular vote in 2008, suffered a serious loss when its charismatic leader,

Mohtarma Benazir Bhutto, was assassinated by militants and the party headed by her husband struggled to keep the democratic rule afloat and was besmirched by many allegations of corruption, and malfeasance, and proactive judicial interventions subjected the government to considerable stress. The PML-N government that came to power in 2013 has done well in stabilizing the economy and attempting to resolve the energy crisis but it has not so far shown any strong resolve to address the institutional reforms required, such as those proposed here.

The focus of Pakistan's leaders in Pakistan, particularly in the post-1990 period, was to capture power and survive. They were, therefore, reluctant to take any serious political risks that deflected them from this. They were aware that any changes they ushered in would have short-term consequences and would upset some powerful entrenched interest groups, i.e. the elite group who held the levers of power. They believed that their opponents would take advantage of the turmoil generated by reforms undertaken during their tenure. The losers from these reforms would organize agitations and protests against them, leading to their defeat in the elections. The benefits that would thereby accrue to the majority of the population through implementation of the reforms over an extended period of time would be appropriated by their opponents who would claim credit for their success. This calculus has, however, been proven wrong in many instances in Pakistan itself and other emerging countries.

In Pakistan, the victory of the PML-N in the 2013 general elections is largely attributed to the relatively good performance of Mian Shahbaz Sharif in Punjab during the 2008–13 period. He carried out far-reaching reforms across a broad spectrum of public services: education, health, roads and infrastructure, public transport, solid waste disposal, and in the recent years, in the energy sector. The record time in which power generating plants were constructed and commissioned have drawn praise and commendation from leaders of China and Turkey. There were very few reports of any corruption when billions of dollars' worth of contracts were awarded. His commitment to get things done was steadfast.

Although his style of leadership was too personality-driven rather than a systematic plan of institution-building, he put in place some elements of good governance. Secretaries and heads of the corporations were selected on the basis of past performance and reputation as doers and without hesitation replaced if they fell short of his expectations. Teachers were recruited on pure merit. Technology was used to bring about transparency, efficiency, and obtain citizen feedback. Although he did not have time to devote to institutional restructuring, he brought about innovation in the public sector by forming corporate entities for various services mimicking the private sector. His ministers, political supporters, and allies didn't pull much weight in his assessments and decision-making. He also became the role model for the chief ministers of other provinces—a hard act to follow.

Karachi, a megalopolis of 20 million people, witnessed two very committed and dedicated mayors from two different political parties which are bitter opponents. Naimatullah Khan, the octogenarian mayor from the right wing religious party Jamaat-i-Islami, was an honest individual who monitored and supervised work underway diligently and regularly and resolved the complaints and grievances of the people judiciously, irrespective of their political affiliations. Young Mustafa Kamal, from the MQM, was energetic and exuberant, and achieved a great deal during his tenure for the collective good of the citizens of Karachi. He alienated some of his party workers and leaders because he did not patronize them as was the case with other MQM office-bearers: ministers and members of parliament and the assembly. The parties of the latter are therefore unlikely to attract much support during any fair and transparent elections held in Karachi as the former.

The new elected government of the KP province has introduced a modern Police Act and also brought about significant change in the functioning of the police department. The non-acceptance and non-filing of First Information Reports (FIRs) by police stations is a main ground of distress for citizens throughout Pakistan. In KP, a citizen can now register an FIR electronically without being subjected to the humiliating and arrogant misbehaviour of the station in-charge. Resources to improve training, mobility, accommodation, welfare of the police force, and the removal from operational functions of corrupt officials of ill repute is a welcome beginning. It is too early to speculate whether these changes are going to survive the present political leadership but it at least partially provides the answer to the earlier question. A far-sighted and committed leadership can indeed become the driver of change. If the people at large in KP see a visible change for better, the prospect of the present party in power—the Pakistan Tehreek-e-Insaf (PTI)—getting re-elected would be considerably enhanced. The demonstration effect of this model may then influence the thinking of other competing political parties.

Why does Pakistan fare so poorly in comparison to India and Bangladesh which also suffer from corruption, poor governance, and weak institutions? Bangladesh was rated not long ago as the most corrupt country in the world. The two *begums* have been constantly engaged in nasty political battles for over two decades. Matters got so out of hand that the military felt obliged to intervene in 2007 and establish a caretaker government for two years to cleanse the political system but without much success. The result after the two-year hiatus was the same: the Awami League and Bangladesh National Party continued to remain the two major political parties with AL winning the elections. Since then, the ruling party has crushed the opposition party with a heavy hand and gradually tamed all institutions of the state, including the judiciary, and is on the path toward a one party government. Even so, Bangladesh has done remarkably well over the past 25 years, with a respectable rate of economic growth and a reasonable improvement in its social indicators.

India's institutional framework is also relatively weak and the performance of India's public institutions has become a matter of concern, with a recent study focusing on the nexus between crime and politics.[7] Several ministers of the union government and chief ministers were accused of corruption and other malpractices and indicted or convicted in recent years. Notwithstanding the frailty of institutions and weak governance, India remains one of the top economic performers amongst emerging economies.

Indonesia under Suharto was cited as a living example of crony capitalism. The family was involved in most large projects and business transactions along with their business partners and no major deal could be consummated without the blessing of the family. However, Suharto's record in turning around Indonesia's economy and lifting nearly a hundred million people out of poverty by 1998 was quite impressive.

A careful comparative analysis of binary pairing of Pakistan vs any of these other three countries is beyond the scope of this study but some tentative and preliminary explanatory hypotheses can be offered. All three countries enjoyed macroeconomic and political stability over a prolonged period of time with a continuity of economic policies and encouragement and promotion of the private sector, signalling to investors that political change would usher in no surprises or unanticipated effect on economic policies. This imbued the private sector with a sense of confidence and predictability which allowed an uninterrupted and orderly journey in the given direction. Rent-sharing amongst private businesses, government officials, and politicians was commonplace and became entrenched as a norm in conducting business. There were no abrupt disruptions in the rent-sharing process when the government changed hands and therefore the practice was growth-enhancing[8] in the sense that the owners used the surplus to invest and expand their domain while the government facilitated and paved the way by removing any bottlenecks and hurdles, making the businesses internationally competitive. This relationship unshackled the entrepreneurial energies of the private sector to contribute to the achievement of higher national growth. Bangladesh, for its part, was able to raise its gross investment ratio from 12 per cent in 1990 to 30 per cent in 2015.

In the case of Bangladesh, an additional feature was the empowerment by the political parties of non-governmental organizations to participate in social development. NGOs were allowed to, and facilitated in, opening schools, health clinics, providing family planning services, and micro-credit. The country made great strides that would not have been possible had the government been the sole provider of these services.

Pakistan, by contrast, stifled private businesses through crude attempts by each ruling party to use the patronage apparatus on a highly selective, partisan, and parochial manner to favour their cronies. The bank loans, permits, and approvals given to them were used, by and large, for ostentatious consumption or transfer of assets abroad and not for expansion of productive capacity or new investment. Consequently, the investment ratios in Pakistan remained in the teens and growth rates since the 1990s have been well below potential. It is clear from this that the nature of rent-seeking and rent-sharing was somewhat different in Pakistan from that in India and Bangladesh. The excess profits thus earned by rentier businessmen and corrupt politicians and bureaucrats were not invested in productive activities in the country as a consequence of political uncertainty, macroeconomic instability, and discontinuity of economic policies. These were either parked outside Pakistan or found their way either into real estate or the stock market. While the initial public offerings (IPOs) were few and far-between, trading in the existing shares was quite hectic and intense. The prices of land in urban areas skyrocketed, making housing unaffordable for middle and low income groups.

The answer to the question posed above can also be partially provided by examples where patronage politics gave way to performance politics and the collective good rather than parochial interests. Some salutary lessons can also be drawn from other emerging and developing countries where progressive and enlightened leadership has shaped sound policies and the establishment of well-conceived institutions which made a significant difference.

Let us keep China out of this discussion as its polity is not democratic and its achievements unparalleled and unprecedented. Very few countries can match its record. There is, however, an example of a country which demonstrates what even hereditary leadership can accomplish for its people within a generation. The most spectacular performance in recent times, apart from China in this respect, is that of Dubai in the United Arab Emirates. A visionary leader, Sheikh Rashid al Maktoum, and his son, Sheikh Muhammad, building on his father's vision, has transformed the city state into a magnet for tourists, shipping, air connections, financial institutions, and international trade. Oil revenues were depleting (now accounting for only 5 per cent of the GDP) and the ruling family saw an alternative opportunity in taking advantage of accelerated globalization. They utilized Dubai's strategic location and easy connectivity to markets in different continents and went about constructing accessible and affordable transportation, logistics, trade, and financial services, and nurturing a relaxed living environment.

They had no hesitation in opening up their country to external actors, to the extent that 85 to 90 per cent of the labour force today comprises expatriates. Liberalization and integration with the rest of the world have led to a GDP growth rate of 11 per cent annually with an average per capita income rising by 126 per cent in 13 years, exports expanding by 575 per cent, and the population growing by 186 per cent.[9] It was inconceivable even 15 years ago that a desert town would become a hub and symbol of globalization. Sheikh Muhammad's dynamic and far-sighted leadership is admired throughout the world as he has shown that rickety infrastructure, bureaucratic inertia, red-tape, and controlled flows of capital in the larger countries surrounding Dubai can prove advantageous to those willing to open up their countries and economies by building efficient institutions and state-of-the-art facilities.

President Recep Tayyip Erdogan and his party, the Justice and Development Party (AKP), got Turkey out of continuing economic setbacks by embarking upon bold reforms and was successful in winning the elections twice on the basis of his economic record. When a coup was organized by a group of military officers to oust him recently, the public came out on to the streets to resist the military force and defeated the coup attempt. Had the benefits of his economic policies been confined to a small group of elite individuals, it is extremely doubtful if ordinary people would have faced them off and sacrificed their lives.

Prime Minister Mahathir Mohamed remained in power for over two decades and won five consecutive general elections. During his long tenure, Malaysia experienced a period of rapid modernization and economic growth. His government privatized airlines, utilities, and telecommunication firms, accelerating to a rate of about 50 privatizations a year by the mid-1990s. He also deftly handled the Asian economic crisis of 1998 and Malaysia emerged from it unscathed while other countries suffered enormously. He was not particularly popular among the Chinese and Indian populations for his Bhumiputra policy but major groups among them formed part of the United Malays National Organisation (UMNO), Mahathir's party.

More recently, the example of President Enrique Pena Nieto of Mexico, is illuminating. According to Jonathan Tepperman, 'he managed to win over his bitterest political enemies and then joined forces with them to bust open Mexico's smothering monopolies, liberalize its rusting energy sector, restructure its failing schools, modernize its banking laws, and much more'.[10] Both major political parties realized that 'the constant obstructionism in Mexico had cost us a lot in the eyes of society'. Over the next 18 months they together passed major reforms, with support from lawmakers averaging 80 per cent. Not only did they crack open Mexico's monopolies, reinvigorate its oil sector, and revamp the tax laws but also took on the powerful teachers' unions. By unshackling the Mexican economy, promoting competition, improving education, and easing foreign investment, the reforms have set the stage for serious growth, especially once oil prices, so critical to Mexico's economy, begin to recover.

As Iftikhar Malik[11] points out, the 'politics and administration of the country [Pakistan] have revolved around strong personalities, so-called strong-men': Ayub Khan, Z. A. Bhutto, Zia ul-Haq, Benazir Bhutto, Nawaz Sharif, and Pervez Musharraf but instead of using their power and office to bring about a transformation of the state, economy, polity, and society, most of these strong men concentrated their efforts on 'the mutilation of political opponents, muzzling of the press, thwarting the judiciary and educational institutions, and the manipulation of power'. Should we keep waiting and praying for a Messiah who can fix things or move along?

The *WDR 2017* argues that the driver for governmental change in a positive direction for development is, (a) when the elite groups adopt rules that constrain their own power, (b) when leaders are selected and sanctioned on the basis of performance in providing public goods, and (c) when international actors introduce norms, standards, and regulations which have direct or indirect effects on governance. How do we apply this prescription in the specific context of Pakistan where citizen engagement has been minimal and elite capture has become entrenched? It is not realistic to expect that the elite would, in any way, soon adopt rules that would constrain their own power. In actuality, they are expanding their sphere of influence by co-opting new and emerging elite groups within their fold, thus reducing contestation and a potential threat to their power.

The negative influence of the patronage politics of the elite can be reversed if the examples of the successful leaders at a subnational level in Pakistan cited above (in delivering basic public services to the people) can be replicated at the larger national canvas. While all efforts should be geared to make this mechanism work, the high degree of political tensions among major political parties, between the federation and the provinces, highly concentrated, and exclusive- and non-participatory decision-making process, and the current controversy about the sources of wealth of the first family, the prospects do not look particularly promising for the present.

The imperatives of globalization and integration are, of course, fuelling some move forward in adopting international conventions, agreements, standards, and practices under the UN, WTO, IMF, World Bank, and Basel, and other global and regional arrangements. The flexibility that the nation states enjoy under these arrangements and lack of enforcement for deviant behaviour do not augur well for this approach to work. In reality, Pakistanis in general are very suspicious of outsiders and the external actors' visible influence can actually be a hindrance rather than an inducement for change. The US has been a long-standing ally of Pakistan but its role is not widely appreciated, and indeed resented. The recent example of Brexit has provided ammunition to those who believe that surrendering elements of national sovereignty to regional or international arrangements is detrimental to the national development goal. Utilization of foreign economic aid as a tool to promote growth and equity and military aid to bolster security in Pakistan has not proved to be effective as it has relieved the state from efforts to mobilize taxes from the elite groups and efficiently manage public expenditure. Past experience shows that the influence of international actors in Pakistan, particularly the US and the IMF, although highly exaggerated in the popular discourse, has not had much success in bringing about the desired deep-rooted reforms. Therefore, this particular instrument cannot be considered a serious contender as a driver of governance reform.

That leaves the only possible driver of change, i.e. of leaders being selected and sanctioned on the basis of performance in providing public goods. How can this happen in Pakistan where patron–client politics has for so long dominated the landscape? As discussed in the section on Drivers of Change in the chapter 'Restructuring Institutions', the emergence of a vocal, assertive, educated middle-class based in urban areas free from links of kinship, caste, tribal affiliations, and feudal subservience has a high probability of triggering this institutional reform. The pathway may zigzag along the following lines:

The constituencies should be delimited on the basis of the 2017 census results, and at the same time administrative powers and resources should be devolved to local governments. Once the new elected representatives come to office, at least half representing the urban areas, performance and delivery of basic public services to their constituents would gradually replace the existing patron–client relationships. In order to survive politically, the elected representatives would be forced to reform the institutions that deliver these services. Otherwise, the prospects of their being thrown out of office by an informed and demanding electorate would be high and this fear of rejection would act as an incentive to support restructuring. This path would by no means be easy and resistance by powerful vested interest groups, who would be the losers in this bargain, is likely to be fierce. These changes are unlikely to happen during one five-year electoral cycle but at least a beginning should now be made by conducting a census and delimiting constituencies. This appears to be the best possible route. Single-factor explanations range from the dominant influence of ideology and religion on the society and body politic; the emergence of Pakistan as a National Security State where fear and insecurity have played a dominant role; and the alliance between Allah, Army, and America that has shaped the affairs of Pakistan.

Notes and References

1. Jalal, A., 'Prologue', *in The Struggle for Pakistan: A Muslim Homeland and Global Politics* (Cambridge: The Belknap Press, 2014).

2. Hasan, P., *Pakistan's Economy at the Crossroads: Past Policies and Present Imperatives* (OUP, 1998).

3. Lieven, *Pakistan: A Hard Country.* (New York: BBS Publications, 2011).

4. Cohen, S., 'Subash Chandra Bose and the Indian National Army', *Pacific Affairs* 36(4) (1988); 'The Military and India's Democracy', *in* Atul Kohli (ed.) *India's Democracy* (Princeton, N. J. 2014).

5. Sethi, N., 'How to Tame the ISI', *Friday Times*, August 2008.

6. Kochanek, S., *Corruption and the Criminalization of Politics in South Asia* (Routledge Handbook of Politics in South Asia, 2010).

7. Kapur, D. and Mehta, P. B., *Public Institutions in India* (New Delhi: OUP, 2005); Vaishnav, M., *When Crime Pays: Money and Muscle in Indian Politics* (Yale University Press, 2017).

8. Khan, M., *Rents, Rent-seeking and Economic Development: An Introduction* (SOAS, 2008).

9. Nasr, V., *The Rise of Islamic Capitalism* (New York: Free Press, 2009).

10. Tepperman, J., 'Can pragmatic, far-sighted leaders really solve the world's crises', *The Washington Post*, 16 October 2016.

11. Malik, I. H., *State and Civil Society in Pakistan: Politics of Authority, Ideology, and Ethnicity* (Macmillan, 1997).

Works Cited

Chapter 1

Abbas, H. (2005). *Pakistan's Drift with Extremism: Allah, then Army and America's War of Terror*. Routledge.

Ayub, M. and T. Hussain (2015). *Candles in the Dark*. OUP.

Baldacci, E., N. Kojo., and A. Hillman (2003). *Growth, Governance, and Fiscal Policy Transmission Channels in Low-Income Countries*. IMF Working Paper WP/03/237.

Barro, R. (1991). 'Economic Growth in a Cross Section of Countries'. *Quarterly Journal of Economics*.

Burki, S. J. (1999). *Pakistan Fifty Years of Nationhood*. Westview Press.

Chong, A. and M. Gradstein (2004). *Inequality and Institutions*. Working paper no. 506. Inter-American Development Bank Research Department.

Dollar, D. and A. Kraay (2002). 'Growth is Good for the Poor'. *Journal of Economic Growth* 7.

Douglas, N. (1991). 'Institutions'. *Journal of Economic Perspectives* 5(1).

Haq, R. and U. Zia (2009). *PIDE* Working paper.

Haqqani, H. (2013). 'Magnificent Delusions'. *Public Affairs*.

————, (2005). *Pakistan: Between Mosque and Military*. Carnegie Endowment for International Peace.

Hasan, P. (1998). *Pakistan's Economy at the Crossroads*. OUP.

Husain, I. (1999). *Pakistan: The Economy of an Elitist State*. OUP.

————, (2011). 'Retooling Institutions' *in* Maleeha Lodhi (ed.). *Pakistan: Beyond the Crisis State*. OUP.

————, (2014). 'Economic Governance and Institutional Reforms' *in* Rashid Amjad and S. J. Burki (eds.). *Pakistan: Moving the Economy Forward*. Cambridge University Press.

Huther, J. and A. Shah (2005). 'Chapter 2: A Simple Measure of Good Governance'. *Public Services Delivery*: 39.

IMF (2016). 'Pakistan Selected Issues Paper'. *IMF Country Report No. 16/2*.

———, (2016). 'Improving Pakistan's Competitiveness and Business Climate'. Selected Issues Paper.

Kaufmann, D. and A. Kraay (2002). *Growth without Governance*. World Bank Policy Research Working Paper 2928. World Bank. Washington DC.

Khattak, M. S. (2016). 'The New COAS'. *Express Tribune*. 28 November.

Kimenyi, M. S. (2005). 'Institutions of Governance. Power Diffusion and Pro poor Growth Policies'. Paper presentation. Cape Town. Johannesburg: VII Senior Policy Seminar at Applied Economics Research Centre.

Kraay, A. (2004). *When is Growth Pro Poor?* Working Paper 3225. Cross-country Experience World Bank Policy Research.

Martinsson, M. (2016). 'Interview of Mattis Martinsson With BR Research'. *Business Recorder*. 5 December.

McCartney, M. (2011). *Pakistan: The Political Economy of Growth, Stagnation and the State, 1951–2009*. Routledge.

Muhammad, A. et al. (2015) 'Human Capital and Economic Growth'. *Pakistan Development Review*. Winter.

Naviwala, N. (2016). *Pakistan's Education Crisis: The Real Story*. Woodrow Wilson Center.

North, D. (1990). *Institutions, Institutional Change, and Economic Performance*. Cambridge University Press.

Olson, M. (2003). 'Big Bills Left on the Sidewalk: Why Some Nations are Rich and Others Poor' *in* S. Knack. (ed.). *Democracy. Governance and Growth*. University of Michigan Press. Ann Arbor.

Olson, M. 1982. *The Rise and Decline of Nations: Economic Growth, Stagflation, and Economic Rigidities*.

Ostry, J., A. Berg, and H. Tsangarides. (2014). *Redistribution, Inequality, and Growth*. IMF Staff Discussion Note. February.

Ostry, J. D. and A. Berg (2011). *Inequality and Unsustainable Growth: Two Sides of the Same Coin?* No. 11/08. International Monetary Fund.

Packer, G. (2011). 'The Broken Contract: Inequality and American Decline'. *Foreign Affairs*. Nov–Dec. 90(6).

Piketty, T. (2015). *Capitalism in the 21st Century.* Harvard University Press.

PILDAT (2017). 'Assessment of the Quality of Democracy in Pakistan'.

Radelet, S. (2016). *The Great Surge: The Ascent of the Developing World.* Simon & Schuster.

Rana, N., I. Idris, and I. Touqeer (2013). *Revamping Governance.* Pakistan Policy Note 13. The World Bank Group South Asia Region. Washington DC.

Rehman, I. A. (2009). 'The Crisis of Institutions in Pakistan'. *The News.* 8 February.

Shah, A. (2014). *The Army and Democracy: Military Politics in Pakistan.* Harvard University Press.

Sherani, S. (2017). *Institutional Reform in Pakistan.* Report submitted to Friedrich Ebert Stiftung (FES).

UNDP (2016). *Human Development Report 2015.* New York.

Wolf, M. (2012). 'Seven Ways to Fix the System's Flaws'. *Financial Times.* 23 January.

Chapter 2

Burki, S. J. (1980). *Pakistan Under Bhutto, 1971–1977.* Macmillan. London.

———, (1969). 'Twenty Years of Civil Service in Pakistan: A Reappraisal'. *Asian Survey* 9(4).

———, (2000). *Changing Perception. Altered Reality: Emerging Economies in the 1990s.* World Bank Publications.

Goodnow, H. F. (1964). *The Civil Service of Pakistan: Bureaucracy in a New Nation.* Yale University Press. New Haven CT.

Hasan, P. (2011). *My Life. My Country: Memoirs of a Pakistani Economist.* Ferozsons.

Husain, I. (2009). 'Governance and Development: A Case Study of Pakistan' *in* Robert Springborg (ed.). *Development Models in Muslim Countries.* Edinburgh University Press.

———, (2012). *Reforming the Government in Pakistan.* Vanguard.

Hyat, K. (2016). 'All That Glitters'. *The News.*

Jalal, A. (1995). *Democracy and Authoritarianism in South Asia.* Sang-e-Meel. Lahore.

Niaz, I. (2010). *The Culture of Power and Governance of Pakistan 1947–2008.* OUP. Islamabad.

Sayeed, K. B. (1980). *Politics in Pakistan: The Nature and Direction of Change.* Praeger. New York.

Shaikh, F. (2009). *Making Sense of Pakistan.* Hurst & Co. London.

Waseem, M. (1989). *Politics and the State in Pakistan.* Progressive Publishers. Lahore.

Wolpert, S. (2005). *Jinnah of Pakistan.* OUP.

Chapter 3

Almeida, C. (2017). 'The Revenge of the State'. *DAWN.* 17 January.

Arif, K. M. (1995). *Working with Zia.* OUP.

Bardhan, P. (1984). *The Political Economy of Development in India.* OUP. New Delhi.

Bari, F. (2016). 'Quest for Solution'. *DAWN.* 26 August.

Easterly, W. and R. Levine (1997). 'Africa's Growth Tragedy: Policies and Ethnic Divisions'. *Quarterly Journal of Economics* 112(4). November.

Easterly, W. (2001). Can 'Civic Institutions Resolve Ethnic Conflict?' *EDCC* 49(4).

Hamid, N. and M. Khan. (2015). 'Pakistan: A Case of Premature Deindustrialization?' *Lahore Journal of Economics* 20(SE). September 2015.

Husain, I. (2009). 'Pakistan's Economy 1999–2000 to 2007–2008'. *Business Review.* January–June.

———, (2010). 'Pakistan's Growth Experience 1947–2007'. *Business Review.* July–December.

———, (2016). 'Economic Reforms in Pakistan'. *Pakistan Development Review Papers and Proceedings.* Winter.

Jahan, R. (1972). *Pakistan: Failure in National Integration.* Columbia University Press.

Kamal, A. and A. W. Qasimi (2012). 'Precise Estimates of the Informal Economy'. *PIDE.*

Ghani, J. (2014). *The Emerging Middle Class in Pakistan: How it Consumes, Earns, and Saves.* KSBL Working Paper Series.

Kemal, A. R. et al. (2006). 'Source of Growth in Pakistan' *in* K. Parikh (ed). *Explaining Growth: A South Asian Perspective.* OUP. New Delhi.

Kharas, H. (2010). *The Unprecedented Expansion of the Global Middle Class.* The Brookings Institute.

_____, (2016). *How a Growing Middle Class Could Save the World's Economy.* Pew Charitable Trusts.

Lieven, A. (2012). 'Pakistan: A Hard Country'. *Public Affairs.* New York.

LIFE Magazine. 31 January 1948.

McCartney, M. (2011). *Pakistan: The Political Economy of Growth, Stagnation and the State, 1951–2009.* Routledge.

_____, (2011). *Pakistan, Growth, Dependency, and Crisis.* School of Oriental and African Studies (SOAS). University of London.

Mohammad, F., G. Badar, and S. A. Hussain (1985). 'Structure of Rural Income in Pakistan: Some Preliminary Estimates [with Comments]'. *Pakistan Development Review* 24(3/4).

Nayab, D. (2011). *Estimating the Middle Class in Pakistan.* PIDE. Working Paper 2011.

Parikh, K. (2006). *Explaining Growth in South Asia.* OUP.

Poverty Reduction and Economic Management Sector Unit South Asia Region (2002). *Pakistan Development Policy Review: A New DAWN?* World Bank.

State Bank of Pakistan (Several Years). *Annual Reports.* Government of Pakistan.

Subohi, A. (2016) 'Resilient Despite All Odds'. *DAWN.* 31 October.

World Bank (2017). *Growth: A Shared Responsibility.* Pakistan Development Update. May.

Zaidi, S. A. (2017). 'Inequality, not Poverty'. *DAWN.* 24 January.

Chapter 4

Economist (2009). London. 24 October.

Bari, S. (2013). 'Elections and Parochialism'. *DAWN.* 20 January.

Cheema, A., H. Javid, and M. F. Naseer (2013). *Dynastic Politics in Punjab: Facts, Myths and their Implications.* IDEAS Working Paper.

Editorial (2017). 'Transition to Democracy'. *DAWN.* 23 March. Accessed at: <https://www.*DAWN*.com/news/1322226>

Hewitt, V. (2010). *International Politics of South Asia. Routledge Handbook of South Asian Politics.*

Javed, U. (2017). 'Electoral Patriarchy'. *DAWN.* 30 January.

Khan, R. M. (2016). 'Bumpy Road to Stability'. *The News.* 10 December.

Lodhi, M. (2009). *The News.* 1 September.

Malik, I. (1996). *State and Civil Society in Pakistan: Politics of Authority. Ideology and Ethnicity.* Springer.

Mufti, M. (2008). *The Friday Times.* 1 April.

Mustafa, S. (2008). *Asian Age.* 5 January.

Rais, R. B. (2007). *The Friday Times.* 31 August–6 September.

Rehman, I. A. (2016). 'Lessons of the Dharna'. *DAWN.* 3 November.

———, (2016). 'Decline of Political Parties'. *DAWN.* 27 October.

Rizvi, H. A. (2009). *Daily Times.* 6 September.

———, (2016). 'The Decisive Confrontation'. *Express Tribune.* 1 November. Accessed at: <https://tribune.com.pk/story/1215486/the-decisive-confrontation/>

Sahi, A. (2009). *The News.* 8 February.

Syed, A. (1982). *Pakistan: Islam, Politics, and National Solidarity or The Idea of a Pakistani Nationhood.* ABC-CLIO. LLC.

Chapter 5

Gilani, Z. (2017). 'Democratic Political Leaders'. *Express Tribune.* 27 May.

Haider, E. (2008). *Daily Times.* 27 July.

Hisham, Z. (2017). 'Work Ethics'. *DAWN.* 5 February.

Husain, I. (2013*)*. 'Regulating the NGO Sector'. *DAWN.* 17 December.

Jaffrelot, C. (2002). *Pakistan: Nationalism without a Nation.* Manshar.

Jalal, A. (2010). *The Friday Times.* 22 October.

Javaid, U. (2016). 'Social immobility in Pakistan'. *DAWN.* 10 October.

Khan, F. S. (2016). 'Shrinking Progress'. *DAWN.* 11 October.

Krepon, M. (2009). *The Friday Times.* 30 October.

Malik, I. H. (1997). *State and Civil society in Pakistan: Politics of Authority, Ideology, and Ethnicity.* Macmillan.

Memon, N. (2017). 'How Extremism reached Sindh'. *The News.* 14 May.

Mumtaz, S., I. Ali, and J. Racine (2002). *Pakistan: The Contours of State and Society.* OUP.

Murtaza, N. (2017). 'Grandmother Cause'. *DAWN.* 14 May.

Myrdal, G. (1968). *Asian Drama: An Inquiry into the Poverty of Nations.* Pantheon.

Qadeer, M. A. Quoted *in* K. Hasan. *The Friday Times.*

_____, (2000). 'Ruralopolises: The spatial organisation and residential land economy of high-density rural regions in South Asia'. *Urban Studies* 37(9).

_____, (1999). Paper presented at the Annual Conference of Pakistan Society of Development Economists. Islamabad.

_____, (2006). *Islam and Social Life*. Accessed at: <http://archives.cerium.ca/IMG/pdf/Qadeer2006.pdf>

_____, (2009). 'Brutalization of Society'. *The News*. 24 August.

Qasim, A. I. (2011). *Questioning the Authority of the Past*. OUP.

Rehman, I. A. (2009). 'Balance of Power'. *The News*. 22 March.

_____, (2016). 'Shades of McCarthyism'. *DAWN*. 22 November.

_____, 'Focus on gender disparity' (2017). *DAWN*. 9 March.

Rizvi, H. A. (2017). 'Conflictual Politics'. *Express Tribune*. 14 February.

Sattar, B. (2017). 'Rule of Law on Trial'. *The News*. 10 June.

State Bank of Pakistan. (2016). *Annual Report 2015–16*.

World Bank (2005). *Economic Growth in 1990s*. World Bank. Washington DC.

Zaidi, A. (2015). *Issues in Pakistan's Economy*. OUP.

Ziauddin, M. (2017). 'Good Governance is the Answer'. *Express Tribune*. 4 March.

Zahab, M. A. 2007. 'The Politicization of the Shia Community in Pakistan in the 1970s and 1980s' *in* Monsutti A. S. Naef and F. Sabahi (eds.). *The Other Shiites: From the Mediterranean to Central Asia*. Bern: Peter Lang AG. International Academic Publishers.

Chapter 6

Asian Development Bank (2016). *Sector Assessment*. June.

Husain, I. (2009). 'A Confused Federalism'. *DAWN*. 21 June.

_____, (2009) 'Public Entities and Political Control'. *DAWN*. 19 October.

_____, (2011). 'Reforming Public Enterprises'. *DAWN*. 2 June.

_____, (2012). 'New Fiscal Federalism'. *DAWN*. 25 June.

Rana, A. (2013). 'Transferred Woman Officer Pays the Price of Resistance'. *Express Tribune*. 22 May. Accessed at: <https://tribune.com.pk/story/552675/transferred-woman-officer-pays-the-price-of-resistance/>

Rana, S. (2013). 'Corruption Charges: Presidential Reference Against AGP Put on Ice'. *Express Tribune*. 31 May. Accessed at: <http://tribune.com.pk/

story/556894/corruption-charges-presidential-reference-against-agp-put-on-ice/>

Chapter 7

Bardhan, P. and D. Mukherjee. (2007). *Decentralization and Local Governance in Developing Countries: A Comparative Perspective*. OUP. Delhi.

Cheema, A., A. Khwaja, and A. Khan (2006). 'Decentralization in Pakistan Context: Content and Causes' *in* P. Bardhan and D. Mookherjee (eds.). *Decentralization in Developing Countries: A Comparative Perspective*. MIT Press.

———— and S. Mohmand. (2006). *Accountability Failures and the Decentralisation of Service Delivery in Pakistan*.

Das, G. (2012). *India Grows at Night*. Penguin.

Hasan, A. (2016). 'Ugly Karachi'. *DAWN*. 6 November.

Husain, I. (2011). 'Maximizing Benefits for Devolution'. *The News*. 25 July.

————, (2012). 'Adapting Public Sector Services to Local Delivery'. *Lahore Journal of Economics* 17(SE). September.

Jamal, H. (2012). *Districts' Indices of Multiple Deprivations for Pakistan, 2011*. SPDC.

Mangi, N. (2016). 'Rural Sindh Agenda'. *DAWN*. 20 September.

Nishtar, S. (2009). 'Equity, Social Justice and the Social Sector'. *The News*. 22 June.

Sattar, B. (2017). 'Race to the Bottom'. *The News*. 7 January.

SPDC (2007). *Annual Review 2007*. Karachi.

————, (2012). *Devolution and Social Development: Annual Review 2011–12*.

Subohi, A. (2016). 'Sindh's Second Chance'. *DAWN*. 29 August.

World Bank (2004). *World Development Report 2004*. World Bank. Washington DC.

————, (1997). *World Development Report 1997: The State in a Changing World*. World Bank. Washington DC.

Zahid, H. (2008). *Devolution, Accountability, and Service Delivery: Some Insights from Pakistan*. Policy Research Working Paper No. 4610. World Bank. Washington DC.

Chapter 8

Ahmed, M. (1964). *The Civil Servant in Pakistan*. OUP.

Artaza, I. (2016). 'Civil Service Reform'. *DAWN*. 15 November.

Braibanti, R. (1966). *Research on the Bureaucracy of Pakistan*. Duke University.

Ghuman, A. (2016). 'Revitalising CSS Performance'. *DAWN*. 31 October.

Government of Pakistan (1958–59). *Administrative Reorganization Committee Report*.

———, *Report of the National Commission for Government Reforms*. Vol I.

Hanif, A. N. et al. (2016). 'Performance Management in Public Sector: A Case Study of Civil service in Pakistan'. *South Asia Studies* 31(1).

Haque, N. U. and I. Khawaja (2007). *Public Service Through the Eyes of Civil Servants*. PIDE Series on Governance and Institutions.

Husain, I. (2013). 'The Nexus of Human Capital and Governance'. *The News*. 23 January.

———, (2013). 'Short run Governance Reforms'. *Express Tribune*. 1 June.

———, (2014). *Bureaucracy Needs Reforms. DAWN*. 25 January.

Jadoon, Z. (2013). 'Administrative Reforms in Pakistan' *in* M. Sabharwal and E. Berman (eds.). *Public Administration in South Asia*. CRC Press.

Khan, M. J. R. (ed.) (1987). *Government and Administration in Pakistan*. Pakistan Public Administration Research Centre.

Kux, D. (2001). *The United States and Pakistan, 1947–2000: Disenchanted Allies*. Johns Hopkins University Press.

Maddison, A. (1971). *Class Structure and Economic Growth*. Allen & Unwin.

Niaz, I. (2010). *The Culture of Power and Governance of Pakistan 1947–2008*. OUP. Islamabad.

———, (2013). 'Corruption and the Bureaucratic Elite in Pakistan: The 1960s and 1970s Revisited'. *Journal of the Royal Asiatic Society* 23(4). Cambridge University Press.

Noman, O. (1998). *A Political and Economic History of Pakistan*. OUP.

Sadat, S. (2016). 'The Bitter Truth'. *DAWN*. 27 October.

Shafqat, S. (1994). 'Pakistani Bureaucracy: Crisis of Governance and Prospects of Reform'. *Pakistan Development Review* 38(4) Part II.

Sherani, S. (2016). 'Poverty of our Reform Ambition'. *DAWN*. 5 August.

Siddiqui, T. A. (2001). *Towards Good Governance*. OUP.

Subohi, A. (2016). 'Public Sector Training'. *Development Advocate* 3(3).

World Bank (1998). *Pakistan: A Framework for Civil Service Reform in Pakistan*. Report no. 18386-PAK. 15 December.

Chapter 9

Ahmed, S. (2016). 'Justice Delayed is Justice Denied'. *DAWN*. 20 December.

Douglas, W. O. (1951). *United States Supreme Court* quoted *in* A. G. Noorani. 'Civil Society'. *DAWN*. 20 August 2016.

Gilani, U. (2016). 'The Pace of Justice'. *The News*. 31 December.

Husain, I. (2012). 'Judicial Reforms and Economic Growth'. *Express Tribune*. 17 March.

———, (2014). *Economic Consequences of Judicial Actions*. Keynote address delivered at the International Judiciary Conference. Islamabad. 9 December.

IMF (2017). *World Economic Outlook*.

Jatoi, B. (2016). 'Parliament or Judiciary: Who is the Grand Inquisitor?' *Express Tribune*. 29 December.

Khan, S. R. et al. (2007). *Initiating Devolution for Service Delivery in Pakistan*. OUP.

Newberg, P. (2010). 'Balancing Act: Prudence, Impunity and Pakistan's Jurisprudence' *in* P. R. Brass. (ed.). *Routledge Handbook of South Asian Politics*. Routledge.

Mehta, (2007). 'India's Judiciary: The Promise of Uncertainty' *in* D. Kapur and P. B. Mehta (eds.). *Public Institutions in India: Performance and Design*. OUP. Delhi.

Khan, M. H. 'Judicial Reforms'. *DAWN*. 1 April 2011.

Khosa, S. (2016). 'Indiscipline Ignored'. *The News*. 16 October.

Lieven, A. (2011). 'Pakistan: A Hard Country'. *Public Affairs*. April.

Malik, T. (2016). 'Judicial Freedom'. *DAWN*. 1 November.

Rahim, P. (2017). 'Justice for Labour'. *DAWN*. 24 January.

Rizvi, H. A. (2016). 'In Search of Genuine Democracy'. *Express Tribune*. 19 September.

Sattar, B. (2017). 'Not Guilty vs Not Proven'. *The News*. 21 January.

———, (2017). 'Rule of Law on Trial'. *The News*. 10 June.

Shinwari, N. A. (2015). *Understanding the Informal Justice System: Opportunities and Possibilities of Legal Pluralism in Pakistan*.

———, (2015). *Understanding the Informal Justice System: Opportunities and Possibilities for Legal Pluralism in Pakistan* cited *in* M. A. Nekokara. 'Access to Justice and Legal Aid'. *DAWN*. 12 December 2016.

Siddiqi, F. (2016). 'Judicial Independence'. *DAWN*. 1 August.

Chapter 10

Constitution of Pakistan amended up to 2016. Article 46: Duties of Prime Minister in Relation to President'. Accessed at: <https://pakistanconstitutionlaw.com/article-46-duties-of-prime-minister-in-relation-to-president/>

DAWN (2016). *ECP Reactivates Political Finance Wing.* 3 October.

Fazal, K. '*Comparative Functions of Parliamentary Committee System in Pakistan. India and Bangladesh*'.

Husain, F. (2017). 'Wisdom without Expiry Date'. *Express Tribune.* 5 February.

Husain, I. (2009). 'Economic Cost of Instability'. *DAWN.* 2 November.

———, (2012). 'The Economics of Corruption'. *The News.* 16 September.

———, (2012). 'Politics vs Economics'. *The News.* 22 October.

———, (2011). 'Parliament's Role in Economic Governance'. *Express Tribune.* 22 December.

Jatoi, B. (2016). 'Parliament or Judiciary?' *Express Tribune.* 29 December.

Khuhro, Z. (2017). 'Reformation'. *DAWN.* 23 January.

Kupchan, C. (2012). 'The Democratic Malaise'. *Foreign Affairs.* January–February.

Lafrance, P. UNESCO Special Envoy. France's Special Representative for Afghanistan and Pakistan.

Mahboob, A. B. (2017). 'Who Pays for the Brawl?' *DAWN.* 7 February.

Noorani, T. (2016). Background paper. Intra party elections.

Rehman, I. A. (2016). 'Standing Committees'. *DAWN.* 10 November.

Sen, A. (1999). 'Democracy as a Universal Value'. *Journal of Democracy* 10(3).

Shafqat, S. (2002). 'Democracy and Political Transformation in Pakistan' *in* Sofia Mumtaz et al. *Pakistan: The Contours of Society and State.* OUP.

Soofi, A. B. (2016). 'Parliament's Inertia'. *DAWN.* 30 August.

Sultana, T. (2014). 'Montesquieu's Doctrine of Separation of Powers: A Case Study of Pakistan'. *Journal of European Studies.* 5 May. Accessed at: <pgil.pk/wp-content.uploads/2014/05/5>

Syed, A. (2007). 'Liberal Tradition in Pakistan'. *DAWN.* 8 July.

Chapter 11

Aziz, M. (2008). *Military Control in Pakistan.* Routledge.

Aziz, S. (2016). *From Banking to the Thorny World of Politics.* Quartet.

Chaudhary, A. Y. (2016). 'Why do coups happen in Pakistan?' *The Diplomat*. 31 August.

Cheema, P. I. (2003). *The Armed Forces of Pakistan*. New York University Press.

Cohen, S. (1998). *The Pakistan Army*. OUP.

Gul, I. (2016). 'The Sharif Exit'. *Express Tribune*. 23 November.

Haqqani, H. (2005). *Pakistan: Between Mosque and Military*. Carnegie Endowment for International Peace.

Humayun, F. (2016). 'Interview of Mahmud Ali Durrani'. *DAWN*. 28 July.

Husain, T. (2017). 'Semi-civilian Rule'. *The News*. 6 March.

Khan, A. (1967). *Friends not Masters*. OUP. Karachi.

Khan, R. M. (2016). 'Bumpy Road to Stability'. *The News*. 10 December.

Lieven, A. (2012). 'Pakistan: A Hard Country'. *Public Affairs*.

Monashipour, M. and A. Samuel (1995). 'Development and Democracy in Pakistan'. *Asian Survey* xxxv(11). November.

Naviwala, N. (2016). *Pakistan's Education Crisis: The Real Story*. Woodrow Wilson Center.

Nawaz, S. (2008). *Crossed Swords*. OUP.

_____, (2011). *Learning by Doing: The Pakistan Army's Experience with Counterinsurgency*. Atlantic Council.

Olson, M. (1993). 'Dictatorship, Democracy and Development'. *American Political Science Review* 87(3). September.

Rashid, A. (2011). 'Ten Years of Rising Resentment'. *International Herald Tribune*. 10–11 September.

Rizvi, H. A. (2016). 'Civil Military Relations'. *Express Tribune*. 17 October.

Sattar, B. (2016). 'Is the Silly Season here?' *The News*. 14 May. Accessed at: <http://tn.thenews.com.pk/print/119826-Is-the-silly-season-here?>

_____, (2017). 'The anti-climax'. *The News*. 14 May.

Shah, A. (2014). *The Army and Democracy: Military Politics in Pakistan*. Harvard University Press.

Syed, A. (2007). 'Extremism on the loose'. *DAWN*. April 8. Accessed at: <https://www.dawn.com/news/1069994/dawn-opinion-april-08-2007>

Chapter 12

Akhtar, A. S. (2014). 'Structural Violence'. *DAWN*. 29 May.

Alam, A. (2016). 'Taking Stock in Increasingly Dangerous Times'. *The News*. 18 August.

Amir, A. (2016). 'The Altaf Cure'. *The News*. 26 August.

———, (2017). 'Pakistan's Problem is Moderation not Extremism'. *The News*. 27 December.

Ashraf, M. M. (2017). 'Taking the Fight to Terror'. *The News*. 7 January.

Ayaz, B. (2013). *What's Wrong with Pakistan?* Hay House.

Basit, A. (2017). 'Urban Jihadists'. *The News*. 7 January.

Burki, Abid A., R. Memon, and K. Mir (2015). 'Multiple Inequalities and Policies to Mitigate Inequality Traps in Pakistan'. *Oxfam Research Report*. Lahore University of Management Sciences and Oxfam Pakistan. Lahore and Islamabad.

Darlymple, W. (2005). 'Inside the Madrasa'. *New York Review of Books*. November.

Haider, Z. (2011). 'Ideologically Adrift' *in* M. Lodhi (ed.). *Pakistan: Beyond the Crisis State*. OUP. Karachi.

Husain, I. (2009). 'The Economics of Fundamentalism'. *Notebook*. May.

Hussain, Z. (2007). *Pakistan*. Vanguard.

———, (2011). *Battling Militancy in Pakistan: Beyond Crisis*. Columbia University Press.

———, (2016). 'A Quintessential Rebel'. *DAWN*. 3 August.

Islam, M. (2008). *Decline of Muslim States and Societies*. Xlibris Corp.

Jalal, A. (1990). *The State of Martial Rule*. Cambridge University Press.

———, (2011). 'The past as present' *in* M. Lodhi. *Pakistan: Beyond the Crisis State*. Columbia University Press.

Khan, Z. (2016). 'The New Raheel Sharif'. *The News*. 16 January.

Lieven, A. (2012). 'Pakistan: A Hard Country'. *Public Affairs*. 1 April.

Milam, W. (2014). *The Friday Times*. 24 October.

Qadeer, M. A. *in* Khalid Hassan. *The Friday Times*. 22–8 October.

Rana, M. A. (2016). 'The Myth of Soft Targets'. *DAWN*. 28 August.

———, (2017). 'Unfolding Madrassah Challenge'. *DAWN*. 1 January.

———, (2013). 'Layers of Complexity'. *DAWN*. 23 September.

———, (2017). 'Challenging Convention'. *DAWN*. 12 February.

———, (2016). 'In search of relevance'. *DAWN*. 13 March.

Rizvi, H. A. (2009). 'Living with delusions'. *Daily Times*. 12 April.

Safi, S. (2016). 'Afghanistan: Our Case'. *The News*. 2 August.

———, (2017). 'How to Strike the Root of Terror'. *The News*. 21 February.

Sheikh, F. (2009). 'Making Sense of Pakistan'. *The Independent*. 20 July.

Yousafzai, M. and C. Lamb (2013). *I Am Malala*. Orion.

Zaidi, A. (2015). *Issues in Pakistan's Economy*. OUP.

Ziauddin, U. (2017) 'The road not taken'. *Express Tribune*. 26 January.

Chapter 13

Acemoglu, D. and S. Johnson (2003). *Unbundling Institutions*. Massachusetts
    Institute of Technology.

Husain, I. (2004). 'Preparing for Privatization: Lessons from Pakistan' *in* G.
    Caprio et al. (eds). *The Future of State-owned Financial Institutions*. Brookings
    Institution Press.

———, (2014). 'State's Role in Business'. *DAWN*. 10 May.

———, (2014). 'Deregulating the Economy'. *DAWN*. 15 November.

———, (2015). 'Public-Private Partnerships'. *DAWN*. 2 June.

———, (2015). 'Markets. Society and Economy'. *Blue Chip Magazine*.
    15 October.

Spielman, D. et al. (2016). *Agriculture and the Rural Economy in Pakistan*.
    University of Pennsylvania Press.

Subohi, A. (2017). 'Productivity'. *DAWN*. 23 January.

Walton, M. (2012). 'Where do India's Billionaires Get their Wealth?' *EPW* 97(40).
    6 October.

World Bank (2017). *Punjab Development Update*.

Chapter 14

The News (2016). 'Corruption and Terrorism'. 24 April.

The News (2016). 21 July.

The News (2017). 20 June.

Alam, I. (2016). 'Stocktaking in Increasingly Dangerous Times'. *The News*.
    18 August.

Arif, K. M. (1995). *Working with Zia*. OUP.

Babakhel, M. A. (2016). 'Building Community Resilience'. *Express Tribune*.
    26 August.

Bayley, D. H. (2015). *The Police and Political Development in India.* Princeton University Press.

Buchanan, J. M. (1975). *The Limits of Liberty.* Chicago University Press.

Committee for the Study of Corruption. (1986).

Das, G. (2000). *India Unbound: The Social and Economic Revolution.* Penguin Books.

Government of Pakistan. *Report of the Committee for the (Stopping) of Corruption.*

Government of Pakistan. *Report of the Pakistan Police Commission 1969–70.*

Gul, I. (2017). 'Integrity and Character'. *Express Tribune.* 24 January.

Hanif, I. (2016). 'Public Prosecutors to be bound by Code of Conduct'. *DAWN.* 3 October.

Husain, I. (2015). 'Coordination Failure'. *DAWN.* 22 December.

Hussain, A. (2016). 'Public safety and the Police'. *The News.*

International Crisis Group (2010). *Reforming the Criminal Justice system in Pakistan.* December.

———, (2011). *Reforming the Criminal Justice System in Pakistan.* Islamabad/ Brussels. October.

Kennedy, C. (1987). *Bureaucracy in Pakistan.* OUP.

Khalid, S. (2016). 'Mature CSS'. *The News.* 28 August.

Khan, J. R. (1987). *Government and Administration in Pakistan.* Pakistan Public Administration Research Centre. O&M Division. Cabinet Secretariat. Government of Pakistan.

Khawar, H. (2016). 'KP Police Law: Reform or Rhetoric'. *Express Tribune.* 30 August.

Khosa, T. (2016). 'Sleeping on the Job'. *DAWN.* 22 August.

———, (2016). 'Between the Devil and the Deep Sea'. *DAWN.* 1 November.

LaPalombara, J. (1967). *Bureaucracy and Political Development.* Princeton University Press.

Nekokara, M. A. (2017). *The News.* 25 January.

———, (2017). 'Rickety Justice System'. *The News.* January.

Rashid, I. (2016). 'Fundamental Reform Required in our Police Force'. *Express Tribune.* 22 November.

Shafqat, S. (1997). *Civil-Military Relations in Pakistan.* Westview.

Shah, N. H. *Judicial Administration.*

Yasin, M. and T. Banuri (2004). *Dispensation of Justice in Pakistan*. OUP.

Chapter 15

Adil, A. (2017). 'A Balancing Act in Afghanistan'. *The News*. 21 January.

Ahmad, E. and A. A. Mohammed. (2012). *Pakistan: the United States and the IMF.* LSE Working paper 57.

Center for Global Development (2011). *Aid to Pakistan by the Numbers*. US Development Strategy. Pakistan.

Cheema, P. I. (1984). 'Pakistani Perspectives on International Security' *in* Donald H. McMillen (ed.). *Asian Perspectives on International Security*. MacMillan.

Goldberg, J. and M. Ambinder (2011). 'Pakistan: The Ally from Hell'. *The Atlantic*. December.

Husain, I. (2007). 'How Critical is US Assistance to Pakistan?' *DAWN*. 17 April.

———, (2009). 'Pakistan-US Economic Ties'. *DAWN*. 8 April.

———, (2011). *Prospects and Challenges for Increasing Trade Between India and Pakistan*. Atlantic Council. Washington DC.

———, (2011). 'US Assistance: Differing Perceptions'. *Express Tribune*. 19 May.

———, (2013). 'Managing India-Pakistan Trade Relations' *in* M. Kugelman and R. Hathaway (eds.). *Pakistan-India Trade*. Woodrow Wilson Center. Washington DC.

———, (2014). *Reviving India-Pakistan Economic Relations*. Keynote address delivered at the Annual Conference of ICRIER. New Delhi. 21 January.

———, (2016). 'Reorienting Pak-US Tie'. *DAWN*. 7 September.

Hasan, P. (1998). *Pakistan's Economy at the Crossroads*. OUP.

Husain, K. (2015). 'Pakistan and the IMF: The Ties that Bind Pakistan'. *DAWN*. 11 January.

IMF and IEO. (2002). *Evaluation of the Prolonged Users of the IMF.* Washington DC. IMF.

McCartney, M. (2011). *Pakistan: The Political Economy of Growth. Stagnation and the State 1951–2009*. Routledge.

Paul, T. V. (2013). *The Warrior State: Pakistan in the Contemporary World*. OUP.

Rashid, A. (2011). 'Ten Years of Rising Resentment'. *I.H.T.* 10 September.

Chapter 16

Acemoglu, D. and S. Robinson (2008). *The Role of Institutions in Growth and Development.* Working paper 10. Growth Commission.

Ali, R. (2015). *The Urban Edge.* SPDC.

Bokhari, F. (2016). 'Poor Food Insecurity'. *DAWN.* 20 November.

Cheema, A., H. Javid, and F. Naseer (2013). *Dynastic Politics in Punjab: Facts. Myths and their Implications.* IDEAS Working Paper 1/13.

Husain, I. (1999). 'Institutions of Restraint'. *Pakistan Development Review.* Winter.

———, (2006). 'Why Reform the Government?' *DAWN.* 9 July.

———, (2007). 'Reforming the Government'. *The News.* 24, 26, and 30 May.

———, (2008). 'Reforming Institutions for Governance'. *DAWN.* 7 January.

———, (2009). 'A Roadmap for Governance Reforms'. *Blue Chip Magazine.* 14 April.

———, (2009). 'Economic Governance in Pakistan'. *Criterion Quarterly.* January–March.

———, (2015). 'Democratic Governance'. *Blue Chip Magazine.* 15 July.

Malik, I. H. (1997). *State and Civil Society in Pakistan.* Macmillan.

Mehta, P. B. (2010). 'It's Land, Stupid'. *Indian Express.* 19 August.

Radelet, S. (2016). *The Great Surge: The Ascent of the Developing World.* Simon & Schuster.

UNDP (2016). 'Civil Service Reforms in Pakistan'. *Development Advocate Pakistan* 3(3).

Chapter 17

Ahmed, F., A. Greenleaf, and A. Sacko (2013–14). 'The Paradox of Export Growth in Areas of Weak Governance: The Case of the Ready-Made Garment Sector in Bangladesh'. *World Development* 56. Accessed at: <dx.doi.org/10.1016/j.worlddev.2013>

Alam, M. B. (2016). 'E-government in India' *in* Meghan Sabharwal and Evan Berman (eds.). *Public Administration in South Asia.* CRC Press.

Chelliah, R. (1999). *Towards Sustainable Growth: Essay in Public Finance and Financial Reforms in India.* OUP. New Delhi.

Diamond, L. (2009). *Democratic Governance and the Performance of Democracy.* CDDRL Working Paper no. 117. November.

Gherzi Textile Organisation (2002). *Executive Summary of the Initial Report on Post-MFA Development Strategy and Technical Assistance for the RMG Sector*. Report submitted to the Ministry of Commerce. Government of Bangladesh.

Hausman, R. (2006). *Economic Growth: Shared Beliefs. Shared Disappointments?* Center for International Development. Harvard.

Husain, I. (2004). 'South Asian Economies: Future Challenge'. *South Asia Journal*. October–December.

———, (2007). 'Pakistan–Indian Economies Compared: Sixty Years Later'. *DAWN*. 2 November.

———, (2010). 'India–Pakistan Economies Compared'. *South Asia Magazine*. 10 August.

Kapur, D. (2005). 'Explaining Democratic Durability and Economic Performance: The Role of Indian Institutions' *in* D. Kapur and P. B. Mehta. *Public Institutions in India*. OUP. 2007.

———, and P. B. Mehta (2005). *Public Institutions in India*. OUP.

———, and P. Nangia (2013). 'A Targeted Approach: India's Expanding Social Safety Net'. *World Politics Review*. 2 September.

Khan, M. H. (2000). *Rents, Rent-seeking and Economic Development: An Introduction*. SOAS.

———, (2011). *The Political Settlement and Its Evolutions in Bangladesh*. SOAS. Working Paper. Accessed at: <http://eprints.soas.ac.uk/12845/1/ThePoliticalSettlementanditsEvolutioninBangladesh.pdf>

Khan, S. R. et al. (2007). *Initiating Devolution of Service Delivery*. OUP.

Kumar, R. (2016). 'Making Reforms Work for the Common People'. *Economic and Political Weekly*. Accessed at: <http://www.epw.in/journal/2016/29/making-reformsworkcommonpeople.html0#>

Rashid, M. A. (2009). *Governance and Development in Bangladesh*. Bangladesh Institute of Development Studies. Dhaka.

Riaz, A. (2016). *Bangladesh: A Political History Since Independence*. I. A. Taurus. New York and London.

Rudolph, L. I. and S. H. Rudolph (2010). 'The Old and New Federalism in Independent India' *in* Paul R. Brass (ed.). *Routledge Handbook of South Asian Politics*.

Singh, M. P. (2013). 'Administrative Reforms in India' *in* Meghan Sabharwal and Evan Berman (eds.). *Public Administration in South Asia.* CRC Press.

Survi, K. C. et al. (2010). 'Support for Democracy in S. Asia'. *Global Barometer Surveys Conference.* Taipei. 15–16 October.

Taslim, M. A. (2009). 'Governance. Policies and Economic Growth in Bangladesh' *in* N. Islam and M. Asaduzzaman (eds.). *Ship Adrift: Governance and Development in Bangladesh.* Bangladesh Institute of Development Studies. Dhaka.

Vaishnav, M. (2017). *When Crime Pays: Money and Muscle in Indian Politics.* Yale University Press.

World Values Survey.

Chapter 18

Cohen, S. (1964). 'Subhas Chandra Bose and the Indian National Army'. *Pacific Affairs* 36(4); (1988) 'The Military and India's Democracy' *in* Atul Kohli (ed.). *India's Democracy.* Princeton. N. J. (2014).

Husain, I. (2011). 'Good Governance for Dummies'. *Newsweek.* 21 February.

———, (2011). 'Bridging the Governance Deficit'. *The News.* 2–3 April.

Kapur, D. and P. B. Mehta (2005). *Public Institutions in India.* OUP.

Khan, M. (2008). *Rents, Rent-seeking and Economic Development: An Introduction.* SOAS.

Kochanek, S. (2010). 'Corruption and the Criminalization of Politics in South Asia'. *Routledge Handbook of Politics in South Asia.*

Lieven, A. (2011). *Pakistan: A Hard Country.* BBS Publications. New York.

Malik, I. H. (1997). *State and Civil Society in Pakistan: Politics of Authority, Ideology, and Ethnicity.* Macmillan.

Nasr, V. (2009). *The Rise of Islamic Capitalism.* Free Press. New York.

Sethi, N. (2008). 'How to Tame the ISI'. *The Friday Times.*

Tepperman, J. (2016). 'Can pragmatic, far-sighted leaders really solve the world's crises?' *The Washington Post.* 11 November.

Vaishnav, M. (2017). *When Crime Pays: Money and Muscle in Indian Politics.* Yale University Press.

Bibliography

Abbas, H. (2005). *Pakistan's Drift into Extremism: Allah, the Army, and America's War on Terror Routledge*.

Acemoglu, D. and Robinson, J. (2014). 'Institutions, Human Capital and Development'. *Annual Review of Economics* 6(1): 875–912.

Acemoglu, D. et al. (2004). *Democracy Causes Growth*. WP 20004, NBER. Accessed at: <www.nber.org/paper/w20004>

Ahluwalia, M. S. (2002). 'Economic Reforms in India since 1991'. *Journal of Economic Perspectives*. Summer. 16(3): 67–88.

Ahmad, E. (2004). *Between Past and Future: Selected Essays on South Asia*. OUP.

Ahmed, I. (2013). *The Garrison State*. OUP.

———— and Rafiq, A. (2017). *Pakistan's Democratic Transition*. Routledge.

Ahmed, S. (1994). *Explaining Pakistan's Huge Growth Performance*. World Bank.

Alavi, H. (1972). 'The State in Post-colonial Societies: Pakistan and Bangladesh'. *New Left Review* I(74) July–August: 59–81.

Alesina A, and Rodrik, D. (1994). 'Distributive politics and Economic Growth'. *The Quarterly Journal of Economics* 109(2).

Ali, C. M. (1967). *The Emergence of Pakistan*. Columbia University Press.

Ali, M. (2008). *Devolution and Governance Reforms in Pakistan*. OUP.

Anderson, K. and Nelgen, S. (2013). *Updated National and Global Estimates of Distortions in Agricultural Incentives, 1955–2011*. World Bank.

Arif, K. M. (2015). *Working with Zia: Pakistan's Power Politics, 1977–1988*. OUP.

Asian Development Bank (ADB). (2009). *Calibrating the Civil Service Institutes for People's Wellbeing in Punjab*.

Azhar, M. (2014). *Voice of Teachers*. Alif Ailaan. Islamabad.

Aziz, M. (2008). *Military Control in Pakistan*. Routledge.

Bano, R. and Lee, J. (2010). *A New Data Set of Educational Attainment in the World 1950–2010*. Working Paper 15902. NBER.

Bardhan, P. (2001). 'Distributive Conflicts, Collective Action and Institutional Economics'. *Frontiers of Developmental Economics.* Meier and Stiglitz (eds.). OUP.

Board of Investment (BOI). (2004). *Pakistan, Investment Policies, Incentives and Facilities.* Islamabad.

Bolman, L. and Deal, T. (1997). *Reforming Organizations.* San Francisco: Jossey-Bass.

Braibanti, R. (1966). 'The Higher Bureaucracy of Pakistan', in Ralph Braibanti (ed.), *Asian Bureaucratic Systems Emergent from the British Imperial Tradition.* Durham, NC: Duke University Press.

_____, (1966). *Research on the Bureaucracy of Pakistan: A Critique of Sources and Issues.* Durham, NC: Duke University Press.

Burki, A. (2011). *Industrial Policy, its spatial aspects and cluster development.* LUMS.

Centre for Policy Dialogue (CPD). (1998). *Crisis in Governance.* Bangladesh Development Studies Vol 28.

Centre for Research and Security Studies (CRSS). (2011). *Pakistan in 2011: The Simmering Crises.*

_____, (2015). *Counter-terrorism and Pakistan Police.*

Cheema, G. S. (2013). *Democratic Local Governance.* Tokyo: UNO Press.

Chen, S. and Ravillion, M. *An Update on World Bank's Estimates.* Accessed at: <http://siteresources.worldbank.org/INTPOVCALNET/Resources/GlobalPovertyUpdate201202-29-12.pdf>

Chowdhury, A. and Mahmud, W. eds. (2008). *Handbook on the South Asian Economies.* Edward Elgar Center for International Development and Conflict Management. University of Maryland. Accessed at: <cidcm.umd.edu/polity/country-reports>

Clemens, M. et al. (2012). *Counting Chickens When They Hatch: Timing and the Effects of Aid in Growth.*

Cohen, S. (1998). *The Pakistani Army.* OUP.

_____, (2004). *The Idea of Pakistan.* Brookings Institution Press.

Constable, P. (2011). *Playing with Fire.* Random House.

Devarajan, S. and Nabi, I. (2006). 'Economic Growth in South Asia'. *EPW Research Foundation* 41(33): 3573–80.

Diamond, L. (2008). *The Spirit of Democracy.* New York: Times Book.

Deolkar, A. et al. (2008). *Governance in Developing Asia*. Bangladesh Institute of Development Studies.

Din, M. (2007).

Easterly, W. (2001). 'The Middle Class Consensus and Economic Development'. *Journal of Economic Growth* 6(4): 317–35.

———, et al. (2006). 'Social Cohesion, Institutions, and Growth'. *Economics and Politics* 18(2): 103–20.

Ellis, P. and Roberts, M. (2015). *Leveraging Urbanization in South Asia 2016*. Global Monitoring Report. Accessed at: <data.worldbank.org>

Erving, A. (1982). 'Administering India: The Indian Civil Service'. *History Today* 32(6).

Esposito, J. *Voices of Resurgent Islam*. New York: OUP.

Faguet, J. P. et al. (2015). *Is Decentralization Good for Development?* OUP.

Fair, C. (2010). *Pakistan: Can the US secure an insecure state?* RAND Corporation.

Freedom House. <freedomhouse.org/uploads/FIWallscne.xls>

Fukuyama, F. (2004). *The End of History and the Last Man*. New York: Free Press.

Goodnow, H. F. (1964). *The Civil Service of Pakistan*. Yale University Press.

Government of Pakistan. Ministry of Finance. *Economic Survey of Pakistan* (various issues).

———, *Statistical yearbooks* (various issues).

———, *Five year Plans and Annual Plans* (various issues).

Gul, I. (2011). *Pakistan's Security Challenges*. HV 6433: 18–85.

Haqqani, H. (2005). *Pakistan: Between Mosque and Military*. Carnegie Institute for Peace.

———, (2013). *Magnificent Delusions*. Perseus Books.

Hasan, L. (2010). *Rule of Law, Legal Development, and Economic Growth: Perspectives for Pakistan*. Archive Paper 2265. Munich Personal, Pakistan Institute of Development Economics.

Hassan, P. (1998). *Pakistan's Economy at the Crossroads*. OUP.

Hathaway, R. et al. (2010). *Hunger Pains*. Washington DC: Woodrow Wilson Center.

Heath, R. and Mubarak, M. (2014). *Manufacturing Growth and the Lives of Bangladeshi Women*. Accessed at: <http://www.nber.org/papers/w20383>

Husain, I. (2003). *Economic Management in Pakistan, 1992–2002*. OUP.

_____, (2015). *Globalization, Governance and Growth*, IBA Press.

Hussain, Z. (2007). *Frontline Pakistan*. Columbia University Press.

Information Management and Mine Action Programs (iMMAP). (2013, 2015). *Pakistan Development Perspective, City District Karachi*, and *City District Lahore*.

Institute of Public Policy. *State of the Economy Annual Reports* (various issues). BHU. Lahore.

Institute of Social and Policy Sciences (I-SAPS). (2013). *Aid Effectiveness in Pakistan*. Accessed at <i-saps.org>

Institute of Social and Policy Sciences (I-SAPS). (2014). *Private Sector Education in Pakistan: Mapping and Musing*.

International Crisis Group (ICG). (2014). *Educational Reform in Pakistan*. Brussels.

_____, (2014). *Policing Urban Violence in Pakistan*. Brussels.

_____, (2010). 'Reforming Pakistan's Justice System'. *Asia Report* No. 196. Accessed at: <https://www.crisisgroup.org/asia/south-asia/pakistan/reforming-pakistan-s-criminal-justice-system>

_____, (2008). 'Reforming Pakistan's Police'. *Asia Report* No. 117. Accessed at: <https://www.crisisgroup.org/asia/south-asia/pakistan/reforming-pakistan%E2%80%99s-police>

_____, (2008). 'Reforming the Judiciary in Pakistan'. *Asia Report* No. 160. Accessed at: <https://www.crisisgroup.org/asia/south-asia/pakistan/reforming-judiciary-pakistan>

_____, (2004). 'Building Judicial Independence in Pakistan'. *Asia Report* No. 86. Accessed at: <http://old.crisisgroup.org/en/regions/asia/south-asia/pakistan/086-building-judicial-independence-in-pakistan.html#>

International Growth Centre (IGC). (2010). *Economic growth and Structural change in South Asia*. WP/10/0859.

International Monetary Fund (IMF). *World Economic Outlook* (various issues).

_____, *Pakistan Staff Reports and Selected Issues papers* (various issues)

Islam, M. *Decline of Muslim States and Societies*. Lahore: Sh. M. Ashraf Publications.

Islam, N. and Azaduzzaman. (2008). A *Ship Adrift*. Bangladesh Institute of Development Studies.

Islam, S. N. (2016). *Governance for Development*. Palgrave Macmillan.

Jaffrelot, C. (2002). *Pakistan: Nationalism without a Nation*. Manshar.

Jalal, A. (1992). *The Sole Spokesman*. Sang-e-Meel Publications.

———, (1995). *Democracy and Authoritarianism in South Asia*. Cambridge University Press.

———, (1999). *The State of Martial Law*. Sang-e-Meel Publications.

———, (2014). *The Struggle for Pakistan*. Harvard University Press.

Johnson, R. and Clark, T. (2015). *At the end of military intervention*. OUP.

Kapur, D. and Mehta, P. (2005). *Public Institutions in India*. OUP.

Kardar, S. (2007). *Punjab Civil Service Reform*. Report for the ADB. November.

Keefer, P. et al. *The Database of Political Institutions*. World Bank.

Kennedy, C. (1987). *Bureaucracy in Pakistan*. OUP.

———, (Winter 1999). 'Pakistan Bureaucracy: Crisis of Governance and Prospects for Reform'. *Pakistan Development Review* 38:4.

Khan, A. (2005). *Politics of Identity*. Sage Publications.

Khan, S. R. et al. (2007). *Initiating Devolution for Service Delivery*. OUP.

Khan, S. A. (2016). *Governance in Pakistan*. OUP.

Kharas, H. (2010). 'The Emerging Middle Class in Developing Countries'. Working Paper 285. *Organisation for Economic Co-operation and Development (OECD)*. Accessed at: <oecd.org/dev/44457738>

Knack, S. P. (1995). 'Institutions of Economic Performance'. *Economics and Politics* 7(3): 207–27.

La Porte, R. (1975) *Power and Privileges*. University of California Press.

Levy, A. and Scott-Clark, C. (2007). *Deception: Pakistan, the U.S. and Secret trade in nuclear weapons*. Walker Books.

Lieven, A. (2011) *Pakistan: A Hard Country*. Public Affairs.

Mahbubani, K. (2013). *The Great Convergence*. New York: Public Affairs.

Mahbubul Haq Center for Human Development. *Human Development in South Asia* (Annual Reports). Islamabad and Lahore.

Mahmood, S. (2007). *Good Governance Reform Agenda in Pakistan*. Nova Science Publishers.

Malik, I. (1997). *State and Civil Society in Pakistan*. London: Macmillan.

McCartney, M. C. (2011) *Pakistan: The Political Economy of Growth, Stagnation and the State*. Routledge.

Michalopoulos, C. (2013). *Trends in Developing Countries Trade 1980–2010*. Policy Research WP 6334. Accessed at: <http://documents.worldbank.org/curated/en/2013/01/17196495/trends-developing-country-trade-1980-2010>

Milanovic, B. (2016). *Global Inequality.* Harvard University Press.

Mullick, H. (2010). *The Pakistani Surge.* Australian Strategic Policy Institute.

Mumtaz, S. et al. (2002). *Pakistan: The Contours of State and Society.* OUP.

Muslehuddin and Khan, A. (2011). *A Dynamic Macroeconomic Model of Pakistan.* PIDE.

Myerson, R. *Rethinking the Fundamentals of State Building.* Accessed at: <uchicago. edu/myerson/research/prism10.pdf>

Naqvi, Z. and Schuler, P. (2007). *The Challenges and Potential of Pak-India Trade.* World Bank.

National Judicial Committee Secretariat. (2009). *National Judicial Policy.* Law and Justice Commission of Pakistan.

Nawaz, S. (2008). *Crossed Swords.* OUP.

Niaz, I. (2010). *The Culture of Power and Governance of Pakistan.* OUP.

North, D. C. (1990). *Institutions, Institutional Change, Economic Performance.* New York: Cambridge University Press.

———, (1991). 'Institutions'. *Journal of Economic Perspectives* 5(1): 97–112

Oldenburg, P. (2010). *India, Pakistan and Democracy.* Routledge.

Pakistan Institute of Development Economics (PIDE). *Papers and Proceedings of papers read at the Annual Conferences* (various issues).

Pakistan Institute of Legislative Development and Transparency (PILDAT). (2016). *Internal Democracy of Major Political Parties of Pakistan.*

———, (2014). *Assessment of the quantity of governance in Pakistan.*

Persson, T. and Tabellini, G. (1994). 'Is Equality Harmful for Growth'. *American Economic Review.* 84, Issue 3.

Perotti, R. (1996). 'Growth, income distribution, and democracy: What the data say'. *Journal of Economic Growth* 1(2): 149–87.

Qadeer, M. A. *Pakistan: Social and Cultural Transformation in a Muslim Nation.* Routledge.

Radelet, S. (2016). *The Great Surge: The Ascent of the Developing World.*

Rama, M. et al. (2015). *Addressing Inequality in South Asia.* Accessed at: <https:// openknowledge.worldbank.org/handle/10986/20395>

Ray, J. K. (2007). *Essays on politics and governance in Bangladesh, India, and Pakistan.* Towards Freedom.

Riaz, A. (2016). *Bangladesh A Political History since Independence.* London/New York: I. A. Taurus.

Riedel, B. (2011). *Deadly Embrace.* Brookings Institution Press.

Rodrik, D. et al. (2004). Institutions Rule. *Journal of Economic Growth* 9(2): 131–65.

Rosengrant, M. and Evanson, R. (1993). *Agricultural Productivity Growth in Pakistan and India.* PIDE Annual General Meeting.

Shah, A. (2012). *Pakistan Military's Role in Governance.* New Delhi: KW Publishers.

Shah, A. (2014). *The Army and Democracy Military Politics in Pakistan.* Harvard University Press.

Shaikh, F. (2009). *Making Sense of Pakistan.* Columbia University Press.

Siddiqui, F. H. (2012). *The Politics of Ethnicity in Pakistan.* Routledge.

Sobhan, R. (1998). *Towards a theory of governance and development.* Dhaka: CPD.

Social Policy Development Centre (SPDC). *Social Development in Pakistan Annual Reports* (various issues). Karachi.

Society for the Advancement of Education (SAHE). (2015). *Education Monitor: The State's Engagement with Private Sector.*

State Bank of Pakistan. *Quarterly and Annual Reports* (various issues).

———, (2016). *Handbook of Statistics of Pakistan.*

Sustainable Development Institute of Pakistan. *Annual Conference proceedings volumes* (various issues).

Tahir, M. R. et al. *Dispatches from Pakistan.* University of Minnesota Press.

The News. (14 March 2012). 'Civil Servants and Politicians'.

Toor, S. (2014). *The Neoliberal Security State.* Accessed at: <researchgate.net/publications/29312758>

United Nations Development Program (UNDP). *Human Development Reports* (various issues).

World Bank. Country reports and Development updates on Pakistan (various issues).

———, World Development Indicators (various issues).

———, Global Governance Indicators (various issues).

White, J. (2008). *Pakistan's Islamic Frontier.* Center on Faith and International Affairs.

Ziring, L. (1980). *Pakistan: The Enigma of Political Development.* Colorado: Westview Press.

Index

472; debt 73, 273; enterprises 24, 75, 97, 167–8, 171, 179, 468; expenditure 9, 13, 17, 28, 158, 188, 192, 266, 285, 311, 319, 449, 508; finances 67, 75, 157, 241, 268, 428, 486; goods 9, 21, 55, 74, 121, 139, 187, 230, 361, 507; health 191, 314, 332; institutions 10, 145, 217, 263, 467, 471, 486, 503, 510; investment 65, 72; monopolies 23, 170; opinion 96, 100, 123, 151, 162, 429–30, 493; ownership 168–70; policy 65, 157, 243, 317, 324, 326, 360, 365, 376–7, 385–6; safety 220, 390; sector 11, 22–4, 26, 45, 53–4, 66–8, 74, 84, 129, 147, 159, 164, 168, 170, 172, 189, 218, 222–3, 225–6, 233–5, 241, 272, 312, 358, 362, 367–9, 426, 472, 475, 481, 502; services 10, 24, 31–2, 35, 39, 42, 45, 57, 72, 88–9, 118, 179, 182, 186–8, 197, 207, 211, 214, 219, 221, 223, 229–32, 245, 272, 323, 328, 389, 393, 426, 447–8, 452, 455, 459, 461, 464–5, 471, 475, 501, 508–9; spending 67, 189; transport 153, 501

Public Sector Development Program (PSDP) 164

Public Representatives Disqualification Order (PRODA) 20

Puritanism 47, 324–6, 332–3

R

Radicalism 47, 134, 136, 330, 340, 342

Recruitment 39, 119, 162, 172, 193, 196, 199, 207, 210–11, 213–14, 216, 221, 223, 230–4, 287, 313, 339, 353, 382, 388–90, 393, 395, 404, 459, 489

Reforms 11–12, 23–6, 28, 37–8, 40, 42–4, 47, 50, 52, 54, 56, 58, 64–5, 68–9, 71–2, 74–6, 78, 94, 96–7, 99, 110, 113–15, 118, 122, 124, 131, 143, 164, 172, 179, 181–2, 184–6, 189, 191, 205–6, 210,

213, 215–18, 229–30, 233, 235, 240, 247, 252, 257–8, 263, 278–80, 284, 305, 323, 353, 359, 369, 381, 384, 389, 391–2, 397, 400, 405, 413, 419–21, 425–6, 435, 443–5, 447, 449–2, 464–6, 468–70, 473–5, 477, 479–80, 486–7, 491, 493–4, 500–1, 506–7, 509

Refugees 1, 14, 35, 38, 47, 60, 79, 100, 126, 324, 333, 343, 348, 438–9, 441

Rehabilitation 1, 38, 149, 194, 407, 435

Religion 10, 46, 133–4, 236, 322–6, 328, 331–2, 340, 342–3, 347, 355–6, 509

Religious edifice 25, 322, 335

Remittances 5, 71, 78, 82, 380, 414

Revenue: administration 447; base 177, 420; collection 220, 277, 363; department 363; generation 384; leakages 381; mobilization 176–7

Rice, Condoleezza 6, 300

S

Sattar, Babar 131, 203, 246, 262, 307

Saudi Arabia 132, 151, 294, 332, 343, 491

Sectarianism 1, 67, 132–4, 136, 155, 327–9, 333, 340–1, 343–6, 349, 352–3, 388, 392, 397, 491, 497

Securities and Exchange Commission of Pakistan (SECP) 383, 452, 454

Sewerage and waste:
Garbage 135, 197, 204, 205, 447
Drainage 80, 194, 204, 205, 374

Sharif, Nawaz 49–51, 68–9, 73, 76, 103, 108, 264, 290, 297, 319, 419, 436, 500, 507

Sheikh Mujibur Rahman 40, 101, 472

Singh, Manmohan 98, 436, 498

Socialism 40, 43–4, 48, 65, 103, 336

Social Policy Development Centre (SPDC) 197–8, 202, 206, 208–9, 466

South Asian cyberspace 329